Course   MGMT 50500
            Rahul Menon
            PURDUE UNIVERSITY
            Krannert School of Management

http://create.mheducation.com

ISBN-10: 1308858353   ISBN-13: 9781308858357

Contents

Credits

About the Author

Jerold L. Zimmerman

Jerold Zimmerman is Professor Emeritus at the William E. Simon Graduate School of Business, University of Rochester. He holds an undergraduate degree from the University of Colorado, Boulder, and a doctorate from the University of California, Berkeley.

While at Rochester, Dr. Zimmerman has taught a variety of courses spanning accounting, finance, and economics. Accounting courses include nonprofit accounting, intermediate accounting, accounting theory, and managerial accounting. A deeper appreciation of the challenges of managing complex organizations was acquired by serving as the Simon School's Deputy Dean and on the board of directors of several public corporations.

Professor Zimmerman publishes widely in accounting on topics as diverse as cost allocations, corporate governance, disclosure, financial accounting theory, capital markets, and executive compensation. His paper "The Costs and Benefits of Cost Allocations" won the American Accounting Association's Competitive Manuscript Contest. He is recognized for developing Positive Accounting Theory. This work, co-authored with colleague Ross Watts, at the Massachusetts Institute of Technology, received the American Institute of Certified Public Accountants' Notable Contribution to the Accounting Literature Award for "Towards a Positive Theory of the Determination of Accounting Standards" and "The Demand for and Supply of Accounting Theories: The Market for Excuses." Both papers appeared in the *Accounting Review.* Professors Watts and Zimmerman are also co-authors of the highly cited textbook *Positive Accounting Theory* (Prentice Hall, 1986). Professors Watts and Zimmerman received the 2004 American Accounting Association Seminal Contribution to the Literature award. Professor Zimmerman's textbooks also include *Managerial Economics and Organizational Architecture* with Clifford Smith and James Brickley, 6th ed. (McGraw-Hill, 2016) and *Management Accounting in a Dynamic Environment* with Cheryl McWatters (Routledge UK, 2016). He is a founding editor of the *Journal of Accounting and Economics,* published by Elsevier. This scientific journal is one of the most highly referenced accounting publications.

He and his wife Dodie have two daughters, Daneille and Amy. Jerry has been known to occasionally engage friends and colleagues in an amicable diversion on the links.

Preface

During their professional careers, managers in all organizations, profit and nonprofit, rely on their accounting systems. Sometimes managers use the accounting system to acquire information for decision making. At other times, the accounting system measures performance and thereby influences their behavior. The accounting system is both a source of information for decision making and part of the organization's control mechanisms—thus, the title of the book, *Accounting for Decision Making and Control.*

The purpose of this book is to provide students and managers with an understanding and appreciation of the strengths and limitations of an organization's accounting system, thereby allowing them to be more intelligent users of these systems. This book provides a framework for understanding accounting systems and a basis for analyzing proposed changes to these systems. The text demonstrates that managerial accounting is an integral part of the firm's organizational architecture, not just an isolated set of computational topics.

Changes in the Ninth Edition

Feedback from reviewers and instructors using the prior editions and my own teaching experience provided the basis for the revision. In particular, the following changes have been made:

- Each chapter has been revised to further enhance readability and remove redundancy.
- References to actual company practices have been updated.
- Users were uniform in their praise of the problem material. They found it challenged their students to critically analyze multidimensional issues while still requiring numerical problem-solving skills.
- The end-of-chapter problem material was revised by adding 45 new problems— including some related to health care and knowledge-based service firms—and removing outdated problems.
- The ninth edition is a more concise revision that presents the same fundamental concepts, learning objectives, and challenging critical thinking end-of-chapter materials as in prior editions.

Overview of Content

Chapter 1 presents the book's conceptual framework by using a simple decision context regarding accepting an incremental order from a current customer. The chapter describes why firms use a single accounting system and the concept of economic Darwinism, among other important topics. This chapter is an integral part of the text.

Chapters 2, 4, and 5 present the underlying conceptual framework. The importance of opportunity costs in decision making, cost–volume–profit analysis, and the difference between accounting costs and opportunity costs are discussed in Chapter 2. Chapter 4 employs the economic theory of organizations and organizational architecture as the conceptual foundation to understand the role of the accounting system as part of the organization's control mechanism. Chapter 5 describes the crucial role of accounting as part of the firm's organizational architecture. Chapter 3 on capital budgeting extends opportunity costs to a multiperiod setting. This chapter can be skipped without affecting the flow of later material. Alternatively, Chapter 3 can be assigned at the end of the course.

Chapter 6 applies the conceptual framework and illustrates the trade-off managers face between decision making and control in a budgeting system. Budgets are a decision-making tool to coordinate activities within the firm and are a device to control behavior. This chapter provides an in-depth illustration of how budgets are an important part of an organization's decision-making and control apparatus.

Chapter 7 presents a general analysis of why managers allocate certain costs and the behavioral implications of these allocations. Cost allocations affect both decision making and incentives. Again, managers face a trade-off between decision making and control. Chapter 8 continues the cost allocation discussion by describing the "death spiral" that can occur when significant fixed costs exist and excess capacity arises. This leads to an analysis of how to treat capacity costs—a trade-off between underutilization and overinvestment. Finally, the chapter describes several specific cost allocation methods such as service department costs and joint costs.

Chapter 9 applies the general analysis of overhead allocation in Chapters 7 and 8 to the specific case of absorption costing in a manufacturing setting. The managerial implications of traditional absorption costing are provided in Chapters 10 and 11. Chapter 10 analyzes variable costing, and activity-based costing is the topic of Chapter 11. Variable costing is an interesting example of economic Darwinism. Proponents of variable costing argue that it does not distort decision making and therefore should be adopted. Nonetheless, it is not widely practiced, probably because of tax, financial reporting, and control considerations.

Chapter 12 discusses the decision-making and control implications of standard labor and material costs. Chapter 13 extends the discussion to overhead and marketing variances. Chapters 12 and 13 can be omitted without interrupting the flow of later material. Finally, Chapter 14 synthesizes the course by reviewing the conceptual framework and applying it to various organizational innovations, such as total quality management, just in time, six sigma, lean production, and the balanced scorecard. These innovations provide an opportunity to apply the analytic framework underlying the text.

Acknowledgments

William Vatter and George Benston motivated my interest in managerial accounting. The genesis for this book and its approach reflect the oral tradition of my colleagues, past and present, at the University of Rochester. William Meckling and Michael Jensen stimulated my thinking and provided much of the theoretical structure underlying the book, as anyone familiar with their work will attest. My long and productive collaboration with Ross Watts sharpened my analytical skills and further refined the approach. He also furnished most of the intellectual capital for Chapter 3, including the problem material. Ray Ball has been a constant source of ideas. Clifford Smith and James Brickley continue to enhance my economic education. Three colleagues, Andrew Christie, Dan Gode, and Scott Keating, supplied particularly insightful comments that enriched the analysis at critical junctions. Valuable comments from Anil Arya, Ron Dye, Andy Leone, Dale Morse, Ram Ramanan, K. Ramesh, Shyam Sunder, and Joseph Weintrop are gratefully acknowledged.

This project benefited greatly from the honest and intelligent feedback of numerous instructors. I wish to thank Mahendra Gupta, Susan Hamlen, Badr Ismail, Charles Kile, Leslie Kren, Don May, William Mister, Mohamed Onsi, Ram Ramanan, Stephen Ryan, Michael Sandretto, Richard Sansing, Deniz Saral, Gary Schneider, Joe Weber, and William Yancey. This book also benefited from two other projects with which I have been involved. Writing *Managerial Economics and Organizational Architecture* (McGraw Hill Education, 2016) with James Brickley and Clifford Smith and *Management Accounting in a Dynamic Environment* (Routledge, 2016) with Cheryl McWatters helped me to better understand how to present certain topics.

To the numerous students who endured the development process, I owe an enormous debt of gratitude. I hope they learned as much from the material as I learned teaching them. Some were even kind enough to provide critiques and suggestions, in particular Jan Dick Eijkelboom. Others supplied, either directly or indirectly, the problem material in the text. The able research assistance of P. K. Madappa, Eamon Molloy, Jodi Parker, Steve Sanders, Richard Sloan, and especially Gary Hurst, contributed amply to the manuscript and problem material. Janice Willett and Barbara Schnathorst did a superb job of editing the manuscript and problem material.

The very useful comments and suggestions from the following reviewers are greatly appreciated:

Urton Anderson	William M. Cready	Steven Huddart
Howard M. Armitage	James M. Emig	Robert Hurt
Vidya Awasthi	Gary Fane	Douglas A. Johnson
Kashi Balachandran	Anita Feller	Lawrence A. Klein
Da-Hsien Bao	Tahirih Foroughi	Thomas Krissek
Ron Barden	Ivar Fris	A. Ronald Kucic
Howard G. Berline	Jackson F. Gillespie	Daniel Law
Margaret Boldt	Irving Gleim	Chi-Wen Jevons Lee
David Borst	Jon Glover	Suzanne Lowensohn
Eric Bostwick	Gus Gordon	James R. Martin
Marvin L. Bouillon	Sylwia Gornik-Tomaszewski	Alan H. McNamee
Wayne Bremser	Tony Greig	Marilyn Okleshen
David Bukovinsky	Susan Haka	Shailandra Pandit
Linda Campbell	Bert Horwitz	Sam Phillips

viii   *Preface*

Frank Probst	Richard Saouma	Clark Wheatley
Kamala Raghavan	Arnold Schneider	Lourdes F. White
William Rau	Henry Schwarzbach	Paul F. Williams
Jane Reimers	Elizabeth J. Serapin	Robert W. Williamson
Thomas Ross	Norman Shultz	Peggy Wright
Harold P. Roth	James C. Stallman	Jeffrey A. Yost
P. N. Saksena	William Thomas Stevens	S. Mark Young
Donald Samaleson	Monte R. Swain	
Michael J. Sandretto	Heidi Tribunella	

To my wife Dodie and daughters Daneille and Amy, thank you for setting the right priorities and for giving me the encouragement and environment to be productive. Finally, I wish to thank my parents for all their support.

Jerold L. Zimmerman
University of Rochester

Chapter One

Introduction

Chapter Outline

A. Managerial Accounting: Decision Making and Control

Managers at Hyundai must decide which car models to produce, the quantity of each model to produce given the selling prices for the models, and how to manufacture the automobiles. They must decide which car parts, such as headlight assemblies, Hyundai should manufacture internally and which parts should be outsourced. They must decide not only on advertising, distribution, and product positioning to sell the cars, but also the quantity and quality of the various inputs to use. For example, they must determine which models will have leather seats and the quality of the leather to be used. Similarly, in deciding which investment projects to accept, capital budgeting analysts require data on future cash flows. How are these numbers derived? How does one coordinate the activities of hundreds or thousands of employees in the firm so that these employees accept senior management's leadership? At Hyundai, and at other organizations small and large, managers must have good information to make all these decisions and the leadership abilities to get others to implement the decisions.

Information about firms' future costs and revenues is not readily available but must be estimated by managers. Organizations must obtain and disseminate the knowledge to make these decisions. Organizations' internal information systems provide some of the knowledge for these pricing, production, capital budgeting, and marketing decisions. These systems range from the informal and the rudimentary to very sophisticated, electronic management information systems. The term **information system** should not be interpreted to mean a single, integrated system. Most information systems consist not only of formal, organized, tangible records such as payroll and purchasing documents but also informal, intangible bits of data such as memos, special studies, and managers' impressions and opinions. The firm's information system also contains nonfinancial information such as customer and employee satisfaction surveys. As firms grow from single proprietorships to large global corporations with tens of thousands of employees, managers lose the knowledge of enterprise affairs gained from personal, face-to-face contact in daily operations. Higher-level managers of larger firms come to rely more and more on formal operating reports.

The **internal accounting system**, an important component of a firm's information system, includes budgets, data on the costs of each product and current inventory, and periodic financial reports. In many cases, especially in small companies, these accounting reports are the only formalized part of the information system providing the knowledge for decision making. Many larger companies have other formalized, nonaccounting–based information systems, such as production planning systems. This book focuses on how internal accounting systems provide knowledge for decision making.

After making decisions, managers must implement them in organizations in which the interests of the employees and the owners do not necessarily coincide. Just because senior managers announce a decision does not necessarily ensure that the decision will be implemented.

Organizations do not have objectives; people do. One common objective of owners of the organization is to maximize profits, or the difference between revenues and expenses. Maximizing firm value is equivalent to maximizing the stream of profits over the organization's life. Employees, suppliers, and customers also have their own objectives—usually maximizing their self-interest.

Not all owners care only about monetary flows. An owner of a professional sports team might care more about winning (subject to covering costs) than maximizing profits. Nonprofits do not have owners with the legal rights to the organization's profits. Moreover, nonprofits seek to maximize their value by serving some social goal such as education or health care.

No matter what the firm's objective, the organization will survive only if its inflow of resources (such as revenue) is at least as large as the outflow. Accounting information is useful to help manage the inflow and outflow of resources and to help align the owners' and employees' interests, no matter what objectives the owners wish to pursue.

Throughout this book, we assume that individuals maximize their self-interest. The owners of the firm usually want to maximize profits, but managers and employees will do so only if it is in their interest. Hence, a conflict of interest exists between owners—who, in general, want higher profits—and employees—who want easier jobs, higher wages, and more fringe benefits. To control this conflict, senior managers and owners design systems to monitor employees' behavior and incentive schemes that reward employees for generating more profits. Not-for-profit organizations face similar conflicts. Those people responsible for the nonprofit organization (boards of trustees and government officials) must design incentive schemes to motivate their employees to operate the organization efficiently.

All successful firms must devise mechanisms that help align employee interests with maximizing the organization's value. All of these mechanisms constitute the firm's **control system**; they include performance measures and incentive compensation systems, promotions, demotions, and terminations, security guards and video surveillance, internal auditors, and the firm's internal accounting system.[1]

As part of the firm's control system, the internal accounting system helps align the interests of managers and shareholders to cause employees to maximize firm value. It sounds like a relatively easy task to design systems to ensure that employees maximize firm value. But a significant portion of this book demonstrates the exceedingly complex nature of aligning employee interests with those of the owners.

Internal accounting systems serve two purposes: (1) to provide some of the knowledge necessary for planning and making decisions (*decision making*) and (2) to help motivate and monitor people in organizations (*control*). The most basic control use of accounting is to prevent fraud and embezzlement. Maintaining inventory records helps reduce employee theft. Accounting budgets, discussed more fully in Chapter 6, provide an example of both decision making and control. Asking each salesperson in the firm to forecast his or her sales for the upcoming year is useful for planning next year's production (decision making). However, if the salesperson's sales forecast is used to benchmark performance for compensation purposes (control), he or she has strong incentives to underestimate those forecasts.

Using internal accounting systems for both decision making and control gives rise to the fundamental trade-off in these systems: A system cannot be designed to perform two tasks as well as a system that must perform only one task. Some ability to deliver knowledge for decision making is usually sacrificed to provide better motivation (control). The trade-off between providing knowledge for decision making and motivation/control arises continually throughout this text.

This book is applications oriented: It describes how the accounting system assembles knowledge necessary for implementing decisions using the theories from microeconomics, finance, operations management, and marketing. It also shows how the accounting system helps motivate employees to implement these decisions. Moreover, it stresses the continual trade-offs that must be made between the decision making and control functions of accounting.

---

[1]*Control* refers to the process that helps "ensure the proper behaviors of the people in the organization. These behaviors should be consistent with the organization's strategy," as noted in K. Merchant, *Control in Business Organization* (Boston: Pitman Publishing Inc., 1985), p. 4. Merchant provides an extensive discussion of control systems and a bibliography. In *Theory of Accounting and Control* (Cincinnati, OH: South-Western Publishing Company, 1997), S. Sunder describes control as mitigating and resolving conflicts among employees, owners, suppliers, and customers that threaten to pull organizations apart.

A survey of senior-level executives (chief financial officers, vice presidents of finance, controllers, etc.) asked them to rank the importance of various goals of their firm's accounting system. Eighty percent of the respondents reported that cost management (controlling costs) was a significant goal of their accounting system and was important to achieving their company's overall strategic objective. Another top priority of their firm's accounting system, even higher than cost management or strategic planning, is internal reporting and performance evaluation. These results indicate that firms use their internal accounting system both for decision making (strategic planning, cost reduction, financial management) and for controlling behavior (internal reporting and performance evaluation).[2]

The firm's accounting system is very much a part of the fabric that helps hold the organization together. It provides knowledge for decision making, and it provides information for evaluating and motivating the behavior of individuals within the firm. Being such an integral part of the organization, the accounting system cannot be studied in isolation from the other mechanisms used for decision making or for reducing organizational problems. A firm's internal accounting system should be examined from a broad perspective, as part of the larger organization design question facing managers.

This book uses an economic perspective to study how accounting can motivate and control behavior in organizations. Besides economics, a variety of other paradigms also are used to investigate organizations: scientific management (Taylor), the bureaucratic school (Weber), the human relations approach (Mayo), human resource theory (Maslow, Rickert, Argyris), the decision-making school (Simon), and the political science school (Selznick). Behavior is a complex topic. No single theory or approach is likely to capture all the elements. However, understanding managerial accounting requires addressing the behavioral and organizational issues. Economics offers one useful and widely adopted framework.

B. Design and Use of Cost Systems

Managers make decisions and monitor subordinates who make decisions. Both managers and accountants must acquire sufficient familiarity with cost systems to perform their jobs. Accountants (often called *controllers*) are charged with designing, improving, and operating the firm's accounting system—an integral part of both the decision-making and performance evaluation systems. Both managers and accountants must understand the strengths and weaknesses of current accounting systems. Internal accounting systems, like all systems within the firm, are constantly being refined and modified. Accountants' responsibilities include making these changes.

An internal accounting system should have the following characteristics:

1. Provide the information necessary to assess the profitability of products or services and to optimally price and market these products or services.
2. Provide information to detect production inefficiencies to ensure that the proposed products and volumes are produced at minimum cost.
3. When combined with the performance evaluation and reward systems, create incentives for managers to maximize firm value.
4. Support the financial accounting and tax accounting reporting functions. (In some instances, these latter considerations dominate the first three.)
5. Contribute more to firm value than it costs.

---

[2]Ernst & Young and IMA, "State of Management Accounting," www.imanet.org/pdf/SurveyofMgtAcctingEY .pdf, 2003.

FIGURE 1-1

The multiple role of accounting systems

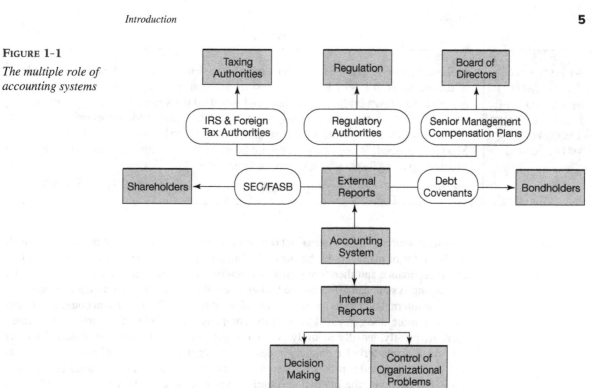

Figure 1–1 portrays the functions of the accounting system. In it, the accounting system supports both external and internal reporting systems. Examine the top half of Figure 1–1. The accounting procedures chosen for external reports to shareholders and taxing authorities are dictated in part by regulators. In the United States, the **Securities and Exchange Commission (SEC)** and the **Financial Accounting Standards Board (FASB)** regulate the financial statements issued to shareholders. The **Internal Revenue Service (IRS)** administers the accounting procedures used in calculating corporate income taxes. If the firm is involved in international trade, foreign tax authorities prescribe the accounting rules applied in calculating foreign taxes. Regulatory agencies constrain public utilities' and financial institutions' accounting procedures.

Management compensation plans and debt contracts often rely on external reports. Senior managers' bonuses are often based on accounting net income. Likewise, if the firm issues long-term bonds, it agrees in the debt covenants not to violate specified accounting-based constraints. For example, the bond contract might specify that the debt-to-equity ratio will not exceed some limit. Like taxes and regulation, compensation plans and debt covenants create incentives for managers to choose particular accounting procedures.[3]

As firms expand into international markets, external users of the firm's financial statements become global. No longer are the firm's shareholders, tax authorities, and regulators domestic. Rather, the firm's internal and external reports are used internationally in a variety of ways.

The bottom of Figure 1–1 illustrates that internal reports are used for decision making as well as control of organizational problems. As discussed earlier, managers use a variety of sources of data for making decisions. The internal accounting system provides one

---

[3]For further discussion of the incentives of managers to choose accounting methods, see R. Watts and J. Zimmerman, *Positive Accounting Theory* (Englewood Cliffs, NJ: Prentice Hall, 1986).

6   *Chapter 1*

| **Managerial Application: Spaceship Lost Because Two Measures Used** | Multiple accounting systems are confusing and can lead to errors. An extreme example of this occurred in 1999 when NASA lost its $125 million Mars spacecraft. Engineers at Lockheed Martin built the spacecraft and specified the spacecraft's thrust in English pounds. But NASA scientists, navigating the craft, assumed the information was in metric newtons. As a result, the spacecraft was off course by 60 miles as it approached Mars and crashed. When two systems are being used to measure the same underlying event, people can forget which system is being used.

SOURCE: A. Pollack, "Two Teams, Two Measures Equaled One Lost Spacecraft," *The New York Times.* October 1, 1999, p. 1. |

important source. These internal reports are also used to evaluate and motivate (control) the behavior of managers in the firm. The internal accounting system reports on managers' performance and therefore provides incentives for them. Any changes to the internal accounting system can affect all the various uses of the resulting accounting numbers.

The internal and external reports are closely linked. The internal accounting system affords a more disaggregated view of the company. These internal reports are generated more frequently, usually monthly or even weekly or daily, whereas the external reports are provided quarterly for publicly traded U.S. companies. The internal reports offer costs and profits by specific products, customers, lines of business, and divisions of the company. For example, the internal accounting system computes the unit cost of individual products as they are produced. These unit costs are then used to value the work-in-process and finished goods inventory, and to compute cost of goods sold. Chapter 9 describes the details of product costing.

Because internal accounting systems serve multiple users and have several purposes, the firm employs either multiple systems (one for each function) or one basic system that serves all three functions (decision making, performance evaluation, and external reporting). Firms can either maintain a single set of books and use the same accounting methods for both internal and external reports, or they can keep multiple sets of books. The decision depends on the costs of writing and maintaining contracts based on accounting numbers, the costs from the dysfunctional internal decisions made using a single system, the additional bookkeeping costs arising from the extra system, and the confusion of having to reconcile the different numbers arising from multiple accounting systems.

Inexpensive accounting software packages and falling costs of information technology have reduced some of the costs of maintaining multiple accounting systems. However, confusion arises when the systems report different numbers for the same concept. For example, when one system reports the manufacturing cost of a product as $12.56 and another system reports it at $17.19, managers wonder which system is producing the "right" number. Some managers may be using the $12.56 figure while others are using $17.19, causing inconsistency and uncertainty. Whenever two numbers for the same concept are produced, the natural tendency is to explain (i.e., reconcile) the differences. Managers involved in this reconciliation could have used this time in more productive ways. Also, using the same accounting system for multiple purposes increases the credibility of the financial reports for each purpose.[4] With only one accounting system, the external auditor monitors the internal reporting system at little or no additional cost.

---

[4]A. Christie, "An Analysis of the Properties of Fair (Market) Value Accounting," in *Modernizing U.S. Securities Regulation: Economic and Legal Perspectives,* K. Lehn and R. Kamphuis, eds. (Pittsburgh, PA: University of Pittsburgh, Joseph M. Katz Graduate School of Business, 1992).

Historical Application: Different Costs for Different Purposes	"... cost accounting has a number of functions, calling for different, if not inconsistent, information. As a result, if cost accounting sets out, determined to discover what the cost of everything is and convinced in advance that there is one figure which can be found and which will furnish exactly the information which is desired for every possible purpose, it will necessarily fail, because there is no such figure. If it finds a figure which is right for some purposes it must necessarily be wrong for others."
	SOURCE: J. Clark, *Studies in the Economics of Overhead Cost.* (Chicago: University of Chicago Press, 1923), p. 234.

Interestingly, a survey of large U.S. firms found that managers typically use the same accounting procedures for both external and internal reporting. More than 80 percent of chief financial officers (CFOs) report using the same accounting methods and report the same earnings internally and externally. In other words, most firms use "one number" for both external and internal communications. One CFO stated, "We make sure that everything that we have underneath—in terms of the detailed reporting—also rolls up basically to the same story that we've told externally."[5] Nothing prevents firms from using separate accounting systems for internal decision making and internal performance evaluation except the confusion generated and the extra data processing costs.

Probably the most important reason firms use a single accounting system is it allows reclassification of the data. An accounting system does not present a single, bottom-line number, such as the "cost of publishing this textbook." Rather, the system reports the components of the total cost of this textbook: the costs of proofreading, typesetting, paper, binding, cover, and so on. Managers in the firm then reclassify the information on the basis of different attributes and derive different cost numbers for different decisions. For example, if the publisher is considering translating this book into Chinese, not all the components used in calculating the U.S. costs are relevant. The Chinese edition might be printed on different paper stock with a different cover. The point is, a single accounting system usually offers enough flexibility for managers to reclassify, recombine, and reorganize the data for multiple purposes.

A single internal accounting system requires the firm to make trade-offs. A system that is best for performance measurement and control is unlikely to be the best for decision making. It's like configuring a motorcycle for both off-road and on-road racing: Riders on bikes designed for both racing conditions probably won't beat riders on specialized bikes designed for just one type of racing surface. Wherever a single accounting system exists, additional analyses arise. Managers making decisions find the accounting system less useful and devise other systems to augment the accounting numbers for decision-making purposes.

Concept Questions		
	Q1–1	What causes the conflict between using internal accounting systems for decision making and control?
	Q1–2	Describe the different kinds of information provided by the internal accounting system.
	Q1–3	Give three examples of the uses of an accounting system.
	Q1–4	List the characteristics of an internal accounting system.
	Q1–5	Do firms have multiple accounting systems? Why or why not?

[5]Dichev, I.D., Graham, J.R., Campbell, H., and Rajgopal, S., 2013. "Earnings quality: evidence from the field," *Journal of Accounting and Economics*, 56 (2–3), pp. 1–33.

8   *Chapter 1*

C. Marmots and Grizzly Bears

Managers often criticize accounting's usefulness for making pricing or outsourcing decisions. Accounting data are based on historical costs rather than current values, and hence contain stale information. Why then do managers persist in using (presumably inferior) accounting information?

Before addressing this question, consider the parable of the marmots and the grizzly bears.[6] Marmots are small groundhogs that are a principal food source for certain bears. Zoologists studying the ecology of marmots and bears observed bears digging and moving rocks in the autumn in search of marmots. They estimated that the calories expended searching for marmots exceeded the calories obtained from their consumption. A zoologist relying on Darwin's theory of natural selection might conclude that searching for marmots is an inefficient use of the bear's limited resources and thus these bears should become extinct. But fossils of marmot bones near bear remains suggest that bears have been searching for marmots for tens of thousands of years.

Because the bears survive, the benefits of consuming marmots must exceed the costs. Bears' claws might be sharpened as a by-product of the digging involved in hunting for marmots. Sharp claws are useful in searching for food under the ice after winter's hibernation. Therefore, the benefit of sharpened claws and the calories derived from the marmots offset the calories consumed gathering the marmots.

What does the marmot-and-bear parable say about why managers persist in using apparently inferior accounting data in their decision making? As it turns out, the marmot-and-bear parable is an extremely important proposition in the social sciences known as *economic Darwinism*. In a competitive world, if surviving organizations use some operating procedure (such as historical cost accounting) over long periods of time, then this procedure likely yields benefits in excess of its costs. Firms survive in competition by selling goods or services at lower prices than their competitors while still covering costs. Firms cannot survive by making more mistakes than their competitors.[7]

Terminology: Benchmarking and Economic Darwinism	*Benchmarking* is defined as a "process of continuously comparing and measuring an organization's business processing against business leaders anywhere in the world to gain information which will help the organization take action to improve its performance."
	Economic Darwinism predicts that successful firm practices will be imitated. Benchmarking is the practice of imitating successful business practices. The practice of benchmarking dates back to 607, when Japan sent teams to China to learn the best practices in business, government, and education. Today, most large firms routinely conduct benchmarking studies to discover the best business practices and then implement them in their firms.
	SOURCE: Society of Management Accountants of Canada, *Benchmarking: A Survey of Canadian Practice* (Hamilton, Ontario, Canada, 1994).

---

[6]This example is suggested by J. McGee, "Predatory Pricing Revisited," *Journal of Law & Economics.* XXIII (October 1980), pp. 289–330.

[7]See A. Alchian, "Uncertainty, Evolution and Economic Theory," *Journal of Political Economy.* 58 (June 1950), pp. 211–21.

Economic Darwinism suggests that in successful (surviving) firms, things should not be fixed unless they are clearly broken. Currently, considerable attention is being directed at revising and updating firms' internal accounting systems because many managers believe their current accounting systems are "broken" and require major overhaul. Alternative internal accounting systems are being proposed, among them **activity-based costing (ABC), balanced scorecards, economic value added (EVA)**, and **Lean accounting systems**. These systems are discussed and analyzed later in terms of their ability to help managers make better decisions, as well as to help provide better measures of performance for managers in organizations, thereby aligning managers' and owners' interests.

Although internal accounting systems may appear to have certain inconsistencies with some particular theory, these systems (like the bears searching for marmots) have survived the test of time and therefore are likely to be yielding unobserved benefits (like claw sharpening). This book discusses these additional benefits. Two caveats must be raised concerning too strict an application of economic Darwinism:

1. Some surviving operating procedures can be neutral mutations. Just because a system survives does not mean that its benefits exceed its costs. Benefits less costs might be close to zero.

2. Just because a given system survives does not mean it is optimal. A better system might exist but has not yet been discovered.

The fact that most managers use their accounting system as the primary formal information system suggests that these accounting systems are yielding total benefits that exceed their total costs. These benefits include financial and tax reporting, providing information for decision making, and creating internal incentives. The proposition that surviving firms have efficient accounting systems does not imply that better systems do not exist, only that they have not yet been discovered. It is not necessarily the case that what is, is optimal. Economic Darwinism helps identify the costs and benefits of alternative internal accounting systems and is applied repeatedly throughout the book.

Historical Application: Sixteenth-Century Cost Records	The well-known Italian Medici family had extensive banking interests and owned textile plants in the fifteenth and sixteenth centuries. They also used sophisticated cost records to maintain control of their cloth production. These cost reports contained detailed data on the costs of purchasing, washing, beating, spinning, and weaving the wool, of supplies, and of overhead (tools, rent, and administrative expenses). Modern costing methodologies closely resemble these fifteenth-century cost systems, suggesting they yield benefits in excess of their costs. Source: P. Garner, *Evolution of Cost Accounting to 192.* (Montgomery, AL: University of Alabama Press, 1954), pp. 12–13. Original source *R de Roover, "A Florentine Firm of Cloth Manufacturers," Speculu. XVI* (January 1941), pp. 3–33.

D. Management Accountant's Role in the Organization

To better understand internal accounting systems, it is useful to describe how firms organize their accounting functions. No single organizational structure applies to all firms. Figure 1–2 presents one common organization chart. The design and operation of the internal and external accounting systems are the responsibility of the firm's chief financial officer. The firm's line-of-business or functional areas, such as marketing, manufacturing,

10 *Chapter 1*

FIGURE 1-2

Organization chart for a typical corporation

and research and development, are combined and shown under a single organization, "operating divisions." The remaining staff and administrative functions include human resources, chief financial officer, legal, and other. In Figure 1–2, the CFO oversees all the financial and accounting functions in the firm and reports directly to the president. The CFO's three major functions include controllership, treasury, and internal audit. Controllership involves tax administration, the internal and external accounting reports (including statutory filings with the Securities and Exchange Commission if the firm is publicly traded), and the planning and control systems (including budgeting). Treasury involves short- and long-term financing, banking, credit and collections, investments, insurance, and capital budgeting. Depending on their size and structure, firms organize these functions differently. Figure 1–2 shows the internal audit group reporting directly to the CFO. In other firms, internal audit reports to the controller, the chief executive officer (CEO), or the board of directors.

The controller is the firm's chief management accountant and is responsible for data collection and reporting. The controller compiles the data to prepare the firm's balance sheet, income statement, and tax returns. In addition, this person prepares the internal reports for the various divisions and departments within the firm and helps the other managers by providing them with the data necessary to make decisions—as well as the data necessary to evaluate these managers' performance.

Usually, each operating division or department has its own controller. For example, if a firm has several divisions, each division has its own division controller, who reports to both the division manager and the corporate controller. In Figure 1–2, the operating divisions have their own controllers. The division controller provides the corporate controller with periodic reports on the division's operations. The division controller oversees the division's budgets, payroll, inventory, and product costing system (which reports the cost of the division's products and services). While most firms have division-level controllers, some firms centralize these functions to reduce staff so that all the division-level controller functions are performed centrally out of corporate headquarters.

The controllership function at the corporate, division, and plant levels involves assisting decision making and control. The controller must balance providing information to other managers for decision making against providing monitoring information to top executives for use in controlling the behavior of lower-level managers.

Historical Application: The Rise of the CFO	In a study of 400 of the largest U.S. corporations, in 1960 none of the firms had a position entitled "Chief Financial Officer." By the year 2000, 80 percent had a person holding the title "CFO." Prior to 1960, most large firms called their top accounting manager "Chief Accountant," who typically was not part of the senior executive team. Several factors caused the elevation of "Chief Accountant" to "CFO," who also became an integral member of the firm's senior executives. First, between 1960 and 2000, large U.S. firms became global, with operations in numerous countries requiring more complex financial transactions involving foreign currency hedging and multinational banking relations. Besides becoming global, large firms began to diversify their operations by entering into new lines of business. These firms became more complex, which necessitated more sophisticated reporting and control systems such as budgeting and monthly reports. To enter new markets, large firms began engaging in mergers and acquisitions as the capital markets developed to finance these transactions. The CFO played an integral role in valuing and financing acquisition targets. In addition, accounting rules became significantly more complicated, requiring sophisticated compliance capabilities. Thus, today's CFOs have a much broader skill set and manage a larger portfolio of activities than their predecessors, and as such, their role and title in their firms has been elevated.

SOURCES: L. Sjoblom and N. Michels-Kim, "Leading Nestle's House of Finance," *Strategic Finance* (September 2011), pp. 29–33 and D. Zorn, "Here a Chief, There a Chief: The Rise of the CFO in the American Firm," *American Sociological Review* (June 2004), pp. 345–364.

Besides overseeing the controllership and treasury functions in the firm, the chief financial officer usually has responsibility for the internal audit function. The internal audit group's primary roles are to seek out and eliminate internal fraud and to provide internal consulting and risk management. The U.S. Sarbanes–Oxley Act of 2002 mandated numerous corporate governance reforms, such as requiring boards of directors of U.S. publicly traded companies to have audit committees composed of independent (outside) directors and requiring these companies to continuously test the effectiveness of the internal controls over their financial statements. This federal legislation indirectly expanded the internal audit group's role. The internal audit group now works closely with the audit committee of the board of directors to help ensure the integrity of the firm's financial statements by testing whether the firm's accounting procedures are free of internal control deficiencies.

The Sarbanes–Oxley Act also requires companies to have corporate codes of conduct (ethics codes). While many firms had ethics codes prior to this act, these codes define honest and ethical conduct, including conflicts of interest between personal and professional relationships, compliance with applicable governmental laws, rules and regulations, and prompt internal reporting of code violations to the appropriate person in the company. The audit committee of the board of directors is responsible for overseeing compliance with the company's code of conduct.

The importance of the internal control system cannot be stressed enough. Throughout this book, we use the term *control* to mean aligning the interests of employees with maximizing the value of the firm. The most basic conflict of interest between employees and owners is employee theft. In fact, one study reports that the typical firm loses 5 percent of its revenues to fraud.[8] To reduce the likelihood of embezzlement, firms install internal

---

[8]Association of Certified Fraud Examiners, "2014 Report to the Nation on Occupational Fraud and Abuse," www.acfe.com.

control systems, which are an integral part of their control system. Internal and external auditors' first responsibility is to test the integrity of the firm's internal controls. Fraud and theft are prevented not just by having security guards and door locks but also through a variety of procedures such as requiring checks above a certain amount to be authorized by two people. Internal control systems include internal procedures, codes of conduct, and policies that prohibit corruption, bribery, and kickbacks. Finally, internal control systems should prevent intentional (or accidental) financial misrepresentation by managers.

| **Concept Questions** | Q1–6 | Define *economic Darwinism.* |
| | Q1–7 | Describe the major functions of the chief financial officer. |

E. Evolution of Management Accounting: A Framework for Change

Management accounting has evolved with the nature of organizations. Prior to 1800, most businesses were small, family-operated organizations. Management accounting was less important for these small firms. It was not critical for planning decisions and control reasons because the owner could directly observe the organization's entire environment. The owner, who made all of the decisions, delegated little decision-making authority and had no need to devise elaborate formal systems to motivate employees. The owner observing slacking employees simply replaced them. Only as organizations grew larger with remote operations would management accounting become more important.

Most of today's modern management accounting techniques were developed in the period from 1825 to 1925 with the growth of large organizations.[9] Textile mills in the early nineteenth century grew by combining the multiple processes (spinning the thread, dying, weaving, etc.) of making cloth. These large firms developed systems to measure the cost per yard or per pound for the separate manufacturing processes. The cost data allowed managers to compare the cost of conducting a process inside the firm versus purchasing the process from external vendors. Similarly, the railroads of the 1850s to 1870s developed cost systems that reported cost per ton-mile and operating expenses per dollar of revenue. These measures allowed managers to increase their operating efficiencies. In the early 1900s, Andrew Carnegie (at what was to become U.S. Steel) devised a cost system that reported detailed unit cost figures for material and labor on a daily and weekly basis. This system allowed senior managers to maintain very tight controls on operations and gave them accurate and timely information on costs for pricing decisions. Merchandising firms such as Marshall Field's and Sears, Roebuck developed gross margin (revenues less cost of goods sold) and stock-turn ratios (sales divided by inventory) to measure and evaluate performance. Manufacturing companies such as Du Pont Powder Company and General Motors developed performance measures to control their growing organizations.

In the period from 1925 to 1975, management accounting was heavily influenced by external considerations. Income taxes and financial accounting requirements (e.g., those of the Financial Accounting Standards Board) were major factors affecting management accounting.

Since 1975, two major environmental forces have changed organizations and caused managers to question whether traditional management accounting procedures

---

[9]P. Garner, *Evolution of Cost Accounting to 1925* (Montgomery, AL: University of Alabama Press, 1954); and A. Chandler, *The Visible Hand* (Cambridge, MA: Harvard University Press, 1977).

(pre-1975) are still appropriate. These environmental forces are (1) factory automation and computer/information technology and (2) global competition. These environmental changes force managers to reconsider their organizational structure and their management accounting procedures.

Managerial Application: Big Data and Data Analytics	According to IBM, "Every day, we create 2.5 quintillion bytes of data—so much that 90% of the data in the world today has been created in the last two years alone. This data comes from everywhere: sensors used to gather climate information, posts to social media sites, digital pictures and videos, purchase transaction records, and cell phone GPS signals to name a few. This data is '**big data**.'"

The future of finance and accounting professionals at many firms is to learn how to apply statistical and computer science techniques called "data analytics" to extract valuable insights about their customers, products, and competitors from their big data. For example, large online retailers constantly monitor the prices of products offered by competitors to adjust their prices dynamically throughout the day. Managers pore over data to uncover the causes behind the company's sales, costs, and profits and to better understand what drive revenues and operating and sales expenses. Where and by which salespeople are different products sold? Why are certain stores or factories more profitable? What are customers Tweeting or Facebook postings saying about our products and our competitors?

SOURCES: www-01.ibm.com/software/data/bigdata/what-is-big-data.html. D. Katz "Accounting's Big Data Problem," CFO. com. (March 4, 2014)

Information technology advances such as the Internet, intranets, wireless communications, and faster microprocessors have had a big impact on internal accounting processes. More data are now available faster than ever before. Electronic data interchange, XHTML, e-mail, B2B (business-to-business) e-commerce, bar codes, data warehousing, and online analytical processing (OLAP) are just a few examples of new technology impacting management accounting. For example, managers now have access to daily sales and operating costs in real time, as opposed to having to wait two weeks after the end of the calendar quarter for this information. Firms have cut the time needed to prepare budgets for the next fiscal year by several months because the information is transmitted electronically in standardized formats.

The history of management accounting illustrates how it has evolved in parallel with organizations' structure. Management accounting provides information for planning decisions and control. It is useful for assigning decision-making authority, measuring performance, and determining rewards for individuals within the organization. Because management accounting is part of the organizational structure, it is not surprising that management accounting evolves in a parallel and consistent fashion with other parts of the organizational structure.

Figure 1–3 is a framework for understanding the role of accounting systems within firms and the forces that cause accounting systems to change. As described more fully in Chapter 14, environmental forces such as technological innovation and global competition change the organization's business strategies. For example, the Internet has allowed banks to offer electronic, online banking services. To implement these new strategies, organizations must adapt their organizational structure or architecture, which includes management accounting. An organization's architecture (the topic of Chapter 4) is composed of three

14   *Chapter 1*

FIGURE 1-3

Framework for organizational change and management accounting

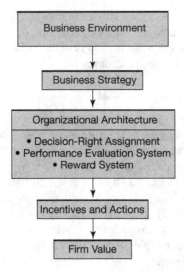

related processes: (1) the assignment of decision-making responsibilities, (2) the measurement of performance, and (3) the rewarding of individuals within the organization.

The first component of the organizational architecture is assigning responsibilities to the different members of the organization. Decision rights define the duties each member of an organization is expected to perform. The decision rights of a particular individual within an organization are specified by that person's job description. Checkout clerks in grocery stores have the decision rights to collect cash from customers but don't have the decision rights to accept certain types of checks. A manager must be called for that decision. A division manager may have the right to set prices on products but not the right to borrow money. The president usually retains the right to issue debt, subject to board of directors' approval.

The next two parts of the organizational architecture are the performance evaluation and reward systems. To motivate individuals within the organization, organizations must have a system for measuring their performance and rewarding them. Performance measures for a salesperson could include total sales and customer satisfaction based on a survey of customers. Performance measures for a manufacturing unit might be number of units produced, total costs, and percentage of defective units. The internal accounting system is often an important part of the performance evaluation system.

Performance measures are extremely important because rewards are generally based on these measures. Rewards for individuals within organizations include wages and bonuses, prestige and greater decision rights, promotions, and job security. Because rewards are based on performance measures, individuals and groups are motivated to act to influence the performance measures. Therefore, the performance measures chosen influence individual and group efforts within the organization. A poor choice of performance measures can lead to conflicts within the organization and derail efforts to achieve organizational goals. For example, measuring the performance of a college president based on the number of students attending the college encourages the president to enroll ill-prepared students, thereby reducing the quality of the educational experience for other students.

As illustrated in Figure 1–3, changes in the business environment lead to new strategies and ultimately to changes in the firm's organizational architecture, including changes in the accounting system to better align the interests of the employees with the objectives of the organization. The new organizational architecture provides incentives for members of the organization to make decisions, which leads to a change in the value of the organization. Within this framework, accounting assists in the control of the organization through the organization's architecture and provides information for decision making. This framework for change is referred to throughout the book.

F. Vortec Medical Probe Example

To illustrate some of the basic concepts developed in this text, suppose you have been asked to evaluate the following decision. Vortec Inc. manufactures a single product, a medical probe. Vortec sells the probes to distributors who then market them to physicians. Vortec has two divisions. The manufacturing division produces the probes; the marketing division sells them to distributors. The marketing division is rewarded on the basis of sales revenues. The manufacturing division is evaluated and rewarded on the basis of the average unit cost of making the probes. The plant's current volume is 100,000 probes per month. The following income statement summarizes last month's operating results.

VORTEC MANUFACTURING
Income Statement
Last Month

Sales revenue (100,000 units @ $5.00)	$500,000
Cost of sales (100,000 units @ $4.50)	450,000
Operating margin	$ 50,000
Less: Administrative expenses	27,500
Net income before taxes	$ 22,500

Medsupplies is one of Vortec's best distributors. Vortec sells 10,000 probes per month to Medsupplies at $5 per unit. Last week, Medsupplies asked Vortec's marketing division to increase its monthly shipment to 12,000 units, provided that Vortec would sell the additional 2,000 units at $4 each. Medsupplies would continue to pay $5 for the original 10,000 units. Medsupplies argued that because this would be extra business for Vortec, no overhead should be charged on the additional 2,000 units. In this case, a $4 price should be adequate.

Vortec's finance department estimates that with 102,000 probes the average cost is $4.47 per unit, and hence the $4 price offered by Medsupplies is too low. The current administrative expenses of $27,500 consist of office rent, property taxes, and interest and will not change if this special order is accepted. Should Vortec accept the Medsupplies offer?

Before examining whether the marketing and manufacturing divisions will accept the order, consider Medsupplies's offer from the perspective of Vortec's owners, who are interested in maximizing profits. The decision hinges on the cost to Vortec of selling an additional 2,000 units to Medsupplies. If the cost is more than $4 per unit, Vortec should reject the special order.

It is tempting to reject the offer because the $4 price does not cover the average total cost of $4.47. But will it cost Vortec $4.47 per unit for the 2,000-unit special order? Is $4.47 the cost per unit for each of the next 2,000 units?

To begin the analysis, two simplifying assumptions are made that are relaxed later:

- Vortec has excess capacity to produce the additional 2,000 probes.
- Past historical costs are unbiased estimates of the future cash flows for producing the special order.

Based on these assumptions, we can compare the incremental revenue from the additional 2,000 units with its incremental cost:

Incremental revenue (2,000 units × $4.00)		$8,000
Total cost @ 102,000 units (102,000 × $4.47)	$455,940	
Total cost @ 100,000 units (100,000 × $4.50)	450,000	
Incremental cost of 2,000 units		5,940
Incremental profit of 2,000 units		$2,060

The estimated incremental cost per unit of the 2,000 units is then

$$\frac{\text{Change in total cost}}{\text{Change in volume}} = \frac{\$455,940 - \$450,000}{2,000} = \$2.97$$

The estimated cost per incremental unit is $2.97. Therefore, $2.97 is the average per-unit cost of the extra 2,000 probes. The $4.47 cost is the average cost of producing 102,000 units, which is more than the $2.97 incremental cost per unit of producing the extra 2,000 probes.

Based on the $2.97 estimated cost, Vortec should take the order. Is this the right decision? Not necessarily. There are some other considerations:

1. Will these 2,000 additional units affect the $5 price of the 100,000 probes? Will Vortec's other distributors continue to pay $5 if Medsupplies buys 2,000 units at $4? What prevents Medsupplies from reselling the probes to Vortec's other distributors at less than $5 per unit but above $4 per unit? Answering these questions requires management to acquire knowledge of the market for the probes.

2. What is the alternative use of the excess capacity consumed by the additional 2,000 probes? As plant utilization increases, congestion costs rise, production becomes less efficient, and the cost per unit rises. Congestion costs include the wages of the additional production employees and supervisors required to move, store, expedite, and rework products as plant volume increases. The $2.97 incremental cost computed from the average cost data provided above might not include the higher congestion costs as capacity is approached. This suggests that the $4.47 average cost estimate is wrong. Who provides this cost estimate and how accurate is it? Management must acquire knowledge of how costs behave at a higher volume. If Vortec accepts the Medsupplies offer, will Vortec be forced at some later date to forgo using this capacity for a more profitable project?

3. What costs will Vortec incur if the Medsupplies offer is rejected? Will Vortec lose the normal 10,000-unit Medsupplies order? If so, can this order be replaced?

4. Does the Robinson-Patman Act apply? The **Robinson-Patman Act** is a U.S. federal law prohibiting charging customers different prices if doing so is injurious to competition. Thus, it may be illegal to sell an additional 2,000 units to Medsupplies at less than $5 per unit. Knowledge of U.S. antitrust laws must be acquired. Moreover, if Vortec sells internationally, it will have to research the antitrust laws of the various jurisdictions that might review the Medsupplies transaction.

We have analyzed the question of whether Medsupplies' 2,000-unit special order maximizes the owners' profit. The next question to address is whether the marketing and manufacturing divisions will accept Medsupplies' offer. Recall that marketing is evaluated based on total revenues, and manufacturing is evaluated based on average unit costs. Therefore, marketing will want to accept the order as long as Medsupplies does not resell the probes to other Vortec distributors and as long as other Vortec distributors do not expect similar price concessions. Manufacturing will want to accept the order as long as it believes average unit costs will fall. Increasing production lowers average unit costs and makes it appear as though manufacturing has achieved cost reductions.

Suppose that accepting the Medsupplies offer will not adversely affect Vortec's other sales, but the incremental cost of producing the 2,000 extra probes is really $4.08, not $2.97, because there will be overtime charges and additional factory congestion costs. Under these conditions, both marketing and manufacturing will want to accept the offer. Marketing increases total revenue and thus appears to have improved its performance. Manufacturing still lowers average unit costs from $4.50 to $4.4918 per unit:

$$\frac{(\$4.50 \times 100,000) + (\$4.08 \times 2,000)}{102,000} = \$4.4918$$

However, the shareholders are worse off. Vortec's cash flows are lower by $160 [or 2,000 units × ($4.00 − $4.08)]. The problem is not that the marketing and manufacturing managers are "making a mistake." The problem is that their measures of performance are creating the wrong incentives. In particular, rewarding marketing for increasing total revenues and manufacturing for reducing average unit costs means there is no mechanism to ensure that the incremental revenues from the order ($8,000 = $4 × 2,000) are greater than the incremental costs ($8,160 = $4.08 × 2,000). Both marketing and manufacturing are doing what they were told to do (increase revenues and reduce average costs), but the firm's cash flow falls because the incentive systems are poorly designed.

Four key points emerge from this example:

1. *Beware of average costs.* The $4.50 unit cost tells us little about how costs will vary with changes in volume. Just because a cost is stated in dollars per unit does not mean that producing one more unit will add that amount of incremental cost.

2. *Use opportunity costs.* Opportunity costs measure what the firm forgoes when it chooses a specific action. The notion of opportunity cost is crucial in decision making. The opportunity cost of the Medsupplies order is what Vortec forgoes by accepting the special order. What is the best alternative use of the plant capacity consumed by the Medsupplies special order? (More on this in Chapter 2.)

3. *Supplement accounting data with other information.* The accounting system contains important data relevant for estimating the cost of this special order from Medsupplies. But other knowledge that the accounting system cannot capture must be assembled, such as what Medsupplies will do if Vortec rejects its offer. Managers usually augment accounting data with other knowledge such as customer demands, competitors' plans, future technology, and government regulations.

4. *Use accounting numbers as performance measures cautiously.* Accounting numbers such as revenues or average unit manufacturing costs are often used to evaluate managers' performance. Just because managers are maximizing particular performance measures tailored for each manager does not necessarily cause firm profits to be maximized.

The Vortec example illustrates the importance of understanding how accounting numbers are constructed, what they mean, and how they are used in decision making and control. The accounting system is a very important source of information to managers, but it is not the sole source of all knowledge. Also, in the overly simplified context of the Vortec example, the problems with the incentive systems and with using unit costs are easy to detect. In a complex company with hundreds or thousands of products or services, such errors are very difficult to detect. Finally, for the sake of simplicity, the Vortec illustration ignores the use of the accounting system for external reporting.

G. Outline of the Text

Internal accounting systems provide data for both decision making and control. The organization of this book follows this dichotomy. The first part of the text (Chapters 2 through 5) describes how accounting systems are used in decision making and providing incentives in organizations. These chapters provide the conceptual framework for the remainder of the book. The next set of chapters (Chapters 6 through 8) describes basic topics in managerial accounting, budgeting, and cost allocations. Budgets not only communicate knowledge within the firm for decision making but also serve as a control device and as a way to partition decision-making responsibility among the managers. Likewise, cost allocations serve decision-making and control functions. In analyzing the role of budgeting and cost allocations, these chapters draw on the first part of the text.

The next section of the text (Chapters 9 through 13) describes the prevalent accounting system used in firms: absorption costing. Absorption cost systems are built around cost allocations. The systems used in manufacturing and service settings generate product or service costs built up from direct labor, direct material, and allocated overheads. After first describing these systems, we critically analyze them. A common criticism of absorption cost systems is that they produce inaccurate unit cost information, which can lead to dysfunctional decision making. Two alternative accounting systems (variable cost systems and activity-based cost systems) are compared and evaluated against a traditional absorption cost system. The next topic describes the use of standard costs as extensions of absorption cost systems. Standard costs provide benchmarks to calculate accounting variances: the difference between the actual costs and standard costs. These variances are performance measures and thus are part of the firm's motivation and control system described earlier.

The last chapter (Chapter 14) expands the integrative approach summarized in section E of this chapter. This approach is then used to analyze four modifications of internal cost systems: quality measurement systems, just-in-time production, six sigma and lean production, and balanced scorecards. These modifications are evaluated within a broad historical context. Just because these systems are new does not suggest they are better. Some have stood the test of time, while others have not.

H. Summary

This book provides a framework for the analysis, use, and design of internal accounting systems. It explains how these systems are used for decision making and motivating people in organizations. Employees care about their self-interest, not the owners' self-interest. Hence, owners must devise incentive systems to motivate their employees. Accounting numbers are used as measures of managers' performance and hence are part of the control system used to motivate managers. Most organizations use a single internal accounting system as the primary data source for external reporting and internal uses. Applying the economic Darwinism principle, the costs of multiple systems likely outweigh the benefits for most firms. The costs are not only the direct costs of operating the system but also the indirect costs from dysfunctional decisions resulting from faulty information and poor performance evaluation systems. The remainder of this book addresses the costs and benefits of internal accounting systems.

Problems

P 1–1: MBA Students

One MBA student was overheard saying to another, "Accounting is baloney. I worked for a genetic engineering company and we never looked at the accounting numbers and our stock price was always growing."

"I agree," said the other. "I worked in a rust bucket company that managed everything by the numbers and we never improved our stock price very much."

Evaluate these comments.

P 1–2: One Cost System Isn't Enough

Robert S. Kaplan in "One Cost System Isn't Enough" (*Harvard Business Review*. January–February 1988, pp. 61–66)

> No single system can adequately answer the demands made by diverse functions of cost systems. While companies can use one method to capture all their detailed transactions data, the processing of this information for diverse purposes and audiences demands separate, customized development. Companies that try to satisfy all the needs for cost information with a single system have discovered they can't perform important managerial functions adequately. Moreover, systems that work well for one company may fail in a different environment. Each company has to design methods that make sense for its particular products and processes.
>
> Of course, an argument for expanding the number of cost systems conflicts with a strongly ingrained financial culture to have only one measurement system for everyone.

Describe the costs and benefits of having a single measurement system.

P 1–3: U.S. and Japanese Tax Laws

Tax laws in Japan tie taxable income directly to the financial statements' reported income. That is, to compute a Japanese firm's tax liability, multiply the net income as reported to shareholders by the appropriate tax rate to derive the firm's tax liability. In contrast, U.S. firms typically have more discretion in choosing different accounting procedures for calculating net income for shareholders (financial reporting) and taxes.

What effect would you expect these institutional differences in tax laws between the United States and Japan to have on internal accounting and reporting?

P 1–4: Using Accounting for Planning

The owner of a small software company felt his accounting system was useless. He stated, "Accounting systems only generate historical costs. Historical costs are useless in my business because everything changes so rapidly."

Required:

    a. Are historical costs useless in rapidly changing environments?

    b. Should accounting systems be limited to historical costs?

P 1–5: Budgeting

Salespeople at a particular firm forecast what they expect to sell next period. Their supervisors then review the forecasts and make revisions. These forecasts are used to set production and purchasing plans. In addition, salespeople receive a fixed bonus of 20 percent of their salary if they meet or exceed their forecasts.

Discuss the incentives of the salespeople to forecast next-period sales accurately. Discuss the trade-off between using the budget for decision making versus using it as a control device.

20   *Chapter 1*

P 1–6:   Golf Specialties

Golf Specialties (GS), a Belgian company, manufactures a variety of golf paraphernalia, such as head covers for woods, embroidered golf towels, and umbrellas. GS sells all its products exclusively in Europe through independent distributors. Given the popularity of Tiger Woods, one of GS's more popular items is a head cover in the shape of a tiger.

GS is currently making 500 tiger head covers a week at a per unit cost of 3.50 euros, which includes both variable costs and allocated fixed costs. GS sells the tiger head covers to distributors for 4.25 euros. A distributor in Japan, Kojo Imports, wants to purchase 100 tiger head covers per week from GS and sell them in Japan. Kojo offers to pay GS 2 euros per head cover. GS has enough capacity to produce the additional 100 tiger head covers and estimates that if it accepts Kojo's offer, the per unit cost of all 600 tiger head covers will be 3.10 euros. Assume the cost data provided (3.50 euros and 3.10 euros) are accurate estimates of GS's costs of producing the tiger head covers. Further assume that GS's variable cost per head cover does not vary with the number of head covers manufactured.

Required:

a. Given the data in the problem, what is GS's weekly fixed cost of producing the tiger head covers?

b. To maximize firm value, should GS accept Kojo's offer? Explain why or why not.

c. Besides the data provided above, what other factors should GS consider before making a decision to accept Kojo's offer?

P 1–7:   Parkview Hospital

Parkview Hospital, a regional hospital, serves a population of 400,000 people. The next closest hospital is 50 miles away. Parkview's accounting system is adequate for patient billing. The system reports revenues generated per department but does not break down revenues by unit within departments. For example, Parkview knows patient revenue for the entire psychiatric department but does not know revenues in the child and adolescent unit, the chemical dependence unit, or the neuropsychiatric unit.

Parkview receives its revenues from three principal sources: the federal government (Medicare), the state government (Medicaid), and private insurance companies (Blue Cross–Blue Shield). Until recently, the private insurance companies continued to pay Parkview's increasing costs and passed these on to the firms through higher premiums for their employees' health insurance.

Last year Trans Insurance (TI) entered the market and began offering lower-cost health insurance to local firms. TI cut benefits offered and told Parkview that it would pay only a fixed dollar amount per patient. A typical firm could cut its health insurance premium 20 percent by switching to TI. TI was successful at taking 45 percent of the Blue Cross–Blue Shield customers. Firms that switched to TI faced stiff competition and sought to cut their health care costs.

Parkview management estimated that its revenues would fall 6 percent, or $3.2 million, next year because of TI's lower reimbursements. Struggling with how to cope with lower revenues, Parkview began the complex process of deciding what programs to cut, how to shift the delivery of services from inpatient to outpatient clinics, and what programs to open to offset the revenue loss (e.g., open an outpatient depression clinic). Management can forecast some of the costs of the proposed changes, but many of its costs and revenues (such as the cost of the admissions office) have never been tracked to the individual clinical unit.

Required:

a. Was Parkview's accounting system adequate 10 years ago?

b. Is Parkview's accounting system adequate today?

c. What changes should Parkview make in its accounting system?

P 1–8:   Montana Pen Company

Montana Pen Company manufactures a full line of premium writing instruments. It has 12 different styles, and within each style, it offers ball point pens, fountain pens, mechanical pencils, and a roller ball pen. Most models also come in three finishes—gold, silver, and black matte. Montana Pen's Bangkok, Thailand, plant manufactures four of the styles. The plant is currently producing the gold clip for the top of one of its pen styles, no. 872. Current production is 1,200 gold no. 872 pens each month at an average cost of 185 baht per gold clip. (One U.S. dollar currently buys 32 baht.) A Chinese manufacturer has offered to produce the same gold clip for 136 baht. This manufacturer will sell Montana Pen 400 clips per month. If it accepts the Chinese offer and cuts the production of the clips from 1,200 to 800, Montana Pen estimates that the cost of each clip it continues to produce will rise from 185 baht to 212.5 baht per gold clip.

Required:

a. Should Montana Pen outsource 400 gold clips for pen style no. 872 to the Chinese firm? Provide a written justification of your answer.

b. Given your answer in part (*a*), what additional information would you seek before deciding to outsource 400 gold clips per month to the Chinese firm?

Chapter Two

The Nature of Costs

Chapter Outline

As described in Chapter 1, accounting systems measure costs that managers use for external reports, decision making, and controlling the behavior of people in the organization. Understanding how accounting systems calculate costs requires a thorough understanding of what **cost** means. Unfortunately, that simple term has multiple meanings. Saying a product costs $3.12 does not reveal what the $3.12 measures. Additional explanation is often needed to clarify the assumptions that underlie the calculation of cost. A large vocabulary exists to communicate more clearly which cost meaning is being conveyed. Some examples include average cost, common cost, full cost, historical cost, joint cost, marginal cost, period cost, product cost, standard cost, fixed cost, opportunity cost, sunk cost, and variable cost, just to name a few.

We begin this chapter with the concept of opportunity cost, a powerful tool for understanding the myriad cost terms and for structuring managerial decisions. In addition, opportunity cost provides a benchmark against which accounting-based cost numbers can be compared and evaluated. Section B discusses how opportunity costs vary with changes in output. Section C extends this discussion to cost–volume–profit analysis. Section D compares and contrasts opportunity costs and accounting costs (which are very different). Section E describes some common methods for cost estimation.

A. Opportunity Costs

When you make a decision, you incur a cost. Nobel Prize–winning economist Ronald Coase noted, "The cost of doing anything consists of the receipts that could have been obtained if that particular decision had not been taken."[1] This notion is called **opportunity cost**—the benefit forgone as a result of choosing one course of action rather than another. Cost is a sacrifice of resources. Using a resource for one purpose prevents its use elsewhere. The return forgone from its use elsewhere is the opportunity cost of its current use. The opportunity cost of a particular decision depends on the other alternatives available.

The alternative actions comprise the *opportunity set*. Before making a decision and calculating opportunity cost, the opportunity set itself must be enumerated. Thus, it is important to remember that opportunity costs can be determined only within the context of a specific decision and only after specifying all the alternative actions. For example, the opportunity set for this Friday night includes the movies, a concert, staying home and studying, staying home and watching television, inviting friends over, and so forth.

The opportunity cost concept focuses managers' attention on the available alternative courses of action. Suppose you are considering three job offers. Job A pays a salary of $100,000, job B pays $102,000, and job C pays $106,000. In addition, you value each job differently in terms of career potential, developing your human capital, and the type of work. Suppose you value these nonpecuniary aspects of the three jobs at $8,000 for A, $5,000 for B, and only $500 for C. The following table summarizes the total value of each job offer. You decide to take job A because it has the highest total pecuniary and nonpecuniary compensation. The opportunity cost of job A is $107,000 (or $102,000 + $5,000), representing the amount forgone by not accepting job B, the next best alternative.

Job Offer	Salary	$ Equivalent of Intangibles	Total Value
A	$100,000	$8,000	$108,000
B	102,000	5,000	107,000
C	106,000	500	106,500

[1]R. Coase, Business Organization and the Accountant, originally published in Accountant, 1938. Reprinted in *L.S.E. Essays in Cost*, ed. J. Buchanan and G. Thirlby (New York University Press, 1981), p. 108.

24 *Chapter 2*

The decision to continue to search for more job offers has an opportunity cost of $108,000 if job offer A expires. If you declined job offer L last week, which had a total value of $109,000, this job offer is no longer in the opportunity set and hence is not an opportunity cost of accepting job A now. Besides jobs A, B, and C, you learn there is a 0.9 probability of receiving job offer D, which has a total value of $110,000. If you wait for job D and you do not get it, you will be forced to work in a job valued at $48,000. Job D has an expected total value of $103,800 (or $110,000 × 0.9 + $48,000 × 0.1). Since job D's opportunity cost of $108,000 (the next best alternative forgone) exceeds its expected value ($103,800), you should reject waiting for job offer D.

1. Characteristics of Opportunity Costs

Opportunity costs are not necessarily the same as payments. The opportunity cost of taking job A included the forgone salary of $102,000 plus the $5,000 of intangibles from job B. The opportunity cost of going to a movie involves both the cash outlay for the ticket and popcorn, and also forgoing spending your time studying or attending a concert. Remember, the opportunity cost of obtaining some good or service is what must be surrendered or forgone in order to get it. By taking job A, you forgo job B at $107,000.

Opportunity costs are forward looking. They are the estimated forgone benefits from actions that could, but *will not,* be undertaken. In contrast, accounting is based on historical costs in general. **Historical costs** are the resources expended for actions actually undertaken. Opportunity cost is based on anticipations; it is necessarily a forward-looking concept. Job offers B, C, and D are part of the opportunity set when you consider job A, but job offer L, which expired, is no longer part of the opportunity set. Your refusal of job L last week is not an opportunity cost of accepting job A now.

Opportunity costs differ from (accounting) expenses. Opportunity cost is the sacrifice of the best alternative for a given action. An (accounting) expense is a cost incurred to generate a revenue. For example, consider an auto dealer who sells a used car for $7,500. Suppose the dealer paid $6,500 for the car and the best alternative use of cars like this one is to sell them at auction for $7,200. The car's opportunity cost in the decision to keep it for resale is $7,200, but in matching expenses to revenues, the accounting expense is $6,500. Financial accounting is concerned with matching expenses to revenues. In decision making, the concern is with estimating the opportunity cost of a proposed decision. We return to the difference between opportunity and accounting costs in section D.

2. Examples of Decisions Based on Opportunity Costs[2]

Several examples illustrate opportunity costs. The first four examples pertain to raw materials and inventories.

Opportunity cost of materials (no other uses)
What is the opportunity cost of materials for a special order if the materials have no other use and a firm has these materials in stock? The firm paid $16,000 for the materials and anticipates no other orders in which it can use these materials. The opportunity cost of these materials is whatever scrap value they may have. If the materials have no alternative use and they have no storage or disposal cost, their opportunity cost is zero. In fact, the opportunity cost is negative if the firm incurs costs for storing the product and if disposal is costly.

Opportunity cost of materials (other uses)
The opportunity cost of materials not yet purchased for a job is the estimated cash outflow necessary to secure their delivery. If the materials are already in stock, their opportunity cost is their highest-valued use elsewhere. If the materials will be used in another order,

---

[2]Some of the examples presented here are drawn from Coase (1938), pp. 10–22.

using them now requires us to replace them in the future. Hence, the opportunity cost is the cost of replacement.

Interest on inventory as an opportunity cost

An automobile manufacturer plans to introduce a new car model. Included in the opportunity cost of the new model are the payments for materials, labor, capital, promotion, and administration. Opportunity cost also contains the interest forgone on the additional inventory of cars and parts the firm carries as part of the normal operations of manufacturing and selling cars. If the average inventory of materials, work in process, and finished cars is $125 million and the market rate of interest for this type of investment is 10 percent, then the opportunity cost of interest on this investment is $12.5 million per year.

The next raw material example introduces the concept of *sunk costs,* expenditures that have already been made and are irrelevant for evaluating future alternatives.

Sunk costs and opportunity costs

A firm paid $15,000 for a coil of stainless steel used in a special order. Twenty percent (or $3,000 of the original cost) of the coil remains. The remaining steel in the coil has no alternative use; a scrap steel dealer is willing to haul it away at no charge. The remaining

| **Managerial Application: Sustainability and Opportunity Costs** | Many large corporations around the world now have sustainability programs that create long-term shareholder value by identifying opportunities and managing risks from economic, environmental, and social developments. For example, in 2013 the catastrophic collapse of the Rana Plaza building in Bangladesh killed more than 1,100 garment workers. This plant produced apparel for some of the world's largest retailers such as H&M, Marks and Spencer, and Zara. Even though the plant was not owned by any of these retailers, they came under intense criticism by the media, governments, and customers for not imposing tighter building inspections of their Bangladesh supplier. Sustainability programs seek to identify, measure, and integrate social, environmental, and economic impacts into corporate strategy and into management decisions to manage those impacts successfully and increase long-run profitability. As such, firms that outsource significant amounts of their products now proactively monitor the workplace safety of their suppliers. Before Nike introduces new footwear, the product design team compares alternative materials in terms of not just cost but also environmental impacts such as energy use, greenhouse gas emissions, water use, land use, and waste and chemical use. By improving the environment, Nike hopes to increase the future demand for its products.

Well-functioning sustainability programs capture the opportunity cost of decisions managers make today on future cash flows of the firm arising from social, environmental, and political processes. For example, Home Depot drops suppliers that violate its workplace standards for safety and child labor. By not doing business with such firms, Home Depot reduces its risk of costly publicity if a supplier has an adverse event. PepsiCo has conservation programs to reduce its water use to minimize future water shortages and scarcity, especially in the arid Middle East and Africa. Because water makes up most of Pepsi's beverages, future water shortages can have a devastating impact on Pepsi's products. In 2013, Pepsi estimated water-flow savings of more than 14 billion liters. Pepsi's water sustainability program views the opportunity cost of not undertaking water conservation programs today to be quite high.

SOURCE: M. Epstein and A. Buhovac, "A New Day for Sustainability," *Strategic Finance* (July 2014) pp. 25–33. www.pepsico.com/Purpose/Environmental-Sustainability/Water |

$3,000 of the original cost is a sunk cost. **Sunk costs** are expenditures incurred in the past that cannot be recovered. The $3,000 is sunk because it has already been incurred and is not recoverable. Because it cannot be recovered, the $3,000 should not influence any decision. In this case, the remaining steel coil has a zero opportunity cost. Sunk costs are irrelevant for future uses of this stainless steel. Suppose the scrap dealer is willing to pay $500 for the remaining coil. Using the remainder in another job now has an opportunity cost of $500.

Remember that sunk costs are irrelevant for decision making unless you are the one who sunk them. However, sunk costs are not irrelevant as a control device. Holding managers responsible for past actions causes them to take more care in future decisions. Suppose $4 million was spent on new software that doesn't work and the firm buys a commercial package to replace it. The manager responsible for the failed software development will be held accountable for the failure and will have incentives to consume more firm resources trying to either fix it or cover up its failure before this knowledge becomes widely known.

The next example applies the opportunity cost concept to evaluating alternatives regarding labor.

Opportunity cost of labor

Suppose a firm's work force cannot be changed because of existing labor agreements. Employees are guaranteed 40 hours of pay per week. For the next three weeks, only 35 hours of work per week per employee exists. What is the cost of taking a special order that will add five hours of work per employee? One is tempted to cost the five hours of labor in the special order at zero because these employees must be paid anyway. But the

| **Managerial Application: The Costs of the Sarbanes–Oxley Act** | Following the accounting scandal at Enron and the demise of Arthur Andersen, the U.S. government enacted the Sarbanes–Oxley Act of 2002, the "Public Company Accounting Reform and Investor Protection Act." This law has many provisions, including the requirement that large public companies and their auditors must report annually that management has "an adequate internal control structure and procedures for financial reporting." This provision, known as section 404 of the act, caused the greatest concern among publicly traded companies.

In a survey of U.S. firms, *CFO* magazine reports that 48 percent of companies will spend at least $500,000 complying with Sarbanes–Oxley, with 52 percent reporting that their compliance has yielded no benefits for their company.

In addition to the direct costs of complying with Sarbanes–Oxley, the act is imposing significant opportunity costs on companies. The CFO of the $5 billion Constellation Energy Group believes that the law makes the "fear of personal liability so great that managers are afraid to take risks on innovation." Some 33 percent of the *CFO*-surveyed companies have delayed or canceled projects so they can comply with the law. Financial executives have less time to make strategic decisions as compliance efforts absorb 10 percent of a CFO's time in 40 percent of the companies. More small, publicly traded companies are going private because the cost of remaining public has increased. This deprives these companies of the benefits of being public, such as access to public equity markets and liquidity for equity investments.

But not everyone has been harmed by Sarbanes–Oxley. The law has been a windfall for auditors, lawyers, and software firms.

SOURCE: A. Nyberg, "Sticker Shock: The True Costs of Sarbanes-Oxley Compliance," *CFO*, September 2003, pp. 51–62. |

question remains: What will these employees do with the five hours if this special order is rejected? If they would do preventive maintenance on the machines or do general maintenance or improve their skills through training, then the opportunity cost of the labor for the special order is not zero but the value of the best forgone alternative use of the employees' time.

Public accounting firms confront this issue. The summer months tend to be low-demand periods relative to year-end. How the firm prices summer (off-peak) audits depends in part on the perceived opportunity cost of the staff's time.

If a firm owns long-lived assets such as buildings and equipment, understanding their opportunity costs involves alternative uses of these assets. The next three examples describe the opportunity costs of capital assets.

Asset depreciation as an opportunity cost

Using assets can affect their value. Suppose a delivery van used four days a week can be sold next year for $34,000. If additional business is taken and the delivery van is used six days a week, its market value next year will be $28,000. Depreciation due to use for the additional business is $6,000 ($34,000 − $28,000). Additional labor for the driver's time, maintenance, gasoline, and oil are required.

The opportunity cost of using an asset is the decline in its value. Accounting depreciation (such as straight-line depreciation) is based on historical costs. Accounting depreciation does not necessarily reflect the opportunity cost of the van (its decline in value from use). However, accounting depreciation can be a reasonably accurate approximation of the decline in the market value of the asset. In any given year, accounting depreciation may not exactly capture the decline in the asset's market value. However, over the asset's economic life, accumulated accounting depreciation equals the decline in value. Holding managers responsible for accounting depreciation commits them to recovering the historical cost of the asset in either additional revenues or cost savings.

Interest on an asset as an opportunity cost

If the asset can be sold, then interest should be included as an opportunity cost. If the asset has no resale value, then obviously no interest is forgone. For example, a local area network and servers are purchased for $100,000. The interest rate is 8 percent. Should interest on the capital tied up in the hardware ($8,000) be included as a cost in the decision to continue to use the system? If the equipment has no market value, then interest is not a cost because the firm is not forgoing selling the hardware and earning interest on the proceeds. If the system can be sold, then the forgone interest on the proceeds is a cost. Chapter 3 presents an expanded discussion of the opportunity cost of a capital investment.

Opportunity cost of excess capacity

Suppose a plant operates at 75 percent capacity. Is the firm forgoing profits on the 25 percent of idle capacity? It is usually optimal to have some "excess" capacity in order to absorb random shocks to normal production, such as machine breakdowns and demand fluctuations, which increase production time and costs. When plants are built, rarely are they expected to run at 100 percent capacity. As plant utilization increases, per-unit costs increase as congestion rises. The opportunity cost of increasing the plant's expected utilization, say from 75 percent to 85 percent of capacity, is the higher production cost imposed on the existing units that currently utilize 75 percent of the capacity.

Consider this illustration. The following table lists the output of a plant in units of production and the average cost per unit. Average costs rise as volume increases because congestion increases. This causes more machine breakdowns, and indirect labor (expediters, material handlers, production schedulers) must be hired to manage the increased

28   *Chapter 2*

congestion. The plant is currently operating at 75 percent capacity (150 units) and incurring average costs of $6.04 per unit.

Units	Capacity	Average Cost
130	65%	$6.00
140	70	6.02
150	75	6.04
160	80	6.06
170	85	6.08
180	90	6.11
190	95	6.15
200	100	6.20

Suppose production increases from 150 units (75 percent capacity) to 170 units (85 percent capacity). Increasing production by an extra 20 units causes the average cost of the base production of 150 units to rise from $6.04 to $6.08, or 4¢ per unit. The opportunity cost of producing 20 more units is not the average cost of $6.08 but the incremental cost of the last 20 units, $6.38 (or $[(170 \times \$6.08) - (150 \times \$6.04)] \div 20$ units). Another way of computing the opportunity cost of the last 20 units is

$$\$6.38 = \$6.08 + (4¢ \times 150) \div 20$$

Or the opportunity cost of producing 20 more units is composed of their average cost ($6.08) plus the cost increase that each of the 20 units imposes on the first 150 units $[(4¢ \times 150) \div 20]$.

The final example describes evaluating the opportunity costs of introducing new products.

Opportunity cost of product line cannibalization

A company that produces tablet computers has 60 percent of a particular market niche. The company plans to introduce a new, high-end, faster tablet with additional features. The major competition for the new tablet is the firm's current high-end tablet. In the first year, management projects sales of the new model to be 20,000 units. Sales of the existing tablet are expected to fall by 7,000 units. Thus, the new tablet "cannibalizes" the old tablet's sales by 7,000 units. Are the forgone profits from the 7,000 units that could have been sold an opportunity cost of introducing the new tablet? It depends on the opportunity set. If management expects competitors to introduce a device that competes with the old tablet, meaning that the company is likely to have lost those units anyway, then the profits forgone on the 7,000 units are not an opportunity cost of introducing the new tablet.

Concept Questions	Q2–1	Define *opportunity cost.*
	Q2–2	What are some characteristics of opportunity costs?
	Q2–3	A firm paid $8,325 last year for some raw material it planned to use in production. When is the $8,325 a good estimate of the opportunity cost of the material?
	Q2–4	Define *sunk cost* and give an example.
	Q2–5	What are avoidable and unavoidable costs? How are they related to opportunity costs?

B. Cost Variation

Managers commonly decide how many units to produce or how much service to provide during a certain time period. Apple must decide how many Apple watches of a particular model to manufacture next quarter. United Airlines must decide whether to fly a 90-passenger jet or a 130-passenger jet between Denver and Palm Springs next month. Making these decisions requires an understanding of how costs change with volume—the topic of this section.

1. Fixed, Marginal, and Average Costs

Cost behavior is defined relative to some activity, such as the number of units produced, hours worked, pounds of ore mined, miles driven, or meals served. Usually, units produced is the measure of activity. For example, consider Figure 2–1, which illustrates the general relation between cost and units produced. Two important points emerge from Figure 2–1. First, even with no units produced, the firm still must incur some costs. The costs incurred when there is no production are called **fixed costs**. If the plant is idle, some costs such as property taxes, insurance, plant management, security, and so on must be incurred to provide production capacity. For example, Intel acquires land and builds a plant to manufacture a specific quantity of microprocessors. It pays annual property taxes of $1.75 million on this land. The $1.75 million expenditure on property taxes is part of the cost Intel pays to have this manufacturing capacity at this plant.

Second, in general the cost curve is not a straight line as output expands, but rather is curvilinear. The particular shape of the curve arises because marginal cost varies with the level of production. **Marginal cost** is the cost of producing one more unit. In Figure 2–1, marginal cost is the slope of a line drawn tangent to the total cost curve. For the first few units, such as to the left of output level *X,* the slope of the tangent is quite steep. The marginal cost for the first few units is high because employees must be hired, suppliers must be found, and marketing channels must be opened. Therefore, the cost of starting operations and producing the first few units may be extremely high. Expanding output beyond the first few units allows the organization to achieve smooth, efficient production techniques. At normal production rates, the marginal cost of making additional units is relatively low. At high levels of output (output level *Y*), additional costs are incurred because of constraints on the use of space, machines, and employees. Machines are more likely to fail when operating at or near capacity. Labor costs increase because employees are paid for overtime. Therefore, the marginal cost of making additional units when operating near capacity is higher than under normal operations.

FIGURE 2-1

Nonlinear cost curve

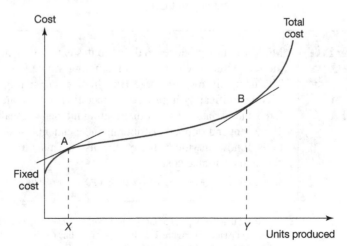

30   *Chapter 2*

FIGURE 2-2

*Average and
marginal cost*

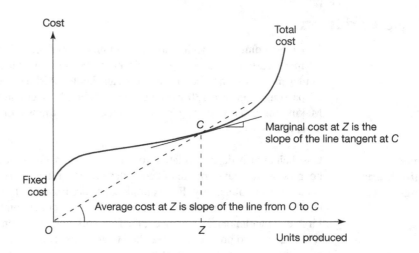

By definition, a fixed cost is not an opportunity cost of the decision to change the level of output. The decision to expand output usually does not affect property insurance premiums. Therefore, property insurance is a fixed cost with respect to volume and is not a cost when deciding to increase output.

The fact that a cost is fixed with respect to volume changes, however, does not mean that it cannot be managed or reduced. A firm can reduce insurance premiums by increasing deductibles or by lowering the risks being insured (installing fire alarms and sprinkler systems). Many fixed costs can be altered in the long run, in the sense that a particular plant can be closed. If a cost is fixed, this does not mean it is a constant and known with certainty. Fixed costs vary over time due to changes in prices. But fixed costs do not vary with changes in the number of units produced.

Another important cost term is **average cost**. Average cost per unit is calculated by dividing total cost by the number of units produced. Average cost is the slope of the line drawn from the origin to the total cost curve and is depicted in Figure 2–2 as the slope of the line from point O through point C.[3] The average cost at output level Z represents the cost *per unit* of producing Z units. For the pattern of costs in Figure 2–2, the average cost per unit is very high at low levels of output but declines as output increases. The average cost per unit only increases as output nears capacity. Notice that at Z units of production, the average cost is larger than the marginal cost. (The slope of OC is steeper than the slope of the tangent at point C.)

Managerial Application: Metro-Goldwyn-Mayer Inc.	MGM Studios produces and distributes entertainment products worldwide, including motion pictures, television programming, home video, interactive media, and music. The company owns a large film library, consisting of approximately 4,000 titles. MGM significantly improved its operating performance after a careful analysis of the fixed and variable costs of distributing movies to local cinemas. It reduced head count 10 percent and stopped distributing independent films through United International Pictures. It now distributes these films itself. This allowed MGM to convert a large fixed cost into a variable cost. SOURCE: L. Calabro, "Everything in Moderation," *CFO*, February 2004, pp. 59–65.

---

[3]Recall that the slope of a line is the ratio of the change in its vertical distance divided by the change in its horizontal distance. In Figure 2–2, the slope of the line OC is the distance CZ divided by the distance OZ. CZ ÷ OZ is the total cost of producing Z units divided by Z units, which is the average cost of producing Z units.

Exercise 2-1

Suppose that a plant making steam boilers has the following costs per month:

Number of Boilers	Total Cost
1	$ 50,000
2	98,000
3	144,000
4	184,000
5	225,000
6	270,000
7	315,000
8	368,000
9	423,000
10	480,000

Required:

 a. What are the marginal and average costs for each level of output?

 b. The plant is currently making and selling eight boilers per month. The company can sell another steam boiler for $53,000. Should the company accept the offer?

Solution:

a. Number of Boilers	Total Cost	Marginal Cost	Average Cost
1	$ 50,000	$50,000	$50,000
2	98,000	48,000	49,000
3	144,000	46,000	48,000
4	184,000	40,000	46,000
5	225,000	41,000	45,000
6	270,000	45,000	45,000
7	315,000	45,000	45,000
8	368,000	53,000	46,000
9	423,000	55,000	47,000
10	480,000	57,000	48,000

 b. The company should reject the offer because the marginal cost of making the ninth boiler is $55,000, whereas the price is only $53,000. The average cost of $47,000 should not be used in this decision.

---

2. Linear Approximations

The cost of changing production levels is not always easy to estimate. Estimating the total cost curve in Figure 2–1 requires knowledge of both fixed cost and how the total costs of facilities, labor, and materials varies as the rate of production increases. Such estimates are difficult to obtain, so managers often approximate these costs. One such approximation assumes the curve is linear instead of curvilinear.

An approximation of total cost in Figure 2–1 using a linear cost curve is displayed in Figure 2–3. In this figure, estimating total cost requires an estimate of the y-axis intercept and the slope of the straight line. The intercept, *FC*, approximates the fixed costs. The slope of the line is the variable cost per unit. **Variable costs** are the additional costs incurred when output is expanded. When Honda expands the production of minivans at a particular

32 *Chapter 2*

FIGURE 2-3

*Linear approximation
of total cost*

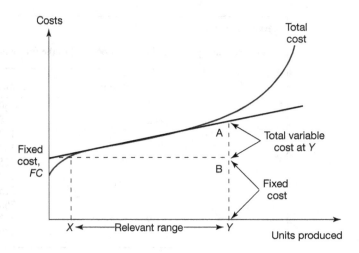

plant from 200 to 250 vans per day, it must buy more parts, hire more employees, use more power, and so forth. All costs that increase when more vans are produced are variable costs.[4]

In Figure 2–3, the straight line is the sum of the fixed and variable cost approximations of total cost. The line is closest to the total cost in the range of normal operations. This range between output levels *X* and *Y* is called the *relevant range*. The **relevant range** encompasses the rates of output for which the sum of fixed and variable costs closely approximates total cost. Because the slopes of the total cost curve and the fixed and variable cost curve are about the same, the variable cost is a close approximation of the marginal cost. In the relevant range, variable cost can be used to estimate the cost of making additional units of output.

Notice that variable cost per unit approximates marginal cost per unit. The slope of the variable cost line is constant as the activity measure increases. Variable cost per unit is usually assumed to be constant. Later chapters relax this assumption. The terms *marginal cost* and *variable cost* are often used interchangeably, but the two are not necessarily the same. Marginal cost refers to the cost of the last unit produced and in most cases varies as volume changes. In some situations, marginal cost per unit does not vary with volume. Then marginal cost (per unit) and variable cost per unit are equal.

The straight-line approximation of total cost can be represented by the following equations:

Total cost = Fixed cost + Variable cost
Total cost = Fixed cost + (Variable cost per unit)(Units produced)
$$TC = FC + VC \times Q$$

where *TC* represents total cost, *FC* represents fixed cost, *VC* is variable cost per unit, and *Q* is the number of units. For example, suppose the fixed cost is $100,000 per month, the variable cost per unit is $3, and 15,000 units are to be manufactured. Total cost is calculated to be $145,000 (or $100,000 + $3 × 15,000 units). The total cost of $145,000 is an estimate of the cost of manufacturing 15,000 units.

---

[4]While most managers understand intuitively the difference between fixed and variable costs, not everyone does. When asked the difference between a fixed cost and a variable cost, one employee replied, "A fixed cost? If it's broke, I fix it and it costs me." See R. Suskind, "Guys Holding Axes and Chainsaws Get to Use Any Name They Like," *The Wall Street Journal*, February 26, 1992, p. B1.

FIGURE 2-4

Step and mixed costs

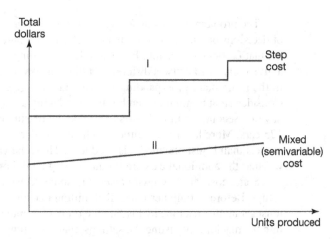

3. Other Cost Behavior Patterns

Some costs vary with output (variable costs) and others do not (fixed costs). Between these two extreme cases are step costs and mixed (semivariable) costs. Each of these is described in turn and illustrated in Figure 2–4.

Step costs

One type of cost behavior involves **step costs**, expenditures fixed over a range of output levels (line I in Figure 2–4). For example, each supervisor can monitor a fixed number of employees. As output expands and the number of supervisors increases with the number of employees, the resulting increases in supervisory personnel expenditures are a step function. Likewise, once the number of transactions a computer system can process is exceeded, a larger machine is required. Expenditures on computers often behave as step costs.

Mixed (semivariable) costs

Many costs cannot be neatly categorized as purely fixed or variable. The cost of electricity used by a firm is a good example. Producing more output requires some additional electricity. But some portion of the electric bill is just for turning on the lights and heating or cooling the plant whether the plant produces 1 unit or 50,000 units. In this case, the cost of electricity is a mixture of fixed and variable costs. **Mixed** or **semivariable costs** are cost categories that cannot be classified as being purely fixed or purely variable (line II in Figure 2–4).

4. Activity Measures

The discussion so far has focused on how total cost varies with changes in output (units produced). Output is the *measure of activity.* Consider a steel mill that makes 1 million tons of two-inch steel plate in one month and 1 million tons of one-inch steel plate in the next month. The cost of the one-inch steel plate will likely be higher because more work is required to roll out the thinner plate. In this factory, costs vary not only with weight of the output but also with its thickness. In general, costs vary based on units produced as well as on the size, weight, and complexity of the product.

In many costing situations, managers choose a single activity measure, such as the total number of toys painted or pounds of toys painted. This activity measure is then assumed to be the primary cost driver. The **cost driver** is that measure of physical activity most highly associated with variations in cost. For example, in the painting department, the quantity of paint used often will be chosen as the cost driver if it has the highest association with total costs in the painting department.

An input measure, such as the quantity of paint used, is often used as a single cost driver to capture the many factors and to simplify the process of estimating total cost. The choice of the activity/volume measure is often critical to the perceived variation of costs. This issue is discussed in greater detail in Chapter 11.

34   *Chapter 2*

The problem with using a single activity measure is that it can be correct for one class of decisions but incorrect for others. Such categorizations indicate how costs vary but only for that particular decision. For example, expanding the volume of an existing product in a given plant will cause a different set of costs to vary than will adding a new product line in the same plant or expanding the volume of a given product by building a new plant. Consider an automobile assembly line producing a single car model. Adding 125 cars per day of a second car model costs more than increasing production of the existing model by 125 cars. More labor is required to schedule, order parts, and store them for two different models than if just one model is produced. Thus, the variable costs of 125 cars depend on whether the additional cars are for an existing model or a new model.

Some costs are fixed with respect to some decisions but not others. Consider machine setups. Before a computer-controlled milling machine can begin milling parts, a technician must set up the machine by loading the proper computer program, loading the correct tools into the machine, adjusting the settings, making a few parts, and checking their tolerances. Once set up, the machine can produce a large number of parts without another machine setup. The cost of the setup is the cost of the technician's time, the material used to check the machine, and the forgone profits of not using the machine while it is being set up. This setup cost is independent of the number of units produced and thus is a fixed cost. However, if the machine produces 1,000 parts per batch, expanding volume from 1,000 parts to 2,000 parts doubles the number of setups and doubles the setup costs. On the other hand, if the plant increases volume to 2,000 parts by doubling batch size, setup costs remain fixed. Therefore, classifying setup costs as being either fixed or variable can be right for some decisions and wrong for others, depending on whether batch sizes change. If some decisions cause batch sizes to change and others do not, then any classification of setup costs as fixed or variable will be wrong for some decisions.

Exercise 2-2

Total cost in the painting department of a toy factory varies not only with the number of toys painted but also with the sizes of the toys, the types of surfaces painted, the kinds of paint applied, and so on.

Paint costs $15 per gallon. To set up the painting machines to paint a part costs $500, which includes cleaning out the old color. Using the paint machine for one hour costs $70, which also includes the labor to operate it.

A particular part with 4,200 pieces in the batch requires 10 gallons of paint and eight hours of paint machine time.

Required:

Calculate the total cost to paint this batch.

Solution:

Using multiple activity bases, the cost of painting this part is calculated as

Setup cost	$ 500
Paint	150
Machine time	560
Total painting cost	$ 1,210

Notice that the cost of painting the parts includes a fixed setup cost of $500, which does not vary with the number of parts painted.

Concept Questions	Q2–6	Define *mixed cost* and give an example.
	Q2–7	Define *step cost* and give an example.
	Q2–8	Define *fixed cost*.
	Q2–9	Define *variable cost*. Is it the same as marginal cost? Explain.

C. Cost-Volume-Profit Analysis

1. Copier Example

Once costs are classified into fixed/variable categories, managers can perform cost–volume–profit analysis. The following example illustrates the essential features of this analysis. Suppose Xerox Corp. has a walk-up copy division that places coin-operated color photocopying machines in public areas such as libraries, bookshops, and supermarkets. Customers pay 25¢ per copy and the store providing the space receives 5¢ per copy. Xerox provides the machine, paper, toner, and service. Machines are serviced every 20,000 copies at an average cost of $200 per service call. Paper and toner cost 4¢ per copy. Xerox's walk-up copy division is charged $150 per month per machine placed (the opportunity cost of the machine). The variable costs per copy are

Paper and toner	$ 0.04
Store owner	0.05
Service ($200 ÷ 20,000)	0.01
Variable costs	$ 0.10

The **contribution margin** is the difference between the price and the variable cost per copy. The contribution margin is the net receipts per copy that are contributed toward covering fixed costs and providing profits. In this example, the contribution margin is calculated as

Price	$ 0.25
Less variable costs	(0.10)
Contribution margin	$ 0.15

Given the contribution margin and monthly fixed costs, the number of copies each machine must sell monthly to recover fixed costs is the ratio of fixed costs to the contribution margin. This quantity of copies is called the **break-even point** and is calculated as

$$\text{Break-even point} = \frac{\text{Fixed costs}}{\text{Contribution margin}} = \frac{\$150}{\$0.15} = 1,000 \text{ copies}$$

In other words, if the copier makes 1,000 copies each month, it produces net receipts (after variable costs) of $150 (or 1,000 × $0.15), which is just enough to recover the fixed costs.

The Xerox copier example illustrates that classifying costs into fixed and variable components provides a simple decision rule as to where to place copiers. If a store is expected to produce (or actually produces) fewer than 1,000 copies per month, a copier should not be located there. The break-even volume provides a useful management tool for where to place machines.

2. Calculating Break-Even and Target Profits

Let us study the cost–volume–profit analysis further. For simplicity, assume that production equals sales (to avoid inventory valuation issues such as the LIFO/FIFO choice). Also assume that the firm produces a single product. Figure 2–5 displays the total cost and revenue of producing various levels of output. The total revenue curve has a decreasing slope beyond some quantity because more unit sales can be achieved only at lower prices. At high prices, volumes are low. As prices fall, volume increases and the slope of the total revenue curve becomes less steep. The total cost curve, also nonlinear, is the same cost curve depicted in Figure 2–1. Break-even occurs when total revenues equal costs. In Figure 2–5, two break-even volumes exist, labeled "Break-even point 1" and "Break-even point 2." The profit-maximizing point of output occurs when marginal revenue equals marginal cost ($MC = MR$). **Marginal revenue** refers to the receipts from the last unit sold. At any point, marginal revenue is the slope of the line just tangent to the total revenue curve.

As described in section B, it is difficult to estimate nonlinear functions. Linear approximations are often used. Figure 2–6 substitutes linear cost and linear revenue approximations for nonlinear curves. Instead of allowing price to vary with quantity, assume a constant price, P. The total revenue function, TR, is then

$$TR = P \times Q$$

where Q is output. If the firm can sell as much as it wants without affecting price, then assuming a linear revenue function, TR, does not distort the analysis. Likewise, total cost is assumed to follow a linear function of the form

$$TC = FC + VC \times Q$$

where FC is the fixed cost and VC is the variable cost per unit. For the moment, ignore income taxes.

FIGURE 2-5

Total cost and revenue curves

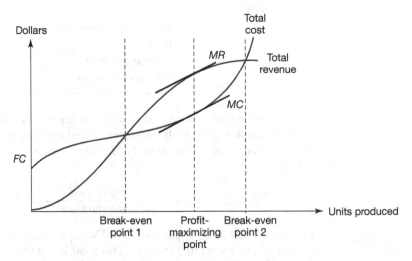

MC: Marginal cost is the slope of the total cost curve.
MR: Marginal revenue is the slope of the total revenue curve.
MC and MR are equal at the profit-maximizing point.

FIGURE 2-6

Linear approximations of cost and revenue curves and cost–volume–profit analysis

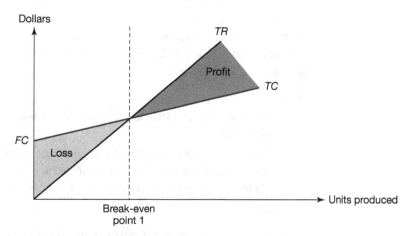

FC: Fixed cost
TR: Total revenue equals a constant price times total output ($P \times Q$)
TC: Total cost equals fixed costs plus the variable cost per unit times output ($FC + VC \times Q$)

Using linear functions allows managers to simplify analyzing how profits vary with output. In particular,

$$\text{Profit} = TR - TC = P \times Q - VC \times Q - FC \qquad (2.1)$$

$$\text{Profit} = (P - VC) \times Q - FC \qquad (2.2)$$

Break-even volume is the number of units sold that just covers fixed and variable costs. To find break-even volume, Q_{BE}, set equation (2.2) equal to zero and solve for Q_{BE}.

$$\text{Profit} = 0 = (P - VC) \times Q_{BE} - FC \qquad (2.3)$$

$$Q_{BE} = \frac{FC}{P - VC} = \frac{FC}{\text{Contribution margin}} = \frac{FC}{CM}$$

Price minus variable costs ($P - VC$), the contribution margin per unit (CM), is the profit per unit sold that can be used to cover fixed costs (FC). Contribution margin is important because it measures the incremental net receipts of selling one more unit. Refer to Figure 2–6. If units produced is less than the break-even point, a loss occurs. If output exceeds break-even quantity, a profit is earned.

Note that the estimated break-even point, Q_{BE}, will not exactly correspond to the "real" break-even point, where total revenue equals total cost. The discrepancy occurs because *TR* and *TC* do not represent exactly total revenue and total costs, respectively.

Suppose we want to make a target after-tax profit of Profit_T and the income tax rate is *t*. We can compute the number of units needed to make an after-tax profit by modifying equation (2.2) and solving for Q_T, target output:

$$\text{Profit}_t = [Q_T \times (P - VC) - FC] \times (1 - t) \qquad (2.4)$$

$$Q_T = \frac{\text{Profit}_t}{(1 - t) \times CM} + \frac{FC}{CM} \qquad (2.5)$$

Instead of memorizing this formula, it is better to start with equation (2.1) or (2.2) and make the necessary modifications to solve the particular problem at hand. Exercise 2–3 illustrates how to modify the formula.

Exercise 2-3

DGA Tile manufactures ceramic flooring tiles. DGA's annual fixed costs are $740,000. The variable cost of each tile is $0.25, and tiles are sold for $6.50. DGA has a combined state and federal tax rate of 45 percent.

Required:

   a. How many tiles does DGA need to make and sell each year to earn an after-tax profit of $85,000?

   b. DGA must pay 10 percent of before-tax profits as a royalty payment to its founder. Now how many tiles must DGA make and sell to generate $85,000 after taxes? (Assume the royalty payment is not a tax-deductible expense.)

Solution:

   a. Let Q denote the number of tiles made and sold that generates $85,000 of after-tax profit. Given the preceding data, we can write

$$(\$6.50\,Q - \$0.25\,Q - \$740,000)(1 - 0.45) = \$85,000$$
$$(6.25\,Q - \$740,000) \times 0.55 = \$85,000$$

Solving for Q:

$$\$3.4375\,Q = \$85,000 + \$740,000 \times 0.55$$
$$Q = 143,127 \text{ tiles}$$

Therefore, to generate an after-tax profit of $85,000, about 143,000 tiles must be sold.

   b. The formula with the royalty payment, R, is

$$(\$6.25\,Q - \$740,000) \times 0.55 - R = \$85,000$$

where

$$R = (\$6.25\,Q - \$740,000) \times 0.10$$

Substituting R into the earlier equation,

$$(\$6.25\,Q - \$740,000)(0.55 - 0.10) = \$85,000$$
$$Q = 148,622$$

The following exercise illustrates another use of contribution margins. It involves choosing the most profitable product to produce when capacity is constrained.

Exercise 2-4

The Ralston Company produces three shirts. It only has 200 machine hours per day to produce shirts and has the following cost and production information:

	Basic	Deluxe	Super
Selling price	$7.50	$9	$13
Variable cost of production	$6.00	$7	$7
Machine hours to complete one shirt	0.6	2	3
Demand per day (shirts)	50	50	50

Ralston has fixed costs of $75 per day. How many shirts of each type should be produced?

Solution:

The opportunity cost of producing one type of shirt arises from not using those machine hours to produce another type of shirt. In this problem, to maximize firm profits in light of a capacity constraint, we must produce those products with the highest contribution margin *per unit of capacity*. First calculate the contribution margin per shirt and then convert this to the contribution margin per machine hour.

	Basic	Deluxe	Super
Selling price	$7.50	$9	$13
Variable cost of production	$6.00	$7	$7
Contribution margin per shirt	$1.50	$2	$6
Hours to complete one shirt	÷ 0.6	÷ 2	÷ 3
Contribution margin per machine hour	$2.50	$1	$2
Demand per day (shirts)	50	50	50
Production schedule (shirts)	50	10	50
× Hours to complete one shirt	0.6	2	3
Hours consumed	30	20	150

To maximize profits, Ralston should produce the shirt(s) with the highest contribution margin per unit of scarce resource (machine hours). This is an application of the opportunity cost principle. Even though super has the highest contribution margin per unit, basic has the highest contribution margin per machine hour. Therefore, to maximize profits, produce 50 units of basic, which will consume 30 hours (or 50 units × 0.6 hours per unit). Next, produce 50 units of super, which consumes 150 hours of capacity. This leaves 20 hours of capacity to be used to produce 10 units of deluxe.

The preceding analysis suggests producing the market demand for basic and super but not for deluxe. Fixed costs never enter the analysis. By definition, fixed costs are fixed and cannot be relevant to the decision, which depends only on selling price, variable cost, and the capacity constraint.[*]

[*]One artificial aspect of this exercise is that the quantity demanded and the price are taken as constants. Clearly, at lower prices, more shirts will be demanded. Fixed demand is assumed to simplify the problem.

The Ralston Company example illustrates a very simple situation in which there is only one constraint. If there are multiple constraints, linear programming is a useful technique for identifying the profit-maximizing mix of products. The next section describes some of the shortcomings of cost–volume–profit analysis.

3. Limitations of Cost-Volume-Profit Analysis

Exercise 2–5

Using equation (2.2), find the output, Q, that maximizes profits.

Solution:

Profits are maximized by setting output to infinity. That is, equation (2.2) cannot be used to maximize profits.

40   *Chapter 2*

<table>
<tr><td>

Managerial Application: Break-Even Analysis of Carbon-Dioxide Emissions of Electric Car Batteries

</td><td>

To manufacture a green, battery-powered automobile generates 30,000 pounds of carbon-dioxide emissions, compared to 14,000 pounds of carbon-dioxide emissions to produce a conventional gasoline-powered car. Much of the difference is due to the additional carbon dioxide needed to mine and produce lithium batteries. Each mile driven by the green car generates six ounces of carbon dioxide to produce the electricity to recharge the batteries, whereas an equivalent size gasoline-powered car generates twelve ounces per mile. Based on these data, one can calculate the number of miles a green car owner must drive before the battery-powered car produces less carbon-dioxide emissions than a conventional car. First, convert pounds of carbon dioxide to ounces of carbon dioxide:

$$30,000 \text{ pounds} = 16 \times 30,000 = 480,000 \text{ ounces}$$

$$14,000 \text{ pounds} = 16 \text{ ounces per pound} \times 14,000 \text{ pounds} = 224,000 \text{ ounces}$$

Next, calculate the break-even number of miles (M) where carbon dioxide is the same for the electric car and a conventional car.

$$480,000 + 6M = 224,000 + 12M$$

Solving for M:

$$256,000 = 6M$$

$$M = 42,667 \text{ miles}$$

If, over the life of the green car, the owner drives less than about 43,000 miles, the green car generates more carbon dioxide than a conventional car.

SOURCE: B. Lomberg, "Green Cars Have a Dirty Little Secret," *Wall Street Journal* (March 11, 2013) p. A15.

</td></tr>
</table>

Exercise 2–5 illustrates that cost–volume–profit analysis is not useful for choosing the profit-maximizing output quantity when both revenues and costs are assumed linear. Given this conclusion, what good is it? Cost–volume–profit analysis offers a useful place to start analyzing business problems. It gives managers an ability to do sensitivity analysis and ask simple what-if questions. And, as we saw in the copier example, break-even analysis can prove useful for certain types of decisions. However, several limitations of cost–volume–profit analysis exist:

1. Price and variable cost per unit must not vary with volume.
2. Cost–volume–profit is a single-period analysis. All revenues and costs occur in the same time period.
3. Cost–volume–profit analysis assumes a single-product firm. All fixed costs are incurred to produce a single product. If the firm produces multiple products, and fixed costs such as property taxes are incurred to produce multiple products, then the break-even point or target profit for any one of the products depends on the volume of the other products. With multiple products and common fixed costs, it is not meaningful to discuss the break-even point for just one product.

Although these limitations are important, cost–volume–profit analysis forces managers to understand how costs and revenues vary with changes in output.

Notice in the earlier Xerox copier example that the assumptions underlying break-even analysis are not violated:

- Price does not vary with quantity.
- Variable cost per unit does not vary with quantity.
- Fixed costs are known.
- There is a single product (copies).
- All output is sold.

4. Multiple Products

As we saw earlier, one limitation of cost–volume–profit analysis is that it applies only to firms making a single product. One way to overcome this limitation is to assume a constant output mix of bundles with fixed proportions of the multiple products. Then a break-even or a target profit number of bundles can be calculated.

For example, suppose a winery produces two types of wine: merlot and chablis. The following table summarizes prices and variable costs of the winery, which has fixed costs of $500,000 per year.

	Merlot	*Chablis*
Price per case	$ 30	$ 20
Variable cost per case	20	15
Contribution margin per case	$ 10	$ 5

For every case of merlot produced, three cases of chablis are produced. Define a wine *bundle* to consist of four cases of which one is merlot and three are chablis. Each wine bundle has revenues of $90 ($1 \times \$30 + 3 \times \$20$), variable costs of $65 ($1 \times \$20 + 3 \times \$15$), and a contribution margin of $25 ($1 \times \$10 + 3 \times \$5$). The number of *bundles* required to break even is:

$$\text{Break-even number of bundles} = \frac{\text{Fixed costs}}{\text{Contribution margin}} = \frac{\$500,000}{\$25} = 20,000 \text{ bundles}$$

Twenty thousand bundles needed to break even translate into 20,000 cases of merlot and 60,000 cases of chablis to break even. Hence, if a firm produces a variety of products in fixed proportions, then break-even analysis can be conducted by creating a standard bundle of products.

Exercise 2-6

Using the preceding winery example, how many cases of merlot and chablis must be produced and sold to make an after-tax profit of $100,000 if the tax rate is 20 percent?

Solution:

The after-tax profit is calculated from the following equation:

$$\text{After-tax profit} = (1 - \text{Tax rate}) \times (\text{Revenues} - \text{Variable cost} - \text{Fixed costs})$$
$$\$100,000 = (1 - 20\%) \times (\$90\,B - \$65\,B - \$500,000)$$

where B is the number of bundles.

continued

Solving for *B* yields:

$$\$100,000 = .8 \times (\$25B - \$500,000)$$
$$\$100,000 = \$20B - \$400,000$$
$$B = \$500,000/\$20$$
$$B = 25,000 \text{ bundles}$$

In other words, 25,000 cases of merlot and 75,000 cases (3 × 25,000) of chablis must be sold to generate $100,000 after taxes. At these production levels, $100,000 of after-tax profit is generated as demonstrated by the following income statement:

Revenue—Merlot	25,000 × $30	$750,000
Revenue—Chablis	75,000 × $20	1,500,000
Total revenue		$2,250,000
Less: Variable costs		
Merlot	25,000 × $20	$500,000
Chablis	75,000 × $15	1,125,000
Fixed costs		500,000
Total costs		$2,125,000
Income before taxes		$ 125,000
Taxes (20%)		25,000
Net income after taxes		$ 100,000

Concept Questions	Q2–10	What are the underlying assumptions in a cost–volume–profit analysis?
	Q2–11	What are the benefits and limitations of cost–volume–profit analysis?

5. Operating Leverage

Separating costs into fixed and variable components is useful for calculating break-even points and for pricing decisions, and for deciding to take new orders. Understanding a product's fixed and variable costs is also useful for strategic reasons.

The higher a firm's fixed costs, the higher its operating leverage, which is the ratio of fixed costs to total costs. Operating leverage measures the sensitivity of profits to changes in sales. The higher the operating leverage, the greater the firm's risk. In firms with high operating leverage, small percentage changes in sales lead to large percentage changes in net cash flows (and profits). Therefore, firms with high operating leverage have greater variability in cash flows and hence greater risk than firms with a lower ratio of fixed costs to total costs. High operating leverage firms face greater risk of failing if volumes stay low because they are unable to continue to generate enough cash to pay their high fixed costs.

To illustrate the importance of operating leverage, consider the illustration in Table 2–1. Two companies, HiLev and LoLev, each sell 10,000 units of an identical product for $8 per unit. At that level of production, both companies have identical total costs of $70,000, and both companies are making $10,000 in profits. Since three-sevenths of LoLev's costs are fixed, whereas five-sevenths of HiLev's costs are fixed, HiLev has more operating leverage.

TABLE 2-1   **Operating Leverage**
(Production and Sales Are 10,000 Units)

		LoLev	HiLev
Revenue	10,000 units @ $8	$80,000	$80,000
Variable costs	10,000 units @ $4	40,000	
	10,000 units @ $2		20,000
Fixed costs		30,000	50,000
Net income		$10,000	$10,000

Suppose volume falls 25 percent. Table 2–2 indicates the impact on net income. In LoLev, net income falls to zero; in HiLev, a loss of $5,000 results. Table 2–3 illustrates that when volume increases 25 percent, HiLev has a greater increase in profits than LoLev. Operating leverage amplifies the earnings impact of a given percentage change in volume.

TABLE 2-2   **Operating Leverage**
(Production and Sales Are 7,500 Units)

		LoLev	HiLev
Revenue	7,500 units @ $8	$60,000	$60,000
Variable costs	7,500 units @ $4	30,000	
	7,500 units @ $2		15,000
Fixed costs		30,000	50,000
Net income (loss)		$ 0	$ (5,000)

TABLE 2-3   **Operating Leverage**
(Production and Sales Are 12,500 Units)

		LoLev	HiLev
Revenue	12,500 units @ $8	$ 100,000	$ 100,000
Variable costs	12,500 units @ $4	50,000	
	12,500 units @ $2		25,000
Fixed costs		30,000	50,000
Net income		$ 20,000	$ 25,000

Firms with low variable costs per unit can sustain larger short-term price cuts when faced with increased competition. For example, a firm selling a product for $10 per unit that has a variable cost of $7 per unit can cut the price to just above $7 (for short periods of time) and still cover the variable costs of each unit. If that same firm has variable costs of $8 per unit, a price cut to below $8 causes a cash drain with each incremental unit. Knowledge of a competitor's cost structure is valuable strategic information in designing marketing campaigns. Estimating a firm's riskiness also requires knowledge of operating leverage.

Exercise 2-7

Two Internet retailers have the following data:

(millions)	BuyEverything.com	SportsWhere.com
Sales	$120	$186
Variable costs	70	150
Fixed costs	40	24
Net income	$ 10	$ 12

Required:

a. Which retailer has more operating leverage?

b. Suppose the sales of each retailer double. Which one's net income shows the greatest percentage increase?

c. Calculate the percentage change in each retailer's net income if sales fall 50 percent.

Solution:

a. BuyEverything.com's operating leverage (as measured by the ratio of fixed to total cost) is .36 ($40/$110), and SportsWhere.com's operating leverage is .14 ($24/$174). Hence, BuyEverything.com has more operating leverage.

b. The following table calculates how net income changes with a doubling of sales:

(millions)	BuyEverything.com	SportsWhere.com
Sales	$240	$372
Variable costs	140	300
Fixed costs	40	24
Net income	$ 60	$ 48
Prior net income	$ 10	$ 12
% change	500%*	300%†

*($60 − $10)/$10
†($48 − $12)/$12

   BuyEverything.com (which has more operating leverage from part *a*) shows the greatest percentage increase in net income.

c. The following table calculates how net income changes when sales fall 50 percent:

(millions)	BuyEverything.com	SportsWhere.com
Sales	$60	$93
Variable costs	35	75
Fixed costs	40	24
Net income	($15)	($ 6)
Prior net income	$10	$12
% change	−250%*	−150%†

*(−$15 − $10)/$10
†(−$6 − $12)/$12

   BuyEverything.com (which has more operating leverage from part *a*) shows the greatest percentage decrease in net income.

D. Opportunity Costs versus Accounting Costs

The theoretically correct way to evaluate choices requires estimating opportunity costs. Estimating opportunity costs requires the decision maker to formulate all possible actions (the opportunity set) and the forgone net receipts from each of those alternatives so that the highest net cash flows from the set of actions not undertaken can be calculated. This yields the opportunity cost of the selected action. Such an exercise requires a special study for every decision, which is a time-consuming and costly activity. And after completing the study, the opportunity cost changes as the opportunity set changes. It is little wonder that managers devise shortcut approximations to estimating opportunity costs. Accounting-based costs are such a shortcut.

Accounting systems record "costs" after making the decisions. Accounting systems track asset conversions. When the firm acquires assets such as raw material, accountants record them in monetary terms (historical cost valuation). As the raw inputs are converted into intermediate products, accountants value the intermediate products at the historical costs of the raw inputs converted into the intermediate products. The in-process, partially completed units flowing through departments are recorded in the accounts at historical costs. If an employee who is paid $20 per hour completes an intermediate product in two hours, the accounting system increases the cost of the intermediate product by $40. Completion and sale of the manufactured unit causes the historical costs attached to it to be transferred from the inventory accounts to the expense account "cost of goods sold." Accounting costs are not forward-looking opportunity costs; they look backward at the historical cost of the resources consumed to produce the product. Accounting systems produce accounting costs, not opportunity costs. However, accounting costs often provide a reasonable approximation of opportunity costs. Over short periods of time, prices and costs do not change very much. Thus, accounting costs can be reasonably accurate estimates of opportunity costs of producing the same products again.

Besides providing data for decision making, internal accounting systems also provide data for controlling the behavior of people in organizations, as well as the data for external financial reporting. The resources consumed to produce this textbook might differ from the opportunity cost of a new textbook. But the historical cost of this book provides information to senior managers as to how well the persons responsible for producing this book discharged their duties. Valuing the ending inventory of books, calculating taxes payable, and computing net income require the historical cost of this textbook.

Managerial Application: New Economy Firms and High Operating Leverage	High-technology firms incur large fixed costs and relatively low variable costs to produce intellectual property such as software and Web sites. This combination creates high operating leverage that causes these firms to be very risky. In good times, they are flying high. In weak times, there is very little they can do to trim expenses. Inktomi Corp. was a high-flying software company. It spent $10 million developing research engines and software to manage Web content. Once those fixed costs were incurred, each additional sale was almost pure profit. The president remarked, "You have no cost of goods. We don't even ship a physical diskette anymore. Next to the federal government, this is the only business that's allowed to print money." All this has changed. Software development costs rose and sales nosedived, causing Inktomi to report a very large loss. Enormous fixed costs were required to research, develop, design, test, and market software. Intense competition and rapid obsolescence required high levels of spending each year. The result was a dramatic reversal of fortune leading to big swings in profits, stock prices, and hiring when sales sagged. Inktomi did not survive the Internet bubble and was sold to Yahoo! in 2002. SOURCE: B. McClure, "Operating Leverage Captures Relationships," *www.investopedia.com*, Dec 28, 2006

Cost systems do not focus on opportunity costs, nor can they, because opportunity costs depend on the particular decision being contemplated. Accounting systems cannot anticipate all future decisions. For example, suppose you purchased land on a busy commercial street last month, paying $1 million. If you open a fast-food restaurant on this land, you estimate it will be worth $1.6 million. If, on the other hand, you open a gas station, its value is estimated at $1.7 million. Using the land for a gas station costs you $1.6 million in terms of the next best forgone opportunity (the fast-food restaurant). The $1 million historical cost of the land, even though only one month old, is not the opportunity cost. Thus, the term *cost* can refer to accounting cost (historical amounts) or to opportunity cost (the amount forgone by some decision), two very different concepts. In some cases, the user's meaning is obvious, but it is always important to question whether the term *cost* means opportunity cost or accounting cost.

1. Period versus Product Costs

To further understand how accounting costs differ from opportunity costs, we distinguish between product costs and period costs. **Product costs** include all those accounting costs incurred to manufacture a product. Product costs are inventoried and expensed only when the product is sold. **Period costs** are those costs that are expensed in the period in which they are incurred. They include all nonmanufacturing accounting costs incurred to sell the product. For example, administration, distribution, warehousing, selling, and advertising expenditures are period costs. Research and development is a period cost. Period costs are not part of the product's cost included in inventory valuation.

Product costs include both fixed and variable manufacturing components. Likewise, period costs, the costs of distributing and selling the product, contain both fixed and variable components. Fixed period costs include salespersons' salaries, advertising, and marketing costs. Examples of variable period costs include distribution costs and sales commissions.

Accounting systems, even those used for internal purposes, distinguish between product and period costs. In most situations, unit cost figures refer to *product* costs excluding all *period* costs. Suppose that the unit manufacturing cost of a particular cell phone is $23. Selling and distributing this product costs an additional $4 per unit. This $4 period cost includes both fixed and variable period costs. The total cost of manufacturing and selling each unit is $27. Many firms refer to the $23 product cost as a *unit manufacturing cost* (UMC). For decision-making purposes, both period ($4) and product ($23) costs must be considered, so it is important to remember that a UMC usually excludes period costs.

Period costs and product costs are historical costs. They are not opportunity costs. However, to the extent that the future looks a lot like the past, these historical costs can be useful predictors of opportunity costs.

2. Direct Costs, Overhead Costs, and Opportunity Costs

The accounting concepts of direct costs versus overhead costs also illustrate the difference between opportunity and accounting costs. Direct costs and overhead costs form the core of this book, to which we will return in later chapters, particularly Chapters 9 through 13. But it is useful to introduce the terms now.

Direct costs of a product or service are those items that are easily traced to the product or service. Direct labor and direct material costs are direct costs. An employee producing a product is classified as direct labor. If this employee is idled by a machine breakdown, that idle time is classified as indirect labor. Indirect materials include those used in maintaining and testing machines as well as those lost in the machine during a breakdown. **Overhead** includes indirect labor and indirect material costs as well as other types of general manufacturing costs that cannot be directly traced, or are not worth tracing, to units being produced. Examples include the cost of the purchasing department; factory property taxes, maintenance, depreciation, insurance, and security guards; and some engineering services. *Indirect cost* is another term for *overhead.*

Direct costs are usually variable. For example, to produce more copies of this book requires additional paper and ink (direct materials) and additional time by the person running the printing press (direct labor). But direct costs can be fixed. For example, the costs associated with a machine (depreciation, electricity, and routine maintenance) dedicated to one product are direct costs of that product and are largely fixed. Or, if the firm has a material supply contract to purchase a fixed amount of noninventoriable input, then this direct material is a fixed cost over the life of the contract. For example, if a steel mill has a long-run supply contract to purchase a fixed amount of natural gas per year over the life of the contract, this direct material (natural gas) is largely a fixed cost. If the company can sell what it does not use, the natural gas is a variable cost. Overhead costs contain both fixed costs and variable costs.

The distinction between overhead and direct costs can be difficult to determine at times. For example, should the 10¢ worth of glue used in each bookcase containing $9 of wood and $30 of direct labor be treated as a direct or an indirect cost? To apply a cost–benefit criterion, we must decide what decisions will be affected if the glue is classified as direct versus indirect. In most cases, small dollar amounts of direct costs are treated as overhead because the costs of tracking and reporting them separately exceed the benefits. Never assume that all direct costs are variable and all overhead costs are fixed costs.

The following chart summarizes the relations among accounting cost terminology:

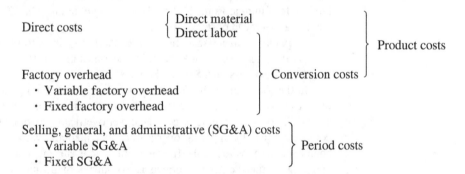

Product costs consist of direct material, direct labor, and overhead. The term conversion costs refers to direct labor and factory overhead. Period costs consist of selling, general, and administrative costs.

By definition, overhead costs cannot be directly traced to products. Instead, they must be *allocated* to products. The most common allocation bases are direct labor hours, direct material, machine hours, and direct labor dollars. Managers usually choose the allocation base that most closely approximates the factors that cause overhead to vary in the long run.

To illustrate the distinction between accounting and opportunity costs with respect to overheads, consider the following example: All expenses in a department containing 10 machines are allocated to the machines in the department. All 10 machines in the department are identical. Utilities, supervision, labor, depreciation, and engineering support are assigned to this department. The total cost divided by machine hours gives an hourly rate for allocating this department's costs to jobs. For example, suppose the total annual cost of this department is $525,000. Each machine normally operates 35 hours per week, 50 weeks per year, for 1,750 (or 35 × 50) hours per year. So the 10 machines normally operate 17,500 hours per year. This department thus has an overhead rate of $30 per machine hour ($525,000 ÷ 17,500 hours). If a particular job takes nine hours on the machines in this

48 Chapter 2

Historical Application: Railroads Develop Unit Cost Data	In the 1870s, the railroads developed detailed and highly accurate cost estimates of hauling one ton of freight one mile. This has come to be known as the *cost per ton mile*. The calculation first involved separating the accounting records into four groups of accounts: costs that did not vary with the volume of traffic (general superintendence), costs that varied with the volume of freight but not the length of the haul (stations and agents), costs that varied with the number of trains run (conductors, engineers, and fuel), and interest on the capital investment. Each of these four costs was converted into a unit rate, and each freight shipment was costed based on its weight and how many miles it was carried.
	These cost data allowed senior managers to monitor costs and to evaluate the performance of the managers responsible for the various segments of track. By studying how the unit cost data varied over time and across various branches of the railroad, managers could evaluate the performance of the parts of the railroad and its managers.
	SOURCE: A. Chandler, *The Visible Hand* (Cambridge, MA: Harvard University Press, 1977), pp. 116–19.

department, it is allocated $270 of "cost" (9 × $30). But did the firm actually incur $270 to process this job in the department? We don't know. The machine-hour rate ($30/hour) is an average accounting cost. It is a mixture of both fixed and variable costs, and it gives a false impression of variability. It does not tell us whether we made money on this job. In bidding for future jobs, the $30 per hour does not tell us what competitors will bid or what additional overhead costs will be incurred.

As plant volumes rise, congestion costs rise. Queues form. More expediters are hired to track inventory. Machine scheduling becomes more difficult. Marginal overhead costs may be more or less than $30 per hour.

In the long run, if the firm cannot charge prices (and generate sales) that cover all overhead costs (including depreciation of the assets), it will not be able to replace its assets. Of course, charging prices that cover overhead may price the firm out of the market completely. But by applying overhead costs (fixed and variable costs) to products, management can see whether the firm is viable under current conditions. The other reason for applying overhead costs to products is to control organizational problems. If the machine-hour rate is $30 this year and rises to $35 next year, senior managers are alerted that something has changed. By reporting the higher overhead cost, managers will investigate the reason for the change and presumably take corrective action.

Concept Questions	Q2–12	Why are opportunity costs costly to estimate?
	Q2–13	Define *direct costs*.
	Q2–14	Define *overhead costs*. How are they allocated?
	Q2–15	What are *period costs*?

E. Cost Estimation

Now that the important concepts of opportunity cost and how opportunity costs vary with changes in output have been introduced, they must be put into practice. Costs must be estimated, either from the accounting records or by some other method. This section describes two approaches to cost estimation: account classification and motion and time studies.

1. Account Classification

The simplest and the most common method of estimating fixed and variable costs is *account classification*. Each account in the accounting system is classified as being either fixed or variable. The sum of all the variable cost accounts, divided by a measure of volume (e.g., units produced), yields variable cost *per unit*. Likewise, the sum of all the accounts classified as fixed costs yields an estimate of the total fixed costs. While this method is quick and simple, it is not very precise. Its accuracy depends on the knowledge and intuition of the person classifying the accounts as fixed or variable.

2. Motion and Time Studies

In motion and time studies, industrial engineers estimate how much time a particular task or work activity requires with the goal of determining the optimal work method. Motion studies involve the systematic analysis of work methods considering the raw materials, the design of the product or process, the process or order of work, the tools, and the activity of each step. Besides estimating how long a particular activity should take, industrial engineers are often able to redesign the product or process to reduce the required time. Time studies employ a wide variety of techniques for determining the duration required for a particular activity under certain standard conditions. Work sampling (one type of time study) involves selecting a large number of observations taken at random intervals and observing how long employees take to perform various components of the job. It tells management how employees are currently spending their time, not how efficiently they could be spending their time. No benchmarks exist to judge performance. Work sampling tends to institutionalize existing inefficiencies. Motion and time studies are often expensive in terms of engineering time used in the studies. They also suffer from potential bias because of employees' incentives to underperform during the study period to set lower quotas.

Most of the problems presented in this and other books furnish the necessary cost data to solve the problem being posed. However, deriving the cost data is often more difficult than making a decision after securing the information. Besides engineering cost estimation techniques, accounting records are often the most prevalent source of cost data. Chapter 9 describes how accounting develops product costs.

Concept Question	Q2–16	What are motion and time studies? What are their objectives?

F. Summary

This chapter emphasizes that decision making requires knowledge of opportunity costs, or the benefits forgone from actions precluded by the alternative selected. Opportunity costs can be determined only within a specific decision context by specifying all the alternative actions. While opportunity cost is the theoretically correct concept to use in decision making, it can be costly to estimate. Special studies are required to identify the alternative actions and forecast their likely consequences. Accounting costs often provide useful and less costly approximations for opportunity costs. However, costs reported by accounting systems are not opportunity costs. Opportunity costs are forward-looking and are usually not recorded by accounting systems.

Accounting costs measure the monetary resources expended for a particular activity. They provide a useful database to begin the process of estimating opportunity costs. Accounting costs also serve the important function of influencing the behavior of the firms' employees and managers. The accounting system reports the accounting cost of making the sofa this month and what the cost was last month to make the same sofa. Senior managers can then assess the performance of sofa

50   *Chapter 2*

production, providing incentives for the sofa-producing managers to pay attention to costs. If the accounting cost of the sofa is $208 this month, this number is not the opportunity cost of making the sofa. But if the same type of sofa had an accounting cost of $150 last month, something has happened that senior management will want to investigate. Chapter 4 explores these organizational control issues in more detail.

Managers must decide how many units of each product to manufacture. This decision also requires opportunity costs. One method of estimating opportunity costs for these decisions assumes that total costs are linear; hence, total costs are the fixed costs and variable costs per unit. A linear cost curve is also useful for cost–volume–profit analyses. These analyses focus managers' attention on how costs and profits vary with some volume measure. However, such analyses require assumptions to be made. These include assuming a single-period, single-product plant and linear cost and revenue curves.

When someone asks what something costs, the first reaction should be to find out for what purpose the cost number is to be used. If the cost number will be used for decision making, an opportunity cost must be generated for that decision context, which requires the decision maker to specify all the relevant alternative actions. If the number is to be used for financial reporting or taxes, a different cost number will be produced. If the cost number is being used to control behavior within the firm, probably a different number will be used. Cost numbers can vary significantly according to the purpose for which they are being produced.[5]

Appendix: Costs and the Pricing Decision

One of the most important decisions managers make involves pricing the firm's goods and services. Clearly, the cost of producing the good or service is a crucial variable entering the pricing decision. This appendix discusses how managers use cost information in setting prices. There are two cases to consider: (1) the firm is a "price taker" and (2) the firm has "market power."

Price Takers

Some markets are very competitive. With many buyers and sellers of the same product, no single producer or consumer can influence the market price. For example, consider wheat farmers. With thousands of wheat farmers, no single farmer can affect the price of wheat by altering the amount of wheat the farmer produces. In this case, wheat farmers are price takers who do not set the price. They do, however, use cost information when deciding to grow (or not to grow) wheat.

While price takers understand that the price is given, they still must decide how much, if any, of the product to produce. Here cost data are extremely important. Suppose a wheat farmer leases land and equipment for $2,200,000 per year and expects to produce 1 million bushels of wheat. The variable cost per bushel is $1.60 and the market price of wheat is expected to be $3.90 per bushel when the wheat is harvested. The farmer expects to make $100,000 of profit (1 million bushels × ($3.90 − $1.60) − $2,200,000). If this is adequate compensation for the farmer's time and risk, she will lease the land and equipment and plant the wheat. So in this case, before the farmer decides to lease the land and plant wheat, she uses cost data to determine if the production decision (growing wheat) is worthwhile.

Suppose the land and equipment have been leased (and paid), but before the wheat is planted and the variable costs have been incurred, the price of wheat is expected to be only $3.65. Taking into account the fixed costs that have already been incurred, the farmer now expects to lose $150,000 (1 million bushels × ($3.65 − $1.60) − $2,200,000). However, the lease payments are sunk. The farmer still generates $2,050,000 of contribution margin, but not enough to recoup her fixed costs. She will still go ahead and plant the wheat. Not doing so will cost her the entire fixed cost of $2.2 million. If she thinks wheat prices next year will remain at $3.65 per bushel, she will not lease the land and equipment again.

---

[5] It has long been recognized that no single cost concept can serve all purposes. J. Clark, writing in *Studies in the Economics of Overhead Costs* (Chicago: University of Chicago Press, 1923), p. 175, states, "We may start with the general proposition that the terminology of costs is in a state of much confusion and that it is impossible to solve this confusion by discovering and adopting the one correct usage, because there is no one correct usage, usage being governed by the varying needs of varying business situations and problems."

To summarize, price takers use cost data to determine whether to undertake production, not to set prices. Fixed costs that have not yet been incurred are relevant in this production decision. Once incurred, the fixed costs are irrelevant in making production decisions.

Market Power

A more complicated pricing situation arises when producers have market power. Firms have market power if perfect substitutes do not exist for their products. This means that they can raise prices without losing all their customers to competitors. For instance, although Colgate and Crest compete directly, many customers do not view these toothpaste brands as perfect substitutes. Each company can raise their price and some consumers will not switch to the other toothpaste. But with higher prices, more customers will defect to competitors. This is not the situation with price takers. If a wheat farmer were to ask for a price above the prevailing market price, no buyers would pay this price because they can purchase identical wheat at a lower price.

When firms have market power, managers must decide not only whether to produce but also what price to charge. The next example illustrates how managers use cost data in the pricing decision.

Consider a tennis racket company with a patent for a unique, high-performance tennis racket. The number of rackets sold depends on the price charged for the racket. At low prices, more rackets can be sold than at higher prices. After extensive study of competitors' prices for high-performance rackets, management expects the relation between price and quantity of rackets sold to be as depicted in Table 2–4. For example, at a price of $1,050 per racket, only 500 are sold, but if the price is dropped to $100 per racket, 10,000 can be sold.

The cost of producing the rackets consists of annual fixed costs of $1.9 million and variable costs of $100 per racket. The fixed costs include all fixed marketing, production, and administration expenses, and the variable costs include all variable production and distribution expenses. Thus, total annual costs, *TC,* can be expressed as:

$$TC = \$1,900,000 + \$100Q \text{ (where } Q \text{ is the number of rackets)}$$

Notice that with this linear cost function, marginal cost (the cost of the last racket) and variable cost are both $100.

Given the data in Table 2–4 and the total cost curve, management can determine the profit-maximizing price to charge for tennis rackets. Table 2–5 provides the calculations.

As Table 2–5 shows, 500 rackets will be sold when the price per racket is $1,050, thereby producing total revenues of $525,000 ($1,050 × 500), total cost of $1,950,000 ($1,900,000 + $100 × 500), and thus a loss of $1,425,000. Clearly, this is not the right price to charge. By calculating profits at all the other price-quantity combinations, we see that profits are maximized at $600,000 when price is set at $600 per racket and 5,000 rackets are sold. Total costs are $2.4 million ($1,900,000 + $100 × 5,000). Notice that profits are *not* maximized where revenues are maximized. Maximum revenues occur at a price-quantity combination of $550 per racket and 5,500 rackets, which is a lower-price–higher-quantity combination than the profit-maximizing combination.

TABLE 2-4 The Relation between the Price per Racket and the Quantity of Rackets Sold at That Price

Price per Racket	Number of Rackets	Price per Racket	Number of Rackets
$1,050	500	$550	5,500
1,000	1,000	500	6,000
950	1,500	450	6,500
900	2,000	400	7,000
850	2,500	350	7,500
800	3,000	300	8,000
750	3,500	250	8,500
700	4,000	200	9,000
650	4,500	150	9,500
600	5,000	100	10,000

TABLE 2-5   **Determining the Profit-Maximizing Price-Quantity Relation**

Price per Racket	Number of Rackets	Total Revenue	Total Cost	Total Profit (Loss)
$1,050	500	$ 525,000	$1,950,000	$(1,425,000)
1,000	1,000	1,000,000	2,000,000	(1,000,000)
950	1,500	1,425,000	2,050,000	(625,000)
900	2,000	1,800,000	2,100,000	(300,000)
850	2,500	2,125,000	2,150,000	(25,000)
800	3,000	2,400,000	2,200,000	200,000
750	3,500	2,625,000	2,250,000	375,000
700	4,000	2,800,000	2,300,000	500,000
650	4,500	2,925,000	2,350,000	575,000
600	5,000	3,000,000	2,400,000	600,000
550	5,500	3,025,000	2,450,000	575,000
500	6,000	3,000,000	2,500,000	500,000
450	6,500	2,925,000	2,550,000	375,000
400	7,000	2,800,000	2,600,000	200,000
350	7,500	2,625,000	2,650,000	(25,000)
300	8,000	2,400,000	2,700,000	(300,000)
250	8,500	2,125,000	2,750,000	(625,000)
200	9,000	1,800,000	2,800,000	(1,000,000)
150	9,500	1,425,000	2,850,000	(1,425,000)
100	10,000	1,000,000	2,900,000	(1,900,000)

Now let's study more closely how fixed and variable costs enter the profit-maximizing pricing decision. We will examine two types of cost changes: an increase in fixed costs and an increase in variable costs.

Increase in fixed costs

Table 2–6 reflects a rise in fixed costs from $1.9 million to $2.4 million, or a $500,000 increase. Suppose that the $2.4 million of fixed costs have not been incurred yet. Will the $500,000 increase in fixed costs change the pricing decision?

In Table 2–6, we see that a change in fixed costs does *not* alter the profit-maximizing pricing decision. Managers still set the price at $600 and expect to sell 5,000 rackets. In general, fixed costs do not enter the pricing decision. Fixed costs only determine whether the firm produces at all. If the contribution margin at the profit-maximizing price-quantity combination fails to cover the fixed costs (and the fixed costs have not yet been paid), the firm should not produce. For example, if fixed costs increased to $2.55 million, the profit-maximizing price-quantity combination would still be $600 and 5,000 rackets. But now the firm loses $50,000 at this price-quantity combination and it should not produce any rackets.

Increase in variable costs

We now consider how variable costs affect the pricing decision. Fixed costs are $1.9 million. If the variable cost of rackets increases from $100 to $200 per racket, the profit-maximizing price rises from $600 to $650 per racket and fewer rackets are sold (4,500 instead of 5,000). See Table 2–7. Notice that only $50 of the $100 variable cost increase is passed on to consumers. If the price were raised to $700 to recover all the $100 variable cost increase, even fewer rackets would be sold and the revenue decline would be greater than the cost increase.

Tables 2–5 to 2–7 illustrate a central point from economics: Only variable cost (which equals marginal cost in our linear cost function) affects the pricing decision. Fixed costs do not affect the pricing decision. Fixed costs only determine whether the firm should produce the product. Economics texts demonstrate that the profit-maximizing price is determined where marginal (variable) cost equals marginal revenue.

TABLE 2-6   Determining the Profit-Maximizing Price-Quantity Relation: Fixed Costs Increased by $500,000

Price per Racket	Number of Rackets	Total Revenue	Total Cost	Total Profit (Loss)
$1,050	500	$525,000	$2,450,000	$(1,925,000)
1,000	1,000	1,000,000	2,500,000	(1,500,000)
950	1,500	1,425,000	2,550,000	(1,125,000)
900	2,000	1,800,000	2,600,000	(800,000)
850	2,500	2,125,000	2,650,000	(525,000)
800	3,000	2,400,000	2,700,000	(300,000)
750	3,500	2,625,000	2,750,000	(125,000)
700	4,000	2,800,000	2,800,000	0
650	4,500	2,925,000	2,850,000	75,000
600	5,000	3,000,000	2,900,000	100,000
550	5,500	3,025,000	2,950,000	75,000
500	6,000	3,000,000	3,000,000	0
450	6,500	2,925,000	3,050,000	(125,000)
400	7,000	2,800,000	3,100,000	(300,000)
350	7,500	2,625,000	3,150,000	(525,000)
300	8,000	2,400,000	3,200,000	(800,000)
250	8,500	2,125,000	3,250,000	(1,125,000)
200	9,000	1,800,000	3,200,000	(1,500,000)
150	9,500	1,425,000	3,350,000	(1,925,000)
100	10,000	1,000,000	3,400,000	(2,400,000)

TABLE 2-7   Determining the Profit-Maximizing Price-Quantity Relation: Variable Costs Increased by $100 per Racket

Price per Racket	Number of Rackets	Total Revenue	Total Cost	Total Profit (Loss)
$1,050	500	$525,000	$2,000,000	$(1,475,000)
1,000	1,000	1,000,000	2,100,000	(1,100,000)
950	1,500	1,425,000	2,200,000	(775,000)
900	2,000	1,800,000	2,300,000	(500,000)
850	2,500	2,125,000	2,400,000	(275,000)
800	3,000	2,400,000	2,500,000	(100,000)
750	3,500	2,625,000	2,600,000	25,000
700	4,000	2,800,000	2,700,000	100,000
650	4,500	2,925,000	2,800,000	125,000
600	5,000	3,000,000	2,900,000	100,000
550	5,500	3,025,000	3,000,000	25,000
500	6,000	3,000,000	3,100,000	(100,000)
450	6,500	2,925,000	3,200,000	(275,000)
400	7,000	2,800,000	3,300,000	(500,000)
350	7,500	2,625,000	3,400,000	(775,000)
300	8,000	2,400,000	3,500,000	(1,100,000)
250	8,500	2,125,000	3,600,000	(1,475,000)
200	9,000	1,800,000	3,700,000	(1,900,000)
150	9,500	1,425,000	3,800,000	(2,375,000)
100	10,000	1,000,000	3,900,000	(2,900,000)

54   *Chapter 2*

Cost-Plus Pricing   A common pricing method used by firms is *cost-plus pricing*. Firms that use this technique calculate average total cost and mark up the cost to yield the selling price. Or,

$$\text{Selling price} = \text{Cost} + (\text{Markup percentage} \times \text{Cost})$$

To solve for the selling price, managers begin by calculating a *unit cost:*

$$\text{Unit cost} = \text{Variable cost} + (\text{Fixed costs/Unit sales})$$

Using our tennis racket example and 5,000 rackets,

$$\text{Unit cost} = \$100 + (\$1,900,000/5,000 \text{ rackets}) = \$480$$

Managers using a markup of 25 percent would set the price as:

$$\text{Selling price} = \$480 + (25 \text{ percent} \times \$480) = \$600$$

In this example, the formula yields the same price as our profit-maximizing price-quantity combination from Table 2–5. However, we started with the profit-maximizing quantity and markup. So by construction, we had to end up with the profit-maximizing price.

Suppose that fixed costs increase to $2 million and variable costs decrease to $80. Managers still expect to sell 5,000 rackets. Unit costs remain at $480 ($80 + $2,000,000/5,000). If managers maintain the same 25 percent markup, they will keep the price at $600. But this is no longer the profit-maximizing price. Variable costs have fallen, so managers should lower the price to $590 and sell 5,100 rackets.[6]

Profit-maximizing pricing considers only variable (marginal) costs and depends on the price sensitivity of customers. Cost-plus pricing appears to ignore both of these considerations. The cost-plus price marks up average total cost (both fixed and variable cost) and seems to ignore the demand for the product. Just because managers target a 25 percent markup on average cost does not mean that customers will necessarily buy the product in the required quantities at the implied price.

Firms that consistently use bad pricing policies find themselves earning lower profits than they could with better pricing techniques and may even go out of business. If cost-plus pricing is so unsound, why is it so widely used? One explanation is that managers implicitly consider market demand in choosing the markup and unit sales in calculating the unit cost. If managers know that they face little competition, more units can be sold and higher markups will be chosen than when facing greater competition. Conceptually, there is always some target volume and markup that produces the profit-maximizing price.

The idea that managers choose markups and unit volumes based on market power when they use cost-plus price is supported empirically. Consider the price markups by a typical grocery store employing cost-plus pricing. One experienced grocery store manager noted that "price sensitivity is the primary consideration in setting margins."[7] Staple products such as bread, hamburger, milk, and soup are relatively price sensitive and carry low margins (markups of under 10 percent above cost). Products with high margins (markups as high as 50 percent or more) tend to be those where consumers are less price sensitive, such as spices, seasonal fresh fruit, and nonprescription drugs.

| **Concept Question** | Q2–17 | How do fixed costs enter the pricing decision? |

---

[6]To derive this new price-quantity combination, note that the price-quantity combinations in Table 2–4 are based on the following formula: Price = $1,100 − 0.1 × Quantity. This equation is used to calculate price-quantity combinations in 100-racket increments.

[7]J. Pappas and M. Hirschey, *Managerial Economics*, 6th ed. (Chicago: Dryden Press, 1990).

Self-Study Problems

Self-Study Problem 1: Exclusive Billiards

In each month, Exclusive Billiards produces between 4 and 10 pool tables. The plant operates one 40-hour shift to produce up to seven tables. Producing more than seven tables requires the craftsmen to work overtime. Overtime work is paid at a higher hourly wage. The plant can add overtime hours and produce up to 10 tables per month. The following table contains the total cost of producing between 4 and 10 pool tables.

Pool Tables	Total Cost
4	$62,800
5	66,000
6	69,200
7	72,400
8	75,800
9	79,200
10	82,600

Required:

a. Prepare a table computing the average cost per pool table for 4 to 10 tables.

b. Estimate Exclusive Billiards' fixed costs per month.

c. Suppose Exclusive Billiards sells its tables for $13,200 each. How many tables must it sell to break even?

d. Next month, Exclusive Billiards has orders for eight tables. Another order for two tables is received. What is the absolute lowest price Exclusive Billiards should accept for the two additional tables?

Solution:

a. Average cost is calculated in the following table:

Tables	Total Cost	Variable Cost	Average Cost
4	$62,800	—	$15,700
5	66,000	$3,200	13,200
6	69,200	3,200	11,533
7	72,400	3,200	10,343
8	75,800	3,400	9,475
9	79,200	3,400	8,800
10	82,600	3,400	8,260

b. Since the variable cost of five to seven pool tables is $3,200, it appears reasonable to assume the first four pool tables also have variable costs equal to $3,200. Hence, we can estimate fixed cost as:

$$FC = TC - VC$$
$$= \$62,800 - 4 \times \$3,200$$
$$= \$50,000$$

56   *Chapter 2*

    c. Variable cost is $3,200 if seven or fewer tables are produced. For seven or fewer tables, the break-even point occurs where

$$(\$13,200 - \$3,200)Q - \$50,000 = 0$$

or

$$\frac{\$50,000}{\$10,000} = \text{tables}$$

    d. The lowest price for two additional tables $= 2 \times \$3,400$

$$= \$6,800$$

Self-Study Problem 2:   Sandler Company

Sandler Company produces circuit boards for various products. Before being shipped to customers, each board is tested to make sure it meets the customers' specifications. Sandler produces 6,400 boards and scraps approximately 10 percent of all boards because of defects. The remaining 5,760 boards are sold for $124,800. Currently, material cost is $42,000. The manager has two options for buying more expensive material to decrease the percentage of bad boards produced. The first option is to buy material for $44,000 that would result in 7 percent being scrapped. The second option is to buy material for $54,000 that would result in only 1 percent being scrapped. The firm can sell as many "good" boards as produced. Production capacity, not demand, is limiting the number of units sold each month.

    Evaluate the two proposals for reducing the defect rates, and recommend which one should be accepted.

Solution:

To begin, notice that the selling price of a board is $21.67 (or $124,800 ÷ 5,760 boards). Under the current situation in which the firm has a 10 percent defect rate, the current margin is $82,800, calculated as

	Current Situation: 10% Defects
Number of boards	5,760
Revenues	$124,800
Cost of raw materials	42,000
Margin	$ 82,800

Sandler currently sells 5,760 boards. A 7 percent defect rate would yield (6,400 × 93%), or 5,952 boards. At a 1 percent defect rate (6,400 × 99%), 6,336 good boards would be produced. The margins on 7 percent and 1 percent defect rates are as follows:

	7% Defects	1% Defects
Number of boards	5,952	6,336
Revenues	$128,960	137,280
Cost of raw materials	44,000	54,000
Margin	$ 84,960	$ 83,280

The profit-maximizing decision is to spend $44,000 on material, resulting in a 7 percent defect rate and an increase in the margin to $84,960. Pushing the defect rate down to 1 percent improves the margin over the status quo but not over the 7 percent defect rate option.

Self-Study Problem 3:   Fast Oil Franchise

Mike Hurst earns $10 per hour as assistant manager at a pet store in the mall. He can work as many hours as he likes but would never consider working more than 72 hours per week. In his will, Mike's Uncle Paul, western New York's oil-change king, leaves him the Jefferson Road Fast Oil Franchise. In an effort to boost its franchising campaign, the Fast Oil Co. has guaranteed that any franchise can be sold back to the parent company for $150,000. Because nobody is willing to offer a higher price for the Jefferson Road franchise, Mike is considering exercising this option.

As part of the franchise agreement, a Fast Oil franchisee must keep the business open 72 hours per week. Furthermore, the franchisee must lease all facilities and equipment on an annual basis, as well as buy all supplies from the parent corporation. The parent company also requires that all franchises be capable of continually operating at full capacity. In the case of the Jefferson Road franchise, this requirement entails having two oil-change technicians and one oil-change manager at the facility at all times.

Fast Oil franchises offer only one service, oil change and lube, at one price, $22.95. Facilities and equipment are leased at $50,000 per year. Materials are sold to franchisees at the following prices: oil at $0.75 per quart, filters at $1 each, and lubrication material at $1 per 16 ounces. Each oil change and lube requires five quarts of oil, one filter, and four ounces of lubrication materials. Oil-change technicians are paid $8 per hour; managers earn $10 per hour. On average, an oil change and lube require one man-hour of work.

According to reliable studies, the number of customers at any given franchise is solely contingent upon the volume of drive-by traffic. On average, one out of every 1,723 cars that drive by a Fast Oil will stop in for an oil change. The Henrietta Chamber of Commerce knowledgeably states that 289,464 cars per week drive by the Jefferson Road franchise at a constant rate during its hours of business. If he keeps the franchise, Mike will work there 72 hours a week as the oil change manager. His sole compensation will be the profits of the business. This will be his only job. If he sells the franchise, Mike will invest the proceeds in Treasury bills that yield 7 percent per annum, with a time to maturity of one year.

Mike lives in a tax-free world and all cash flows are risk free. Assume a one-year time horizon, and assume exactly 52 weeks per year.

Required:

  a. How many oil changes is the Jefferson Road franchise expected to perform in a year? Assuming that Mike keeps the franchise and ignoring opportunity costs of Mike's time and the interest on the proceeds from selling the franchise, what is the annual break-even point (in oil changes) for the franchise?

  b. Define Mike's alternatives. If opportunity costs excluded in (a) are considered, calculate his break-even point (in number of oil changes).

  c. If opportunity costs mentioned in (a) are *not* considered, calculate Mike's profit/loss. What would it be if opportunity costs were considered? What alternative should Mike choose?

Solution:

  a. Given that 289,464 cars pass by weekly and one out of every 1,723 will stop in for an oil change and lube, the franchise is expected to perform 289,464/1,723 × 52 = 8,736 oil changes per year. The rest of the solution requires identification of the fixed and variable components of the franchise's costs.

   The most obvious fixed cost is the annual lease cost of $50,000 per year. Since employee pay does not vary with output, labor costs are fixed. Employees must be paid simply for being at work, and the quantity of labor required is defined by the franchise agreement. (The time required to perform an oil change is relevant only as a capacity constraint. Because there are 216 man-hours per week, 52 weeks per year, and each oil change requires one man-hour, total capacity for the facility is 11,232 changes per year.) Mike will work as oil-change manager, so the labor cost will apply only to the two oil-change technicians (2 technicians × $8/hour × 72 hours/week × 52 weeks per year = $59,904 per year).

   The only variable costs are materials costs. Cost per oil change is the most logical unit to consider, and one year is the obvious time horizon for consideration.

Variable Costs per Oil Change

Oil costs:	
$0.75/quart × 5 quarts	$3.75
Lubrication costs:	
$1/pound × 4/16	0.25
Oil filter	1.00
	$5.00

The price of an oil change is $22.95. The accompanying table summarizes the break-even analysis:

Fixed costs (annual)		
Lease	$50,000	
Technicians	59,904	
Total fixed costs		$109,904
÷ **Contribution margin** (per unit)		
Price	$ 22.95	
Variable cost	5.00	
Contribution margin per unit		$ 17.95
Break-even (in oil changes)		6,123

b. Opportunity costs are defined as "the benefits forgone from actions that are precluded by the alternative selected." To assess the opportunity costs of a particular action, the set of mutually exclusive opportunities must be considered. Mike faces two choices:

- Quit his present job, work as oil-change manager, and keep the profits of the franchise.
- Keep his present job, sell the franchise to the parent company, and invest the proceeds in Treasury bills.

If Mike keeps the franchise, the following benefits are forgone:

- Income from the pet store job and value of free time given up. Mike earns $10 per hour. Therefore, the annual opportunity cost of the time he gives up to work at the oil-change franchise is $10 × 72 × 52 = $37,440 per year.
- Income lost from not selling the franchise and investing in Treasury bills. At 7 percent per year, $150,000 would provide income of $10,500.

The total opportunity cost of keeping the franchise is:

Opportunity cost of Mike's time	$37,440
Investment proceeds from sale of franchise	10,500
	$47,940

This cost should be considered a fixed cost, bringing break-even volume to 8,794 oil changes [($109,904 + $47,940) ÷ $17.95].

c. Ignoring Mike's opportunity costs, annual fixed costs for the business are covered at the 6,123rd oil change. The franchise "profit," therefore, is the contribution margin of all additional oil changes done during the year. For Mike, the profit is (8,736 − 6,123) × $17.95 = $46,907. Since $46,907 is far more than Mike could earn at the pet store, he might be tempted to keep and operate the oil-change franchise. However, when opportunity costs are considered, it would be better for Mike to sell the franchise back to the parent company. Since his opportunity costs are $47,940, Mike would in reality lose $1,033 by keeping the franchise.

This analysis ignores a number of additional factors that Mike should consider before making a final decision:

- How much growth is likely to occur in the oil-change business?
- What is the likelihood of losing the pet store job?
- Is it likely that technological or market changes will reduce the value of the franchise?
- How do the alternatives differ in risk?
- Does Mike like working in the pet store or would he prefer managing the oil-change franchise?

Problems

P 2–1: Darien Industries

Darien Industries operates a cafeteria for its employees. The operation of the cafeteria requires fixed costs of $4,700 per month and variable costs of 40 percent of sales. Cafeteria sales are currently averaging $12,000 per month.

Darien has an opportunity to replace the cafeteria with vending machines. Gross customer spending at the vending machines is estimated to be 40 percent greater than current sales because the machines are available at all hours. By replacing the cafeteria with vending machines, Darien would receive 16 percent of the gross customer spending and avoid all cafeteria costs. How much does monthly operating income change if Darien Industries replaces the cafeteria with vending machines?

P 2–2: Negative Opportunity Costs

Can opportunity costs be negative? Give an example.

P 2–3: NPR

In its radio fund-raising campaign, National Public Radio (NPR) stated, "On-air radio membership campaigns are the most cost-effective means we have for raising the funds necessary to bring you the type of programming you expect." NPR is commercial-free, member-supported radio. Most of its operating funds come from private individuals, corporations, and foundations. Twice a year, it interrupts its regularly scheduled programming for fund-raising pledge campaigns where listeners are encouraged to call in and make pledges.

Critically evaluate the passage quoted above.

P 2–4: Silky Smooth Lotions

Silky Smooth lotions come in three sizes: 4, 8, and 12 ounces. The following table summarizes the selling prices and variable costs per case of each lotion size.

Per Case	4 Ounce	8 Ounce	12 Ounce
Price	$36.00	$66.00	$72.00
Variable cost	13.00	24.50	27.00

Fixed costs are $771,000. Current production and sales are 2,000 cases of 4-ounce bottles; 4,000 cases of 8-ounce bottles; and 1,000 cases of 12-ounce bottles. Silky Smooth typically sells the three lotion sizes in fixed proportions as represented by the preceding sales amounts.

Required:

How many cases of 4-, 8-, and 12-ounce lotion bottles must be produced and sold for Silky Smooth to break even, assuming that the three sizes are sold in fixed proportions?

60   *Chapter 2*

P 2–5: J.P. Max Department Stores

J.P. Max is a department store carrying a large and varied stock of merchandise. Management is considering leasing part of its floor space for $72 per square foot per year to an outside jewelry company that would sell merchandise. Two areas currently in use are being considered: home appliances (1,000 square feet) and televisions (1,200 square feet). These departments had annual profits of $64,000 for appliances and $82,000 for televisions after allocated fixed occupancy costs of $7 per square foot were deducted. Allocated fixed occupancy costs include property taxes, mortgage interest, insurance, and exterior maintenance for the department store.

Required:

Considering all the relevant factors, which department should be leased and why?

P 2–6: Vintage Cellars

Vintage Cellars manufactures a 1,000-bottle wine storage system that maintains optimum temperature (55–57 °F) and humidity (50–80 percent). The system has a backup battery for power failures and can store red and white wines at different temperatures. The following table depicts how average cost varies with the number of units manufactured and sold (per month):

Quantity	Average Cost
1	$12,000
2	10,000
3	8,600
4	7,700
5	7,100
6	7,100
7	7,350
8	7,850
9	8,600
10	9,600

Required:

a. Prepare a table that computes the total cost and marginal cost for each quantity between 1 and 10 units.

b. What is the relation between average cost and marginal cost?

c. What is the opportunity cost of producing one more unit if the company is currently producing and selling four units?

d. Vintage Cellars sells the units for $9,000 each. This price does not vary with the number of units sold. How many units should Vintage manufacture and sell each month?

P 2–7: ETB

ETB plans to manufacture a slim bamboo hard case for the Apple iPad, which will be sold for $65. ETB estimates that it can produce and sell between 3,000 and 5,000 bamboo cases a month. The following data summarize ETB's cost structure at various output (sales) levels:

Production (Units)	3,000	3,500	4,500	5,000
Variable manufacturing cost	$36,000	$35,000	$36,000	$60,000
Fixed manufacturing cost	$60,000	$60,000	$60,000	$60,000
Variable selling and admin cost	$26,100	$28,000	$31,500	$35,000
Fixed selling and admin cost	$40,000	$40,000	$40,000	$40,000

Required:

    a. What monthly production (sales) level minimizes the average cost of the bamboo iPad case?

    b. How many bamboo iPad cases should ETB produce monthly?

P 2–8: Taylor Chemicals

Taylor Chemicals produces a particular chemical at a fixed cost of $1,000 per day. The following table displays how marginal cost varies with output (in cases):

Quantity (Cases)	Marginal Cost
1	$500
2	400
3	325
4	275
5	325
6	400
7	500
8	625
9	775
10	950

Required:

    a. Given the preceding data, construct a table that reports total cost and average cost at various output levels from 1 to 10 cases.

    b. At what quantity is average cost minimized?

    c. Does marginal cost always intersect average cost at minimum average cost? Why?

P 2–9: Emrich Processing

Emrich Processing is a small custom stainless steel parts processor. Customers send new and used stainless steel parts to Emrich for cleaning in various acid baths to remove small imperfections or films on the surface. These parts are used in a variety of applications, ranging from nuclear reactors to chemical and medical applications. Depending on the foreign substance to be removed, Emrich chooses the acid bath mixture and process.

Such chemical cleaning operations require highly skilled technicians to handle the dangerous acids. Environmental Protection Agency (EPA) and Occupational Safety and Health Administration (OSHA) regulations are closely followed. Once the part is treated in the proper chemical bath using other chemicals, a benign waste solution results that can be disposed of via the city sewer system.

On May 12, Emrich ordered a 50-gallon drum of a specialty acid known as GX-100 for use in a May 15 job. It used 25 of the 50 gallons in the drum. The 50 gallons cost $1,000. GX-100 has a shelf life of 30 days after the drum is opened before it becomes unstable and must be discarded. Because of the hazardous nature of GX-100 and the other chemicals Emrich uses, Emrich works closely with Environ Disposal, a company specializing in the disposal of hazardous wastes. At the time of ordering the GX-100, Emrich anticipated no other orders in the May–June time period that could use the remaining 25 gallons of GX-100. Knowing it would have 25 gallons remaining, it built $1,000 into the cost of the job to cover the cost of the GX-100 plus an additional $400 to cover the cost of having Environ dispose of the remaining 25 gallons.

On June 1, a customer called and asked for a price bid for a rush job to be completed on June 5. This job will use 25 gallons of GX-100. Emrich is preparing to bid on this order. What cost amount for the GX-100 must be considered in preparing the bid? Justify your answer.

62   *Chapter 2*

P 2–10:   Verdi Opera or Madonna?

You won a free ticket to see Verdi's *Aida* opera. The ticket has no resale value, but since you enjoy Verdi operas, you would be willing to pay $30 for the ticket had you not received it for free. Madonna is performing on the same night. There is absolutely nothing else you can do that night other than either attending the Verdi opera or the Madonna concert. Tickets to the Madonna concert cost $160. On any given day, you would be willing to pay up to $200 to see Madonna because you are such a big fan. Assume there are no other costs of seeing either the Verdi opera or Madonna. What is the opportunity cost of attending the Verdi opera?

P 2–11:   Dod Electronics

Dod Electronics manufactures various RFID (radio-frequency identification) chips for medical device companies. The RFID chips track the location and movement of medical personnel. A non-medical device company, Xtron Systems, has approached Dod Electronics for a one-time special order of 10,000 RFID chips. The RFID chip that Xtron is seeking to purchase is virtually identical to Dod's existing RFID chip model FQ4503. The Dod manufacturing cell that produces model FQ4503 currently is producing 60,000 FQ4503 chips for medical customers and has excess capacity to run the 10,000 special order without disrupting Dod's regular production/delivery schedule. Xtron will purchase the chips for $38 per chip. If Dod accepts this special order, assume that it will have NO impact on the pricing of Dod's existing FQ4503 contracts/customers. Dod's average cost of producing its current level of 60,000 RFID chips is $35 per chip. Management does not know precisely what it will cost to produce the extra 10,000 chips for Xtron.

Required:

a.   Management is very confident that the average cost of FQ4503 chips is falling at their current production level of 60,000. Should Dod accept Xtron's offer to purchase the 10,000 chips for $38 per chip? Explain the logic supporting your answer.

b.   Management is very confident that the average cost of FQ4503 chips is rising at their current production level of 60,000. Should Dod accept Xtron's offer to purchase the 10,000 chips for $38 per chip? Explain the logic supporting your answer.

P 2–12:   Napoli Pizzeria

Gino Potestio, owner of Napoli Pizzeria, is evaluating leasing an espresso/cappuccino machine. A number of patrons have inquired about espresso and cappuccino beverages. Napoli currently does not offer these beverages. Gino believes adding these beverages will increase the demand for his pizzas. A good espresso/cappuccino machine can be leased for $300 month. Each espresso/cappuccino will sell for $3 and the coffee and milk will average $1 per serving. No additional labor cost is needed because the restaurant staff has enough idle time to prepare and serve the espresso/cappuccino. Gino estimates that the machine will add about $75 of additional pizza profits per month.

Required:

a.   How many espresso/cappuccino beverages must Napoli sell to break even?

b.   Gino doesn't want to offer espresso/cappuccino beverages unless he makes at least $1,000 per month after taxes including the additional sales of pizzas from adding espresso/cappuccino beverages. Napoli's income tax rate is 35 percent. How many servings of espresso/cappuccino must Gino sell to meet his after tax profit goal?

P 2–13:   JLT Systems

JLT Systems sells and installs a firewall program to protect mobile apps from hacking an e-tailer's servers. Each sale and installation requires JLT to incur a variable cost to sell and install the JLT firewall. JLT has a linear cost structure meaning that JLT has a fixed cost each month and a variable cost per sale and installation that does not vary with the number of sales and installs. At 200 sales and installs per month, JLT's average cost is $2,700 per sale and install. JLT incurs fixed costs of $400,000 per month.

Required:

a. What is JLT's variable cost per sale and install?

b. JLT Systems sets the price for its firewall software at the market price of $2,000 per sales and installation. Being a small competitor in this market, JLT is a price taker, and varying the number of JLT sales and installs does not affect the market price of $2,000. JLT Systems wants to show an after-tax profit of $18,000 per month and has an income tax rate of 40 percent. How many sales and installs per month does JLT need to make to achieve its after-tax profit goals?

c. Instead of being a price taker as in part b, now assume that JLT faces the following demand schedule.

Quantity	Price
250	$2,100
275	$2,050
300	$2,000
325	$1,950
350	$1,900
375	$1,850
400	$1,800
425	$1,750
450	$1,700
475	$1,650
500	$1,600
525	$1,550
550	$1,500

(JLT's demand curve is represented by the equation: $P = 2600 - 2Q$)

What is JLT Systems' profit maximizing number of sales and installs of its firewall software per month?

P 2–14: Volume and Profits

Assuming the firm sells everything it produces and assuming that variable cost per unit does not change with volume, total profits are higher as volume increases because fixed costs are spread over more units.

Required:

a. True or false?

b. Explain your answer in part (*a*).

P 2–15: American Cinema

American Cinema shows first-run movies. It pays the company distributing the movies a fixed fee of $1,000 per week plus a percentage of the gross box office receipts. In the first two weeks a movie is released, the theater pays the fixed fee of $1,000 per week plus 90 percent of gross box office receipts to the distributor. If the theater keeps the movie for weeks 3 and 4, the theater pays the distributor $1,000 per week plus 80 percent of its gross box office receipts received during those two weeks. American Cinema charges $6.50 per ticket for all movies, including those shown for two weeks and those shown for four weeks.

American Cinema must decide what movies to show and for how many weeks to show each movie (either two weeks only or four weeks) before the movie is released. For most movies, the audience demand is higher in the first two weeks than in the next two weeks.

American Cinema is evaluating two similar comedies. The first one, *Paris Is for Lovers*, is scheduled for release on October 1. The second comedy, *I Do*, is scheduled for release on October 14. American Cinema has decided to rent *Paris Is for Lovers* but must decide whether to run it for four weeks or to run it for two weeks and then replace it with *I Do*. Based on all the information about the stars in the movie, production costs, and prerelease publicity, management expects the two movies will have the same demand in the first two weeks and will have the same (lower) demand in weeks 3 and 4.

Required:

a. The only movie being released on October 14 is *I Do*. How should management go about deciding whether to rent *Paris* for four weeks or to rent it for two weeks and then replace it with *I Do*? In other words, provide American Cinema management with a decision-making rule to use in choosing between renting *Paris* for four weeks or just two weeks. American Cinema's tax rate is zero. Be sure to justify your advice with clearly described analysis.

b. How does your answer in part (*a*) change if American Cinema's income tax rate is 30 percent?

c. American Cinema's average movie patron purchases soda, popcorn, and candy that yields profits of $2 after supplies and labor. How does profit on these concession items affect your answer to part (*a*)? (Ignore taxes.)

P 2–16:   Home Auto Parts

Home Auto Parts is a large retail auto parts store selling the full range of auto parts and supplies for do-it-yourself auto repair enthusiasts. The store is arranged with three prime displays in the store: front door, checkout counters, and ends of aisles. These display areas receive the most customer traffic and contain special stands that display the merchandise with attractive eye-catching designs. Each display area is set up at the beginning of the week and runs for one week. Three items are scheduled next week for special display areas: Texcan Oil, windshield wiper blades, and floor mats. The accompanying table provides information for the three promotional areas scheduled to run next week:

Planned Displays for Next Week

	Ends of Aisles	Front Door	Checkout Counter
Item	Texcan Oil	Wiper blades	Floor mats
Sales price	69¢/can	$9.99	$22.99
Projected weekly volume	5,000	200	70
Unit cost	62¢	$7.99	$17.49

Based on past experience, management finds that virtually all display-area sales are made by impulse buyers. The display items are extra purchases by consumers attracted by the exhibits.

Before the store manager sets up the display areas, the distributor for Armadillo car wax visits the store. She says her firm wants its car wax in one of the three display areas and is prepared to offer the product at a unit cost of $2.50. At a retail price of $2.90, management expects to sell 800 units during the week if the wax is on special display.

Required:

a. Home Auto has not yet purchased any of the promotion items for next week. Should management substitute the Armadillo car wax for one of the three planned promotion displays? If so, which one?

b. A common practice in retailing is for the manufacturer to give free units to a retail store to secure desirable promotion space or shelf space. The Armadillo distributor decides to sweeten the offer by giving Home Auto 50 free units of car wax if it places the Armadillo wax on display. Does this change your answer to part (*a*)?

P 2–17: Stahl Inc.

Stahl produces and sells a single product and faces an inelastic demand curve, meaning it can sell as many units as it wants without affecting the selling price. Stahl has a cost structure consisting of fixed costs that are incurred each month, and a variable cost of $12 per unit produced that is independent of (i.e., does not vary with) the number of units produced. Stahl's income tax rate is 30 percent, and its break-even quantity is 24,000 units each month. If Stahl produces 30,000 units during the month, it has an after-tax net income of $33,600. Calculate Stahl's selling price and monthly fixed costs.

P 2–18: Affording a Hybrid

With gasoline prices at $3.00 per gallon, consumers are flocking to purchase hybrid vehicles (with a combination of gasoline and electric motors) that get 50 miles per gallon of gasoline. The monthly payment on a three-year lease of a hybrid is $499 compared to $399 per month on a conventional, equivalent traditional gasoline car that gets 25 miles per gallon. Both vehicles require a one-time $1,500 payment for taxes, license, and dealer charges. Both vehicles have identical lease terms for the residual value, maximum number of miles allowed without penalty, and so forth.

Required:

a. Calculate how many miles the consumer must drive per year to make the hybrid the economical choice over the conventional gasoline-only vehicle.

b. How does your answer to part (a) change if the price of gasoline is $4.00 per gallon?

P 2–19: Easton Diagnostics

Easton Diagnostics is a large medical testing laboratory that services a four-county region. Easton runs a van that picks up specimens from clinics and hospitals and takes them to the Easton laboratory where various tests are conducted. Easton currently has a large chemical blood analysis system. This system runs a battery of standard tests for which Easton is reimbursed $750 per blood sample. The cost structure of the current blood analysis system consists of annual fixed costs (lease payment of $1.6 million, supervisory costs of $400,000, and occupancy costs of $100,000) and variable costs per blood sample (direct labor, including transporting the blood samples, technicians, and so forth of $175, direct materials of $125, and a royalty fee of $150). [*Note:* The current equipment is leased for $1.6 million per year plus $150 (royalty) for every blood sample analyzed.]

A competing vendor has approached Easton Diagnostics with a comparable system that performs the same set of tests. The reliability and quality of both the proposed and the existing systems are the same. The competing vendor is willing to lower the annual lease payment to $1.2 million but raise the royalty fee by $30 per blood sample to $180. Both the existing and proposed leases have the same contractual terms in all other respects. If Easton adopts the competing vendor's proposal, the current fee it charges ($750) and the direct labor costs per blood sample ($175) are unaffected. However, the proposed equipment adds $10 per blood sample analyzed to direct materials.

Required:

a. How does Easton Diagnostic's break-even point for standard blood tests change if the competing vendor's proposal is accepted?

b. Easton Diagnostic currently analyzes 10,300 blood samples per year, and this number has remained constant over the past few years. Moreover, Easton management does not foresee any growth in the number of standard blood tests it performs. Make a recommendation to management as to whether Easton should stay with its existing blood analysis equipment or accept the competing vendor's proposal. Justify your recommendation. (Assume that there are no cancellation payments on the existing equipment and there are no costs of converting from the existing equipment to the new equipment other than the costs described in the problem.)

P 2–20:   Spa Salon

The Spa Salon is a full-service day spa specializing in massage and manicures. One out of every three massage clients also purchases a manicure. Last month, Spa Salon did 90 massages and 30 manicures and reported the following net loss:

Revenues:	
Massage	$ 8,100
Manicures	1,500
	$ 9,600
Variable costs:	
Massage	$ (3,600)
Manicures	(600)
	$ (4,200)
Fixed costs	(7,020)
Net income (loss)	$ (1,620)

After reviewing the income statement for last month, the owner was quite upset about the net loss. She thought the spa was making money.

Required:

How many massages and manicures does Spa Salon have to conduct each month to break even, assuming that the prices and the variable costs of massages and manicures remain the same as last month's, as do the fixed costs?

P 2–21:   Manufacturing Cost Classification

A company makes DVD players and incurs a variety of different costs. Place a check in the appropriate column if the cost is a product cost or a period cost. Further, classify each product cost as direct materials, direct labor, or manufacturing overhead.

	Period Cost	Product Cost	Direct Labor	Direct Materials	Overhead
Advertising expenses for DVD					
Depreciation on PCs in marketing department					
Fire insurance on corporate headquarters					
Fire insurance on plant					
Leather carrying case for the DVD					
Motor drive (externally sourced)					
Overtime premium paid assembly workers					
Factory building maintenance department					
Factory security guards					
Plastic case for the DVD					
Property taxes paid on corporate headquarters					
Salaries of public relations staff					
Salary of corporate controller					
Wages of engineers in quality control					
Wages paid assembly line employees					
Wages paid employees in finished goods warehouse					

P 2–22: Australian Shipping

In the 1800s, Australia was a colony of England and most of its trade was with England. Australia primarily exported agricultural products such as wheat and imported manufactured goods such as steel, machinery, and textiles. The volume of trade measured in British pounds (£) was roughly equal in the sense that exports equaled imports. (Imports were slightly larger as there were net positive investments being made in Australia.) However, in cubic feet of cargo being shipped, exports to England exceeded imports. A British pound (£) of wheat required more cubic feet than £1 of manufactured goods. Hence, an imbalance of shipping existed. Numerous ships would carry agricultural products to England but return to Australia empty because no cargo of manufactured goods existed.

Large sail-powered ships required substantial ballast (weight) in the hold to keep the ship sailing properly, especially in rough seas. Before leaving England empty, the ships would purchase stone from local quarries for ballast. However, once in Australia, the stone had no market value, and in fact had to be hauled from the harbor area.

Consider the following facts for a particular ship in England with a shipment of Australian cargo for England.

1. The ship has contracted to sail to Australia and return with a cargo of Australian wheat. The ship has no cargo scheduled for London to Sydney.
2. The wheat-shipping contract calls for paying the captain and crew £4,900 for the round trip. The wheat seller will arrange for and pay Australian dock hands £250 to load the wheat in Sydney, and the wheat purchaser will arrange for and pay English dock hands to unload the wheat in London. The ship's crew does not load or unload the cargo.
3. To sail to Australia, the ship requires 10 tons of ballast. (1 ton = 2,000 pounds)
4. Stone can be quarried in England, transported to the docks, and loaded as ballast for £40 per ton. In Sydney, the stone can be unloaded and hauled away for £15 per ton.
5. Wrought iron bars of 10-foot lengths can also be used as ship ballast. Wrought iron bars can be purchased in England at £1.20 per bar. Each bar weighs 20 pounds. Wrought iron bars sell for £0.90 per bar in Sydney. The cost of loading the wrought iron in London is £15 per ton, and the cost of unloading it and transporting it to the Sydney market is £10 per ton.

Required:

a. Write a memo to the ship's captain describing what actions he should take with respect to using stone or wrought iron as ballast. Assume that interest rates are zero and all prices and quantities are known with certainty. Support your recommendation with a clearly labeled financial analysis.
b. Why do you think the price of wrought iron is lower in Sydney than in London?

P 2–23: iGen3

The Xerox DocuColor iGen3 digital production press is a high-volume, on-demand, full-color printer capable of producing up to 6,000 impressions (pages) per hour. It weighs nearly 3 tons, stretches 30 feet long, and holds more than 40 pounds of dry ink. It sells for over $500,000, and its principal market is print shops that produce mail order catalogs (e.g., L.L.Bean). Xerox offers two leasing options for the iGen3. Option A requires a three-year agreement with a monthly lease fee of $10,000 plus $0.01 per impression. Option B (also a three-year agreement) does not include a monthly lease fee but requires a charge of $0.03 per impression.

ColorGrafix is a print shop considering leasing the iGen3 to begin producing customized mail-order catalogs. Besides leasing the iGen3, ColorGrafix estimates that it will have to buy ink for the iGen3 at a cost of $0.02 per impression and hire an operator to run the iGen3 to produce the customized catalogs at a cost of $5,000 per month. ColorGrafix estimates that it can charge $0.08 per impression for customized color catalogs. (*Note:* The customer provides the paper stock on which the color impressions are printed.)

68   *Chapter 2*

Required:

    a. If ColorGrafix leases the iGen3 and chooses Option A, how many impressions per month will ColorGrafix have to sell and produce to break even?

    b. If ColorGrafix leases the iGen3 and chooses Option B, how many impressions per month will ColorGrafix have to sell and produce to break even?

    c. Should ColorGrafix choose Option A or Option B? Explain why.

    d. ColorGrafix is a fairly new firm (only three years old) and has a substantial amount of debt that was used to help start the company. ColorGrafix has positive net cash flow after servicing the debt, but the owners of ColorGrafix have not felt it wise to withdraw any cash from the business since its inception, except for their salaries. ColorGrafix expects to sell and produce 520,000 impressions per month. Which lease option would you recommend ColorGrafix choose? Explain why.

P 2–24:   Adapt Inc.

You work for the strategy group of Adapt Inc., a firm that designs and manufactures memory cards for digital cameras. Your task is to gather intelligence about Adapt's key competitor, DigiMem, a privately held company. Your boss has asked you to estimate DigiMem's fixed costs. Industry sources, such as trade associations, provide the following information on DigiMem:

DigiMem	Last Fiscal Year
Revenues (millions)	$6.200
Net income after taxes (millions)	$1.700
Income tax rate	40%
Operating margin*	70%

*Ratio of revenues less variable costs divided by revenues.

Required:

    a. Using the preceding data, estimate DigiMem's annual fixed costs.

    b. Why might your boss be interested in knowing DigiMem's fixed costs?

P 2–25:   Tesla Motors

You work in the long-run strategic planning group of a large automotive firm and are tasked with following the development of electric vehicles. Your firm has electric cars in development but has not yet decided to enter the battery-powered car market. One company you follow is Tesla Motors, founded by Silicon Valley engineers, that specializes in high-performance luxury electric vehicles. A recent article in *The Wall Street Journal,* entitled "Tesla Motors Approaches Crossroad," describes Tesla's current and expected operating performance. Last quarter, Tesla lost $49 million when it was making 200 cars a week. To break even, Tesla needs to make 400 cars a week. Tesla operates its plant 50 weeks out of the year and is shut down for the remainder of the days in the year for holidays and planned maintenance. While the list price of a Tesla ranges between $60,000 and $100,000 depending on battery capacity and other options, the average price is $75,000.

Required:

    a. What is the variable cost of a Tesla automobile and what are Tesla's quarterly fixed costs?

    b. Why would your firm be interested in knowing about Tesla's fixed and variable cost structure?

P 2–26:   Oppenheimer Visuals

Oppenheimer Visuals manufactures state-of-the-art flat-panel plasma display screens that large computer companies like Dell and Gateway assemble into flat-panel monitors. Oppenheimer produces just the display panels, not any of the electronics, cases, or stands needed to make a complete unit. It is about to launch a new product employing TN polarized glass with a unique microscopic groove pattern. Two different technologies exist that can produce the unique groove pattern. One technology has a fixed cost of $34,000 per day and a variable cost of $200 per panel. The second technology has a fixed cost of $16,000 per day and a variable cost of $400 per panel. The fixed costs of the two technologies consist entirely of three-year leases for equipment to produce the panels. Both technologies are equally reliable and produce panels of equal quality. The only difference between the two technologies is their cost structures.

Because Oppenheimer holds a patent on the new YN polarized glass flat-panel displays, it has some market power and expects to sell the new display panels to computer companies based on the following demand schedule:

Price per Display Panel	Quantity (per Day)
$760	60
740	65
720	70
700	75
680	80
660	85
640	90
620	95
600	100
580	105
560	110

In other words, if Oppenheimer sets the price per panel at $760, it expects to sell 60 panels per day. If it sets the price at $560, it expects to sell 110 panels per day.

Required:

    a. To maximize firm value, should Oppenheimer Visuals choose technology 1 or technology 2 to manufacture the new flat-panel display?

    b. Given the technology choice you made in part (*a*), what price should Oppenheimer charge for the new flat-panel display?

    c. Using Oppenheimer Visuals as an example, explain what is meant by the often used expression, "All costs are variable in the long run."

P 2–27: Eastern University Parking

Eastern University faces a shortage of parking spaces and charges for parking. For nearby parking (e.g., behind the business school), faculty and staff pay $180 per year. Parking in lots Z and B, which are north and south of the campus and involve about a 10-minute walk to the business school, costs $124 per year. In setting these prices, the university seeks to recover the costs of parking and to manage the queue of people wishing to park on campus. The current $180 and $124 fees cover the costs of surface spaces. Lots Z and B have lower fees to compensate people for the longer walks and to encourage them to park in outlying lots. University officials say this fee structure, when multiplied by the number of parking stickers of each type sold, covers the cost of running the parking office and building new spaces.

The cost of providing a parking space consists of costs of construction of the space, maintenance, and security. The construction cost is the annual amount required to repay the cost of grading, draining, and asphalting the space. Maintenance includes snow removal, line painting, fixing the gates after the arms are broken by irate faculty members searching for a space, and patching the asphalt. Security costs include all costs of the parking officers who ticket the cars of staff and students parked illegally.

The university recently evaluated a proposal to construct an enclosed, multifloor parking facility. Design estimates place the construction cost at $12,000 per enclosed space. The equivalent cost of a surface space is $900. The university uses a 10 percent cost of capital. (Assume that this is an appropriate interest rate.) To compensate the university for the cost of the capital involved in building

70   *Chapter 2*

parking garages, parking fees would have to be at least $1,200 per space per year, as opposed to $90 per space per year for the surface space. Because the university does not believe that faculty, staff, and students are willing to pay more than $1,200 per year for a covered parking space, no plans exist to build a parking building.

Required:

Critically evaluate Eastern University's costing of parking permits. What do you think accounts for the university administration's reluctance to build a parking garage?

P 2–28:   GRC

GRC currently manufactures and sells computer-controlled gear-cutting machines used by automobile companies to produce gears for car and truck transmissions and differentials. GRC has decided to produce gear-cutting machines that wind-powered, electric-generating turbine companies (e.g., Siemens and General Electric) will purchase to manufacture gear sets used in their turbines. Because of the tremendous torque generated by the 160-foot blades on the windmills, the gears in the electric power generators must be able to withstand unusually large forces. GRC has designed a gear-cutting machine to produce gears that can withstand such forces.

The following table describes the demand curve for the number of wind-powered turbine gear-cutting machines GRC expects to sell per year.

Price ($000s)	Quantity
$440	3
420	4
400	5
380	6
360	7
340	8
320	9
300	10
280	11
260	12

(*Note:* The demand curve in the table can be represented as $P = 500 - 20Q$.)

GRC can produce its new gear-cutting machines for wind-powered turbines using one of two technologies. One technology (HI Automation) involves more capital investment but results in lower variable costs. The other technology (LO Automation) requires less capital investment but results in higher variable costs. The following table summarizes how the average costs of the two technologies vary with different production levels of wind-powered turbine gear-cutting machines.

Number of Machines Produced	Average Cost Hi Auto	Average Cost Low Auto
3	$525.00	$308.33
4	425.00	300.00
5	365.00	295.00
6	325.00	291.67
7	296.43	289.29
8	275.00	287.50
9	258.33	286.11
10	245.00	285.00
11	234.09	284.09
12	225.00	283.33

(All numbers in thousands)

In other words, if five wind-powered turbine gear-cutting machines are produced, the average cost of each machine is $365 using the Hi Automation technology but only $295 if the Low Automation technology is used. On the other hand, if 10 machines are produced, the Hi Automation technology is less expensive ($245) than the Low Automation technology ($285). (*Note:* The average cost estimates above include the annual lease cost of the automation technology.)

Required:

    a. Should GRC purchase the Hi Automation or the Low Automation technology? Justify your answer with convincing supporting analyses.

    b. Given your choice of production technology (Hi or Low Automation) in part (*a*), what price should GRC set for its gear-cutting machines for wind-powered turbines and how many machines will GRC expect to sell at this price?

P 2–29: Mastich Counters

Mastich Counters manufactures a material used to fabricate kitchen counters. It is a very durable, high-fashion, and expensive product that is installed in luxury homes. The manufacturing process is complicated and requires highly skilled employees, supervisors, and engineers. Mastich employs 450 people in its manufacturing operation. Most of the production employees are cross-functionally trained to perform several manufacturing tasks.

The firm's vacation policy gives employees three hours of paid vacation for every week of work. An employee who works 52 weeks accrues 156 hours or 3.9 weeks (156 ÷ 40) of paid vacation. In the past, Mastich allowed employees unlimited accumulation of vacation time. Some long-time employees had accumulated six months of vacation. When they retired from the firm, they continued to be paid for six months after leaving.

Management decided that allowing employees unlimited accumulation of vacation was costing the firm too much money when they left. Not only were the employees who left being paid, but so were their replacements. To correct this problem, management instituted a policy that an employee could not accumulate more than 156 hours of vacation. Once an employee's accumulated vacation exceeded 156 hours, these additional hours would not be added to his or her account. In addition, employees with more than 156 hours of accrued vacation had two years from the date of the policy change to bring their balance down to the maximum 156 hours. After the two-year phase-in period, the "take it or lose it" policy was strictly enforced.

While there was much grumbling about the "take it or lose it" policy, after the two-year phase-in period, the following comments were collected at a focus group held by the personnel department to assess the new policy:

   • *Manager A:* "In some cases it has been very beneficial. Some of our people in high-stress positions were burned out. These people never took all their vacation. One woman took every Friday off for six months to use her excess vacation time. For the four days she worked, she was like a new person—refreshed, invigorated, and enthused."

   • *Manager B:* "Well, that may be true, but this new policy, especially during the phase-in period, has been hell on our staffing. Some days, especially around weekends and holidays, we've had 30 percent of the plant on vacation. What impact do you think this has had on our production schedule and quality programs?"

   • *Manager C:* "I have looked at the data and very few employees lose any accrued vacation. Fewer than 1 percent of the accrued vacation hours were lost last year after the phase-in period because employees did not use them."

Required:

Evaluate the costs and benefits of the new policy that limits accumulated vacation to 156 hours.

P 2–30: Prestige Products

Prestige manufactures a line of female cosmetics, including lipsticks, face creams, eyeliners, and so forth. Prestige manufactures its own products to maintain proprietary information and to assure high-quality standards. They have just developed a new exfoliating masque face cream in a unique

72   *Chapter 2*

tube and applicator that they expect to sell for $12.00 per unit. To manufacture the new face cream, Prestige will have to lease new equipment. Only two companies manufacture the necessary equipment for producing the face cream, a German company and a Swedish company. The following table lists the two alternative production technologies that Prestige can use to produce the new face cream.

Technology	*German*	*Swedish*
Fixed cost (annual)	$500,000	$900,000
Variable cost/unit	$8.00	$6.00
Maximum annual capacity (units)	215,000	380,000

The German equipment has an annual capacity of 215,000 units per year, whereas the Swedish equipment can produce up to 380,000 units per year. Both companies require Prestige Products to sign a five-year, non-cancelable lease for the annual lease payment ($500,000 for the German equipment and $900,000 for the Swedish equipment). The variable costs include the labor and material ($8 if the German equipment is used and $6 if the Swedish equipment is used).

Required:

    a. Calculate the break-even point if Prestige were to lease the German equipment.

    b. Calculate the break-even point if Prestige were to lease the Swedish equipment.

    c. Which equipment (German or Swedish) should Prestige lease (and why)?

    d. Suppose that Prestige management expects to sell 180,000 masques per year. Calculate the average cost (fixed plus variable cost) of the German and Swedish equipment at 180,000 units.

    e. What is operating leverage and what is the relation between operating leverage and firm value?

P 2–31: JLE Electronics

JLE Electronics is an independent contract manufacturer of complex printed circuit board assemblies. Computer companies and other electronics firms engage JLE to assemble their boards. Utilizing computer-controlled manufacturing and test machinery and equipment, JLE provides manufacturing services employing surface mount technology (SMT) and pin-through-hole (PTH) interconnection technologies. The customer purchases the subcomponents and pays JLE a per-board fee to assemble the components.

JLE has a new one-of-a-kind, state-of-the-art board assembly line. The line can be operated 20 hours per day, seven days a week, in each three-week (21-day) period. Four customers have asked that their boards be manufactured on this line over the next three-week period. The following table summarizes the number of units of each board requested, the price JLE will charge for each board, JLE's variable and fixed cost per board, and the number of assembly line minutes each board requires. Fixed cost per board is the allocated cost of property taxes, fire insurance, accounting, depreciation, and so forth.

Customers

	A	B	C	D
Number of boards requested	2,500	2,300	1,800	1,400
Price	$ 38	$ 42	$ 45	$ 50
Variable cost/board*	23	25	27	30
Fixed cost/board	9	10	10	15
Number of machine minutes/board	3	4	5	6

*Allocated based on both machine minutes and direct labor cost.

Make the following assumptions:

- The four customer orders can be produced only on the new JLE line.
- If JLE rejects an order, future orders from that customer are not affected.
- There is no setup or downtime between orders.
- Customers are willing to have any number of boards produced by JLE up to the number of units specified in the preceding table. For example, customer A has requested 2,500 boards in the 21-day period, but would accept a smaller number.
- The four customers comprise the entire set of potential customers who would want to use the new JLE line in the next 21-day period.

Required:

Which customer orders should be accepted? In other words, complete the following table:

Customers

	A	B	C	D
Number of boards requested to be produced in the next 21 days	2,500	2,300	1,800	1,400
Number of boards scheduled to be produced in the next 21 days	?	?	?	?

P 2–32: News.com

News.com is a website that offers users access to current national and international news stories. News.com does not charge users a fee for accessing the site, but rather charges advertisers $0.05 per hit to the website. A "hit" is a user that logs on the website.

News.com is considering two alternate ISPs that will link News.com's computer system to the World Wide Web—NetCom and Globalink. These firms are identical in access speeds and the number of users able to connect to the site per minute. Both ISPs are equally reliable. NetCom proposes to charge $3,000 per month plus $0.01 per hit to News.com. Globalink proposes to charge $2,000 per month plus $0.02 per hit. Assume that the only costs News.com incurs are the access fees charged by the ISP.

Required:

a. Calculate the number of hits to its website needed to break even if News.com uses NetCom.

b. Calculate the number of hits to its website needed to break even if News.com uses Globalink.

c. Which ISP do you recommend that News.com use? Explain why.

d. Monthly demand (in number of hits) for News.com is expected to be either 50,000 if the economy is slumping or 150,000 if the economy is booming, each equally probable. Which ISP should News.com choose and why?

P 2–33: Rowe Waste Removal (A)

Rowe Waste Removal now only collects garbage from private residences (houses) because it does not own trucks with the capability of lifting and emptying garbage dumpsters used by apartment complexes. Rowe currently is reassessing this decision. To lease, license, insure, and get the various permits to operate a refuse collection truck with a fork-lift capable of emptying a dumpster costs $54,000 per month. This includes the cost of the driver, fuel, and oil. Rowe prices each apartment complex based on the number of apartment units in the complex based on a standard of 25 units. The following table indicates how Rowe expects the number of apartment customers to vary with the price (per 25 apartment units)

Number of Customers	Price per Month
100	1,560
105	1,538
110	1,516
115	1,494
120	1,472
125	1,450
130	1,428
135	1,406
140	1,384
145	1,362

(Table is based on the demand curve: $P = 2000 - 4.4Q$.)

In other words, if Rowe wants 100 apartment customers, it will set the price at $1,560 per 25 units per month. If an apartment has 50 units, then at this price point, this apartment complex pays $3,120 ($2 \times \$1,560$) per month. Since garbage is collected once per week at each apartment complex, the single truck has the capacity to handle up to 145 25-unit apartment complexes per month.

Rowe uses a landfill in the county to dispose of the waste. The landfill charges $1,750 per truck load of garbage the size Rowe would acquire. Rowe estimates that 10 apartment complexes (each with 25 units) will fill the truck once and will require dumping at the landfill. And, Rowe will remove the refuse at each 25-unit complex exactly four times per month. Each 25-unit apartment complex requires Rowe to lease a dumpster that can be lifted and emptied by its fork-lift–equipped garbage truck. Rowe can lease these dumpsters for $200 per month per 25-unit dumpster.

Required:

   a. What is Rowe's monthly fixed cost of adding an apartment-complex refuse disposal service to its existing residential services? And what is Rowe's monthly variable cost of servicing each 25-unit apartment complex?

   b. Given the demand curve Rowe expects to face in the apartment refuse collection business, what price should it choose to maximize profits, and how much profit will it make at this price?

   c. Based on the profit maximizing price computed in part (*b*), what is the break-even point at this price?

   d. After preparing the analysis in part (*b*), Rowe discovers it has forgotten to include an additional cost of $72,000 per year to cover the cost of the new person needed to contact potential apartment complexes, sign contracts for waste removal, and manage the apartment refuse collection business. After incorporating the $72,000 cost of the manager to market and manage the apartment collection business, how do your answers to parts (*b*) and (*c*) change? In other words, what price should Rowe set to maximize profits, how much profit will Rowe make at this price, and what is the break-even point at this new price?

   e. Discuss why your answers in parts (*a*) and (*c*) are either the same or differ from your answers in part (*d*).

P 2–34: Littleton Imaging

Dr. Na Gu plans to open a radiology office that provides CAT scans. She can lease the CAT scanner for $1,200 per month plus $45 for each imaging session. In addition to the $45 lease cost per imaging session, Dr. Gu must purchase film for each session at a cost of $55. She plans to charge $250 for each session. Dr. Gu has identified a suitable office that she can rent for $1,400 per month. The monthly cost of a receptionist is $2,400 and two radiology technicians are $3,200 each per month. Office furnishings, phones, and office equipment cost $600 per month. She expects that her salary will be $15,000 per month.

The Nature of Costs   **75**

Required:

  a. How many imaging sessions per month must Littleton Imaging conduct in order for the office to break even?

  b. How many imaging sessions per month must Littleton Imaging conduct in order for the office to yield an after-tax profit of $5,000 if the tax rate is 40 percent?

  c. Dr. Gu expects that the office will perform 200 imaging sessions per month. How much must she charge per session to break even?

P 2–35: Candice Company

Candice Company has decided to introduce a new product that can be manufactured by either of two methods. The manufacturing method will not affect the quality of the product. The estimated manufacturing costs of the two methods are as follows:

	Method A	Method B
Raw materials	$5.00	$5.60
Direct labor	6.00	7.20
Variable overhead	3.00	4.80
Directly traceable incremental fixed manufacturing costs per year	$2,440,000	$1,320,000

Candice's market research department has recommended an introductory unit sales price of $30. The incremental selling expenses are estimated to be $500,000 annually plus $2 for each unit sold, regardless of manufacturing method.

Required:

  a. Calculate the estimated break-even point in annual unit sales of the new product if Candice Co. uses

  (i) Manufacturing method A.

  (ii) Manufacturing method B.

  b. Which production technology should the firm use and why?

P 2–36: Cost Behavior Patterns

For each of the following questions draw a graph that depicts how costs vary with volume. Completely label each graph and axis.

  a. Plant XXX works a 40-hour week. Management can vary the number of employees. Currently, 200 employees are being paid $10 per hour. The plant is near capacity. To increase output, a second 40-hour shift is being considered. To attract employees to the second shift, a 20 percent wage premium will be offered. Plot total labor costs as a function of labor hours per week.

  b. Plant YYY has a contract with the Texas Gas Company to purchase up to 150 million cubic feet of natural gas per month for a flat fee of $1.5 million. Additional gas can be purchased for $0.0175 per cubic foot. Plant YYY manufactures aluminum cans. One thousand cans require 10 cubic feet of gas. Plot total gas costs as a function of can production.

  c. Use the same facts as in (b), but plot the gas cost per can as a function of can production.

P 2–37: Royal Holland Line

Royal Holland is a cruise ship company. It currently has six ships and plans to add two more. It offers luxury passenger cruises in the Caribbean, Alaska, and the Far East. Management is currently addressing what to do with an existing ship, the *S.S. Amsterdam,* when she is replaced by a new ship.

76   *Chapter 2*

The *S.S. Amsterdam* was built 20 years ago for $100 million. For accounting purposes, she was assumed to have a 20-year life and hence is now fully depreciated. To replace the *S.S. Amsterdam* would cost $500 million, but her current market value is $371,250,000. The Holland Line can borrow or lend money at 10 percent.

The *S.S. Amsterdam* is now sailing the Caribbean and will be replaced next year by a new ship. The *S.S. Amsterdam* might be moved to the Mediterranean for a new seven-day Greek island tour. A seven-day cruise would depart Athens Sunday night, stop at four ports before returning to Athens Sunday morning, and prepare for a new cruise that afternoon. The *S.S. Amsterdam* can carry as many as 1,500 passengers. The accompanying data summarize the operating cost for this seven-day cruise.

Estimated Operating Cost of Seven-Day Greek Island Cruise
(S.S. Amsterdam)

	Variable Cost[*]	Fixed Cost[†]
Labor	$ 60,000	$ 80,000
Food	236,000	10,500
Fuel		177,000
Port fees and services		62,000
Marketing, advertising, promotion		240,000
Supplies	28,000	38,000
Totals	$324,000	$607,500

[*]Based on 1,200 passengers.

[†]Fixed costs per weekly cruise. Assume there are 50 weeks (and hence 50 cruises) in a year.

Required:

 a. Assuming the seven-day Greek island cruise can be priced at an average of $1,620, calculate the break-even number of passengers per cruise using the data provided.

 b. What major cost component is not included in management's estimates?

 c. If you were to include the omitted cost component identified in part (*b*), recalculate the break-even point for the *S.S. Amsterdam*'s Greek island cruise.

 d. Passengers purchase beverages, souvenirs, and services while on the ship. The ship makes money on the purchases. If the ship line has a margin of 50 percent on all such on-board purchases, how much would the average passenger have to purchase for the break-even point to be 900 passengers?

P 2–38: Roberts Machining

Roberts Machining specializes in fabricating metal racks that hold electronic equipment such as telephone switching units, power supplies, and so forth. Roberts designs and produces the metal stamping dies used to fabricate the racks. It is currently fabricating several racks for GTE. A new rack, the 1160, is scheduled to begin production. The die used to fabricate this rack cost Roberts $49,000 to design and build. This die was completed last week, and production of the 1160 is scheduled to begin next week. Rack 1160 is a specialized custom product only for GTE. GTE and Roberts have a one-year contract whereby Roberts agrees to manufacture and GTE agrees to purchase a fixed number of 1160 racks over the next 12 months for a fixed price per rack. The 1160 rack will not be produced beyond one year. This contract generates profits of $358,000 (after deducting the die's cost of $49,000). Roberts's accounting system recorded all expenditures for the 1160 die as a fixed asset with a one-year life. If this die is scrapped today or in one year's time, it has a scrap value of $6,800.

Easton, another metal fabricator, has offered to buy the 1160 die from Roberts for $588,000 and will supply 1160 racks to GTE. GTE has agreed to this supplier substitution. Roberts estimates that if it sells the 1160 tools and dies to Easton, it will lose a current cash equivalent of $192,000 of future profits that would have been generated from GTE and similar customers, but now this business will go to Easton. (Ignore all tax effects.)

Required:

a. List all the alternatives in Roberts's opportunity set with respect to the 1160 die.

b. Calculate the net cash flows associated with each alternative in Roberts's opportunity set listed in part (*a*).

c. What is the opportunity cost of each alternative in the opportunity set listed in part (*a*)?

d. What action should Roberts take with respect to the 1160 die?

P 2–39: Fuller Aerosols

Fuller Aerosols manufactures six different aerosol can products (room deodorants, hair sprays, furniture polish, and so forth) on its fill line. The fill line mixes the ingredients, adds the propellant, fills and seals the cans, and packs the cans in cases in a continuous production process. These aerosol products are then sold to distributors. The following table summarizes the weekly operating data for each product.

Fuller Aerosols Weekly Operating Data

	AA143	AC747	CD887	FX881	HF324	KY662
Price/case	$37	$54	$62	$21	$34	$42
Fill time/case (minutes)	3	4	5	2	3	4
Fixed cost per product per week	$900	$240	$560	$600	$1,800	$600
Cases ordered per week	300	100	50	200	400	200
Variable cost/case	$28	$50	$48	$17	$28	$40

Each product has fixed costs that pertain only to that product. If the product is discontinued for the week, the product's fixed costs are not incurred that week.

Required:

a. Calculate the break-even volume for each product.

b. Suppose the aerosol fill line can operate only 70 hours per week. Which products should be manufactured?

c. Suppose the aerosol fill line can operate only 50 hours per week. Which products should be manufactured?

P 2–40: Happy Feet

Dr. Lucy Zang, a noted local podiatrist, plans to open a retail shoe store specializing in hard-to-find footwear for people with feet problems such as bunions, flat feet, mallet toes, diabetic feet, and so forth. Because of the wide variety of foot ailments and shoe sizes needed, Dr. Zang estimates that she would have to stock a large inventory of shoes, perhaps as much as $1.5 million (at her cost). She found a 4,000-square-foot store in a popular mall that provides adequate retail space and storage for her inventory. Store improvements including carpeting, lighting, shelving, computer terminals, and so forth, require an additional $0.2 million investment. Initial advertising, hiring expenses, legal fees, and working capital are projected to add another $0.1 million of initial investment. To finance this $1.8 million investment, Dr. Zang and her family will invest $0.4 million, and the balance of the $1.4 million will be borrowed from a bank.

The mall charges rent of $40 per square foot per year, payable in equal monthly install-ments, plus 3 percent of her retail sales. So, to rent the 4,000-square-foot store, the annual rent is $160,000, or $13,333 per month PLUS 3 percent of her sales. Besides the rent, Dr. Zang estimates other monthly expenses for labor, utilities, and so on to be $38,000. These expenses will not vary with the amount of shoe sales. She plans to mark up the shoes 100 percent, so a pair of shoes she buys wholesale for $110 will be sold at retail for $220. Based on her research, she expects monthly retail sales to be $150,000, but in any given month, total sales can be $80,000 or $220,000 with equal probability.

Dr. Zang talks to her local banker and lays out her business plan; the banker tells her the bank would make a three-year interest-only loan at 10 percent interest, with the principal of $1.4 million due in three years (or it could be refinanced). The high interest rate of 10 percent was caused by the rather large risk of default due to the substantial fixed costs in the business plan. The banker explains that the monthly rent ($13,333), other expenses ($38,000), and interest ($11,667), or $63,000, require the shoe store to generate a fairly large minimum level of sales to pay these expenses.

Required:

  a. Calculate the amount of sales the Happy Feet store must do each month to break even.

  b. After calculating the break-even point in part (*a*), Dr. Zang still believes that her Happy Feet store can be commercially successful and provide a valuable service to her patients. She goes back to the mall leasing agent and asks if the mall would take a lower fixed monthly rental amount and a larger percentage fee of her sales. The mall leasing agent (who happens to have sore feet and believes the Happy Feet store will drive new customers to his mall) says the mall would accept a rental fee of $1,000 per month plus 12.5 percent of her monthly sales. While Dr. Zang likes the idea of dropping her monthly rent from $13,333 to $1,000, she feels that raising the percentage of sales from 3 percent to 12.5 percent is a bit steep. But she goes back to the bank and presents the revised rental agreement. The banker says the bank would lower the annual interest rate from 10 percent to 9 percent if Dr. Zang accepts the new lease agreement. Both the original lease and the new lease are for three years and can be renegotiated at the end of the three years. Should Dr. Zang accept the new lease agreement ($1,000 per month plus 12.5 percent) or the original lease terms ($13,333 per month plus 3 percent)? Support your recommendation with both a written analysis and a quantitative analysis backing up your recommendation. (*Hint:* First, conduct an analysis comparing the two options, using the expected monthly sales of $150,000. Second, conduct an analysis comparing the two options, using the two extreme sales of $80,000 and $220,000.)

P 2–41:   Digital Convert

Digital Convert (DC) is a three-year-old startup company with most of its capital coming from banks and personal investments by the founders. DC manufactures a high-resolution scanner (MXP35). At the heart of the MXP35 is a photoelectric light sensor that converts light into digital pixels. DC currently produces the MXP35 for $480 (variable cost) per unit and incurs virtually no fixed manufacturing costs. All of its equipment is leased, and the leases are structured whereby DC only pays for the actual units produced. DC operates out of a building that is provided free by New York State for entrepreneurial startups. New York State also pays utilities, taxes, insurance, and administrative costs. DC does have fixed financing costs to service its existing loans, and these financing costs consume most of its profits from sales of the MXP35.

DC faces the following monthly demand schedule for the MXP35 (where price is the wholesale price DC receives):

Quantity	Price
19	$1,278
20	1,240
21	1,202
22	1,164
23	1,126
24	1,088
25	1,050
26	1,012

The equation of the demand curve for the preceding table is $P = \$2,000 - 38Q$. In other words, if DC wants to sell 20 MXP35s per month, it would charge a wholesale price of $1,240 per unit.

Required:

a. Given DC's current cost structure of $480 variable cost and zero fixed costs, what is its profit-maximizing price-quantity combination for MXP35?

b. DC learns of a new manufacturing process for their photoelectric light sensor that lowers the variable cost from $480 per unit to $100 per unit. But the equipment must be leased for $7,000 per month for 24 months. If DC leases the new equipment, then over the next 24 months DC commits to paying $7,000 each month. If DC installs the new equipment, what is the price-quantity combination that maximizes profits? (Assume the quality and quantity of sensors produced by the existing and new technologies are identical.)

c. Before deciding to adopt the new photoelectric light sensor production technology, DC does some further research into its cost of financial distress. While the demand curve DC faces represents its normal demand, random monthly variation can cause demand to shift up or down unexpectedly. Given its existing bank loans, its variable costs of $480 per unit, no fixed manufacturing costs, and its small cash balances, DC faces a 15 percent chance of defaulting on its loans sometime over the next 24 months. If DC defaults on its loans, the owners of DC estimate the costs of default (legal costs, bank fees, lost sales, and so forth) to be $500,000. With the additional fixed leasing cost of the new sensor manufacturing technology, the owners of DC predict that the likelihood of defaulting on their fixed monthly commitments (bank loans and the $7,000 equipment lease) increases to 25 percent over the next 24 months. Prepare an analysis supporting your recommendation as to whether DC should adopt the new sensor manufacturing process or stay with their current manufacturing technology. (To simplify your analysis, assume a zero discount rate.)

P 2–42:   APC Electronics

APC is a contract manufacturer of printed circuit board assemblies that specializes in manufacturing and test engineering support of complex printed circuit boards for companies in the defense and medical instruments industries. The assembly process begins with raw printed circuit boards, into which preprogrammed robotic machines insert various integrated circuits and other components, and then these parts are soldered onto the board. The board is then tested before shipment to the customer.

Four separate assembly lines, each with roughly the same type of equipment, are used to assemble the circuit boards. Before running a particular board assembly, the insertion equipment must be loaded with the correct components, and the equipment programmed and tested before production begins. Setup time varies between 3 to 6 hours depending on the complexity of the board being assembled. Setup labor costs APC $40 per hour, and technicians assembling and testing the completed boards cost $28 per hour. Not every assembly line can manufacture every type of board. Some lines have older insertion and testing equipment inappropriate for more complex assemblies. The assignment of boards to assembly lines depends on the number and complexity of the component insertions, the type of soldering to be applied, and the testing required.

Each assembly line has an hourly cost consisting of the accounting depreciation on the equipment (straight line) and occupancy costs (factory depreciation, taxes, insurance, and utilities). Occupancy costs are fixed with respect to volume changes. Direct labor to set up and test the line as well as the direct labor to manufacture the complete board assemblies and the testing of each board is tracked separately to each batch of boards. The following table summarizes the costs of operating each line and the annual number of hours each line is expected to run assembling boards (excluding setup and testing time).

	Line I	Line II	Line III	Line IV
Equipment depreciation	$ 840,000	$1,300,000	$480,000	$ 950,000
Occupancy costs	213,000	261,000	189,000	237,000
Total annual line costs	$1,053,000	$1,561,000	$669,000	$1,187,000
Expected hours of operations	1,800	2,200	1,600	2,000

The equipment depreciation cost varies widely across the two lines because some of the lines (especially Line III) have older machines, some of which are fully depreciated.

Required:

a. Calculate the hourly cost of operating each of the four lines.

b. One of APC's customers, Healthtronics, has requested a special order for one of its boards APC currently builds. Healthtronics needs 150 boards by next week. These boards have to be run on Line I because that is the only one with the specialized soldering capability needed for these boards. Healthtronics will ship APC the raw boards and components to be inserted, so APC will not have to buy any of the parts. Setup time is expected to be four hours, and run time for these boards is expected to be 30 hours. Three technicians, each working 30 hours, are needed to staff Line I while the Healthtronics boards are being assembled and tested. Healthtronics splits the production of this particular board between APC and another contract manufacturer. So, if APC refuses this special offer, the customer will take the work to the other manufacturer. APC does not expect refusing this order to adversely affect Healthtronics' demand for future APC work. If APC accepts the special order, the line will be set up next Monday during the day. The job will start Monday afternoon and be finished by Wednesday. Sixteen of the 30 hours of run time will be during an evening shift when the technicians are paid time and a half, or $42 an hour ($28 × 1.5). Calculate the cost APC will record as cost of goods sold when it ships the special order to Healthtronics.

c. Assume that accepting this special order from Healthtronics does not adversely affect the delivery schedules of any of APC's other customers. What is APC's out-of-pocket cash flow of accepting this Healthtronics special order?

d. Instead of assuming no other APC customers' deliveries are affected by accepting the special order from Healthtronics as in part (*c*), assume that another APC customer, SonarTech, will be affected. SonarTech's boards are currently running on Line I. They will have to be pulled from the line (two hours of tear-down time using setup technicians to unload the automatic parts feeders and return the parts to the storeroom), and Line I will have to be set up and tested as described in part (*b*). Healthtronics boards are run as in part (*b*). Then on Wednesday, six hours of setup time is needed to unload the remaining Healthtronics parts and reload and retest the SonarTech parts. To partially catch up on the SonarTech job, 14 hours of line run time that would have been done during the day is shifted to the evening, when the four technicians needed to run the SonarTech boards are paid time and a half ($42 per hour). Instead of shipping all the SonarTech boards in one shipment, two overnight shipments will be made—the first occurring when the first half is produced, and the second batch when the order is completed, costing an additional $2,300 of freight. SonarTech is willing to have its boards delayed a few days, as long as it can receive the boards in two overnight shipments. But SonarTech is unwilling to pay the additional freight. What is the opportunity cost of accepting the Healthtronics special order?

P 2–43: Amy's Boards

Amy Laura is opening a snowboard rental store. She rents snowboards for skiing on a weekly basis for $75 per week, including the boots. The skiing season is 20 weeks long. Laura can buy a snowboard and boots for $550, rent them for a season, and sell them for $250 at the end of the season.

The store rent is $7,200 per year. During the off-season, Laura sublets the store for $1,600. Salaries, advertising, and office expenses are $26,000 per year.

On average, 80 percent of the boards in any given week are rented. After each rental, the boards must be resurfaced and the boots deodorized. Labor (not included in the $26,000) and materials to prepare the board and boots to be re-rented cost $7.

Required:

   a. How many boards must Laura purchase in order to break even?

   b. Suppose that Laura purchases 50 boards. What profit does she expect?

   c. Laura purchases 50 boards. What fraction of her boards must she rent each week to break even (including covering the cost of the boards)?

   d. Explain why the percentage utilization you calculated in part (*c*) differs from the expected rental rate of 80 percent.

P 2–44: Blue Sage Mountain

Blue Sage Mountain produces hinged snowboards. The price charged affects the quantity sold. The following equation captures the relation between price and quantity each month:

$$\text{Selling price} = \$530 - .2 \times \text{Quantity sold}$$

In other words, if they wish to sell 500 boards a month, the price must be \$430 (\$530 − .2 × 500). Fixed costs of producing the boards are \$70,000 a month and the variable costs per board are \$90.

Required:

   a. Prepare a table with quantities between 100 and 2,000 boards in increments of 100 that calculates the price, total revenue, total costs, and profits for each quantity-price combination.

   b. Determine the profit-maximizing quantity-price combination.

   c. Fixed costs fall from \$70,000 a month to \$50,000 a month. Should Blue Sage change its pricing decision?

   d. Variable costs fall from \$90 per unit to \$50 per unit. Should Blue Sage change its pricing decision?

Cases

Case 2–1: Old Turkey Mash

Old Turkey Mash is a whiskey manufactured by distilling grains and corn and then aging the mixture for five years in 50-gallon oak barrels. Distilling requires about a week and aging takes place in carefully controlled warehouses. Before it ages, the whiskey is too bitter to be consumed. Aging mellows the brew (and ultimately the consumer). The cost of the product prior to aging is \$100 per barrel (direct plus indirect costs of distilling). In the aging process, each barrel must be inspected monthly and any leaks repaired. Every six months the barrels are rotated and sampled for quality. Costs of direct labor and materials in the aging process (excluding the cost of oak barrels) amount to \$50 per barrel per year (all variable). As the whiskey ages, evaporation and leakage cause each 50-gallon barrel to produce only 40 gallons of bottled whiskey. New oak barrels cost \$75 each and cannot be reused. After aging, they are cut in half and sold for flowerpots. The revenues generated from sales of the pots just cover the costs of disposing of the used barrels. As soon as the whiskey is aged five years, it is bottled and sold to wholesalers.

While domestic consumption of whiskey is falling, an aggressive international marketing campaign has opened up new international markets. The firm is in the third year of a five-year campaign to double production. Because it takes five years to increase production (an additional barrel of mash produced today does not emerge from the aging process for five years), the firm is adding 100,000 gallons of distilled product each year. Prior to the expansion, 500,000 distilled gallons were produced each year. Distilled output is being increased 100,000 gallons a year for five years until it reaches 1 million gallons. Distilled output is currently 800,000 gallons and is projected to rise to 900,000 gallons next year. The accompanying table describes production, sales, and inventory in the aging process.

82   *Chapter 2*

	Base Year	Year 1	Year 2	Year 3
Production (distilled gallons)	500,000	600,000	700,000	800,000
Aged gallons sold	400,000	400,000	400,000	400,000
Warehouse Inventory at Beginning of Year				
4-year-old bbls	10,000	10,000	10,000	10,000
3-year-old bbls	10,000	10,000	10,000	10,000
2-year-old bbls	10,000	10,000	10,000	12,000
1-year-old bbls	10,000	10,000	12,000	14,000
New bbls added	10,000	12,000	14,000	16,000
Total bbls to be aged in year	50,000	52,000	56,000	62,000

(bbls = barrels)

Warehousing rental costs to age the base-year production of 10,000 barrels per year are $1 million per year. Additional warehouse rental costs of $40,000 per year must be incurred to age each additional 20,000 barrels (100,000 distilled gallons). All costs incurred in warehousing are treated as handling or carrying costs and are written off when incurred. Bottled Old Turkey is sold to distributors for $15 per gallon. These income statements summarize the firm's current operating performance:

	Base Year	Year 1	Year 2	Year 3
Revenues	$6,000,000	$6,000,000	$6,000,000	$6,000,000
Less:				
Cost of goods sold:				
10,000 bbls @ $100/bbl	1,000,000	1,000,000	1,000,000	1,000,000
Oak barrels	750,000	900,000	1,050,000	1,200,000
Warehouse rental	1,000,000	1,040,000	1,120,000	1,240,000
Warehouse direct costs	2,500,000	2,600,000	2,800,000	3,100,000
Net income (loss) before taxes	$750,000	$460,000	$30,000	$(540,000)
Income taxes (30%)	225,000	138,000	9,000	(162,000)
Net income after taxes	$525,000	$322,000	$21,000	$(378,000)

Management is quite concerned about the loss that is projected for the third year of the expansion (the current year). The president has scheduled a meeting with the local bank to review the firm's current financial performance. This bank has been lending the firm the capital to finance the production expansion.

Required:

a. Instead of writing off all the warehousing and oak barrel costs, prepare revised income statements for years 1 through 3, treating the warehousing and barrel costs as product costs.

b. Which set of income statements (those given or the ones you prepared) should the president show the bank at the meeting? Justify your answer.

Case 2–2: Mowerson Division

The Mowerson Division of Brown Instruments manufactures testing equipment for the automobile industry. Mowerson's equipment is installed in several places along an automobile assembly line for component testing and is also used for recording and measurement purposes during track and road tests. Mowerson's sales have grown steadily, and revenue will exceed $200 million for the first time in 2001.

Mowerson designs and manufactures its own printed circuit boards (PCBs) for use in the test equipment. The PCBs are manually assembled in the Assembly Department, which employs 45 technicians. Because of a lack of plant capacity and a shortage of skilled labor, Mowerson is considering having the printed circuit boards manufactured by Tri-Star, a specialist in this field. Quality control restrictions and vendor requirements dictate that all PCBs be either manufactured

The Nature of Costs

83

by Mowerson or contracted to an outside vendor. The per-board cost of outside manufacture is higher than the in-house cost; however, management thinks that savings could also be realized from this change.

Jim Wright, a recently hired cost analyst, has been asked to prepare a financial analysis of the outside manufacturing proposal. Wright's report includes the assumptions he used in his analysis, along with his recommendation. His financial analysis appears next, and his notes and assumptions follow the analysis.

Required:

a. Discuss whether Jim Wright should have analyzed only the costs and savings that Mowerson will realize in 2002.

b. For each of the 10 items listed in Wright's financial analysis, indicate whether

  (i) The item is appropriate or inappropriate for inclusion in the report. If the item is inappropriate, explain why it should not be included in the report.

  (ii) The amount is correct or incorrect. If the amount is incorrect, state what the correct amount is.

c. What additional information about Tri-Star would be helpful to Mowerson in evaluating its manufacturing decision?

Annual Cost Savings Analysis for Tri-Star Contract

Savings
1. Reduction in assembly technicians
   ($28,500 × 40) — $1,140,000
2. Assembly supervisor transferred — 35,000
3. Floor space savings
   [(1,000 × $9.50) + (8,000 × $6.00)] — 57,500
4. Purchasing clerk, 1/2 time on special project — 6,000
5. Purchase order reduction
   (2,000 orders @ $1.25 each) — 2,500
6. Reduced freight expense — 7,500
   Total savings — $1,248,500

Costs
7. Increased production cost
   [($60.00 × 52.00) × 100,000 units] — $800,000
8. Hire junior engineer — 20,000
9. Hire quality control inspector — 22,000
10. Increased storage cost for safety stock
   (Expected value of 4,200 units @ $2.00/unit) — 8,400
   Total costs — 850,400
   Net annual savings — $ 398,100

Notes and Assumptions

Personnel Assembly department technicians will be reduced by 40 at an annual savings (salary plus benefits) of $28,500 each. Five assemblers will remain to assist the field service department with repair work on the printed circuit boards; assemblers have always assisted in repair work. The supervisor of the assembly department will remain with Mowerson because he has only two years until retirement; a position will be created for him in the machining department, where he will serve as a special consultant.

Because of the elimination of purchasing and stocking of component parts required for PCB assembly, one purchasing clerk will be assigned half-time to a special project until his time can be more fully utilized.

A junior engineer will be hired to act as liaison between Mowerson and the manufacturer of the PCBs. In addition, a third quality control inspector will be needed to monitor the vendor's adherence to quality standards.

84   *Chapter 2*

Floor Space   For the past two years, Mowerson has rented, on a month-to-month basis, 1,000 square feet of space for $9.50 per square foot in a neighboring building to accommodate the overflow of assembly work. The 8,000 square feet currently being used in Mowerson's main plant by the assembly department will be used for temporary stockroom storage. However, this space could be reclaimed for manufacturing use without overloading the stockroom facilities. This floor space is valued at $6 per square foot.

Production Costs and Volume   Mowerson's cost for manufacturing printed circuit boards is as follows:

Direct material	$24.00
Direct labor	12.50
Variable overhead	6.25
Fixed overhead	9.25
Total cost	$52.00

The direct material cost includes normal scrap and other such material-related costs as incoming freight and issuing costs. Mowerson's annual cost for incoming freight attributed to PCBs is $7,500. Tri-Star will charge $60 per board, including the cost of delivery.

Mowerson's production volume of printed circuit boards for the past two years has been 80,000 and 90,000 boards, respectively. Projected production volumes for the next three years are:

2002	100,000
2003	120,000
2004	130,000

Storage Costs   Because Mowerson will not have direct control over the manufacture of the PCBs, the level of safety stock will be increased over the current level of 1,800 boards. The supervisor of the assembly department has provided the accompanying probabilities associated with reductions in Tri-Star's ability to produce and/or deliver PCBs.

Percentage of Time Tri-Star Deliveries Will Be Late	Probability (1)	Safety Stock of PCBs (2)	Expected Value (1) × (2)
4%	0.30	2,500	750
6	0.40	4,000	1,600
8	0.25	6,000	1,500
10	0.05	7,000	350
	New safety stock level		4,200

The variable cost to store the PCBs is $2 per board per year.

Other   The variable cost of executing a purchase order at Mowerson is $1.25 for items such as postage, forms, and telephone. Since Mowerson will no longer have to purchase all the component parts required for the printed circuit boards, there will be a reduction of 2,000 purchase orders prepared annually.

Recommendation   Based on the annual savings of $398,100 projected above, Mowerson should enter into an agreement with Tri-Star to manufacture the printed circuit boards.

Chapter Four

Organizational Architecture

Chapter Outline

Chapter 2 described the important concept of opportunity cost and its relation to other costing terms. Understanding the nature of costs is critical to making decisions. Internal accounting systems are used not only in decision making but also for influencing the behavior of individuals within organizations.

This chapter addresses the general problem of controlling behavior. Individuals working in firms will maximize their welfare, sometimes to the detriment of the organization's objectives, unless provided incentives to do otherwise. Accounting systems are often used to provide these incentives. For example, incentive bonuses are often based on accounting earnings. Section A presents some building blocks underlying the analysis. Section B describes how the firm's organizational architecture creates incentives for employees to maximize the organization's objectives. Sections C and D describe how accounting controls conflicts of interest inside the organization. The next chapter discusses two more accounting tools that are used to resolve organizational problems: responsibility accounting and transfer pricing.

A. Basic Building Blocks[1]

Before describing the general problem of how to motivate and control behavior in organizations (the economics of organizations), this section first describes some underlying concepts:

1. Self-interested behavior, team production, and agency costs.
2. Decision rights and rights systems.
3. Role of knowledge and decision making.
4. Markets versus firms.
5. Influence costs.

1. Self-Interested Behavior, Team Production, and Agency Costs

One of the fundamental tenets of economics is that individuals act in their self-interest to maximize their utility. Employees, managers, and owners are assumed to be rational, utility-maximizing people. Individuals have preferences for a wide variety of not only goods and services but also intangibles such as prestige, love, and respect, and they are willing to trade one thing they value for another. People evaluate the opportunities they face and select those that they perceive will make them better off. Moreover, individuals are not generally able to satisfy all their preferences. Limited resources (time, money, or skills) force people to make choices. When confronted with constraints or a limited set of alternatives, individuals will use their resourcefulness to relax the constraints and generate a larger opportunity set. For example, when the highway speed limit was reduced to 55 miles per hour, the CB radio and radar detector industries emerged to help resourceful, self-interested people circumvent the new law.[2]

Individuals coalesce to form a firm because it can (1) presumably produce more goods or services collectively than individuals are capable of producing alone and (2) thus generate a larger opportunity set. Team production is the key reason that firms exist. Firms are contracting intermediaries. They facilitate exchanges among resource owners who

---

[1]Much of the next two sections is based on M. Jensen and W. Meckling, "Specific and General Knowledge and Organizational Structure," *Contract Economics,* ed. L. Werin and H. Wijkander (Oxford: Blackwell, 1992), pp. 251–74. Also see J. Brickley, C. Smith, and J. Zimmerman, *Managerial Economics and Organizational Architecture,* 6th ed. (Boston: McGraw-Hill, 2016).

[2]W. Meckling, "Values and the Choice of the Model of the Individual in the Social Sciences," *Schweizerische Zeitschrift Für Volkswirtschaft und Statistik,* December 1976.

Managerial Application: Shirking, Surfing, and Social Media while at Work	Depending on the study, most employees spend between one and three hours a day while at work on personal social media or surfing the Web. The time spent on such non-work-related matters is increasing, causing many senior executives to worry about the loss of productivity. Surfing and social media are nothing more than employee shirking, and firms are adopting a variety of policies and systems to control this "on-the-job leisure" activity. Firms are purchasing software that resides on the corporate network that scans for signs of social-media activity and catches inappropriate activity. Some firms require employees to access social-media sites via company-controlled technology. In some cases, these technologies cost as much as $20 a month per employee.

SOURCE: J. Hyatt, "Spies Like You," *CFO* (July/August 2011), p. 16.

voluntarily contract among themselves to benefit each party.[3] People choose to enter contracts because they are made better off by the exchange; there are gains to each party in contracting.

Team production implies that the productivity of any one resource owner is affected by the productivity of all the other team members, because output is a joint product of all the inputs. Suppose Sally and Terry can produce more working together than working separately because they assist each other. Hence, Sally can increase Terry's output and vice versa. This interdependency has important implications for organizations and internal accounting. For one thing, measuring the productivity of one team member requires observing the inputs of all the other team members. However, inputs (such as effort) are typically difficult to observe. If two people are carrying a large, awkward box and it slips and falls, which employee do you blame? Did one of them let it go? Or did it slip out of one employee's hands because the other employee tripped?

In most cases, a resource owner's input cannot be directly observed. Hence, team members have incentives to shirk their responsibilities. If it is difficult to observe Sally's effort, she has incentives to shirk when working with Terry. She can always blame either Terry or random uncontrollable events such as bad weather or missing parts as the reason for low joint output. If Sally and Terry are paid based on their joint output, each still has an incentive to shirk because each bears only half the cost of the reduced output. As the team size is increased, the incentive to shirk becomes greater because the reduced output is spread over more team members. The incentive to shirk in team production is called the *free-rider problem*. Teams try to overcome the free-rider problem through the use of team loyalty—pressure from other team members—and through monitoring. Team production clearly has advantages, but it also causes a variety of organizational problems, in particular the free-rider problem.[4]

Another organizational problem arises when principals hire agents to perform tasks for them. For example, the chief executive officer (CEO) is the agent of the board of directors, who are in turn the elected agents of the shareholders. Vice presidents of the firm are agents of the president, managers are agents of vice presidents, and employees are agents

---

[3]C. Barnard, *The Functions of the Executive* (Cambridge, MA: Harvard University Press, 1938), p. viii, defines organizations as "a system of consciously coordinated activities or forces of two or more persons." See also M. Jensen and W. Meckling, "Theory of the Firm: Managerial Behavior, Agency Costs and Ownership Structure," *Journal of Financial Economics* 3 (1976), pp. 305–60.

[4]A. Alchian and H. Demsetz, "Production, Information Costs, and Economic Organization," *American Economic Review* 62 (1972), pp. 777–95.

Managerial Application: Agency Problems at General Electric	General Electric's (GE) former CEO Jack Welch received a lavish retirement package that attracted considerable public attention when the details became public. The package promised Welch lifetime access to such perks as use of office space in New York and Connecticut, access to GE aircraft, and a chauffeured limousine. Mr. Welch received lifetime use of a $15 million apartment facing Central Park, floor-level seats to New York Knicks basketball games, Yankees tickets, a box at the Metropolitan Opera, free flowers, free toiletries, and free satellite TV at his four homes. The exact details of Mr. Welch's retirement perks came to light when his wife filed for divorce. The perks, valued at $2.5 million a year, were a fraction of Welch's total retirement package, estimated at $20 million to $50 million. After an investigation by securities industry regulators and public outcry, GE revoked some of Welch's privileges, and he said he would pay for the rest.

SOURCES: L. Browning, "Executive Pay: A Special Report; The Perks Still Flow (But With Less Fizz)," *The New York Times,* April 6, 2003, and A. Borrus, "Exposing Execs' 'Stealth' Compensation," *BusinessWeek,* September 12, 2004. http://www.businessweek.com/bwdaily/dnflash/sep2004/nf20040924_8648_db016.htm.

of supervisors. Most employees in a chain of command are both principals to those who report to them and agents to those to whom they report. These principal–agent relationships pervade all organizations: profit and nonprofit firms and governments.

When hired to do a task, agents maximize their utility, which may or may not maximize the principal's utility. Agents' pursuit of their self-interest instead of the principal's is called the *principal–agent problem* or simply the *agency problem*.[5] The extreme example of an agency problem is employee theft of firm property. If undetected, such theft benefits the agent at the expense of the principal. The agent would prefer to see firm resources directed into activities that improve the agent's welfare even if these expenditures do not benefit the principal to the same degree. For example, agents prefer excessive perquisites such as gourmet company-provided lunches and on-the-job leisure. Differences among employees' risk tolerances, working horizons, and desired levels of job perks generate **agency costs**—the decline in firm value that results from agents pursuing their own interests to the detriment of the principal's interest. Agency costs can also arise when agents seek larger organizations to manage (empire building) for the sole purpose of increasing either their job security or their pay. (Many firms base pay on the number of employees reporting to the manager.)

In general, agency problems arise because of information asymmetries. The principal possesses less information than the agent. In the classic principal–agent problem, the principal hires the agent to perform some task, such as managing the principal's investment portfolio. If the agent works hard, the portfolio grows more than if the agent shirks. But the principal cannot observe how hard the agent is working (information asymmetry). Moreover, the investment portfolio's performance depends not just on how hard the agent works, but also on random events, such as general market movements or embezzlement by managers in a company in the investment portfolio. If the principal were able to observe the agent's effort, then a simple contract that pays the agent for effort expended could be used to force the agent to work hard. But since the agent's effort is not observable by

[5]M. Jensen and W. Meckling (1976); H. Simon, "A Formal Theory of the Employment Relationship," *Econometrica* 19 (1951), pp. 293–305; S. Ross, "The Economic Theory of Agency: The Principal's Problem," *American Economic Review* 63 (1973), pp. 134–39; and O. Williamson, *The Economic Institutions of Capitalism* (New York: The Free Press, 1985).

the principal, the principal must contract on some other basis. One such contract could pay the agent a fraction of the portfolio's growth. But since part of the portfolio's performance depends on random factors, the agent could work hard, but adverse random events outside the agent's control could negate that hard work. While this contract induces hard work, it also imposes risk on the agent for which he or she must be compensated. Hence, most agency problems involve balancing stronger incentives for the agent to work hard against the higher risk premium required by the agent to compensate for the additional risk imposed on the agent.

Consider another example of an agency problem, that of senior executives paid a fixed salary. Because executives have less incentive to maximize shareholder value than if they owned the entire firm themselves, incentive compensation plans are introduced to tie the executive's welfare more closely to shareholder welfare. The agent may have a lower tolerance for risk than the principal and therefore will choose more conservative actions. Principal–agent problems can also arise because most supervisors find it personally unpleasant to discipline or dismiss poorly performing subordinates. Instead of taking these unpopular actions, supervisors allow underperforming subordinates to remain in their positions, which reduces firm value. The difference between the value of the firm with and without the poorly performing subordinate is the agency cost imposed on the owners of the firm by the shirking supervisor.

If the agent expects to leave the organization before the principal, the agent will tend to focus on short-run actions. This leads to the *horizon problem:* Managers expecting to leave the firm in the near future place less weight than the principal on those consequences that may occur after they leave. As an example of the horizon problem, consider the case of a divisional manager, Henry Metz, who expects to retire in three years. Henry is paid a fixed salary plus 5 percent of his division's profits. To simplify the example, make the unrealistic assumption that Henry cares only about cash compensation. He can spend $100,000 on process improvements this year and next year that will yield $150,000 of cost savings for each of the following four years. Table 4–1 illustrates the cash flows.

The process improvements are clearly profitable, so they should be accepted.[6] But Henry, who has a three-year horizon, rejects the project because it reduces his total bonus. He bears much of the cost while his successor receives most of the benefits in years 4, 5, and 6. Nonpecuniary interests of the manager, such as peer pressure, tend to reduce the horizon problem. However, the basic point remains: Agents facing a known departure date place less weight on events that occur after they leave than on events that occur while they are still there; the short-term consequences of current decisions will matter far more to them than the long-term consequences.

TABLE 4–1 Example of the Horizon Problem

Year	Outlay	Cost Savings	Effect on Henry Metz's Bonus Compensation
1	$100,000	—	−$5,000
2	100,000	—	−5,000
3	0	$150,000	+7,500
4	0	150,000	0
5	0	150,000	0
6	0	150,000	0

[6]These process improvements have a positive net present value unless the discount rate is greater than 45 percent. Hence, under most market discount rates, they are profitable.

Managerial Application: Agency Problems at Société Générale	Société Générale was founded in the 1860s and in 2008 was France's second largest bank. It pioneered some of the most complex international financial instruments, earned billions of dollars, and gained the respect of bankers throughout the world. In January 2008, the bank discovered fraudulent securities trading by one of its low-level traders, Jérôme Kerviel. The fraud was estimated to cost a staggering $7.14 billion, making it one of the largest financial frauds in history. The bank asserted that the fraud was the result of one employee's illegal activities, did not involve other employees at the bank, and represented the aberrant and unexplainable actions of one "rogue trader."
	Kerviel's job involved arbitraging small differences between various stock market indexes, such as the CAC in France and the DAX in Germany, by selling a security on the exchange with the higher price and simultaneously buying an equivalent instrument on the exchange with the lower price. Small price differences on the two exchanges can produce a substantial profit when done in sufficient volume. Purchasing and selling equal amounts on the two exchanges should produce little net exposure to price changes. However, Kerviel had bought securities on both markets, betting that European stock prices would increase. When they fell, the bank incurred a substantial loss. Kerviel told investigators that all he wanted was to be respected and to earn a large bonus.
	Prior to becoming a trader, Kerviel had worked in the bank's trading accounting office, where he gained knowledge of the bank's risk-management system. This allowed him to conceal the trades and bypass the firm's control system. An investigation of this incident concluded that Société Générale "allowed a culture of risk to flourish, creating major flaws in its operations" that enabled Kerviel's actions to proceed. Traders were rewarded for making risky investments with the bank's money. Top executives at the bank received large bonuses because of the bank's successful trading operations.
	This example illustrates that agency problems (including fraud) can impose enormous costs on firms.
	SOURCE: Adapted from J. Brickley, C. Smith, and J. Zimmerman (2009), p. 13.

To reduce agency costs such as employee theft and the free-rider and horizon problems, firms incur costs. These costs include hiring security guards to prevent theft, hiring supervisors to monitor employees, installing accounting and reporting systems to measure and reward output, and paying legal fees to enforce compliance with contracts. However, as long as it is costly to monitor agents' actions, some divergence of interests between agents and principals will remain. It is usually not cost-efficient to eliminate all divergent acts.

Managerial Application: Agency Problems with Corporate Jet Pilots	Corporate jets often have to refuel on intercontinental flights, usually in Kansas or Nebraska. Refuelers at the same airport compete by offering pilots frozen steaks, wine, or top-of-the-line golf gear. These freebies are usually offered only if the pilot forgoes discounts on fuel, and they are almost always given in a covert manner—so that the corporation owning the plane never knows why the pilot has chosen that particular refueler. Suppose the pilot chooses a refueler who charges $150 more than the least-cost option because the pilot gets $80 worth of gifts. This wealth transfer from the owners of the jet to the pilot is an example of an agency problem.
	SOURCE: S. McCartney, "We'll Be Landing So the Crew Can Grab a Steak," *The Wall Street Journal,* September 8, 1998, p. A1.

Academic Application: Adverse Selection and Moral Hazard Problems	Two types of agency problems have been given specific names. *Adverse selection* refers to the tendency of individuals with private information about something that benefits them to make offers that are detrimental to the trading partner. For example, individuals have more information regarding their health than do life insurance companies. If unconstrained, people who buy life insurance are likely to have more severe health problems than the average person assumed by the insurance company when setting its rates. After the insurance company sets its rates based on an average person, an adverse group of individuals will buy the insurance and the insurance company will lose money. To protect itself from adverse selection, insurance companies require medical exams to exclude the overly ill or to charge them higher prices (e.g., smokers).
	Moral hazard problems arise when an individual has an incentive to deviate from the contract and take self-interested actions because the other party has insufficient information to know if the contract was honored. An example of a moral hazard problem often occurs in automobile accident claims. The insured may claim that the door was dented in the accident when in fact it was already damaged. To reduce moral hazard problems, a variety of solutions exist, including inspections and monitoring.

Agency costs are also limited by the existence of a job market for managers, the market for corporate control, and competition from other firms. The job market for managers causes managers to limit their divergent actions to avoid being replaced by other (outside) managers.[7] Replacements will occur if the board of directors has access to these job markets and incentives to replace the managers. If the board fails to reduce the firm's agency costs, the firm's stock price declines. Low stock prices encourage takeovers. The market for corporate control will then limit the agency costs of existing management via unfriendly takeovers. Finally, if both the job and corporate control markets fail, other firms in the same product market will supply better products at lower prices and eventually force firms with high agency costs out of business. However, to the extent that there are transactions costs in all these markets, it will not be cost-beneficial to drive agency costs to zero. For example, if the transactions costs of a corporate takeover, including legal, accounting, and underwriting fees, are 3 percent of the value of the firm, then it will not pay outsiders to acquire the firm if the magnitude of the agency costs they hope to eliminate are less than 3 percent. Thus, this level of agency costs will persist.

Agents maximize their utility, not the principal's. This problem is commonly referred to as **goal incongruence**, which simply means that individual agents have different goals from their principal. The term is misleading, because it suggests that the firm can secure congruence by changing personal preferences (i.e., utility functions) so that all individuals in the organization adopt the principal's goal. However, self-interested individuals' preferences are not easily altered. The firm can reduce the agency problem, if not goal incongruence, by structuring agents' incentives so that when agents maximize their utility (primarily incentive-based compensation), the principal's utility (or wealth) is also maximized. In other words, the agents' and principals' goals become congruent through the agents' incentive scheme, not through a change in the agents' underlying preferences.

2. Decision Rights and Rights Systems

All economic resources or assets are bundles of decision rights with respect to how they can or cannot be used. For example, ownership of a car includes a bundle of decision rights

---

[7]E. Fama, "Agency Problems and the Theory of the Firm," *Journal of Political Economy,* April 1980, pp. 288–307.

over its use, although not unrestricted use. The car owner can drive, sell, paint, or even destroy the car, but it is illegal to drive the car over the speed limit. The police powers of the state enforce private decision rights over assets; the threat of legal sanctions is brought to bear against someone interfering with another's rights. If someone prevents you from driving your car by stealing it, the thief can be imprisoned. Our system of private property rights, including the courts and the police, enforces and limits individual decision rights.

Decision rights over the firm's assets are assigned to various people within the firm who are then held accountable for the results. If an individual is given decision-making authority over some decision (such as setting the price of a particular product), we say that person has the *decision right* for that product's price. Throughout the remainder of the book, we describe the importance of assigning decision rights to various individuals within the organization and the role of accounting in the assignment process. Who or what group of individuals has the decision rights to set the price, hire employees, accept a new order, or sell an asset? A key decision for many managers is whether to retain the right to make a particular decision or delegate the right to someone else. The question of whether the organization is centrally managed or decentralized is an issue of decision right assignment. **Employee empowerment** is a term that means assigning more decision rights to employees (i.e., decentralization). Accounting-based budgets assign decision rights to make expenditures to specific employees.

3. Role of Knowledge and Decision Making

Although they are rational and self-interested, individuals have limited capacities to gather and process knowledge. Since information (knowledge) is costly to acquire, store, and process, individual decision-making capacities are limited. Steve Jobs did not make all of the decisions at Apple because he lacked the time to acquire the knowledge necessary for decision making. The process of generating the knowledge necessary to make a decision and then transferring that knowledge within the firm drives the assignment of decision rights.[8]

Because knowledge is valuable in decision making, knowledge and decision making are generally linked; the right to make the decision and the knowledge to make it usually reside within the same person. In fact, a key organizational architecture issue is *whether and how to link knowledge and decision rights.* Some knowledge, such as price and quantity, is easy (inexpensive) to transfer. In these cases, the knowledge is transferred to the person with the right to make the decision. Other knowledge is more difficult and hence costlier to transfer. Technical knowledge, such as how to design a computer chip, is costly to transfer. Knowledge that changes quickly, such as whether a machine is idle for the next hour, is costly to transfer in time to be useful; therefore, the decision right to schedule the machine is transferred to the person with the knowledge.

Ideally, knowledge and decision rights are linked, but they do not always reside with the same person. Suppose it is very difficult to transfer knowledge and very difficult to monitor the person with the knowledge. Moreover, suppose large agency costs arise if the person with the knowledge has the decision rights. Firm value might be higher if another manager with less knowledge makes the decision. This will occur if the costs from the inferior decisions made by the manager with less knowledge are smaller than the agency costs that result from giving the decision rights to the person with the better knowledge. For example, in many firms, salespeople do not have the decision right to negotiate prices directly with the customer, even though they have specialized knowledge of the customer's demand curve. Pricing is determined centrally by managers with less information, perhaps to reduce the likelihood that the salesperson will offer a low price and receive a kickback from the customer.

---

[8]M. Jensen and W. Meckling, *Contract Economics*, ed. L. Werin and H. Wijkander (Oxford: Blackwell, 1992), pp. 251–74.

Managerial Application: Use of Specific Knowledge at Apple Computer	Apple's PowerBook was among the first portable Macs. It had so many bells and whistles that it weighed 17 pounds. It did not do well in the market. Apple began completely reworking the design of the computer from the consumer's viewpoint. The entire product-development team of software designers, industrial engineers, marketing people, and industrial designers was sent into the field to observe potential customers using other products. The team discovered that people used laptops on airplanes, in cars, and at home in bed. Users wanted mobile computers, not just small computers. In response, Apple redesigned the PowerBook so it was easy to use and distinctive. Sales improved. The knowledge of what customers really wanted in a laptop was acquired by a team who interacted closely with customers. The team also had important knowledge that allowed them to use this information to design a marketable product. Finally, they had the authority to modify the product based on their findings. It is less likely that this specific knowledge would have been incorporated in product design in a large centrally planned firm—in which a central office is in charge of making literally thousands of decisions. SOURCE: "Hot Products, Smart Design Is the Common Thread," *BusinessWeek*, June 7, 1993, pp. 54–57.

Managerial Application: Linking Knowledge and Decision Rights at Safety-Cleen Systems	How do high-ranking managers with the decision rights acquire the knowledge to make good decisions? One common way is by visiting customers. Safety-Cleen, a $1.3 billion recycler of oil and environmental services provider, hired a new CFO. He visited customers with "ride-alongs" to pick up oil and containerized waste and, thereby, to "really get to learn the company." As the new CFO explains, "To make proper investment decisions on capital expenditures, marketing, business development, and so on, the CFO has to know the business. It's easier to approve a capital project related to a facility when you've actually been to the facility and you know the facility manager and understand his opportunity. It's easier to support and approve a marketing campaign when you know the strategy of the product and how it fits with the strategy of the company as a whole." SOURCE: S. Leibs, "Going for the Green," *CFO Magazine*, April 15, 2012, pp. 37–38.

Within all organizations, decision rights and knowledge must be linked. As we will see, accounting systems, especially budgets (Chapter 6) and standard costs (Chapter 12), are important devices for transferring knowledge to the individuals with the decision rights or giving the decision rights to individuals with the knowledge.

4. Markets versus Firms

Production occurs either within a firm or across markets. For example, some computer software is produced by computer hardware companies and bundled with the computer, while other software is produced and sold separately. As another example, stereos can be purchased as entire systems. Here, the manufacturer designs, assembles, and ships complete units composed of a tuner-amplifier, CD player, and speakers. Alternatively, the consumer can purchase the components separately and assemble a complete system.

Nobel Prize winner in economics Ronald Coase argued that firms lower certain transactions costs below what it would cost to acquire equivalent goods or services in a series of market transactions.[9] He conjectured that firms exist when they have lower costs than

---

[9]R. Coase, "The Nature of the Firm," *Economica* 4 (1937), pp. 386–405. Also, see R. Watts, "Accounting Choice Theory and Market-Based Research in Accounting," *British Accounting Journal* 24 (1992), pp. 242–46.

136   *Chapter 4*

Historical Application: Firms versus Markets when Markets Ruled	Much of the world's economic activity is conducted within firms. In fact, it is hard to envision a world where large firms do not play an important role in the production and distribution of products. The importance of firms, however, is a relatively recent phenomenon. Prior to the middle of the nineteenth century, there were almost no large firms. Most production was conducted by small owner-managed operations. The activities of these operations were coordinated almost entirely through market transactions.

> The traditional American business (before 1950) was a single-unit business enterprise. In such an enterprise an individual or a small number of owners operated a shop, factory, bank, or transportation line out of a single office. Normally, this type of firm handled only a single economic function, dealt in a single product line, and operated in one geographic area. Before the rise of the modern firm, the activities of one of these small personally owned and managed enterprises were coordinated and monitored by market and price mechanisms.
>
> The large firm became feasible only with the development of improved energy sources, transportation, and communications. In particular, coal provided a source of energy that made it possible for the factory to replace artisans and small mill owners, while railroads enabled firms to ship large quantities of goods to newly emerging urban centers. The telegraph allowed firms to coordinate activities of employees over larger geographic areas. These developments made it less expensive to coordinate production and distribution using administrative controls, rather than relying on numerous market transactions among numerous small firms.

SOURCE: A. Chandler, *The Visible Hand: The Managerial Revolution in American Business* (Cambridge, MA: Harvard University Press, 1977).

markets. Team production, discussed earlier, is one way firms can have lower costs than markets. When a firm can substitute one transaction that occurs inside the firm for a series of external market contracts, total contracting costs usually are lower.

The longer the term of a contract, the more difficult and costly it is to negotiate and to specify the respective parties' tasks. Firms eliminate a series of short-term market contracts and replace them with a single long-term contract. For example, if the firm has a long-term project to develop a sophisticated piece of computer software, it is likely that such software will be developed inside the firm as opposed to being purchased from an outside firm.

The costs of acquiring knowledge and enforcing contracts drive some production to occur within firms and other production to occur in markets. If knowledge were costless to acquire and process and there were no transactions costs, there would be no multiperson firms. To purchase an automobile, the consumer would enter into thousands of separate contracts with individual assemblers. If knowledge were free, these contracts would be costless. But knowledge is not free; our ability to acquire and process it is limited. Firms emerge because they economize on repetitive contracting. For example, individuals usually hire general contractors to build custom homes. The general contractor has specialized knowledge of the various skilled tradespeople (plumbers, carpenters, and electricians) and can monitor these subcontractors more cheaply than the individual home owner.

Coase's analysis has led to an important proposition in economics. Firms that survive in competition must have a comparative advantage in constructing contracts for internal production. Surviving firms have lower transactions costs than the market. This is an application of economic Darwinism (discussed in Chapter 1).

Managerial Application: Markets versus Firms: Taxicabs	To illustrate how markets help to control human behavior, consider the example of privately owned and operated cabs versus cabs owned by a taxi company and driven by different-salaried drivers. Which cabs will have a higher market value after being driven 50,000 miles? The owners of privately owned cabs have a greater incentive to maintain their cabs than the drivers of company-owned cabs. The resale price of each cab reflects wear and tear and maintenance. Since private cab drivers, as the sole drivers, bear all the financial consequences of their actions, they have an incentive to provide the correct amount of maintenance and generally drive the cab in such a way as to maximize the market value of the cab at resale. Drivers for the taxi company do not bear the consequences of any abusive driving and/or poor maintenance, unless the taxi company implements costly procedures to monitor the condition of the cabs after each driver's shift. To provide incentives for the cabbies not to damage the cabs, the taxi company must install monitoring devices, but it is prohibitively costly to detect all abuse (such as transmission damage).

Nonetheless, markets perform certain functions far better than firms. Ultimately, markets exist because of the right to transfer ownership of an asset and receive the proceeds. As noted earlier, individuals or firms have decision rights with respect to resources they own, including the right to use those resources as they see fit (within the limits of the law), the right to sell the resources, and the right to the sales proceeds. Markets discipline those who have the resources to use them in their highest-valued way. If owners lower the value of their assets by not properly maintaining them, markets punish them by lowering the resale price. Thus, markets not only measure decision-makers' performance but also reward or punish that behavior. In fact, markets do three things automatically that organizations (firms) can accomplish only through elaborate administrative devices: (1) measure performance, (2) reward performance, and (3) partition rights to their highest-valued use. When Adam Smith described the invisible hand of the market and how the market allocates resources to their most highly valued use, he was describing how the market influences behavior and assigns decision rights.[10]

Because an asset's current price reflects the future cash flows associated with it, decision rights over how assets will be used in the future tend to be assigned to those who value them the highest. In markets, decision rights are linked with knowledge. Individuals or firms with "better" knowledge in using the asset will be willing to pay a higher price for the asset, thereby linking knowledge with decision rights.

5. Influence Costs

Up to this point, we have assumed that when decision-making authority is granted to an individual or a team within the firm, that agent or team is then actively involved in decision making (subject to ratification and monitoring from others). Sometimes, however, firms use bureaucratic rules that purposely limit active decision making. For example, airlines allocate routes to flight attendants based on seniority—there is no supervisor deciding who gets which route. Similarly, some firms base promotions solely on years worked with the firm.

One potential benefit of limiting discretion in making decisions is that it reduces the resources consumed by individuals in trying to influence decisions. Employees are often very concerned about the personal effects of decisions made within the firm. For example, flight attendants care about which routes they fly. Employees are not indifferent to which

---

[10]A. Smith, *The Wealth of Nations,* 1776, Cannan edition (New York: Modern Library, 1937).

Managerial Application: Frauds	Fraud and embezzlement remain major problems in all organizations. Bernie Madoff's $65 billion Ponzi scheme where he pleaded guilty and was sentenced to 150 years in prison continues to be a prominent example. The PwC 2014 Global Fraud Report of over 5,000 firms found that 37 percent of the respondents reported that their firm had experienced economic crime in 2013. Fifty-three percent of CEOs surveyed reported being concerned about bribery and corruption. And 48 percent reported the risk of cybercrime had increased. Among firms reporting economic crime, 69 percent involved stolen assets, 29 percent were procurement frauds, 27 percent involved bribery and corruption, 24 percent were cybercrimes, and 22 percent were accounting frauds. The most likely targets of fraud are firms in financial services, communication, and retail, as well as small and mid-sized firms.

SOURCE: *"PwC 2014 Global Economic Crime Survey" at www.pwc.com/gx/en/economic-crime-survey/downloads.jhtm*

colleagues are laid off in an economic downturn. These concerns motivate politicking and other potentially nonproductive activities. For instance, employees might waste valuable time trying to influence decision makers. In vying for promotions, employees might take dysfunctional actions to make other employees look bad.

By not assigning the decision right to a specific individual, influence costs are lowered because there is no one to lobby. This policy, however, can impose costs on an organization. For example, consider individuals who are competing for a promotion. Each of these individuals has an incentive to provide evidence to the supervisor that he or she is the most qualified person for the promotion. Such information is often useful in making better promotion decisions. However, the information comes at a cost—employees spend time trying to convince the supervisor that they are the most qualified candidate rather than performing some other activity such as selling products.

In some cases, the firm's profits are largely unaffected by decisions that greatly affect individual employee welfare. For example, firm profits might be invariant as to which flight attendant gets the Hawaii route versus the Sioux Falls route. It is in this setting that bureaucratic rules for decision making are most likely. The firm benefits from a reduction in influence costs but is little affected by the particular outcome of the decision process.

Concept Questions	Q4–1	What generates agency costs?
	Q4–2	How are agency costs reduced, and what limits them?
	Q4–3	Define *goal incongruence*.
	Q4–4	How does one achieve goal congruence?
	Q4–5	Why are knowledge and decision making linked within a firm?
	Q4–6	Name three things markets do automatically that must be replaced with elaborate administrative systems in the firm.
	Q4–7	What are influence costs?
	Q4–8	Why do firms exist?

Managerial Application: Gaming Objective Performance-Evaluation Systems	This example illustrates how members of one local management team who did not want to lose their jobs successfully gamed the performance-evaluation system their company used in deciding when to close unprofitable mines.
	In this particular company, mines were shut down after the yield per ton of ore dropped below a certain level. One old marginal mine managed to stay open for several years because of the strategic behavior of its management. It happened that the mine contained one very rich pocket of ore. Instead of mining this all at once, the management used it as its reserve. Every time the yield of the ore it was mining fell below an acceptable level, it would mix in a little high-grade ore so the mine would remain open.
	SOURCE: E. Lawler and J. Rhode, *Information and Control in Organizations* (Santa Monica, CA: Goodyear Publishing, 1976), pp. 87–88.

B. Organizational Architecture

When firms undertake certain repetitive transactions instead of contracting for them in outside markets, market prices for resources used inside the firm no longer exist. For example, the firm can be thought of as a bundle of resources used jointly to produce a product. Suppose one of the many jointly used resources is a machine used in manufacturing. There is not a specific market price for the machine used inside the firm. There is not a price for an hour of time on the machine because the firm does not engage in selling time on this machine. There may be market prices for leasing time on other firms' machines, but if buying outside machine time was cheaper than using the internal machine, the machine would not exist inside the time. The cost of buying outside services includes the external price and the transactions costs of using the market. Even if prices for seemingly equivalent transactions occurring in markets exist, they are unlikely to represent the opportunity cost for transactions within the firm. The transaction exists within the firm because the firm can perform the transaction more cheaply than the market. Hence, the external market price for the machine, while indicative of what the firm can charge for time on its machine, does not capture the opportunity cost of using the machine inside the firm. The market price does not entirely capture the transactions cost savings of owning the machine.[11]

1. Three-Legged Stool

The firm cannot always use the external market's price (even if available) to guide internal transactions. More important, in the absence of the discipline of the market, the parties to the firm must design administrative devices to (1) measure performance, (2) reward performance, and (3) partition decision rights. These three activities (called **organizational architecture**) are performed automatically by markets but must be performed by (costly) administrative devices inside the firm.[12]

Performance evaluation can involve either objective or subjective performance measures or combinations of both. Objective criteria include explicit, verifiable measures such as paying employees on piece rates or sales. Subjective criteria focus on multiple hard-to-measure factors. For example, subjective performance measures include a variety of factors such as improving team spirit, getting along with peers, meeting budgets and

---

[11]"Observed market prices cannot directly guide the owner of the input to perform in the same manner as if every activity he performs were measured and priced." S. Cheung, "The Contractual Nature of the Firm," *Journal of Law & Economics* 26 (April 1983), p. 5.

[12]Jensen and Meckling (1992), p. 265.

schedules, and affirmative action hiring. Firms use implicit, subjective performance measures because jobs typically have multiple dimensions. If a few explicit characteristics are chosen to reward performance, employees will ignore the hard-to-quantify aspects of their work. Although firms must measure and reward performance, the performance measure need not be objective. Firms that use objective performance measures supplement them with subjective measures to ensure that employees do not focus entirely on the objective criteria to the detriment of their other responsibilities.

Besides measuring performance, organizations must reward favorable performance and in some cases punish unwanted behaviors (sometimes by firing employees). Agents meeting or exceeding performance expectations are rewarded with pay increases, bonuses, promotions, and perquisites. Superior performance is rewarded with both monetary and nonmonetary compensation. Monetary rewards involve salary, bonus, and retirement benefits. Nonmonetary rewards include prestigious job titles, better office location and furnishings, reserved parking spaces, and country club memberships.

Another administrative device in firms is partitioning decision rights. Within organizations, all decision rights initially reside with the board of directors. The vast majority of these rights are assigned to the chief executive officer (CEO), with the exception of the right to replace the CEO and set his or her pay. The CEO retains some rights and reassigns the rest to subordinates. This downward cascading of decision rights within an organization gives rise to the familiar pyramid of hierarchies. Centralization and decentralization revolve around the issues of partitioning decision rights between higher versus lower levels of the organization and linking knowledge and decision rights.

Ultimately, all organizations must construct three systems:

1. A system that measures performance.
2. A system that rewards and punishes performance.
3. A system that assigns decision rights.

These three systems make up the firm's organizational architecture. They are like the legs of a three-legged stool. For the stool to remain level, all three legs must balance. Similarly, each of the three systems that compose the organization's architecture must be coordinated with the other two. The performance measurement system must measure the agent's performance in areas over which he or she has been assigned the decision rights. Likewise, the reward system must be matched to those areas over which performance is being measured. A person should not be assigned decision rights if the exercise of these rights cannot be measured and rewarded. Though this sounds obvious, changing one system often requires changing the other two systems.

The internal accounting system is a significant part of the performance measurement system. Changes are often made to this system without regard to their impact on the performance-reward and decision-assignment systems. Managers making changes to the accounting system are surprised when the stool is no longer level because one leg is now a different length than the other two.

Performance measurement systems generally use financial and nonfinancial measures of performance. Nonfinancial metrics include percentage of on-time deliveries, order completeness, excess inventory, employee turnover, manufacturing quality, percentage of defects and units of scrap, and customer complaints. Financial indicators are collected and audited by the firm's accountants, whereas nonfinancial measures are more likely to be self-reported. Therefore, financial measures are usually more objective and less subject to managerial discretion. Nonfinancial indicators usually relate to important strategic factors. For example, airline profitability is very sensitive to the fraction of airline seats occupied. Thus, load factors are an important strategic measure in airlines. Nonfinancial measures

Managerial Application: Objective and Subjective Performance Criteria at Lincoln Electric Company	Lincoln Electric manufactures electric arc welding machines and welding disposables (electrodes). At the heart of Lincoln Electric's success is a strategy of building quality products at a lower cost than its competitors and passing the savings on to customers. Lincoln implements this strategy, in part, by fostering labor-productivity increases via a pay-for-performance compensation plan.

The two components of Lincoln's performance evaluation scheme are pieces produced and merit rating. The first component is an objective, readily quantifiable performance measure for each production employee (i.e., the number of good units produced). The employee's wage is equal to the piece rate times the number of good units produced. (Employees are not paid for defects.) By working hard, in some cases even through lunch and breaks, employees can double and sometimes triple their pay.

The second component of Lincoln's evaluation scheme is the employee's merit rating. These ratings are used to determine the employee's share of the bonus pool. The size of the bonus pool approximately equals wages and is about twice Lincoln's net income after taxes, although there is substantial annual variation in the size of the pool. Each employee's merit evaluation is based on employee dependability, quality, output, and ideas and cooperation, assessed primarily by the employee's immediate supervisor.

Two important observations emerge from Lincoln Electric. First, the output from the performance evaluation system is used as an input by the performance reward system; the two systems are linked. Second, Lincoln uses highly objective, explicit measures of performance (piecework) as well as subjective measures (ideas and cooperation).

SOURCE: www.lincolnelectric.com.

Managerial Application: Performance Evaluation and Rewards at the Haier Group	Haier, one of China's fastest-growing firms, stresses customer service, product quality, efficiency, and speed to market. It manufactures more than 15,000 different home appliances such as refrigerators, air conditioners, microwaves, and washing machines that are sold in 160 countries through 59,000 sales outlets. In the 1980s, it was near bankruptcy. What explains Haier's phenomenal success?

Haier utilizes sophisticated employee performance measurement and reward systems. Each day, every factory worker receives a detailed report card outlining his or her production quantity, quality, defects, equipment use, and safety record. Each employee is expected to improve 1 percent over the previous day. Realizing these improvements results in higher wages, bonuses, more job training, and additional social benefits. People not achieving their targets are demoted and eventually fired. Managers are reviewed weekly based on their achieving both qualitative and quantitative goals such as process improvement and innovation. Managers, like factory workers, are rewarded with additional pay and promotions for meeting their targets or demoted or even fired for poor performance. Dozens of Haier employees are fired every month. "Whoever tarnishes the brand of the company will be dismissed by the company."

SOURCE: T. Lin, "Haier Is Higher," *Strategic Finance*, December 2009, pp. 41–49; http://www.haier.com.pk/.

provide information for making decisions. Financial measures of performance tend to be for controlling behavior.

One problem with using nonfinancial measures is that they tend to proliferate to the point that managers can no longer jointly maximize multiple measures. Numerous

Managerial Application: VA Administrators Game Their Performance Measures	Most federal agencies pay executive bonuses to increase accountability in government by tying pay to performance. Federal bonuses are designed to retain and reward knowledgeable and professional career public servants. While bonuses can help retain key employees, performance-based bonuses can be gamed, leading to counterproductive actions.
	The Secretary of the U.S. Department of Veterans Affairs, General Eric Shinseki, was forced to resign following the disclosure of secret waiting lists at several V.A. hospitals serving former U.S. military personnel, many of whom were wounded in action. Administrators at veterans' hospitals were told to alter data to make patient-access numbers look good for their supervisors. These superiors did not want long reported wait times because their bonuses were tied directly to the waiting times of the veterans. Reporting long wait times generated unfavorable performance reviews and, hence, a lower bonus. In one hospital, many veterans were not entered into the official electronic waiting list, thereby distorting actual delays in providing care. Another V.A. clinic changed its bonus system, whereby bonuses would be paid only to doctors who limited patient follow-up visits to an average of two a year as a way to reduce waiting times by persuading veterans to make fewer appointments.
	This example illustrates that pay-for-performance creates incentives to game the system. In other words, employees will attempt to game all performance measures, especially when they are used to determine rewards. The critical managerial question is: "By how much?"
	SOURCE: R. Oppel and A. Goodnough (2014), "Doctor Shortage Is Cited in Delays at V.A. Hospitals," *NY Times* (May 29).

performance measures dilute attention. If several key indicators are used, senior managers must implicitly specify the relative weights for each indicator for performance evaluation. Which indicator is really the most important in assessing performance? If senior management does not specify the weights, subordinates are uncertain which specific goal should receive the most attention. Chapter 14 describes the Balanced Scorecard, and specifically the problem of using multiple performance measures.

Managerial Application: When the Legs of the Stool Don't Balance	This example illustrates how dysfunctional decisions can result when the three legs of the stool do not match. A plane was grounded for repairs at an airport. The nearest qualified mechanic was stationed at another airport. The decision right to allow the mechanic to work on the airplane was held by the manager of the second airport. The manager's compensation, however, was tied to meeting his own budget rather than to the profits of the overall organization. The manager refused to send the mechanic to fix the plane immediately because the mechanic would have had to stay overnight and the hotel bill would have been charged to the manager's budget. The mechanic was dispatched the next morning so that he could return the same day. A multimillion-dollar aircraft was grounded, costing the airline thousands of dollars. The manager, however, avoided a $100 hotel bill. The mechanic would probably have been dispatched immediately had the manager been rewarded on the overall profit of the company or had the decision right been held by someone else with this objective.
	SOURCE: M. Hammer and J. Champy, *Reengineering the Corporation* (New York: Harper Business, 1993).

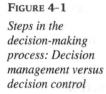

FIGURE 4-1

Steps in the decision-making process: Decision management versus decision control

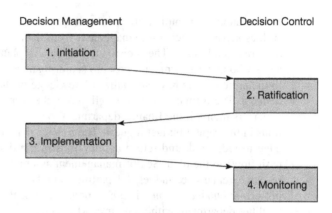

Decision Management   Decision Control

1. Initiation

2. Ratification

3. Implementation

4. Monitoring

2. Decision Management versus Decision Control

Markets automatically control behavior and partition decision rights. The firm must design administrative devices to do what the market does. These mechanisms include hierarchies to separate decision management from control, budgeting systems, periodic performance evaluation systems, standard operating rules and policy manuals, executive compensation schemes, and accounting systems. Some of these administrative devices, such as hierarchies and performance evaluation systems, are described in greater detail next. Budgeting systems and accounting systems are deferred to later chapters.

Perhaps the most important mechanism for resolving agency problems is a hierarchical structure that separates decision management from decision control.[13] All organizations have hierarchies with higher-level managers supervising lower-level employees. **Decision management** refers to those aspects of the decision process in which the manager either *initiates* or *implements* a decision. **Decision control** refers to those aspects of the decision process whereby managers either *ratify* or *monitor* decisions. See Figure 4–1. Managers rarely have all the decision rights to make a particular decision. Rather, an elaborate system of approvals and monitoring exists. Consider a typical decision to hire a new employee. First, a manager requests authorization to add a new position. This request is reviewed by higher-level managers. Once the position is authorized, the manager making the request usually begins the recruiting and interviewing process. Eventually a new employee is hired. After a certain period, the employee's performance is evaluated. In general, the following steps in the decision process occur (categorized according to decision management or decision control): (1) initiation (management), (2) ratification (control), (3) implementation (management), and (4) monitoring (control). *Initiation* is the request to hire a new employee. *Ratification* is the approval of the request. *Implementation* is hiring the employee. *Monitoring* involves assessing the performance of the hired employee at periodic intervals to evaluate the person who hires the employee.

Individual managers typically do not have the authority to undertake all four steps in this decision process. The manager requesting a new position does not have the decision right to ratify (approve) the request. There is a *separation of decision management from control.* The same principle in the U.S. Constitution separates the powers of the various branches of government. The executive branch requests spending, which is approved by the legislature. The executive branch is then charged with making the expenditures. The judicial branch ultimately monitors both the executive and legislative branches.

---

[13]See E. Fama and M. Jensen, "Separation of Ownership and Control," *Journal of Political Economy,* June 1983, pp. 301–25.

As another example of how knowledge is linked with initiation rights and how hierarchies separate decision management from decision control, consider the decision to acquire capital assets. The decision to build a new plant usually begins with division managers who make a formal proposal to senior management. This is decision *initiation*. The initiating managers have specialized knowledge of their production process and product demand. The formal proposal usually takes the form of a capital budget request. Senior managers then ask the finance department to evaluate the discounted cash flow assumptions in the capital budget request. The finance department possesses specialized knowledge to judge risk-and-return assumptions in the discount rate and the analysis of the cash flows in the plan. Senior management assembles other knowledge from the human resource, real estate, and legal departments in the *ratification* process. Construction of the project—*implementation*—is the responsibility of the proposing managers or a separate facilities department within the firm. After construction is completed, accountants prepare monthly, quarterly, and annual reports on the division requesting and operating the capital project. This is part of the *monitoring* process.

Organizations separate decision management from decision control. Before implementing a decision, someone higher up in the organization must ratify it. Management and control are not separated, however, when it is too costly to separate them. For example, managers are often assigned the decision rights to make small purchases (perhaps under $500) without ratification because the cost of separating management from control exceeds the benefits. Since it takes time to receive ratification, lost opportunities or other adverse consequences can occur. The most vivid illustration of delay costs is in the military. Fighter pilots flying in noncombat situations do not have the decision rights to fire at unauthorized or potential enemy planes. They first must notify their superiors and seek authority to shoot. But in combat situations, decision management and decision control are not separated because to do so would hamper the pilots' ability to respond in situations when delays can be catastrophic. In combat, pilots have the authority to fire at enemy aircraft. An example of avoiding a delay that could possibly be deadly: In some states, paramedics can administer certain drugs in life-threatening situations without first getting a physician's approval.

Managerial Application: Capital Project Monitoring at Caterpillar	Most large firms have internal audit groups, and one important function of these groups is to monitor capital investment projects. For example, Caterpillar Inc. monitors strategic capital projects such as a new plant over the life of each project. Once a capital project is approved and installed, the internal auditors review it every six months. Only large strategic projects (often composed of several individual capital assets), such as an axle factory or an assembly line, are evaluated. The internal auditors prepare a report that compares the actual results with the budgeted results. Reasons for any differences are listed, including a detailed report that reconciles why the project's current results differ from what was expected at the time the capital project was approved. In addition, the monitoring team issues a list of recommendations to improve the performance of the project. The monitoring team's findings are distributed to the manager of the project being evaluated, the plant manager, the group presidents, and the corporate board of directors.

SOURCES: J. Hendricks, R. Bastian, and T. Sexton, "Bundle Monitoring of Strategic Projects," *Management Accounting*, February 1992, pp. 31–35; and Ernst & Young, "The Future of Internal Auditing Is Now," July 2012.

Concept Questions	Q4–9	Define *decision management* and *decision control*, and give an example of each.
	Q4–10	Describe the three systems all organizations must construct to control agency problems.
	Q4–11	Describe the four major steps in the management decision process. How are agency problems reduced in this process?

C. Accounting's Role in the Organization's Architecture

The preceding section described the separation of decision management from decision control. One way to limit agency costs is to separate the decision rights to initiate and implement decisions (decision management) from the ratifying and monitoring functions (decision control). Accounting systems play a very important role in monitoring as part of the performance evaluation system. Accounting numbers are probably more useful in decision monitoring and often least useful in decision initiation and implementation. For decision management, managers want opportunity costs (described in Chapter 2). Accounting

Historical Application: Performance Measures in Retailing

Large department stores with multiple lines of goods such as clothing, furniture, jewelry, and glassware began to appear in the United States in the latter half of the 1800s (Lord & Taylor in 1858 and Macy's in 1870). These successful retailers had high volume and high inventory turnover by selling at low prices and low margins. They marked down slow-moving lines and did extensive local advertising.

In rural areas, mass marketing was done by mail-order houses. Montgomery Ward began in 1872; Sears and Roebuck began in 1887. The 1887 Montgomery Ward mail-order catalog was 540 pages long and contained 24,000 items. The success of the mail-order houses, like the department stores, was due to low prices and high volumes. Mail-order houses could process 100,000 orders per day.

At the heart of both the department stores and mail-order houses were the operating departments (such as women's and children's clothing, furniture, and housewares) and their buyers. The buyers had to acquire specialized knowledge of their customers' preferences. They committed their departments to purchase millions of dollars of goods before they knew whether the items could be sold.

Two types of information generated by the accounting department were used to evaluate the operating managers and their buyers: gross margin and stock turn. *Gross margin* is income (sales less cost) divided by sales. *Stock turn* or *inventory turnover* is sales divided by average inventory; it measures the number of times stock on hand is sold and replaced during the year. Departments with higher stock turns are using their capital invested in inventories more efficiently. For example, the large Chicago merchandiser Marshall Field's had a stock turn of around five in the 1880s. The development of gross margin and stock turn illustrates how accounting-based performance-evaluation measures develop to match the decision rights partitioned to particular managers. Critical to the success of large mass distributors was partitioning decision rights to the buyers with the specialized knowledge and then evaluating and rewarding them based on their decision rights.

SOURCE: A. Chandler, *The Visible Hand: The Managerial Revolution in American Business* (Cambridge, MA: Harvard University Press, 1977), pp. 223–36.

data are often criticized as not being useful for decision management, but their usefulness for decision control is frequently overlooked.

As a monitoring device, the accounting function is usually independent of operating managers whose performance the accounting report is measuring. The reason for this separation is obvious. Accounting, as part of the firm's monitoring technology, is designed to reduce agency costs, including theft and embezzlement. Since accounting reports bring subordinates' performance to the attention of their superiors, the reports should not be under the control of the subordinates. Internal accounting reports provide an overall review of subordinates' performance by giving senior managers reasonably objective and independent information. Shareholders and the board of directors use the accounting system to check on the performance of the CEO and senior managers. The CEO often has substantial influence over the accounting system since the corporate controller usually reports ultimately to the CEO. Some firms have the controller report to the independent audit committee of the board of directors. To use the accounting system for control of the CEO and senior management, the shareholders and outside directors on the board insist on an external, third-party audit of the financial results.[14]

To the extent financial measures are used for decision control and nonfinancial measures are used for decision management, the following implications arise:

1. Financial measures are not under the complete control of the people being monitored (i.e., the operating managers).

2. Nonaccounting measures, such as customer complaints and defect rates, are often more timely than accounting measures. Nonfinancial data can be reported more frequently than quarterly or monthly, as is usually the case for accounting data.

3. Not every decision requires ratification or monitoring. Decision control can be based on aggregate data to average out random fluctuations. Instead of monitoring every machine setup, it is usually cost-efficient to aggregate all setups occurring over the week and make sure the average setup time or cost is within acceptable levels.

4. Operating managers tend to be dissatisfied with financial measures for making operating decisions. The accounting numbers are not especially timely for operating decisions. They often are at too aggregate a level and do not provide sufficient detail for the particular decision. In response, these operating managers develop their own, often nonfinancial, information systems to provide the more timely knowledge they require for decision management. But at the same time, they rely on accounting data to monitor the managers who report to them.

A number of specific internal accounting procedures, such as standard costs, budgeting, and cost allocations (described in later chapters), help reduce agency problems. Many accounting procedures are better understood as control mechanisms than as aids in decision management. For example, economists have long cautioned against using accountants' allocation of fixed costs to compute "average" unit costs in making short-term decisions. These unit costs bear little relation to short-term variable cost, which is necessary for determining the short-term profit-maximizing level of output. However, average unit accounting costs can be useful as a control mechanism for detecting changes in a subunit's cost performance.

The economic Darwinism (discussed in Chapter 1) suggests that these seemingly irrational accounting procedures must be yielding benefits in excess of their costs. Economists describe

---

[14]R. Watts and J. Zimmerman, "Agency Problems, Auditing and the Theory of the Firm: Some Evidence," *Journal of Law & Economics,* October 1983, pp. 613–33.

the dysfunctional output/pricing decision that can result when accounting average costs are used instead of variable costs. These dysfunctional decisions are the indirect costs of using the accounting procedures. Reducing the firm's agency problems provides the necessary offsetting benefits to explain the preponderance of so-called irrational accounting procedures. In addition to the benefits provided via organizational reasons, such procedures can provide benefits (or costs) via external reporting, tax reporting, and/or as a cost control device (see Figure 1–1).

So far, this chapter has focused on the conflicts of interest between shareholders and managers of the firms, and how accounting numbers can be used to measure the performance of the managers to help align the shareholders' and managers' interests. Another important agency conflict exists between the shareholders and debt holders of the firms. Debt holders in corporations worry about the shareholders paying excessive dividends and eventually driving the firm into bankruptcy at their expense. To protect debt holders (including banks and insurance companies), the loan agreements contain provisions that prevent excessive dividend payments by tying dividends to accounting earnings. These agreements also contain covenants that often link the interest rate on the loan to accounting-based ratios, prevent future borrowings unless earnings are above a certain multiple of interest charges, and require the firm to maintain minimum ratios of current assets to current liabilities. Again, we observe accounting numbers used in debt contracts to better align the interests of shareholders and debt holders.

The next section provides a specific example of how accounting earnings are used in executive compensation plans to better align managers' and shareholders' interests.

D. Example of Accounting's Role: Executive Compensation Contracts

Executive compensation contracts illustrate how accounting numbers help reduce agency costs. To better align the interests of shareholders and senior managers, most large U.S. corporations have incentive compensation contracts. This section briefly describes the design of these contracts and their reliance on accounting numbers. It illustrates how accounting performance measures are used to reduce agency problems.

Senior executives in most publicly held firms typically are paid a salary plus an annual bonus; the bonus is often 100 percent of the salary. The compensation committee of the board of directors, which usually consists of outside nonmanagement directors, administers the annual bonus and the annual salary adjustment. The committee annually sets performance goals for each senior executive and establishes how large a bonus each will receive if the goals are achieved. The goals often consist of earnings growth targets, market share, new product introduction schedules, affirmative action hiring targets, and other strategic measures appropriate for the particular manager. If executives meet their targets, they receive some combination of cash, stock options, restricted stock, or deferred compensation.

To protect shareholders from excessive payouts to senior executives and to give senior executives a sense of the whole organization rather than just their own part, the total bonus payout to all eligible managers is limited to some fraction of accounting earnings. Besides defining who is eligible for awards and how they are administered and paid, these contracts constrain the total annual bonus payments to be paid out of an annual fund.

Accounting numbers enter executive compensation in two ways. First, accounting earnings are often used as individual performance measures (such as divisional profits). Second, accounting earnings constrain the total amount of compensation paid out to executives.

Surveys of compensation practices in publicly traded firms find that almost all of them rely on some measure of accounting profit to measure and reward the performance of senior executives.[15] Large-scale empirical studies routinely find a strong positive association between changes in accounting profits and changes in executive pay. In these studies, accounting profits are usually one of the most important explanatory variables of executive pay among firm size, stock returns, and industry classification. Thus, it appears as if accounting profits either are used directly in setting executive compensation or are highly correlated with performance measures used in setting pay.

E. Summary

Besides providing information for making operating decisions, accounting numbers are also used in controlling conflicts of interest between owners (principals) and employees (agents). Agency problems arise because self-interested employees maximize their welfare, not the principal's welfare, and principals cannot directly observe the agents' actions.

The free-rider problem, one specific agency problem, arises because, for agents working in teams, the incentive to shirk increases with team size. Usually it is more difficult to monitor individual agents as team size increases. Also, each agent bears a smaller fraction of the reduced output from his or her shirking. The horizon problem, another agency problem, arises when employees expecting to leave the firm in the future place less weight than the principal does on those consequences occurring after they leave.

Transactions that occur across markets have fewer agency problems because the existence of market prices gives owners of an asset the incentive to maximize its value by linking knowledge with decision rights. But once transactions occur within firms, administrative devices must replace market-induced incentives. In particular, firms try to link decision rights with knowledge and then provide incentives for people with the knowledge and decision rights to maximize firm value.

To maximize firm value, which involves minimizing agency costs, managers design the organization's architecture—three interrelated and coordinated systems that measure and reward performance and assign decision rights. The analogy of the three-legged stool illustrates how important it is that the three legs be matched to one another. Changing one leg usually requires changing the other two to keep the stool balanced.

The internal accounting system, used to measure agents' performance, provides an important monitoring function. Hence, the accounting system usually is not under the control of those agents whose performance is being monitored. Primarily a control device, accounting is not necessarily as useful for decision making as managers would like.

The performance evaluation system, one leg of the stool, consists of both financial and nonfinancial measures of performance. Executive compensation plans routinely use accounting earnings as a performance measure both to evaluate managers and to reduce agency costs by constraining the total bonus payouts to managers. Chapter 5 describes two more accounting tools that are used to reduce agency problems: responsibility accounting and transfer pricing.

Self-Study Problem

Self-Study Problem 2–1: Span of Control

Span of control is defined as the number of subordinates whom a superior directly controls. Whether the span of control is large or small depends on several factors, including training. "(I)f a person was well trained, he or she would need little supervision. The span of control would be wide. If personnel were not well trained, they would need more supervision, and the span of control would be narrow and the hierarchy higher." But the evidence shows "the more qualified the people, the less the span of control" and the higher the hierarchy.

---

[15]J. Core, W. R. Guay, and D. Larcker, "Executive Equity Compensation and Incentives: A Survey," *Federal Reserve Bank of New York Economic Policy Review,* April 2003, pp. 27–50.

In some situations, we observe a span of control of 40 or 50 (e.g., the faculty in a business school). In other situations, we observe spans of control of two to five (e.g., card dealers in a casino). What factors would you expect to be important in determining the optimum span of control? Give examples where appropriate.

Solution:

Span of control (or the height/shape of the organization chart) is a central feature of the control problem faced by organizations. The amount of monitoring required by each individual in the firm affects the span of control. High levels of monitoring decrease the span of control because supervisors have limited processing capacities.

A number of factors will affect the span of control:

1. Knowledge—it is useful to try to link knowledge and decision rights. If decision management rights are delegated, decision control rights are usually retained, thereby decreasing the span of control.

2. If monitoring costs are reduced, span of control increases, other things being equal. A case of reduced monitoring costs is grouping subordinates close to the supervisor. Performance evaluation and reward systems that reduce agency costs (including monitoring costs) increase the span of control. If agency costs are high because the residual loss is large (e.g., bank tellers or card dealers in casinos), the span of control is smaller, other things being equal.

3. Perrow argues that one can change behavior via training to induce people to behave in the organization's interest. This is inconsistent with the view that people are self-interested, rational maximizers.

Problems

P 4–1: Empowerment

It is frequently argued that for empowerment to work, managers must "let go of control" and learn to live with decisions that are made by their subordinates. Evaluate this argument.

P 4–2: Pay for Performance

Communities are frequently concerned about whether or not police are vigilant in carrying out their responsibilities. Several communities have experimented with incentive compensation for police. In particular, some cities have paid members of the police force based on the number of arrests that they personally make. Discuss the likely effects of this compensation policy.

P 4–3: Course Packets

Faculty members at a leading business school receive a budget to cover research expenditures, software and hardware purchases, travel expenses, photocopying for classroom use, and so forth. The budget is increased $250 for each class taught (independent of the number of students enrolled). For example, a faculty member receives a base budget of $14,000 for this year and teaches three courses—hence, the faculty's total budget is $14,750.

Finance professors teach much larger classes than any other functional area (e.g., accounting) and they tend to have larger course packets per student. Faculty can photocopy their course packets and have their budgets reduced by the photocopying charges. Or the faculty can distribute course materials via the school's network where students can download them and print them on their personal printers.

Required:

a. Which faculty members are more likely to put course packets and lecture notes on their Web pages, and which faculty are more likely to photocopy the material and distribute it to their students?

b. Is this partitioning of faculty members distributing materials electronically versus making paper copies efficient?

P 4–4:   Allied Van Lines

Why are drivers for long-haul (cross-country) moving companies (e.g., Allied Van Lines) often franchised, while moving companies that move households within the same city hire drivers as employees? Franchised drivers own their own trucks. They are not paid a fixed salary but rather receive the profits from each move after paying the franchiser a fee.

P 4–5:   Voluntary Financial Disclosure

Prior to the Securities Acts of 1933 and 1934, corporations with publicly traded stock were not required to issue financial statements, yet many voluntarily issued income statements and balance sheets. Discuss the advantages and disadvantages of such voluntary disclosures.

P 4–6:   University Physician Compensation

Physicians practicing in Eastern University's hospital have the following compensation agreement. Each doctor bills the patient (or Blue Cross Blue Shield) for his or her services. The doctor pays for all direct expenses incurred in the clinic, including nurses, medical malpractice insurance, secretaries, supplies, and equipment. Each doctor has a stated salary target (e.g., $100,000). For patient fees collected over the salary target, less expenses, the doctor retains 30 percent of the additional net fees. For example, if $150,000 is billed and collected from patients, and expenses of $40,000 are paid, then the doctor retains $3,000 of the excess net fees [30 percent of ($150,000 – $40,000 – $100,000)] and Eastern University receives $7,000. If $120,000 of fees are collected and $40,000 of expenses are incurred, the physician's net cash flow is $80,000 and Eastern University receives none of the fees.

Required:
Critically evaluate the existing compensation plan and recommend any changes.

P 4–7:   American InterConnect I

Employee satisfaction is a major performance measure used at American Inter Connect (AI), a large communications firm. All employees receive some bonus compensation. The lower-level employees receive a bonus that averages 20 percent of their base pay, whereas senior corporate officers receive bonus pay that averages 80 percent of their base salary. Bonus payments for all employees are linked to their immediate work group's performance on the following criteria: income, revenue growth, customer satisfaction, and employee satisfaction. Managers can have these criteria supplemented with additional specific measures, including hiring targets and some other specific objective for each manager, such as meeting a new product introduction deadline or a market share target.

Employee satisfaction usually has a weight of between 15 and 20 percent in determining most employees' overall bonus. To measure employee satisfaction, all employees in the group complete a two-page survey each quarter. The survey asks a variety of questions regarding employee satisfaction. One question in particular asks employees to rate how satisfied they are with their job using a seven-point scale (where 7 is very satisfied and 1 is very dissatisfied). The average score on this question for all employees in the group is used to calculate the group's overall employee satisfaction score.

Required:
Describe what behaviors you would expect to observe at AI.

P 4–8:   Raises

A company recently raised the pay of employees by 20 percent. The productivity of the employees, however, remained the same. The CEO of the company was quoted as saying, "It just goes to show that money does not motivate people." Provide a critical evaluation of this statement.

P 4–9:   Vanderschmidt's

Jan Vanderschmidt was the founder of a successful chain of restaurants located throughout Europe. He died unexpectedly last week at the age of 55. Jan was sole owner of the company's common stock and was known for being very authoritarian. He made most of the company's personnel decisions himself. He also made most of the decisions on the menu selection, food suppliers, advertising programs, and so on. Employees throughout the firm are paid fixed salaries and have been heavily monitored by

Mr. Vanderschmidt. Jan's son, Joop, spent his youth driving BMWs around the Netherlands and Germany at high speeds. He spent little time working with his dad in the restaurant business. Nevertheless, Joop is highly intelligent and just received his MBA degree from a prestigious school. Joop has decided to follow his father as the chief operating officer of the restaurant chain. Explain how the organization's architecture might optimally change now that Joop has taken over.

P 4–10: Sales Commissions

Sue Koehler manages a revenue center of a large national manufacturer that sells office furniture to local businesses in Detroit. She has decision rights over pricing. Her compensation is a fixed wage of $23,000 per year plus 2 percent of her office's total sales. Critically evaluate the organizational architecture of Koehler's revenue center.

P 4–11: Formula 409

"I used to run the company that made Formula 409, the spray cleaner. From modest entrepreneurial beginnings, we'd gone national and shipped the hell out of P&G, Colgate, Drackett, and every other giant that raised its head. From the beginning, I'd employed a simple incentive plan based on 'case sales': Every month, every salesman and executive received a bonus check based on how many cases of 409 he'd sold. Even bonuses for the support staff were based on monthly case sales. It was a happy time, with everyone making a lot of money, including me."

"We abandoned our monthly case-sales bonus plan and installed an *annual* profit-sharing plan, based on personnel evaluations. It didn't take long for the new plan to produce results."

SOURCE: Wilson Harrell, "Inspire Action: What Really Motivates Your People to Excel?" *Success*, September 1995.

Required:

What do you think happened at this company after it started the annual profit-sharing plan?

P 4–12: Pratt & Whitney

A *Wall Street Journal* article (December 26, 1996) describes a series of changes at the Pratt & Whitney plant in Maine that manufactures parts for jet engines. In 1993, it was about to be closed because of high operating costs and inefficiencies. A new plant manager overhauled operations. He broadened job descriptions so inspectors do 15 percent more work than they did five years ago. A "results-sharing" plan pays hourly employees if the plant exceeds targets such as cost cutting and on-time delivery. Now, everyone is looking to cut costs.

Hourly employees also helped design a new pay scheme that is linked to the amount of training, not seniority, that an employee has. This was after the plant manager drafted 22 factory-floor employees, gave them a conference room, and told them to draft a new pay plan linked to learning.

Shop-floor wages vary between $9 and $19 per hour with the most money going to people running special cost studies or quality projects, tasks previously held by managers.

This text emphasizes the importance of keeping all three legs of the stool in balance. Identify the changes Pratt & Whitney made to all three legs of the stool at its Maine plant.

P 4–13: Theory X–Theory Y

A textbook on organization theory says:

Drawing upon the writings of Maslow, McGregor presented his Theory X–Theory Y dichotomy to describe two differing conceptions of human behavior. Theory X assumptions held that people are inherently lazy, they dislike work, and that they will avoid it whenever possible. Leaders who act on Theory X premises are prone to controlling their subordinates through coercion, punishment, and the use of financial rewards; the use of external controls is necessary, as most human beings are thought to be incapable of self-direction and assuming responsibility. In contrast, Theory Y is based on the assumption that work can be enjoyable and that people will work hard and assume responsibility if they are given the opportunity to achieve personal goals at the same time.[16]

Using the framework presented in the text, critically analyze Theory X–Theory Y.

[16]V. K. Narayanan and R. Nath, *Organization Theory: A Strategic Approach* (Burr Ridge, IL: Richard D. Irwin, 1993), p. 403.

P 4–14:   American InterConnect II

Employee bonuses at American InterConnect (AI), a large communications firm, depend on meeting a number of targets, one of which is a revenue target. Some bonus is awarded to the group if it meets or exceeds its target revenue for the year. The bonus is also tied to meeting targets for earnings, employee satisfaction, hiring goals, and other specific objectives tailored to the group or manager.

AI has several product development groups within the firm. Each is assigned the task of developing new products for specific divisions within the firm. Product developers, primarily engineers and marketing people, are assigned to a new product development team to develop a specific new product. Afterward, they are assigned to new development teams for a different division or are reassigned back to their former departments. Sometimes they become product managers for the new product. Product development teams take roughly 18 months to develop and design the product. For example, Network Solutions is one group of products AI sells. The employees in the product development group for Network Solutions receive part of their bonus based on whether Network Solutions achieves its revenue target for that year.

It typically takes AI three years from the time a product development team is formed until the product reaches the market. Once a new product idea is identified and researched, a prototype must be built and tested. Finally, it is introduced. Another 18 months is required for approval, manufacturing design, further testing, and marketing. These functions are performed after the product development team has been reassigned.

Required:

Analyze the incentives created by basing a portion of each current product developer's bonus on revenues for products now being sold.

P 4–15:   Tipping

One of the main tenets of economic analysis is that people act in their narrow self-interest. Why then do people leave tips in restaurants? If a study were to compare the size of tips earned by servers in restaurants on interstate highways with those in restaurants near residential neighborhoods, what would you expect to find? Why?

P 4–16:   White's Department Store

Employees at White's Department Store are observed engaging in the following behavior: (1) They hide items that are on sale from the customers and (2) they fail to expend appropriate effort in designing merchandise displays. They are also uncooperative with one another. What do you think might be causing this behavior, and what might you do to improve the situation?

P 4–17:   Coase Farm

Coase Farm grows soybeans near property owned by Taggart Railroad. Taggart can build zero, one, or two railroad tracks adjacent to Coase Farm, yielding a net present value of $0, $9 million, or $12 million.

Value of Taggart Railroad (in millions) as a Function of the Number of Train Tracks (before any damages)	
Zero tracks	$ 0
One track	9
Two tracks	12

Coase Farm can grow soybeans on zero, one, or two fields, yielding a net present value of $0, $15 million, or $18 million before any environmental damages inflicted by Taggart trains.

Environmental damages inflicted by Taggart's trains are $4 million per field per track. Coase Farm's payoffs as a function of the number of fields it uses to grow soybeans and the number of tracks that Taggart builds are shown next.

	Value of Coase Farm (in millions) as a Function of the Number of Fields Planted and the Number of Train Tracks		
	Zero Fields	*One Field*	*Two Fields*
Zero tracks	$0	$15	$18
One track	0	11	10
Two tracks	0	7	2

It is prohibitively expensive for Taggart Railroad and Coase Farm to enter into a long-term contract regarding either party's use of its land.

Required:

    a. Suppose Taggart Railroad cannot be held liable for the damages its tracks inflict on Coase Farm. Show that Taggart Railroad will build two tracks and Coase Farm will plant soybeans in one field.

    b. Suppose Taggart Railroad can be held fully liable for the damages that its tracks inflict on Coase Farm. Show that Taggart Railroad will build one track and Coase Farm will plant soybeans in two fields.

    c. Now suppose Taggart Railroad and Coase Farm merge. Show that the merged firm will build one track and plant soybeans in one field.

    d. What are the implications of the merger for the organizational architecture of the newly merged firm in terms of decision rights, performance measurement, and employee compensation?

SOURCE: R. Sansing.

P 4–18: Rothwell Inc.

Rothwell Inc. is the leader in computer-integrated manufacturing and factory automation products and services. The Rothwell product offering is segmented into 15 product categories, based on product function and primary manufacturing location.

Rothwell's sales division sells all 15 product categories and is composed of 25 district offices located throughout the United States. The company is highly decentralized, with district offices responsible for setting sales price, product mix, and other variables.

District offices are rewarded based on sales. Some large customers have plants in more than one of Rothwell's sales districts. In cases where sales are made to these customers, the district offices participate jointly and sales credits are shared by each district involved.

The sales division compensation plan designed by L. L. Rothwell, founder of the firm, was structured so that the staff would pursue sales in each of the 15 product categories. The selling program has the following features:

- Each sales representative receives a commission based on a percentage of the sales revenue generated.
- Each district (approximately 160 sales reps) is assigned a quota for each product line, defined in terms of dollar sales.
- In addition to commission, sales reps are eligible for an annual bonus. The company calculates individual bonuses by multiplying the number of bonus points earned by the individual target bonus amount. Points are credited at the district level.

- In order for all sales reps in a district to qualify for a bonus, the district must achieve 50 percent of quota in all 15 product groups and 85 percent of quota in at least 13 groups.
- Bonus points are awarded for sales greater than 85 percent of quota.
- Five product groups have been identified as strategic to Rothwell. These "pride-level" products are weighted more heavily in bonus point calculations.

Over the past three years, Rothwell generated exceptionally high sales—and awarded record bonuses. Profits, however, were lackluster. L. L. was befuddled!

Required:

   a. Evaluate the compensation situation at Rothwell.

   b. Identify the types of behavior the existing system promotes and explain how such behavior may be contributing to the firm's declining profitability. Suggest improvements.

P 4–19: Gong-Fen

"It was in Deyang in 1969 that I came to know how China's peasants really lived. Each day started with the production team leader allocating jobs. All the peasants had to work, and they each earned a fixed number of 'work points' (*gong-fen*) for their day's work. The number of work points accumulated was an important element in the distribution at the end of the year. The peasants got food, fuel, and other daily necessities, plus a tiny sum of cash, from the production team. After the harvest, the production team paid part of it over as tax to the state. Then the rest was divided up. First, a basic quantity was meted out equally to every male, and about a quarter less to every female. Children under three received a half portion."

"The remainder of the crop was then distributed according to how many work points each person had earned. Twice a year, the peasants would all assemble to fix the daily work points for each person. No one missed these meetings. In the end, most young and middle-aged men would be allocated 10 points a day, and women 8. One or two whom the whole village acknowledged to be exceptionally strong got an extra point. 'Class enemies' like the former village landlord and his family got a couple of points less than the others, in spite of the fact that they worked no less hard and were usually given the toughest jobs."

"Since there was little variation from individual to individual of the same gender in terms of daily points, the number of work points accumulated depended mainly on how many days one worked, rather than how one worked."

SOURCE: J. Chang, *Wild Swans: Three Daughters of China,* (New York: Anchor Books, 1991), pp. 414–15.

Required:

What predictable behavior do you expect the Chinese agricultural system will generate?

P 4–20: International Computer Company

International Computer Company (ICC) has annual revenues of $2 billion primarily from selling and leasing large networked workstation systems to businesses and universities. The manufacturing division produces the hardware that is sold or leased by the marketing division. After the expiration of the lease, leased equipment is returned to ICC, where it is either disassembled for parts by the field service organization or sold by the international division. Internal studies have shown that equipment leased for four years is worth 36.5 percent of its original manufacturing cost as parts or sold overseas. About half of ICC's systems are leased and half are sold, but the fraction being leased by ICC is a falling proportion of total sales.

The leasing department is evaluated on profits. Its annual profits are based on the present value of the lease payments from new leases signed during the year, less

1. The unit manufacturing cost of the equipment.
2. Direct selling, shipping, and installation costs.
3. The present value of the service agreement costs.

Organizational Architecture **155**

Each leased piece of equipment will be serviced over its life by ICC's field service organization. The leasing division arranges a service contract for each piece of leased equipment from the field service organization. The field service organization commits to servicing the leased equipment at a fixed annual cost, determined at the time the lease is signed. The leasing department then builds the service cost into the annual lease payment.

The leasing department negotiates the lease terms individually for each customer. In general, the leasing division sets the annual lease terms to recover all three cost components plus a 25 percent markup (before taxes). The 25 percent markup for setting the annual lease payment seemed to work well in the past and provided the firm with a reasonable return on its investment when ICC had dominance in the workstation market niche. However, in recent years, new entrants have forced the ICC leasing department to reduce its markup to as low as 10 percent to sign leases. At this small margin, senior management is considering getting out of the lease business and just selling the systems.

The following lease to Gene Science is being priced by the leasing department. A four-year lease of a small network of three workstations is being negotiated. The unit manufacturing cost of the network is $30,000. The service costs, which are payable to the field service department at the beginning of each year, are $2,000 (payable at installation), $3,000, $4,000, and $5,000 (payable at the beginning of each of the next three years, respectively). Selling, shipping, and installation costs are $7,000. The leasing department has an 8 percent cost of capital.

To simplify the analysis, ignore all tax considerations.

Required:

a. Using a 25 percent markup on costs and an 8 percent discount rate, calculate the fixed annual lease payment for the four-year lease to Gene Science.

b. Comment on some likely reasons why a 25 percent markup on leased equipment is proving more difficult to sustain. Should ICC abandon the lease market? What are some alternative courses of action?

P 4–21: Repro Corporation

Repro Corporation is the leading manufacturer and seller of office equipment. Its most profitable business segment is the production and sale of large copiers. The company is currently organized into two divisions: manufacturing and sales. Manufacturing produces all products; sales is responsible for the distribution of all finished products to the final customers. Each division is evaluated on profits. Market research shows an existing demand for a facilities management service whereby Repro installs its equipment and personnel at a client's site and operates the client's copy center. To meet this demand, Repro is considering a proposal to expand its operations to include a service division responsible for contracting with firms to install Repro's equipment in a copy service agreement. This copy service is named Facilities Management (FM).

A contract for FM includes the leasing of a complete copy center from the service division, including all necessary equipment and personnel. The client provides space for FM on site.

The value offered by the service division is threefold. The service division will be organized so that a base center in each city covered will be responsible for acting as both an independent copy center and a backup to the FMs contracted in the local area. Any FM processing shortfalls due to equipment failure or shop overflows would result in a transfer of copy needs to the center. Additionally, since the equipment used in FM contracts is leased and not purchased, contracting companies are not strapped with showing a return on assets for this equipment (allowing the flexibility of adjusting the lease as company needs vary). Nor are they responsible for equipment maintenance. Finally, the personnel to run the equipment in the FM sites are service division employees, not employees of the client. Thus, no additional headcount is needed by the client. For this complete value-added service, firms are charged based on projected monthly copy volume, with an agreed-upon surcharge for copies processed in excess of the contracted volume.

With the introduction of this new division, Repro would reorganize itself into three divisions: *manufacturing, products,* and *service.* The responsibility of selling business equipment (copiers, fax machines, etc.) would be assigned to the products division, and the service division would become responsible for the sale of FM sites (products and services would utilize separate sales forces). Both divisions would buy hardware from manufacturing at similar costs.

Currently, Repro's sales comprise approximately 80 percent repeat-purchase customers (who are either replacing existing equipment with similar equipment or upgrading to new Repro products) and 20 percent new customers. It has been estimated that 30 percent of the current market base would, given the opportunity, choose a Facilities Management contract rather than purchase equipment outright.

Repro's current sales force compensation is a function of a fixed salary plus a commission based on a percentage of sales. The average salesperson's compensation consists of a $25,000 base salary and a 2 percent sales commission. Over the last four years, the average piece of copy equipment from Repro sold for $80,000 and the average salesperson sold $1 million of equipment (adjusted for inflation). If the proposal for a service division is undertaken, this compensation scheme will be applied to both the products and service divisions' sales force.

Required:

    a. Discuss the conflict that will result if the service division is introduced.

    b. Propose a solution to solve this conflict.

Cases

Case 4–1: Christian Children's Fund

Christian Children's Fund, Inc. (CCF), established in 1938, is an international, nonsectarian, non-profit organization dedicated to assisting children. With program offices around the world, it provides health and educational assistance to more than 4.6 million children and families through over 1,000 projects in 30 countries, including the United States. CCF's programs promote long-term development designed to help break the cycle of poverty by improved access to health care, safe water, immunizations, better nutrition, educational assistance, literacy courses, skills training, and other services specific to improving children's welfare.

Most of CCF's revenues come from individual donors who are linked with a specific child. About 75 percent of the sponsors are in the United States, and in 2003, CCF had total revenues of about $143 million. (See Exhibit 1.)

In 1995, CCF began developing an evaluation system, nicknamed AIMES (Annual Impact Monitoring and Evaluation System), to assess the performance of its programs and whether they are making a positive, measurable difference in children's lives. A working group of national directors, program managers, CCF finance and audit managers, and outside consultants developed a series of metrics that allowed CCF to be more accountable to its sponsors, as well as an evaluation tool to continually assess the impact of its programs on children. The working group wanted metrics that (1) captured critical success factors for CCF's projects; (2) focused on a program's impact, not its activities; (3) measured the program's impact on children; and (4) could be measured and tracked.

The following indicators were chosen:

Under 5-year-old mortality rate
Under 5-year-old moderate and severe malnutrition rate
Adult literacy
One-to-two-year-old immunizations
Tetanus vaccine-protected live births
Families that correctly know how to manage a case of diarrhea
Families that correctly know how to manage acute respiratory infection
Families that have access to safe water
Families that practice safe sanitation
Children enrolled in a formal or informal educational program

Each family in a community with a CCF program is given a family card that tracks each of the preceding 10 indicators for that family. In 1997, the first year of implementation, AIMES captured the health status of about 1.9 million children in approximately 850 projects in 18 countries. Annual visits by project staff or volunteers update each family's card. The family cards are aggregated at the community level, national level, and then in total for CCF, and provide a reporting system. CCF managers then track trends and compare performance at the community, national, and organizational levels.

It took CCF two years to develop these metrics, test them, and train the staff in all the national offices in how to use the system. AIMES does not prescribe the strategy each community should adopt but rather allows each community to design programs that promote the well-being of children in that community. Program directors can use the AIMES data as a tool to monitor and manage their programs. If child mortality is high, local program directors decide how best to reduce the rate. The 10 AIMES metrics have made project managers more focused and better able to concentrate resources in those areas that make a measurable difference in children's health. CCF uses the information to make program and resource allocation decisions at the community level. The family card has promoted better nutrition via appropriate feeding and child care practices because there is now more direct contact between CCF staff and volunteers and families.

Required:

Using this chapter's organizational architecture framework, discuss the strengths and weaknesses of CCF's AIMES project.

SOURCES: D. Henderson, B. Chase, and B. Woodson, "Performance Measures for NPOs," *Journal of Accountancy* (January 2002), pp. 63–68; and www.christianchildrensfund.org.

Case 4–2: Woodhaven Service

Background

Woodhaven Service is a small, independent gas station located in the Woodhaven section of Queens. The station has three gasoline pumps and two service bays. The repair facility specializes in automotive maintenance (oil changes, tune-ups, etc.) and minor repairs (mufflers, shock absorbers, etc.). Woodhaven generally refers customers who require major work, such as transmission rebuilds and electronics, to shops that are better equipped to handle such repairs. Major repairs are done in-house only when both the customer and mechanic agree that this is the best course of action.

During the 20 years that he has owned Woodhaven Service, Harold Mateen's competence and fairness have built a loyal customer base of neighborhood residents. In fact, demand for his services has been more than he can reasonably meet, yet the repair end of his business is not especially profitable. Most of his competitors earn the lion's share of their profits through repairs, but Harold is making almost all of his money by selling gasoline. If he could make more money on repairs, Woodhaven would be the most successful service station in the area. Harold believes that Woodhaven's weakness in repair profitability is due to the inefficiency of his mechanics, who are paid the industry average of $500 per week. While Harold does not think he overpays them, he feels he is not getting his money's worth.

Harold's son, Andrew, is a student at the university, where he has learned the Socratic dictum, "To know the Good is to do the Good." Andrew provided his father with a classic text on employee morality, Dr. Weisbrotten's *Work Hard and Follow the Righteous Way*. Every morning for two months, Harold, Andrew, and the mechanics devoted one hour to studying this text. Despite many lively and fascinating discussions on the rights and responsibilities of the employee, productivity did not improve one bit. Harold figured he would just have to go out and hire harder-working mechanics.

The failure of the Weisbrotten method did not surprise Lisa, Harold's daughter. She knew that Andrew's methods were bunk. As anyone serious about business knows, the true science of productivity and management of human resources resides in Professor von Drekken's masterful *Modifying Organizational Behavior through Employee Commitment*. Yes, employee commitment was the answer to everything! Harold followed the scientific methods to the letter. Yet, despite giving out gold stars, blowing up balloons, and wearing a smiley face button, he found Lisa's approach no more successful than Andrew's.

EXHIBIT 1
CHRISTIAN CHILDREN'S FUND, INC.
Consolidated Statements of Activities and Changes in Net Assets
For the Years Ended June 30, 2003, and 2002

	Total	
	2003	*2002*
Public support		
Sponsorships:		
U.S. sponsors	$ 76,838,477	$ 74,077,556
International sponsors	22,086,375	18,151,969
Special gifts from sponsors for children	12,351,284	11,838,912
Total sponsorships	$111,276,136	$104,068,437
Contributions:		
General contributions	$ 13,657,676	$ 13,642,476
Major gifts and bequests	4,712,032	4,751,059
Gifts in kind	804,247	637,977
Total contributions	$ 19,173,955	$ 19,031,512
Grants:		
Grants and contracts	$ 10,164,264	$ 7,768,755
Total public support	$140,614,355	$130,868,704
Revenue		
Investment and currency transactions	$ 264,893	$ 350,841
Service fees and other	1,636,717	1,522,652
Total revenue	$ 1,901,610	$ 1,873,493
Net assets released from restrictions		
Satisfaction of program and time restrictions	—	—
Total public support and revenue	$142,515,965	$132,742,197
Expenses		
Program:		
Basic education	$ 41,263,708	$ 40,964,478
Health and sanitation	28,767,904	29,442,196
Nutrition	13,824,871	15,635,046
Early childhood development	11,850,954	10,717,133
Micro enterprise	14,555,029	9,183,004
Emergencies	2,802,575	2,861,528
Total program expenses	$113,032,041	$108,803,385
Supporting services		
Fund-raising	$ 16,777,149	$ 15,484,634
Management and general	12,651,014	11,156,134
Total supporting services	29,428,163	26,640,768
Total expenses from operations	142,493,204	135,444,153
Change in net assets from operations	$ 22,761	$ (2,701,956)
Non-operating revenues (expenses)		
Realized (loss) gain on investments	$ (602,619)	$ 387,223
Unrealized gain (loss) on investments	696,584	(1,967,114)
Total non-operating revenues (expenses)	93,965	(1,579,890)
Change in net assets	$ 116,726	$ (4,281,847)

Compensation Plans

Harold thinks that his neighbor Jack Myers, owner of Honest Jack's Pre-Enjoyed Autorama, might be helpful. After all, one does not become as successful as Jack without a lot of practical knowledge. Or maybe it is Jack's great radio jingle that does it. Jack tells Harold,

> It's not the jingle, you idiot! It's the way I pay my guys. Your mechanics make $500 a week no matter what. Why should they put out for you? Because of those stupid buttons? My guys—my guys get paid straight commission and nothing more. They do good by me and I do good by them. Otherwise, let 'em starve.
>
> Look, it's real simple. Pay 'em a percent of the sales for the work they do. If you need to be a nice guy about it, make that percent so that if sales are average, then they make their usual $500. But if sales are better, they get that percent extra. This way they don't get hurt but got real reason to help you out.

This hurt Harold. He really liked those buttons. Still, Jack did have a point. Straight commission, however, seemed a little radical. What if sales were bad for a week? That would hurt the mechanics.

Harold figured that it would be better to pay each mechanic a guaranteed $300 a week plus a commission rate that would, given an average volume of business, pay them the extra $200 that would bring their wage back to $500. Under this system, the mechanics would be insulated from a bad week, would not be penalized for an average week, and would still have the incentive to attempt to improve sales. Yes, this seemed more fair.

On the other hand, maybe Jack knows only about the used car business, not about business in general. Harold figured that he should look for an incentive pay method more in line with the way things are done in the auto repair business. Perhaps he should pay his mechanics as he is paid by his customers—by the job. It is standard practice for service stations to charge customers a flat rate for the labor associated with any job. The number of labor hours for which the customer is charged is generally taken from a manual that outlines expected labor times for specific jobs on specific vehicles. The customer pays for these expected hours regardless of how many actual labor hours are expended on the job. Many shops also pay their mechanics by the job. Harold thinks that this approach makes sense because it links the mechanic's pay to the labor charges paid by the customer.

Required:

a. This case presents some popular approaches to alleviating agency costs. Although certain aspects of each of these methods are consistent with the views presented in the text, none of these methods is likely to succeed. Discuss the similarities and differences between the ideas of the chapter and

   (i) Dr. Weisbrotten's approach.

   (ii) Harold Mateen's idea of hiring "harder-working" mechanics.

b. Discuss the expected general effect on agency costs at Woodhaven Service of the new incentive compensation plans. How might they help Woodhaven? Assuming that Harold wants his business to be successful for a long time to come, what major divergent behaviors would be expected under the new compensation proposals? How damaging would you expect these new behaviors to be to a business such as Woodhaven Service? Also, present a defense of the following propositions:

   (i) Harold's plan offers less incentive for divergent behavior than Honest Jack's.

   (ii) Limiting a mechanic's pay by placing an upper bound of $750 per week on his or her earnings reduces the incentive for divergent behavior.

c. Suppose Harold owned a large auto repair franchise located in a department store in a popular suburban shopping mall. Suppose also that this department store is a heavily promoted, well-known national chain that is famous for its good values and easy credit. How should Harold's thinking on incentive compensation change? What if Harold did not own the franchise but was only the manager of a company-owned outlet?

160 *Chapter 4*

  d. In this problem, it is assumed that knowledge and decision rights are linked. The mechanic who services the car decides what services are warranted. Discuss the costs and benefits of this fact for Woodhaven Service and the independently owned chain-store repair shop.

  e. Suppose that Woodhaven's problems are not due to agency costs. Briefly describe a likely problem that is apparent from the background description in this problem.

Responsibility Accounting and Transfer Pricing

Chapter 4 described the general *agency problem* of motivating and thereby influencing individual behavior. Chapter 4 also described how the organization's architecture can reduce this problem. The firm's organizational architecture consists of three interrelated systems: the performance evaluation system, the performance reward system, and the system that assigns decision rights. The accounting system plays an integral part in most firms' performance evaluation. This chapter discusses two additional examples of how accounting systems can be applied to reduce agency problems: responsibility accounting and transfer pricing.

While this chapter and other chapters in the text focus on the use of accounting numbers as performance measures, it is important to recognize that publicly traded firms also use their stock price as a performance measure. Executives in these firms usually receive (and hold) stock and stock options as part of their compensation packages as a way to align the interests of shareholders and managers. Accounting earnings create incentives for managers to take actions in the current period that increase the current period's revenues, decrease expenses, or use assets more efficiently. Accounting earnings do not reflect actions taken by managers in the current period that will increase future period revenues or decrease future period expenses. For example, investments in research and development, new product development, or marketing that enhance earnings next year or the year after are not incorporated into this year's accounting earnings. Only when the additional revenues are generated or expenses are reduced will accounting earnings reflect these changes. On the other hand, the stock market will reflect these investments in the form of higher stock prices as soon as the market becomes aware of the nature of the investment. Because stock prices are forward looking, they reflect the future anticipated benefits of actions taken in the current period. Accounting earnings are not forward looking and, hence, do not incorporate the effect of managerial actions taken today that will affect future periods. To reward managers for current actions that will impact future periods, publicly traded firms include stock and stock options in their managers' compensation packages.

A. Responsibility Accounting[1]

All but the smallest organizations are divided into subunits, each of which is granted decision rights and then evaluated based on performance objectives for that subunit. For example, the firm might be organized into marketing, manufacturing, and distribution departments. Manufacturing is further subdivided into parts manufacturing and assembly, and assembly is further organized by product assembled. These basic building blocks of the organization form the work groups that define and characterize what each part of the firm does. Assigning decision rights to the subunits is a critical part of solving the limited processing capacity of humans discussed in Chapter 4. **Responsibility accounting** begins with formal recognition of these subunits as responsibility centers. A responsibility accounting system is part of the performance evaluation system used to measure the operating results of the responsibility center.

The decision rights assigned to a subunit categorize the unit as a cost center, a profit center, or an investment center. The particular decision rights assigned to a subunit are the key determinants of how the unit's performance is evaluated and rewarded. Each of these categories implies a different assignment of decision rights and, accordingly, a different performance metric. In each case, decision rights are linked with the specialized knowledge necessary to exercise them. Responsibility accounting then dictates that the

[1]This section draws heavily on M. Jensen and W. Meckling, "Divisional Performance Measurement," manuscript (Boston: Harvard Business School, 1986); and J. Brickley, C. Smith, and J. Zimmerman, *Managerial Economics and Organizational Architecture,* 6th ed. (New York: McGraw-Hill/Irwin, 2016).

TABLE 5-1　Operating Leverage (Production and Sales Are 10,000 Units)

	Decision Rights	*Performance Measures*	*Typically Used When*
Cost center	• Input mix (labor, materials, supplies)	• Minimize total cost for a fixed output • Maximize output for a fixed budget	• Central manager can measure output, knows the cost functions, and can set the optimal quantity and appropriate rewards • Central manager can observe the quality of the cost center's output • Cost center manager has knowledge of the optimal input mix
Profit center	• Input mix • Product mix • Selling prices (or output quantities)	• Actual profits • Actual compared to budgeted profits	• Profit center manager has the knowledge to select the optimal price/quantity
Investment center	• Input mix • Product mix • Selling prices (or output quantities) • Capital invested in center	• Actual ROI • Actual residual income • Actual compared with budgeted ROI or residual income	• Investment center manager has the knowledge to select the optimal price/quantity • Investment center manager has the knowledge to select the optimal product mix • Investment center manager has knowledge about investment opportunities

performance measurement system (the accounting system) measures the performance that results from the decision rights assigned to the responsibility center. For example, if an agent is assigned decision rights to sell products to customers in New York, the performance metric of this agent should not include sales to customers in Maine.

　　Matching the decision rights assigned to a subunit to its performance measure reduces the agency problems described in Chapter 4. A subunit is assigned a set of decision rights, a performance measure designed to evaluate the exercise of those rights, and rewards based on the measures. In this way, the subunit focuses on those tasks the principal wants performed. Table 5–1 describes the various responsibility centers. (In all cases, accounting numbers are used in the performance measurement system.)[2]

1. Cost Centers　　**Cost centers** are established whenever a subunit is assigned the decision rights to produce some stipulated level of output and the unit's efficiency in achieving this objective is to be measured and rewarded. Cost center managers are assigned decision rights for determining the mix of inputs (labor, outside services, and materials) used to produce the output. Managers of cost centers are evaluated on their efficiency in applying inputs to produce outputs. Since they are not responsible for selling the final services or products, they are not judged on revenues or profits.

　　To evaluate the performance of a cost center, its output must be measurable. Moreover, some higher unit in the organization with the specialized knowledge and decision rights must specify the department's output or budget. Manufacturing departments like a parts manufacturing department in a factory are usually cost centers. The output of a parts

---

[2]In this chapter, we focus on three centers (cost, profit, and investment centers). Other types, such as expense and revenue centers, are not as prevalent as the three discussed. For discussion of these additional types of centers, see Jensen and Meckling (1986), and Brickley et al. (2016).

Historical Application: Respon- sibility Accounting Not New	In 1922, James O. McKinsey, founder of the consulting firm McKinsey & Co., described responsibility accounting:

> In the modern business organization, control is exercised through individuals who compose the organization. If control of expenses is to be effected through members of the organization, it is necessary that they be classified so as to show responsibility for each class. If responsibility is taken as the controlling factor in an expense classification, each department will be charged with those expenses over which the executive head of the department exercises control. In addition it may be charged with some items of expense the amount of which is fixed or at least beyond the control of any officer.
>
> To illustrate, the production department will be charged for the supplies used in production, for these are under the control of the production manager, and in addition it will be charged with the depreciation on production equipment, the estimated amount of which is determined in most cases by others than the production manager.*

Notice that McKinsey advocates the use of responsibility accounting and he also argues in favor of charging not only expenses over which managers have direct control but also expenses they control indirectly, such as depreciation.

*J. McKinsey, Budgetary Control (New York: Ronald Press, 1922), p. 281.

department is measured by counting the number of parts produced. Cost centers are also used in service organizations for functions such as check processing in a bank (number of checks processed) or food services in a hospital (number of meals served). In addition to measuring the quantity of output, its quality must be monitored effectively. If not, cost center managers who are evaluated on costs can meet their targets by cutting quality.

Various objectives are used for evaluating cost center performance. One is to minimize costs for a given output; another is to maximize output for a given budget. Minimizing costs for a given output is consistent with profit maximization, as long as central management has selected the profit-maximizing level of output. For example, the manager of a metal stamping department is told to produce 10,000 stampings per day of a fixed specification and quality. The manager is evaluated on meeting the production schedule and on reducing the cost of the 10,000 stampings while maintaining quality. The cost center manager does not have the decision rights to set the price or scale of operations.

Another possible evaluation criterion, maximizing output for a specified budget, provides incentives equivalent to the first criterion, as long as the specified budget is the minimal budget necessary for producing the profit-maximizing quantity of output. For example, the manager has a fixed budget ($27,500 per week) and is evaluated based on the number of metal stampings produced that meet quality specifications within the fixed budget.

For both objectives, the manager is constrained either by total output or by budget. The two objectives are optimal if the central management chooses (1) the profit-maximizing output level or (2) the correct budget for efficient production of this output level. Nonetheless, under both cost center arrangements, the cost center manager has incentives to reduce costs (or increase output) by lowering quality. Therefore, the quality of the cost center's output must be monitored.

Sometimes cost center managers are evaluated based on minimizing average cost. In this case, the manager has the incentive to choose the output at which average costs are minimized and to produce this output efficiently. It is important to emphasize that profit maximization need not occur when average costs are minimized. In general, minimizing average unit cost is not the same as maximizing profit. For example, suppose a cost center

TABLE 5-2 **Example Demonstrating that Minimizing Average Cost May Not Yield the Profit-Maximizing Level of Sales**

Quantity	Price	Revenue	Total Cost	Total Profits	Average Cost
1	$35	$35	$78	$–43	$78.0
2	33	66	83	–17	41.5
3	31	93	90	3	30.0
4	29	116	99	17	24.8
5	27	135	110	25	22.0
6	25	150	123	27	20.5
7	23	161	138	23	19.7
8	21	168	155	13	19.4
9	19	171	174	–3	19.3
10	17	170	195	–25	19.5

has some fixed costs and constant variable costs per unit. In this case, average unit costs will continue to fall with increases in output. To illustrate, assume total costs are

$$TC = \$300,000 + \$6Q$$

Here, fixed costs are $300,000 and variable costs are a constant $6 per unit. Given this equation, average costs are derived by dividing both sides of the equation by Q to get

$$AC = \frac{TC}{Q} = \frac{\$300,000}{Q} + \$6$$

With a constant variable cost, the average cost falls as the quantity produced increases. In this situation, a cost center manager who is evaluated based on minimizing average unit costs has incentives to increase output, even as inventories mount. Focusing on minimizing average unit cost can provide incentives for cost center managers to either overproduce or underproduce; it depends on how the profit-maximizing output level compares to the quantity where average costs are minimized.

Table 5–2 provides another simple example that minimizing average cost is not equivalent to profit maximization. This table shows that profits are maximized by selling six units, while minimum average cost occurs by producing nine units.

Cost centers work most effectively if (1) the central managers have a good understanding of the cost functions, can measure quantity, and can set the profit-maximizing output level and appropriate rewards; (2) the central managers can observe the quality of the cost center's output; and (3) the cost center manager has specific knowledge of the optimal input mix.

2. Profit Centers

Profit centers are often composed of several cost centers. Profit center managers are given a fixed capital budget and have decision rights for input mix, product mix, and selling prices (or output quantities). Profit centers are most appropriate when the knowledge required to make the product mix, quantity, pricing, and quality decisions is specific to the division and costly to transfer.

Profit centers are usually evaluated on the difference between actual and budgeted accounting profits for their division. Although measuring profit centers' profits seems straightforward, two complications often consume managers' attention: how to price transfers of goods and services between business units (transfer pricing) and which corporate overhead costs to allocate to business units. Managers constantly debate these two issues. We examine the transfer pricing problem in the next section. Chapters 7 and 8 discuss the allocation of corporate overhead costs to responsibility centers.

When interdependencies exist among business units, motivating individual profit centers to maximize their unit's profits will not generally maximize profits for the firm as a whole. For example, individual units focusing on their own profits frequently ignore how their actions affect the sales and costs of other units. One division might free-ride on another division's quality reputation, thereby reaping short-run gains at the expense of the other division. For example, Chevrolet and Buick are two profit centers within General Motors. Suppose Chevrolet, in pursuit of higher profits, decides to raise the quality of its cars. This might affect consumers' perceptions of the average quality of all General Motors cars, including Buick's perceived quality. An enhanced reputation for all General Motors cars helps Buick. But if Chevrolet receives no credit for Buick's profits, Chevrolet managers will likely ignore the positive effects they generate for Buick and tend to underinvest in quality enhancements. To help managers internalize both the positive and negative effects that their actions impose on other profit center managers, firms often base incentive compensation not just on the manager's own profit center profits but also on a group of related profit centers' profits and/or firm wide profits. Unless the entire firm makes a certain profit target, no individual profit center manager earns a bonus.

3. Investment Centers

Investment centers are similar to profit centers. However, they have additional decision rights for capital expenditures and are evaluated on measures such as return on investment (ROI). Investment centers are most appropriate when the manager of the unit has specific knowledge about investment opportunities as well as information relevant for making operating decisions for the unit.

Several profit centers often comprise one investment center. They have all the decision rights of cost and profit centers, as well as the decision rights over the amount of capital invested. For example, suppose the consumer electronics group of an electronics firm consists of three profit centers: the television division, the Blu-ray division, and the stereo division. Consumer electronics has decision rights over the amount of capital invested in the group.

Academic Application: How Firms Match Performance Measures and Decision-Making Authority	A study of 140 large European companies examined how performance measures are chosen to capture the manager's decision-making authority. Key findings include:

A study of 140 large European companies examined how performance measures are chosen to capture the manager's decision-making authority. Key findings include:

- Accounting return measures receive more weight in performance evaluation, bonus calculation, and promotion decisions when managers have more decision-making authority.
- Accounting return measures are more pronounced when managers have more influence on *investment* decisions.
- Accounting return measures become more important compared to profit measures as decision-making authority increases.

In other words, the importance and type of performance measure is tailored to the decision-making authority assigned to managers.

SOURCE: J. Bouwens and L. Van Lent, "Assessing the Performance of Business Unit Managers," *Journal of Accounting Research*, September 2007, pp. 667–97.

Investment center managers do not have decision rights over the quality of products they can sell and the market niches they can enter. These constraints prevent investment center managers from debasing the firm's reputation (also called its *brand-name capital*). Debasing the firm's reputation by lowering the quality of its products is one example of an adverse effect that one responsibility center can have on another. Responsibility centers can interact in many ways and can have adverse or favorable impacts on other centers. A plant's operating efficiency can be affected by the quantity and timing of the orders it receives from the marketing department. A purchasing department can affect the manufacturing department's operations by the timing and quality of the raw materials purchased. A responsibility center sharing a newly discovered cost-saving idea or R&D development with other centers is an example of a favorable (or positive) interaction. Managing these interactions (eliminating the negative ones and encouraging the positive ones) is critical to the successful linking of decision rights to individual(s) with the specialized knowledge. As discussed throughout the remaining chapters, the firm's internal accounting system can play a powerful role in either enhancing the positive interactions or exacerbating the negative ones.

In all of the responsibility centers in Table 5–1, the measure of performance is linked to the decision rights vested in the management. Investment center performance can be measured in at least three ways: net income, return on investment, and residual income. Each of these is described next.

Net income

The simplest of the three performance measures is accounting **net income** generated by the investment center (revenues minus expenses). However, net income does not consider all the investment used in the investment center to generate that income. Net income usually incorporates interest on any debt used to finance the assets, but it does not include any equity financing charge. Measuring investment center performance using net income creates dysfunctional incentives in investment centers to overinvest. Managers have incentives to overinvest as long as the new investment yields positive net income, no matter how small it is relative to the investment. Two investment centers can have the same net income, but if one has more investment than the other, the one with the smaller investment is yielding a higher rate of return. If investment center managers have the decision rights over capital investments but are not held accountable for how efficiently that capital is employed, they likely will over invest.

Return on investment

A commonly used investment center performance measure is **return on investment** (ROI). ROI is the ratio of accounting net income generated by the investment center divided by the total assets invested in the investment center. The other variants of ROI are ROA (return on total assets) and RONA (return on net assets, where net assets are total assets less current liabilities). Exactly how the denominator is measured is unimportant for understanding the key conceptual issues. In subsequent discussion, ROI, ROA, and RONA are used interchangeably.

ROI reduces the overinvestment problem of net income by holding the investment center manager responsible for earning a return on the capital employed in the center. It has intuitive appeal because ROI can be compared with external market-based yields to provide a benchmark for a division's performance. However, using ROI creates problems. ROI is not a measure of the division's economic rate of return because accounting net income (the numerator) excludes some value increases, such as land value appreciation, until the land is sold. Accounting net income tends to be conservative in that it recognizes most losses and defers most gains. The denominator of ROI, total assets invested, excludes many intangible assets such as patents and the firm's brand-name capital.

<table>
<tr><td>

Historical Application: The Du Pont Company ROI Method

</td><td>

The E.I. Du Pont de Nemours Powder Company, the leading firm manufacturing high explosives in the early 1900s, would later grow into one of the world's largest chemical companies. To control and evaluate its operations, Du Pont managers developed the concept of *return on investment*.

The financial staff traced the cost and revenues for each product produced. This gave management accurate information on profits, which provided a more precise way of evaluating financial performance. However, managers found product-line profits to be an incomplete measure of performance because these did not indicate the rate of return on capital invested. One manager said, "The true test of whether the profit is too great or too small is the rate of return on the money invested in the business and not the percent of profit on the cost."

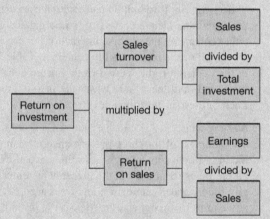

Developing a rate of return on each segment of business required accurate data on investment. Du Pont undertook a careful valuation of each of its plants, properties, and inventories by product line. These data, along with profits, allowed management to track ROI by product line. In addition, Du Pont managers decomposed ROI (Profits ÷ Investment) into its component parts. The accompanying figure illustrates this decomposition.

ROI is the product of sales turnover (Sales ÷ Total investment) and return on sales (Earnings ÷ Sales). These data allowed managers to determine the causes of a product's change in ROI. Also, these data benchmarked new capital appropriations by establishing the policy that there "be no expenditures for additions to the earnings equipment if the same amount of money could be applied to some better purpose in another branch of the company's business."

SOURCE: A. Chandler, *The Visible Hand: The Managerial Revolution in American Business* (Cambridge, MA: Harvard University Press, 1977), pp. 445–49.

</td></tr>
</table>

Whereas net income as an investment center performance measure creates an overinvestment problem, using ROI typically creates an underinvestment problem. Managers have incentives to reject profitable projects with ROIs below the mean ROI for the division because accepting these projects lowers the division's overall ROI. For example, suppose the division has an average ROI of 19 percent, 4 percent above its 15 percent cost of capital.[3] A new investment project that is 10 percent the size of the combined division is available. Its

---

[3]Cost of capital is the rate of return the firm must pay the market to raise capital. If the firm can raise money at 15 percent and invest in projects earning 16 percent, the firm's value increases.

ROI is 16 percent, which is above the cost of capital of 15 percent, so that taking this project would increase the value of the firm. However, accepting this project lowers the division's average ROI to 18.7 percent (or 0.90 × 19% + 0.10 × 16%). If the division is evaluated based on increasing ROI, the division management will reject the project, even though its return exceeds the opportunity cost of capital. Underinvesting results. In some cases, overinvestment also can occur using ROI. For example, suppose a division has a 15 percent cost of capital, but only a 10 percent ROI. This division has incentive to seek out and accept a 12 percent ROI project. Doing so raises the division's ROI. But clearly this project is unprofitable because it is earning less than its cost of capital.

Riskier projects require a higher cost of capital to compensate investors for bearing this risk. If managers are rewarded solely for increasing their division's ROI without being charged for any additional risk imposed on the firm, they have an incentive to plunge the firm into risky projects. Also, a manager with a short time horizon who is evaluated based on ROI would prefer projects that boost ROI in immediate years (the horizon problem) even if they were expected to be unprofitable over the life of the project.

Residual income

To overcome some of the incentive deficiencies of ROI, such as over- or underinvesting, some firms use residual income to evaluate performance. **Residual income** measures divisional performance by subtracting the opportunity cost of capital employed from division profits (after excluding any interest expense included in division profits). The opportunity cost of capital is measured using the firm's weighted-average cost of capital, which reflects the cost of equity and debt. The cost of equity is the price appreciation and dividends that the shareholders could have earned in a portfolio of companies of similar risk. This is the opportunity cost that the shareholders bear by buying the company's stock. The cost of debt is the current market yield on debt of similar risk. The costs of debt and equity are weighted by the relative amounts of debt and equity. Suppose the cost of equity is 18 percent, the cost of debt is 10 percent, and the firm's capital structure is 40 percent debt and 60 percent equity. Then the weighted-average cost of capital is 14.8 percent (or 0.60 × 18% + 0.40 × 10%). Suppose a division has profits of $20 million and investment (total assets) of $100 million. This division also has a cost of capital of 15 percent. Its ROI is 20 percent, which is in excess of its cost of capital (15 percent). Residual income is $5 million (or $20M – 15% × $100M). Under the residual income approach, divesting a project with an ROI of less than 20 percent, but above 15 percent, lowers residual income, although it raises average ROI.

Managerial Application: Strattec Security Corp Uses EVA	Strattec Security, with sales of $350 million, manufactures and markets automotive access control products, including mechanical locks and keys and steering column and instrument panel ignition locks. It uses EVA to measure and reward managers. As described in its proxy statement,

> Our "Economic Value Added Bonus Plan for Executive Officers and Senior Managers" provides for annual bonus payouts based on (1) the achievement of specific company-wide objective financial criteria, including minimum financial performance targets that must be met as a condition to payouts under the Plan, and (2) achievement of individual performance objective. . . . We believe that an improvement in the Economic Value Added measure is the financial performance measure most closely correlated with increases in our shareholder value. . . . In general, Economic Value Added (EVA) is our net operating profit after cash basis taxes, less a capital charge. The capital charge is intended to represent the return expected by the providers of our capital.

Source: www.strattec.com/files/2714/2115/9258/2014Proxy.pdf

TABLE 5-3　**Comparison of Residual Income with ROI ($000,000)**

	Division A	Division B
Invested capital	$100	$1,000
Net income	30	250
Capital charge (20%)	20	200
Residual income	10	50
ROI	30%	25%

Nonetheless, residual income is not without its own problems. Residual income is an absolute number, and thus larger divisions typically have larger residual incomes than smaller divisions, making relative performance-evaluation comparisons across investment centers of different sizes more difficult. To implement residual income measures, senior managers must estimate the cost of capital for each division. In principle, each division will have a different cost of capital to allow more precise performance evaluations by controlling for risk differences.

Like ROI, residual income measures performance over one year. It does not measure the impact of actions taken today on future firm value. For example, cutting maintenance increases current period residual income (and ROI) but jeopardizes future cash flow and hence firm value.

Table 5–3 illustrates the differences between ROI and residual income. Division B has 10 times the invested capital and more than 8 times the net income of Division A. Which division is better? Division B has five times the residual income of Division A, but Division A has the higher ROI. Does this mean Division A is better? The larger division, B, is more important to the firm, because more of the firm's income is from Division B. Division A, if younger than B, will have a higher ROI partly because it has taken its most profitable projects first. As firms (or divisions) grow, their ROI tends to fall to the extent they invest in the most profitable projects first. Therefore, Division A's higher ROI does not imply that it is the better-managed division or has the best investment prospects.

Identifying the "better" division requires establishing a benchmark. Suppose Divisions A and B had budgeted residual incomes of $12 million and $45 million, respectively. We would likely conclude that Division B was the better performer because it exceeded its budget by $5 million, whereas Division A fell short of its budget by $2 million. Of course, these conclusions depend on whether, at the end of the year, we still believe the beginning-of-year budgets ($12 and $45 million) to be valid performance benchmarks.

4. Economic Value Added (EVA®)

A number of large companies, including AT&T, Best Buy, Coca-Cola Company, DirecTV, Kaiser Aluminum, and Whirlpool Corp., use **economic value added**, or **EVA®**, as a measure of performance.[4] Other EVA-like terms have been created such as *economic profit, shareholder value added, total business return,* and *cash-flow return on investment.* And like EVA, these other metrics are variants of residual income. The formula for EVA is:

$$\text{EVA} = \frac{\text{Adjusted accounting}}{\text{earnings}} - \left(\begin{array}{c} \text{Weighted−average cost of} \\ \text{capital} \times \text{Total capital} \end{array} \right)$$

---

[4]EVA is a registered trademark of Stern Stewart & Co.

This formula is basically the same as residual income. EVA, like residual income, measures the total return after deducting the cost of all capital employed by the division or firm. Even though the formula is the same as the residual income formula, the two differ in a couple of ways. First, different accounting procedures are often used to calculate "adjusted accounting earnings" than are used in reporting to shareholders.[5] For example, U.S. accounting rules require that the entire amount spent on research and development each year be deducted from earnings. This creates incentives for managers with a short horizon to cut R&D spending. One adjustment to accounting earnings that EVA advocates suggest is adding back R&D spending and treating it as an asset to be amortized, usually over three to seven years. Total capital in the EVA formula consists of all the division's or firm's assets, including the amount of capitalized R&D and other capitalized accounting adjustments. However, many firms using EVA choose not to make any accounting adjustments.

Exercise 5-1

R&D spending at one company was $1.2 million in 2014, $1.5 million in 2015, $1.8 million in 2016, and $2.4 million in 2017. Calculate the amount of R&D assets and R&D expense from 2014 to 2017 under two alternative accounting procedures: (1) all current-year R&D is expensed immediately, and (2) R&D is capitalized and then amortized over three years. (Assume that all R&D spending for the year occurs on the first day of the year.)

Solution:

If R&D is expensed immediately, the R&D asset on the balance sheet is $0 and the 2017 expense is $2.4 million. The following table amortizes R&D spending over three years. For example, $1.2 million was spent on R&D in 2014. If this amount is capitalized, its annual amortization would be $0.4 million per year. But this $1.2 million would have been completely amortized before 2017 begins; none of its amortization would be in 2017. The amortization expense of $1.9 million in 2017 consists of one-third of the R&D spending in 2015, 2016, and 2017 $(1/3 \times \$5.7$ million).

	R&D Spending	Amortization of R&D Spending Incurred in				Total R&D Amortization Expenses in 2017
		2014	*2015*	*2016*	*2017*	*2017*
2014	$1.2	$0.4				
2015	1.5	0.4	$0.5			
2016	1.8	0.4	0.5	$0.6		
2017	2.4		0.5	0.6	$0.8	$1.9

continued

---

[5]For a more complete description of EVA, see B. Stewart, *The Quest for Value* (New York: Harper Business, 1991).

172   *Chapter 5*

Using the amortization amounts in the previous table, the next table calculates the amount of the R&D asset at the end of the current year.

	Balance of the R&D Asset Acquired in				*Total R&D Asset in 2017*
	2014	*2015*	*2016*	*2017*	
Beginning of 2014	$1.2				
Beginning of 2015	0.8	$1.5			
Beginning of 2016	0.4	1.0	$1.8		
Beginning of 2017	0.0	0.5	1.2	$2.4	
End of 2017	0.0	0.0	0.6	1.6	$2.2

The $2.2 million of R&D asset remaining after the end of 2017 consists of the remaining unamortized portion of 2016's R&D spending ($0.6 million) plus the unamortized portion from 2017's R&D spending ($1.6 million). The $1.2 million spent in 2014 and $1.5 million spent in 2015 are fully amortized, and hence no remaining portion of these amounts is in the R&D asset balance at the end of 2017.

Exercise 5-2

The company in Exercise 5–1 has EVA before R&D of $15.2 million and a weighted-average cost of capital of 20 percent. Calculate its EVA under two alternative accounting procedures: (1) All current year R&D is expensed immediately, and (2) R&D is capitalized and then amortized over three years.

Solution:

1. If all R&D is expensed immediately, the company's EVA is $12.8 million ($15.2 – $2.4).

2. If R&D is capitalized and then amortized, the company's EVA is $12.86 million ($15.2 – $1.9 – 20% × $2.2).

Managerial Application: Boosting Return on Capital	Eaton, a maker of transmissions for large trucks, divided its transmission components into three categories: those for which other firms were more cost-effective because they had economies of scale, those for which Eaton was the most efficient producer or for which it had proprietary technology, and all other component parts of its transmissions. Eaton then outsourced the manufacturing of all component parts other than those for which it was the most efficient producer or for which it had proprietary technology. By doing this, Eaton significantly decreased the asset intensity of its business, thereby leading to better returns on capital.

SOURCE: D. Katz, "Lite Makes Right," *CFO*, November 2010, pp. 35–36.

Responsibility Accounting and Transfer Pricing   **173**

Second, many companies implementing EVA not only adopt EVA as their performance measure but also link compensation to performance measured by EVA. For example, bonuses are paid only if managers achieve pre-stated EVA targets. Usually, firms adopting EVA put more of the total compensation paid to managers at risk. Instead of the bonus being 10 percent of the base salary, it becomes 30 percent or more. The pool of managers eligible to earn bonuses is expanded. Thus, firms adopting EVA increase the sensitivity of their managers' pay to performance. While adopting EVA-based compensation plans imposes more risk on managers, EVA also increases their incentives to maximize firm value.

Adopting EVA as a performance measure and then linking pay to EVA performance is a complicated process. Employees receiving EVA-based bonuses must be trained in how EVA is measured and how their actions affect EVA. For example, EVA creates incentives for managers to reduce unused assets, plant, equipment, and inventory. Eliminating underutilized assets lessens the capital charge applied to these assets and hence increases EVA. Consulting firms that help companies adopt EVA train their employees to understand EVA and how to manage the firm to increase EVA.

Accounting earnings, ROI, residual income, and EVA enhance goal congruence by aligning managers' and shareholders' interests. But the four performance measures have subtle differences in achieving goal congruence. Earnings create incentives to increase revenues and decrease expenses. But earnings do not create incentives for managers to use assets efficiently. ROI gives managers incentives to shed unproductive assets (i.e., by decreasing the denominator, the ratio increases). Residual income and EVA charge managers for the capital employed, thereby providing incentives to use assets efficiently. However, all four metrics focus on short-run accounting earnings. They do not reward managers for actions taken today that improve future accounting earnings. Some of the accounting adjustments, such as capitalizing R&D, help reduce this problem. Nonetheless, the future cash inflows from the R&D are not recognized in EVA (or ROI or residual income) until they are received. Thus, a company can be making very profitable investments, but the returns from these investments will not show up in EVA (or earnings, ROI, and residual income) until the cash inflows from these investments are received.

5. Controllability Principle

Responsibility accounting seeks to identify the objectives of each part of the organization and then develop performance measures that report the achievement of those objectives. For example, the department handling customer complaints might be evaluated based on how long customers wait for a representative or how many callers hang up. Holding managers responsible for only those decisions for which they have authority is called the **controllability principle. Controllable costs** are all costs affected by a manager's decisions. Uncontrollable costs are those that are not affected by the manager.

Some people argue that the performance of managers should be judged solely on those items under their control, not on costs over which they have no influence. However, a strict application of the controllability principle has two major drawbacks. First, holding managers accountable for only those variables directly under their control does not give them an incentive to take actions that can affect the consequences of the uncontrollable event. For example, if the marina manager is not held accountable for damage done by hurricanes, the manager has less incentive to prepare the marina for severe storms. While managers cannot influence the likelihood of hurricanes, they can certainly influence the costs incurred when a hurricane strikes.[6]

---

[6]G. Baker, M. Jensen, and K. Murphy, "Compensation and Incentives: Practice vs. Theory," *Journal of Finance* 43 (July 1988), p. 611. Also see K. Merchant, *Rewarding Results: Motivating Profit Center Managers* (Boston: Harvard Business School Press, 1989), pp. 87–141.

Managerial Application: Gaming in Call Centers	At one call center, operators taking queries from customers about their accounts were evaluated on the number of calls answered per day. Customers with difficult, time-consuming questions had their calls forwarded to other departments. Customer satisfaction fell. Now most call centers record all calls and base operator performance on a subjective evaluation of a random sampling of their calls.
	SOURCE: C. Day, *Call Center Operations: Profiting from Teleservices* (McGraw-Hill Professional, 2000).

Consider whether profit center managers should be evaluated based on their profits before or after taxes. One argument is that since profit center managers cannot control changes in state and federal tax policies, they should not be evaluated on after-tax profits. However, profit center managers' decisions affect corporate tax payments in a variety of ways. Export sales affect tax credits. Charitable contributions and inventory write-offs affect taxes. One company reports that before it started charging taxes to profit center managers, the corporation's income taxes were 46 to 48 percent of its profits. After it started charging taxes to the profit center managers, the average tax rate fell to 40.5 percent.[7] This example illustrates an important point. Evaluating managers on items that they can at least influence, if not control, such as corporate taxes, changes the managers' incentives regarding those items.

The second drawback of the controllability principle is that it ignores the often useful role of relative performance evaluation, in which performance is judged relative to how some comparison group performed instead of by absolute standards. The comparison group helps control for random events that affect both the person being evaluated and the comparison group. For example, many instructors curve grades. Instead of awarding As for scores of 94 to 100, they give As to the top 15 percent of the class. Curving grades controls for unusually easy or hard exams and removes some of the risk from students.

Whenever the controllability principle is applied and managers are held accountable for their actions, dysfunctional actions can occur. All of the performance measures in Table 5–1 are prone to managerial opportunism in the form of accounting manipulations. Managers can choose depreciation methods or estimates that reduce expenses and increase reported earnings (e.g., straight-line depreciation or longer estimated asset lives). These accounting choices artificially raise ROI. Investment center managers can increase ROI by rejecting or divesting profitable projects with ROIs below the division average. All of the accounting measures in Table 5–1 are short-term measures of performance that suffer from the horizon problem, whereby managers emphasize short-term performance at the expense of long-term returns. Each measure requires careful monitoring by senior managers to reduce dysfunctional suboptimal subordinate behavior from the viewpoint of the owners.

Two important points must be stressed regarding the controllability principle:

1. Performance measurement schemes (including accounting-based methods) used mechanically and in isolation from other measures are likely to produce misleading results and induce dysfunctional behavior. For example, in the former Soviet Union, Moscow cab drivers were evaluated on the number of miles driven. This scheme caused cab drivers to circle the city on the uncongested outer highways while most of the demand for cabs remained in the congested center of Moscow, where there were no cabs.

---

[7]Merchant (1989), p. 99.

2. No performance measurement and reward system works perfectly. There always remains some managerial action that enhances the manager's welfare at the expense of the shareholders. In other words, all incentive schemes will be gamed. One should avoid discarding a system because some managerial opportunism exists and the system proves to be less than perfect. The key question is whether the current system outperforms the next best alternative after considering all costs and benefits.

Concept Questions		
	Q5–1	What is responsibility accounting?
	Q5–2	What role does the firm's internal accounting system play in resolving organizational problems?
	Q5–3	Describe three different types of responsibility centers. Include any shortcomings the centers might have.
	Q5–4	How does EVA differ from residual income?
	Q5–5	What is the controllability principle and what are its limitations?
	Q5–6	What two points must be kept in mind when examining performance-based measurement systems?

B. Transfer Pricing

When goods are transferred from one profit (or investment) center to another, an internal price (the **transfer price**) is assigned to the units transferred. If Chevrolet manufactures an engine that is installed in a Buick, the transfer price is the internal charge paid by the Buick division of General Motors to the Chevrolet division of General Motors. Transfer prices are much more prevalent in organizations than most managers realize. Consider the charge that the advertising department receives from the maintenance department for janitorial service, or the monthly charge for telephones, security services, e-mail, legal and personnel services, and so on. Most firms use cost allocations as a method of charging internal users for goods or services received from another part of the organization. These cost allocations are, in reality, transfer prices. Hence, transfer pricing and cost allocations are two closely related topics. (The specifics of cost allocations are discussed in Chapters 7 and 8.)

There are basically two main reasons for transfer pricing within firms: international taxation and performance measurement of profit and investment centers. Each of these is described next.

1. International Taxation

When products are transferred overseas, the firm's corporate tax liability in both the exporting and importing country is affected if the firm files tax returns in both jurisdictions. For example, when a copier is manufactured in Rochester, New York, by Xerox Corp. and shipped to England to be sold, U.S. and British taxes paid by Xerox are affected. The transfer price of the copier is a revenue for U.S. tax purposes and a tax-deductible expense in England. To the extent allowed by the tax regulations, the firm will set a transfer price that minimizes the joint tax liability in the two countries. If the two tax jurisdictions tax income at different rates, then the firm will set the transfer price to shift as much of the profit into the lower-rate jurisdiction as possible, subject to the taxing authorities' guidelines.

For example, suppose Bausch & Lomb manufactures a box of contact lenses in the Netherlands and ships the lenses to an Australian subsidiary that sells them for

85 Australian dollars. The variable out-of-pocket cost of manufacturing the contact lenses is 50 euros. The exchange rate is 0.70 Australian dollars to 1 euro. Suppose the Dutch corporate tax rate is 30 percent and the Australian corporate tax rate is 40 percent. Bausch & Lomb will want to set the transfer price on the lenses as high as permissible to recognize more profits in the lower tax-rate jurisdiction, which is the Netherlands in this case. The transfer price of the contacts can vary, depending on what fixed costs are allocated to them and how. Suppose Australian and Dutch tax treaties allow Bausch & Lomb to set a transfer price at anywhere between 80 and 110 euros. Table 5–4 illustrates how the combined tax liability varies with the transfer price.

By choosing the highest allowed transfer price, 110 euros, Bausch & Lomb can recognize more profits in the country with the lowest corporate income tax rate. If Australia had the lower tax rate, then Bausch & Lomb would select the lowest transfer price, 80 euros, thereby reducing its Dutch tax liability and raising its Australian tax liability. But the higher taxes paid in Australia would be offset by the lower taxes paid in the Netherlands.

Each country has tax regulations that define how companies in its jurisdiction calculate the price of goods transferred in and out of the country. Section 482 of the U.S. Internal Revenue Code authorizes the Internal Revenue Service to regulate the allocation of revenues and costs to prevent tax evasion. International tax treaties regulate allowable transfer pricing methods. Because tax codes vary across jurisdictions, we ignore the role of international taxation in setting transfer prices in this chapter and focus instead on the organizational issues. Small differences in tax rates can generate large cash flow differences, depending on the transfer prices. Thus, in many firms international taxation is the primary factor determining the firm's transfer pricing policy.

TABLE 5-4   Bausch & Lomb: Effect of Transfer Pricing on Combined Tax Liability

		Transfer Price at 80 Euros		*Transfer Price at 110 Euros*
Taxes Paid in the Netherlands				
Revenue (transfer price)		€80		€110
Variable cost		–50		–50
Taxable income		€30		€60
Tax rate		30%		30%
Dutch taxes		€9		€18
Taxes Paid in Australia				
Revenue[†]		A$85		A$85
Transfer price in euros	€80		€110	
× Exchange rate 0.70 A$/Euro	× 0.70		× 0.70	
Transfer price as A$[†]		–A$56		–A$77
Taxable income		A$29		A$8
Tax rate		40%		40%
Australian taxes		A$11.6		A$3.2
Converted to euros (÷ 0.70)		€16.57		€4.57
Sum of Dutch and Australian taxes		€25.57		€22.57

[†]A$ denotes Australian dollars.

Managerial Application: Dual Transfer Pricing Systems?	Some consultants advocate using two separate transfer pricing systems, one for tax purposes and another for internal decision making, even though maintaining two systems can be costly. For example, one consultant believes in having two systems provide senior management with more accurate information about profitability. However, a partner at Ernst & Young advises against having two systems because if the single transfer pricing system reflects economic reality, the firm does not need to have two systems. If the firm has two systems because the one used for taxes does not reflect the firm's economic reality, the tax authorities may disallow the transfer prices used for tax calculations.

SOURCES: I. Springsteel, "Separate But Unequal," *CFO*, August 1999, pp. 89–91

Firms can have two sets of transfer prices: one for taxes and one for internal purposes. However, maintaining two such systems is costly. Additional bookkeeping costs are incurred and are confusing to users. In addition, some tax jurisdictions may argue that the transfer prices used for internal purposes should also be used for taxes, especially if they result in higher taxes than the transfer prices used for taxes.

2. Economics of Transfer Pricing

As discussed earlier, firms are organized into responsibility centers. Whenever responsibility centers transfer goods or services among themselves, measuring their performance requires that a "transfer price" be established for the goods and services exchanged. For example, suppose a large chemical company is organized into profit centers. Besides producing for and selling to outside customers, these profit centers also sell intermediate products to other profit centers within the company, which then further process the intermediate products into final products that are sold to outside customers. To measure the performance of the profit centers, each of these internal transactions requires a transfer price. The purchasing division pays the transfer price and the producing division receives the transfer price.

Some managers mistakenly view the transfer pricing problem as unimportant. They think that alternative transfer pricing methods merely shift income among divisions and that, except for relative performance evaluation, little else is affected. But this is a mistake: *The choice of transfer pricing method does not merely reallocate total company profits among business units; it also affects the firm's total profits.* Think of the firm's total profit as a pie. Choice among transfer pricing methods not only changes how the pie is divided among responsibility centers, it also changes the size of the pie to be divided.

Managers make investment, purchasing, and production decisions based on the transfer prices they face. If, from the firm's perspective, these transfer prices do not reflect the true value of the resources, managers will make inappropriate decisions and the value of the firm will be reduced. For example, if the opportunity cost to the firm of producing an intermediate chemical is $20 per kilogram but the transfer price is $30, the purchasing division will consume too little of the chemical relative to the quantity it would purchase if the transfer price were $20, and total firm profits will be reduced. Purchasing-unit managers will have the incentive to shift away from using the chemical toward using other inputs that, in reality, are more expensive for the firm. Also, because transfer prices affect the managers' performance evaluations, incorrect transfer prices can result in inappropriate promotion and bonus decisions.

Managerial Application: Transfer Pricing and Taxes	Judicious transfer pricing can allow companies to cut their international tax bill by a third. For example, one U.S.-headquartered firm manufactures products in Ireland, sells them primarily in the United States, and uses subsidiaries in the Netherlands and Bermuda to recognize the income tax. Setting high transfer prices between the United States and Ireland shifts the income first to Ireland. Then, transfer prices shift that income to the Netherlands and Bermuda, which have even lower tax rates than Ireland. By not returning the profits to the United States in the form of cash, firms legally avoid most U.S. taxes on their income. Apple Inc. reduces its federal tax bill by billions of dollars. Apple conducts most of its research in the United States, and most of its key employees, long-lived assets, and retail stores are in the United States. But by employing legal transfer pricing rules, Apple reports only 30 percent of its profits as being from the United States, which has one of the highest tax rates on corporate earnings (35 percent), while Apple's actual worldwide effective tax rate is closer to 13 percent.

But not all schemes go smoothly. Taxing authorities have become much more aggressive in challenging multinational firms' tax returns. UK-based GlaxoSmithKline (GSK) agreed to settle its transfer pricing dispute with the U.S. IRS by paying $3.4 billion. At issue was how GSK treated the transfer price of making its popular ulcer drug Zantac. In fact, 30 percent of all U.S. corporate tax adjustments made each year involve transfer-pricing disputes.

In an attempt to streamline the transfer-pricing dispute-resolution process, the IRS has an Advance Pricing Agreement (APA) program. The taxpayer and the IRS work together prospectively to develop the transfer-pricing method the taxpayer will use. As long as the taxpayer complies with the agreement, the IRS usually will not challenge subsequent years' transfer prices.

SOURCES: www.irs.gov/pub/irs-utl/apa03.pdf; M. Sullivan, "Apple Reports High Rate but Saves Billions on Taxes," *Tax. com*, February 13, 2012; Ernst & Young, "Navigating the choppy waters of international tax," 2013 Global Transfer Pricing Survey (2013) www.EY.com

Because transfer prices (including chargeback systems) are widespread in many firms and because transfer pricing affects performance evaluation and hence the rewards managers receive, disputes over the transfer price between divisions are inevitable. Transfer pricing is a constant source of tension within firms. It is not uncommon for managers in most multidivisional firms to be involved in transfer pricing disputes over the course of their careers.

The transfer price that maximizes firm value is quite simple to state: The optimal transfer price for a product or service is its opportunity cost—it is the value forgone by not using the transferred product in its next best alternative use. Unfortunately, as we will see, this simple rule is often difficult to implement in practice.

Transfer pricing with perfect information

To illustrate the concept of using opportunity cost to set the transfer price, suppose the firm has two profit centers: Manufacturing and Distribution. Senior management is considering making a product in Manufacturing and transferring it to Distribution. Assume also that Manufacturing's variable cost of production is $3 per unit, and that it has excess capacity. If the product is transferred to Distribution, Distribution can sell it and receive $5 for each unit, net of its own variable cost. Also, everyone knows each division's cost and revenue data.

If the unit is not manufactured, the firm saves $3 but forgoes $5, thus reducing profits by $2. If the unit is manufactured and transferred, the firm forgoes $3 (variable cost to produce) and receives $5 for a net receipt of $2. The better alternative is to manufacture and transfer the unit. The resources forgone by transferring the unit from Manufacturing to Distribution—and hence the opportunity cost of such a transfer—is $3 per unit, the same as Manufacturing's variable cost of production.

As this example is meant to suggest, the variable cost of producing the unit is often the opportunity cost. But this is not always the case. Sometimes, the opportunity cost is the revenue of selling the intermediate good externally. For example, suppose Manufacturing can produce one unit for $3 and can either transfer that unit to Distribution or sell it for $5.50 outside the firm—but, because of limited capacity, it cannot do both. In this case, by having Manufacturing transfer the unit to Distribution, the firm forgoes selling the intermediate good in the market. Even though the variable cost of producing the unit is $3, the opportunity cost of the transfer is $5.50. Thus, it is now optimal to sell it externally rather than transfer it to Distribution. Selling it externally yields profits of $2.50 ($5.50 − $3.00). Transferring it to Distribution, who sells it for $5, yields profits of only $2 ($5 − $3).

When opportunity cost is used to set the transfer price, Manufacturing will produce to the point at which the variable cost of the last unit equals the transfer price. Likewise, Distribution will buy units from Manufacturing as long as Distribution's net receipts just cover the transfer price. When opportunity cost is used to set the transfer price and both Manufacturing and Distribution are maximizing their respective profits, assuming there are no interdependencies between the business units (a case we consider later), total firm profits are maximized. If the transfer price is too high or too low relative to opportunity cost, too few units are transferred and firm profits are not maximized.

Transfer pricing with asymmetric information

The preceding discussion assumes everyone knows (1) Manufacturing's variable production cost, (2) Distribution's revenue, and (3) whether Manufacturing has excess capacity. Yet if all of this knowledge were readily available, there would be no reason to decentralize decision making within the organization. Central management would have the knowledge to make the decision and could either retain the decision rights or, if the decision rights were delegated, monitor the process at low cost. In reality, much of the information is not readily available to central management. Especially in large, multidivisional firms, such knowledge generally resides at lower levels of the firm where it is private knowledge, costly to either transfer or verify by senior management. In some circumstances, lower-level managers have incentives to distort the information they pass up to senior managers. To illustrate these incentives, we consider the role of market power.

Consider a situation where the manager of Manufacturing is the only person with knowledge of his division's variable costs, and assume that Burt seeks to maximize the profits of his division. Even if Distribution is allowed to purchase the product on the outside, if Manufacturing has market power in setting the transfer price, it will attempt to set the price above its variable cost to increase its *measured* profits. When this happens, the firm manufactures and sells too few units of the product. The Manufacturing division, possessing what amounts to monopoly rights in information, behaves like a monopolist. Just as monopolists earn "monopoly profits" by raising prices and restricting output, Manufacturing's higher profits lead to lower-than-optimal production levels and lower total firm profits. Example 5–1 illustrates how firm profits are reduced when the transfer price is not set at opportunity cost.

Example 5-1

There are two profit centers: the Seller and Buyer divisions. The Seller division produces and sells an intermediate product (electric motors) to the Buyer Division. The Buyer Division uses the motors in making a toy car. Both divisions are profit centers and maximize their division's profits. The following outlines the cost structure of the two divisions:

Cost Structure of the Two Divisions

	Selling Division (Seller)	Buying Division (Buyer)
Fixed costs	$150/day	$100 (1st 100 units per day)
Variable costs	$0.10/unit	$0.20/unit (over 100 units)

The Buyer Division faces a downward-sloping demand curve for its final product (the toy car), which includes the intermediate product with the following price-quantity relationship:

Demand for Buyer Division's Toy Car

Quantity Sold	Price/Car	Total Revenue
100	$2.00	$200
200	1.80	360
300	1.50	450
400	1.30	520
500	1.20	600
600	1.04	624

Suppose the transfer price is set at $0.95 per unit and 200 motors are transferred. The $0.95 was set by taking Seller's variable cost of $0.10 per unit and adding $0.75 for fixed costs (Unit fixed cost = $0.75 = $150/200) and $0.10 for profits. Seller's profit is $20 = 200 × $0.10.

The Buyer Division produces 200 cars and maximizes profits at $50. These relations are summarized in the next table.

Buying Division's Costs and Revenues

Output (Units)	Buyer's Own Cost ($100 + .20/Unit over 100)	Cost from Seller ($0.95/Unit)	Total Cost (Buyer's Own Cost + Transfer)	Total Revenue (Price × Quantity)	Profit (Revenue − Cost)
100	$100	$ 95	$195	$200	$ 5
200	120	190	310	360	50
300	140	285	425	450	25
400	160	380	540	520	−20
500	180	475	655	600	−55
600	200	570	770	624	−146

Both divisions seem to be operating well, and both are making a profit. The Buyer Division is maximizing its profit. The selling division, Seller, is making $20 profit and could make more motors if only the Buyer Division would buy more. But the company is not maximizing firm-wide profits.

continued

Company profits are maximized at 500 motors. The accompanying table indicates the total companywide costs and revenues at the various output levels.

Firm Profits

Output	Seller Costs	Buyer Costs	Total Costs	Total Revenue	Firm Profit
100	$160	$100	$260	$200	$–60
200	170	120	290	360	70
300	180	140	320	450	130
400	190	160	350	520	170
500	200	180	380	600	220
600	210	200	410	624	214

Company profits rise from $70 at 200 motors per day to $220 at 500 motors per day. In this example, the correct transfer price is at variable cost ($0.10). Transferring at $0.10/motors maximizes company profits. Charging more than variable cost causes the Buyer Division to purchase too few motors. But the Seller Division shows a loss (its fixed costs, if the transfer price is set at variable cost).

3. Common Transfer Pricing Methods

The correct transfer price is opportunity cost. But, as noted earlier, determining opportunity costs is difficult—in part because the information necessary to calculate such costs resides with operating managers who have incentives to distort it. To address this problem, companies sometimes commission special studies of the firm's cost structure by outside experts. However, not only are such studies costly but their findings become outdated whenever the firm's business opportunities or productive capacities change. On the other hand, if senior management simply vests the right to set the transfer price with either Manufacturing or Distribution, these opportunistic managers will set the transfer price to maximize their division's profits, not firm-wide profits. Hence, too few units get transferred, and the firm's value will be lower than it could be.

Because determining opportunity costs is itself an expensive undertaking, managers resort to various lower-cost approximations. There are at least four different methods that firms regularly use to approximate the opportunity cost of the units transferred: market price, variable production cost, full cost, and negotiated pricing. As discussed next, each one of these four methods is better than the others in some situations, but not in others. For example, if the divisions operate in different countries with different tax rates, then the choice of method will be driven in part by tax considerations. The remainder of this section describes the various methods and their advantages and disadvantages.

Market-based transfer prices

The standard transfer pricing rule offered by most textbooks is: Given a competitive external market for the good, the product should be transferred at the external market price. If Manufacturing cannot make a long-run profit at the external price, then the company is better off not producing internally and instead should purchase in the external market. If the purchasing division cannot make a long-run profit at the external price, then the company is better off not processing the intermediate product and instead should sell it in the external market. Using the external market price of goods and services transferred internally is often an objective way to set transfer prices. Such external prices are not subject to manipulations by managers in the selling division as are accounting-based transfer prices. (Discussed later.)

The use of market-based transfer prices is often assumed to produce the correct make-versus-buy decisions. In many situations, however, market prices will not provide an accurate reflection of opportunity cost. If the firm and the market both are making the intermediate good, the fundamental question arises, *Can both survive in the long run?* If one can produce the good at a lower, long-run, average cost than the other, the high-cost producer should not be producing the intermediate product.

Transactions generally take place inside rather than outside firms whenever the cost of repetitive internal contracting is cheaper than outsourcing.[8] For example, firms often produce products inside even though they could purchase them externally. Firms produce internally when there are important interdependencies or synergies among those products. And, of course, the more valuable these synergies, the more likely the firm will continue producing internally.

As the synergies from internal production increase, the external market price becomes a more inaccurate reflection of the opportunity cost of internal production. For example, it is often the case that an intermediate good is not being produced by other firms or that the good produced externally is not identical to the good produced internally. In the first case, there is no market price; in the second, the market price is often an unreliable guide to opportunity cost. And, even when there are virtually identical "cheaper" external products, producing internally can still make sense insofar as it provides greater quality control, more timely supply, or better protection of proprietary information. When these factors are included in the analysis, the external market may no longer be "cheaper."

In such cases, using the market price as the transfer price may understate the profitability of the product and its contribution to the value of the firm. Suppose, for example, that an intermediate product can be purchased but not sold externally for $3 per unit. Synergies such as high transactions costs of using the market make it beneficial to produce the item internally. Internal production avoids the costs of writing and enforcing contracts. Suppose there are $0.50 worth of synergies, so that the "correct" transfer price is $2.50 in the sense that $2.50 is the opportunity cost to the firm. But, if the market price of $3.00 is used as the transfer price, Distribution will purchase fewer units than if $2.50 were used, and the value of the firm will not be maximized.

Variable-cost transfer prices
If no external market for the intermediate good exists or if large synergies that exist from internal production cause the market price to be an inaccurate measure of opportunity cost,

Academic Application: Why Transfer Pricing Is So Hard	"The economist's first instinct is to set the transfer price equal to marginal cost. But it may be difficult to find out marginal cost. As a practical matter, marginal cost information is rarely known to anybody in the firm, because it depends on opportunity costs that vary with capacity use. And even if marginal cost information were available, there is no guarantee that it would be revealed in a truthful fashion for the purpose of determining an optimal transfer price." SOURCE: B. Holmstrom and J. Tirole, "Transfer Pricing and Organizational Form," *Journal of Law, Economics, & Organizations* 7 (1991), pp. 201–28.

[8]Advantages to internal transactions include the elimination of credit risk, lower marketing costs, and learning from production. See R. Coase, "The Nature of the Firm," *Economica* 4 (1937), pp. 386–405; and R. Watts, "Accounting Choice Theory and Market-Based Research in Accounting," *British Accounting Journal* 24 (1992), pp. 242–46.

then variable production cost may be the most effective alternative transfer price. As we saw earlier, variable cost represents the value of the resources forgone to produce one more unit.

As with other transfer-pricing methods, however, there are problems with variable cost as a measure of opportunity cost. One is that Manufacturing does not necessarily recover its fixed costs. If Manufacturing's entire output is transferred internally and variable cost is below its average total cost, Manufacturing's fixed costs are not recovered. Thus, Manufacturing appears to be losing money.[9]

One variant of variable-cost transfer pricing is to price all transfers at variable cost while also charging Distribution a fixed fee for these services. Distribution pays the variable cost for the additional units and buys the number of units that maximizes firm profits. Unlike straight variable-cost pricing, however, this variant allows Manufacturing to cover its full cost and earn a profit. The fixed fee represents the right of Distribution to acquire the product at variable cost and is set to cover Manufacturing's fixed cost plus a return on equity.

Another problem with variable-cost transfer pricing occurs in situations where the variable cost per unit is not constant as volume changes. Suppose the variable cost per unit increases as volume expands (say, a night shift is added at a higher hourly wage). If variable cost is greater than average cost and all users are charged the higher variable cost, the total cost charged to all the users is greater than the total cost incurred by the firm. Users who did not expand their volume will still see their costs increase. In such cases, conflicts are likely within the firm over the appropriate measure of variable cost and whether all users should pay variable cost or just those users who expanded output, thereby prompting the addition of the night shift.

A similar problem arises when Manufacturing approaches capacity. To illustrate the problem, assume that Manufacturing is considering a $2.5 million outlay to add more capacity. These additional capacity costs of $2.5 million are variable in the long run but become

Managerial Application: The Costs of the Sarbanes-Oxley Act	Teva Pharmaceutical Industries Ltd. in Israel implemented a variable-cost transfer pricing system defined as only material cost. Labor was largely fixed because of the high cost of firing and hiring employees in Israel. Manufacturing produced drugs that several geographic marketing divisions sold. These marketing divisions could also sell other producers' pharmaceuticals. Market-based transfer pricing was rejected because many of Teva's products did not sell in intermediate markets. Senior executives rejected negotiated transfer pricing because they believed it would lead to endless arguments.

Variable-cost transfer pricing proved very unpopular. Senior managers worried that marketing divisions would show extremely high profits because they were not being charged for fixed costs. They also worried that manufacturing would have little incentive to control labor and other so-called fixed expenses. Finally, if manufacturing was less efficient than outside suppliers, variable-cost transfer pricing would provide little incentive to the marketing divisions to buy internally.

Teva replaced the variable-cost transfer pricing system with one based on full cost, including materials, labor, and overhead.

SOURCE: R. Kaplan, D. Weiss, and E. Desheh, "Transfer Pricing with ABC," *Management Accounting*, May 1997, pp. 20–28 and A. Ovadia, Restructuring Can Help Teva's Copaxone Woes," Globes, November 17, 2013.

[9]Of course, if central management knows the magnitude of the fixed costs, they can budget for this loss. But, once again, if central management knows the magnitude of the fixed costs, then they know variable cost, and thus there is little reason to have a separate responsibility center and transfer pricing system in the first place.

184   *Chapter 5*

short-run fixed costs (depreciation and higher utilities and maintenance). Thus, conflicts arise between Manufacturing and Distribution as to whether these additional capacity costs should be included in the transfer price or not. Such conflicts are difficult to resolve because no indisputably objective method exists for calculating variable costs. They are not reported in *The Wall Street Journal.* Instead, they have to be estimated from accounting records. Although most of the components of variable cost are easily observed, such as the cost of direct labor and direct material, some components are difficult to estimate. For example, the additional costs incurred by the purchasing department when additional units are manufactured are not easily observed and hence difficult to estimate precisely.

Variable-cost transfer pricing also creates incentives for Manufacturing to distort variable cost upward, perhaps by misclassifying fixed costs as variable costs. For example, how much of the electricity bill is fixed and how much is variable? Since these classifications are to some extent arbitrary, influence costs are generated as managers in Manufacturing and Distribution debate various cost terms and their applications—and as senior managers are forced to spend time arbitrating such disputes.

Moreover, under variable-cost transfer pricing, Manufacturing can have an incentive to convert a dollar of fixed costs into more than a dollar of variable costs—for example, by using high-priced outsourcing of parts instead of cheaper internal manufacturing—even though this clearly reduces the value of the firm. For Manufacturing, the use of outsourcing can remove the burden of any fixed costs while Distribution, as well as the firm as a whole, bears the extra cost of such decisions.

Exercise 5-3

Scoff Division of Worldwide Paint is currently losing money, and senior management is considering selling or closing Scoff. Scoff's only product, an intermediate chemical called Binder, is used principally by the latex division of the firm. If Scoff is sold, the latex division can purchase ample quantities of Binder in the market at sufficiently high-quality levels to meet its requirements. Worldwide requires all of its divisions to supply product to other Worldwide divisions before servicing the external market.

Scoff's statement of operations for the latest quarter is:

SCOFF DIVISION
Profit/Loss
Last Quarter
($ thousands)

Revenues		
Inside	$200	
Outside	75	$275
Operating expenses		
Variable costs	$260	
Fixed costs	15	
Allocated corporate overhead	40	315
Net income (loss) before taxes		($40)

NOTES:
1. Worldwide Paint has the policy of transferring all products internally at variable cost. In Scoff's case, variable cost is 80 percent of the market price.
2. All of Scoff's fixed costs are avoidable cash flows if Scoff is closed or sold.
3. $4,000 of the $40,000 allocated corporate overhead will be avoided if Scoff is closed or sold.

continued

Required:

Calculate the annual net cash flows to Worldwide Paint of closing or selling Scoff.

Solution:

The key to this problem is recognizing that the variable cost transfer price is very favorable to Latex and is causing Scoff to appear unprofitable. If Scoff is closed or sold, Latex will have to pay the market price for Binder, which is higher than the current transfer price. Also, not all the corporate overhead is saved by closing or selling Scoff.

Selling or closing Scoff changes the potential synergies within the firm. Can Worldwide Paint maintain the same quality/delivery times on Binder? One question to raise is what these are worth. Analyzing these "intangibles" will be necessary only if an outside offer is larger than the value of the cash flows forgone from selling Scoff. The following table indicates that Scoff is generating positive cash flow to Worldwide despite the operating losses reported.

SCOFF DIVISION
Quarterly Net Cash Flows to Worldwide Paint of Closing
Last Quarter Ending
($ thousands)

Operating expenses saved:		
Variable costs	$260	
Fixed costs	15	
Allocated corporate overhead	4	
Scoff's operating expenses avoided		$279
Revenues forgone:		
Outside		(75)
Market purchases by Latex Division		
of Binder ($200 ÷ 80%)		(250)
Decline in quarterly cash flows ×		($46)
4 quarters per year		× 4
Annual decline in Worldwide cash flows		($184)

Full-cost transfer prices

The information and incentive problems described earlier can lead the firm to select simple, objective, hard-to-change transfer price rules where responsibility center managers cannot easily game the transfer price. Objective transfer pricing rules such as those based on full accounting cost are often adopted primarily to avoid unproductive disputes over measuring variable costs. Full cost includes both direct materials and labor, as well as a charge for overhead. Since full cost is the sum of fixed and variable cost, full cost cannot be changed simply by reclassifying a fixed cost as a variable cost.

The problem, however, is that full-cost transfer pricing frequently overstates the opportunity cost to the firm of producing and transferring one more unit internally, especially if Manufacturing has excess capacity. And so Distribution usually will buy too few units internally. Full cost also allows Manufacturing to transfer any of its inefficiencies to Distribution. Thus, Manufacturing has less incentive to be efficient under a full-cost transfer price rule.[10]

---

[10]To be sure, variable-cost transfer prices also allow the selling division to export some of its inefficiencies to the purchasing division, but the problem is not as pronounced as under full cost. Nevertheless, the problem of exporting inefficiencies to the buying division through cost-based transfer prices is reduced if the purchasing division can purchase externally, as well as from the selling division. This forces the selling division to remain competitive.

Despite all these problems, however, full-cost transfer pricing is quite common. Various surveys of firms report 40–50 percent usage of full-cost transfer prices. One reason for the popularity of full-cost transfer prices is their ability to deal with the problem of changes in capacity. As a plant begins to reach capacity, opportunity cost is likely to rise because of congestion and the cost of alternative uses of now-scarce capacity. Hence, opportunity cost is likely to be higher than direct materials and labor costs. In this case, full cost might be a closer approximation to opportunity cost than just variable cost.

Perhaps the most important benefit of full-cost transfer pricing is its simplicity and hence low cost of implementation. Because operating managers have much less ability to manipulate full-cost than variable-cost calculations, senior management arbitrate fewer disputes over calculating the transfer price. Nevertheless, managers should consider carefully whether full-cost pricing is optimal for their particular situation. If the opportunity cost is substantially different from full cost, the firm's forgone profits can be large.

Negotiated transfer prices

Transfer prices can be set by negotiation between Manufacturing and Distribution. This method can result in transfer prices that approximate opportunity cost because Manufacturing will not agree to a price that is below its opportunity cost and Distribution will not pay a price that is above the product's price elsewhere.

With negotiated transfer prices, the two divisions have the incentive to set the number of units to maximize the combined profits of the two divisions. Once the value-maximizing number of units is agreed upon, the negotiated transfer price determines how the total profits are divided between the two divisions. If the two divisions negotiate both price and quantity, they have the joint incentive to maximize the total profit to be split. Yet, if the two divisions only negotiate the price, there is no guarantee that they will arrive at the transfer price that maximizes firm value.

While negotiation is a fairly common method, it too has drawbacks. It is time-consuming and can produce conflicts among divisions. Divisional performance measurement becomes sensitive to the relative negotiating skills of the two division managers. Moreover, if the two divisions negotiate a transfer price without at the same time agreeing on the quantity to be transferred at that price, there is no guarantee that they will arrive at the transfer price that maximizes the firm's value.

4. Reorganization: The Solution if All Else Fails

In some cases, transfer pricing conflicts among responsibility centers can become sufficiently divisive as to impose large costs on the firm. These costs arise when other than firm-value-maximizing transfer prices are chosen. Costly transfer pricing disputes usually occur when the relative volume of transactions among divisions is large. In such cases, a small change in the transfer price can have a large effect on the division's reported profits. Hence, destructive effects of opportunistic transfer pricing actions by operating managers are substantial.

If transfer pricing becomes sufficiently dysfunctional, reorganize the firm. For example, senior management could combine two profit centers with a large volume of transfers into a single division. Alternatively, it might make more sense to convert Manufacturing into a cost center rather than a profit center and compensate the operating head based on efficiency in production. Or both divisions might be reorganized as cost centers and keep the pricing and quantity decisions at a higher level in the firm.

5. Recap

To review the discussion on transfer pricing, firms decentralize and create responsibility centers to take advantage of the divisional manager's specialized knowledge of local conditions. Incentives must then be provided for these managers to use their specialized knowledge to make profit-maximizing decisions for their firms. Forming responsibility

TABLE 5-5   **Advantages and Disadvantages of Common Transfer Pricing Methods**

Method	Advantages	Disadvantages
Market-based transfer prices	• Objective • Less subject to manipulation • Often leads to correct long-run make/buy decisions	• Might not exist for specialty items • Might not capture interdependencies among divisions
Variable-cost transfer prices	• Can approximate the opportunity cost of transferring one more unit • Gives the buying division incentive to purchase the correct number of units if the selling division has excess capacity	• Does not allow the selling division to recover its fixed costs • Variable cost might vary with output • The selling division has the incentive to classify fixed costs as variable costs
Full-cost transfer prices	• Avoids disputes over which costs are fixed and which are variable • Simplicity	• The selling division can export its inefficiencies to the buying division • The buying division purchases too few units
Negotiated transfer prices	• Both selling and buying divisions have incentives to transfer the number of units that maximize their combined profits	• Time-consuming • Depends on the relative negotiating skills of the two divisions
Reorganize the buying and selling divisions	• Eliminates costly disputes over transfer pricing	• Reduces the benefits from having two decentralized responsibility centers

centers and linking performance measures to their decision rights (as described in Table 5–1) provides these incentives. When one responsibility center buys or sells goods or services from another center, a transfer price must be established for this internal transaction in order that each center's performance measures, such as earnings, can be calculated. This gives each center the incentive to engage in internal transactions that benefit the firm. Hence, transfer pricing permits managers to exploit the specialized information they possess about local opportunities.[11] Various methods exist for calculating transfer prices. Table 5–5 summarizes the advantages and disadvantages of each method.

No single method is best in all circumstances. Since each method has its advantages and disadvantages, managers must choose the method that trades off decision making, control, and taxes given their unique circumstances. Market-based transfer pricing is objective, but might not capture interdependencies that exist within the firm. While variable-cost transfer pricing approximates the opportunity cost of producing one more unit when excess capacity exists, it is not commonly used. While we do not know exactly why variable costing is used infrequently, we can speculate on some plausible reasons. Full-cost transfer pricing approximates the costs of adding fixed capacity (in the absence of inflation and productivity changes). Also, with variable-cost transfer pricing it is difficult to separate fixed and variable costs. Finally, as discussed earlier, variable costing gives the selling division significant discretion in altering the transfer price by reclassifying fixed costs as variable costs.

The trade-off between decision making and control discussed in Chapter 1 also applies to transfer prices. The transfer price that most accurately measures the opportunity cost to the firm of transferring one more unit inside the firm may not be the transfer pricing method that gives internal managers the incentive to maximize firm value. For

---

[11]For an expanded discussion of transfer pricing, see R. Eccles, *The Transfer Pricing Problem: A Theory for Practice* (Lexington, MA: Lexington Books, 1985); and B. Holmstrom and J. Tirole, "Transfer-Pricing and Organizational Form," *Journal of Law, Economics, & Organizations* 7 (1991), pp. 201–28.

example, if the transfer pricing method that most accurately measures the opportunity cost of transferred units also requires managers producing these units to reveal privately held and hard-to-verify data of their costs, then these managers have considerable discretion over the transfer prices. If these transfer prices are important in rewarding managers, the producing managers can distort the transfer price to their benefit. Alternatively, a transfer pricing scheme that measures opportunity cost less accurately but more objectively might produce a higher firm value than a transfer pricing scheme that more closely approximates opportunity costs.

Managers often have authority for external sourcing. The ability to buy/sell outside is an important control device on the transfer pricing scheme. No matter how the internal transfer price is set, the ability to go outside limits the monopoly profits that can be earned by one responsibility center at the expense of another.

Changing transfer-pricing methods does more than shift income among responsibility centers. The level of the firm's output changes, as does firm-wide profitability. The transfer price not only changes how the total profit pie is divided among responsibility centers; it also affects the size of the pie.

Finally, transfer pricing is more ubiquitous in organizations than many managers realize. Most organizations recharge inside users for information technology, telecommunications, janitorial service, maintenance, and so forth. In effect, these recharge schemes, based on cost allocations, are cost-based transfer prices. Since much of management accounting and cost accounting deals with cost allocations, many of the same issues that apply to transfer pricing also arise in later chapters.

Concept Questions		
	Q5–7	What are the two main reasons for transfer pricing within firms?
	Q5–8	Name four alternative methods for determining transfer prices.
	Q5–9	Is the choice of transfer pricing methods a zero-sum game?

C. Summary

Besides making operating decisions that involve pricing, marketing, and financing, managers must also ensure that employees perform tasks that add value to the firm. Chapter 4 described the general agency problem and how the firm's organizational architecture can provide incentives for self-interested employees to take value-adding actions. In particular, the organizational architecture, which consists of the three legs of the stool (the performance evaluation system, the performance reward system, and the partitioning of decision rights), helps align employees' and owners' interests. Accounting systems are an integral part of the firm's organizational architecture. This chapter described two central ways in which accounting systems are used: responsibility accounting and transfer pricing.

In responsibility accounting, decision rights within the firm are partitioned to cost, profit, and investment centers. Cost centers usually have decision rights over the mix of inputs used to produce the product or service. Cost centers are then evaluated based on the ability of the center to maximize output for a given cost or to minimize cost for a predetermined amount of output. Profit centers have decision rights over input mix and pricing and are evaluated based on profits. Investment centers have all the decision rights of profit centers plus the rights over how much capital is invested in the center. They are evaluated based on either return on investment or residual income.

Also, accounting is often used in transfer pricing. Whenever goods or services are transferred across responsibility centers and the performance of these centers is measured, a transfer price for the transferred item must be calculated. Market prices, cost-based transfer prices, or negotiated transfer prices are used. Cost-based transfer prices include both variable costs and full costs (variable plus fixed costs). Each transfer pricing scheme has pros and cons that depend on the particular circumstances of the firm. Hence, each firm must determine the transfer pricing scheme that is best for its situation. In general, no transfer pricing scheme, just as no particular organizational architecture, is best for all firms or even best for a single firm over time. In transfer pricing schemes, as in other internal accounting methods, a trade-off exists between decision making and control. Transfer price schemes that are best for decision making are not always the best for control and vice versa.

Chapter 6 describes another example of how accounting systems are used to reduce agency problems: budgeting systems.

Self-Study Problems

Self-Study Problem 1:   Tam Burger

In the past five years, Tam Burger has expanded to more than 200 stores, 80 percent of which are franchised. Two of the company-operated units, Northside and Southside, are among the fastest-growing stores. Both are considering expanding their menus to include pizza. Purchase and installation of the necessary equipment costs $180,000 per store. The current investment in the Northside store totals $890,000. Store revenues are $1,100,500 and expenses are $924,420. Expansion of the Northside's menu should increase profits by $30,600. The current investment in the Southside store totals $1,740,000. The store's revenues are $1,760,800 and expenses are $1,496,680. Adding pizza to Southside's menu should increase its profits by $30,600.

Tam Burger evaluates its managers based on return on investment. Managers of individual stores have decision rights over the pizza expansion.

Required:

a. Calculate the return on investment for both stores before pizza is added, for the pizza project only, and for the stores after expansion.

b. Assuming a 14 percent cost of capital, calculate residual income for both stores before and after the potential expansion.

c. Will the Tam Burger stores choose to expand? How would the answer change if the stores were franchised units?

Solution:

a. Return on investment before and after the pizza expansion:

	Northside	Southside
ROI before Pizza		
Revenue	$1,100,500	$ 1,760,800
Expenses	924,420	1,496,680
Net income	$ 176,080	$ 264,120
÷ Assets	890,000	1,740,000
ROI	19.78%	15.18%
ROI of Pizza Only		
Increased profits from pizza	$ 30,600	$ 30,600
÷ Expansion cost	180,000	180,000
ROI of project	17.00%	17.00%
ROI after Pizza		
Total income	$ 206,680	$ 294,720
4 Total assets	1,070,000	1,920,000
Total ROI	19.32%	15.35%

b. Residual income before and after the pizza expansion:

	Northside	Southside
Cost of capital	14.00%	14.00%
Residual Income before Pizza		
Net income	$176,080	$264,120
Less: Assets × 14%	(124,600)	(243,600)
Residual income	$ 51,480	$ 20,520
Residual Income of Pizza Only		
Increased profits from pizza	$ 30,600	$ 30,600
Less: 14% × Expansion cost	(25,200)	(25,200)
Residual income	$ 5,400	$ 5,400
Residual Income after Pizza		
Net income	$206,680	$294,720
Less: 14% × Assets	(149,800)	(268,800)
Residual income	$ 56,880	$ 25,920

c. The two units currently have different ROIs. The smaller Northside store is earning an ROI of just under 20 percent, while the larger Southside store is earning an ROI of just over 15 percent. Since the project's ROI is 17 percent, adding the project to the Northside store lowers its average ROI; adding the project to the Southside store raises its average ROI. The Northside manager will avoid adding pizza to the menu, because the store's ROI would drop as a result. The Southside manager, however, will want to add pizza since the store's ROI would subsequently rise.

If the stores were franchised units, both owners would definitely expand. The ROI of the project is higher than the cost of capital. This ensures a positive residual income for the project. As long as the residual income is positive, any franchise owner would jump at the opportunity. Franchise owners would not care if the store's ROI dropped, as long as the residual income increased.

Self-Study Problem 2:   BioScience

Tomato beetles, a major pest to the tomato crop, are now being controlled by toxic pesticides. The firm BioScience invested $5 million in R&D over the last five years to produce a genetically engineered, patented microbe, MK-23, which controls tomato beetles in an environmentally safe way. BioScience built a plant with capacity to produce 10,000 pounds of MK-23 per month. The plant cost $12 million and has a 10-year life. MK-23 has a variable cost of $3 per pound. Fixed costs are $50,000 per month for such costs as plant management, insurance, taxes, and security. Plant depreciation is not included in the $50,000 fixed cost.

The following table summarizes the full cost of producing MK-23:

Depreciation per month ($12 million ÷ 120 months)	$100,000
Other fixed costs	50,000
Total fixed costs	$150,000
÷ Capacity per month (pounds)	10,000
Fixed costs per unit of capacity (pound)	$ 15.00
Variable costs per pound	3.00
Full cost per pound	$ 18.00

MK-23 is sold for $30 per pound. BioScience is currently selling 8,000 pounds per month to tomato farmers.

Another division of BioScience, Home Life, wants to secure 1,000 pounds per month of MK-23 that it will process further into a consumer product, Tomato Safe, for gardeners. Home Life is willing to pay an internal transfer price of $5 per pound. Home Life will incur an additional $4 of variable cost per pound of MK-23 in packaging and reducing the potency of MK-23 to make Tomato Safe more appropriate for home gardeners. Tomato Safe will sell for $20 per pound of MK-23.

Required:

   a. Should the internal transfer be allowed?

   b. What happens if the transfer price is set at full cost, $18? What happens if the transfer price is set at variable cost, $3?

   c. After deciding to use variable cost as the transfer price, new farm orders for 2,000 pounds of MK-23 at $30 per pound per month are received. Suppose plants come only in fixed sizes of 10,000-pound capacities of $12 million each. Analyze the various options facing BioScience.

   d. What is the opportunity cost of the excess capacity prior to producing MK-23 for Tomato Safe?

   e. What happened to the $5 million R&D costs incurred to invent MK-23?

Solution:

   a. The following table indicates that BioScience generates incremental cash flow of $13 for every pound of MK-23 it transfers to Home Life to be converted to Tomato Safe, assuming it does not forgo selling this pound of MK-23 directly to farmers for $30 per pound.

Contribution Margins for MK-23 and Tomato Safe

	MK-23	Tomato Safe
Selling price	$30.00	$20.00
Variable costs		
Manufacturing MK-23	3.00	3.00
Additional processing		4.00
Contribution margin	$27.00	$13.00

Clearly, if BioScience has excess capacity of 2,000 pounds of MK-23 production per month, then transferring 1,000 pounds of MK-23 enhances overall firm profits.

   b. If a full-cost transfer price of $18 per pound is charged for MK-23, Home Life will not accept the transfer because its total cost of $22 ($18 transfer price plus $4 for further processing) is above the market price of $20. If the firm has unused capacity, then transferring at full cost causes it to forgo selling Tomato Safe and receiving $13 per pound for its unused capacity. Transferring at variable cost ($3) allows Tomato Safe to be produced. In the case where the firm has unused excess capacity, full-cost transfer pricing leads to the wrong decision.

     If variable-cost transfer pricing is used, each month 1,000 pounds of MK-23 are transferred to Home Life.

   c. After receiving new farm orders for 2,000 pounds of MK-23, management has three options. First, it can fill 1,000 pounds of the 2,000-pound order, because this is all the capacity available after transferring 1,000 pounds to Home Life. Second, management can cancel the 1,000 pounds transferred for Tomato Safe and fill all 2,000 pounds of the new farm order. Or third, management can build a new plant to increase capacity. Canceling the 1,000-pound transfer to Home Life and using this production capacity to fill the new farm orders increases BioScience's cash flows:

Contribution from new order	2,000 × $27	$54,000
Contribution forgone from Tomato Safe	1,000 × $13	13,000
Additional contribution		$41,000

Every additional pound of MK-23 sold to farmers instead of converted to Tomato Safe contributes $14 (or $27 2 $13) to BioScience's cash flows, assuming the firm does not have enough capacity to meet demand in the farm market. The third option of adding capacity to meet both farm and home demand is not profitable. Each pound, including new capacity for MK-23, costs $18, and Tomato Safe cannot recover these costs. Therefore, full-cost transfer pricing includes the cost of adding additional capacity.

The managers of Home Life will object to canceling the internal transfer because their divisional profits will fall. They will most likely construct reasons that such a decision will adversely affect their other products. Undoing the decision to transfer MK-23 will require senior managers' time and patience. Thus, influence costs are likely to be generated. In general, internal transfers tend to be permanent and difficult to change.

d. Prior to accepting the internal transfer of MK-23 to produce Tomato Safe, BioScience has 2,000 pounds of unused capacity. If the demand for MK-23 is growing, then either consuming this capacity with an internal transfer causes the firm to forgo the contribution margin on lost sales of MK-23 or else the firm has to add capacity. The decision to permanently consume fixed capacity should not be based on the short-run incremental cost of the transfer unless it is highly likely that the internal transfer is the only long-run use of the unused capacity. Full-cost transfer pricing includes an estimate of the cost of adding capacity and reveals the past (historical) cost of a unit of capacity. A new unit of capacity will cost more than historical cost if there has been construction cost inflation. However, a unit of capacity can cost less than the historic cost if adding a second plant creates productivity enhancements or synergies.

e. These R&D costs were not included in the manufacturing costs of MK-23. The accounting system writes these costs off when incurred. The firm has an unrecorded but real economic asset, the patent on MK-23. The profit of $12 per pound of MK-23 ($30 – $18) represents the firm's return on this investment.

Problems

P 5–1:   Canadian Subsidiary

The following data summarize the operating performance of your company's wholly owned Canadian subsidiary for 2009 to 2011. The cost of capital for this subsidiary is 10 percent.

	($000,000)		
	2009	2010	2011
Subsidiary net income	$14.0	$14.3	$14.4
Total assets in subsidiary	125	130	135
Return on net investment* in subsidiary	20%	22%	24%

*Net investment is calculated as total assets less all liabilities.

Responsibility Accounting and Transfer Pricing   **193**

Required:

Critically evaluate the performance of this subsidiary.

P 5–2: Phipps Electronics

Phipps manufactures circuit boards in Division Low in a country with a 30 percent income tax rate and transfers them to Division High in a country with a 40 percent income tax. An import duty of 15 percent of the transfer price is paid on all imported products. The import duty is not deductible in computing taxable income. The circuit boards' full cost is $1,000 and variable cost is $700; they are sold by Division High for $1,200. The tax authorities in both countries allow firms to use either variable cost or full cost as the transfer price.

Required:

Analyze the effect of full-cost and variable-cost transfer pricing methods on Phipps' cash flows.

P 5–3: Sunder Properties

Brighton Holdings owns private companies and hires professional managers to run its companies. One company in Brighton Holdings' portfolio is Sunder Properties. Sunder owns and operates apartment complexes, and has the following operating statement.

SUNDER PROPERTIES
(Last Fiscal Year)
(Millions)

Revenues	$86.50
Expenses*	(72.30)
Net income before taxes	$14.20

*Includes interest expense of $2.6 million.

Brighton Holdings estimates Sunder Properties' before-tax weighted average cost of capital to be 15 percent. Brighton Holdings rewards managers of their operating companies based on the operating company's before-tax return on assets. (The higher the operating company's before-tax ROA, the more Sunder managers are paid.) Sunder Properties' total assets at the end of the last fiscal year are $64 million.

Required:

a. Calculate Sunder's ROA last year.

b. Sunder management is considering purchasing a new apartment complex called Valley View that has the following operating characteristics (millions $):

Revenues	$16.60
Expenses*	$13.30
Total assets of new apartment	$20.00

*Includes interest expense of $0.71.

Will the managers of Sunder Properties purchase Valley View?

c. If they had the same information about Valley View as Sunder's management, would the shareholders of Brighton Holdings accept or reject the acquisition of Valley View in part (*b*)?

d. What advice would you offer the management team of Brighton Holdings?

P 5–4: Economic Earnings

A large consulting firm is looking to expand the services currently offered its clients. The firm has developed a new performance metric called "Economic Earnings," or EE for short. The performance metric is argued to be a better measure of both divisional performance and firmwide performance, and hence "a more rational platform for compensating employees and managers." The consulting firm is seeking to convince clients they should replace their current metrics, such as accounting net income, ROA, EVA, and so forth, with EE.

EE starts with traditional accounting net income but then makes a series of adjustments. The primary adjustment is to add back depreciation and then subtract a required return on invested capital. The consultants argue for adding accounting depreciation back because it is a sunk cost. It does not represent a current cash flow. For example, suppose a client has accounting net income calculated as:

**Client's Traditional
Income Statement**

Revenues	$5,700
Cost of goods sold	(2,000)
Gross margin	$3,700
Depreciation	(900)
Selling, general, other	(700)
Interest	(500)
Earnings before taxes	$1,600
Income taxes (40%)	(640)
Net income	$ 960

Suppose the client has total assets of $6,000 and a risk-adjusted weighted-average cost of capital (WACC) of 25 percent. Then this client's EE is calculated as follows:

Client's Economic Earnings

Net income	$ 960
Depreciation	900
Capital charge*	(1,500)
Economic earnings	$ 360
*Total assets	$6,000
WACC	25%
Capital charge	$1,500

Required:

Critically evaluate EE as a performance measure. What are its strengths and weaknesses?

P 5–5: Performance Technologies

Sylvia Zang is president of the Wilson Division of Performance Technologies, a multinational conglomerate. Zang manages $100 million of assets and is currently generating earnings before interest (EBI) of $12 million. The corporate office of Performance Technologies has determined that Wilson's existing assets have a risk-adjusted cost of capital of 11 percent. All division presidents (including Zang) are rewarded based on their individual division's ROA. If Zang is able to increase the Wilson Division's current ROA, she can earn a substantial bonus whereby the larger the increase in the division's ROA, the larger is Zang's bonus. Performance Technology computes ROA as EBI divided by total assets.

Currently, Zang is considering two new investment opportunities: Project A and Project B. She can accept one or the other, or both, or neither. Each project, A and B, has a risk profile that differs from that of her existing portfolio of assets. Project A (with a risk-adjusted cost of capital of 15 percent) requires her purchasing new assets for $25 million that will generate EBI of $3.5 million. Project B (with a risk-adjusted cost of capital of 9 percent) requires her purchasing new assets for $30 million that will generate EBI of $3 million.

Assume there are no synergies between Wilson's existing assets and either project A and B, and there are no synergies between project A and project B.

Required:

    a. Assuming that Zang is rewarded based on improving the ROA of the Wilson Division, will she accept or reject projects A and B? Support your answer with detailed computations.

    b. Instead of basing divisional managers' bonuses on ROA, Performance Technologies switches to residual income as the methodology used to measure divisional performance and reward divisional managers, including Ms. Zang. Assuming that Zang is rewarded based on improving the residual income of the Wilson Division, what decision(s) will she make regarding accepting or rejecting projects A and B? Support your answer with detailed computations.

    c. Discuss why your answers differ or are the same in parts (*a*) and (*b*).

    d. Should Performance Technologies use ROA or residual income to evaluate and reward division managers? Justify your recommendation with sound logical analysis.

P 5–6: Metal Press

Your firm uses return on assets (ROA) to evaluate investment centers and is considering changing the valuation basis of assets from historical cost to current value. When the historical cost of the asset is updated, a price index is used to approximate replacement value. For example, a metal fabrication press, which bends and shapes metal, was bought seven years ago for $522,000. The company will add 19 percent to this cost, representing the change in the wholesale price index over the seven years. This new, higher cost figure is depreciated using the straight-line method over the same 12-year assumed life (no salvage value).

Required:

    a. Calculate depreciation expense and book value of the metal press under both historical cost and price-level-adjusted historical cost.

    b. In general, what is the effect on ROA of changing valuation bases from historical cost to current values?

    c. The manager of the investment center with the metal press is considering replacing it because it is becoming obsolete. Will the manager's incentives to replace the metal press change if the firm shifts from historical cost valuation to the proposed price-level-adjusted historical cost valuation?

P 5–7: ICB, Intl.

ICB has four manufacturing divisions, each producing a particular type of cosmetic or beauty aid. These products are then transferred to five marketing divisions, each covering a particular geographic region. Manufacturing and marketing divisions are free to negotiate among themselves the transfer prices for products transferred internally. The manufacturing division that produces all the hair care products wants a particular hair conditioner it developed and produces for Asian markets priced at full cost plus a 5 percent profit markup, which amounts to $105 per case.

The South American marketing division believes it can sell this conditioner in South America after redesigning the labels. However, most South American currencies have weakened against the dollar, putting further pressure on the prices of U.S.–produced products. The South American marketing division estimates it can make money on the hair conditioner only if it can buy it from manufacturing at $85 per case.

Manufacturing claims that it cannot make a profit at $85 per case. Moreover, the other ICB marketing divisions that are paying around $105 per case will likely want to renegotiate the $105 transfer price if South America marketing buys it for $85.

You work for the corporate controller of ICB, Intl. She has asked you to write a short, nontechnical memo to her that spells out the key points she should consider in her upcoming meeting with the two division heads regarding transfer pricing. You are not being asked to recommend a particular transfer price, but rather to list the important issues the controller should be aware of for the meeting.

P 5–8: Shop and Save

Shop and Save (S&S) is a large grocery chain with 350 supermarkets. Twenty-eight S&S stores are located within the Detroit metropolitan region and serviced by the S&S Detroit Bakery, a large central bakery producing all of the fresh-baked goods (breads, rolls, donuts, cakes, and pies) sold in the 28 individual S&S stores in the Detroit region. Besides selling S&S baked goods, the stores also sell other nationally branded commercial baked goods both in the baked goods section of the store and in the frozen section as well. But all freshly baked items sold in the 28 S&S stores come from the S&S Detroit Bakery. Each store orders all the baked goods from the S&S Detroit Bakery the day before. The S&S Detroit Bakery also is a profit center and sells only to the 28 Detroit S&S stores. Each store pays the bakery 60 percent of the retail selling price. So, for example, if a store manager orders from the bakery a loaf of whole grain bread that has a retail price of $5.00, that store is charged $3.00 (60% × $5.00) and the Detroit Bakery records revenues of $3.00.

Each store manager is evaluated and compensated as a profit center and has some decision rights over the particular items stocked in each store. But roughly 85 percent of all SKUs (stock keeping units) carried by each store and the retail price of each SKU are dictated centrally by the S&S Detroit Regional headquarters, which oversees both the 28 stores and the bakery. Each store manager has decision rights over the quantity of the various baked goods ordered from the S&S Detroit Bakery. The retail price of each freshly baked item produced by the S&S Detroit Bakery and sold in the grocery stores is set by the Detroit Regional headquarters, not the individual grocery stores or the S&S Detroit Bakery.

The manager of the Detroit Bakery complains that the reason her central bakery loses money is that the 60 percent rate is too low to cover her costs. The individual grocery store managers complain that the quality and variety of fresh baked goods they receive from the S&S Detroit Bakery are not competitive with high-end private specialty bake shops in the Detroit area.

Required:

a. Evaluate the advantages and disadvantages of the S&S policy of each S&S grocery store paying the S&S Detroit Bakery 60 percent of the retail price of the bakery item.

b. Suggest ways that S&S can improve the relationship between its grocery stores and its central bakery.

P 5–9: Microelectronics

Microelectronics is a large electronics firm with multiple divisions. The circuit board division manufactures circuit boards, which it sells externally and internally. The phone division assembles cellular phones and sells them to external customers. Both divisions are evaluated as profit centers. The firm has the policy of transferring all internal products at market prices.

The selling price of cellular phones is $400, and the external market price for the cellular phone circuit board is $200. The outlay cost for the phone division to complete a phone (not including the cost of the circuit board) is $250. The variable cost of the circuit board is $130.

Required:

a. Will the phone division purchase the circuit boards from the circuit board division? (Show calculations.)

b. Suppose the circuit board division is currently manufacturing and selling externally 10,000 circuit boards per month and has the capacity to manufacture 15,000 boards. From the standpoint of Microelectronics, should 3,000 additional boards be manufactured and transferred internally?

c. Discuss what transfer price should be set for part (*b*).

d. List the three most important assumptions underlying your analysis in parts (*b*) and (*c*).

P 5–10: US Copiers

US Copiers manufactures a full line of copiers including desktop models. The Small Copier Division (SCD) manufactures desktop copiers and sells them in the United States. A typical model has a retail price of less than $500. An integral part in the copier is the toner cartridge that contains the black powder used to create the image on the paper. The toner cartridge can be used for about 10,000 pages and must then be replaced. The typical owner of an SCD copier purchases four replacement cartridges over the life of the copier.

SCD buys the initial toner cartridges provided with the copier from the Toner Division (TD) of US Copiers. TD sells subsequent replacement cartridges to distributors that sell them to U.S. retail stores. Toner cartridges sell to the end consumer for $50. TD sells the cartridges to distributors for about 70 percent of the final retail price paid by the consumer. The Toner Division manager argues that the market price to TD of $35 (70% × $50) is the price SCD should pay to TD for each toner cartridge transferred.

Required:

a. Why does US Copiers manufacture both copiers and toner cartridges? Why don't separate firms specialize in either copiers or toner cartridges like Intel specializes in making computer chips and Gateway specializes in assembling and selling PCs?

b. You work for the president of SCD. Write a memo to your boss identifying the salient issues she should raise in discussing the price SCD should pay TD for toner cartridges included in SCD copiers.

P 5–11: Cogen

Cogen's Turbine Division manufactures gas-powered turbines for generating electric power and hot water for heating systems. Turbine's variable cost per unit is $150,000 and its fixed cost is $1.8 million per month. It has excess capacity. Cogen's Generator Division buys gas turbines from Cogen's Turbine Division and incorporates them into electric steam-generating units. Both divisional managers are evaluated and rewarded as profit centers.

The Generator Division has variable cost of $200,000 per completed unit, excluding the cost of the turbine, and fixed cost of $1.4 million per month. The Generator Division faces the following monthly demand schedule for its complete generating unit (turbine and generator):

Quantity	Price ($000)	Quantity	Price ($000)
1	$1,000	5	$800
2	950	6	750
3	900	7	700
4	850	8	650

Required:

a. If the transfer price of turbines is set at Turbine's variable cost ($150,000), how many turbines will the Generator Division purchase to maximize its profits?

b. The Turbine Division expects to sell a total of 20 turbines a month, which includes both external and internal sales. Calculate the (average) full cost of a turbine (fixed cost plus variable cost) at this level of sales.

c. If the transfer price of turbines is set at Turbine's (average) full cost calculated in part (*b*), how many turbines will the Generator Division purchase?

d. Should Cogen use a variable-cost transfer price or a full-cost transfer price to transfer turbines between the Turbine and Generator divisions? Why?

P 5–12:   Wegmans

Wegmans, a privately owned regional supermarket chain founded in Rochester, New York, in 1916, focuses on the more affluent market by providing a unique shopping experience and value. Wegmans' much larger stores stock roughly twice as many items as other supermarkets and offer more displays of fresh produce, artisan breads, fresh seafood, and take-out or in-store dining of restaurant-quality entrees. The company currently operates more than 80 stores and 10 regional distribution centers in five states stretching from New York to Virginia. Their most recent expansion is into Virginia with three new stores and a new Wegmans Virginia distribution center serving the three new stores, but with capacity to serve more Virginia stores as they are opened.

As Wegmans expands geographically, it must open regional distribution centers that are responsible for accurate and on-time selection, inventorying, and delivery of the thousands of products (fresh produce, meats, seafood, frozen goods, etc.) sold in the stores in that distribution center's region. Each store in the region is allocated a share of the costs of its distribution center based on total store revenues served by the distribution center.

Senior management uses residual income to evaluate the performance of each store (and reward store management). All Wegmans stores face the same weighted-average cost of capital (13 percent) applied to direct investment in each store (working capital and property, building, and fixtures). The following table summarizes last year's operations of the newest Virginia store (Virginia 3), Wegmans flagship store (Rochester 1), and the Wegmans store with median revenues across the entire 80-store chain (Median). Virginia 3's results in the table represent the first complete year of operations since opening the store. "Rochester 1" is Wegmans' first megastore, rebuilt and expanded in 1990, with a very large and loyal customer base. All figures are in thousands of dollars.

	Last Year		
(000s)	*Virginia 3*	*Rochester 1*	*Median*
Working capital*	$1,100	$1,500	$1,300
Revenues	59,300	110,250	70,000
Property, building, and fixtures†	58,300	28,740	44,000
Cost of goods sold	41,510	74,970	48,300
Store administration‡	5,930	8,820	6,300
Distribution center charges§	5,100	4,900	3,900

*Current assets less current liabilities of the store.

†Net of accumulated depreciation.

‡Includes all other costs of operating the store, including utilities, occupancy, and store management.

§Allocation of the fixed and variable costs of the regional distribution center to all the stores served by the distribution center. Allocation based on the store revenues served by the center.

Required:

a. Compute the residual incomes for the Virginia 3, Rochester 1, and the Median stores.

b. Write a memo to senior Wegmans management evaluating the performance of Virginia 3 relative to Rochester 1 and to the Median store. Be sure to provide credible explanations for all material differences in performance between Virginia 3 and the other two Wegmans stores.

P 5–13: Zee Spin Wedges

Zee Spin manufactures a line of golf club wedges (sand wedge, pitching wedge, lob wedge, and attack wedge) that vary with loft and club head sole design. The wedges have become very popular among professional and serious golfers because of their unique club head design and shafts. All Zee Spin wedges consist of three parts: club head, shaft, and grip. Zee Spin manufactures the club heads and shafts and purchases the grips. The three components are assembled to produce a wedge that is sold to distributors, who then sell them to golf pro shops and websites. The shafts are specially designed to match the playing characteristics of the Zee Spin wedge club head.

The following table summarizes the total costs of producing a complete Zee Spin wedge. All the various models of Zee Spin wedges (sand wedge, pitching wedge, lob wedge, and attack wedge) have the same cost structure.

	Club Head	Shaft	Total
Variable manufacturing cost	$16.05	$11.48	$27.53
Variable selling cost			5.43
Fixed manufacturing cost	4.17	6.52	10.69
Other common fixed costs			6.43
Grip			2.50
Total cost			$52.58

Zee Spin traditionally only sold complete wedges (club head, shaft, and grip), and the company was treated as a single profit center. But with the success of the Zee Spin brand and recent inquiries from other club makers about purchasing just Zee Spin shafts, which are unique in the industry, Zee Spin is going to sell both complete wedges (as they do now) and individual shafts. To implement this strategy, Zee Spin will create two profit centers: Wedges and Shafts. The Shaft profit center will produce shafts for external customers, as well as for the Zee Spin Wedge profit center. There will be two profit center managers in Zee Spin that will be rewarded based on the profits of their respective profit centers. The Zee Spin wedges will continue to be sold for $75 per complete wedge, while the shafts will be sold for $23 per shaft.

Shafts that are sold externally will incur variable selling costs of $2.43 (primarily sales commission and shipping). These costs are not incurred for shafts sold internally to the Wedge profit center.

Required:

a. The owners of Zee Spin want to maximize profits and realize that, to properly motivate the managers of the Wedges and Shafts profit centers, they need to set the proper transfer price for the shafts produced by the Shafts profit center and sold to the Wedges profit center. Using the actual data provided in the problem, what transfer price should be used for the shafts produced by the Shafts profit center and sold to the Wedges profit center? (Your answer should be a specific number, such as $18.00.)

b. After implementing the transfer price policy you described in part (*a*), what problems should the owners of Zee Spin anticipate? Stated differently, what non-firm-value maximizing behaviors by the two profit center managers should the owners of Zee Spin expect to occur?

P 5–14: Creative Learning Centers

Creative Learning Centers (CLC), a for-profit firm, operates over 100 preschools primarily located in the northeast for children ages 4–6. CLC's innovative curriculum utilizes the latest technology and offers young minds creative expression, language and social skills, physical movement, music, and number skills—all provided by professional trained teachers. CLC leases buildings for their schools and invests substantial resources in leasehold improvements for classrooms, technology, and playground equipment. CLC's cost of capital is 12 percent. Typical tuition is about $6,300 per year for a five-day-a-week, four-hour-per-day program. Maria Schnelling manages 15 CLC schools in the state of Virginia. She has decision-making responsibility for staffing and operating her schools, as well as the responsibility for recommending adding new schools and closing existing schools. The following table provides current operating data on all of her 15 preschools, and breaks out her top- and bottom-performing schools:

	After-Tax Operating Income	Total Investment
All 15 Virginia preschools	$1,811,250	$11,625,000
Best 3 Virginia performers		
VA4	$184,230	$801,000
VA12	$156,030	$743,000
VA9	$151,000	$755,000
Worst 3 Virginia performers		
VA2	$34,000	$680,000
VA8	$14,200	$710,000
VA5	–$23,700	$790,000

"After-tax operating income" represents all revenues less all expenses (including depreciation and taxes but excluding any interest on debt to finance the investment) of running a school for the last 12 months.

Ms. Schnelling has identified three possible locations for new CLC preschools in Virginia (denoted as NVA1, NVA2, and NVA3).The following table provides current projected data on the three new preschools:

	After-Tax Operating Income	Total Investment
NVA1	$132,000	$880,000
NVA2	$110,500	$850,000
NVA3	$79,200	$720,000

Required:

a. If Maria Schnelling is evaluated and rewarded based on after-tax operating income, which of her 15 existing schools will she recommend closing, and which of her three new schools will she recommend opening? (Justify your answers.)

b. If Maria Schnelling is evaluated and rewarded based on return on investment, which of her existing 15 schools will she recommend closing, and which of her three new schools will she recommend opening? (Show computations.)

c. You have been hired as a consultant to the board of directors to advise the board as to how CLC should measure and reward the performance of CLC managers, such as Ms. Schnelling in Virginia. How should CLC measure and reward its state managers? Provide a compelling rationale to support your recommendation. (Support your recommendation with relevant computations.)

P 5–15:   Warm Boots

Warm Boots manufactures and sells a patented ski boot with 9-volt batteries designed to keep a skier's feet warm even when the outside temperature reaches –10 °Celsius. Warm Boots is organized into three divisions: Administration (accounting, finance, human resources, CEO, and CFO), Manufacturing, and Marketing and Sales. To promote cost efficiency, Manufacturing is treated as a cost center, where its manager is evaluated and paid a bonus based on minimizing the actual average cost of manufacturing boots in the week. The manager of Manufacturing has the discretion to choose its production level. Marketing and Sales (M&S) is treated as a profit center, where its profits are computed as the sales revenue it generates less the manufacturing cost of the boots. The manufacturing cost of the boots is the number of boots sold in the week times the actual average cost of manufacturing the boots in that week. The manager of M&S has the discretion to set the price per pair of boots and is paid a bonus based on M&S reported profits.

The following table summarizes how price and total cost varies with the number of boots produced and sold PER WEEK. "Total Cost" includes both fixed and variable cost where the fixed cost is the annual fixed cost divided by 52 (the number of weeks in the year).

Quantity	Price	Total Manufacturing Cost
20	$300	$645.00
21	290	672.30
22	280	700.20
23	270	728.70
24	260	757.80
25	250	787.50
26	240	817.80
27	230	848.70
28	220	880.20
29	210	912.30
30	200	945.00
31	190	978.30
32	180	1012.20
33	170	1046.70
34	160	1081.80
35	150	1117.50

Required:

a. As the head of Manufacturing, how many boots will you manufacture if given the discretion to set production levels? Show calculations to support your answer.

b. If you managed the M&S Division of Warm Boots, and given the production level (and its resulting average cost) chosen by the Manufacturing manager in part a, what price (and quantity level) would you choose for a pair of boots that maximizes your bonus? Show calculations to support your answer.

c. Given the decisions of the Manufacturing and M&S managers in parts (a) and (b), is the firm maximizing profits? Explain why profits are or are not being maximized.

P 5–16: University Lab Testing

Joanna Wu manages the University Lab Testing department within the University Hospital. Lab Testing, a profit center, performs most of the standard medical tests (such as blood tests) for other university clinical care units as well as for outside health care providers (independent hospitals, clinics, and physician groups). These outside health care providers are charged a price for each lab test using a predetermined rate schedule. University Hospital health care providers reimburse University Lab Testing using a transfer price formula. Roughly 70 percent of all Lab Testing procedures are performed for University Hospital units and the remainder for outside health care providers. Other lab testing firms in the community perform many of the same tests as Lab Testing. Lab Testing operates at about 85 percent capacity, on average. But when Lab Testing is operating at 100 percent of capacity, it must refuse outside work and even sends some inside- (University Hospital–) generated specimens to other community testing labs.

A standard blood test (code Q796) performed by Lab Testing has the following cost structure:

Cost Structure for Q796

Variable Costs		
Chemical and supplies	$ 8.90	
Labor	13.15	$22.05
Fixed Costs		
Equipment	$17.20	
Supervision and administration	2.05	
Occupancy	6.68	25.93
Total Cost		$47.98

The predetermined rate paid by the outsiders (non–University Hospital health care providers) for this test (Q796) is $68.90.

Required:

a. Suppose Lab Testing has excess capacity. What transfer price maximizes University Hospital's profits?

b. Using the transfer price you chose in part (*a*), how much profit does Joanna Wu generate for her department if she performs one more Q796 test for an internal University Hospital user?

c. Suppose Lab Testing has no excess capacity. What transfer price maximizes University Hospital's profits?

d. Using the transfer price you chose in part (*c*), how much profit does Joanna Wu generate for her department if she performs one more Q796 test for an internal University Hospital user?

e. What transfer pricing policy should University Hospital implement regarding other University Hospital clinical care units reimbursing Lab Testing for Q796 blood tests? Be sure to describe the logic (and any administrative problems that you considered) underlying your proposed transfer pricing policy for Q796.

P 5–17:   Beckett Automotive Group

Beckett is a large car dealership that sells several automobile manufacturers' new cars (Toyota, Ford, Lexus, and Subaru). Beckett also consists of a Pre-owned Cars Department and a large service department. Beckett is organized into three profit centers: New Cars, Pre-owned Cars, and Service. Each profit center has a manager who is paid a fixed salary plus a bonus based on the net income generated in his or her profit center.

When customers buy new cars, they first negotiate a price with a new car salesperson. Once they have agreed on a price for the new car, if the customer has a used car to trade in, the Pre-owned Cars Department manager gives the customer a price for the trade in. If the customer agrees with the trade-in price offered by Pre-owned Cars, the customer pays the difference between the price of the new car and the trade-in price.

Suppose a customer buys a new car for $47,000 that has a dealer cost of $46,200. The same customer receives and accepts $11,000 for the trade-in of her used car and pays the balance of $36,000 in cash (ignoring taxes and license). In this case, New Cars shows a profit of $800 (before any commission to the salesperson). If the customer does not accept the trade-in value, she does not purchase the new car from Beckett.

Once the deal is struck, the trade-in is then either sold by Pre-owned Cars to another customer at retail or is taken to auction where it is sold at wholesale. Continuing the preceding example, suppose the customer accepts $11,000 as the trade-in for her used car. The Pre-owned Cars Department can sell it on its used car lot for $15,000 at retail or sell it at auction for $12,000. If the trade-in is sold for

$15,000, Pre-owned Cars would have a profit of $4,000 ($15,000 – $11,000). If it is sold at auction, Pre-owned Cars reports a profit of $1,000 ($12,000 – $11,000).

Required:

    a. Describe some of the synergies that exist within Beckett. In other words, why does Beckett consist of three departments (New Cars, Pre-owned Cars, and Service) as opposed to just selling new cars, or just selling used cars, or just providing service?

    b. What potential conflicts of interest exist between the New Cars and Pre-owned Cars department managers? For example, describe how in pursuing their own self-interest, the manager of New Cars or Pre-owned Cars will behave in a way that harms the other manager.

    c. Suggest two alternative mechanisms to reduce the conflicts of interest you described in part (*b*).

P 5–18: WBG

WBG manufactures and sells electronic transducers that are used in military and commercial products. WBG has three divisions: Transducer Division, Military Division, and Commercial Division. The Transducer Division designs and produces transducers that are sold externally as well as internally to the Military Division and the Commercial Division. Both the Military Division and the Commercial Division incorporate transducers in their final products that are sold to non-WBG end users. Because of the unique proprietary design of the WBG transducers, Military and Commercial Divisions only use WBG transducers in their products. All of WBG's sales are in the United States.

The three divisions are profit centers and about 50 percent of the Transducer Division output is sold externally, while the remainder is sold internally to the Military Division and the Commercial Division. WBG currently uses a full-cost transfer pricing policy for the transducers. The senior managers of the three divisions receive about 40 percent of their compensation tied to the performance of their division and the balance is received as base salary.

Because of the incessant bickering among WBG's three divisions' management teams over its current transfer pricing policy, the CEO of WBG attended a seminar on transfer pricing. After attending the seminar, the CEO proposed the following new policy for transducers: "Each month the transfer price of transducers will be the same as the external market price the Transducer Division receives for transducers sold to external customers, if, and only if, the Transducer Division is at capacity for the month. Otherwise, the transfer price is the Transducer Division's variable cost for the month."

Required:

You work for the CEO. Write a memo to the CEO that (*a*) explains the benefits of the proposed policy, (*b*) explains the likely changes in behavior among the three divisions that the new policy is likely to produce, and (*c*) states what additional data the CEO and you should collect and how you would analyze the data before making a decision regarding whether or not the new transfer pricing policy should be adopted.

P 5–19: CJ Equity Partners

CJ Equity Partners is a privately held firm that buys small family-owned firms, installs professional managers to run the firms, and then sells them three to five years later, often for a substantial profit. CJ Equity is owned by four partners who raise capital from wealthy investors and invest this money in unrelated firms. Their aim is to provide a 15 percent rate of return on their investors' capital after paying the partners of CJ Equity a management fee. CJ Equity currently owns three operating companies: a tool and die company (Jasco Tools), a chemical bottling company (Miller Bottling), and a janitorial supply company (JanSan). The professional managers running these three companies are paid a fixed salary and bonus based on the performance of their company. Currently, CJ Equity is measuring and rewarding its three professional managers based on the net income after taxes of their

204 *Chapter 5*

individual companies. The following table summarizes the current year's operations of each of the three companies (all dollar amounts in millions):

	Jasco Tools	Miller Bottling	JanSan
Weighted average cost of capital	14%	12%	10%
CJ Equity management fee*	$0.200	$0.200	$0.200
Number of employees	84	120	85
Interest expense*	$1.600	$1.800	$0.800
Income tax rate	40%	40%	40%
Operating expenses	$33.600	$36.800	$18.200
Revenues	$38.600	$42.900	$21.200
Total assets	$20.1	$31.2	$16.3

*Not included in the operating expenses of the three companies.

CJ Equity charges each of the three operating companies an annual management fee of $200,000 for managing the companies, including filing the various tax returns. The weighted average cost of capital represents CJ Equity's estimate of the risk-adjusted, after-tax rate of return of similar companies in each operating company's industry.

You have been hired by CJ Equity as a consultant to recommend whether CJ Equity should change the way it measures the performance of the three companies (net income after taxes), which is then used to compute the professional managers' bonuses.

Required:

a. Design and prepare a performance report for the three operating companies that you believe best measures each operating company's performance and which will be used in computing the three professional managers' bonuses. In other words, using your performance measure, compute the performance of each of the three operating companies.

b. Write a short memo explaining why you believe the performance measure you chose in part (*a*) best measures the performance of the three professional managers.

P 5–20: R&D Inc.

R&D Inc. has the following financial data for the current year (millions):

Earnings before R&D expenditures	$21.5
Interest expense	$0.0
R&D expenditures	$6.0
Total invested capital (excluding R&D assets)	$100.0
Weighted average cost of capital	14%

Assume the tax rate is zero.

Required:

a. R&D Inc. writes off R&D expenditures as an operating expense. Calculate R&D Inc.'s EVA for the current year.

b. R&D Inc. decides to capitalize R&D and amortize it over three years. R&D expenditures for the last three years have been $6.0 million per year. Calculate R&D Inc.'s EVA for the current year after capitalizing the current year and previous years' R&D and amortizing the capitalized R&D balance.

c. In the specific case of R&D Inc., how does capitalizing and amortizing R&D expenditures instead of expensing R&D affect the incentive for managers approaching retirement to underspend on R&D at R&D Inc.

P 5–21: Flat Images

Flat Images develops and manufactures large, state-of-the-art flat-panel television screens that consumer electronic companies purchase and incorporate into a complete TV unit by adding the case, mounting brackets, tuner, amplifier, other electronics, and speakers. Flat Images has just introduced a new high-resolution, high-definition 60-inch screen. Flat Images is composed of two profit centers: Manufacturing and Marketing. Manufacturing produces sets that are sold internally to Marketing. Each profit center has the following cost structure:

	Manufacturing	*Marketing*
Fixed cost (per month)	$300,000	$150,000
Variable cost per screen	$800	$200

Note that Marketing's fixed cost of $150,000 and variable cost of $200 per screen do not contain any transfer price from Manufacturing. The numbers in the preceding table consist only of their own costs, not any costs transferred from the other department.

The selling price that Marketing receives for each 60-inch screen depends on the number of screens sold that month, according to the following table:[12]

Quantity	*Price*
50	$8,000
75	7,500
100	7,000
125	6,500
150	6,000
175	5,500
200	5,000
225	4,500
250	4,000
275	3,500

Required:

a. Suppose that Manufacturing sets a transfer price for each screen at $4,800. How many screens will Marketing purchase to maximize Marketing's profits (after Marketing pays Manufacturing $4,800 per screen) and how much profit will Marketing make?

b. At a transfer price of $4,800 per screen, and assuming Marketing buys the number of screens you calculated in part (*a*), how much profit is Manufacturing reporting?

c. At an internal transfer price of $4,800, and assuming Marketing purchases the number of screens you calculate in part (*a*), what is Flat Images' profit?

d. Given the cost structures of Manufacturing and Marketing, and the price-quantity relation given in the problem, how many 60-inch screens should Flat Image manufacture and sell to maximize firmwide profits?

e. If parts (*c*) and (*d*) are the same, explain why they are the same. If they are different, explain why they are different.

f. What transfer price should Flat Images set to maximize firmwide profits? (Give a quantitative number.)

P 5–22: Premier Brands

Premier Brands buys and manages consumer personal products brands such as cosmetics, hair care, and personal hygiene. Premier management purchases underperforming brands and redesigns

---

[12]An equivalent way to express the price-quantity relation in the table is $P = \$9,000 - 20\,Q$, where P = price and Q = quantity.

their marketing strategy and brand equity positioning, and then promotes the repositioned brand to the mega–retail chains (Walmart and Kmart). Each product line manager is evaluated and rewarded based on return on net assets (RONA). RONA is calculated as net income divided by net assets where net assets is total assets invested in the product line less current liabilities in the product line [RONA = Net income/(Total assets – Current liabilities)]. For every 1 percent of RONA (or fraction thereof) in excess of 12 percent of the product line returns, the product line manager receives a bonus of $250,000. So, if a manager's RONA is 13.68 percent, his or her bonus is $420,000 [(13.68% – 12.00%) × 100 × $250,000]. Premier's weighted average cost of capital (WACC) is 12.43 percent.

Amy Guttman, one of Premier's three product line managers, manages a portfolio of four brands in the hair care business. These four brands currently generate a net income of $708,000, requiring $6.5 million of total assets and $1.3 million of current liabilities. Guttman is evaluating two possible brand acquisitions: Brand 1 and Brand 2. The following table summarizes the salient information about each brand (thousands).

	Brand 1	*Brand 2*
Current liabilities	$ 82	$ 498
Net assets	522	1,546
Net income	67	228
Total assets	604	2,044

Required:

a. Given Premier's incentive plan, will Amy Guttman acquire Brand 1 and/or Brand 2, or neither? Justify your answer with supporting calculations.

b. Suppose that Premier's WACC is 15.22 percent instead of 12.43 percent, and the bonus system remains as described in the problem. How do Amy's decisions in part (*a*) change? Explain your answer.

c. Given the facts as stated in the problem, if you were the sole owner of Premier Products, would you acquire Brand 1 and/or Brand 2, or neither? Justify your answer with supporting calculations.

d. Given the facts as stated in the problem, except that Premier's WACC is 15.22 percent instead of 12.43 percent, if you were the sole owner of Premier Products, would you acquire Brand 1 and/or Brand 2, or neither? Justify your answer with supporting calculations.

e. Why do some companies use RONA instead of ROA (net income/total assets)? In other words, describe how the incentives generated by using RONA differ from the incentives from using ROA.

P 5–23: Easton Electronics

Easton Electronics in Irvine, California, is a contract manufacturer that assembles complex solid-state circuit boards for advanced technology companies in the aerospace and health sciences industries. The contract manufacturing industry is very competitive in terms of pricing and performance (quality and on-time delivery). Outsourcing clients specialize in the design of sophisticated electronics products and then rely on their contract manufacturing partners (like Easton) to produce their designs. Once a new product is designed, the advanced technology firm solicits firm, fixed-price bids for the electronic components.

A completed electronic component consists of several assembled circuit boards, a box containing the boards, cables connecting the boards inside the box, cables connecting the box to other components, and exhaustive testing of the complete box build. The technology firm either solicits bids for each separate component (box, boards, and cables) or selects an integrated supplier that can deliver a completely assembled box that has been tested. After receiving the initial bids but prior to selecting the winning bidder, the technology firm selects two or three finalists and then spends considerable resources to qualify new suppliers by sending teams of engineers and purchasing specialists to inspect the bidders' manufacturing facility, procurement process, and quality programs.

Once a contract manufacturer is chosen, most clients are reluctant to switch to new suppliers because of the high search and startup costs of moving to a new supplier. Although some Easton customers source their metal boxes, boards, and cables from different contractors and then assemble the final electronic components into a complete unit that they test, most of Easton clients rely on Easton to provide a complete unit (box, circuit boards, connecting cabling, and final testing).

Easton has recently acquired a wholly owned cable company (TT Cabling). With the acquisition, Easton has two profit centers: Irvine (which manufactures the boards, builds the complete box, and assembles and tests it) and TT Cabling (which only makes and tests the cables). Currently, TT sells most of its cables to a different set of customers than those who have their boards built by Easton. After the acquisition, Easton has a single sales force that sells board assembly, box build, and cables.

Easton assembles the electronic controller for a particular health imaging system for Scopics Imaging (SI). Easton manufactures the circuit boards, buys a sheet metal box designed specifically to house the boards, buys the cables to connect the boards within the box and other cables to connect the box to other components, tests the box, and delivers the completed unit to SI to plug the box into its imaging system.

Irvine currently purchases four cables for the SI program. The following table summarizes Irvine's cost for ONE complete SI box:

	Fixed Costs	Variable Costs	Total Costs
Metal box		$347	$347
Circuit boards	$1,460*	9,375	10,835
Cable harnesses		1,275	1,275
Box build and test	998*	720	1,718
Total	$ 2,458	$11,717	$14,175

*Represents the proportionate utilization of both equipment necessary to populate the circuit boards with components and the testing equipment.

Although Irvine purchases the cables for the SI program from an outside cable company, Easton senior managers are analyzing whether to have TT Cabling supply these cables. The managers of TT Cabling have submitted a bid to Irvine of $1,700 for the four cables in the SI assembly. The Irvine managers oppose buying the cables from TT because the TT bid of $1,700 is significantly higher than the outside cable supplier ($1,275). The bid of $1,700 submitted by TT for the four SI cables consists of variable costs of $1,000, fixed manufacturing costs of $300, and profits of $400. The quality of the TT cables (including reliability of delivery schedule) is the same for both the TT cables and the outside supplier of cables.

When bidding on new proposals that involve complete box builds, Easton management wonders whether they should continue to solicit price quotes from outside cable suppliers only, solicit bids from both outside cable suppliers and TT, or only get price quotes from TT Cabling.

Required:

Write a memo to the senior managers of Easton electronics proposing a policy that describes how Easton should decide whether to purchase cables externally or internally (through TT). The memo should describe the decision-making process, the relevant considerations, and the underlying objectives of such a policy. Use the SI cables as an example of how your Easton cable sourcing policy should be applied.

P 5–24: Evergreen Nursery and Landscape

Evergreen Nursery and Landscape has two profit centers: Nursery and Landscape. Nursery buys young evergreen trees, grows them for a year, and then sells them to Landscape. Landscape then sells and plants them for residential customers. Nursery only sells its trees to Landscape, and Landscape only buys trees from Nursery. Landscape faces the following demand curve per month for planted trees by residential customers:

Trees Sold	Price per Tree
2	$260
3	240
4	220
5	200
6	180
7	160
8	140
9	120

(*Note:* The demand curve in the table can be represented as $P = 300 - 20Q$.)

Nursery has variable costs of $10 per tree and fixed costs of $210 per month. Landscape has variable costs of $50 per tree (before paying Nursery a transfer price for the tree) and fixed costs of $290 per month.

Required:

a. Assume the owner of Evergreen Nursery and Landscape knows all the costs of both divisions and the demand curve. If the owner sets the price for trees planted by Landscape, what final price for a planted tree would the owner set to maximize her profits and how many trees per month get planted?

b. Suppose the owner does not know the demand curve faced by Landscape, but she does know each division's fixed and variable costs. What transfer price would the owner set to maximize her profits?

c. Suppose that Nursery sets the transfer price at $75 per tree. How many trees will Landscape purchase from Nursery and plant per month in order to maximize Landscape's profits (including the transfer price of $75 per tree)?

d. What is Nursery's profit from setting a transfer price of $75, assuming Landscape maximizes its profits as in part (*c*)?

e. Compare the firmwide profits that result from the transfer price chosen in part (*b*) and the firmwide profits that result from a $75 transfer price chosen in part (*c*), and explain why they are either the same or different.

P 5–25: Transfer Price Company

The Transfer Price Company has two divisions (Intermediate and Final) that report to the corporate office (Corporate). The two divisions are profit centers. Intermediate produces a proprietary product (called "*intermed*") that it sells both inside the firm to Final and outside the firm. Final can only purchase *intermed* from Intermediate because Intermediate holds the patent to manufacture *intermed*. *Intermed's* variable cost is $15 per unit, and Intermediate has excess capacity in the sense that it can satisfy demand from both its outside customers and Final. Final buys one *intermed* from Intermediate, incurs an additional variable cost of $5 per unit, and sells the product (called "*final* ") to external consumers. Final faces the following demand schedule for *final.*

Quantity	Price
4	$420
5	400
6	380
7	360
8	340
9	320
10	300
11	280
12	260
13	240

(The preceding demand schedule can be represented algebraically as: $P = \$500 - 20Q$.)

Required:

a. Calculate the quantity-price combination of *final* that maximizes firm value. In other words, if Corporate knew the variable costs of the two divisions, for what price would they sell *final,* and how many units of *intermed* would Corporate tell Intermediate to produce and transfer to Final?

b. Assume that the managers in Corporate do not know the variable costs in the two divisions. Intermediate has the decision rights to set the transfer price of *intermed* to Final. Intermediate knows Final's variable cost of $5 and the demand schedule Final faces for selling *final* to its customers. Intermediate, therefore, knows that the following schedule explains how many units of *intermed* Final will purchase given the transfer price Intermediate sets:

Transfer Price	Quantity of intermed Purchased by Final
$220	7
230	7
240	6
250	6
260	6
270	6
280	5
290	5

In other words, if Intermediate sets a transfer price of $260, Final will purchase six units of *intermed* and produce 6 units of *final.* Given the above schedule of possible transfer prices that Intermediate can choose, what transfer price will Intermediate set to maximize its profits?

c. While Corporate does not know *intermed's* variable cost, it does know that the total cost of *intermed* is $48 per unit. This $48 per unit cost consists of both the variable costs to manufacture *intermed* plus the allocated fixed manufacturing costs. Intermediate allocates all its fixed costs over all the products it produces, including *intermed.* If Corporate sets the transfer price of *intermed* at $48, how many units of *intermed* will Final purchase?

d. What is the dollar impact on Intermediate's profits if Final purchases the number of *intermeds* calculated in part (c)?

e. Should Corporate allow Intermediate to set the transfer price for *intermed* that you calculated in part (b), or should Corporate set the transfer price at $48 as in part (c)? Support your recommendation with a quantitative analysis.

P 5–26: XBT Keyboards

The keyboard division of XBT, a personal computer manufacturing firm, fabricates 50-key keyboards for both XBT and non-XBT computers. Keyboards for XBT machines are included as part of the XBT personal computer and are also sold separately. The keyboard division is a profit center. Keyboards included as part of the XBT PCs are transferred to the PC division at variable cost ($60) plus a 20 percent markup. The same keyboard, when sold separately (as a replacement part) or sold for non-XBT machines, is priced at $100. Projected sales are 50,000 keyboards transferred to the PC division (included as part of the XBT PC) and 150,000 keyboards sold externally.

The keys for the keyboard are fabricated by XBT on leased plastic injection-molding machines and then placed in purchased key sockets. These keys and sockets are assembled into a base, and connectors and cables are attached. Ten million keys are molded each year on four machines to meet the projected demand of 200,000 keyboards. Molding machines are leased for $500,000 per year per machine; maximum practical capacity is 2.5 million keys per machine per year. The variable overhead account includes all of the variable factory overhead costs for both key manufacturing and assembly. Studies have shown that variable overhead is more highly correlated with direct labor dollars than any other volume measure.

Cost Data per XBT Keyboard		
Variable Costs		
Materials		
Plastic for keys	$ 3.00	
Base	11.00	
Key sockets	13.00	
Connectors and cables	9.00	
Direct labor, keys	4.00	
Direct labor, assembly	12.00	
Variable overhead*	8.00	$60.00
Fixed Costs[†]		
Key injection molding	$10.00	
Fixed overhead	18.00	28.00
Unit manufacturing cost		$88.00

*Based on direct labor dollars.
[†]At projected production of 200,000 keyboards.

Sara Litle, manager of the keyboard division, is considering a proposal to buy some keys from an outside vendor instead of fabricating them inside XBT. These keys (which do not include the sockets) will be used in the keyboards included with XBT PCs but not in keyboards sold separately or sold to non-XBT computer manufacturers. The lease on one of XBT's key injection-molding machines is about to expire and the capacity it provides can be easily shifted to the outside vendor.

The outside vendor will produce keys for $0.39 per key and will guarantee capacity of at least 2.5 million keys per year. Litle is compensated based on the profits of the keyboard division. She is considering returning one of the injection-molding machines when its lease expires and purchasing keys from the outside vendor.

Required:

    a. How much will XBT save per key if it outsources the 2.5 million keys rather than producing them internally?

    b. What decision do you expect Sara Litle to make? Explain why.

    c. If you were a large shareholder of XBT and knew all the facts, would you make the same decision as Litle? Explain.

    d. What changes in XBT's accounting system and/or organizational structure would you suggest, given the facts of the case? Explain why.

P 5–27: Infantino Toyota

Infantino Toyota is a car dealership that has been in business for 40 years at the same 20-acre location selling and servicing new and "pre-owned" (used) Toyotas. Two years ago, Infantino Toyota replaced its aging showroom and service center with a new, state-of-the-art facility. When Ms. Infantino's father started the dealership, the business was on the outskirts of town. Now with city sprawl, the dealership is located on a busy commercial street surrounded by other dealerships, restaurants, and shopping centers.

The market for new cars is very competitive because many buyers shop on the Internet before visiting new car dealers. Once customers decide to purchase a new car from a dealer, they usually trade in their used car to avoid the hassle of selling the car themselves, and hence these new car buyers are willing to accept lower prices from car dealers for their trade-ins. Also, pre-owned cars have higher margins because there is less competition for used cars, as each used car differs in terms of mileage, condition, and options. Suppose a new car is sold for $45,000 ($500 over dealer cost) and the buyer receives a trade-in allowance on his old car of $8,000 and pays the difference in cash. That used car is then sold for $10,800. The dealer makes $500 on the new car and $2,800 on the used car. Infantino also offers parts and service for the new and pre-owned cars it sells.

Infantino Toyota is organized into three departments: New Cars, Pre-owned Cars, and Service. All three share the same building and lot where the new and used cars are displayed. Ms. Infantino compensates her three department heads based on residual income. After careful analysis by her financial manager, they determine that all three departments should be charged for the capital invested in their departments at 16 percent.

The new building cost $12 million and the land cost $900,000. The following table summarizes the land and building utilization by each department, each department's net income, and other net assets invested in each department:

	New Cars	Pre-owned Cars	Parts and Service	Total
Percent of land	50%	40%	10%	100%
Percent of building	30%	10%	60%	100%
Department income	$600,000	$1,725,000	$1,813,000	$4,138,000
Other assets	$2,500,000	$6,700,000	$1,300,000	$10,500,000

For example, the new car department occupies 50 percent of the land and 30 percent of the building. It had net income of $600,000 and other assets of $2,500,000. Other assets consist of all inventories and receivables invested in the department. For example, the new car department has a substantial inventory of new cars. Each department's income consists of all revenues and expenses directly traceable to that department. Income taxes are not included in each department's net income reported in the table. Infantino Toyota uses the trade-in allowance of used cars taken in trade as the transfer price of used cars in calculating the net incomes of the new and pre-owned car departments.

Required:

a. Calculate the residual income of each of the three divisions of Infantino Toyota.
b. Discuss the relative profitability of the three departments. Which is making the most money and which is making the least amount of money?
c. Discuss whether the residual incomes of the three departments capture the true profitability of each department. What problems do you see in the way Ms. Infantino is evaluating the performance of the three department managers and of Infantino Toyota as a whole?

P 5–28:   Wujo

Wujo is a Shanghai company that designs high-end software to enhance and edit digital images. Its software, EzPhoto, is more powerful and easier to use than Adobe Photoshop, but sells at a much lower price. Currently, EzPhoto is written in Chinese for the Chinese market, but Wujo is entering the English-speaking market. This requires a substantial investment to convert EzPhoto to English. Wujo has established a UK wholly owned subsidiary (Wujo UK, or WUK for short) to sell EzPhoto to North American and European consumers—professional and serious amateur photographers. The following table displays the various combinations of prices and quantities it expects in sales of EzPhoto to English-speaking users:

Price (euros)	Quantity (000)
270	130
265	135
260	140
255	145
250	150
245	155
240	160
235	165
230	170
225	175

For example, at a price of €270 it expects to sell 130,000 units of EzPhoto, or at €225 it can sell 175,000 units. To enter this market, WUK must spend €15 million to convert EzPhoto from Chinese to English, advertise EzPhoto, establish a website where purchasers can download EzPhoto, and hire an administrative staff to market and maintain the website. For each English version of EzPhoto sold, WUK expects to incur costs of €70 for sales commissions paid to third parties who market EzPhoto (e.g., Amazon, ZDNet.com, and Buy.com) and technical support for customers purchasing EzPhoto. EzPhoto will be distributed only via the WUK website. There are no packaging or CD-ROM costs.

WUK is evaluated and its managers compensated based on reported WUK profits. Wujo China, the parent company, is considering charging WUK a transfer price (actually a royalty) for each unit of EzPhoto WUK sells.

Required:

a. If Wujo China does not charge WUK a royalty for each unit of EzPhoto WUK sells (i.e., the transfer price is zero), what price-quantity combination will WUK select and how much profit will WUK make?

b. If Wujo China charges WUK a royalty of €50 for each unit of EzPhoto WUK sells (i.e., the transfer price is €50), what price-quantity combination will WUK select and how much profit will WUK make?

c. Ignoring any income taxes, what is the firm-value maximizing royalty (either zero euros or €50) that Wujo should charge WUK for each unit of EzPhoto WUK sells? Explain your answer.

d. Wujo (the parent) has to pay income taxes to the People's Republic of China (PRC) at the rate of 15 percent on any royalty payments it receives from WUK, while WUK faces a UK tax rate of 33 percent on profits of EzPhoto. Note that WUK's taxable income is calculated after deducting any transfer price (royalties) paid to Wujo. What is the firm-value maximizing royalty (either zero euros or €50) that Wujo should charge WUK for each unit of EzPhoto WUK sells? Whichever transfer price Wujo charges WUK (zero or €50), that transfer price is used to (1) measure and reward WUK managers, and (2) calculate income taxes in the PRC and the UK. Provide a detailed explanation supported by calculations justifying your answer.

e. Suppose that Wujo is able to use a different transfer price for determining WUK's profits (and hence the compensation paid to WUK management) than it uses for calculating income taxes on its PRC and UK tax returns. What transfer prices should Wujo use for calculating WUK's net income in determining WUK's managers' bonuses and for use on its two tax returns? The same transfer price has to be used on the two tax returns, but this transfer price need not be the same transfer price used for calculating WUK's income for management bonuses.

f. Why might you expect Wujo will be unable to implement the two transfer prices you propose in part (*e*)?

Cases

Case 5–1:   Celtex

Celtex is a large and very successful decentralized specialty chemical producer organized into five independent investment centers. Each of the five investment centers is free to buy products either inside or outside the firm and is judged based on residual income. Most of each division's sales are to external customers. Celtex has the general reputation of being one of the top two or three companies in each of its markets.

Don Horigan, president of the synthetic chemicals (Synchem) division, and Paul Juris, president of the consumer products division, are embroiled in a dispute. It all began two years ago when Juris asked Horigan to modify a synthetic chemical for a new household cleaner. In return, Synchem would be reimbursed for out-of-pocket costs. After Synchem spent considerable time perfecting the chemical, Juris solicited competitive bids from Horigan and some outside firms and awarded the contract to an outside firm that was the low bidder. This angered Horigan, who expected his bid to receive special consideration because he developed the new chemical at cost and the outside vendors took advantage of his R&D.

The current conflict involves Synchem's production of chemical Q47, a standard product, for consumer products. Because of an economic slowdown, all synthetic chemical producers have excess capacity. Synchem was asked to bid on supplying Q47 for the consumer products division. Consumer products is moving into a new, experimental product line, and Q47 is one of the key ingredients. While the order is small relative to Synchem's total business, the price of Q47 is very important in determining the profitability of the experimental line. Horigan bid $3.20 per gallon. Meas Chemicals, an outside firm, bid $3.00. Juris is angry because he knows that Horigan's bid contains a substantial amount of fixed overhead and profit. Synchem buys the base raw material, Q4, from the organic chemicals division of Celtex for $1.00 per gallon. The organic chemical division's out-of-pocket costs (i.e., variable costs) are 80 percent of the selling price. Synchem then further processes Q4 into Q47 and incurs additional variable costs of $1.75 per gallon. Synchem's fixed manufacturing overhead adds another $0.30 per gallon.

Horigan argues that he has $3.05 of cost in each gallon of Q47. If he turned around and sold the product for anything less than $3.20, he would be undermining his recent attempts to get his sales-people to stop cutting their bids and start quoting full-cost prices. Horigan has been trying to enhance the quality of the business he is getting, and he fears that if he is forced to make Q47 for consumer products, all of his effort the last few months will be for naught. He argues that he already gave away the store once to consumer products and he won't do it again. He asks, "How can senior managers expect me to return a positive residual income if I am forced to put in bids that don't recover full cost?"

Juris, in a chance meeting at the airport with Debra Donak, senior vice president of Celtex, described the situation and asked Donak to intervene. Juris believed Horigan was trying to get even after their earlier clash. Juris argued that the success of his new product venture depended on being able to secure a stable, high-quality supply of Q47 at low cost.

Required:

    a. Calculate the incremental cash flows to Celtex if the consumer products division obtains Q47 from Synchem versus Meas Chemicals.

    b. What advice would you give Debra Donak?

Case 5–2: Executive Inn

Sarah Adams manages Executive Inn of Toronto, a 200-room facility that rents furnished suites to executives by the month. The market is for people relocating to Toronto and waiting for permanent housing. Adams's compensation contains a fixed component and a bonus based on the net cash flows from operations. She seeks to maximize her compensation. Adams likes her job and has learned a lot, but she expects to be working for a financial institution within five years.

Adams's occupancy rate is running at 98 percent, and she is considering a $10 million expansion of the present building to add more rental units. She has very good private knowledge of the future cash flows. In year 1, they will be $2 million and will decline $100,000 a year. The following table summarizes the expansion's cash flows:

Year	Net Cash Flow (Millions)	Year	Net Cash Flow (Millions)
0	$(10.0)	6	1.5
1	2.0	7	1.4
2	1.9	8	1.3
3	1.8	9	1.2
4	1.7	10	1.1
5	1.6		

Based on the preceding data, Adams prepares a discounted cash flow analysis of the addition, which is contained in the following report:

Year	Net Cash Flow (Millions)	Discount Factor	Present Value of Cash Flow
0	$(10.0)	1.000	$(10.00)
1	2.0	0.893	1.79
2	1.9	0.797	1.51
3	1.8	0.712	1.28
4	1.7	0.636	1.08
5	1.6	0.567	0.91
6	1.5	0.507	0.76
7	1.4	0.452	0.63
8	1.3	0.404	0.53
9	1.2	0.361	0.43
10	1.1	0.322	0.35
Total			$ (0.73)

The discount factors are based on a weighted-average cost of capital of 12 percent, which accurately reflects the inn's nondiversifiable risk.

Adams's boss, Kathy Judson, manages the Inn Division of Comfort Inc., which has 15 properties located around North America, including Executive Inn of Toronto. Judson does not have the detailed knowledge of the Toronto hotel/rental market as Adams does. Her general knowledge is not as detailed or as accurate as Adams's. (For the following questions, ignore taxes.)

Required:

a. The Inn Division of Comfort Inc. has a very crude accounting system that does not assign the depreciation of particular inns to individual managers. As a result, Adams's annual net cash flow statement is based on the operating revenues less operating expenses. Neither the cost of expansion nor depreciation on expanding her inn is charged to her operating statement. Given the facts provided so far, what decision do you expect her to make regarding building the $10 million addition? Explain why.

b. Adams prepares the following report for Judson to justify the expansion project:

Year	Net Cash Flow (Millions)	Discount Factor	Present Value of Cash Flow
0	$(10.0)	1.000	$(10.00)
1	2.0	0.893	1.79
2	1.9	0.797	1.51
3	1.9	0.712	1.35
4	1.8	0.636	1.14
5	1.8	0.567	1.02
6	1.8	0.507	0.91
7	1.8	0.452	0.81
8	1.8	0.404	0.73
9	1.7	0.361	0.61
10	1.7	0.322	0.55
Net present value			$ 0.42

Judson realizes that Adams's projected cash flows are most likely optimistic, but she does not know how optimistic or even whether or not the project is a positive net present value project. She decides to change Adams's performance measure used in computing her bonus. Adams's compensation will be based on residual income (EVA). Judson also changes the accounting system to track asset expansion and depreciation on the expansion. Adams's profits from operations will now be charged for straight-line depreciation of the expansion using a 10-year life (assume a zero salvage value). Calculate Adams's expected residual income from the expansion for each of the next 10 years.

    c. Based on your calculations in part (*b*), will Adams propose the expansion project? Explain why.

    d. Instead of using residual income as Adams's performance measure in part (*b*), Judson uses net cash flows from operations less straight-line depreciation. Will Adams seek to undertake the expansion? Explain why.

    e. Reconcile any differences in your answers for parts (*c*) and (*d*).

Case 5–3: Royal Resort and Casino

Royal Resort and Casino (RRC), a publicly traded company, caters to affluent customers seeking plush surroundings, high-quality food and entertainment, and all the "glitz" associated with the best resorts and casinos. RRC consists of three divisions: hotel, gaming, and entertainment. The hotel division manages the reservation system and lodging operations. Gaming consists of operations, security, and junkets. Junkets offers complimentary air fare and lodging and entertainment at RRC for customers known to wager large sums. The entertainment division consists of restaurants, lounges, catering, and shows. It books lounge shows and top-name entertainment in the theater. Although many of those people attending the shows and eating in the restaurants stay at RRC, customers staying at other hotels and casinos in the area also frequent RRC's shows, restaurants, and gaming operations. The following table disaggregates RRC's total EVA of $12 million into an EVA for each division:

ROYAL RESORT AND CASINO
EVA by Division
(Millions $)

	Entertainment	Hotel	Gaming	Total
Adjusted accounting profits	$ 5	$ 10	$30	$ 45
Invested capital	$40	$120	$60	$220
Weighted-average cost of capital	15%	15%	15%	15%
EVA	$ (1)	$ (8)	$21	$ 12

    Based on an analysis of similar companies, it is determined that each division has the same weighted-average cost of capital of 15 percent.

    Across town from RRC is a city block with three separate businesses: Big Horseshoe Slots & Casino, Nell's Lounge and Grill, and Sunnyside Motel. These businesses serve a less affluent clientele.

Required:

    a. Why does RRC operate as a single firm, whereas Big Horseshoe Slots, Nell's Lounge and Grill, and Sunnyside Motel operate as three separate firms?

    b. Describe some of the interdependencies that are likely to exist across RRC's three divisions.

    c. Describe some of the internal administrative devices, accounting-based measures, and/or organizational structures that senior managers at RRC can use to control the interdependencies that you described in part (*b*).

    d. Critically evaluate each of the "solutions" you proposed in part (*c*).

Chapter Six

Budgeting

Chapter Outline

A. Generic Budgeting Systems

    1. Country Club

    2. Large Corporation

B. Trade-Off between Decision Management and Decision Control

    1. Communicating Specialized Knowledge versus Performance Evaluation

    2. Budget Ratcheting

    3. Participative Budgeting

    4. New Approaches to Budgeting

    5. Managing the Trade-Off

C. Resolving Organizational Problems

    1. Short-Run versus Long-Run Budgets

    2. Line-Item Budgets

    3. Budget Lapsing

    4. Static versus Flexible Budgets

    5. Incremental versus Zero-Based Budgets

D. Summary

Appendix: Comprehensive Master Budget Illustration

Chapter 4 described the firm's organizational architecture as consisting of three integrated systems: assigning decision rights, measuring performance, and rewarding performance. The firm's organizational architecture reduces conflicts of interest among the various parties contracting with the firm. This chapter describes how budgeting is used for decision making and to control conflicts of interest. A **budget** is management's formal quantification of the operations of an organization for a future period. It is an aggregate forecast of all transactions expected to occur.

Giving a manager an advertising budget of $8 million authorizes that manager to consume $8 million of firm resources on advertising. Put another way, the advertising budget authorizes the manager to spend $8 million on advertising by assigning these decision rights to the manager. At the end of the year, actual spending on advertising can be compared with the budget; any difference is a measure of the manager's performance and can be used in determining the manager's performance rewards. Budgets are thus part of the firm's organizational architecture; they partition decision rights and control behavior.

Dwight D. Eisenhower, Supreme Commander of the Allied Forces in Europe during World War II and the 34th president of the United States, is quoted as saying, "In preparing for battle, I have always found that plans are useless but planning is indispensable."[1] Budgets are a form of planning. And as expressed by Eisenhower, in many cases their value lies more in the process of planning than in the actual budgets produced. Many times, budgets are obsolete before they can be implemented because the world has changed in some unexpected manner. However, the process of budgeting remains vital.

Budgets are an integral part of decision making by assembling knowledge and communicating it to the managers with the decision rights. Budgets are developed using key planning assumptions or basic estimating factors that are widely accepted forecasts of strategic elements faced by the firm. Typical planning assumptions are product prices, unit sales, foreign currency exchange rates, and external prices of key inputs. Budgets help assemble and then communicate these key planning assumptions. Various managers throughout the firm must accept these planning assumptions as reasonable and likely. Key planning assumptions represent those factors that are, to some extent, beyond management control and that set a limit on the overall activities of the firm.

Each key planning assumption must be forecast using past experience, field estimates, and/or statistical analysis. Making these forecasts involves accumulating the collective knowledge of numerous individuals in the firm. No single manager has detailed knowledge of total expected sales, but individual salespeople have knowledge of likely unit sales in their districts. Because salespersons have specific knowledge of their customer's future purchases, the firm develops an accurate estimate of the planning assumption (firmwide sales) by adding sales forecasts from all the salespeople. From these key planning assumptions, a complete set of management plans is developed regarding raw materials acquisition, labor requirements, financing plans, and distribution and marketing budgets.

James McKinsey, founder of the consulting firm McKinsey & Co., describes budgetary control as involving the following:

1. The statement of the plans of all departments of the business for a certain period of time in the form of estimates.
2. The coordination of these estimates into a well-balanced program for the business as a whole.

---

[1]Quoted by Richard Nixon in *Six Crises* (Garden City, NY: Doubleday, 1962), http://en.wikipedia.org/wiki/Dwight_D._Eisenhower#_note-34.

Managerial Application: Budgeting at General Electric	GE's forecasting and budgeting process focuses on understanding how its various businesses will perform in the future. The budgeting process begins in the spring of each year as each profit center develops a three- to five-year plan describing the macroeconomic factors that are expected to affect supply and demand in each profit center's business. It begins bottom-up with each of the 45 profit centers presenting a most probable outcome and worst-case and best-case scenarios. Senior managers challenge the profit centers' assumptions and analyses. In July, the financial projections for each of GE's businesses is presented to the board of directors aggregated around 12 main business segments.

In the fall, all of the spring forecasts are updated using another six months of data. Each profit center provides detailed operating budgets for its business for the next fiscal year. These updated forecasts and budgets in summary form are presented to GE's board, and they also provide the basis for the annual update with investors each December when GE senior managers present their outlook for the next year.

In the middle of every quarter, each business unit submits income and cash-flow statements and balance sheets for the current quarter, the following quarter, and the entire year, thereby creating a "rolling" look at their future performance. During the second and third months of each quarter, the CEO and CFO review each of the businesses. The last month of each quarter involves a weekly call to discuss the performance of each business versus expectations.

Notable aspects of GE's budgeting process include the following:

- Provides a long-range (three-year) financial plan.
- Serious, highly involved, externally focused review by the most senior managers.
- Generates internal forecasts of growth in earnings and cash flow and of returns on capital.
- Identifies risks to GE's business plan and ways to manage them.
- Involves a bottoms-up and top-down process whereby business unit managers "propose" and senior managers "challenge" the proposals, thereby ensuring that specific knowledge dispersed throughout the firm is assembled in the forecasts.

SOURCE: K. Sherin, "Financial Planning and Investor Communications at GE (With a Look at Why We Ended Earnings Guidance)," *Journal of Applied Corporate Finance*, Fall 2010, pp. 8–16.

3. The preparation of reports showing a comparison between the actual and the estimated performance, and the revision of the original plans when these reports show that such revision is necessary.[2]

Because budgeting performs such critical functions involving decision management and decision control, it is ubiquitous—virtually all organizations prepare budgets. This chapter first describes some generic budgeting systems used by different organizations (section A). It then discusses how budgeting involves the trade-off between decision management and decision control (section B). Section C describes how budgets help reduce conflicts of interest between owners and managers. A comprehensive budget example is provided in the appendix.

---

[2]J. McKinsey, *Budgetary Control* (New York: Ronald Press, 1922), p. 8.

A. Generic Budgeting Systems

The following discussion illustrates the essential aspects of budgeting using a simple organizational form (a hypothetical private country club) and a large corporation. In both examples, budgeting is part of the system whereby decision rights are partitioned and performance is measured and rewarded.

1. Country Club

This example illustrates the use of budgets to assign decision rights and create incentives for employees to act in the owners' interests.

Bay View Country Club is a private club with 350 members. Members pay a one-time initiation fee of $45,000 and dues of $385 per month. They have access to the golf course, pool, tennis courts, and restaurant.

Bay View Country Club has three departments (each managed by a full-time employee): the restaurant, the golf course, and the pro shop. The restaurant is managed by the club manager; the maintenance of the golf course is supervised by the golf course superintendent; and the pro shop is operated by the golf professional. The restaurant is treated as a profit center and the golf course and pro shop are treated as cost centers. The club manager is responsible for revenues and expenses in operating the restaurant, whereas the golf course superintendent and golf professional are responsible primarily for controlling expenses in their operations.

Table 6–1 is the operating statement for the club. Bay View Country Club is essentially a cash business. All of the members pay their dues on time, and there are negligible inventories of food and liquor. Because it is a cash business, revenues are equivalent to cash receipts, while expenses are equivalent to cash disbursements. Table 6–1 lists the

TABLE 6-1

	BAY VIEW COUNTRY CLUB			
	Operating Results			
	September 2017			
	Actual September	*Budget September*	*Favorable (Unfavorable) Variance*	*Last Year*
Revenues				
Dues	$133,350	$134,750	$ (1,400)	$129,600
Guest fees	2,900	2,500	400	2,200
Food and bar	46,000	44,500	1,500	45,000
Golf carts	2,200	1,900	300	2,100
Miscellaneous	1,600	1,800	(200)	1,700
Total revenue	$186,050	$185,450	$ 600	$180,600
Expenses				
Food & bar	$ 57,000	$ 51,300	$ (5,700)	$ 49,700
Golf course	79,500	80,000	500	75,000
Administration & maintenance	47,050	45,350	(1,700)	45,600
Interest on debt	8,500	8,500	0	9,000
Total expenses	$192,050	$185,150	$ (6,900)	$179,300
Net operating surplus (deficit)	$ (6,000)	$ 300	$ (6,300)	$ 1,300

220 *Chapter 6*

revenues and expenses for September 2017 and September 2016, and the budget for September 2017, including variances from budget. Parentheses denote negative numbers and unfavorable variances from budget. An unfavorable budget variance occurs when actual expenses exceed budgeted expenses or when actual revenues are less than budgeted revenues. The annual operating budget and monthly operating statement are the principal control devices used in most organizations, including Bay View Country Club.

At the beginning of the operating year, the board of directors submits an operating budget to the general membership for approval. This plan shows projected revenues (including dues) and projected expenses. To prepare the budget, management and the board examine each revenue and expense item for the previous year and adjust it for expected inflation and any change in operating plans. For example, the golf course superintendent reviews last year's spending on labor and supplies. The superintendent decides how to change the golf course maintenance schedule and forecasts how these changes, adjusted for price changes, translate into a total operating budget for the year. Knowing the maintenance program for each month, the superintendent estimates how the annual amount will be spent each month.

The annual budget, after approval by the members, authorizes the board and club management to operate the club for the next year under the limits it specifies. For example, the budgeted amount to be spent on the golf course in September 2017 is $80,000. The members (who are the owners of the club) control the operations by authorizing the board of directors, and hence the management, to spend club resources according to the plan. If there is a major unanticipated cost during the year (e.g., the swimming pool heater breaks), the board of directors can either pay for this out of cash generated from prior years' accumulated surpluses or call a special meeting of the membership and propose an assessment from each member.

Table 6–1 reports the actual amounts received and spent in September 2017. The club had a net operating deficit of $6,000 in September. The budget projected a surplus of $300. Thus, September's operations were $6,300 below budget. Last year in September, actual revenue exceeded actual expenses by $1,300. Comparing budget with actual for individual line items indicates that most of this September's $6,300 unfavorable variance is from food and bar expenses, which were $5,700 over budget. At this point, additional information is needed to determine the reasons for the unfavorable variance in food and bar expenses. The operating statement merely identifies a budget variance. Additional analysis is required to identify its causes and any corrective action needed to solve the problem.

Table 6–2 provides additional information on the food and bar operations. It indicates that actual expenses exceeded actual revenues by $11,000. The budget called for only a $6,800 deficit. Thus, there was an unfavorable budget variance of $4,200 in the net operating deficit. September's unfavorable variances occurred because party revenue was $3,200 under budget and party expenses were $5,000 over budget. Further investigation reveals that the assistant manager in charge of parties quit in August. A large party was canceled in September, but no one at the club canceled the additional staff, food, and flower orders. The board criticized the club manager for not supervising these parties more closely during the absence of the assistant manager. A new assistant manager for parties was hired, and these problems were solved.[3]

---

[3]A well-known agency problem with private clubs (and other nonprofit organizations) is that the board of directors has little financial incentive to oversee the club. Board members receive no cash compensation for serving on the board. Thus, firing the manager imposes costs on them because they have to spend their time replacing the manager. All the members gain from the improved operations with the new (better) manager. Each board member receives 1/350th of the benefit (if there are 350 members) but incurs 1/15th of the cost (if there are 15 board members). This free-rider problem is one of the reasons member-owned country clubs usually are run less efficiently than for-profit clubs. Members are willing to bear these higher agency costs because of the prestige and exclusivity of belonging to the club and because of social interactions from associating with a stable membership.

TABLE 6-2

BAY VIEW COUNTRY CLUB				
Food and Bar Operations				
September 2017				
	Actual September	*Budget September*	*Favorable (Unfavorable) Variance*	*Last Year*
Revenues				
Parties	$ 8,300	$ 11,500	$ (3,200)	$11,000
Food	24,000	22,000	2,000	21,500
Bar	12,700	10,500	2,200	10,500
Miscellaneous	1,000	500	500	2,000
Total revenue	$ 46,000	$ 44,500	$ 1,500	$45,000
Expenses				
Parties	$ 9,000	$ 4,000	$ (5,000)	$ 5,000
Food	44,000	43,000	(1,000)	40,000
Bar	4,000	4,300	300	4,700
Total expenses	$ 57,000	$ 51,300	$ (5,700)	$49,700
Net operating surplus (deficit)	$(11,000)	$ (6,800)	$ (4,200)	$(4,700)

Chapter 4 described organizational architecture as consisting of administrative systems that assign decision rights and evaluate and reward performance. Bay View Country Club's budgeting system illustrates how each of these three administrative systems is used to reduce agency problems at Bay View. *Decision rights,* which are initially held by the members, are assigned to the board of directors. The board hires professional managers who have the specialized knowledge to operate the various club functions: the club manager, the golf course superintendent, and the golf professional. These individuals submit their operating plans for the upcoming year via the budget.

Their budgets translate the plans for the next year into financial terms—the dollars of revenue and expenses that are expected to occur when their plans are implemented. The board reviews and modifies these plans to reflect member preferences and to ensure that monies are available to implement the plans. Once the membership approves the budget, the three managers have the decision rights to spend monies as specified in the budget. Decision rights are linked with knowledge. For example, the golf course superintendent has the specialized knowledge of the golf course as well as the available chemicals and maintenance procedures to maintain the course. The budget assigns to the superintendent the decision rights to implement a specific set of actions.

Notice the bottom-up nature of the budgeting process. The operating managers submit their budgets to the board of directors, who adjust the budgeted figures and recommend the budget to the membership. The members then have final approval rights over the budget.

Budgets are also a *performance measurement system.* Monthly operating statements for each manager are prepared. Table 6–2 is the operating statement for the club manager's food and bar operation. This statement is only one component of the club manager's performance. It shows whether the club manager met revenue and expense targets. Another indication of the manager's performance is the level of member satisfaction with the food and bar operation. Member satisfaction will ultimately show up in revenues and expenses if quality falls and members stop using the restaurant. Similarly, it does little good for the golf course superintendent to meet financial targets if the golf course condition deteriorates. Also, the condition of the course relative to other courses in the area is an important consideration in evaluating the superintendent's performance.

Budget variances are indicators of whether managers are meeting expectations and they are used in the *performance reward system* to determine pay increases or, in the case of extremely unfavorable variances, the need to terminate the responsible manager. The large unfavorable variance in party operations caused the board of directors to search for reasons, which led to the discovery that the manager did not supervise the parties. The lack of supervision caused the board to criticize the club manager. If unfavorable variances continue and the board determines that they are the fault of the manager, they may be grounds for dismissal or for not granting a pay increase. On the other hand, favorable budget variances need not indicate superior performance. If less was spent than was budgeted, quality may have been sacrificed.

One danger inherent in annual budgets such as the Bay View Country Club example is their tendency to focus managers' attention on next year's operations only, ignoring the long-term well-being of the organization. For example, if budgeted expenses exceed budgeted revenues, there is pressure to reduce maintenance expenditures. Reducing maintenance and repairs brings the one-year budget into line, but the long-term goals of the organization are compromised. To reduce the tendency of short-term budgets to focus managers too narrowly on short-term performance, many organizations prepare long-term budgets of three- to five-year duration along with a short-run budget. A budget for five years is more likely to reveal the effects of reducing short-run maintenance than a one-year budget. Section C discusses short-run versus long-run budgets in greater detail.

Bay View Country Club's budget separates decision management (decision initiation and implementation) from decision control (decision ratification and monitoring):

1. *Decision initiation* (budget preparation) is done by the operating managers.
2. *Decision ratification* (budget approval) is done by the board and the members.
3. *Decision implementation* (operating decisions) is done by the managers.
4. *Decision monitoring* (reviewing monthly operating statements) is done directly by the board and indirectly by the members.

The managers prepare the budget and make day-to-day operating decisions in their area (decision management rights). The board of directors approves budget requests and monitors operations (decision control rights). The board not only examines financial operating variances (the favorable and unfavorable variances on the operating statements) but also monitors member satisfaction with the club's food and golf operations.

In the country club example, the budget and the monthly operating statements are an integral part of the various administrative mechanisms that reduce the club's organizational problems. We now turn to a large complex organization—namely, a global corporation. Again, the budget is a key device in resolving organizational problems.

2. Large Corporation

The previous example described budgeting primarily as a process by which knowledge is assembled *vertically,* from both lower levels and higher levels in the organization's hierarchy. But budgeting is also an important device for assembling specialized knowledge *horizontally* within the firm. In a large, complex corporation, it is a major challenge to disseminate specific knowledge. Getting managers to share their knowledge among superiors and subordinates (vertically) as well as among peers in other parts of the organization

Managerial Application: "Budgeting for Curve Balls"	The Chicago White Sox baseball team has an annual budget of more than $200 million. Budget assumptions are set in August/September, and by October the new budget is prepared for the next year. The team owner first sets guidelines for the total player salary budget; this is the largest single expense category. Department heads assemble assumption sheets, books of 1,500–2,000 pages, one for every account. These sheets contain details—such as the number of security people for each game based on expected attendance levels, their pay rates, and union contracts—and explain any recommended changes from last year. Then the vice president of finance, the accounting manager, and the controller review the budgets with each department head. These meetings ensure consistent assumptions are being made across departments and that the budget requests are realistic. The team owner then reviews the budget requests. Once the budget is set, department heads must explain cost overruns and underruns.

SOURCE: A. Dennis, "Budgeting for Curve Balls," *Journal of Accountancy*, September 1998, pp. 89–92; www.usatoday.com/sports/baseball/salaries

(horizontally) and giving managers incentives to acquire valuable knowledge are important aspects of the budgeting system. Consider the case of Xerox Corporation.

Xerox produces, sells, leases, and services a wide range of copiers with different copy output rates, features, and sales and rental plans. The field organization consists of branch offices with sales, service, and administrative personnel. The manufacturing organization produces copiers at sites around the world and is treated as a cost center. Besides manufacturing copiers, Xerox also sells supplies, such as toner. The field offices that are part of marketing are cost centers; the supplies division is a profit center.

Each year, Xerox must plan how many new copiers of each type will be placed in service and how many old copiers will be returned. These numbers drive the manufacturing plans for the year. The number of various types of copiers currently in the field, which is called the *installed base,* affects the number of service personnel in the field, the training programs they require, and the stock of spare parts needed to service the base. The installed base also affects the amount and types of supplies Xerox sells.

Each part of Xerox must communicate with the other parts of the firm. Manufacturing wants to know how many of each type of copier marketing expects to install. Marketing wants to know what prices will be charged for each type of copier. Copier placements depend on the market's expectation of new product introductions. In setting their forecasts, manufacturing and marketing managers want to know about new products. Likewise, the supplies division needs to know the size of the installed base and its composition so it can plan the production of supplies for the year.

Not only must the various parts of Xerox share their specialized knowledge, but they must have incentives to acquire it. The sales force must acquire the knowledge about the forecasted quantities and prices of particular copiers to be sold (or leased). These estimates must be transmitted to manufacturing with enough lead time to build the projected quantities of new copiers.

An important part of the budgeting process is sharing and assembling knowledge about such key planning assumptions as unit placements, prices, and copier returns. Knowledge of these numbers is widely dispersed throughout the firm. In the process of assembling the knowledge, people will change their expectations of the key planning assumptions. In addition, all managers affected by a key planning assumption are usually required to approve it and then build their budgets using it. Each manager's approval helps ensure that expectations are consistent throughout the firm.

> **Managerial Application: Budgeting at Nestlé Waters Division**
>
> The Nestlé Waters Division was created to manage the two Nestlé water businesses: the French brands of Perrier, Vittel, and Contrex and the Italian brands of Pellegrino and Acqua Panna. These brands are sold worldwide through the Nestlé Waters distribution system. The French and Italian units start the budgeting process by developing a multiyear, long-term global brand strategy that includes positioning, pricing, and brand development. Next, the Nestlé Waters headquarters approves the global strategy. This strategy then generates a plan for each Nestlé distributor that defines market priorities, volumes, and price targets, as well as budgets to implement the plan. Each distributor prepares a budget for achieving its piece of the global strategy and discusses it with the French and Italian Nestlé Waters producers until all parties are in agreement. Once approved by the French and Italian units and distributors, the first year of the plan becomes the operating plan (budget).
>
> Monthly, quarterly, and annual reports provide actual sales statistics, outlook by brand, actual profits by brand, and variances from budget. Prior to implementing the new organization and budgeting system, very limited information flowed laterally among the French and Italian producers and distributors, and there was no integrated international brand strategy. The new structure and budgeting system forces Nestlé Waters producers and distributors to think strategically in terms of joint profitability. A Pellegrino finance manager said, "The new performance measurement and accountability . . . has brought a new end-to-end mentality, fostering the (business unit) integration through shared goals between the producer and the distributor. On the one hand, it improved the producer's control over the distributors' activities. On the other hand, it links the distributors and the producer to a common faith as they have a shared goal to achieve, and, in so doing, it favors identification around a global brand commitment."
>
> SOURCE: C. Busco, M. Frigo, E. Giovannoni, A. Riccaboni, and R. Scapens, "Integrating Global Organizations through Performance Measurement Systems," *Strategic Finance*, January 2006, pp. 31–35.

The corporate budgeting system is also a communication device through which some of the specialized knowledge and key planning assumptions are transmitted. It also involves a process by which various individuals arranged vertically and horizontally in the organization negotiate the terms of trade among the various parts of the organization. For example, for a given price schedule, the marketing organization estimates the quantity of each type of copier placed. Manufacturing agrees to produce this quantity of copiers and estimates the cost at which they will be produced. Usually, price schedules are adjusted to bring manufacturing (supply) in line with marketing (demand). In principle, when sales forecasts and production plans are produced, knowledge of cost (from manufacturing) and revenue (from marketing) is transferred to those agents with the decision rights to set prices, who ideally set the price for each product to maximize profits. Likewise, the supplies and service organizations accept their targets. Senior management ensures that all parts of the budget are consistent: Marketing and manufacturing are in agreement, the financing is in place, the parts inventory is adequate to meet service requirements, and so on. Moreover, senior management likely has specialized knowledge to forecast some assumptions such as interest rates and salary levels and to arbitrate disputes that arise between departments during the budgeting process.

Many budgeting systems involve a bottom-up, top-down approach. Usually, some key planning assumptions are announced. Then, the lowest levels in the decision hierarchy submit budgets for the next year. For example, product prices or the general inflation rate for next year is announced by a budget officer at the beginning of the budget process. These first-round, lowest-level projections are accumulated at the next level up in the organization, revised and submitted again to the next level, and so on up the hierarchy. At each level, managers ensure that the budget assumptions are consistent across their departments and that each department's forecast is reasonable. Each manager also modifies subordinates' plans with any specialized knowledge the manager has acquired. In most firms, lower-level managers have a significant role in both the initial and revision stages of the budget's preparation.

Exercise 6-1

Shocker Company's sales budget shows quarterly sales for next year as follows:

Quarter 1	10,000 units
Quarter 2	8,000 units
Quarter 3	12,000 units
Quarter 4	14,000 units

Company policy is to have a finished goods inventory at the end of each quarter equal to 20 percent of the next quarter's sales.

Required:

Compute budgeted production for the second quarter of next year.

Solution:

Quarter 2 sales	8,000 units
+ Ending Inventory: 20% of Quarter 3 sales (12,000 × 20%)	2,400 units
− Beginning Inventory: 20% of Quarter 2 sales (8,000 × 20%)	(1,600) units
Budgeted production	8,800 units

As the budget is passed from one level of the organization up to a higher level, potential bottlenecks are uncovered before they occur. For example, if one department's budget calls for 10,000 units of a part and the parts fabrication department can produce only 7,500 units, this bottleneck is identified before production actually begins. At some point, the key assumptions may be challenged by managers with better specialized knowledge. On occasion, the assumptions are revised and the budgets updated.

The budget is revised at the top and passed back down through the organization. Either lower-level managers with specialized knowledge will agree with the changes and adapt to the new plan or they will disagree. If there is enough disagreement and it is made known to senior management, another round of budget revisions will occur.

In summary, organizations use budgets to

1. Assign decision rights.
2. Communicate and coordinate information both vertically and horizontally.
3. Set goals through negotiation and internal contracting.
4. Measure performance.

Concept Questions	Q6–1	How are budgets developed?
	Q6–2	How are key planning assumptions derived?
	Q6–3	Define *budget variance*.
	Q6–4	Are budgets part of the performance measurement system or the performance reward system?
	Q6–5	What are some of the synergies that budgets provide within a large corporation?
	Q6–6	How do budgets partition decision rights within a firm?
	Q6–7	What purposes are served by the budgeting process in a large firm?

B. Trade-Off between Decision Management and Decision Control

The budgeting process plays an important role in both decision management and decision control in organizations. In one survey, over 50 percent of managers agreed that budgets are indispensable in running their business.[4]

1. Communicating Specialized Knowledge versus Performance Evaluation

As the earlier examples describe, budgeting systems perform several functions within firms, including decision management and decision control. In decision management, budgets serve to communicate specialized knowledge about one part of the organization to another part, thereby improving decision making. In decision control, budgets are part of the performance measurement system. Because budgets serve several purposes, trade-offs must be made when a budgeting system is designed or changed. The budget becomes the benchmark against which to judge actual performance. If too much emphasis is placed on the budget as a performance benchmark, then managers with the specialized knowledge will stop disclosing unbiased forecasts of future events and will report conservative budget figures ex ante that enhance their performance measure ex post.

The trade-off between decision management and decision control is best illustrated in marketing. Salespeople usually have specialized knowledge of future sales. This information is important in setting production plans. But if budgeted sales are used to evaluate sales reps at the end of the year (i.e., actual sales are compared with budget), then sales reps have an incentive to ex ante underforecast future sales, thus improving their ex post performance evaluation. However, production plans will then be too low and the firm will not be able to plan the most efficient production schedules.[5] For example, suppose the salespeople underforecast sales by 20 percent. When actual sales are higher than the plant expects, overtime must be paid to produce the extra units. It would have been cheaper to expand the plant's permanent work force.

An important lesson from this chapter is that whenever budgets are used to evaluate managers' performance and then to compensate (or promote) them based on their

---

[4]T. Libby and M. Lindsay, "Beyond Budgeting or Better Budgeting," *Strategic Finance,* August 2007, pp. 47–51.

[5]In some cases, it is possible to structure an incentive contract that induces managers to disclose their private information in an unbiased fashion. See J. Gonik, "Tie Salesmen's Bonuses to Their Forecasts," *Harvard Business Review,* 1978, pp. 116–23; M. Weitzman, "The New Soviet Incentive Model," *Bell Journal of Economics,* Spring 1976, pp. 251–57; and A. Kirby, S. Reichelstein, P. Sen, and Y. Paik, "Participation, Slack, and Budget-Based Performance Evaluation," *Journal of Accounting Research,* Spring 1991, pp. 109–28.

performance relative to the budget target, strong incentives are created for these managers to game the system. Even subjective performance evaluations based on meeting or exceeding the budget create dysfunctional behavior. Gaming occurs in both the budget-setting process and in the actions managers take during the year to achieve the budgeted targets. Most companies report that budgeting induces dysfunctional behaviors, including negotiating easier targets to help ensure they will receive bonuses ("sandbagging"), spending money at the end of the year to avoid losing it in the next budget period, deferring needed spending (maintenance and advertising) to meet the budget, accelerating sales near the end of the period to achieve the budget, and taking a "big bath" when budgets cannot be achieved in order to lower next year's budgets. In rare cases, trying to achieve budget targets has induced managers to commit fraud by recording fictitious revenues or misclassifying expenses as assets.[6]

2. Budget Ratcheting	Using historical data on past performance is a common mechanism for setting next year's budget. Unfortunately, it often leads to a perverse incentive called the *ratchet effect*. The ratchet effect refers to basing next year's budget on this year's actual performance. However, performance targets are usually adjusted in only one direction—upward. A bad year usually does not cause subsequent years' targets to fall. For example, if this year's sales budget is $1 million and the salesperson sells $1.3 million, next year's sales budget becomes $1.3 million. However, if actual sales are only $0.9 million, next year's budget is not cut back to $0.9 million.

H. J. Heinz, a producer of processed food (best known for its catsup) sets next year's profit center budgets at the greater of 115 percent of either last year's budget or last year's actual results. For example, if last year's budgeted earnings were $10 million and actual earnings were $11 million in a particular profit center, next year's profit for this center would be budgeted at $12.65 million ($11 million × 115%). However, if earnings last year were only $9 million, next year's budget would be $11.5 million ($10 million × 115%). Thus, at Heinz budgeted earnings only increase. One study of a large international conglomerate found that when the actual earnings of a subsidiary exceed budgeted earnings by, say, $100,000, the next year's budget is increased by $90,000. However, if actual earnings fall short of the budget by $100,000, next year's budget is only reduced by $40,000.[7] Hence, favorable budget variances are more likely to lead to larger increases than unfavorable variances are to lead to decreases.

This "ratcheting up" of budgets causes employees to temper this year's better-than-budgeted performance to avoid being held to a higher standard in future periods. Many illustrations of dysfunctional behavior induced by the ratchet effect exist:

- In the former Soviet Union, central planners would set a plant's production quota based on past experience. Plant managers meeting their targets received various rewards and those missing the target were punished. This created incentives for managers to just barely exceed their quota.
- Companies often base a salesperson's bonus on meeting a sales target that is based on last year's sales. If salespeople expect an unusually good year, they will try to defer some sales into the next fiscal year. They may take a customer's order but delay processing it until the next fiscal year.
- Budget ratcheting can create incentives for managers to defer making big productivity improvements in any one year, preferring instead to spread them over several years.

---

[6]T. Libby and M. Lindsay, "Beyond Budgeting or Better Budgeting," *Strategic Finance,* August 2007, p. 50.
[7]A. Leone and S. Rock, "Empirical Tests of Budget Ratcheting and Its Effect on Managers' Discretionary Accrual Choices," *Journal of Accounting and Economics,* February 2002.

Managerial Application: Budgeting Practices	Surveys of CFOs, VPs of finance, and controllers about their companies' budgeting practices consistently reveal the following:

Surveys of CFOs, VPs of finance, and controllers about their companies' budgeting practices consistently reveal the following:

- 97 percent of firms prepare annual budgets.
- 75 percent use a combination of top-down and bottom-up methods to build their budgets.
- Most companies take four to eight weeks for their annual budgeting process.
- Companies use budgets as financial planning and business planning tools for decision making, to meet bank disclosure requirements, to manage cash flow, and to tie compensation to achieving budget goals.
- 82 percent of very large companies and 50 percent of small companies tie compensation to meeting budget goals.
- 80–90 percent of companies prepare actual-to-budget variance analysis monthly.

Three interesting insights emerge from these surveys. First, budgeting is pervasive. Second, budgets are used for decision management (planning and coordination) and for decision control (performance evaluation, motivation, and compensation). Third, given the widespread use of a combination of top-down and bottom-up budgeting methods, budgets assemble knowledge.

SOURCES: Centage/Ioma, "Budgeting Survey: Benchmarks & Issues," www.centage.com (2007).

In one survey, nearly 70 percent of respondents report using budget ratcheting.[8] Why do firms ratchet up their budgets given the perverse incentives induced? One possible reason is that even more perverse incentives might arise if they don't. For example, one simple solution to the dysfunctional incentives arising from the ratchet effect is to eliminate budget targets completely and simply base salespeople's salary on actual sales. Assume that budgeted sales next year are $1 million. Instead of paying a commission of 10 percent on all sales of more than $1 million, pay a commission of 2 percent on total sales. Suppose that both commission schemes have the same expected compensation. The 10 percent commission gives the employee five times the incentive (10 percent versus 2 percent) to make an additional sale. Thus, eliminating the $1 million target reduces the commission rate and hence the employee's marginal incentives.

Managerial Application: Budgeting at Best Buy	At Best Buy, with more than 1,100 retail stores across the United States, Canada, and China, budgeting was a nightmare.

At Best Buy, with more than 1,100 retail stores across the United States, Canada, and China, budgeting was a nightmare. It was time consuming and was not helpful at assembling knowledge. Corporate-level planners made broad assumptions about what each store would sell and the resources needed to meet their targets. Best Buy spent four years revamping its budgeting and planning system. First, Best Buy pushed the planning down to the district managers, and then to the stores. The districts and the stores have firsthand knowledge of what the customers want and where the opportunities for cost savings lie. A senior finance analyst at Best Buy states, "There is a gap between what the store managers know about their operations and what corporate knows."

SOURCE: D. Durfee, "The Last Mile," *CFO*, January 2007, pp. 49–55.

---

[8]Grant Thornton and APQC, "Financial Planning and Analysis," www.GrantThornton.com (2015).

Asking the salespeople to estimate next year's sales instead of ratcheting up next year's target eliminates the perverse incentives of the ratchet effect. However, this alternative creates another problem. In particular, salespeople will forecast next year's sales far below what they expect to sell, thereby increasing their expected compensation and communicating too low an expected sales forecast to manufacturing.

Or, instead of ratcheting up to set next year's budget, a central planning group can prepare top-down budgets by using past sales and cost patterns, macroeconomic trends, and customer surveys. But this central forecasting group might be more expensive than simple ratcheting. The direct costs of preparing budgets centrally (personnel and occupancy costs) could exceed the indirect costs from dysfunctional decision making induced by the ratchet effect.

Another way to reduce the problems caused by ratcheting up each year's performance targets is more frequent job rotation. If you know that next year someone else has to meet the sales figures you achieve this year, you will sell more now. However, job rotation destroys job-specific human capital such as customer-specific relationships.

In summary, while the ratchet effect creates dysfunctional behavior, the alternatives might prove more costly. In essence, one agency problem is replaced with another one. Depending on the particular situation, senior managers must choose the lesser of the two evils.

3. Participative Budgeting

The trade-off between decision management and decision control is often viewed as a trade-off between bottom-up and top-down budgeting. Bottom-up budgets are those submitted by lower levels of the organization to higher levels and usually imply greater decision management. An example of a bottom-up budget is the field sales offices' submission of their forecasts for next year to the marketing department. A top-down budget would be the marketing department's use of aggregate data on sales trends to forecast sales for the entire firm and then disaggregate this firmwide budget into field office targets. This top-down budget provides greater decision control. Bottom-up budgeting, in which the person ultimately being held responsible for meeting the target makes the initial budget forecast, is called *participative budgeting*.

Managerial Application: Improving Budgeting

Budgeting is the bane of many executives. About 55 percent of executives say budgeting is too time-consuming, 65 percent believe budgets are slow to detect problems, 50 percent think they quickly get out of date, and 35 percent see budgets as disrupting cooperation within their firms. And 30 percent report budgets not being aligned with the firm's changing business strategy. But over 60 percent of financial executives say their budgets achieve their objectives.

Technology is improving budgeting. Web-based software is replacing numerous nonstandard spreadsheets submitted by operating divisions that often have to be reentered and consolidated with other divisions' spreadsheets. Browser-based budgeting software now allows divisions to enter and revise data remotely using a standard format and allows corporate managers access to the consolidated numbers instantly. Conexant Systems, Inc., a supplier of semiconductor products, uses a Web-based budgeting tool to manage 1,200 cost centers with up to 500 accounts per cost center. Cost center managers enter their own budget data with less help from financial analysts.

SOURCES: T. Reason, "Building Better Budgets," CFO, December 2000, pp. 91–98; D. Dufee, "Alternative Budgeting," *CFO*, June 2006, p. 28; and T. Libby and M. Lindsay, 2007, p. 49.

230   *Chapter 6*

Participative budgeting supposedly enhances the motivation of the lower-level managers by getting them to accept the targets. Whether budgeting is bottom-up or top-down depends in part on where the knowledge is located. If the field salespeople have the knowledge, this would tend to favor a bottom-up approach to link the knowledge and decision rights. If the central marketing organization has better knowledge, a top-down budget is likely to prove better. Which budgeting scheme provides better motivation ultimately depends on the design of the performance measurement and performance reward systems.

A survey of 98 Standard & Poor's 500 U.S. companies found that these firms use participative budgeting more frequently when lower-level managers have more knowledge than central management.[9] Participative budgeting is more frequently observed when managers' rewards are based on the performance against the budget. Likewise, the use of budget-based incentives and the extent of specialized knowledge held by lower-level managers are positively correlated. This evidence is consistent with budgets and performance reward systems being designed to link decision-making rights and specialized knowledge.

Once the budget is set, it becomes the target by which performance is evaluated and rewarded. Some experts argue the budget should be "tight" but achievable. If budgets are too easily achieved, they provide little incentive to expend extra effort. If budgets are unachievable, they provide little motivation. As discussed earlier, most budgets are set in a negotiation process involving lower- and higher-level managers. Lower-level managers have incentives to set a loose target to guarantee they will meet the budget and be favorably rewarded. Higher-level managers have incentives to set a tight target to motivate the lower-level managers to exert additional effort. A study of 54 profit center managers in 12 corporations found that budgeted profits were set so that they were achieved 8 or 9 years out of 10.[10] These managers reported that these loose budgets improved resource planning, control, and motivation.

4. New Approaches to Budgeting

The trade-off between decision management and decision control in budgeting creates tension between the two roles, and these tensions lead to criticism. Budgets are criticized often because they are time consuming to construct and add little value, are developed and updated too infrequently. are based on unsupported assumptions and guesswork, constrain responsiveness and act as a barrier to change, are rarely strategically focused and often contradictory, concentrate on cost reduction and not value creation, encourage gaming and perverse behaviors, reinforce departmental barriers rather than encourage knowledge-sharing, and make people feel undervalued.

These criticisms fail to recognize that budgeting systems are almost universally used and have survived. Thus, they must be yielding benefits at least as large as their costs. The question is whether even more dysfunctional behavior arises when budgets are not used. The fact that so many firms use budgets suggests that forgoing budgets is an unlikely formula for success. One reason firms retain their budgets is because budgets often remain the only central coordinating mechanism within the firm.

Two different approaches are proposed to improve the budgeting process.[11] One method involves building the budget in two distinct steps. The first step, which involves the lowest levels of the organization, is to construct budgets in operational, not financial terms. At this step, budgeting requires data about estimated demand for resources and

[9]M. Shields and S. Young, "Antecedents and Consequences of Participative Budgeting: Evidence on the Effects of Asymmetrical Information," *Journal of Management Accounting Research,* 1993, pp. 265–80.

[10]K. Merchant and J. Manzoni, "The Achievability of Budget Targets in Profit Centers: A Field Study," *Accounting Review* 64 (July 1989), pp. 539–58.

[11]S. Hansen, D. Otley, and W. Van der Stede, "Practice Developments in Budgeting: An Overview and Research Perspective," *Journal of Management Accounting Research* 15 (2003), pp. 95–116.

outputs stated in nonfinancial terms such as units of output, hours of various types of labor, and consumption rates of resources. Operational budgets are in balance when resource consumption requirements equal the resources available for each resource required to operate the firm. The second step develops a financial plan based on the operational plans developed in step one. This two-step process makes the budgeting process more representative of how the organization actually operates by balancing operational requirements. The first step provides a more sophisticated model for balancing capacity. Lower-level managers more easily understand and communicate information in operational rather than financial terms. Lower-level managers' specific knowledge is usually couched in nonfinancial terms, and the first step of the process utilizes their specific knowledge directly.

However, this approach is more costly than traditional budgets (which are stated in financial terms only) because the additional detailed information about individual resources must be collected and managed. Also, this approach, at least as described by its proponents, does not involve a third step whereby the organization iterates between steps one and two until all the various inconsistencies are resolved. For example, consider a package delivery company. Assume that a particular resource such as the number of delivery vans and the number of orders expected to be delivered are in balance. During budget construction, senior executives learn that the average size of each shipment is expected to increase. This increase in the average shipment size must be communicated to the executive responsible for managing the fleet. With a larger average package size, the firm might not have enough capacity to deliver the same number of packages. The firm has to decide whether to increase fleet size, acquire larger trucks, raise the price of deliveries (to reduce the quantity shipped), or some combination of the three. A cost-benefit trade-off must be made somewhere in the firm. Exactly how and where this analysis and decision occurs is not specified by the proponents of the two-step approach to improving budgeting.

Managerial Application: Microsoft's Budgeting System

Microsoft reorganized the company around seven distinct businesses. The budgeting system also changed. Prior to the change, Microsoft's centralized management proved too unwieldy, and its software engineering groups had little responsibility for sales. After the reorganization, each business group had its own CFO responsible for that group's strategy, budgeting, and analysis of market performance and operating expenses. Each of the seven businesses has a budget based on its own product-development strategy and on the firmwide corporate strategy.

The budget process consists of the following steps:

1. Each business reviews its strategy, proposed changes, and investments at the end of June with the CEO.
2. July involves a "deep midyear review" that examines operational trends by geography, business lines, and channels. Based on this evaluation, the corporate office begins setting targets for each group.
3. Once preliminary targets are set by the corporate office, the CEO meets with each business group about the "ambition" for the next year. "Ambition" is the Microsoft CEO's expectation for that business group in terms of revenue growth, earnings, and product development.
4. After the CEO and each business group reach a consensus on the overall targets, then the detailed budgeting begins—roughly an eight-week effort.

SOURCE: T. Reason, "Budgeting in the Real World," *CFO*, July 2005, pp. 43–48

A second approach to improve budgeting involves breaking the so-called annual performance trap. This approach does not use budgets as performance targets. Budgets are still constructed for financial planning, but they are not used for performance evaluation. Rather, firms use relative performance targets of other units or firms and compare these peer-units' performance to the actual performance achieved by the unit being judged. First a peer benchmark group is set for each budget unit. The benchmarks are either different units in the same firm or their leading competitors. Then the unit's actual achieved performance is compared to the actual performance achieved by the benchmark. Actual rewards are then determined subjectively, taking into account not just the benchmark's performance but other financial and nonfinancial performance measures. This approach to improving the budget process decouples financial planning, information communication, and coordination (decision management) from performance evaluation and performance rewards (decision control). Proponents of this approach claim that by decoupling decision management and decision control, decision management is improved because executives have less incentive to game the initial budget estimates. However, the use of relative performance evaluations and subjective evaluations are not without problems. Managers still have incentives to game how the benchmarks are chosen. There are no guarantees that the managers making the subjective evaluations will do so in an unbiased way, and therefore there is no guarantee that the person being evaluated based in part on the performance of some peer group will accept such an assessment without undue griping or without exerting undue influence costs.

No simple "one-size-fits-all" panacea exists for resolving the conflict between decision management versus decision control when it comes to budgeting. Nor is such a solution ever likely to be found. Budgets perform both decision management and decision control roles, and each firm must find the solution that best fits its unique circumstances at that point in time. Budgeting processes (and associated compensation schemes) evolve as the firm's circumstances change.

5. Managing the Trade-Off

To manage the trade-off between decision management and decision control, many organizations put the chief executive officer in charge of the budgeting process. While the actual collection of data and preparation of the budget are formal responsibilities of the chief financial officer or controller, the president or CEO has the final decision rights. There are several reasons for the chief executive to have ultimate control. First, it signals the importance of the budgeting process. Second, the CEO has the specialized knowledge and the overall view of the entire firm to make the trade-offs needed to resolve disagreements among departments regarding key planning assumptions or coordination of activities. McKinsey writes,

> [T]he sales department may desire to sell more than the production department thinks it can produce profitably, or the production department may desire to produce articles which the sales department does not think it can sell, or both the sales and production departments may desire to increase their activities beyond what the financial department thinks can be financed. Obviously the only authority who can decide these questions is the chief executive who is superior to all executives interested in the controversy.[12]

In addition to placing the chief executive in charge of the budgeting process, many firms use a budget committee consisting of the major functional executives (vice presidents of sales, manufacturing, finance, and personnel), with the CEO as chair. This committee seeks to facilitate the exchange of specialized knowledge and reach consensus on disputed issues. In essence, no budget or estimate is accepted until the budget committee approves.

---

[12]McKinsey (1922), pp. 44–45.

Then all the various parts of the organization agree to the inherent exchanges among the various parts of the organization. The budget is the informal set of contracts between the various units of the organization.

Concept Questions		
	Q6–8	Why would managers bias their forecasts when preparing a budget?
	Q6–9	What is a bottom-up budgeting system?
	Q6–10	What is the *ratchet effect?*
	Q6–11	Describe participative budgeting.

C. Resolving Organizational Problems

As the two examples in section A illustrate, budgeting systems are an administrative device used to resolve organizational problems. In particular, these systems help (1) link knowledge with the decision rights and (2) measure and reward performance. The Bay View Country Club example illustrates how budgets provide performance measurements. The Xerox Corporation example illustrates the linking of knowledge and decision rights. This section further describes various budgeting devices, such as short-run versus long-run budgets, line-item budgets, budget lapsing, flexible budgets, and incremental versus zero-based budgets.

1. Short-Run versus Long-Run Budgets

The budgeting examples in section A described annual budgeting processes. Starting in the prior year, firms develop detailed plans of how many units of each product they expect to sell at what prices, the cost of such sales, and the financing necessary for operations. These budgets then become the internal "contracts" for each responsibility center (cost, profit, and investment center) within the firm. These annual budgets are short-run in the sense that they project only one year at a time. But most firms also project 2, 5, and sometimes 10 years in advance. These long-run budgets are a key feature of the organization's strategic planning process.

Strategic planning refers to the process whereby managers select the firm's overall objectives and the tactics to achieve them. It involves deciding what markets to be in, what products to produce, and what price-quality combinations to offer. For example, Time Warner faces the strategic question of whether to provide local telephone service in its cable markets. Making this decision requires specialized knowledge of the various technologies Time Warner and its competitors face, in addition to knowledge of the demand for various future products. Strategic planning also addresses questions of what the organization's future structure must be to support the strategy, including future R&D and capital spending and the financial structure.

Like short-run budgets, long-run budgets force managers with specialized knowledge to communicate their forecasts of future expected events under various scenarios. Long-run budgets contain future capital budgeting forecasts (and thus financing plans) required to implement the strategy. R&D budgets are long-run plans of the multiyear spending required to acquire and develop the technologies to implement the strategies.

In short-run budgets, the key planning assumptions involve quantities and prices. All parts of the organization must accept these annual key assumptions. In long-run budgets, the key planning assumptions involve what markets to be in and what technologies to acquire.

234   *Chapter 6*

Managerial Application: Lenders Want Five-Year Budgets	Firms prepare long-run budgets for a variety of reasons. One reason is that their bankers demand to see budgets that cover the period of the loans extended to the company. Many bank loans are for three to five years. Bank of America often requires borrowers to produce forecasts that cover the duration of the loan request: "We're looking for the cash-flow perspective and how we're getting paid. We build our loan agreements and covenants on that information. We're obviously asking so we understand the risk of a deal." SOURCE: K. Frieswick, "The Five-Year Itch," *CFO*, February 2003, pp. 68–70.

Managerial Application: Rolling Budgets	Many companies, such as Unilever, American Century Investments, and Norwegian StatOil, are replacing their static annual budgets with rolling eight-quarter budgets. Static annual budgets often become out of date. Annual budgets encouraged managers to spend because it was allocated or defer critical spending to meet the annual budget. Rolling budgets enable managers to set more ambitious goals. Unlike static annual budgets, managers are encouraged to react more quickly to changing economic or business conditions. Rolling budgets force managers to better integrate target setting, forecasting, and resource allocation. However, many companies continue to rely on annual budgets because they keep people focused on the end game. SOURCE: R. Banham, "Let it Roll," *CFO*, May 2011, pp. 43–47.

A typical firm integrates short-run and long-run budgeting into a single process. As next year's budget is being developed, a five-year budget is also produced. Year 1 of the five-year plan is next year's budget. Years 2 and 3 are fairly detailed and year 2 becomes the base to establish next year's one-year budget. Years 4 and 5 are less detailed but begin to look at new market opportunities. Each year, the five-year budget is rolled forward one year and the process begins anew.

The short-run (annual) budget involves both decision management and decision control functions, and, as discussed earlier, a trade-off arises between these two functions. Long-run budgets are hardly ever used for decision control (performance evaluation). Rather, long-run budgets are used primarily for decision management. Five- and 10-year budgets force managers to think strategically and to communicate the specialized knowledge of their future markets and technologies. Thus, long-run budgets emphasize decision management more than decision control because less reliance is placed on using them as a performance measurement tool.

Long-run budgets also reduce managers' focus on short-term performance. Without long-term budgets, managers have an incentive to cut expenditures such as maintenance, advertising, and R&D to improve short-run performance or to balance short-term budgets at the expense of the long-term viability of the organization. Budgets that span five years help alert top management and/or the board of directors to the long-term trade-offs being taken to accomplish short-run goals.

Some firms use rolling budgets. A rolling budget covers a fixed time period, such as one or two years. A future period is added as the current period concludes. For example, suppose a two-year rolling budget is used with quarterly intervals. When the current quarter is concluded, a new quarter (two years ahead) is added. In this way, management is always looking at a two-year planning horizon.

Exercise 6-2

Two Internet-based, e-commerce companies were started about two years ago and both went public last month. They have about the same number of employees, but they offer different services (i.e., they are not competitors). Both firms use a one-year budgeting process, but only one firm supplements its annual budget with a three-year budget.

Required:

Offer some plausible reasons why one firm uses only an annual budget and the other firm uses both an annual and a three-year budget.

Solution:

One-year (or short-term) budgets are used as both decision management and decision control mechanisms. They help assemble knowledge for decision making and are also used as benchmarks in performance evaluation. Obviously, these two functions involve trade-offs. Three-year budgets are used almost exclusively as planning documents to help assemble information for decision making. The executives in the company using both one- and three-year budgets must believe first that they have substantial specialized knowledge of long-term (three-year) cash flows and trends, and second that the benefits of assembling this knowledge outweighs the costs of preparing the three-year budget. The nature of the knowledge held by the managers in the other company must be of shorter duration.

Also, the company with the three-year budget might be worried that only using a one-year budget creates short-run incentives for managers to cut spending on R&D and advertising.

---

2. Line-Item Budgets

Line-item budgets refer to budgets that authorize the manager to spend only up to the specified amount on each line item. For example, consider Table 6–3. In this budget, the manager is authorized to spend $12,000 on office supplies for the year. If the supplies can be purchased for $11,000, the manager with a line-item budget cannot spend the $1,000 savings on any other category such as additional office equipment. Because the manager cannot spend savings from one line item on another line item without prior approval, the manager has less incentive to look for savings. If next year's line item is reduced by the amount of the savings, managers have even less incentive to search for savings.

Line-item budgets reduce agency problems. Managers responsible for the line-item budgets cannot reduce spending on one item and divert the savings to items that enhance their own welfare. By maintaining tighter control over how much is spent on particular items, the organization reduces possible managerial opportunism.

TABLE 6-3   **Line-Item Budget Example**

Line Item	Amount
Salaries	$185,000
Office supplies	12,000
Office equipment	3,000
Postage	1,900
Maintenance	350
Utilities	1,200
Rent	900
Total	$204,350

Line-item budgets are quite prevalent in governments. They also are used in some corporations, but with fewer restrictions. Line-item budgets provide more control. The manager does not have the decision rights to substitute resources among line items as circumstances change. To make such changes during the year requires approval from a higher level in the organization.

Line-item budgets illustrate how the budgeting system partitions decision rights, thereby controlling behavior. In particular, a manager given the decision rights to spend up to $3,000 on office equipment does not have the decision rights to substitute office equipment for postage.

3. Budget Lapsing

Another common feature is **budget lapsing**, in which unspent funds do not carry over to the next year. Budget lapsing creates incentives for managers to spend all their budget. Otherwise, not only do managers lose the benefits from the unspent funds, but next year's budget may be reduced by the amount of the underspending.

Budgets that lapse provide tighter controls on managers than budgets that do not lapse. However, the opportunity cost of lapsing budgets can be less-efficient operations. Managers devote substantial time at the end of the year spending their remaining budget, even if it means buying items that have lower value (and a higher cost) than they would purchase if they could carry the remaining budget over to the next fiscal year. Often the firm incurs substantial warehousing costs to hold the extra end-of-year purchases. In one example, a Navy ship officer purchased an 18-month supply of paper to spend the remaining budget. The paper weighed so much that it had to be stored evenly around the ship to ensure the ship did not list to one side.

In addition, budgets that lapse reduce managers' flexibility to adjust to changing operating conditions. For example, if managers have expended all of their budget authority and the opportunity to make a bargain purchase arises, they cannot borrow against next year's budget without getting special permission.

Without budget lapsing, managers could accumulate substantial balances in their budgets. Toward the end of their careers or before taking a new job in the same firm, these managers would then be tempted to make very large expenditures on perquisites. For example, they could take their staff to Hawaii for a "training retreat." Budget lapsing also prevents risk-averse managers from saving their budget for a rainy day. If it is optimum for a manager to spend a certain amount of money on a particular activity, then saving part of that amount as a contingency fund is not optimum. One way to prevent these agency problems is for budgets to lapse.

As in the case of budget ratcheting, the use of budget lapsing (or not) involves a choice between two evils. Agency costs can not be driven to zero; they can only be minimized.

4. Static versus Flexible Budgets

All of the examples in this chapter so far have presented **static budgets**, which do not vary with volume. Each line item is a fixed amount. In contrast, a **flexible budget** is stated as a function of some volume measure and is adjusted for changes in volume. Flexible budgets provide different incentives than do static budgets.

As an example of flexible budgeting, consider a concert where a band is hired for $20,000 plus 15 percent of the gate receipts. The auditorium is rented for $5,000 plus 5 percent of the gate receipts. Security guards costing $80 apiece are hired, one for every 200 people. Advertising, insurance, and other fixed costs are $28,000. Ticket prices are $18 each. A flexible budget for the concert is presented in Table 6–4.

Each line item in the budget is stated in terms of how it varies with volume (ticket sales in this case). Budgets are then prepared at different volume levels. At ticket sales of 3,000, an $11,000 loss is projected. At sales of 4,000 and 5,000 tickets, $3,000 and $17,000 of profits are forecasted, respectively.

Flexible budgets are better than static budgets for gauging the actual performance of a person or venture *after controlling for volume effects*—assuming, of course, that the

TABLE 6-4   **Concert Operating Results**

		Ticket Sales		
	Formula	*3,000*	*4,000*	*5,000*
Revenues	$18N*	$ 54,000	$ 72,000	$ 90,000
Band	$20,000 + 0.15(18N)	(28,100)	(30,800)	(33,500)
Auditorium	$5,000 + 0.05(18N)	(7,700)	(8,600)	(9,500)
Security	$80(N/200)	(1,200)	(1,600)	(2,000)
Other costs	$28,000	(28,000)	(28,000)	(28,000)
Profit/(loss)		$(11,000)	$ 3,000	$ 17,000

*N is the number of tickets sold.

individual being evaluated is not responsible for the volume changes. For example, 5,000 people attended the concert. Table 6–5 compares actual results with the flexible budget for 5,000 tickets. Total profits were $4,100 less than expected. Most of the difference—$3,000— resulted from not being able to sell all 5,000 tickets at $18 each. To sell 5,000 tickets, some were sold at a discount. The actual cost of the auditorium was $9,900 instead of the $9,500 estimated by the flexible budget. The additional $400 was for damage. The budget for the auditorium is automatically increased to $9,500 due to the 5,000 ticket sales, and the manager is not held responsible for volume changes. However, the manager is held responsible for the $400 difference that resulted from damage. Finally, "other costs" were higher by $700 because the promoters underestimated the cost of the rented sound system.

The key question is: Should managers be held responsible for volume changes if the factors that cause the volume changes are outside their control? The initial reaction is no. Managers should be held responsible for volume effects only if they have some control over volume. However, this reasoning is incomplete. Recall the discussion of the controllability principle in Chapter 5. If the manager's actions influence the effects of volume changes, then the manager should not be insulated from the volume effects. For example, if managers can reduce inventory holdings of perishable inventories during economic downturns, they should be held accountable for the entire inventory amount. This creates an incentive to take actions that mitigate or enhance the effect on the organization of the uncontrollable volume.

When should a firm or department use a static budget and when should it use a flexible budget? Because static budgets do not adjust for volume effects, volume fluctuations are passed through and show up in the variances. Thus, static budgets force managers to be responsible for volume fluctuations. If the manager has some control over volume or the consequences

TABLE 6-5   **Concert Operating Results**

	Flexible Budget at 5,000 Tickets	*Actual Results*	*Favorable (Unfavorable) Variance*
Revenues	$ 90,000	$ 87,000	$ (3,000)
Band	(33,500)	(33,500)	0
Auditorium	(9,500)	(9,900)	(400)
Security	(2,000)	(2,000)	0
Other costs	(28,000)	(28,700)	(700)
Profit/(loss)	$ 17,000	$ 12,900	$ (4,100)

238   *Chapter 6*

of volume, then static budgets should be used as the benchmark to gauge performance. And because flexible budgets do adjust for volume effects, volume fluctuations are not passed through and do not show up in the variances. Flexible budgets do not hold managers responsible for volume fluctuations. Therefore, if the manager does not have any control over either volume or the consequences of volume, then flexible budgets should be used as the benchmark to gauge performance. Flexible budgets reduce the risk of volume changes borne by managers.

Flexible budgets are more widely used in manufacturing departments than in distribution, marketing, or administration. Flexible budgets are more widely used in manufacturing than other parts of the firm, because volume measures are readily available.

The preceding examples illustrate how budgets can be adjusted for different levels of volume, but flexible budgeting is more general. Budgets can be adjusted for variables other than volume levels, such as market share, foreign currency fluctuations, inflation, or any other variable outside of the manager's control that can cause the budget to vary.

Exercise 6-3

August Company's budget for the month just ended called for producing and selling 5,000 units at $8 each. Actual units produced and sold were 5,200, yielding revenue of $42,120. Variable costs were budgeted at $3 per unit and fixed costs were budgeted at $2 per unit. Actual variable costs were $3.30 and fixed costs were $12,000.

Required:

  a. Prepare a performance report for the current month's operation.
  b. Write a short memo analyzing the current month's performance.

Solution:

  a. The performance report for the month is given below:

AUGUST COMPANY
Performance Report
Current Month

	I	II	III	IV	V
				Flexible	
	Static		*Variance*	*Budget*	*Variance*
	Budget	*Actual*	*(II – I)*	*(at 5,200)*	*(II – IV)*
Revenue	$40,000	$42,120	$2,120F	$41,600*	$ 520F
Less:					
Variable costs	15,000	17,160	2,160U	15,600†	1,560U
Contribution margin	$25,000	$24,960	$ 40U	$26,000	$1,040U
Less:					
Fixed costs	10,000	12,000	2,000U	10,000	2,000U
Profits	$15,000	$12,960	$2,040U	$16,000	$3,040U

Note: F = Favorable; U = Unfavorable.
*5,200 × $8
†5,200 × $3

continued

> *b.* The question is whether performance should be gauged against a static budget or a flexible budget. Column III in the preceding report benchmarks current performance against the static budget and shows that while revenues were better than planned, variable costs more than consumed the favorable revenue variance. When the unfavorable variance in fixed costs is considered, profits were $2,040 below budget.
>
> The last two columns in the table present a different perspective. Here the benchmark is not the static budget at 5,000 units but rather what the results should have been given the volume of 5,200 units. In this case, profits fell $3,040 short of the flexible plan. If our cost structure stayed the same, then a volume of 5,200 units should have generated profits of $16,000. But variable costs per unit rose more than prices, causing an unfavorable contribution margin variance of $1,040. When the $2,000 unfavorable fixed cost variance is included, there is an unfavorable variance in profits from the flexible budget of $3,040.

5. Incremental versus Zero-Based Budgets

Most organizations construct next year's budget by starting with the current year's budget and adjusting each line item for expected price and volume changes. Because most budgeting processes are bottom up, where the detailed specialized knowledge resides, lower-level managers submit a budget for next year by making incremental changes in each line item. For example, the manager calculates the line item in next year's budget for "purchases" by increasing last year's purchases for inflation and including any incremental expenditures for volume changes and new programs. Only detailed explanations justifying the increments are submitted as part of the budget process. These incremental budgets are reviewed and changed at higher levels in the organization, but usually only the incremental changes are examined in detail. The core budget (i.e., last year's base budget) is taken as given.

Under **zero-based budgeting** (ZBB), each line item in total must be justified and reviewed annually. Departments must defend the entire expenditure (or program expenditure) each year, not just the changes. For example, the Chicago White Sox baseball team uses zero-based budgets whereby all departments must re-justify the necessity of all expenditure. In a zero-based budget review, the following questions are usually asked: Should this activity be provided? What will happen if the activity is eliminated? At what quality and quantity level should the activity be provided? Can the activity be achieved in some other way, such as hiring an outside firm to provide the goods or service (outsourcing)? How much are similar companies spending on this activity?

In principle, zero-based budgeting causes managers to maximize firm value by identifying and eliminating those expenditures whose total cost exceeds total benefits. Under incremental budgeting, in which incremental changes are added to the base budget, incremental expenditures are deleted when their costs exceed their benefits. But inefficient base budgets can continue to exist.

In practice, ZBB is infrequently used. It is supposed to overcome traditional incremental budgeting, but it often deteriorates into incremental budgeting. Under ZBB, the same rationales and justifications as last year's are submitted and adjusted for incremental changes. Because the volume of detailed reports is substantially larger under ZBB than under incremental budgeting, higher-level managers tend to focus on the changes from last year. Moreover, firms usually promote people from within the firm rather than hiring from outside. Promotions tend to be vertical within the same department or division. Internally promoted managers bring with them specific knowledge of their previous job, including

Managerial Application: Budgeting during a Global Economic Crisis	The economic meltdown that started in 2008 with the U.S. housing markets quickly spread to virtually all sectors of the global economy. When asked why the Federal Reserve did not foresee the pending problems, Alan Greenspan, the former Chairman of the Fed, remarked, "We're not smart enough as people. We just cannot see events that far in advance." Greenspan's comments capture the sentiment of CFOs and their ability to prepare accurate forecasts. A survey found that 39 percent of finance executives said they can't forecast more than one quarter out, 15 percent said they can't forecast more than two weeks ahead, and an equal number said, "We are in the dark."

Because preparing accurate one-year-ahead budgets is so difficult, some firms identify a wide range of potential situations that help managers think about plausible, challenging events and how they might respond if blow-ups occur. As one executive stated, "Plan for the worst and hope for the better."

The Principal Financial Group, a life and health insurer, uses a comprehensive forecasting process that includes short- and long-term components. It develops 5-quarter, 5-year, and 10-year forecasts and then introduces variances to these forecasts to understand the impact on earnings, sales, and assets.

Generating timely, reliable financial forecasts requires managers to identify the key drivers of their business. These drivers consist of those operational measures (such as hours of temporary labor required and associated labor rates in a manufacturing plant) that capture how changes in the environment affect the firm. Identifying these drivers helps executives implement decisions quickly when unexpected events occur. While identifying these drivers sounds simple, it can be quite complicated, because it requires management to really understand their firm's business model. For example, the most important driver of satellite service provider Hughes Communication's profitability is new consumer subscriptions. Profit and loss and cash flow forecasts depend critically on new consumer subscriptions. Forecasted new subscriptions affect whether Hughes launches its own satellite (a $400 million project) or continues to lease transponders on other satellites.

SOURCES: V. Ryan, "Future Tense," *CFO*, December 2008, pp. 36–42; and K O'Sullivan, "From Adversity, Better Budgets," *CFO*, June 2010, pp. 45–48.

knowledge of previous budgets. Thus, managers reviewing detailed lower-level budgets have substantial knowledge of those operations, having earlier had decision management rights over at least some of the operations.

ZBB is most useful in organizations with considerable turnover in middle- and senior-level ranks. Management turnover destroys specialized knowledge. Also, ZBB is useful in cases where there has been substantial strategic change or high uncertainty. For example, a defense contractor shifting into civilian markets might want to use ZBB. In these cases, re-justifying each line item annually helps to inform managers with decision control rights of the total costs and benefits of each department or program. However, ZBB is significantly more costly to perform than incremental budgeting.

ZBB is often used in governments because managers with decision management rights tend to be career civil servants in the departments and agencies. Decision control rights are vested in elected officials in the executive and legislative branches. Elected officials have short tenures in monitoring a specific agency and therefore lack detailed specialized knowledge of the department's functions. Zero-based budgets are useful in helping these elected officials make trade-offs between programs, as opposed to just making trade-offs among increments to programs.

Budgeting **241**

Managerial Application: McKinsey & Company's Five Myths and Realities about Zero-Based Budgeting	McKinsey & Company, a global management Consulting firm, encourages firms to adopt ZBB, and thereby become more cost efficient. In promoting ZBB, McKinsey seeks to debunk several myths about ZBB.

Myth one: ZBB simply means building your budget from zero.

Reality: ZBB is a repeatable process to build a sustainable culture of cost management.

Myth two: Implementing ZBB requires cutting "to the bone."

Reality: The degree of cost reduction is based on the company's top-down target.

Myth three: ZBB will overwhelm your business and prevent it from doing anything else.

Reality: Initial rollout of a new ZBB program can be led by a central team and completed in 4 to 10 months.

Myth four: ZBB only focuses on SG&A (Selling, General, and Administrative expenses).

Reality: ZBB can be applied to any type of cost: capital expenditures; operating expenses; sales, general, and administrative costs; marketing costs; variable distribution; or cost of goods sold.

Myth five: ZBB is not designed for growth-oriented companies.

Reality: ZBB is successfully used by growing companies to redirect unproductive costs to more productive areas that drive growth.

Missing from the previous discussion is the necessary changes in the decision rights assignments, performance evaluation, and reward systems (i.e., the organization's architecture) to motivate the managers to identify and eventually cut unproductive costs. But many of these so-called unproductive costs likely benefit existing managers through empire building and perquisite consumption such as corporate jets, lavish team-building retreats, and so forth.

SOURCE: S. Callaghan, K. Hawke, and C. Mignerey, "Five Myths (and Realities) about Zero-Based Budgeting," McKinsey & Company, October 2014.

Concept Questions	Q6–12	What are short-run and long-run budgets?
	Q6–13	What are the advantages and disadvantages of line-item budgets?
	Q6–14	Why do some organizations practice budget lapsing? What are the disadvantages?
	Q6–15	Define *static* and *flexible budgets*. Discuss their advantages and weaknesses.
	Q6–16	Define *incremental* and *zero-based budgeting*. Discuss their advantages and weaknesses.

D. Summary

Budgets are an important mechanism for resolving firms' organizational problems. Budgets help partition decision rights and provide a benchmark against which performance can be measured. By preparing a budget, each unit in the organization implicitly recognizes the decision rights it has authority to exercise.

242   *Chapter 6*

Budgets perform a number of important functions:

1. Coordination of sales, production, marketing, finance, and so forth.
2. Formulation of a profitable sales and production program.
3. Coordination of sales and production with all other activities of the business.
4. Control of expenditures.
5. Formulation of a financial program including investment and financing.

The process of building a budget via a bottom-up, top-down iterative procedure involves assembling specialized knowledge. Budgeting is a negotiation and consensus-building exercise. Thus, budgeting is part of the decision management process. Budgets are also used in decision control. In practice, budgeting involves a trade-off between decision making and control. Ideally, the budget system helps link specialized knowledge and decision rights, thus improving decision making. But if the budget is also used for control and incentives are provided for meeting it, then managers will bias their forecasts during budget preparation to enhance their reported performance relative to their forecast. Again, designers of the budgeting and performance evaluation systems must trade off more accurate forecasts (transfers of specialized knowledge) for incentive effects (control). We return to these incentive effects of budgeting and variance analysis again in Chapters 12 and 13.

One way to prevent lower-level managers from biasing their budgets is to set the budgets at the top, and one top-down method is referred to as the ratchet effect. Here, next year's budget is set based on last year's deviation of actual from budget. When last year's actual results are better than budget, next year's budget increases by more than it would fall were last year's actual results to fall short of last year's budget. This simple ratcheting up of budgets means that managers no longer need to set their own budgets, but it creates incentives for them to withhold effort when they are having a good year to prevent next year's budget from being too challenging.

Short-run budgets involve both decision management and decision control. Long-run budgets (3 to 10 years) place less emphasis on decision control. Managers are less likely to be held responsible for meeting long-term budget targets than short-term budget goals because long-term budgets are used for information sharing.

Line-item budgeting and budget lapsing are devices that constrain managers' decision rights. Line-item budgets prevent managers from shifting resources across different line items in the budget. Budgets that lapse prevent managers from shifting unspent funds from the current year into future years. Both line-item budgeting and budget lapsing reduce managers' incentives to search for cost savings because it is less likely that the manager can spend the savings.

Static budgets hold managers responsible for changes in volume, whereas flexible budgets do not. Even though they might not be able to control volume, managers evaluated under flexible budgets have less incentive to control the consequences of volume changes.

Finally, most budgeting processes are incremental in the sense that managers need only justify changes from last year's budgets. Under zero-based budgeting, managers must justify the entire budget. ZBB is most useful when those managers with decision ratification and monitoring rights over the budget do not have the specific knowledge of the operations. If managers with decision control rights have the knowledge because they have been promoted from within the organization, ZBB usually becomes incremental budgeting.

Appendix: Comprehensive Master Budget Illustration

Chapter 6 discussed the important conceptual issues of budgeting. This appendix illustrates how the various departments of a firm communicate their specialized knowledge via a firmwide master budget. This example demonstrates how various parts of the organization develop their budgets, the importance of coordinating the volume of activity across the different parts of the organization, and how budgets are then combined for the firm as a whole.

1. Description of the Firm: NaturApples

NaturApples is an upstate New York apple processor with two products: applesauce and apple pie filling. The applesauce is eaten as is, and the pie filling is used to make apple pies. Two types of apples are purchased from local growers, McCouns and Grannys. They are processed and packed in tin cans as either applesauce or pie filling. Principal markets are institutional buyers, such as hospitals, public schools, military bases, and universities. NaturApples is a small processor. Its market is regional and is serviced by four sales reps who call on customers in a four-state area. A fifth salesperson markets the products to food distributors, who then sell them directly to restaurants.

The firm is organized into two departments: processing and marketing. Each is headed by a vice president who reports directly to the president. The vice president of finance is responsible for all financial aspects of the firm, including preparing budgets. The three vice presidents and the president make up NaturApples's executive committee, which oversees the budgeting process.

Apples are harvested in the fall of each year. The firm has long-term contracts with a number of local apple growers for their crops. If the local harvest is smaller than expected, additional apples can be purchased in the spot market. Likewise, if more apples are delivered than NaturApples wants to process, the extra apples can be sold in the spot market. Long-term contracts with local farmers and spot-market purchases and sales are the responsibility of the president and the vice president of finance.

Once harvested, the apples are stored either in coolers at NaturApples or in third-party warehouses until NaturApples processes them. Processing takes nine months. In October, the plant starts up after a three-month shutdown. Workers first thoroughly clean and inspect all equipment. The apples begin arriving in the middle of October. By the end of November, the apple harvest is in warehouses or started in production. By June, all of the apples have been processed and the plant shuts down for July, August, and September. NaturApples has a fiscal year starting October 1 and ending September 30.

Each of the two products (applesauce and pie filling) uses a combination of the two types of apples (McCouns and Grannys). The production process consists of inspection, washing, peeling, and coring. The apples are either mashed for applesauce or diced for pie filling and then are combined with other ingredients such as spices and chemical stabilizers and cooked in vats. Both products are immediately canned on a single canning line in five-pound tins and packed in cases of 12 cans per case. The product has a two-year shelf life and is inventoried until ordered by the customer. Independent truckers deliver apples to NaturApples and deliver finished product to customers.

2. Overview of the Budgeting Process

The budgeting process begins in August for the next fiscal year's budget, which will begin in 14 months. That is, even though the current fiscal year beginning in October has not yet started, the preparation of next year's budget begins in August. In August, the coming fall harvest is reasonably well known. The president and the vice president of finance forecast the following year's crop harvest under long-term contract. The vice president of marketing begins forecasting sales that will be made from the harvest a year from this fall. Likewise, the processing vice president forecasts production costs and capacity. Every 2 months for the next 14 months, these budgets are revised with regard to marketing, processing, and apple procurement in light of any new information, and all three vice presidents and the president meet for a morning to discuss their revisions. In June of each year, the final master budget for the next fiscal year, which begins October 1, is adopted by the executive committee and approved by the board of directors. The executive committee also meets weekly to review current-year operations as compared with budget and to discuss other operational issues.

Figure 6–1 is a schematic that illustrates the relations among component budgets and the NaturApples master budget. The master budget encompasses the budgeted income statement, budgeted balance sheet, and budgeted cash flows at the bottom of Figure 6–1. All the other budgets provide the supporting detail, including the various key planning assumptions underlying the master budget.

Three key pieces in NaturApples's budgeting process include apple procurement, sales, and production. These three components must be internally consistent with respect to the amount of each type of apple purchased and the volume of each product produced and sold. Once these three component budgets are determined, the budgeted ending inventory can be calculated. Given the production budget, the direct labor and factory overhead budgets can be generated. These last two budgets and the direct materials budget (from the apple procurement estimates) determine the cost-of-goods-sold budget. The budgeted income statement can then be prepared using these budgets and the budget for administration, which includes senior officer salaries and other administrative expenses not included elsewhere.

Toward the bottom of Figure 6–1 is the capital investment budget, which is based on an analysis of investment proposals. All profitable projects are in the capital investment budget, including those projects started in previous years but not yet completed. The capital investment budget and budgeted income statement are used to prepare NaturApples's budgeted balance sheet and then the cash flow budget. The remainder of this appendix illustrates the preparation of these various component budgets.

244   *Chapter 6*

FIGURE 6-1

Logical flow of components of the master budget

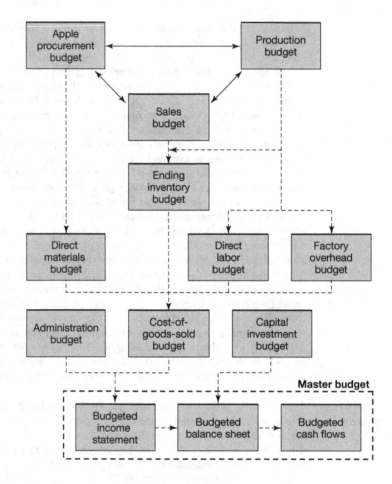

NaturApples uses the following accounting conventions:

1. FIFO is used for inventory accounting.
2. Factory overhead is estimated using a flexible budget.

Variable overhead varies with the number of direct labor hours in the plant. Total overhead is then assigned to product costs using the number of hours of direct labor in the product. Chapter 9 further explains how overhead is assigned to products.

Table 6–6 provides the basic data for the budgeting illustration. This table contains some primary operating data, such as the beginning inventory figures. The bottom half of the table also shows the amount of each type of apple required to make a case of applesauce and a case of pie filling.

By June, the executive committee has agreed on next year's volumes. The sales budget for the next fiscal year is given in Table 6–7. These data are examples of the *key planning assumptions* described in the chapter. The executive committee agrees that the firm should be able to sell 140,000 cases of sauce at $68.95 per case and 60,000 cases of pie filling at $53.95 per case. These quantities and prices were derived after exploring alternative price-quantity combinations. In particular, these price-quantity points represent the managers' best judgment of where profits are maximized. Presumably, higher prices (and thus lower sales) or lower prices (and higher sales) would both result in lower profits than the combinations in Table 6–7.

3. Departmental Budgets

Table 6–8 presents the apple procurement budget. Given the harvest projections and the production plans, NaturApples plans to purchase an additional 50,000 pounds of McCoun apples and sell 910,000 pounds of Granny apples. The total cost of apples is projected to be $6,344,200. The average

TABLE 6-6   **NaturApples**

Basic Data for Budgeting Example for Fiscal Year Beginning 10/1/17

	Cases	Cost/Case	Total
Beginning Inventory			
Sauce	13,500	$57.96	$782,460
Pie filling	2,300	$48.81	$112,263
	McCoun	*Granny*	
Pounds of Apples/Case			
Sauce	60	40	
Pie filling	50	30	

TABLE 6-7   **NaturApples**

Sales Budget for Fiscal Year Beginning 10/1/17

	Budgeted Cases	*Budgeted Price/Case*	*Budgeted Revenue*
Sauce	140,000	$68.95	$ 9,653,000
Pie filling	60,000	53.95	3,237,000
Total			$12,890,000

cost per thousand pounds is $380.32 for McCoun apples and $307.43 for Granny apples. These average cost figures are used later in Table 6–12 to calculate the cost of applesauce and pie filling.

The third major budget component is the production budget presented in Table 6–9. The production budget, the apple procurement budget, and the sales budget must satisfy the following inventory-production-sales identity:

$$\text{Beginning inventory} + \text{Production} = \text{Sales} + \text{Ending inventory}$$

The total units in beginning inventory and this period's production must be either sold or in ending inventory. The beginning inventory numbers are known in advance. Choosing two of the remaining three parameters uniquely determines the third. Given the number of apples purchased, the sales budget, and minimum inventory levels, the production budget is derived from the inventory-production-sales identity as long as the processing department has the capacity.

In the production budget in Table 6–9, notice first that the number of cases budgeted for production is different from the number of cases budgeted for sales in Table 6–7. Ten thousand fewer cases of sauce are planned to be produced than sold. Management has decided to reduce the applesauce inventory. On the other hand, the inventory of pie filling is being increased by 3,000 cases. The last two columns in Table 6–9 display the number of pounds of McCoun and Granny apples needed to produce the budgeted cases. The total pounds of each type of apple (10.95 million of McCouns and 7.09 million of Grannys) is the same as in the procurement budget in Table 6–8, reflecting the coordination process involved in budgeting. All the various parts of the organization end up agreeing on the volume of production.

Tables 6–7, 6–8, and 6–9 correspond to the top three boxes in Figure 6–1. Given these three key component budgets, the remainder of the master budget can be prepared. The next budget to compute is the ending inventory budget. This is presented in Table 6–10. The ending inventory of sauce is budgeted to be 3,500 cases and the ending inventory of pie filling is budgeted at 5,300 cases.

Next is the set of direct labor, direct materials, and factory overhead budgets. These budgets are presented in Tables 6–11, 6–12, and 6–13, respectively. Direct labor, as opposed to indirect labor, represents the time employees are actually working to produce a particular product. Indirect labor represents the time workers are maintaining machines or are idle. (Chapter 9 explains these

TABLE 6-8   NaturApples
Apple Procurement Budget for Fiscal Year Beginning 10/1/17

	Pounds (in 000s)		Price		Cost ($ in 000s)		
	McCoun	Granny	McCoun	Granny	McCoun	Granny	Total
Long-term contracts	10,900	8,000	$380	$310	$4,142.0	$2,480.0	$6,622.0
Market purchases (sales)	50	(910)	450	330	22.5	(300.3)	(277.8)
Total	10,950	7,090			$4,164.5	$2,179.7	$6,344.2
Pounds used					10,950	7,090	
Cost per thousand pounds					$ 380.32	$307.43	

TABLE 6-9   NaturApples
Production Budget for Fiscal Year Beginning 10/1/17

	Budgeted Cases	Pounds of McCouns	Pounds of Grannys
Sauce	130,000	7,800,000	5,200,000
Pie filling	63,000	3,150,000	1,890,000
Total		10,950,000	7,090,000

TABLE 6-10   NaturApples
Ending Inventory Budget for Fiscal Year Beginning 10/1/17 (Cases)

	Sauce	Pie Filling
Beginning inventory	13,500	2,300
Plus: Production	130,000	63,000
Available for sale	143,500	65,300
Less: Cases sold	140,000	60,000
Ending inventory	3,500	5,300

distinctions in greater detail.) Table 6–11 provides the number of direct labor hours needed to per-form each of the processing functions to produce sauce and pie filling. Sauce requires 0.60 direct labor hour (36 minutes) per case and pie filling requires 0.54 labor hour (32.4 minutes). Multiplying these hours per case times budgeted cases determines the total number of direct labor hours for each product for next year (78,000 for sauce and 34,020 for pie filling).

The direct materials budget in Table 6–12 is a straightforward extension of the procurement budget for apples and includes the spices and other ingredients that are added to the sauce and pie filling. The average cost of 1,000 pounds of each type of apple from Table 6–8 is used to cost the quantity of each type of apple in sauce and pie filling. To the cost of apples is added the cost of other ingredients: $0.45 per case for sauce and $0.33 per case for pie filling. Management estimates these costs by taking the known quantities of these other ingredients from the recipes and forecasting any price changes. The total cost of direct materials for sauce is budgeted at $4,623,632, and the total cost of direct materials for pie filling is budgeted at $1,799,841.

Budgeting

TABLE 6-11 NaturApples
Direct Labor Budget for Fiscal Year Beginning 10/1/17

	Direct Labor Hours/Case	
	Sauce	*Pie Filling*
Inspection, washing, peeling, coring	0.30	0.24
Saucing	0.10	0.00
Dicing	0.00	0.04
Cooking	0.10	0.16
Canning	0.10	0.10
Total hours per case	0.60	0.54
× Budgeted cases	130,000	63,000
Budgeted labor hours	78,000	34,020
× Budgeted labor rate	$8.75	$8.75
Budgeted labor cost	$682,500	$ 297,675

TABLE 6-12 NaturApples
Direct Materials Budget for Fiscal Year Beginning 10/1/17

	Sauce		*Pie Filling*	
Cost of Apples				
Thousands of pounds of McCouns	7,800		3,150	
× Average cost of McCouns	$ 380.32	$2,966,496	$380.32	$1,198,008
Thousands of pounds of Grannys	5,200		1,890	
× Average cost of Grannys	$ 307.43	$1,598,636	$307.43	$ 581,043
Total cost of apples		$4,565,132		$1,779,051
Cost of Other Ingredients				
Cost per case	$ 0.45		$ 0.33	
× Number of cases	130,000	$ 58,500	63,000	$ 20,790
Total direct materials cost		$4,623,632		$1,799,841

Table 6–13 presents the factory overhead budget for each product. The top part of Table 6–13 provides the flexible budget for factory overhead. Fixed factory overhead, which contains $650,000 of depreciation, is budgeted to be $1.3 million and variable overhead is budgeted at $13 per direct labor hour. Chapter 9 expands on how these parameters are forecasted. Given these forecasts and the number of direct labor hours from Table 6–11, management calculates the budgeted factory overhead as $2,756,260. This quantity is then divided by the budgeted direct labor hours (112,020 hours) to compute the budgeted overhead rate per hour of direct labor ($24.61). The $24.61 represents the average overhead cost assigned to sauce and pie filling per direct labor hour.

Panel B of Table 6–13 calculates the factory overhead for sauce and pie filling. Since sauce is budgeted to use 78,000 direct labor hours, sauce is allocated $1,919,580 of factory overhead ($24.61 × 78,000 direct labor hours) and pie filling is assigned $837,232 (or $24.61 × 34,020).

Refer to Figure 6–1. Given the direct labor, direct materials, factory overhead, ending inventory budgets, and beginning inventory levels, management can now prepare the budget for cost of goods sold, as shown in Table 6–14. The beginning inventory cost is from Table 6–6. The direct labor and

TABLE 6-13   **NaturApples**

Factory Overhead Budget for Fiscal Year Beginning 10/1/17

A. Factory Overhead Flexible Budget

Fixed factory overhead			$1,300,000
Variable overhead per direct labor hour		$13	
Direct labor hours			
Sauce	78,000		
Pie filling	34,020		
× Budgeted direct labor hours		112,020	
Budgeted variable overhead			$1,456,260
Budgeted factory overhead			$2,756,260
÷ Budgeted direct labor hours			112,020
Budgeted overhead rate per direct labor hour			$ 24.61

B. Factory Overhead

	Sauce	Pie Filling
Direct labor hours	78,000	34,020
Overhead rate per labor hour	× $24.61	× $24.61
Factory overhead cost	$1,919,580	$ 837,232

material and factory overhead costs are taken directly from Tables 6–11, 6–12, and 6–13. Added to these previous data is the cost of cans and packaging materials, $1.20 per case (see Table 6–14). The sum of the beginning inventory and the cost of goods processed is the amount available for sale. From this is deducted the ending inventory to arrive at the cost of goods sold. Because the firm uses FIFO, the ending inventory is valued at the cost of the current units processed. The current processing cost is the total cost of units processed divided by the units processed. The footnote to Table 6–14 indicates that the average cost to process a case of sauce is budgeted at $56.78 and the average cost to process a case of pie filling is budgeted at $47.78. These unit cost figures are used to value the ending inventory.

The administration budget in Table 6–15 contains the remaining operating expenses, including the marketing and finance departments' expenses, trucking costs, and the costs of the president's office. The total of all these administrative costs is $1.19 million.

4. Master Firmwide Budget

The budgeted income statement in Table 6–16 assembles the various pieces from all the earlier statements. The only additional data in Table 6–16 are interest on debt ($380,000) and the provision for corporate income taxes (a 42 percent combined state and federal rate is used). It projects net income after taxes to be $281,420. Clearly, an important question to ask is whether this budgeted profit is high or low, acceptable or unacceptable. To answer this question requires a benchmark for comparison. As we have seen, last year's budget and actuals can provide such a benchmark.

Some managers end their budgeting process with the budgeted income statement, as in Table 6–16. But this statement does not address the firm's cash needs. Just because the firm forecasts positive profits does not mean there will be sufficient cash flow to finance operations. In NaturApples's case, the cost of apples represents about half of total revenues. The apples are harvested and paid for in the fall, but the revenue from selling the processed apples is received over the next 12 months. Therefore, NaturApples must find a source of operating cash to finance its apple procurement.

Table 6–17 presents the budgeted statement of cash flows by quarter. NaturApples must borrow $3,385,722 in the first quarter to finance operations, including the apple purchases. Its beginning

Budgeting

TABLE 6-14 **NaturApples**
Cost-of-Goods-Sold Budget for Fiscal Year Beginning 10/1/17

	Sauce		Pie Filling	
Beginning inventory		$ 782,460		$ 112,263
Cost of goods processed:				
Direct labor cost	$ 682,500		$ 297,675	
Direct materials cost	4,623,632		1,799,841	
Canning ($1.20/case)	156,000		75,600	
Factory overhead cost	1,919,580		837,232	
Total cost of processing		7,381,712		3,010,348
Available for sale		$8,164,172		$3,122,611
Less: Ending inventory*		(198,738)		(253,251)
Cost of goods sold		$7,965,434		$2,869,360

*Calculation of ending inventory (costs per case are not rounded for calculating ending inventories):

	Sauce	Pie Filling
Total cost of processing	$7,381,712	$3,010,348
÷ Cases produced	130,000	63,000
Cost per case	$ 56.78	$ 47.78
× Cases in ending inventory	3,500	5,300
Ending inventory	$ 198,730	$ 253,251

TABLE 6-15 **NaturApples**
Administration Budget for Fiscal Year Beginning 10/1/17

	Administrative Cost
Marketing	$ 470,000
Finance	160,000
Trucking	380,000
President's office	180,000
Total administration	$ 1,190,000

TABLE 6-16 **NaturApples**
Budgeted Income Statement for Fiscal Year Beginning 10/1/17

	Sauce	Pie Filling	Total
Revenue	$9,653,000	$3,237,000	$12,890,000
Less:			
Cost of goods sold	(7,965,434)	(2,869,359)	(10,834,793)
Gross margin	$1,687,566	$ 367,641	$ 2,055,207
Less:			
Administration costs			(1,190,000)
Interest on debt			(380,000)
Net income before taxes			$ 485,207
Taxes (42%)			(203,787)
Net income			$ 281,420

250 *Chapter 6*

TABLE 6-17 **NaturApples**
Budgeted Statement of Cash Flows for Fiscal Year Beginning 10/1/17

	Quarter 1	Quarter 2	Quarter 3	Quarter 4	Annual
Sales in the quarter	$ 3,222,500	$ 3,222,500	$3,222,500	$3,222,500	$12,890,000
80% collected in this quarter	2,578,000	2,578,000	2,578,000	2,578,000	10,312,000
20% collected from last quarter	630,000	644,500	644,500	644,500	2,563,500
Cash from sales	$ 3,208,000	$ 3,222,500	$3,222,500	$3,222,500	$12,875,500
Less:					
Apple purchases	$ 6,344,200	$ 0	$ 0	$ 0	$ 6,344,200
Direct labor	326,725	326,725	326,725	0	980,175
Other ingredients	26,430	26,430	26,430	0	79,290
Variable overhead	485,420	485,420	485,420	0	1,456,260
Fixed factory overhead	162,500	162,500	162,500	162,500	650,000
Administrative costs	297,500	297,500	297,500	297,500	1,190,000
Income taxes	50,947	50,947	50,947	50,947	203,787
Total cash expenses before interest	$ 7,693,722	$ 1,349,522	$1,349,522	$ 510,947	$10,903,712
Cash flows from operations	$(4,485,722)	$ 1,872,978	$1,872,978	$2,711,553	$ 1,971,788
Beginning cash balance	$ 1,500,000	$ 400,000	$ 400,000	$ 613,290	
Less: minimum cash reserves	400,000	400,000	400,000	400,000	
Cash available for operations	$ 1,100,000	$ 0	$ 0	$ 213,280	
New short-term borrowings	$ 3,385,722	$ 0	$ 0	$ 0	
Repayment of loan and interest	0	1,872,978	1,659,698	0	
Outstanding loan balance	$ 3,385,722	$ 1,512,744	$ 0	$ 0	
Interest at 3% per quarter	$ 101,572	$ 45,382	$ 0	$ 0	
Capital expenditures	$ 0	$ 0	$ 0	$ 900,000	
Ending cash balance	$ 400,000	$ 400,000	$ 613,280	$2,424,833	

NOTES:

1. Sales, fixed factory overhead, administrative costs, and income taxes are incurred uniformly over four quarters.
2. Apple purchases are paid in quarter 1.
3. Direct labor, other ingredients, and variable overhead are incurred uniformly over the first three quarters.
4. One-half of the fixed factory overhead is depreciation.
5. 80 percent of sales are collected in the quarter; the other 20 percent are collected in the next quarter.
6. There are no uncollectible accounts.
7. $630,000 of accounts receivable from last year, quarter 4, are collected in quarter 1.
8. All interest in the first two quarters is paid in the third quarter.
9. Minimum cash reserves are $400,000.
10. Beginning cash balance is $1.5 million.
11. Interest on short-term borrowing is 3 percent per quarter.
12. Capital expenditures of $900,000 are paid in quarter 4.
13. Interest expense of $380,000 in Table 6–16 includes interest on short-term borrowing and long-term debt.

cash balance of $1.5 million is insufficient to finance all the apple purchases and production costs. Of this $1.5 million, $400,000 must be kept as minimum cash reserves, leaving only $1.1 million to finance operations. In quarter 2, NaturApples repays $1,872,978 of the loan, leaving a balance of $1,512,744 to be repaid in quarter 3. Interest of 3 percent per quarter is paid in quarter 3 on the outstanding balances in quarters 1 and 2 ($101,572 + $45,382). In quarter 4, capital expenditures of $900,000 are budgeted. The budgeted ending cash balance is $2,424,834. The notes to Table 6–17 explain the quarterly timing of the various cash flows.

Having completed the budgeted statement of cash flows, NaturApples can prepare the budgeted statement of financial position (balance sheet) listing all the assets, liabilities, and equities

TABLE 6-18 NaturApples
Statement of Financial Position for Years Ending 9/30/17 and 9/30/18

	Year Ending 9/30/17	Year Ending 9/30/18
Cash	$1,500,000	$2,424,834
Accounts receivable	630,000	644,500
Inventory:		
Sauce	782,460	198,738
Pie filling	112,263	253,251
Total inventory	894,723	451,989
Fixed assets	2,755,000	3,005,000
Total assets	$5,779,723	$6,526,323
Accounts payable	$1,300,000	$1,765,180
Long-term debt	1,950,000	1,950,000
Shareholder equity	2,529,723	2,811,143
Total liabilities	$5,779,723	$6,526,323

(see Table 6–18). Cash is budgeted to increase from $1,500,000 to $2,424,834. There is no provision at this time to budget a dividend to shareholders, which would decrease the budgeted cash amount and the ending balance in shareholder equity. Budgeted fixed assets are increased by budgeted capital expenditures ($900,000) and decreased by depreciation ($650,000), for a net increase of $250,000. Accounts payable is budgeted to increase from $1,300,000 to $1,765,180. Shareholder equity is budgeted to increase by budgeted net income of $281,420.

Self-Study Problems

Self-Study Problem 1: GAMESS Inc.

GAMESS Inc. develops, markets, packages, and distributes multimedia computer games. GAMESS has outsourced production because it does not believe it can manufacture the games competitively. Its most recent development is an interactive adventure game. Because its multimedia games are different from other computer games in both the physical size of the package and price, GAMESS established a new profit center for the adventure game and future Blu-ray computer games.

GAMESS is in the process of selecting the profit-maximizing price for the new adventure game. Management estimates demand for the new game at various wholesale prices. The retail stores then set the retail price of the game sold to the public. Estimated demand is shown in Table 1.

The manufacturer of the Blu-rays charges GAMESS $9 per Blu-ray produced (assume Blu-rays produced equal Blu-rays sold). Packaging expense is $5 per unit sold. Distribution, which includes the amount paid to distributors for selling the game to retailers, is $3 per unit sold.

Advertising contains fixed and variable elements. The fixed portion is $1 million. The variable portion is computed using the ratio of $1 advertising expense for each $500 of expected sales. Fixed overhead, which includes administration and management salaries, is projected at $2.5 million.

Required:

a. Compute the production, packaging, distribution, advertising, and fixed overhead expenses for the various sales prices and quantities in Table 1. Explain why GAMESS would not consider selling its adventure game for any price other than $44.

b. Actual data for the year are shown in Table 2. Calculate the budget variances.

252 *Chapter 6*

TABLE 1 **Price and Quantity Demanded for Adventure Game**

Wholesale sales price	$40	$44	$48	$52
Sales volume (units)	435,000	389,000	336,000	281,000

TABLE 2 **First-Year Operating Results for Adventure Game**

Sales price	$ 44
Sales volume (units)	389,000
Revenues	$17,116,000
Production costs	3,501,000
Packaging	1,798,700
Distribution	1,633,800
Advertising	1,148,232
Fixed overhead	2,506,200
Net income	$ 6,528,068

Solution:

    a. $44 is the profit-maximizing price, as seen in Table 3.

    b. The variances from the flexible budget are computed as follows:

Sales price	$ 44		
Sales volume (units)	389,000		
	Actual	*Budgeted*	*Variance*
Sales	$17,116,000	$17,116,000	$0
Production	3,501,000	3,501,000	0
Packaging	1,798,700	1,945,000	146,300
Distribution	1,633,800	1,167,000	(466,800)
Advertising	1,148,232	1,034,232	(114,000)
Fixed overhead	2,506,200	2,500,000	(6,200)
Net income	$ 6,528,068	$ 6,968,768	$(440,700)

TABLE 3 **Sales Price**

	$40	*$44*	*$48*	*$52*
Sales volume (units)	435,000	389,000	336,000	281,000
Sales	$17,400,000	$17,116,000	$16,128,000	$14,612,000
Production	3,915,000	3,501,000	3,024,000	2,529,000
Packaging	2,175,000	1,945,000	1,680,000	1,405,000
Distribution	1,305,000	1,167,000	1,008,000	843,000
Advertising	1,034,800	1,034,232	1,032,256	1,029,224
Fixed overhead	2,500,000	2,500,000	2,500,000	2,500,000
Net income	$ 6,470,200	$ 6,968,768	$ 6,883,744	$ 6,305,776

Budgeting **253**

Self-Study Problem 2: Sandy Cove Bank

Sandy Cove is a new small commercial bank in Sandy Cove, Michigan. The bank limits interest rate risk by matching the maturity of its assets to the maturity of its liabilities. By maintaining a spread between interest rates charged and interest rates paid, the bank plans to earn a small income. Management establishes a flexible budget based on interest rates for each department.

The Boat and Car Loan Department offers five-year loans. It matches certificates of deposit (CDs) against car and boat loans. Given all the uncertainty about interest rates, management believes that five-year savings interest rates could vary between 2 percent and 16 percent for the coming year. The savings rate is the rate paid on CD savings accounts. The loan rate is the rate charged on auto and boat loans. Table 1 shows the expected new demand for fixed-rate, five-year loans and the new supply of fixed-rate, five-year savings accounts at various interest rates. There are no loans from previous years. Note that the department maintains a 4 percent spread between loan and savings rates to cover processing, loan default, and overhead.

The amount of new loans granted is always the lesser of the loan demand and loan supply. For simplicity, this bank may lend 100 percent of deposits. Although rates are set nationally, the bank may pay or charge slightly different rates to limit demand or boost supply as needed in its local market.

The Boat and Car Loan Department incurs processing, loan default, and overhead expenses related to these accounts. The first two expenses vary, depending on the dollar amount of the accounts. The annual processing expense is budgeted to be 1.5 percent of the loan accounts. Default expense is budgeted at 1 percent of the amount loaned per year. Again, loans and savings would ideally be the same. Overhead expenses are estimated to be $30,000 for the year, regardless of the amount loaned.

Required:

a. Calculate the processing, loan default, and overhead expenses for each possible interest rate.

b. Create an annual budgeted income statement for five-year loans and deposits for the Boat and Car Loan Department given a savings interest rate of 4 percent. Remember to match supply and demand.

c. Table 2 shows the actual income statement for the Boat and Car Loan Department. Included are the actual loans and savings for the same period. Calculate the variances and provide a possible explanation.

TABLE 1   Demand and Supply of Five-Year Funds

Loan Rate	Loan Demand	Savings Rate	Savings Supply
6%	$12,100,000	2%	$ 4,700,000
7	10,000,000	3	5,420,000
8	8,070,000	4	8,630,000
9	6,030,000	5	9,830,000
10	4,420,000	6	11,800,000

TABLE 2   Actual Income Statement of the Boat and Car Loan Department

Interest income	$ 645,766
Interest expense	314,360
Net interest income	$ 331,406
Fixed overhead	30,200
Processing expense	130,522
Default expense	77,800
Net income	$ 92,884
Loans	$8,062,000
Deposits	$8,123,000

254 *Chapter 6*

Solution:

a. Flexible budget for the Boat and Car Loan Department:

	($ in Millions)					
Savings Rate	Loan Demand	Savings Supply	New Business	Loan Processing	Default Expense	Overhead Expense
2%	$12.10	$4.70	$4.70	$70,500	$47,000	$30,000
3	10.00	5.42	5.42	81,300	54,200	30,000
4	8.07	8.63	8.07	121,050	80,700	30,000
5	6.03	9.83	6.03	90,450	60,300	30,000
6	4.42	11.80	4.42	66,300	44,200	30,000

b. Budgeted income statement, 4 percent savings rate for the Boat and Car Loan Department:

Interest income	$645,600*
Interest expense	322,800[†]
Net interest income	$322,800
Fixed overhead	30,000
Processing expense	121,050
Default expense	80,700
Net income	$ 91,050

*$645,600 = $8,070,000 × 8%
[†]$322,800 = $8,070,000 × 4%

c. Variance report:

	Actual	Budget @ 4%	Fav. (Unfav.) Variance
Interest income	$ 645,766	$ 645,600	$ 166
Interest expense	314,360	322,800	8,440
Net interest income	$ 331,406	$ 322,800	$ 8,606
Fixed overhead	30,200	30,000	(200)
Processing expense	130,522	121,050	(9,472)
Default expense	77,800	80,700	2,900
Net income	$ 92,884	$ 91,050	$ 1,834
Loans	$8,062,000	$8,070,000	$ (8,000)
Deposits	$8,123,000	$8,070,000	$(53,000)

Even though loans were lower and deposits were higher than expected, interest income was higher and interest expense was lower than expected. The answer can be obtained by calculating the average interest rates earned and paid. On $8,062,000 worth of loans, Sandy Cove earned $645,766 interest, or 8.01 percent (0.01 percent more than expected). Similarly, it paid only 3.87 percent (0.13 percent less) on deposits. Therefore, the net interest income variance of $8,606 is a combination of two effects: the variance in the actual loans and deposits (quantity) and the variance in the interest rates (price). The combined effects are a favorable interest income variance, a favorable interest expense variance, and an overall favorable net interest income variance.

At a savings interest rate of 4 percent, there is an excess supply of deposits over demand for loans. The Boat and Car Loan Department lowered the interest rate on deposits to stem additional deposits. The increase in the interest rate on loans can be attributed only to an increase in the demand for loans, which resulted in the department charging a slightly higher average interest rate.

The higher processing expense could be related to the higher number of accounts processed and improvements in the default rate. That is, the favorable default expense could be attributed to an improved screening process—related to spending more on processing.

Problems

P 6–1:   G. Bennett Stewart on Management Incentives

I've given a good deal of thought to this issue of how companies . . . go about negotiating objectives with their different business units. The typical process in such cases is that once the parent negotiates a budget with a unit, the budget then becomes the basis for the bonus. And they are also typically structured such that the bonus kicks in when, say, 80 percent of the budgeted performance is achieved; and the maximum bonus is earned when management reaches, say, 120 percent of the budgeted level. There is thus virtually no downside and very limited upside.

Now, because the budget is negotiated between management and headquarters, there is a circularity about the whole process that makes the resulting standards almost meaningless. Because the budget is intended to reflect what management thinks it can accomplish—presumably without extraordinary effort and major changes in the status quo—the adoption of the budget as a standard is unlikely to motivate exceptional performance, especially since the upside is so limited. Instead it is likely to produce cautious budgets and mediocre performance.

So, because of the perverse incentives built into the budgeting process itself, I think it's important for a company to break the connection between the budget and planning process on the one hand and the bonus systems on the other hand. The bonuses should be based upon absolute performance standards that are not subject to negotiation.

Required:

Critically evaluate this quotation.

SOURCE: B. Stewart, "CEO Roundtable on Corporate Structure and Management Incentives," *Journal of Applied Corporate Finance*, Fall 1990, p. 27.

P 6–2:   Investment Banks

Rogers Petersen and Cabots are two of the five largest investment banks in the United States. Last year, there was a major scandal at Cabots involving manipulation of some auctions for government bonds. A number of senior partners at Cabots were charged with price fixing in the government bond market. The ensuing investigation led four of the eight managing directors (the highest-ranking officials at Cabots) to resign. A new senior managing director was brought in from outside to run the firm. This individual recruited three outside managing directors to replace the ones who resigned. There was then a thorough housecleaning. In the following six months, 15 additional partners and more than 40 senior managers left Cabots and were replaced, usually with people from outside the firm.

Rogers Petersen has had no such scandal, and almost all of its senior executives have been with the firm for all of their careers.

Required:

    a. Describe zero-based budgeting.

    b. Which firm, Rogers Petersen or Cabots, is most likely to be using ZBB? Why?

256   *Chapter 6*

P 6–3:   Ice Storm

In March, a devastating ice storm struck Monroe County, New York, causing millions of dollars of damage. Mathews & Peat (M&P), a large horticultural nursery, was hit hard. As a result of the storm, $653,000 of additional labor and maintenance costs were incurred to clean up the nursery, remove and replace damaged plants, repair fencing, and replace glass broken when nearby tree limbs fell on some of the greenhouses.

Mathews & Peat is a wholly owned subsidiary of Agro Inc., an international agricultural conglomerate. The manager of Mathews & Peat, R. Dye, is reviewing the operating performance of the subsidiary for the year. Here are the results for the year as compared with budget:

MATHEWS & PEAT
Summary of Operating Results for the Current Year ($000s)

	Actual Results	*Budgeted Results*	*Actual as % of Budget*
Revenues	$32,149	$31,682	101%
Less			
Labor	13,152	12,621	104
Materials	8,631	8,139	106
Occupancy costs*	4,234	4,236	100
Depreciation	2,687	2,675	100
Interest	1,875	1,895	99
Total expenses	$30,579	$29,566	103%
Operating profits	$ 1,570	$ 2,116	74%

After thinking about how to present the performance of M&P for the year, Dye decides to break out the costs of the ice storm from the individual items affected by it and report the storm separately. The total cost of the ice storm, $653,000, consists of additional labor costs of $320,000, additional materials of $220,000, and additional occupancy costs of $113,000. These amounts are net of the insurance payments received due to the storm. The alternative performance statement follows:

MATHEWS & PEAT
Summary of Operating Results for the Current Year ($000s)

	Actual Results	*Budgeted Results*	*Actual as % of Budget*
Revenues	$32,149	$31,682	101%
Less			
Labor	12,832	12,621	102
Materials	8,411	8,139	103
Occupancy costs	4,121	4,236	97
Depreciation	2,687	2,675	100
Interest	1,875	1,895	99
Total expenses	29,926	29,566	101%
Operating profits before ice storm costs	2,223	2,116	105%
Ice storm costs	653	0	
Operating profits after ice storm costs	$ 1,570	$ 2,116	74%

Required:

    a. Put yourself in Dye's position and write a short, concise cover memo for the second operating statement summarizing the essential points you want to communicate to your superiors.

    b. Critically evaluate the differences between the two performance reports as presented.

P 6–4: Budget Lapsing versus Line-Item Budgets

    a. What is the difference between budget lapsing and line-item budgets?

    b. What types of organizations would you expect to use budget lapsing?

    c. What types of organizations would you expect to use line-item budgets?

P 6–5: DMP Consultants

You work in the finance department of a telecommunications firm with a large direct sales force selling high-speed fiber optics access lines to companies wanting telephone and Internet access. Your firm uses a top-down budget that sets the sales quota for each of its 180 salespeople. The salespeople are compensated based on a commission as well as a bonus whenever actual sales exceed their individual budgeted sales quota. Each salesperson's quota is estimated by senior marketing managers in the corporate office based on the size of each customer in that salesperson's geographic territory and projected growth of business in that territory.

DMP Consultants specializes in redesigning antiquated budgeting systems. DMP has made a presentation to your finance department after conducting a thorough analysis of your firm's sales force budgeting system. DMP Consultants has emphasized that your current budgeting system does not take advantage of what your salespeople know about future sales to their customer regions. By ignoring this information, your firm does not effectively plan for this growth, and you are at a competitive disadvantage when deciding to add capacity to your fiber optic network in a timely and efficient way. Moreover, DMP points to extensive research documenting that when people participate in setting budgets that are used to evaluate their performance, these people more readily accept the budgets and there is an increase in employee morale. That is, "participative budgeting" (where employees who are judged against the budget participate in setting the budget) results in happier, more motivated employees. DMP Consultants has made a proposal to implement a bottom-up, participative budgeting scheme to replace your top-down system.

You have been asked to write a short memo to the head of the finance department that analyzes the pros and cons of DMP's proposal.

P 6–6: Federal Insurance

Two years ago, Federal Insurance was charged with making misleading marketing claims about the way it was selling its insurance products. In response to these allegations and subsequent investigations, Federal's board of directors fired the chief executive officer (CEO), the chief financial officer (CFO), and the senior vice presidents of marketing and underwriting. They replaced these managers last year with other managers from within the insurance industry, but from firms other than Federal.

A similar insurance firm, Northeast, is about the same size as Federal, operates in the same states, and writes the same lines of insurance (home, auto, life). Both firms prepare detailed annual budgets.

Which of the two firms, Federal or Northeast, is more likely to use zero-based budgeting and why?

P 6–7: Golf World

Golf World is a 1,000-room luxury resort with swimming pools, tennis courts, three golf courses, and many other resort amenities.

The head golf course superintendent, Sandy Green, is responsible for all golf course maintenance and conditioning. Green also has the final say as to whether a particular course is open or closed due to weather conditions and whether players can rent motorized riding golf carts for use on a particular course. If the course is very wet, the golf carts will damage the turf, which Green's maintenance crew will have to repair. Because she is out on the courses every morning supervising the maintenance crews, she knows the condition of the courses.

Wiley Grimes is in charge of the golf cart rentals. His crew maintains the golf cart fleet of more than 200 cars, cleans them, puts oil and gas in them, and repairs minor damage. He also is responsible for leasing the carts from the manufacturer, including the terms of the lease, the number of carts to lease, and the choice of cart vendor. When guests arrive at the golf course to play, they pay greens fees to play and a cart fee if they wish to use a cart. If they do not wish to rent a cart, they pay only the greens fee and walk the course.

Grimes and Green manage separate profit centers. The golf cart profit center's revenue is composed of the fees collected from the carts. The golf course profit center's revenue is from the greens fees collected. When the results from April were reviewed, golf cart operating profits were only 49 percent of budget. Wiley argued that the poor results were due to the unusually heavy rains in April. He complained that there were several days when, though only a few areas of the course were wet, the entire course was closed to carts because the grounds crew was too busy to rope off these areas.

To better analyze the performance of the golf cart profit center, the controller's office recently implemented a flexible budget based on the number of cart rentals:

GOLF WORLD
Golf Cart Profit Center
Operating Results—April

	Static Budget	Actual Results	Variance from Static Budget	Flexible Budget	Variance from Flexible Budget
Number of cart rentals	6,000	4,000	2,000	4,000	0
Revenues (@ $25/cart)	$150,000	$100,000	$50,000U	$100,000	0
Labor (fixed cost)	7,000	7,200	200U	7,000	200U
Gas and oil (@ $1/rental)	6,000	4,900	1,100F	4,000	900U
Cart lease (fixed cost)	40,000	40,000	0	40,000	0
Operating profit	$ 97,000	$ 47,900	$49,100U	$ 49,000	$1,100U

NOTE: F = Favorable; U = Unfavorable.

Required:

    a. Evaluate the performance of the golf cart profit center for the month of April.

    b. What are the advantages and disadvantages of the controller's new budgeting system?

    c. What additional recommendations would you make regarding the operations of Golf World?

P 6–8: Coating Department

The coating department of a parts manufacturing department coats various parts with an antirust, zinc-based material. The parts to be processed are loaded into baskets; the baskets are passed through a coating machine that dips the parts into the zinc solution. The machine then heats the parts to ensure that the coating bonds properly. All parts being coated are assigned a cost for the coating department based on the number of hours the parts spend in the coating machine. Prior to the beginning of the year, cost categories are accumulated by department (including the coating department). These cost categories are classified as either fixed or variable and then a flexible budget for the department is constructed. Given an estimate of machine hours for the next year, the coating department's projected cost per machine hour is computed.

Here are data for the last three operating years. Expected coating machine hours for 2017 are 16,000 hours.

COATING DEPARTMENT
Operating Data

	2014	2015	2016
Machine hours	12,500	8,400	15,200
Coating materials	$ 51,375	$ 34,440	$ 62,624
Engineering support	27,962	34,295	31,300
Maintenance	35,850	35,930	36,200
Occupancy costs (square footage)	27,502	28,904	27,105
Operator labor	115,750	78,372	147,288
Supervision	46,500	47,430	49,327
Utilities	12,875	8,820	16,112
Total costs	$317,814	$268,191	$369,956

Required:

   a. Estimate the coating department's flexible budget for 2017. Explicitly state and justify the assumptions used in deriving your estimates.

   b. Calculate the coating department's cost per machine hour for 2017.

P 6–9: Marketing Plan

Robin Jensen, manager of market planning for Viral Products of the IDP Pharmaceutical Co., is responsible for advertising a class of products. She has designed a three-year marketing plan to increase the market share of her product class. Her plan involves a major increase in magazine advertising. She has met with an advertising agency that has designed a three-year ad campaign involving 12 separate ads that build on a common theme. Each ad will run in three consecutive monthly medical magazines and then be followed by the next ad in the sequence. Up to five medical journals will carry the ad campaign. Direct mail campaigns and direct sales promotional material will be designed to follow the theme of the ad currently appearing. The accompanying table summarizes the cost of the campaign:

	Year 1	Year 2	Year 3	Year 4
Number of ads	4	4	4	12
Number of magazines	5	5	4	
Cost per ad	$ 6,000	$ 6,200	$ 6,500	
Advertising cost	$120,000	$124,000	$104,000	$348,000

The firm's normal policy is to budget each year as a separate entity without carrying forward unspent monies. Jensen is requesting that, instead of just approving the budget for next year (Year 1 above), the firm approve and budget the entire three-year project. This would allow her to move forward with her campaign and give her the freedom to apply any unspent funds in one year to the next year or to use them in another part of the campaign. She argues that the ad campaign is an integrated project stretching over three years and should be either approved or rejected in its entirety.

Required:

Critically evaluate Jensen's request and make a recommendation as to whether a three-year budget should be approved per her proposal. (Assume that the advertising campaign is expected to be a profitable project.)

P 6–10: Potter-Bowen

Potter-Bowen (PB) manufactures and sells postage meters throughout the world. Postage meters print the necessary postage on envelopes, eliminating the need to affix stamps. The meter keeps track of the postage, the user takes the meter's counter to a post office and pays money, and the post office initializes the meter to print postage totaling that amount. The firm offers about 30 different postage systems, ranging from small manual systems (costing a few hundred dollars) to large automated ones (costing up to $75,000).

PB is organized into Research and Development, Manufacturing, and Marketing. Marketing is further subdivided into four sectors: North America, South America, Europe, and Asia. The North American marketing sector has a sales force organized into 32 regions with approximately 75 to 200 salespeople per region.

The budgeting process begins with the chief financial officer (CFO) and the vice president of marketing jointly projecting the total sales for the next year. Their staffs look at trends of the various PB models and project total unit sales by model within each marketing sector. Price increases are forecast and dollar sales per model are calculated. The North American sector is then given a target number of units and a target revenue by model for the year. The manager of the North American sector, Helen Neumann, and her staff then allocate the division's target units and target revenue by region.

The target unit sales for each model per region are derived by taking the region's historical percentage sales for that machine times North America's target for that model. For example, model 6103 has North American target unit sales of 18,500 for next year. The Utah region last year sold 4.1 percent of all model 6103s sold in North America. Therefore, Utah's target of 6103s for next year is 758 units ($4.1\% \times 18,500$). The average sales price of the 6103 is set at $11,000. Thus, Utah's revenue budget for 6103s is $8,338,000. Given the total forecasted unit sales, average selling prices, and historical sales of each model in all regions, each region is assigned a unit target and revenue budget by model. The region's total revenue budget is the sum of the individual models' revenue targets.

Each salesperson in the region is given a unit and revenue target by model using a similar procedure. If Gary Lindenmeyer (a salesperson in Utah) sold 6 percent of Utah's 6103s last year, his unit sales target of 6103s next year is 45 units ($6\% \times 758$). His total revenue target for 6103s is $495,000 (or $45 \times \$11,000$). Totaling all the models gives each salesperson's total revenue budget. Salespeople are paid a fixed salary plus a bonus. The bonus is calculated based on the following table:

% of Total Revenue Target Achieved	Bonus
< 90%	No bonus
90–100%	5% of salary
101–110	10% of salary
111–120	20% of salary
121–130	30% of salary
131–140	40% of salary
141–150	50% of salary
>150%	60% of salary

Required:

Critically evaluate PB's sales budgeting system and sales force compensation system. Describe any potential dysfunctional behaviors that PB's systems are likely to generate.

P 6–11: Feder Purchasing Department

The purchasing department at Feder buys all of its raw materials, supplies, and parts. This department is a cost center. It uses a flexible budget based on the number of different items purchased each month to forecast spending and as a control mechanism.

At the beginning of February, the purchasing department expected to purchase 8,200 different items. Given this expected number of purchased items, purchasing calculated its flexible budget for February to be $1,076,400. In reviewing actual spending in February, the purchasing department was over its flexible budget by $41,400 (unfavorable) when calculated using the actual number of items purchased. Actual spending in February was $1,175,000, and the department purchased 9,300 units.

Budgeted fixed cost and budgeted variable cost per item purchased remained the same in the flexible budgets calculated at the beginning and end of February.

Required:

Calculate the fixed cost and the variable cost per item purchased used in the purchasing department's flexible budget in February.

P 6–12: Access.Com

Access.Com produces and sells software to libraries and schools to block access to websites deemed inappropriate by the customer. In addition, the software also tracks and reports on websites visited and advises the customer of other websites the customer might choose to block. Access.Com's software sells for between $15,000 and $20,000.

Three account managers (V. J. Singh, A. C. Chen, and P. J. Martinez) sell the software and are paid a fixed salary plus a percentage of all sales in excess of targeted (budgeted) sales. Vice President of Marketing S. B. Ro sets the budgeted sales amount for each account manager. The following table reports actual and budgeted sales for the three account managers for the past five years.

	A. C. Chen		V. J. Singh		P. J. Martinez	
	Actual	*Budget*	*Actual*	*Budget*	*Actual*	*Budget*
2003	$1.630	$1.470	$2.240	$2.400	$2.775	$2.695
2004	1.804	1.614	2.586	2.384	2.995	2.767
2005	1.685	1.785	2.406	2.566	2.876	2.972
2006	1.665	1.775	2.600	2.550	2.698	2.963
2007	1.924	1.764	2.385	2.595	3.107	2.936

Required:

a. Based on the data in the table, describe the process used by Ro to set sales quotas for each account manager.

b. Discuss the pros and cons of Access.Com's budgeting process for setting account managers' sales targets.

P 6–13:   Videx

Videx is the premier firm in the security systems industry. Martha Rameriz is an account manager at Videx responsible for selling residential systems. She is compensated based on beating a predetermined sales budget. The last seven years' sales budgets and actual sales data follow. Videx sets its sales budgets centrally in a top-down fashion.

Year	Budget	Actual	Difference
1	$ 850,000	$ 865,000	$ 15,000
2	862,000	888,800	26,800
3	884,000	852,000	–32,000
4	884,000	895,000	11,000
5	893,000	878,000	–15,000
6	893,000	902,000	9,000
7	901,000		
Average	881,000	880,133	2,467
Standard deviation	18,385	18,970	21,715
Median	884,000	883,400	10,000

Required:

a. Martha Rameriz sells $908,000 in year 7. What budget will she be assigned for year 8?

b. Suppose Rameriz sells $900,000 of systems in year 7. What budget will she be assigned in year 8?

P 6–14:   New York Fashions

New York Fashions owns 87 women's clothing stores in shopping malls. Corporate headquarters of New York Fashions uses flexible budgets to control the operations of each of the stores. The following table presents the August flexible budget for the New York Fashions store located in the Crystal Lakes Mall:

NEW YORK FASHIONS—CRYSTAL LAKES MALL STORE
Flexible Budget
August

Expense	Fixed	Variable
Cost of goods sold		45%
Management	$ 7,000	1
Salespersons	2,000	8
Rent	12,000	5
Utilities	900	
Other	1,500	

Variable costs are based on a percentage of revenues.

Required:

 a. Revenues for August were $80,000. Calculate budgeted profits for August.

 b. Actual results for August are summarized in the following table:

**NEW YORK FASHIONS—CRYSTAL LAKES
MALL STORE**
Actual Results from Operations
August

Revenues	$ 80,000
Cost of goods sold	38,000
Management	7,600
Salespersons	9,800
Rent	16,000
Utilities	875
Other	1,400

Prepare a report for the New York Fashions—Crystal Lakes Mall store for the month of August comparing actual results to the budget.

 c. Analyze the performance of the Crystal Lakes Mall store in August.

 d. How does a flexible budget change the incentives of managers held responsible for meeting the flexible budget as compared to the incentives created by meeting a static (fixed) budget?

P 6–15: International Telecon

You are working in the office of the vice president of administration at International Telecon (IT) as a senior financial planner. IT is a Fortune 500 firm with sales approaching $1 billion. IT provides long-distance satellite communications around the world. Deregulation of telecommunications in Europe has intensified worldwide competition and has increased pressures inside IT to reduce costs so it can lower prices without cutting profit margins.

IT is divided into several profit and cost centers. Each profit center is further organized as a series of cost centers. Each profit and cost center submits a budget to IT's vice president of administration and then is held responsible for meeting that budget. The VP of administration described IT's financial control, budgeting, and reporting system as "pretty much a standard, state-of-the-art approach where we hold our people accountable for producing what they forecast."

Your boss has assigned you the task of analyzing firmwide supplies expenditures, with the goal of reducing waste and lowering expenditures. Supplies include all consumables ranging from pencils and paper to electronic subcomponents and parts costing less than $1,000. Long-lived assets that cost under $1,000 (or the equivalent dollar amount in the domestic currency for foreign purchases) are not capitalized (and then depreciated) but are categorized as supplies and written off as expenses in the month purchased.

You first gather the last 36 months of operating data for both supplies and payroll for the entire firm. The payroll data help you benchmark the supplies data. You divide each month's payroll and supplies amount by revenues in that month to control for volume and seasonal fluctuations. The accompanying graph plots the two data series.

Payroll fluctuates from 35 to 48 percent of sales, and supplies fluctuate from 13 to 34 percent of sales. The graph contains the last three fiscal years of supplies and payroll, divided by the vertical lines. For financial and budgeting purposes, IT is on a calendar (January–December) fiscal year.

International Telecon monthly payroll and supply expenses, last 36 months

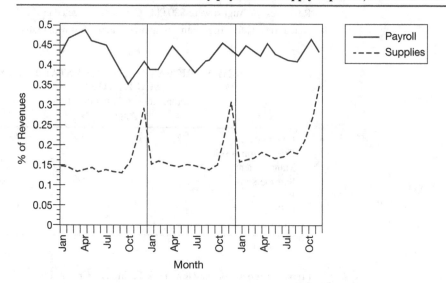

Besides focusing on consolidated firmwide spending, you prepare disaggregated graphs like the one shown, but at the cost and profit center levels. The general patterns observed in the consolidated graphs are repeated in general in the disaggregated graphs.

Required:

a. Analyze the time-series behavior of supplies expenditures for IT. What is the likely reason for the observed patterns in supplies?

b. Given your analysis in part (*a*), what corrective action might you consider proposing? What are its costs and benefits?

P 6–16:   Adrian Power

Adrian Power manufactures small power supplies for car stereos. The company uses flexible budgeting techniques to deal with the seasonal and cyclical nature of the business. The accounting department provided the accompanying data on budgeted manufacturing costs for the month of January:

ADRIAN POWER
Planned Level of Production for January

Budgeted production (in units)	14,000
Variable costs (vary with production)	
Direct materials	$140,000
Direct labor	224,000
Indirect labor	21,000
Indirect materials	10,500
Maintenance	6,300
Fixed costs	
Supervision	24,700
Other (depreciation, taxes, etc.)	83,500
Total plant costs	$510,000

Actual operations for January are summarized as

ADRIAN POWER
Actual Operations for January

Actual production (in units)	15,400
Actual costs incurred	
Direct materials	$142,400
Direct labor	259,800
Indirect labor	27,900
Indirect materials	12,200
Maintenance	9,800
Supervision	28,000
Other costs (depreciation, taxes, etc.)	83,500
Total plant costs	$563,600

Required:

    a. Prepare a report comparing the actual operating results with the flexible budget at actual production.

    b. Write a short memo analyzing the report prepared in part (*a*). What likely managerial implications do you draw from this report? What are the numbers telling you?

P 6–17: Panarude Airfreight

Panarude Airfreight is an international air freight hauler with more than 45 jet aircraft operating in the United States and the Pacific Rim. The firm is headquartered in Melbourne, Australia, and is organized into five geographic areas: Australia, Japan, Taiwan, Korea, and the United States. Supporting these areas are several centralized corporate function services (cost centers): human resources, data processing, fleet acquisition and maintenance, and telecommunications. Each responsibility center has a budget, negotiated at the beginning of the year with the vice president of finance. Funds unspent at the end of the year do not carry over to the next fiscal year. The firm is on a January-to-December fiscal year.

After reviewing the month-to-month variances, Panarude senior management became concerned about the increased spending occurring in the last three months of each fiscal year. In particular, in the first nine months of the year, expenditure accounts typically show favorable variances (actual spending is less than budget), but in the last three months, unfavorable variances are the norm. In an attempt to smooth out these spending patterns, each responsibility center is reviewed at the end of each calendar quarter and any unspent funds can be deleted from the budget for the remainder of the year. The accompanying table shows the budget and actual spending in the telecommunications department for the first quarter of this year.

At the end of the first quarter, telecommunications' total annual budget for this year can be reduced by $7,000, the total budget underrun in the first quarter. In addition, the remaining nine monthly budgets for telecommunications are reduced by $778 (or $7,000 ÷ 9). If, at the end of the

PANARUDE AIRFREIGHT
Telecommunications Department: First Quarter
Budget and Actual Spending (Australian Dollars)

	Monthly Budget	Cumulative Budget	Actual Spending	Cumulative Spending	Monthly Variance*	Cumulative Variance*
Jan.	$110,000	$110,000	$104,000	$104,000	$6,000F	$6,000F
Feb.	95,000	205,000	97,000	201,000	2,000U	4,000F
Mar.	115,000	320,000	112,000	313,000	3,000F	7,000F

*F = Favorable; U = Unfavorable.

second quarter, telecommunications' budget shows an unfavorable variance of, say, $8,000 (after the original budget is reduced for the first-quarter underrun), management of telecommunications is held responsible for the entire $8,000 unfavorable variance. The first-quarter underrun is not restored. If the second-quarter budget variance is also favorable, the remaining six monthly budgets are each reduced further by one-sixth of the second-quarter favorable budget variance.

Required:

a. What behavior would this budgeting scheme engender in the responsibility center managers?
b. Compare the advantages and disadvantages of the previous budget regime, where any end-of-year budget surpluses do not carry over to the next fiscal year, with the system of quarterly budget adjustments just described.

P 6–18: Veriplex

Veriplex manufactures process control equipment. This 100-year-old German company has recently acquired another firm that has a design for a new proprietary process control system. A key component of the new system to be manufactured by Veriplex is called the VTrap, a new line of precision air-flow gauges.

Veriplex uses tight financial budgets linked to annual bonuses to control its manufacturing departments. Each manufacturing department is a cost center. The VTrap gauge is being manufactured in Veriplex's gauge department, which also manufactures an existing line of gauges. The gauge department's budget for the current year consists of two parts: 6.60 million for manufacturing the existing line of gauges and 0.92 million to develop and manufacture VTrap.

The gauge department is responsible for introducing VTrap, which has been in development in the gauge department since the beginning of the year. The new gauge will be manufactured using much of the same equipment and personnel as the existing gauges. VTrap is an integral part of the proprietary process control system that Veriplex hopes will give it a sustainable competitive advantage. Senior management is heavily committed to this strategy. Senior engineering staff members are always in the gauge department working with the manufacturing personnel to modify and refine both the gauges' design and the production processes to produce them. (*Note:* Engineering department costs are not assigned to the gauge department.)

By the end of the fiscal year, the gauge department had spent 1.30 million on the VTrap program and 6.39 million on existing gauge production. Both the new and existing gauge lines achieved their target production quotas and quality goals for the year.

Required:

a. Prepare a financial statement for the gauge department that details its financial performance for the fiscal year just completed.
b. Upon further investigation of previous new product introductions, you discover the same patterns in other departments between new and existing products and their budgets and actual costs. What are some possible reasons why the pattern in the gauge department is not an isolated occurrence but has occurred with other new product introductions and is likely to occur with future new product introductions?

P 6–19: Madigan Modems

Madigan produces a single high-speed modem. The following table summarizes the current month's budget for Madigan's modem production:

Projected production and sales	4,000 units
Variable costs	$ 640,000
Fixed costs	$ 480,000
Total production budget	$1,120,000

Actual production and sales for the month were 3,900 units. Total production costs were $1,114,800, of which $631,800 were variable costs.

Required:

    a. Prepare an end-of-month variance report for the production department using the beginning-of-month static budget.

    b. Prepare an end-of-month variance report for the production department using the beginning-of-month flexible budget.

    c. Write a short memo evaluating the performance of the production manager based on the variance report in part (*a*).

    d. Write a short memo evaluating the performance of the production manager based on the variance report in part (*b*).

    e. Which variance report—the one in part (*a*) or (*b*)—best reflects the performance of the production manager? Why?

P 6–20: Webb & Drye

Webb & Drye (WD) is a New York City law firm with over 200 attorneys. WD has a sophisticated set of information technologies—including intranets and extranets, e-mail servers, the firm's accounting, payroll, and client billing software, and document management systems—that allows WD attorneys and their expert witnesses access to millions of pages of scanned documents that often accompany large class action lawsuits. Bev Piccaretto was hired at the beginning of last year to manage WD's IT department. She and her staff maintain these various systems, but they also act as an internal consulting group to WD's professional staff. They help the staff connect to and use the various IT systems and troubleshoot problems the staff may encounter.

The IT department is a cost center. Piccaretto receives an annual operating budget and believes she is accountable for not exceeding the budget while simultaneously providing high-quality IT services to WD. Piccaretto reports to Marge Malone, WD's chief operating officer. Malone is responsible for IT, accounting, marketing, human resources, and finance functions for Webb & Drye. She reports directly to WD's managing partner, who is the firm's chief executive officer.

The fiscal year has just ended. The following table contains IT's annual budget, actual amounts spent, and variances from the budget.

Malone expresses her concern that the IT department had substantial deviations from the original budgeted amounts for software licenses and salaries, and that Piccaretto should have informed Malone of these actions before they were implemented. Piccaretto argues that because total spending

WEBB & DRYE
IT Department
Budgeted and Actual Expenditures and Variances from Budget Last Year

	Budget	Actual	Variance	Fav./Unfav.
Salaries	$ 350,000	$ 336,000	$ 14,000	F
Benefits*	140,000	134,400	5,600	F
Software site licenses	143,000	168,000	(25,000)	U
Hardware leases	630,000	635,000	(5,000)	U
Travel	59,000	57,000	2,000	F
Supplies	112,000	110,000	2,000	F
Training	28,000	20,000	8,000	F
Occupancy costs	195,000	198,000	(3,000)	U
Total	$1,657,000	$1,658,400	$ (1,400)	U

*40% of salaries

within the IT department was in line with the total budget of $1,657,000 she managed her budget well. Furthermore, Piccaretto points out that she had to buy more sophisticated antivirus software to protect the firm from hacker attacks and that, in paying for these software upgrades, she did not replace a staff person who left in the fourth quarter of the year. Malone counters that this open position adversely affected a large lawsuit because the attorneys working on the case had trouble downloading the scanned documents in the document management system that IT is responsible for maintaining.

Required:

Write a short memo analyzing the disagreement between Malone and Piccaretto. What issues underlie the disagreement? Who is right and who is wrong? What corrective actions (if any) do you recommend?

P 6–21: Spa Ariana

Spa Ariana promotes itself as an upscale spa offering a variety of treatments, including massages, facials, and manicures, performed in a luxurious setting by qualified therapists. The owners of Spa Ariana invested close to $450,000 of their own money three years ago in building and decorating the interior of their new spa (six treatment rooms, relaxation rooms, showers, and waiting area). Located on the main street in a ski resort, the spa has a five-year renewable lease from the building owner. The owners hire a manager to run the spa.

The average one-hour treatment is priced at $100. Ariana has the following cost structure:

	Variable Cost/Treatment	Fixed Cost/Month
Therapist	$40	
Supplies/laundry	4	
Management		$ 5,500
Utilities		1,600
Rent	7	6,000
Repairs/upkeep/cleaning	6	1,500
Total	$57	$14,600

Assume that all treatments have the same variable cost structure depicted in the table.

Required:

a. Calculate the number of treatments Spa Ariana must perform each month in order to break even.

b. In April, the owners of Ariana expect to perform 550 treatments. Prepare a budget for April assuming 550 treatments are given.

c. In April, Spa Ariana performs 530 treatments and incurs the following actual costs. Prepare a performance report for April comparing actual performance to the static budget in part (*b*) based on 550 treatments.

d. Prepare a performance report for April comparing actual performance to a flexible budget based on the actual number of treatments performed in April of 530.

Actual Operating Results for April		
Revenue		$53,000
Therapists	$21,280	
Supplies/laundry	1,795	
Management	5,125	
Utilities	1,725	
Rent	9,710	
Repairs/upkeep/cleaning	5,080	$44,715
Actual profit		$ 8,285

    e. Which of the two performance reports you prepared in parts (*c*) and (*d*) best reflect the true performance of the Spa Ariana in April? Explain your reasoning.

    f. Do the break-even calculation you performed in part (*a*) and the budgeted and actual profits computed in parts (*a*)–(*d*) accurately capture the true economics of the Ariana Spa? Explain why or why not.

P 6–22: St. Ashton Maui Resort

St. Ashton Resorts operates high-end, all-inclusive vacation destinations in 12 locations, including Maui, Hawaii; Los Cabos, Mexico; and the Great Barrier Reef, Australia. At St. Ashton properties, the guest pays a flat daily rate that includes lodging, all meals and beverages, golf, and spa treatments.

Each resort is treated as a profit center, and the managers of the resort receive bonuses for achieving or beating the budget. Under the profit center approach, each resort management team is rewarded based on the difference between budgeted and actual profits.

Last year, St. Ashton switched its budgeting methodology. Previously, the CFO's office of St. Ashton set each property's annual budget based on the projected occupancy rate and expected costs. The annual budget was then broken down into monthly budgets adjusted for the number of days in the month and any seasonal fluctuation in the occupancy rate.

The new CFO, hired in the middle of last year, felt the old budget approach, which was set before the year began, did not take into account the dynamic nature of the tourism market. Travelers used to plan their leisure travel 6–9 months ahead, which allowed resorts to develop reasonably accurate forecasts of demand and hence accurate budgets. The Internet and global markets caused the once-predictable demand to become more unpredictable. The old budget was out of date shortly after the new year began, causing managers rewarded under the budget great consternation. The new CFO changed the budgeting system for the current fiscal year to a monthly rolling model. Before the current fiscal year began, the CFO's office sets the spending targets per guest room occupied for each department in each resort (lodging, food and beverage, golf, and spa) as well as annual budgets to cover each department's fixed costs. The annual departmental budgets are converted to monthly budgets by taking the annual budget, dividing it by 365, and multiplying that by the number of days in the month. The following table illustrates the new budget model for the St. Ashton Maui Resort for the current year.

	Budget
Revenue per room day	$1,700
Number of rooms	500
Average occupancy rate	75%
Expected occupancy	375
Total expected revenue per day	$637,500
Variable costs per room	
Food and beverage	$300
Golf	$30
Spa	$200
Lodging	$70
Total variable cost per room day	$600
Total expected variable cost @ average occupancy	$225,000
Fixed cost per year	
Food and beverage	$18,000,000
Golf	$2,300,000
Spa	$1,600,000
Lodging	$88,000,000
Administration	$14,000,000
Grounds	$1,700,000
Total annual fixed cost	$125,600,000
Total annual fixed cost per day (365 days)	$344,110
Total profit per day	$68,390

270   *Chapter 6*

Required:

  a. What is the St. Ashton Maui Resort's break-even occupancy rate?

  b. Prepare the St. Ashton Maui Resort monthly budget for October (with 31 days) for the current year before the current year begins.

  c. To evaluate and reward the performance of the St. Ashton Maui managers under the new budget model, St. Ashton uses the actual number of guest days in the month, the budgeted variable costs per room, and budgeted fixed costs to establish what the target expenses for the month should have been. This is then compared to the actual expenses incurred. Managerial bonuses are paid based on the difference between the target and the actual expenses. For October of the current year, the St. Ashton Maui had 10,500 guest days at $1,700 per day and reported the following revenues and expenses:

Actual results for October

Guest days	10,540
Revenue	$17,918,000
Variable costs	
Food and beverage	$ 3,035,520
Golf	305,660
Spa	2,002,600
Lodging	685,100
Total variable costs	$ 6,028,880
Fixed costs	
Food and beverage	$ 1,421,753
Golf	175,808
Spa	119,583
Lodging	7,175,013
Administration	1,212,821
Grounds	135,720
Total fixed cost	$10,240,701

Prepare the performance report of the St. Ashton Maui Resort for October that compares actual to budgeted results.

  d. Based on the performance report you prepared in part (c), briefly evaluate the performance of the St. Ashton Maui Resort management team.

  e. In reviewing the performance of the St. Ashton Maui Resort since the beginning of the current year, St. Ashton's CFO noticed that while favorable cost variances have resulted in most months, an alarming trend in occupancy rates is emerging:

Jan	Feb	Mar	Apr	May	Jun	Jul	Aug	Sept	Oct
79%	74%	76%	72%	73%	74%	69%	70%	67%	68%

The St. Ashton Maui Resort managers attribute the falling occupancy rate to new luxury resorts opening in the Hawaiian Islands. However, similar trends in cost variances and occupancy rates exist at other St. Ashton resorts where the budgeting system has been changed to the system used at the St. Ashton Maui Resort.

Discuss possible reasons for the declining occupancy rate at the St. Ashton Maui resort.

P 6–23: City Hospital Nursing

City Hospital is a city government–owned and operated hospital providing basic health care to low-income people. Most of the hospital's revenues are from federal, state, county, and city governments. Some patients covered by private insurance are also admitted, but most of the patients are covered by government assistance programs (Medicare and Medicaid).

Maxine Jones is the director of nursing for the 40-bed pediatrics unit at City Hospital. She is responsible for recruiting nurses, scheduling when they work (days, evenings, weekends), and preparing the nursing budget for the pediatrics unit. A variety of different nursing skills is needed to staff the unit: There are nursing aides, nurse practitioners, registered nurses, nursing supervisors, and clinical nurses. Each type of nurse provides different patient care services (care and feeding, drawing blood samples, giving injections, changing dressings, supervising, etc.). Not all types of nurses can provide all services, and each type of nurse has a different wage rate. Minimum nurse staffing levels per patient must be maintained. If the minimums are violated, new patients cannot be admitted.

More than 45 full-time nurses are required to staff the pediatrics unit. The number of each type of nurse is set in the budget (8 nurses aides, 12 nurse practitioners, 14 registered nurses, etc.). To change the mix of nurse types or their wage rates during the year requires time-consuming approval from the nursing administration, the hospital administration, and finally the city council. The director can change the staffing mix and pay scales in the next budget year by submitting a budget with the revised staffing levels and wage rates and having the budget approved through a lengthy review process that ultimately requires the city council's agreement.

In selecting where to work, nurses evaluate working conditions, pay, and amenities, as all employees do. A key working condition for nurses is flexibility in choosing their schedule. Because of the shortage of nurses in the community, all hospitals have become competitive in terms of work schedules and hours. Some private hospitals allow nurses to schedule when they want to work and how many hours a week they are willing to work. City Hospital often finds its nurses being hired away by private hospitals. If a nurse practitioner is hired away, Jones must replace her or him with another nurse practitioner. The private hospitals do not have such a constraint. If a nurse practitioner position is open, a private hospital will temporarily move a registered nurse with a higher level of skills into the position until a nurse practitioner can be found.

Required:

    a. What type of specialized knowledge does Maxine Jones acquire in preparing the nursing schedule for the upcoming month?

    b. What are some of the consequences of the constraints Jones must operate under?

    c. Explain why City Hospital does not allow Jones as much freedom in her staffing decisions as her counterparts in private hospitals.

P 6–24: Madden International

Madden International is a large ($7 billion sales), successful international pharmaceuticals firm operating in 23 countries with 15 autonomous subsidiaries. The corporate office consists of five vice presidents who oversee the operations of the subsidiaries. These five vice presidents report to two executive vice presidents, who in turn report to the president of the firm.

The 15 subsidiaries specialize by pharmaceutical type and in some cases by country. The pace of innovation in this industry is very fast. In addition, each country has its own elaborate regulatory environment that controls new drug introduction, pricing, and distribution. Each market has its own peculiarities concerning hospital drug purchases. It is an understatement to say that Madden International operates in a very complex world that changes daily.

The corporate office requires each subsidiary to maintain an elaborate, detailed budget and control system. The following points summarize the budget and control system in each subsidiary:

- One-, three-, and five-year budgets are prepared each year.
- The vice president overseeing the subsidiary looks for three- and five-year budgets that stretch the subsidiary's capabilities. That is, subsidiaries are pushed to devise programs that increase value.

- These budgets are developed and approved first at the subsidiary level, then by corporate headquarters.
- Every three months the subsidiaries must reconcile actual performance to budget and write detailed reports to the corporate office explaining variances and corrective actions to be taken.
- The corporate vice president assigned to the subsidiary makes quarterly visits for three days of meetings that involve extensive reviews of the budgets and operating results. These meetings involve all the senior managers in the subsidiary.
- Subsidiary senior managers are not compensated or rewarded for meeting budget targets. Rather, they are evaluated on their ability to develop new markets, solve short-run problems, add value to their organization and to Madden International, and manage and motivate their subordinates. These performance evaluation criteria are quite subjective. But the corporate vice presidents have a great deal of in-depth personal contact with each of the senior people in their subsidiaries and are able to arrive at suitable performance evaluations.
- Preparing for these meetings with the corporate vice president and developing the budgets requires the involvement of all the senior managers in the subsidiary. One manager remarked, "I'd hate to see how much more money we could be making if we didn't have to spend so much time in budget and financial review meetings."

It turns out that Madden International is not unique in the amount of senior management time spent on budgeting and financial reviews. A survey of large, publicly traded U.S. firms supports the Madden system. Researchers found that innovative firms in complex environments characterized by high uncertainty and change used much more elaborate formal financial control (budgeting) systems than did firms in more stable, mature industries. Innovative firms seem to employ more financial controls than less-innovative firms.

Required:

a. List the strengths and weaknesses of the budgeting and control system at Madden International.

b. Why might you expect firms like Madden International to rely so heavily on formal financial control systems?

P 6–25: Brehm Vineyards

Brehm Vineyards grows a unique white pinot noir grape that it uses to produce a white wine that is in high demand. Brehm uses all the grapes it can grow to produce its own white pinot noir wine. Brehm pinot noir wine contains 100 percent Brehm-grown grapes. The company neither buys nor sells grapes. Because of the uniqueness and difficulty of growing white pinot grapes, Brehm can only produce 8,000 cases (12 bottles per case) in a normal year. A good growing season might yield 10,000 cases, whereas bad weather can cut production to 5,000 cases. In a normal year, Brehm expects to sell its wine to wholesalers for $120 per case.

The following table summarizes how Brehm managers expect their costs to vary with the number of cases produced.

	Fixed Cost (per year)	Variable Cost (per case)
Grape costs	$240,000	$2.10
Labor	75,000	2.15
Packaging		14.00
Selling and administrative costs	36,000	
Utilities	4,000	0.75

Budgeting   **273**

Required:

   a. Prepare a flexible budget (including budgeted net income), assuming Brehm produces and sells 8,000 cases of wine.

   b. Calculate the break-even number of cases.

   c. How many cases does Brehm have to produce if it wants an after-tax profit of $300,000 and the income tax rate is 40 percent?

   d. Bad weather this year cut Brehm's production and sales to only 6,000 cases. The low yield drove up wholesale prices of the white pinot wine from $120 to $140 per case. Brehm's actual expenses for the year were:

Actual Costs for the Year

Grape costs	$ 260,000
Labor	98,000
Packaging	83,000
Selling and administrative costs	39,000
Utilities	8,800

Design and prepare a table that reports the performance of Brehm for the year.

   e. Write a short memo summarizing Brehm's performance during the past year. Did management do a good or bad job?

P 6–26: Republic Insurance

Republic Insurance has a direct sales force that sells life insurance policies. All salespeople at the beginning of the year forecast the number of policies they expect to sell that year. At the end of the year, they are evaluated based on how many policies they actually sell. The compensation scheme is based on the following formula:

$$\text{Total compensation} = \$20,000 + \$100B + 20(S - B) \qquad \text{if } S \geq B$$

$$= \$20,000 + \$100B - \$400(B - S) \quad \text{if } S < B$$

where

$B = $ *Budgeted number of policies reported by the manager*

$S = $ *Actual number of policies sold*

Required:

   a. Suppose a particular salesperson expects to sell 100 policies. This salesperson is considering reporting budgeted policies of 90, 99, 100, 101, 102, and 110. What level of budgeted policy sales should this person report at the beginning of the year?

   b. Critically analyze the Republic Insurance compensation scheme.

P 6–27: M&S Mortgage

Jillian Taylor manages the Colorado mortgage processing office of M&S Financial Services. M&S generates mortgage applications via Internet leads that are followed up by a sales force that reports to a manager other than Jillian. Once the salespeople secure a mortgage application from a client, Jillian's office prepares all the various mortgage documents required to close the mortgage for M&S and provide the financing to the client. In preparing her budget for next year, she estimates the following budgeted amounts:

	Fixed Costs/Month	*Variable Costs/Mortgage*
Salaries	$7,500	$120
Supplies	100	18
Legal		50
Telecom/IT	280	8
Occupancy	3,200	

All of Jillian's expenses are for mortgage processors. The costs of the salespeople and marketing expenses are in a different budget. Since the number of mortgages expected to be processed each month does not vary over the fiscal year, Jillian and M&S prepare a budget for a typical month and use it for all 12 months in the fiscal year.

Required:

  a. Jillian and M&S senior management forecast 90 mortgages per month will be processed in the Colorado office. Prepare the monthly budget for Jillian's office for next year, assuming 90 mortgages per month.

  b. After the budget is prepared, the economy slips into a severe recession and home sales, new mortgages, and mortgage refinancings fall dramatically. In May (the fifth month of the fiscal year), Jillian's office processes 70 mortgages and has the following operating expenses:

	Actual Costs
Salaries	$17,500
Supplies	1,550
Legal	4,100
Telecom/IT	920
Occupancy	3,100

Based on the budget from part (*a*), prepare a performance report for Jillian's operations for the month of May.

  c. Write a short memo summarizing Jillian's performance based on the performance report prepared in part (*b*).

  d. Does the performance report in part (*b*) accurately measure Jillian's performance in May? What (if any) changes in the performance report would you recommend?

P 6–28:   Troika Toys

Adrian and Pells (AP) is an advertising agency that uses flexible budgeting for both planning and control. One of its clients, Troika Toys, asked AP to prepare an ad campaign for a new toy. AP's contract with Troika calls for paying AP $120 per design hour for between 150 and 200 hours.

AP has a staff of ad campaign designers who prepare the ad campaigns. Customers are billed only for the time designers work on their project. Partner time is not billed directly to the customer. As part of the planning process, Sue Bent, partner-in-charge of the Troika account, prepared the following flexible budget. "Authorized Design Hours" is the estimated range of time AP expects the job to require and what the client agrees to authorize.

AP's executive committee reviewed Bent's budget and approved it and the Troika contract. After some preliminary work, Troika liked the ideas so much it expanded the authorized time range to be between 175 and 250 hours.

TROIKA TOYS
Flexible Budget

	Fixed Component	Variable Component	Authorized Design Hours		
			150	175	200
Revenues		$120	$18,000	$21,000	$24,000
Design labor	$ 0	45	6,750	7,875	9,000
Artwork	1,700	11	3,350	3,625	3,900
Office and occupancy costs*	0	6	900	1,050	1,200
Total costs	$1,700	$ 62	$11,000	$12,550	$14,100
Budgeted profits			$ 7,000	$ 8,450	$ 9,900

*Consists of rent, phone charges, fax costs, overnight delivery, and so on.

Bent and her design team finished the Troika project. Two hundred and twenty design hours were logged and billed to Troika at the contract price ($120 per hour). Upon completion of the Troika campaign, the following revenues and costs had been accumulated:

TROIKA TOYS
Actual Costs Incurred

Revenue ($120 × 220)	$26,400
Design labor	10,320
Artwork	4,350
Office and occupancy costs	1,690
Total costs	$16,360
Profits	$10,040

AP's accounting manager keeps track of actual costs incurred by AP on each account. AP employs a staff of designers. Their average salary is $45 per hour. New designers earn less than the average; those with more experience earn more. The actual design labor costs charged to each project are the actual hours times the designer's actual hourly cost. Artwork consists of both in-house and out-of-house artists who draw up the art for the ads designed by the designers. Office and occupancy costs consist of a charge per designer hour to cover rent, photocopying, and phones, plus actual long-distance calls, faxes, and overnight delivery services.

Required:

Prepare a table that reports on Sue Bent's performance on the Troika Toys account and write a short memo to the executive committee that summarizes her performance on this project.

P 6–29: Cellular First

The sales department of a cellular phone company pays its salespeople $1,500 per month plus 25 percent of each new subscriber's first month's billings. A new subscriber's first-month bill averages $80. Salespeople work 160 hours a month (four weeks at 40 hours per week). If salespeople work more than 160 hours per month, they receive $12 per hour for hours in excess of 160.

Sales leads for the sales department are generated in a variety of ways—direct mailings to potential customers who then call to speak to a salesperson, lists of prospective customers purchased from outside marketing firms, and so forth. The manager of the sales department reviews potential leads and assigns them to particular salespeople who contact them. The manager of the sales department is expected to oversee the time spent by each salesperson per assigned lead and to approve overtime requests to work beyond the 40 hours per week. Each new customer added requires, on average, 2 hours of salesperson time to make the sale.

Last month, the sales department was budgeted for eight full-time salespeople. However, because of a new ad campaign, an additional salesperson was hired and overtime was approved, bringing actual hours worked up to 1,580. The department added 725 new customers.

Required:

    a. Prepare a performance report comparing actual performance to budgeted performance using a static budget based on eight salespeople and no budgeted overtime.

    b. Prepare a performance report comparing actual performance to budgeted performance using a flexible budget based on nine salespeople selling 725 new accounts.

    c. Discuss when you would expect to see the report prepared in part (*a*) used and when you would expect to see the report in part (*b*) used.

CASES

Case 6–1: Artisans Shirtcraft

Background

Artisans Shirtcraft manufactures and sells hand-painted shirts of original design. The company was founded in 2005 by three sisters: Cathy, Linda, and Valerie Montgomery. Shirtcraft started out as a means of financing a hobby; profits from shirt sales were used to pay the cost of supplies. However, word of the sisters' appealing products spread quickly, eventually creating strong and widespread demand for Shirtcraft shirts. By 2009, the year of Shirtcraft's incorporation, the company no longer relied on selling at the occasional crafts fair. It now earned almost all of its revenues through sales to upscale boutiques and department stores. Shirtcraft had grown into a legitimate business, but the hobby mentality remained. The company retained a simple approach that had served it well: Buy quality materials when available at a bargain price and turn them into shirts. At this time, the sisters had a ready market for whatever they could produce.

In 2010, the sisters loosely organized Shirtcraft into three functional areas, each based around a talent at which one of them excelled. Cathy would hunt high and low for the best prices, Linda would oversee the painting of the original designs, and Valerie would sell the shirts and deal with the general annoyances of business administration. No separate departmental financial records were kept.

Demand for Shirtcraft shirts continued to grow. To finance additional production, the company had become increasingly dependent upon debt. By 2013, bankers had become an integral part of life at Shirtcraft. The sisters were devoting themselves primarily to executive administration, leaving most day-to-day operations to hired managers.

By the end of 2015, more than 75 employees were on the payroll. However, some of Shirtcraft's creditors began to get cold feet. Given the sluggish economy, some felt that continued investment in a company such as Shirtcraft would be foolish. In light of the scrutiny under which their industry presently operated, the bankers wondered about the prudence of increased and continued commitment to a company that was virtually devoid of financial controls. The bankers were particularly concerned by Shirtcraft's continuing reliance on the bargain purchase strategy. They thought the company would inevitably vacillate between periods of incurring excessive inventory holding costs for overpurchased materials and periods of lost sales due to underpurchasing. If Shirtcraft wanted the banks to commit long term to a rapidly growing credit line, the sisters would have to demonstrate their willingness to establish organizational structures and controls such as those found in larger companies.

Plan

In April 2016, a plan was established. Three functional areas were organized: purchasing, production, and sales and administration. Purchasing and production would be cost centers, each monitored by comparisons of actual costs to budgeted costs. Compensation for key personnel of the cost centers would be tied to the results of this comparison. The sisters would officially be employees of the sales and administrative department, which would hold final responsibility for all executive and corporate decisions. Key employees of sales and administration would be judged and compensated based on overall firm profitability.

For the 12 months beginning in September 2016, the sisters expected to sell 192,000 shirts at an average price of $23 per shirt. Expenses for the sales and administrative department are estimated at $750,000 for the year. Interest expenses for the period are estimated at $550,000. Incentive pay to the various departments is expected to amount to $75,000 per functional area. Under the plan, all expenses are charged to the individual department that incurs them, except for interest expenses, taxes, and incentive pay. These are treated as corporate profit and loss items. Taxes are expected to be 40 percent of corporate pretax income.

After considerable negotiations between the sisters and the purchasing manager, it was agreed that direct materials costs should average about $7 per shirt if purchases are made based on production department demand. Although this approach results in higher direct materials costs than a bargain purchase strategy, the demand-based purchase strategy is cheaper when opportunity costs such as inventory holding costs and contribution margin forgone due to lost sales are considered. Salaries and other overhead for the purchasing department are expected to amount to $150,000 for the year.

Discussions with the production manager led to estimates that production will use fixed overhead costing $240,000. Production's variable overhead consists wholly of direct labor. An average of 1/2 hour of direct labor, at a cost of $6 per hour, is needed for each shirt.

Previously, financial records were kept only on a corporate level. Under the new plan, cost records, both budgeted and actual, will be kept for each department. Of Shirtcraft's sales, 40 percent are expected to occur during September, October, November, and December. Sales are divided equally between months within each group of months. All costs that do not vary with shirt production are divided equally throughout the year. All monthly purchasing and production are based on that month's orders and are assumed to be completely sold during that month. Only negligible inventory is held.

Required:

a. Considering only costs, prepare budgeted annual and monthly financial statements for purchasing and production. (Assume that production is not responsible for any costs already assigned to purchasing.) Prepare an annual budgeted income statement for Artisans Shirtcraft for the period September 2016 through August 2017. Annual costs for income statement purposes consist of the following:

> Cost of goods sold
> Administrative expenses
> Interest
> Taxes

All salaries and overhead for purchasing and production are treated as product costs and assigned to individual units. Therefore, these costs should be included in Shirtcraft's annual income statement under cost of goods sold.

b. In general terms, consider the changes in Shirtcraft due to growth. How is the company different from an organizational standpoint? What role do budgeting and cost centers have in attempting to meet the challenges presented by this growth?

SOURCE: G. Hurst.

Case 6–2:   Scion Corp.

Scion Corp. manufactures earth-moving equipment. Department A303 produces a number of small metal parts for the equipment, including specialized screw products, rods, frame fittings, and some engine parts. Scion uses flexible budgeting. The budget for each line item is based on an estimate of the fixed costs and variable costs per unit of volume for that item. The volume measure chosen

278   *Chapter 6*

for each line item is the one with the greatest cause-and-effect relation to the item. For example, the volume measure for utilities is machine hours, whereas the volume measure for supervision is direct labor hours of hourly employees.

At the beginning of the year, the plant is given an annual production quota consisting of the number of each piece of earth-moving equipment to produce. These equipment quotas are exploded into the total number of parts each department must produce, using data about what parts are required for each unit of equipment. Each department has a detailed set of standards, developed over a number of years, that translate each part produced into the number of machine hours, direct labor hours, raw materials, and so on. Table 1 summarizes the operating results of department A303—specifically, the budgeted cost per batch of 100 parts for part number UAV 672.

TABLE 1   **Part Number UAV 672**
Budgeting Standards per 100 Parts per Batch

Raw materials	$26.72
Direct labor, salaried	2.5 hours
Direct labor, hourly	3.2 hours
Machine hours	6.3 hours

Given the production quotas and the detailed set of quantities of each input required to produce a particular part, Department A303's financial budget for the year can be developed. At the end of the year, the actual number of each type of part produced times the budgeting standards for each part can be used to calculate the flexible budget for that line item in the budget. That is, given the actual list of parts produced in Department A303, the flexible budget in Table 2 reports how much should have been spent on each line item. Price fluctuations in raw materials are not charged to the production managers. If low-quality materials are purchased and cause the production departments to incur higher costs, these variances are not charged to the production departments.

TABLE 2   **Scion Corporation**
Machining Department A303 Operating Results for Last Year

	Actual Last Year	Budget*–Last Year	Favorable (Unfavorable) Variance
Volume Measures			
Machine hours	238,654	265,000	
Direct labor hours	146,400	152,000	
Parts machined	33,565,268	35,759,000	
Departmental Financial Performance			
Raw materials	$ 8,326,875	$ 8,150,000	$(176,875)
Direct labor, salaried	1,546,729	1,643,000	96,271
Direct labor, hourly	1,465,623	1,375,000	(90,623)
Supervision	451,597	460,000	8,403
Maintenance	315,864	325,000	9,136
Engineering	279,780	285,000	5,220
Utilities	69,539	82,000	12,461
Training	85,750	53,000	(32,750)
Factory overhead	188,500	210,000	21,500
Total operating expenses	$12,730,257	$12,583,000	$(147,257)

The manager of Department A303 does not have any say over which parts to produce. The manager's major responsibilities include delivering the required number of good parts at the specified time while meeting or bettering the cost targets. The two most important components of the manager's compensation and bonus depend on meeting delivery schedules and the favorable cost variances from the flexible budget.

Senior management of the plant is debating the process used each year to update the various budgeting standards. Productivity increases for labor would cause the amount of direct labor per part to fall over time. One updating scheme would be to take the budgeting standards from last year (e.g., Table 1) and reduce each part's direct labor standard by an average productivity improvement factor estimated by senior plant management to apply across all departments in the plant. The productivity improvement factor is a single plantwide number. For example, if the average productivity factor is forecast to be 5 percent, then for part UAV 672 the budgeting standard for "Direct labor, salaried" becomes 2.375 hours (95 percent of 2.5 hours). This is termed "adjusting the budget."

An alternative scheme, called "adjusting the actual," takes the actual number of direct labor hours used for each part and applies the productivity improvement factor. For example, suppose part UAV 672 used an average of 2.6 hours of salaried direct labor last year for all batches of the part manufactured. The budgeting standard for "Direct labor, salaried" for next year then becomes 2.47 hours (95 percent of 2.6 hours).

Under both schemes, last year's actual numbers and last year's budgeted numbers are known before this year's budget is set.

Required:

Discuss the advantages and disadvantages of the two alternative schemes (adjusting the budget versus adjusting the actual).

Chapter Seven

Cost Allocation: Theory

Chapter Outline

A central issue in all internal accounting systems is **cost allocation**, the assignment of indirect, common, or joint costs to different departments, processes, products or services. Cost allocations, in fact, are a form of transfer pricing within the firm and are thus an integral part of the organization's architecture described in Chapter 4. This chapter presents a general framework for analyzing cost allocations, using the earlier framework of costing for decision making (Chapter 2) and costing for control (Chapter 4).

Consider the following two examples. In the first example, a patient with abdominal pain is admitted to the hospital. After five days, a series of tests, and an operation to remove an ulcer, the patient is discharged. During the patient's stay, she used a variety of services: physicians, nurses, laboratory technicians, food workers, and laundry services. Indirect services include the hospital's admitting and billing offices, building maintenance and security, information technology, and senior hospital administrators. What was the cost of this patient's stay in the hospital? One could just examine the incremental (or marginal) cost of the patient's stay or the "full" cost, including all the indirect services. Calculating the full cost of the patient's stay requires allocating the costs of food workers, laundry services, hospital administrators, and so forth, to patients.

In the second example, the drilling department in a manufacturing plant drills holes in the sheet-metal chassis that forms the base for a desktop printer. Several types of printer chassis are drilled in the department, each with its own configuration and sizes of holes. The drilling department costs consist of labor, tools, supplies, space occupancy (utilities, maintenance, accounting, and plant administration), and accounting depreciation of the drilling machines. Last month, the department drilled 2,100 units of a particular chassis model. Calculating the "full" cost of drilling holes in this particular type requires allocating the drilling department costs to each chassis model produced.

Both organizations face a similar problem: allocating a set of costs to a **cost object**. A cost object is a product, process, department, or program that managers wish to cost. In the two examples, a patient and a chassis are the cost objects. Corporate-level R&D expenses are allocated to the Chevrolet division of General Motors because senior executives at General Motors want to assess the total profitability of Chevrolet net of corporate R&D. The Chevrolet division is the cost object. Managers allocate common costs to cost objects for several reasons, including decision making and/or control. The framework developed in Chapters 2 and 4 will be used to illustrate the trade-off between decision management and decision control in designing cost allocations. Because cost allocations are used for multiple purposes, we will again see that no single way of allocating costs is always right or always wrong. Trade-offs must be made in choosing whether and how to allocate a given common cost. As we will see later, the cost allocation methodology chosen depends on what purposes the allocation serves.

Section A in this chapter describes several institutional settings in which cost allocation takes place. Costs are allocated for a variety of reasons, including taxes, financial reporting, cost-based reimbursement, decision making, and control. The various reasons for allocating costs, including organizational control reasons, are described in section B. The incentive effects of cost allocations are further examined in section C. Allocated costs are intended as proxies for certain hard-to-observe opportunity costs. While allocated costs measure the opportunity cost with error, they are much less easier to compute than opportunity costs.

A. Pervasiveness of Cost Allocations

The vast majority of organizations allocate common costs. A **common cost** arises when a resource is shared by several users. For example, human resource department costs are a common cost because all employees in the firm utilize its services. Common costs of shared services, like a firmwide e-mail system, arise because it is less expensive for the firm to provide the service than for each individual user or department in the company to acquire the service. Hospitals allocate the common costs of shared medical equipment to departments that use it. Telecommunications costs are allocated to users. Purchasing department costs are allocated to products.

Common costs are sometimes called **indirect costs** because they cannot be directly traced to units produced or cost objects precisely because such costs are incurred in providing benefits to different cost objects. Likewise, "overhead" refers to indirect, common costs. Following general practice, we will use the terms *common costs, indirect costs,* and *overhead* interchangeably.

The terms *cost allocation, cost assignment, cost apportionment,* and *cost distribution* are synonyms. All describe the process of taking a given common cost and dividing it between various cost objects (patients or printer chassis). Direct costs do not have to be allocated because they can be directly traced to the cost object. For example, if the firm's intranet is used only by the sales department, then the intranet costs are a direct cost of the sales department. However, if both the sales and the manufacturing departments share the same intranet, the intranet costs are not a direct cost of either department, but rather a common cost that can be allocated to the cost objects—the two departments.

Cost allocation requires the following steps:

1. *Define the cost objects.* The organization must decide what departments, products, or processes to cost. For example, intranet users may be defined as cost objects. The cost object is often a subunit of the organization, such as a cost or profit center. Costs are often allocated to subunits to better evaluate the subunit's performance and to assess product-line profitability. Or costs are allocated as a control device.

2. *Accumulate the common costs to be assigned to the cost objects.* Suppose intranet costs are to be assigned to the intranet users. This step requires the identification and accumulation of the common costs such as the cost of the hardware, personnel expenditures, utilities, and software costs of the intranet that will be distributed to the users.

3. *Choose a method for allocating common costs accumulated in step 2 to the cost objects defined in step 1.* An **allocation base**, a measure of activity associated with the pool of common costs being distributed to the cost objects, must be selected. The allocation base to distribute intranet center costs to users can be time used, computer memory, or some combination of these. As discussed later in this chapter, common costs usually are allocated to cost objects using an allocation base that approximates how the cost objects consume the common resources.

For example, to provide e-mail services for its employees a firm incurs expenses of $575,000 per year consisting of a computer lease ($273,000), labor ($195,000), software ($78,000), and other costs ($29,000). Four departments use various amounts of disk space for e-mail messages measured in terabytes (trillion characters). Table 7–1 shows disk space usage for the four departments.

Terabytes of storage are used as the allocation base to distribute the annual e-mail cost of $575,000 to the departments. The allocation rate is $2,875 per terabyte per year ($575,000 ÷ 200). Table 7–2 displays the resulting allocated costs to each user department.

TABLE 7-1 E-Mail Users of Disk Space
(in Terabytes of Memory)

Users	Terabytes of Memory
Manufacturing	40
Sales	80
Research and development	20
Administration	60
Total	200

TABLE 7-2 Allocation of Annual E-Mail Cost to User Departments

Users	Cost per Terabytes	Terabyte of Memory	Allocated Cost
Manufacturing	$2,875	40	$115,000
Sales	2,875	80	230,000
Research and development	2,875	20	57,500
Administration	2,875	60	172,500
Total		200	$575,000

Most firms allocate a significant fraction of corporate overhead back to their profit centers. Frequently, allocated costs include research and development, information technology, marketing and advertising, distribution expense, income taxes, and finance and accounting costs.

The next three examples illustrate the prevalence of cost allocations in both profit and nonprofit organizations and another role of cost allocations: cost-based reimbursement.

1. Manufacturing Organizations

Cost allocations are quite prevalent in manufacturing. Manufacturers cannot deduct all their manufacturing costs for financial reporting and tax purposes. Rather, they must trace their direct manufacturing costs and allocate their indirect manufacturing costs between units sold and units remaining in inventory. Hence, for calculating cost of goods sold, net income, and inventories, financial reporting and taxes often mandate that indirect manufacturing costs be allocated. Cost allocations also arise whenever the firm has a cost-based reimbursable contract. In this case, the firm's revenues depend on reported costs, including allocated costs. For example, certain government defense contracts are cost-based. The contractor's revenues are contractually tied to reported costs. In these circumstances, the contractor has an incentive to allocate as much cost to the government work as is permitted under the terms of the contract. Suppose an aircraft company manufactures both military and commercial aircraft. Military aircraft are produced under a cost-based contract. Subject to the contractual stipulations, the firm has an incentive to find the

284   *Chapter 7*

allocation basis that maximizes the fraction of the president's salary allocated to the military contract.

2. Hospitals

Hospitals rely on reimbursement by the government and by private medical insurance companies. At one time in the United States, these payments depended on the costs reported by the hospital. In some states, nursing home reimbursement under Medicaid is still based on reported costs. Under cost-based reimbursements, cost allocation becomes an important determinant of revenue. For example, suppose a hospital serves two patient populations: poor elderly cases and affluent maternity cases. Suppose the medical costs for the elderly are paid by the government at a fixed amount per case, whereas private insurance companies reimburse the hospital for maternity cases at "cost." Given these patient populations and reimbursement rules, the hospital administrator has an incentive to choose a cost allocation method that loads as much cost as permitted onto the maternity cases in order to maximize revenues. For example, laundry costs can be assigned using various allocation bases: patient days, floor space, nursing hours, and so on. The hospital administrator wants to use the allocation base that allocates as much laundry cost as possible to maternity because this maximizes hospital revenue.

Today, hospital reimbursement in the United States is less tied to reported costs than previously. Hospitals basically are reimbursed at a flat amount for a given medical procedure (diagnostic-related groups, or DRGs). This change in hospital reimbursement rules has reduced the opportunity to maximize hospital revenues using cost allocations.

3. Universities

Universities also allocate costs. A recurring debate at most campuses concerns *indirect cost pools*. Research-oriented universities derive significant revenues from government contracts and grants. Grants from organizations such as the National Science Foundation and the National Institutes of Health pay for basic research. University scientists submit research proposals to a government funding agency describing their experiments, anticipated contribution, and costs of the project. Besides the direct cost of the experiment, the research grant is expected to pay for the indirect costs of research such as building occupancy, library facilities, administration, and security. University research proposals include a reimbursable cost item for such indirect costs. The university estimates the total cost of all indirect expenses attributable to government-sponsored research, as well as the total direct costs of government-sponsored research. The ratio of these estimates is the *indirect cost rate*. If a cancer researcher seeks $250,000 of direct cost support for laboratory staff, supplies, and salaries, and the university has a 50 percent indirect cost rate, the grant proposal includes an additional $125,000 of indirect cost recovery.

Universities have an incentive to recover as much indirect cost as possible. Stanford University received about $400 million to support research in 1988, which included about $91 million of overhead costs. A September 14, 1990, *Wall Street Journal* article reported that the federal government claims that Stanford "officials may have engaged in 'fraudulent acts' and made 'false claims' in its billing practices including 'excessive library cost reimbursement' amounting to $30 million to $40 million from 1983 to 1986." In 1991, the president, provost, and chief financial officer of Stanford resigned. The U.S. government cut Stanford's indirect cost recovery rate from 78 percent to 55.5 percent, which reduced government payments to Stanford by $22 million per year. This Stanford example, while an isolated case, illustrates that cost allocations can at times have serious consequences for organizations and their leaders.

| **Managerial Application: The $18 Aspirin** | Hospitals routinely justify the prices they charge for services and procedures based on costs. For example, one hospital explained the $18 price for two aspirin tablets as follows: |

Two aspirin tablets	$ 0.040
Direct labor	
Physician	$ 1.050
Pharmacist	$ 1.330
Nurse	$ 0.321
Indirect labor (recordkeeping and orderly)	$ 0.800
Cup	$ 0.025
Shared and shifted costs	
Unreimbursed Medicare	$ 0.450
Indigent care	$ 0.332
Malpractice insurance and uncollectible receivables	$ 0.380
Excess bed capacity	$ 0.429
Other administrative and operating costs	$ 0.688
Product cost	$ 5.845
Hospital overhead costs @ 53.98%	$ 3.16
Full cost (incl. overhead)	$ 9.000
Profit	$ 9.000
Price (per dose)	$18.000

While the $18 price of the aspirin might at first appear ridiculous, this is the amount necessary to recover both the direct and indirect costs of prescribing the aspirin, costs that the hospital cannot recover from its other patients, and to provide a profit.

Source: D. McFadden, "The Legacy of the $7 Aspirin," *Management Accounting*, April 1990, pp. 38–41, and S. Jaffe, "$18 for a Baby Aspirin? Hospitals Hike Costs for Everyday Drugs for Some Patients," Kaiser Health News, www .kaiserhealth news.org, April 30, 2012.

Cost allocations also affect the resources available to the various colleges and departments. Within a university setting, if each college within the university is treated as a profit center, then cost allocations become relevant. If the business school must operate within a balanced budget, in which revenues equal expenditures plus allocated costs, then the amount of central administration, library, security, or human resource department costs allocated to the business school affects its other spending. A college within the university with more net cash flows can be "taxed" and these cash flows used to subsidize colleges within the university with less net cash flows. This is accomplished by allocating more university overhead to colleges with more net cash flow and less overhead to colleges with less net cash flow. By allocating more overhead to the cash-rich colleges and less to the cash-poor colleges, this allows the university to subsidize those colleges within the university with less net cash-flow. Cost allocations are no longer an idle academic speculation in such settings; they often consume a considerable amount of the deans' and central administration's time.

This discussion is not a thorough listing of all cost allocation situations, but it illustrates that cost allocations are important in many types of organizations. Cost allocations can affect real resource utilization and cash flows.

286   *Chapter 7*

Historical Application: The Allocation of Overhead Has Been Contentious for Decades	The allocation of overhead has received more attention than any other cost accounting topic and has been a hotly debated problem ever since accountants began recording indirect expenses. One commentator writing in 1916 described the situation as follows:

> Indirect expense is one of the most important of all the accounts appearing on the books of the manufacturer. Methods of handling its [allocation] have given rise to more arguments than the problem of the descent of man. It is the rock upon which many a ship of industry has been wrecked.

SOURCE: C. Thompson, How to Find Factory Costs (Chicago, IL: A. W. Shaw Co., 1916), p. 105. Quoted by P. Garner, Evolution of Cost Accounting to 1925 (Montgomery, AL: University of Alabama Press, 1954), pp. 170–71.

B. Reasons to Allocate Costs

Most organizations allocate costs. However, some responsibility accounting proponents argue that managers should only be allocated a cost if they have some control over that cost. For example, the maintenance department is a cost center. Its budget contains allocated costs such as a charge for office space over which the maintenance manager has no control. Why give the budget center manager a budget and then take some of it back via a cost allocation? Why not just give the manager a smaller budget?

This section describes three possible reasons why organizations allocate costs: external reporting (including taxes), cost-based reimbursements, and internal decision making and control.

1. External Reporting/Taxes

External financial reports and tax accounting rules require that inventory be stated at cost, including indirect manufacturing costs. For example, inventory includes not only direct labor and direct material, but also a fraction of factory depreciation, property taxes, and the salaries of security guards at the factory. Manufacturing overhead costs, including indirect costs, must be allocated to products. This does not require the firm to use cost allocations for internal reports. To avoid the extra bookkeeping costs of a second set of accounts that exclude the allocated costs, firms use the same accounts internally as externally. However, additional bookkeeping costs would likely be small and offset by the costs of dysfunctional decisions from using the external system for internal operating decisions. Thus, external reporting requirements are not likely to explain the widespread use of cost allocations for internal reporting, such as divisional performance evaluation.

EXERCISE 7-1

Network Systems (NS) offers telecommunications design and consulting services to organizations. The firm offers two types of contracts to its clients: a cost-plus 25 percent contract and a fixed-fee contract where NS offers a fixed price for the job. For cost-plus contracts, total cost includes both direct costs and indirect overheads. NS completes 10 cost-plus contracts at a total direct cost of $450,000 and 15 fixed-fee contracts. Revenues collected from the fixed-fee contracts totaled $2,400,000. The total direct cost of the fixed-fee contracts amounted to 75 percent of the collected revenues. NS has indirect overheads of $350,000.

continued

Required:

a. Allocate the indirect overhead of $350,000 to the fixed-fee and cost-plus 25 percent contracts using direct cost as the overhead allocation base.

b. Allocate the indirect overhead of $350,000 to the fixed-fee and cost-plus 25 percent contracts using number of contracts as the overhead allocation base.

c. Should NS allocate overhead using direct cost or number of contracts? Explain why.

Solution:

a. Indirect overhead allocated using direct cost as the overhead allocation base.

	Fixed Fee	Cost-Plus	Total
Direct cost	$1,800,000*	$450,000	$2,250,000
% of direct cost	80%	20%	100%
Allocated overhead based on direct cost	$280,000	$70,000	$350,000

*75% × $2,400,000.

b. Indirect overhead allocated using contracts as the overhead allocation base.

	Fixed Fee	Cost-Plus	Total
Number of contracts	15	10	25
% of contracts	60%	40%	100%
Allocated overhead based on number of contracts	$210,000	$140,000	$350,000

c. Assuming that (1) the only use of overhead allocations is the computation of total cost for pricing cost-plus contracts and (2) the total number of cost-plus contracts is insensitive to the final price, NS should allocate overhead using number of contracts. Using number of contracts leads to $70,000 ($140,000 – $70,000) more indirect costs allocated to the cost-plus contracts and hence to $87,500 (1.25 × $70,000) of additional revenues on these contracts.

2. Cost-Based Reimbursement

Cost-based reimbursement is another reason for cost allocations. Government cost-based contracts and medical reimbursements for cost give rise to cost allocations. The U.S. Department of Defense purchases billions of dollars of goods a year under cost-plus contracts. Most new weapons systems are procured under negotiated contracts in which the producer's revenues are in part a function of reported costs. To help regulate the cost allocations contractors use in government contracts, the federal government established the Cost Accounting Standards Board (CASB). The CASB has issued standards covering the cost accounting period, capitalization of tangible assets, accounting for insurance and pension costs, and the allocation of direct and indirect costs.

The revenues of public utilities such as electric and gas companies are also tied to reported costs. States often grant public utilities exclusive monopolies over service territories. In return, the state regulates the rates the utility can charge customers. In many cases, the regulated

| **Historical Application: Incentive Effects of Cost Allocations** | James McKinsey, founder of the consulting firm bearing his name, wrote |

James McKinsey, founder of the consulting firm bearing his name, wrote

> [O]ne of the largest items of expense to be allocated in a department store is advertising. The usual method of allocating this to the various departments of the store is on the basis of sales. This practice leads to two undesirable results. First, some departments profit more than others by advertising, since it is devoted to articles sold by some departments much more than to articles sold by other departments. . . . This gives inaccurate (departmental profit) figures. . . . Secondly, if advertising is distributed on the basis of sales, each department head will try to secure as much advertising as possible, since he will feel that each of the other departments must pay part of its cost which results in his department's paying only a small part of the total. He naturally concludes that he must certainly get more benefit from the advertising than it costs him; therefore he will request and urge it. He will be more apt to do this because he knows every other department is seeking advertising, for which his department must pay its proportionate part.

After discussing the allocation of expenses, McKinsey concludes

> [C]are should be exercised to allocate (costs) in such a manner as to attain two results:
>
> 1. Greatest possible accuracy.
> 2. The fixing of responsibility in such a manner that those responsible for the expense will desire to decrease and not to increase it.

McKinsey recognized that cost allocations affect managers' incentives.

SOURCE: J. McKinsey, c (New York: *Ronald Press*, 1922), pp. 283–84.

prices are based on reported costs, including allocated costs. In public utility regulation, the major issue is deciding how to allocate the common costs of capacity, such as the electricity-generating plant, among the different classes of users (residential versus commercial customers). In many public utility rate-setting cases, cost allocation is the preeminent issue.

In firms whose revenues depend on reported costs, cost allocations can have a large impact on cash flows. But relatively few firms have revenues contractually based on costs, and cost allocations are prevalent in firms without cost-based revenues. Therefore, the widespread use of cost allocations cannot be explained solely by the existence of cost-based reimbursement contracts.

3. Decision Making and Control

Decision making and control are the most likely explanation for the prevalence of cost allocations. Cost allocations are an important part of the organization's budget system (by which resources are allocated within the firm) and an important part of the organization's performance evaluation system.

Cost allocations change how decision rights are partitioned within the firm and hence managers' incentives and thus their behavior. For instance, in the university example discussed earlier, the university president constrains the deans of the cash-rich colleges by allocating more costs to them; they receive fewer resources and, therefore, fewer decision rights. Hence, the allocation of more costs to one school and less to another transfers decision rights over the amount of other spending each school can do. Or consider the following example. You are at an expensive restaurant with four friends. Before ordering, it is agreed that you will split the bill evenly—equal cost allocations. What are your incentives under this cost allocation method? Overconsumption. With equal cost allocation, you only bear $0.20 of each additional dollar you eat and drink. The other $0.80 of your incremental consumption is paid by your colleagues. Likewise, you pay 20 percent for each of your friends' bill. Hence, each of you has an incentive to spend more than you would had you agreed upon separate checks. The simple solution is for everyone to pay for only what they consume. But this requires either separate bills (which servers dislike) or one of you to calculate each person's actual cost. Moreover, separate bills do not solve the problem of shared items like wine or appetizers, whose cost must be allocated. This example illustrates that how the bill is allocated affects how the parties will order. Cost allocations affect behavior.

The next section elaborates on the various organizational reasons for allocating costs.

Concept Questions	Q7–1	What are some of the reasons for allocating costs?
	Q7–2	Describe some ways cost allocations can affect cash flows.

C. Incentive/Organizational Reasons for Cost Allocations[1]

1. Cost Allocations Are a Tax System

Cost allocations act as an internal tax system. Like a tax system, they change behavior. For example, consider a computer company with 38 branch offices around the world. Each branch is treated as a profit center and is thus evaluated on total sales less expenses. The branch manager chooses the number of salespeople and the number of ads to place on websites such as Google and Yahoo. The firm incurs substantial R&D, distribution, and administration expenses. Should these costs be allocated to the 38 sales offices?

Table 7–3 summarizes the various combinations of salespeople required to sell $10 million of computers per month in one of the 38 sales offices. Salespeople cost $4,000 per month, and a banner ad costs $2,000 per ad for one hour. To sell $10 million of computers a month, the manager can hire 30 salespeople and buy 182.57 ads or can hire 31 salespeople and buy 179.61 banner ads. More salespeople require fewer ads to produce the same level of sales. Likewise, more ads require fewer salespeople to yield the same sales.

To select the combination of salespeople and advertising, the branch manager will choose the one that minimizes total costs. Therefore, the cost of the first combination is

$$30 \times \$4,000 + 182.57 \times \$2,000 = \$485,140$$

Likewise, the cost of the second combination is

$$31 \times \$4,000 + 179.61 \times \$2,000 = \$483,220$$

The cost of the second allocation is less than the first combination, so it is preferred. From Table 7–3, we see that 40 salespeople and 158.11 ads is the lowest cost combination needed to produce $10 million of sales per month. The calculations so far do not involve any cost allocations.

Suppose corporate expense is allocated based on the number of salespeople. In particular, for each salesperson in the branch, that branch is allocated $1,000 of corporate overhead. The branch manager's reported costs for the first combination now becomes

$$30 \times \$4,000 + 182.57 \times \$2,000 + 30 \times \$1,000 = \$515,140$$

The first combination is $30,000 more expensive than the earlier one before cost allocations.

The "price" the branch manager now "pays" for salespeople includes both the wage ($4,000) and the overhead rate ($1,000). The last column in Table 7–3 calculates the total cost of each combination including the $1,000 cost allocation per salesperson. With cost allocations, the lowest cost combination consists of 34 salespeople and 171.5 ads. This

---

[1]This section is based on J. Zimmerman, "The Costs and Benefits of Cost Allocations," *Accounting Review* 54 (July 1979), pp. 504–21.

TABLE 7-3   **Number of Salespeople and Number of Internet Banner Ads before Cost Allocation Required to Sell $10 Million of Computers per Month**

Number of Salespeople	Number of Banner Ads	Total Cost (before allocations)	Total Cost (after allocations)
30	182.57	$485,140	$515,140
31	179.61	483,220	514,220
32	176.78	481,560	513,560
33	174.08	480,160	513,160
34	171.50	479,000	513,000
35	169.03	478,060	513,060
36	166.67	477,340	513,340
37	164.40	476,800	513,800
38	162.22	476,440	514,440
39	160.13	476,260	515,260
40	158.11	476,220	516,220
41	156.17	476,340	517,340
42	154.30	476,600	518,600

combination has six fewer people but 13.39 more ads. With cost allocations, the branch manager uses more advertising and fewer salespeople than when there was no overhead allocation. The branch manager uses less of the now relatively more expensive input, salespeople, and more of the relatively cheaper input, advertising.

The overhead rate, $1,000, is a tax on salespeople (labor). Like all taxes on consumption items (such as beer, gasoline, and cigarettes), the tax discourages use of the item levied with the tax. Overhead rates and cost allocations are de facto tax systems in firms. The factor input used as the allocation base is being taxed (salespeople in the example). The tax also "distorts" the price of the factor input. Instead of viewing the price of labor as $4,000 per month, the branch manager sees the price for salespeople as $5,000 ($4,000 + $1,000) per month. If the opportunity cost of salespeople is $4,000, but the branch manager is charged $5,000 (including the $1,000 of overhead), the manager will employ too few salespeople.

There are two important lessons from this example. Compared with no allocations, cost allocations

- Reduce the manager's reported profits.
- Change the mix of factor inputs; less of the input taxed by the cost allocation is used (salespeople), and more of the untaxed factor inputs are used (banner ads).

Senior managers and their accountants want to distort the price of salespeople by allocating costs if the price of salespeople is not the total cost to the firm of salespersons. Taxing salespeople induces operating managers to use fewer salespeople. Cost allocations also change the pattern of other incentives within the firm. Each of these reasons is explored in more detail next.

2. Taxing an Externality

One reason for taxing the use of salespeople in the computer company example is that the cost of another salesperson is really not $4,000 per month, but something larger. The $4,000 includes all the direct costs of the salesperson: wages, medical benefits, payroll taxes, pensions, and the like. But the $4,000 does not include the indirect costs of the human resource office, which hires the person, maintains records, and administers benefits. It does not include the legal costs the firm incurs when employees are injured on the job or sue the firm for other reasons. Nor does $4,000 per month include the data processing costs, security costs, and other overhead costs required to support the additional salesperson. It does not include the **externalities** the sales department imposes on other parts of the organization by hiring an additional salesperson.

Externalities in economics are costs or benefits imposed on other individuals without their participation in the decision and without compensation for the costs or benefits imposed on them. The price of an apple compensates the growers and distributors for providing the apple. But the apple's price does not pay for the refuse collection if the apple core is discarded on the street and someone else has to pay to cart it away. Similarly, the price paid for a lawnmower does not reflect the annoyance to the neighborhood of the noise it makes when in use. Discarding an apple core on the street and using a lawnmower cause externalities. If the apple's purchase price includes a sales tax that helps pay the municipality's cost of street cleaning and refuse collection, then the apple's disposal cost has been paid for.

Externalities can be positive or negative. Pollution is a **negative externality**. Automobile exhaust pollutes the air, yet car drivers do not pay for the costs they impose on others by their pollution (except via gasoline taxes). The consumers of polluted air are not compensated directly for the pollution they consume. Education contains a **positive externality** in that people derive benefits from having more educated citizens with whom to interact. Well-manicured lawns of private homes create positive externalities as people pass and enjoy the sight and property values of neighboring homes are increased.

When the computer company branch manager hires an additional salesperson, a negative externality is imposed on the firm. More human resources, security, and legal services will be demanded. Buying another personal computer that sits on a desk imposes few significant externalities. But adding an additional employee who consumes human resource and security services and who can sue the firm and steal property imposes externalities that are not captured in the direct cost of this newly hired person. Employees' direct cost consists of wages, payroll taxes, and benefits. The cost of the externalities generated by hiring one more employee is very difficult to estimate, especially when the employee is hired. But one way to handle this externality is to tax it via a cost allocation, like the sales tax on the apple.

Cost allocation can be used to approximate these hard-to-observe externalities. Consider the case of the human resource department of a sales division. The human resource department maintains the records and answers employee questions regarding retirement and medical benefits. The human resource department is represented by the step function in Figure 7–1. Total human resource department costs behave as a step function that

FIGURE 7-1

Total cost of human resource department

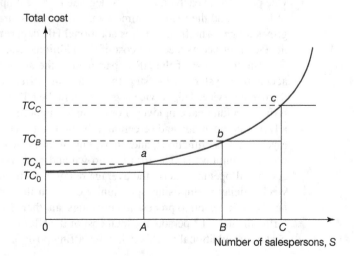

Managerial Application: Examples of Externalities within Organizations	*Positive Externalities* • Customer purchases of particular items are entered into a database by point-of-sale terminals. These data allow market research into customer buying habits and better-designed marketing programs. • If the group at Apple responsible for Apple's computer operating system (OS), improves the software, this has a positive effect on the demand for other Apple hardware and software products. *Negative Externalities* • The purchasing department, trying to reduce costs, purchases substandard raw materials. More manufacturing labor is required to produce acceptable final products. • Suppose some managers wish to use Apple computers, while others wish to use Microsoft Windows PCs. The lack of a uniform standard imposes a series of costs on the firm: File exchange is more difficult, helping each other learn to operate new software/hardware is impeded, and technical service is more costly since consultants must know both operating systems. • In a law firm, if the lawyer handling a client's divorce does a poor job, this lowers the client's perceived quality of the entire law firm. This negative quality externality reduces this client's demand for other law services of this firm (e.g., taxes, wills, and estates) and lowers the demand for the law firm by other clients if the dissatisfied client complains to friends.

depends on the number of salespeople, S, employed in the sales division. The scale (i.e., capacity) of the human resource department is added in large fixed increments rather than continuously in small amounts.

When the firm is small, it is spending TC_0 on the human resource function. This spending remains constant until the number of salespeople reaches A. Then a larger human resource (HR) department is required and spending is increased. The human resource (HR) department is expanded at A because as salespeople are hired between 0 and A, the service provided to each employee is degraded. More employees are sharing a fixed amount of service, and the response time by the human resource department to service a request grows longer. The firm acquires additional HR department capacity when the cost of the degraded service exceeds the cost of the additional capacity.

The total cost of the HR department is the smooth curve. The cost reported by the accounting system is the step function. The difference is the opportunity cost of the degraded service. This service degradation in the HR department is an exterality created by hiring an additional employee. For example, suppose the HR department is responsible for advertising openings and screening job applicants. The department is spending $500,000 a year on these functions, and on average it takes two weeks to place an ad and identify potential employees. The firm has grown and more position openings now occur. These additional openings cause the average delay to increase to three weeks. If the additional week's delay is imposing opportunity costs on the firm in excess of the cost of hiring another HR person to process job openings, another HR employee should be hired. Before hiring the new HR person, the total cost of the HR department is the reported cost plus the cost of the additional week's delay in staffing positions in the firm.

The shape of the total cost varies across departments. The particular shape of the curve drawn in Figure 7–1 is chosen to illustrate the general analysis and is not intended to represent how overhead costs vary in general.

Focusing only on the accounting costs (the step function in Figure 7–1) would lead to the conclusion that the opportunity cost in the HR department of an additional salesperson was zero, unless the salesperson just happened to be at a step. But the opportunity cost in the HR department of an additional salesperson is the slope of the smooth curve. The slope of the smooth curve represents the incremental delay cost in the HR department imposed on all the other internal users of the HR department by adding one more salesperson.

Should HR department costs be allocated back to the branch manager to tax the manager for the externality of degraded service in the HR department caused by the branch manager's hiring an additional salesperson? It depends on the exact shape of the total cost curve and where the firm happens to be on the curve. There are three cases to consider.

Case 1 (*Figure 7-2*)

At point c, the overhead rate, R_c, is

$$R_c = \frac{TC_c}{C} < MC_c$$

Here, MC denotes the marginal cost in the HR department and is the slope of the smooth curve. The slope of the line from the origin through point c is the overhead rate at point c, R_c. The slope of this line, R_c, is the average cost of the HR department when there are C salespeople. The slope of this line is not as steep as the marginal cost line at point c (solid line). At point c, or whenever $R < MC$, the cost allocation rate, which is the average cost, understates the marginal cost of the externality. Whenever the average cost (the cost allocation rate) is less than the marginal cost of the HR department, using a cost allocation to tax the externality is better than no allocation. With no allocation, the branch manager will not attach any cost to the externality imposed on other users of the HR department when salespeople are hired. Since $R_c < MC_c$, the branch manager does not "pay" the entire marginal cost of the externality. Nonetheless, some tax is better than no tax. Whenever a service department's average cost is less than its marginal cost, allocating the service department costs strictly dominates not allocating them. Each user should be charged the marginal cost, MC, but the firm does not know this number without special studies. However, average cost is easily approximated as the ratio of accounting cost divided by salespeople.

FIGURE 7-2

Total cost of human resource department: Relation between overhead rate and marginal cost (overhead allocation dominates no allocation)

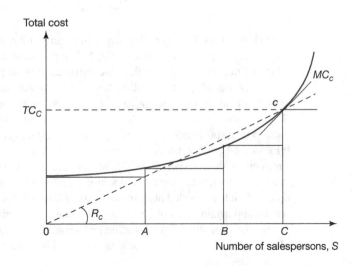

FIGURE 7-3

Total cost of human resource department: Relation between overhead rate and marginal cost (cost allocation equals marginal cost)

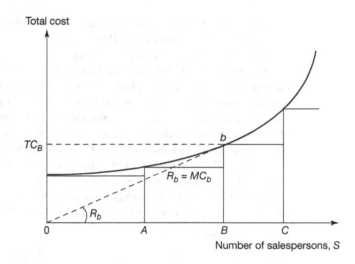

Case 2 (*Figure 7-3*)

At point b, the overhead rate, R_b, is

$$R_b = \frac{TC_B}{B} = MC_b$$

The slope of the line from the origin through point b is the average cost of the HR department when B salespeople are employed. The slope of this line also happens to be the marginal cost in the HR department of adding one more employee in the firm. At this point, the cost allocation rate (the average cost) and the marginal cost are equal. It is highly unlikely that the firm will be operating at this point. But if it is, cost allocations perfectly mimic the correct opportunity cost. Clearly, if the firm happens to be at point b, it should allocate overhead (the HR department), because the overhead rate is exactly equal to the marginal cost in the HR department of hiring one more salesperson. Unfortunately, there is no guarantee that the firm will be at point b.

Case 3 (*Figure 7-4*)

At point a, the overhead rate, R_a, is

$$R_a = \frac{TC_A}{A} > MC_a$$

The slope of the line from the origin through point a is the overhead rate at point a, R_a. Again, R_a is the average cost of the HR department when there are A salespeople. The slope of this line is steeper than the marginal cost at point a (solid line). At point a, or wherever $R > MC$, the cost allocation rate overstates the marginal cost of the externality. Taxing the branch manager R_a might cause too large a reduction in salespeople. Whenever $R > MC$, cost allocations might do more harm than good. For example, suppose the overhead rate, R, on an additional salesperson is $2,000, yet the externality from degraded service in the HR department of hiring the salesperson is $100. Suppose the additional profit from hiring the salesperson is $55,500 and her wages and benefits are $55,000. The profit-maximizing sales manager will not hire the person because the additional profit of $55,500 is less than the reported accounting costs of $57,000 (or $55,000 + $2,000). However, the actual opportunity cost of $55,100 is less than the benefits. Therefore (unlike in Case 1, in which the firm should always allocate overhead), we cannot unambiguously demonstrate that human resource costs should be allocated in Case 3.

FIGURE 7-4

Total cost of human resource department: Relation between overhead rate and marginal cost (no allocation may dominate cost allocation)

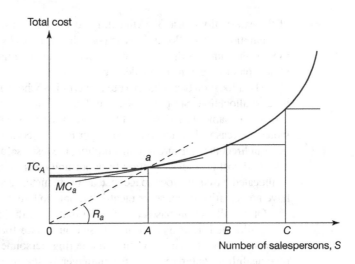

The analysis presented in Figures 7–1 through 7–4 demonstrates that situations do exist where allocating overhead (i.e., allocating human resource department costs) is better than not allocating. Whenever average cost is less than marginal cost, the costs allocated are less than the marginal cost incurred by the firm. Although the firm is not allocating enough cost, it is probably better to impose some tax than no tax on the managers who cause HR department costs to rise. Unfortunately, a simple rule such as "always allocate" or "never allocate" does not exist. The allocation decision depends on the exact shape of the cost curve of the overhead department and where the firm is on the curve. It also depends on whether other inputs are allocated and the relation among inputs. The only guidance, without more knowledge of the cost structure, is to consider allocating whenever marginal cost is above average cost; if marginal cost is below average cost, allocating may not be a good idea.

While knowledge of marginal costs is often difficult to obtain without special studies, the following relations hold for all cost curves:

1. Marginal cost equals average cost when average cost is at a minimum (point b).
2. Marginal cost is above average cost when average cost is increasing (point c).
3. Marginal cost is below average cost when average cost is decreasing (point a).[2]

Given these relations between average and marginal costs, the firm should consider allocating overhead when average cost is increasing, because in this case we also know that marginal cost is always above average cost. Hence, the decision to allocate or not does not require knowledge of marginal costs, but of whether the average cost is falling or rising as output expands.

To summarize, cost allocations are average costs and are a proxy for difficult-to-observe marginal costs. This is an example of using cost allocations to improve decision making. However, some care should be exercised in using cost allocations as internal taxes. In some situations, the cost allocation rate can be significantly larger than the marginal cost

---

[2]Consider average and marginal baseball batting averages. If a professional baseball player has a season batting average of .300 and has two at-bats and gets one hit and one strike-out, his marginal batting average that day is .500 and his season's batting average rises. If he strikes out both times at bat, his marginal batting average for the day is .000 and his seasonal average falls.

of the externality (Case 3). Allocating costs in this case might cause managers to reduce consumption of the allocation base (say, direct labor) by too much. Firm profits might fall more if they underutilize salespeople than if they overutilize salespeople when there is no allocation of human resource department costs.

The allocation base chosen often determines whether firm value is enhanced or harmed by cost allocation. Suppose a service department's output can be directly metered to the user in the same way that a public utility measures electric consumption using electric meters. A reasonably accurate "cost" per unit of service can be established. However, the more indirect the measure of consumption, the less useful is the cost allocation because the allocated cost bears less relation to opportunity cost. For example, if power consumption is allocated based on floor space instead of on meter readings, the consuming departments have no incentive to conserve electricity, only to reduce square footage.

Often, allocation bases are chosen that have the greatest association with the cost being allocated. Rent is allocated based on square footage. Allocating advertising and marketing expense using the time marketing personnel spend on the marketing for the responsibility center reminds the manager of the responsibility center that marketing is not free. Cost allocations also affect managers' incentives in other ways, which are discussed next.

3. Insulating versus Noninsulating Cost Allocations

As discussed at the beginning of this chapter, a common cost arises because it is less expensive for some resource to be provided centrally and shared among the users than for each user to procure the resource individually; human resource department costs are a common cost. Suppose two distinct manufacturing divisions share a common plant location and share common costs, including property taxes, security costs, grounds and building maintenance, and human resource department costs. One division manufactures computer routers and the other manufactures computer disk drives. Although the two divisions share a common building, each is treated as a separate profit center.

Two questions arise:

1. Should the common costs be allocated to the two divisions?
2. If so, how should they be allocated?

The following discussion assumes that both profit center managers' compensation is based on accounting profits, which have deducted any allocated common cost. That is, cost allocations affect the managers' welfare. If common costs are not allocated, the managers in the two divisions have less incentive to invest in the specialized knowledge necessary to determine the optimum level of the common costs. If the decision rights over the level of common costs do not reside with the managers of the two divisions and the common costs are not allocated back to the two divisions, the division managers will demand more common resources. If these managers individually or collectively have the decision rights over the common resources but are not charged for the common costs, these costs will grow rapidly as the managers invent ways to substitute off-budget common costs for currently consumed inputs included in their budget. For example, security guards are a common cost. Suppose security costs are not charged to either division. The division managers have an incentive to use security guards to perform maintenance or even operate machines, thereby reducing the amount of direct labor charged to each division's budget.

Most firms allocate common costs, presumably to prevent individual divisions from overconsuming the common resource. The next question becomes choosing an allocation base. Choosing an allocation base causes it to be taxed and, as demonstrated earlier, managers will reduce their consumption of the taxed item. But this creates other incentives. Consider the following illustration.

Suppose our two manufacturing divisions have a significant amount of interaction: They hire from a common local workforce, they use common shippers, and they deal with the same government officials for building permits, air quality standards, and safety standards. Ideally, the two division managers should cooperate with each other. However, within their firm, they are probably competitors, vying for the same promotion. If one division does poorly, it might enhance the other manager's chances when a promotion opportunity arises.

Cost allocations can promote or discourage cooperation between the two managers, depending on the type of allocation method. With an **insulating allocation**, the costs allocated to one division do not depend on the operating performance of the other division. With a **noninsulating allocation**, the allocated costs of one division do depend on the other division's operating performance. For example, our two divisions share the same factory building and both are profit centers. Assume that the common costs of the shared factory space are $1 million per month. In both January and February, the computer router division has profits of $8 million before allocations. The router division has profits of $8 million in January and $2 million in February. If common costs are allocated using actual profits, then profits after cost allocations for one division depend on the performance of the other division, as illustrated in Table 7–4. This is a noninsulating cost allocation.

In part A of Table 7–4, common costs of $1 million per month are allocated based on actual profits. The router division has the same level of division profits before allocation each month: $8 million. Yet its profits after cost allocation are smaller by $300,000 in February. This reduction occurs because the router division is allocated more common costs when the disk drive division's profits fall; at the same time, the disk drive division receives lower allocated costs.

In Table 7–4, part A's allocation method is noninsulating because each division's allocation depends on the performance of the other. An insulating allocation method is presented in part B of Table 7–4 in which common costs are allocated using floor space. The router division has 60 percent of the floor space and is therefore allocated $600,000 of common costs. To the extent that floor space does not vary with performance, at least in the short run, the performance of one division is not affected by the other division's

TABLE 7–4   Noninsulating and Insulating Cost Allocation Methods ($000s)

	January		February	
	Router Division	*Disk Drive Division*	*Router Division*	*Disk Drive Division*
A. Noninsulating Method				
Division profits before allocation	$8,000	$8,000	$8,000	$2,000
Allocated common costs*	(500)	(500)	(800)	(200)
Net income	$7,500	$7,500	$7,200	$1,800
B. Insulating Method				
Division profits before allocation	$8,000	$8,000	$8,000	$2,000
Allocated common costs†	(600)	(400)	(600)	(400)
Net income	$7,400	$7,600	$7,400	$1,600

*Common costs are allocated based on actual division profits before allocated costs.

†Common costs are allocated based on square footage. The router division has 60 percent of the square footage.

performance. In the long run, if one division expands floor space relative to the other, it will receive a larger fraction of the common costs. Using floor space to allocate the common costs insulates each division's profits from the performance of the other division.

Noninsulating systems can use sales or head count (employment) instead of profits. Either of these allocation bases will cause one division's profits to vary with the actual results of the other division. Insulating allocation systems use predetermined allocation rates that do not vary with actual results.

Both insulating and noninsulating methods give the division managers an incentive to economize on common costs. The noninsulating method (Table 7–4, part A) provides each division manager with incentives to increase the other division's profitability, thereby increasing the other division's share of the common costs. In this sense, noninsulating allocations create incentives for mutual monitoring and cooperation by managers. Noninsulating cost allocations are examples of cost allocations used for control purposes.

The disadvantage of a noninsulating method is that it distorts the performance measure of one division by tying it to another division's performance. Some argue that managers should be held responsible for only those revenues and expenses over which they have decision rights and hence control. (This controllability principle was discussed in Chapter 5.) In the preceding example, the common costs are jointly controllable by both managers. If there is a large interaction effect between the two managers in that one can significantly affect the other's performance, then each manager is held responsible for the other's performance through a noninsulating allocation method.

While noninsulating allocations distort the performance measure by basing one division's share of overhead on another division's performance, they can reduce the risk managers bear. Suppose two divisions are affected by random events outside their control. Moreover, suppose these random events affecting the two divisions are not perfectly positively correlated. If one division has an unusually unfavorable random shock, the other division is unlikely to have such an adverse shock and will absorb more overhead in that period. The division with the adverse event will absorb less overhead and will show a larger profit after common costs are allocated than it would if an insulating allocation method were used. Likewise, a highly favorable random event in one division is likely to occur when the other division does not have such a good period. The division with the good fortune will absorb more overhead, and its performance measure will not be as large as it would if overhead were allocated using an insulating method.

Noninsulating methods act like shock absorbers for random events and reduce the variability of all managers' performance measures. If managers were risk-neutral, such risk sharing would not matter. Variations in allocated costs due to noninsulating allocations wash out over time. And since a risk-neutral manager does not care about variability, the lower risk imposed by noninsulating cost allocation does not matter. But decreased variability does matter to risk-averse managers. Noninsulating methods reduce the variability of their performance measures.[3]

In the previous example, the two divisions shared common factory resources and controlled the level of common costs. Now consider corporate headquarters expenses, such as the president's staff expenditures. The divisions do not have decision rights over the level of corporate headquarters expenses, but noninsulating allocations still create incentives for mutual monitoring. Although they cannot directly control the level of the costs being allocated, subordinate managers can pressure senior management to control staff growth.

---

[3]As long as the random events are not perfectly positively correlated, then noninsulating methods diversify some of the risk managers bear. The analysis is a straightforward application of portfolio theory as to why risk-averse investors want to hold a diversified portfolio of securities.

To summarize the discussion,

1. Common costs should be allocated for decision making and control whenever the marginal cost of a common resource, such as the human resource department, is equal to or greater than the resource's reported average cost.

2. Common costs should be allocated using an allocation base that does not insulate subunits whenever interactions among the subunits are high and cooperation is important. If interaction is unimportant, an allocation base should be chosen that does not fluctuate with other subunits' performance.

3. Noninsulating cost allocations can reduce the risk managers bear by diversifying that risk across other managers.

4. Noninsulating allocations cause one manager's performance (after including the allocation) to be distorted by other managers' performance.

Concept Questions		
	Q7–3	How do cost allocations act as a tax system?
	Q7–4	Define *externality* and give an example of one.
	Q7–5	What is the difference between a positive and a negative externality?
	Q7–6	How are externalities reduced within a firm?
	Q7–7	Describe the three cases to consider when determining if a cost allocation is beneficial.
	Q7–8	Should common costs be allocated?
	Q7–9	Describe how a noninsulating allocation promotes cooperation among managers and encourages mutual monitoring.
	Q7–10	Why would senior managers want to distort factor prices by using cost allocations?

D. Summary

Cost allocations pervade all organizations. Managers allocate costs for a variety of reasons, including: financial reporting, taxes, cost-reimbursement contracts, and government regulation. But it appears that many organizations allocate costs for decision making and control. The important lessons from this chapter are:

1. Cost allocations act as an internal tax on the factor input being used as the allocation base. And, like taxes in general, cost allocations change managers' incentives and hence the decisions they make.

2. Certain inputs, used to produce the firm's goods or services, notably labor, impose externalities on the firm in the sense that when more of that input is used, other costs in the firm also rise. Managers will want to tax that input if its reported cost does not fully reflect its cost plus the externality it generates. The way to tax the input is to use it as the allocation base for allocating some other cost to the manager with the decision rights over the taxed input. For example, labor can be taxed by allocating corporate overhead to departments based on the number of employees in each department.

3. Costs can be allocated in ways that increase or decrease managers' mutual monitoring and cooperation with each other. Noninsulating cost allocations increase mutual monitoring and coordination; insulating methods do the opposite.

300   *Chapter 7*

4. Noninsulating cost allocations can reduce the risk managers face. For example, if a division's profits are unusually low, fewer costs are allocated to this division, thereby softening the full impact of the lower profits. Hence, noninsulating allocations induce risk-sharing among managers and can diversify the risk borne by managers.

Self-Study Problems

Fitzhugh Investors

Fitzhugh Investors sells, manages, and operates three mutual funds: Money Market, Blue Chip, and Fixed Income. Each fund's prospectus specifies a schedule of fees payable to Fitzhugh Investors for its services. The company derives all of its revenue from two fees. The first fee Fitzhugh receives from each fund is based on the net assets in the fund. The second fee is based on the number of accounts. Table 1 itemizes the fee structure for each fund.

Each fund is operated as a separate line of business, incurring avoidable direct expenses for sales and administration, fund management, and transfer agency functions (brokerage fees, maintaining customer accounts, and safekeeping securities). Additionally, the funds employ several common corporate resources, such as a Web site, computer facilities, telephone representatives, security analysts, and corporate staff. Fitzhugh Investors allocates these corporate expenses to the respective funds based on the number of accounts. Corporate expenses total $2,595,000. Management estimates that closing any one fund could avoid $125,000 and any two funds $200,000 of the corporate expenses. Table 2 presents the direct expenses for each fund.

Required:

 a. Prepare an income statement that shows the direct expenses and the allocated corporate expenses by mutual fund for Fitzhugh.

 b. Fitzhugh's managers are reviewing the income statement prepared in part (*a*). Some of the funds are reporting a loss. What actions should management take?

Solution:

 a. Revenues of each fund are composed of the asset-based fee times the net assets plus the per-account fee times the number of accounts. Corporate expenses are allocated based on the number of accounts.

TABLE 1   **Fitzhugh Investors Product Line Summary Data**

	Money Market	Blue Chip	Fixed Income	Total Funds
Asset-based fees	0.75%	1.75%	1.25%	—
Per-account fee	$25	$8	$9	—
Net assets (millions)	$1,050	$1,150	$1,824	$4,024
Accounts (thousands)	275	110	185	570

TABLE 2   **Fitzhugh Investors Direct Expenses by Fund**

	Money Market	Blue Chip	Fixed Income
Sales and administration	$ 2,696,000	$2,332,000	$ 6,838,000
Fund management	1,400,000	2,750,000	1,800,000
Transfer agency	10,465,000	7,224,000	18,911,000

FITZHUGH INVESTORS
Net Income by Fund Both Before and After
Allocated Corporate Expenses

	Money Market	*Blue Chip*	*Fixed Income*	*Total Funds*
Revenues				
Asset-based fees	$ 7,875,000	$20,125,000	$22,800,000	$50,800,000
Per-account fees	6,875,000	880,000	1,665,000	9,420,000
Direct Expenses				
Sales and administration	2,696,000	2,332,000	6,838,000	11,866,000
Fund management	1,400,000	2,750,000	1,800,000	5,950,000
Transfer agency	10,465,0001	7,224,000	18,911,000	36,600,000
Gross profit	$189,000	$8,699,000	$(3,084,000)	$5,804,000
Corporate expense	1,252,000	501,000	842,000	2,595,000
Net income (loss)	$ (1,063,000)	$ 8,198,000	$(3,926,000)	$3,209,000

b. Based on the current accounting system, the money market and fixed income funds are reporting losses after allocating corporate expenses. If the money fund is closed, Fitzhugh does not
avoid losing $1,063,000 because this includes allocated corporate expense. Only $125,000 of
corporate expense is avoided by closing one fund. The money fund is generating $189,000 of
gross profit before corporate expenses. If this fund is eliminated, Fitzhugh forgoes $189,000
of cash flow but saves only $125,000. Thus it should not eliminate the money fund.

The fixed income fund is losing more than $3 million before any corporate expense is
allocated. Therefore, it appears that if this fund is closed, Fitzhugh would save this loss
plus corporate expenses of $125,000.

However, the preceding analysis fails to account for the positive externalities associated with having related funds. Exchange privileges between the funds—specifically,
the ability to shift money across funds—are valued by investors. Before dropping the
fixed income fund, Fitzhugh must consider how many blue chip and money market
accounts such action would sacrifice now and in the future. An accounting system such as
Fitzhugh's offers no real way of assessing the impact of such externalities.

Problems

P 7–1:   MRI

Magnetic resonance imaging (MRI) is a noninvasive medical diagnostic device that uses magnets
and radio waves to produce a picture of an area under investigation inside the body. A patient is
positioned in the MRI and a series of images of the area (say, the knee or abdomen) is generated.
Radiologists then read the resulting image to diagnose cancers and internal injuries. The MRI at
Memorial Hospital has the following projected operating data for next year.

	Fixed Cost	*Variable Cost*	*Total Cost*
Equipment lease	$350,000		$350,000
Supplies		$ 97,000	97,000
Labor	145,000	182,000	327,000
Hospital administration	63,000		63,000
Occupancy	48,000		48,000
Total projected costs	$606,000	$279,000	$885,000
Number of images			33,600
Number of hours			2,800

Memorial Hospital serves two types of patients: elderly, whose hospital bills are covered by
governments (state and federal reimbursement), and other patients, who are covered by private

insurance (such as Blue Cross and Blue Shield). About one-third of Memorial's patients are elderly. Elderly patients using MRI services normally require more time per MRI image. The typical elderly patient requires one hour of MRI time to produce the 10 MRI images needed for the radiologist. Other patients only require about 45 minutes per patient to generate the 10 MRI images.

Governments reimburse MRI imaging based on the reported cost by the hospital. Reimbursable costs include both the fixed and variable costs of providing MRIs. Private insurers reimburse MRI imaging based on a standard fee schedule set by the insurance company. These fee schedules are independent of the hospitals' cost of providing MRI services.

Required:

a. Calculate Memorial Hospital's projected cost per MRI image.

b. Calculate Memorial Hospital's projected cost per hour of MRI time.

c. Suppose a typical elderly patient at Memorial Hospital requires 10 MRI images and takes one hour of MRI time. Calculate the cost of providing this service if Memorial Hospital calculates MRI costs based on cost per image.

d. Suppose a typical elderly patient at Memorial Hospital requires 10 MRI images and takes one hour of MRI time. Calculate the cost of providing this service if Memorial Hospital calculates MRI costs based on cost per hour of MRI time.

e. Should Memorial Hospital calculate the cost of MRI services based on the cost per image or the cost per MRI hour? Explain why.

P 7–2:   Fair Allocations

Choosing among alternative cost allocation methodologies typically is based on one of the following criteria: cause-and-effect, benefits derived, fairness, or ability to bear. Discuss how the "fairness" criterion can be used in selecting a cost allocation methodology.

P 7–3:   Slawson

Slawson is a publicly traded Argentine company with three operating companies located in Argentina, the United States, and Germany. Slawson's corporate headquarters in Buenos Aires oversees the three operating companies. The annual cost of the corporate headquarters, including office expenses, salaries, and legal and accounting fees, is 2.4 million pesos. The following table summarizes operating details of each of the three operating companies.

	Argentina	*United States*	*Germany*
Number of employees	1,500	300	200
Net income (loss) in pesos (millions)	(100)	400	500

Required:

a. Allocate the 2.4 million pesos corporate headquarters cost to the three operating companies using number of employees in each operating company.

b. Allocate the 2.4 million pesos corporate headquarters cost to the three operating companies using net income of each operating company as the allocation base.

c. Discuss the advantages and disadvantages of allocating corporate headquarters costs using (1) employees and (2) net income.

P 7–4:   The Corporate Jet

A large corporation maintains a fleet of three 30-passenger corporate jets that provide (weather permitting) daily scheduled service between Detroit and several cities that are home to its production facilities. The jets are used for business, not personal, travel. Corporate executives book reservations through a centralized transportation office. Because of the limited number of seats available, the planes almost always fly full, at least in the nonwinter months. Excess demand for seats is assigned by executive rank within the firm. The executive's budget is charged for the flight at the end of the month. The charge is based on the jet's total operating expenses during the month (including fuel, pilot's salary and fringes, maintenance, licensing fees, landing fees, and 1/12 of the annual accounting depreciation) divided by the actual passenger miles logged in the month. This rate per passenger mile is multiplied by each passenger's mileage flown in the month.

Required:

   a. Describe the formula being used to calculate the cost per passenger mile flown.
   b. As passenger miles flown increases, what happens to the cost per passenger mile?
   c. Describe what causes the monthly charge per passenger mile flown to fluctuate.
   d. What other problems are present in the current system and what improvements do you suggest making?

P 7–5: Massey Electronics

Massey Electronics manufactures heat sinks. Heat sinks are small devices attached to solid-state circuit boards that dissipate the heat from the circuit board components. Made of aluminum, the devices consist of many small fins cut in the metal to increase its surface area and hence its ability to dissipate the heat. For example, Intel Pentium and Celeron processors are first mounted onto heat sinks and then attached to circuit boards. These processors generate heat that will ultimately destroy the processor and other components on the circuit board without a heat sink to disperse the heat.

Massey has two production facilities, one in Texas and the other in Mexico. Both produce a wide range of heat sinks that are sold by the three Massey lines of business: laptops and PCs, servers, and telecommunications. The three lines of business are profit centers, whereas the two plants are cost centers. Products produced by each plant are charged to the lines of business selling the heat sinks at full absorption cost, including all manufacturing overheads. Both plants supply heat sinks to each line of business.

The Texas plant produces more complicated heat sinks that require tighter engineering tolerances. The Texas workforce is more skilled, but also more expensive. The Mexico plant is larger and employs more people. Both facilities utilize a set of shared manufacturing resources: a common manufacturing IT system that schedules and controls the manufacturing process, inventory control, and cost accounting, industrial engineers, payroll processing, and quality control. These shared manufacturing overhead resources cost Massey $9.5 million annually.

Massey is considering four ways to allocate this $9.5 million manufacturing overhead cost pool: direct labor hours, direct labor dollars, direct material dollars, or square footage of the two plants. The following table summarizes the operations of the two plants:

	Texas	Mexico
Direct labor hours	3,000,000	4,000,000
Direct labor dollars	$60,000,000	$40,000,000
Direct material dollars	$180,000,000	$200,000,000
Square footage	200,000	300,000

Massey has significant tax loss carryforwards due to prior losses and hence expects no income tax liability in any tax jurisdiction where it operates for the next five years.

Required:

   a. Prepare a table showing how the $9.5 million would be allocated using each of the four proposed allocation schemes (direct labor hours, direct labor dollars, direct material dollars, and square footage of the two plants).
   b. Discuss the advantages and disadvantages of each of the four proposed allocation methods (direct labor hours, direct labor dollars, direct material dollars, and square footage of the two plants).

304   *Chapter 7*

P 7–6:   Avid Pharmaceuticals

Avid, a small, privately held biotech pharmaceutical manufacturing firm, specializes in developing and producing a set of drugs for rare classes of cancers. Avid has two divisions that share the same manufacturing and research facility. The two divisions, while producing and selling two different classes of products to different market segments, share a common underlying science and related manufacturing processes. It is not unusual for the divisions to exchange technical know-how, personnel, and equipment. The following table summarizes their most current year's operating performance:

	Division A	*Division B*
Number of employees	80	20
Plant square footage (000)	80	120
Revenues (000)	$2,000	$1,000
Operating expenses (000)	600	500
Operating profits (000)	$1,400	$ 500

Avid's corporate overhead amounts to $900,000 per year. Management is debating various ways to allocate the corporate overhead to the two divisions. Allocation bases under consideration include: number of employees, plant square footage, revenues, operating expenses, and operating profits. Each division is treated as a separate profit center with each manager receiving a bonus based on his or her division's net income (operating profits less allocated corporate overhead).

Required:

a. For each of the five proposed allocation bases, compute Division A's and Division B's net income (operating income less allocated corporate overhead).

b. Recommend one of the five methods (or no allocation of corporate overhead) to allocate corporate overhead to the two divisions. Be sure to justify your recommendation.

P 7–7:   Wasley

Wasley has three operating divisions. Each manager of a division is evaluated on that division's total operating income. Managers are paid 10 percent of operating income as a bonus.

The AB division makes products A and B. The C division makes product C. The D division makes product D. All four products use only direct labor and direct materials. However, a fixed (unavoidable) $1,784 corporate overhead is applied to each division (or product) based on direct labor dollars. In the following operating income statement for the first quarter of the year, all numbers are in 000s.

	Income Statement			
	Product A	*Product B*	*Product C*	*Product D*
Net sales	$1,250	$850	$1,250	$1,650
Direct labor	450	600	540	640
Direct materials	250	0	125	160
Corporate overhead				

Required:

a. Allocate the corporate overhead and compute divisional operating income (after allocating corporate overhead) for each of the three divisions.

b. One day, the manager of the AB division, Shirley Chen, announces that starting in the second quarter she will be discontinuing product B (replacing it with nothing and letting the labor go, cutting all direct costs attributable to the product). She reasons that product B is losing money for her division and the company. Recompute first-quarter operating income for both division AB and the corporation without division AB's product B (as though the manager had already dropped product B).

    c. Is Shirley Chen, the manager of the AB division, better off this way? Why or why not?

    d. Is the corporation better off this way? Why or why not?

    e. What problems do you see with the reporting/evaluation/incentive system currently in place?

SOURCE: Charles Kile.

P 7–8: Hallsite Imaging

Hallsite Imaging produces hardware and software for imaging the structures of the human eye and the optic nerve. Hallsite systems are in most major medical centers and leading ophthalmology clinics. Hallsite has three divisions: Hardware, Software, and Marketing. All three are profit centers, and the three divisional presidents are compensated based on their division's profits. The Hardware Division produces the equipment that captures the images, which are then viewed on desktop PCs. The Software Division produces the software that runs on both Hallsite imaging equipment and the users' PCs to view, manipulate, and manage the images. Hallsite hardware only works with the Hallsite software, and the software can only be used for images captured by Hallsite hardware.

The Marketing Division produces the marketing materials and has a direct sales force of 1,000 Hallsite people that sells both the hardware and software in the United States (Hallsite operates only in the United States). To assess the profits of the Hardware and Software Divisions, the costs of the Marketing Division are allocated back to the Hardware and Software Divisions based on the revenues of the two divisions. The following table summarizes the divisional sales and divisional expenses (before allocation of Marketing Division costs) for the Hardware and Software Divisions for last quarter and this quarter. (All figures are in millions of dollars.)

	Last Quarter		This Quarter	
	Hardware Division	*Software Division*	*Hardware Division*	*Software Division*
Revenue	$500.00	$700.00	$510.00	$400.00
Division expenses	315.00	308.00	321.30	176.00

The Marketing Division reported divisional costs of $320 million last quarter and $370 million this quarter.

Required:

    a. Allocate the Marketing Division's costs to the Hardware and Software Divisions for last quarter and this quarter.

    b. Calculate the Hardware and Software Divisions' profits for this quarter and last quarter after allocating the Marketing Division's expenses to each division.

    c. After receiving her division's profit report for this quarter (which included the Hardware Division's share of the Marketing Division's costs), the president of the Hardware Division called Hallsite's chief financial officer (whose office prepared the report) and said, "There must be something wrong with my division's profit report. Hardware's sales rose and our expenses were in line with what they should have been given last quarter's operating margins. But my profits tanked. Now I know that there was a major problem with Software's new version 7.0 that hurt new sales of upgrades to version 7.0 and required more Marketing resources to address our customers' concerns with this new software. But why am I getting hammered? I didn't cause the software problems. My hardware continues to sell well because version 6.8 of the software still works great. This is really very unfair."

306 *Chapter 7*

Write a memo from Hallsite's chief financial offer to the Hardware Division president explaining that the Hardware Division's current quarter profit report (which includes the Division's share of the Marketing expenses) is in fact correct and outlining the various rationales as to why Hallsite allocates the Marketing Division's expenses to the other two divisions.

P 7–9: Rowe Waste Removal (B)

Continuing the problem started in Rowe Waste Removal (A) in Chapter 2, Rowe Waste Removal hires Sue Lingle to manage the apartment complex collection service and enters the apartment refuse removal market. To provide Lingle incentives to maximize Rowe's profit, she will receive a bonus tied to the profits of her apartment waste collection business. Apartment profits are calculated based on the apartment waste collection revenues less the costs of the apartment waste service (truck lease, dumpsters, driver, fuel, oil, licensing, landfill charges, and Lingle's salary and benefits). (*Note:* Any bonus paid to Lingle is not included in calculating the profits of the apartment waste service.) In addition to these direct costs of the apartment refuse collection service, Lingle is charged a fee of $50 per 25-unit apartment complex to cover her share of the billing, accounting, legal costs, and general operating expenses of Rowe.

Required:

    a. Assume all the costs in Rowe Waste Removal (A) in Chapter 2 remain the same and in addition to the $54,000 per month cost of the truck, driver, etc., Lingle's salary and benefits are $72,000 per year. What price-quantity combination will Lingle select to maximize her bonus?

    b. Explain why the price-quantity combination Sue Lingle chooses in part (*a*) is the same or differs from the firm-profit maximizing price-quantity combination chosen in part (b) of Rowe Waste Removal (A) in Chapter 2.

    c. In computing Sue Lingle's apartment waste collection profits for determining her bonus, should she be charged a fee of $50 per 25-unit apartment complex to cover her share of the billing, accounting, legal costs, and general operating expenses of Rowe?

P 7–10: Winterton Group

The Winterton Group is an investment advisory firm specializing in high-income investors in upstate New York. Winterton has offices in Rochester, Syracuse, and Buffalo. Operating as a profit center, each office receives central services, including information technology, marketing, accounting, and payroll. Winterton has 20 investment advisors, 7 each in Syracuse and Rochester, and 6 in Buffalo. Each investment advisor is paid a fixed salary, a commission based on the revenue generated from clients, plus 2 percent of regional office profits and 1 percent of firm profits. One of the senior investment advisors in each office is designated as the office manager and is responsible for running the office. The office manager receives 8 percent of the regional office profits instead of 2 percent.

Regional office expenses include commissions paid to investment advisors. The following regional profits are calculated before the 2 percent profit sharing. Firm profits are the sum of the three regional office profits.

This table summarizes the current profits per office after allocating central service costs based on office revenues.

WINTERTON GROUP
Profits by Office
Current Year (Millions)

	Rochester	Syracuse	Buffalo
Revenue	$16.00	$14.00	$20.00
Operating expenses	(12.67)	(11.20)	(16.30)
Central services*	(1.92)	(1.68)	(2.40)
	$ 1.41	$ 1.12	$ 1.30

*Allocated on the basis of revenue.

The manager of the Buffalo office sent the following e-mail to the other office managers, the president, and the chief financial officer:

> One of the primary criteria by which all cost allocation schemes are to be judged is fairness. The costs allocated to those bearing them should view the system as fair. Our current system, which allocates central services using office revenues, fails this important test of fairness. Receiving more allocated costs penalizes those offices generating more revenues. A fairer, and hence more defensible, system would be to allocate these central services based on the number of investment advisors in each office.

Required:

a. Recalculate each office's profits before any profit sharing assuming the Buffalo manager's proposal is adopted.

b. Do you believe the Buffalo manager's proposal results in a fairer allocation scheme than the current one? Why or why not?

c. Why is the Buffalo manager concerned about fairness?

P 7–11: National Training Institute

Five departments of National Training Institute, a nonprofit organization, share a rented building. Four of the departments provide services to educational agencies and have little or no competition for their services. The fifth department, Technical Training, provides educational services to the business community in a competitive market with other nonprofit and private organizations. Each department is a cost center. Revenues received by Technical Training are based on a fee for services, identified as tuition.

All five departments have dedicated space as listed in the accompanying table. Common shared space, including hallways, restrooms, meeting rooms, and dining areas, is not included in these allocations. National Training Institute rents space at $10 per square foot.

Allocation Table

Department	Square Footage	Percentage of Space	Revenue
Administration	13,500	9.0%	$ 3,600,000
Support services	46,500	31.0	11,000,000
Computer services	12,000	8.0	8,800,000
Technical training	6,000	4.0	1,900,000
Transportation	72,000	48.0	4,700,000
Total allocated	150,000	100.0%	$30,000,000
Common space	50,000		

In addition to its assigned space, the technical training department offers training during off-hours using many of the areas allocated to other departments. Technical Training also uses off-site facilities for the same purpose. About 50 percent of its training activities are in off-site facilities, which have excess capacity, charge no rent, and are available only during off-hours.

John Daniels, the administration department's business manager, proposed a rental allocation plan based on each department's percentage of dedicated square footage plus the same percentage of the common space. The technical training department would be charged an additional amount for the space it uses during off-hours that is dedicated to other departments. This additional amount would be based on planned usage per year.

Jane Richards, director of technical training, claims this allocation method will cause her to increase the price of services. As a result, she will lose business to competition. She would rather see the allocation method use the percentage of department revenue in relation to total revenue.

Required:

Comment on Daniels's and Richards's proposed rent allocation plans. Make appropriate recommendations.

P 7–12: Colorado BBQ

Colorado BBQ makes a unique barbecue sauce that involves slow roasting very spicy chili peppers from India, pureeing the peppers to remove the seeds, and then flash frying the roasted peppers with the other ingredients before bottling. The sauce is sold throughout the United States. Colorado BBQ is considering entering the Canadian BBQ market with a slightly different recipe and bottle design and label. In order to be able to export its Colorado BBQ sauce into Canada without paying Canadian customs duty at 7 percent of the wholesale price (U.S. $8.99), Colorado BBQ must certify that at least 90 percent of the total manufacturing cost of the Canadian BBQ sauce is from products sourced entirely within the North American Free Trade Agreement or NAFTA (Canada, Mexico, and the United States). If more than 10 percent of the total product cost is determined to be from ingredients sourced outside of NAFTA (Canada, Mexico, and United States), then the product is subject to a 7 percent Canadian import duty. Given the competitive nature of the Canadian BBQ market, Colorado BBQ is unable to pass any Canadian customs duty on to its Canadian importer.

The current breakdown of the direct costs (excluding allocated manufacturing overheads) of the U.S. and Canadian BBQ sauces is (all amounts are U.S. dollars):

	U.S. BBQ Sauce	CDN BBQ Sauce
Bottle and label	$0.09	$0.14
Non-chili ingredients	$0.48	$0.80
Indian chilies	$0.74	$0.76
Direct labor	$0.11	$0.12

The manufacturing overhead for the factory that may produce both the U.S. and Canadian Colorado BBQ sauces is $383,000 per year, and 65,000 bottles will be produced for the U.S. market and 22,000 bottles for the Canadian market. Manufacturing overhead will be allocated to the two BBQ sauces using direct labor cost. All of the manufacturing costs, ingredients, and packaging (except the Indian chilies) are sourced entirely within the NAFTA countries.

Required:

   a. Calculate the manufacturing overhead allocated per bottle of the Canadian BBQ sauce.

   b. Calculate what, if any, Canadian import customs duty Colorado BBQ must pay on the importation of its BBQ sauce based on NAFTA.

   c. Before beginning the production of its Canadian sauce, Colorado BBQ learns of a very similar chili pepper from Mexico that can be used in the Canadian BBQ sauce without altering the sauce's flavor or consistency. The cost of the Mexican chili is $1.26 per Canadian bottle of BBQ sauce instead of the $0.76 per bottle for the Indian chili. Substituting the Mexican chilies for the Indian chilies in the Canadian sauce does not alter any of the other costs of the Canadian sauce. Should Colorado BBQ substitute the Mexican chili for the Indian chili in its Canadian BBQ sauce it plans to export to Canada? What advice would you give to the managers of Colorado BBQ regarding the production, cost certification for Canadian customs under NAFTA, and exportation of its Canadian Colorado BBQ sauce?

P 7–13: Ball Brothers Purchasing Department

The purchasing department of Ball Brothers purchases raw materials and supplies for the various divisions in the firm. Most of the purchasing department's costs are labor costs. The costs of the purchasing department depend on the number of items purchased. The manager of the purchasing department estimates how her department's costs will vary with different levels of demand by the divisions. The following table provides her estimates of how the costs of purchasing vary with the aggregate number of items purchased by all divisions.

Number of Items Purchased per Week	Total Cost per Week
100–199	$1,000
200–299	1,100
300–399	1,200
400–499	1,400
500–599	1,700
600–699	2,100
700–799	2,600
800–999	3,200

In deriving this table, the manager of purchasing projects expanding the size of the department in order to keep roughly constant the time to purchase an item and the quality of the purchasing department's services at all levels of demand placed on the department. That is, if the department is processing 750 items per week, it will provide the same quality of services given a budget of $2,600 as it would processing 250 items per week given a budget of $1,100.

Required:

    a. Suppose the purchasing department is currently purchasing 610 items per week. Should the department's costs of $2,100 per week be allocated back to the divisions, making the purchases at a charge of $3.44 per item purchased ($2,100 ÷ 610)? Explain why or why not.

    b. Suppose the purchasing department is currently purchasing 210 items per week. Should the department's costs of $1,100 per week be allocated back to the divisions, making the purchases at a charge of $5.23 per item purchased ($1,100 ÷ 210)? Explain why or why not.

    c. Reconcile (explain) why your answers to parts (*a*) and (*b*) are either the same or different.

P 7–14:   Dewan Locks

Dewan Locks produces and sells a keyless bicycle lock that uses a small wireless fob to lock and unlock the lock without the need of a key. Dewan produces two models: one for the European market (EU) and one for North America (NA). Dewan started producing the North American lock at its Eastbury plant, and then introduced the EU model, which was also assembled in the Eastbury plant. When demand for both models grew and exceeded the capacity of Eastbury, Dewan leased the Westbury plant. Following the weakening global economy, Dewan saw the demand for its locks from both Europe and North America fall. This caused Dewan's total profits to plummet. The following table summarizes operations for the last fiscal quarter.

	Westbury (EU Lock)	Eastbury (NA Lock)	Total
Units produced and sold	11,000	17,000	
Selling price	$90.00	$95.00	
Variable cost per unit	$65.00	$50.00	
Fixed manufacturing overhead	630,000	510,000	1,140,000
Operating income	–$355,000	$255,000	–$100,000

To address the current operating loss of $100,000, Dewan owners are moving the EU lock production from the Westbury plant to the Eastbury plant where it now has excess capacity due to the declining sales of the NA lock, and since the lease on the Westbury plant is expiring soon. By canceling the lease of the Westbury plant and moving the EU locks back to the Eastbury plant, the fixed manufacturing overhead of producing EU locks will fall from its current level of $630,000 to $210,000. In other words, Dewan will save the lease and occupancy cost of the Westbury plant ($630,000) but will have to incur additional fixed manufacturing cost of $210,000 in Eastbury to produce the EU locks in Eastbury. Stated differently, with both plants in operation, Dewan's total fixed manufacturing overhead is $1,140,000 ($630,000 + $510,000). Total manufacturing overhead will be $720,000 ($510,000 + $210,000) by consolidating both NA and EU lock production into the Eastbury plant.

The EU and the NA locks are separate profit centers with the managers of the two profit centers evaluated and compensated based on the operating income of their respective profit centers.

Required:

   a. Dewan still expects to sell 11,000 locks in Europe and 17,000 in North America. By closing the Westbury plant and producing both the NA and the EU locks in Eastbury, what happens to Dewan's operating income?

   b. After consolidating production of the NA and EU locks in the Eastbury plant, Dewan needs to allocate the $720,000 of common fixed manufacturing overhead of the Eastbury plant to the two profit centers (NA locks and EU locks). The $720,000 of Eastbury's common fixed manufacturing overhead to the two profit centers is to be allocated using total contribution margin (unit sales times the difference between selling price and variable cost per unit) as the allocation base. Using total contribution margin to allocate the manufacturing overhead to the two profit centers, prepare operating income statements for the NA locks and EU locks profit centers for last quarter as if the Westbury plant has closed and all locks are produced in Eastbury.

   c. After seeing the operating income statements prepared in part b, the manager of the NA lock profit center argues, "Something must be wrong in these operating income statements. Why should the NA lock operating income change just because EU locks are now being produced in Eastbury? I haven't done anything differently, so why is NA Locks being penalized for closing Westbury plant and moving the EU locks into Eastbury? All of the benefits of closing Westbury seem to accrue to EU Locks and none to NA Locks." Write a memo to Dewan's president explaining whether the arguments by the manager of the NA Locks profit center have any merits.

   d. Would you recommend using the overhead allocation scheme described in part (*b*), or would you propose an alternative allocation scheme? And if so, what scheme would you recommend, and why?

P 7–15:   Diagnostic Imaging Software

Diagnostic Imaging Software (DIS) is the leading producer of imaging software for the health sciences. DIS develops, writes, produces, and sells its software through two direct selling organizations: North America and South America. Each of these direct selling forces is evaluated and rewarded as profit centers. The remaining world sales of DIS software are handled through independent distributors in Europe, Asia, and Africa. DIS has a software development group that designs, writes, and debugs the software before turning it over to the direct sales organizations (North and South America) and the independent distributors who then sell the software. The cost of designing, writing, and debugging the software is $12 million this year.

The following table presents the income statements of the two divisions (millions of $) for this year:

	North America	South America
Revenues	$17.800	$6.700
Operating expenses*	5.340	3.015
Profit before software development cost	$12.460	$3.685

*Does not include any costs of developing, writing, or debugging the software.

Senior management of DIS wants to allocate the software costs to the two direct-selling forces in order to evaluate and reward their performance.

Required:

a. Calculate the profits of the two direct selling organizations (North and South America) after allocating the software costs of $12 million based on the relative revenues of the two organizations. (Round all decimals to three significant digits.)

b. Calculate the profits of the two direct selling organizations (North and South America) after allocating the software cost of $12 million based on the relative profits before software development cost of the two organizations. (Round all decimals to three significant digits.)

c. Calculate the profits of the two direct selling organizations (North and South America) after allocating the software cost of $12 million where 75 percent of the cost is assigned to North America and 25 percent to South America. (Round all decimals to three significant digits.)

d. Discuss the advantages and disadvantages of each of the three allocation methods used in parts (*a*), (*b*), and (*c*).

P 7–16: Fuentes Systems

Fuentes Systems provides security software to law enforcement agencies. It has a sales force of 70 and has plans to add another 10–15 salespeople. Fuentes allocates corporate administrative costs based on the number of salespeople. The current total administrative cost of $2,184,000 comprises the costs of the human resources, payroll, accounting, and information technology departments.

You manage the western region of Fuentes Systems with 18 salespeople and you plan to add one or two more salespersons. Each salesperson you hire costs $120,000, which includes salary, benefits, and payroll taxes. If you hire one additional salesperson, you expect that person will generate $185,000 of net operating margin for your region. Net operating margin is revenues less cost of sales and less travel and entertainment expenses associated with that salesperson. Net operating margin does *not* include the salary, benefits, and payroll taxes of the salesperson. If you hire two salespeople, the combined additional net operating margin added to your region is expected to be $323,000. You are evaluated and rewarded as a profit center, where profits are calculated as net operating margin less the total salaries, benefits, and payroll taxes of all salespeople employed in the region, plus allocated corporate administrative costs.

Required:

a. What is the current allocated administrative cost per salesperson?

b. Assuming that your hiring of additional salespeople does not alter the allocated cost per salesperson, how many salespersons will you hire in the western region?

c. Suppose that Fuentes hires an additional 10 salespeople, and the total corporate administrative cost rises from $2,184,000 to $2,640,000. Should Fuentes continue to allocate corporate administrative costs to the regions? Explain why or why not.

d. Now suppose that Fuentes hires an additional 10 salespeople and the total corporate administrative cost rises from $2,184,000 to $2,200,000. Should Fuentes continue to allocate corporate administrative costs to the regions? Explain why or why not.

P 7–17: Vorma

Vorma manufactures two proprietary all-natural fruit antioxidant food additives that are approved by the U.S. Food and Drug Administration. One is for liquid vitamins (LiqVita) and the other is used by dry cereal producers (Dry). Both of these products are sold only in the United States, and although they both share common chemistry and manufacturing, their end markets are completely separated. Both are produced in the same plant and share common manufacturing processes, such as purchasing, quality control, human resources, and so forth. These common fixed overhead costs amount to $1,500,000 per month. Each product also has its own directly traceable fixed costs, such as dedicated equipment leases used only by one of the two products, dedicated product engineers, and so forth. The following table summarizes the operations of Vorma for a typical month.

	LiqVita	Dry
Units	200,000	75,000
Price per unit	$10	$21
Variable cost per unit	$6	$11
Own fixed costs per month	$90,000	$110,000

Again, the "Own fixed costs" consist of all fixed costs that can be traced directly to one of the two products (LiqVita and Dry), and these costs do not vary with the number of units produced.

Required:

a. Prepare a typical monthly income statement for LiqVita and Dry after allocating the common fixed overhead costs of $1,500,000 per month to the two product lines based on the relative proportions of total variable costs generated by each product.

b. Which of the two products in part (*a*) is the most profitable and which is the least profitable? (*Note:* You are not being asked to analyze or explain the relative profitablities of LiqVita and Dry.)

c. Vorma is planning to introduce a tablet version of its vitamin into China, with a selling price of $9 and a variable cost per unit of $7. At a price of $9, Vorma managers believe they will sell 950,000 units per month in China. Introducing the new product (called China) will require additional "Own fixed costs" (just for China) of $800,000. As in part (*a*), prepare monthly income statements, computing the monthly net income for the three products (LiqVita, Dry, and China). Allocate the common fixed overhead of $1,500,000 based on the relative proportions of total variable costs generated by each product.

d. As in part (*b*), list the order of the most profitable to least profitable products. Do not do any analysis.

e. Compare the relative profitability of the two products (LiqVita and Dry) before introducing China [part (*b*)] and after introducing China [part (*d*)]. Analyze and discuss why the relative profitability of the two preexisting products (LiqVita and Dry) does or does not change with the introduction of the new product (China).

P 7–18: Easton Taylor & Beckett LLC

Easton Taylor & Beckett, LLC (ETB), an enterprise risk management (ERM) firm, offers IT and security consulting services including network and IT security risk assessment, computer forensic services, IT audit services, regulatory compliance, and attestation services for clients in the food processing industry.

Until recently, ETB has been organized around three regional offices (Boston, Chicago, and Atlanta), each treated as a separate profit center. The corporate office manages the three regional offices (human resources, accounting, payroll, marketing, etc.), develops the specialized enterprise risk management products, and makes them available for use by the three regional offices. The following table summarizes the operations of ETB when it had only three regional offices.

	Boston	Atlanta	Chicago
Revenue	$3,450,000	$2,900,000	$3,440,000
Direct cost	1,035,000	1,015,000	1,238,400
Own indirect cost	345,000	464,000	584,800

Direct cost represents the cost incurred by the regional office to provide ERM services to clients, such as consulting labor, travel, etc. "Own indirect costs" represents costs incurred by the regional office (occupancy costs, training, etc.) that are not directly traceable to a particular client. In addition to the costs incurred by the regional offices (direct and indirect costs), ETB incurs corporate expenses (executive officers, occupancy costs, IT, tax compliance) of $3,780,000 to manage the entire firm and to maintain and develop the ERM tools offered to ETB clients through the regional offices.

Required:

a. Calculate the profitability of each of the three regional offices after allocating the corporate expenses to the three offices using revenues as the allocation base.

b. What is the relative profitability of the three regional offices (first, second, and third most profitable) after allocating corporate expenses?

c. At the end of last year, ETB acquired a similar ERM consulting firm in San Francisco. To support the expanded operations, ETB expects to incur an additional $500,000 of corporate expenses. The following table provides information regarding the operations of ETB as if the San Francisco office had been part of ETB for the entire year.

	Boston	Atlanta	Chicago	San Francisco
Revenue	$3,450,000	2,900,000	3,440,000	3,100,000
Direct cost	1,035,000	1,015,000	1,238,400	1,240,000
Own indirect cost	345,000	464,000	584,800	558,000

Calculate the profitability of each of the four regional offices after allocating the total corporate expenses ($4,280,000) to the four offices using revenues as the allocation base.

d. What is the relative profitability of the four regional offices (first, second, third, and fourth most profitable) after allocating corporate expenses?

e. Compare the relative profitability of the three original offices (Boston, Chicago, and Atlanta) before [part (b)] and after the acquisition of the San Francisco office [part (d)]. Analyze and discuss why the relative profitability of the three original offices (Boston, Chicago, and Atlanta) does or does not change with the acquisition of the San Francisco office.

f. Comment on the appropriateness or inappropriateness of ETB's current cost allocation methodology.

P 7–19: World Imports

World Imports buys products from around the world for import into the United States. The firm is organized into a number of separate regional sales districts that sell the imported goods to retail stores. The eastern sales district is responsible for selling the imports in the northeastern region of the country. Sales districts are evaluated as profit centers and have authority over what products they wish to sell and the price they charge retailers. Each sales district employs a full-time direct sales force. Salespeople are paid a fixed salary plus a commission of 20 percent of revenues on what they sell to the retailers.

The eastern district sales manager, J. Krupsak, is considering selling an Australian T-shirt that the firm can import. Krupsak has prepared the following table of his estimated unit sales at various prices and costs. The cost data of the imported T-shirts were provided by World Imports's corporate offices.

WORLD IMPORTS
Eastern Sales District
Proposed Australian T-Shirt
Estimated Demand and Cost Schedules

Quantity (000s)	Wholesale Price	T-Shirt Price Imported Cost
10	$6.50	$2.00
20	5.50	2.20
30	5.00	2.50
40	4.75	3.00

The unit cost of the imported shirts rises because the Australian manufacturer has limited capacity and will have to add overtime shifts to produce higher volumes. Corporate headquarters of World Imports is considering allocating corporate expenses (advertising, legal, interest, taxes, and administrative salaries) back to the regional sales districts based on the sales commissions paid in the districts. It estimates that the corporate overhead allocation rate will be 30 percent of the commissions (for every $1 of commissions paid in the districts, $0.30 of corporate overhead will be allocated). District sales managers receive a bonus based on net profits in their district. Net profits are revenues less costs of imports sold, sales commissions, other costs of operating the districts, and corporate overhead allocations.

The corporate controller, who is proposing that headquarters costs be allocated to the sales regions and included in bonus calculations, argues that all of these costs must ultimately be covered by the profits of the sales districts. Therefore, the districts should be aware of these costs and must price their products to cover the corporate overhead.

Required:

a. Before the corporate expenses are allocated to the sales districts, what wholesale price will Krupsak pick for the Australian T-shirts and how many T-shirts will he sell? Show how you derived these numbers.

b. Does the imposition of a corporate overhead allocation affect Krupsak's pricing decision on the Australian T-shirts? If so, how? Show calculations.

c. What are the arguments for and against the controller's specific proposal for allocating corporate overhead to the sales districts?

P 7–20:   Painting Department

You are manager of a painting department of a large office complex. The painting department is responsible for painting the buildings' exteriors and interiors. Your performance is judged in part on minimizing your department's operating costs, which consist of paint and labor, while providing a high-quality and timely service.

The job of painting the halls of a particular building is being evaluated. Paint and labor are substitutes. To provide the quality job demanded, you can use less paint and more labor, or more paint and less labor. The accompanying table summarizes this trade-off. Paint costs $10 per gallon and labor costs $6.40 per hour.

Paint (Gallons)	Labor (Hours)
50	200
80	125
100	100
125	80
200	50

Required:

a. How much paint and how much labor do you choose in order to minimize the total cost of the hall painting job? (Show calculations in a neatly labeled exhibit.)

b. The accounting department institutes an overhead allocation on labor. For every dollar spent on labor, $0.5625 of overhead is allocated to the paint department to cover corporate overhead items, including payroll, human resources, security, legal costs, and so forth. Now how much labor and paint do you choose to minimize the total accounting cost of the hall painting job? (Show calculations in a neatly labeled exhibit.)

c. Explain why your decisions differ between parts (a) and (b).

d. Explain why the accounting department might want to allocate corporate overhead based on direct labor to your painting department.

P 7–21:   Scanners Plus

Scanners Plus manufactures and sells two types of scanners for personal computers, the Home Scanner and the Pro Scanner. The Home model is a low-resolution model for small-office applications. The Pro model is a high-resolution model for professional use. The two models are manufactured in separate facilities and each model is treated as a profit center. This table summarizes the prices and costs of each model.

	Home Scanner	Pro Scanner
Selling price to retailers	$ 1,600	$ 8,800
Variable cost	600	2,800
Fixed cost (annual)	800,000	2,400,000

Both models are sold through large office supply and computer stores and through computer catalogs. The marketing department of Scanners Plus sells both models. It has a direct sales force that sells to retail stores and an advertising group that prepares and places ads in computer magazines and computer catalogs. The annual operating budget of the marketing group is $1,000,000. The marketing costs can be allocated to the two profit centers in one of two ways: either on the basis of total revenues or on the basis of 24 percent to the Home model and 76 percent to the Pro model.

At a selling price of $1,600, the Home model division projects the number of units it expects to sell next year to be either 1,000 units or 1,400 units, each equally likely. Similarly, at $8,800, either 600 or 800 units of the Pro model are equally likely to be sold. The demand for Pro scanners is independent of the demand for Home scanners. That is, one can be in high demand while the other one can be in either low or high demand.

Required:

a. Calculate total revenues under various scenarios for the Home model.

b. Calculate total revenues under various scenarios for the Pro model.

c. Suppose the marketing department costs of $1 million are allocated to Home and Pro models using the predetermined, fixed proportions of 24 percent to Home and 76 percent to Pro. Prepare a table projecting all the various total profits of Home and Pro after allocating marketing costs using these predetermined rates.

d. Calculate all the possible overhead proportions that can result from allocating the marketing department costs using the revenues in each profit center as the allocation base. (Round all overhead proportions to two significant digits, e.g., 44.67 percent rounds to 45 percent.)

e. Same as in part (c), except calculate profits for the two profit centers using the overhead rates computed in part (d).

f. Parts (c) and (e) asked you to compute divisional profits for the Home and Pro models using two different methods for allocating marketing costs. Comment on the relative advantages and disadvantages of the two methods.

P 7–22:   Taylor Connect

Taylor Connect operates dedicated call services for a variety of global customers in financial services, consumer products, and health sciences. Conner Beckett manages the call center in Omaha, Nebraska. This call center takes customer queries from a consumer products client. Taylor Connect employees are trained to handle calls from customers of this client in such a way that the callers believe they are talking to employees of the consumer products firm and not those of an outsourced provider of the call center (Taylor Connect). This consumer products client generates 1,200 calls a day at the Omaha call center. To handle this volume of calls, Conner requires both human operators and sophisticated technology (hardware and software). Technology allows many typical questions to be answered by prerecorded messages and by routing specific questions to agents trained to answer these queries. The following table shows how operators (also called agents) and technology can be substituted for each other in order to handle the 1,200 calls per day.

Number of Agents	Number of Technology Units
8	150.0
9	133.3
10	120.0
11	109.1
12	100.0
13	92.3
14	85.7
15	80.0
16	75.0
17	70.6
18	66.7
19	63.2
20	60.0

To process 1,200 calls per day, Conner can either hire eight agents and purchase 150 technology units or hire 20 agents and purchase 60 technology units (and various combinations between these two). A technology unit consists of hardware and software that can route and process calls. The various combinations of agents and technology units in the above table yield the same "quality" in the sense that callers (and the consumer products client) are indifferent among the various combinations. Agents cost $160 per day (salary, fringe benefits, taxes, etc.), and one technology unit costs $30 per day.

Conner is evaluated as a cost center and has decision rights over how many agents to hire and how many technology units to purchase. His performance is evaluated on several criteria, including the total cost of operating his call center.

Required:

a. How many agents and technology units will Conner choose to minimize the daily operating cost of the call center?

b. The chief financial officer (CFO) of Taylor Connect decides to allocate corporate overhead (human resources, legal, accounting, etc.) to the call centers to better judge the profitability of the firm's various decentralized call centers. Each call center will be charged $40 per operator (agent) per day as the mechanism to allocate this corporate overhead. Will Conner change the number of agents and technology units chosen to process the 1,200 calls per day after corporate overhead of $40 per agent per day is allocated? And if so, how many of each will he select?

    c. The CFO justifies the allocation of overhead by arguing, "The corporate overheads have to be paid for by our operations. So it is natural to charge our call centers for these costs." Critically evaluate the CFO's justification for charging the call centers corporate overhead.

    d. Should the call centers be charged corporate overhead? Explain.

P 7–23: Economic Experts

Economic Experts (EE) provides economic consulting and litigation support in complex legal cases. One of EE's current clients, USClient, had a contract with ForeignCO to design and build a plant for ForeignCO. Before the plant was completed (and before ForeignCO made any payments to USClient), ForeignCO notified USClient that it was canceling the contract. USClient filed a lawsuit claiming that ForeignCO breached the contract and as a result of this contract breach USClient was claiming damages of $220 million. These damages consist of $170 million of out-of-pocket expenses that USClient spent designing and building the ForeignCO plant and $50 million of fixed overhead that USClient allocated to the ForeignCO project.

At the time it was building the ForeignCO plant, USClient had several other construction projects. As part of USClient's normal accounting practice, it allocates all overhead costs not incurred directly on particular projects to all projects, using total direct costs as the allocation base. Using this allocation methodology, the total overhead costs allocated to the ForeignCO project totaled $50 million.

ForeignCO hired an expert who wrote a report rejecting the $50 million of overhead as damages. Specifically, the expert for ForeignCO argued:

> "Costs included as damages must be incremental to the contract in order to be damages. As such, those costs must be directly related and necessary to the activities caused by the breach and reflect expenditures that would not have been made but for the breach. Based on my review of USClient's overhead, it is my opinion that the $50 million of overhead claimed as damages by USClient are either unrelated to the ForeignCo project or are fixed in nature and needed for the general operations of USClient. The $50 million of overhead costs would have been incurred by USClient and are not incremental to the ForeignCO project. Therefore, the damages claimed by USClient of $50 million of fixed overhead should not be included as damages."

EE has been engaged by USClient to provide an expert witness to comment on ForeignCO's expert report cited above. You have been hired by EE as the expert witness to rebut ForeignCO's opinion. The legal definition of damages resulting from a breach of contract by a defendant are usually calculated under the principle that compensation awarded to the plaintiff as damages should place the plaintiff in the economical position equivalent to the plaintiff's position had the harmful event never occurred.

Required:

Write a rebuttal report that critiques the ForeignCO expert witness. In other words, do you agree with ForeignCO's expert that the $50 million of fixed overhead should be excluded as damages claimed by USClient? If you disagree, explain why the ForeignCO expert's opinion is wrong. Note: For the purposes of your report, you should assume that the $50 million of overhead consists of allocated fixed indirect charges such as the salaries of the senior executives (CEO, CFO, etc.), the human resource department, accounting, information technology, depreciation on the corporate office, and so forth.

P 7–24: Finsys

Finsys offers Web design and website maintenance and hosting for the mutual fund industry. Finsys clients are small mutual funds that do not have scale economies to design and maintain their own Web portals that their mutual fund investors can access to check account information, receive performance reports on their investments in the fund, and manage their accounts. Finsys uploads real-time information feeds and interfaces with their mutual fund clients' IT systems. The Finsys product line consists of various tools and software modules that enable their clients to control their data and content by automating Web content, print production, and securities regulation compliance.

Finsys has four departments: marketing, Web design, website maintenance, and website hosting. The marketing department contacts potential customers to sell Finsys services, prepares bids, and negotiates final contract details. The typical contract is for three years. (Finsys' Web design services are priced very competitively to win the initial bid.) The Web design department works with clients to design the Web client's initial website to create the client's brand (i.e., the look and feel of the client's website). The website maintenance department provides day-to-day and end-of-quarter website revisions and data feeds so the mutual fund client's customers have access to the latest information about their accounts. Finally, the website hosting department maintains the secure servers that contain the client's mutual fund's data and provides security against hackers and backup. Mutual fund clients of Finsys pay separately for Web design services, website maintenance, and website hosting.

Web design, website maintenance, and website hosting are profit centers, and the managers of these profit centers are rewarded based on their department's operating income. In addition to the four departments, Finsys has an administration department consisting of the CEO, CFO, human resources, and accounting. The following data summarize Finsys's current operating performance:

	Web Design	Web Maintenance	Web Hosting	Total
Revenue	$ 650,000	$1,240,000	$1,180,000	$3,070,000
Operating expenses	(610,000)	(887,000)	(239,000)	(1,826,000)
Operating income	$ 40,000	$ 353,000	$ 851,000	$1,244,000
Marketing				(446,000)
Administration				(698,000)
Net income				$ 100,000

Currently, Finsys does not allocate the marketing and administration costs to the three profit centers. The CEO and CFO believe that the three profit centers' operating profits are not indicative of the real profits of these profit centers because the profit centers are not bearing any of the marketing and administration expenses. The CEO and CFO propose allocating the marketing and administration costs back to the three profit centers based on the percentage of the profit centers' revenues to Finsys's total revenue.

Required:

a. Prepare a revised set of financial statements that report each profit centers' net income after allocating the marketing and administration costs back to the three profit centers using revenues as the allocation base.

b. Briefly discuss the relative profitability of the three profit centers after allocating marketing and administration expenses using revenues as the allocation base.

c. Analyze the CEO's and CFO's proposal to allocate marketing and administration expenses using revenues as the allocation base. What, if any, changes would you suggest to their proposal of allocating marketing and administration expenses using revenues as the allocation base?

P 7–25: Allied Adhesives

Allied Adhesives (AA) manufactures specialty bonding agents for very specialized applications (electronic circuit boards, aerospace, health care, etc.). AA operates a number of small plants around the world, each one specializing in particular products for its niche market. AA has a small plant in

St. Louis that manufactures aerospace epoxy resins and a larger plant in Atlanta that manufactures epoxies for electronics. Each produces somewhat similar epoxy resins that are sold to different customers. The manufacturing processes of the aerospace and electronic adhesives are quite similar, but the selling processes and the types of customers are very different across the two divisions. The St. Louis plant is being closed and moved to Atlanta to economize on duplicative selling, general, and administrative costs (SGA). Aerospace and Electronics will continue to operate as separate divisions. The following table summarizes the current operations of the two plants:

	Aerospace (St. Louis)	Electronics (Atlanta)
Revenue	$16.800	$42.100
Manufacturing cost	8.568	23.155
Manufacturing margin	$ 8.232	$18.945
SGA–variable	5.376	12.630
SGA–fixed	1.900	2.500
Net income	$ 0.956	$ 3.815
Return on sales	5.69%	9.06%

NOTE: Costs in millions.

After Aerospace moves to the Atlanta facility, each division continues to operate as a separate profit center, and neither Aerospace nor Electronics is expected to have its revenues, manufacturing cost, or variable SGA affected. The only change projected from moving Aerospace to Atlanta is that the total fixed SGA will fall from $4.4 million to $3.0 million through elimination of redundant occupancy, administrative, and human resource expenses.

AA evaluates its divisional managers based on return on sales (net income divided by sales).

Required:

    a. Prepare separate financial statements reporting *net income* and *return on sales* for Aerospace and Electronics after the move where the expected lower fixed SGA of $3 million is allocated to the two divisions using:

        (1) Revenues as the allocation base.

        (2) Manufacturing cost as the allocation base.

        (3) Manufacturing margin as the allocation base.

        (Round all allocations to the nearest $1,000.)

    b. Discuss how moving Aerospace into Atlanta affects the relative profitability of the Aerospace and Electronics divisions.

    c. Which of the three possible allocation schemes in part (*a*) will each division manager (Aerospace and Electronics) prefer? Why?

    d. Which allocation scheme should AA adopt? Explain why.

    e. Should AA be using return on sales as the performance measure for its divisional managers?

P 7–26: Plastic Chairs

Plastic Chairs manufactures plastic lawn chairs using a combination of new and recycled plastic. Varying amounts of each type of plastic can be used to produce a batch of 100 chairs. The following table lists the various combinations of recycled and new plastic required to produce one batch of 100 chairs.

320   *Chapter 7*

**Pounds of New and Recycled Plastic Required
to Manufacture One Batch of 100 Chairs**

Pounds of New Plastic	*Pounds of Recycled Plastic*
20	72
24	60
30	48
32	45
36	40
40	36
45	32
48	30
60	24
72	20

New plastic costs $16 per pound and recycled plastic costs $10 per pound. The manager of the chair manufacturing department receives a bonus based on minimizing the cost per batch of 100 chairs.

Required:

a. What combination of new and recycled plastic will the manager of the chair manufacturing department choose?

b. Overhead (including plant administration, utilities, property taxes, and insurance) is allocated to the chair manufacturing department based on the number of pounds of recycled plastic used in each batch. For each pound of recycled plastic used, the chair manufacturing department is charged $30 of plant overhead. What combination of new and recycled plastic will the manager of the chair manufacturing department select if the manager's bonus is based on minimizing the total cost per batch, which includes new and recycled plastic and plant overhead?

c. Why are your answers to parts (*a*) and (*b*) either the same or different?

d. Should the plastic chairs manufacturing manager's bonus be based on minimizing only the plastic costs or should it also be based on minimizing plastic costs plus allocated plant overhead?

P 7–27:   Law Firm Merger

The managing partners of the law firms Spencer, Spinelli, and Howe (SSH) and Gilbert and Lenz (GL) are discussing a possible merger. The two firms specialize in different areas of law, but focus on the same corporate client pool. The proposed merger offers two benefits: higher revenues and lower combined overhead costs. Higher revenues are forecast through cross selling (current SSH clients will start to use GL and vice versa). Three percent more billable hours per attorney in each firm is expected, and these additional billable hours will not require adding any more staff or other costs (such as higher lawyer salaries) because both firms have excess capacity across their professional staffs. Moreover, the billing rates of the two firms will not change following the merger. All attorneys in each firm are paid a flat annual salary and a share of any profits.

Combined overhead costs will fall 25% by merging and eliminating duplicate service functions such as accounting, IT, marketing, and so forth. The following table summarizes the pre-merger operating data for each firm.

	SSH	GL
Number of attorneys	140	165
Average hours billed per attorney per year	1,700	1,900
Average billing rate per hour	$155	$143
Average attorney cost* per year	$155,000	$148,000
Overhead per year	$13,580,000	$11,055,000

*Salary and benefits.

Overhead consists of all other costs except the cost of attorneys (salary and benefits). Each firm now distributes any profits among its lawyers using formulas based on seniority and revenues generated by the attorney.

Post-merger, the new firm will be known as Spinelli and Gilbert (SG) and will consist of two profit centers: SSH and GL. All attorneys in the two pre-merged firms will remain and will be assigned to the corresponding post-merger profit center. Each profit center will distribute its profits to the lawyers in that profit center using the same pre-merger distribution formula. Post-merger, the overhead of the two firms will be pooled and allocated back to the two profit centers based on the number of billable hours generated in each profit center.

Required:

a. Prepare a table that reports the current profits of each firm before the merger and the total profits of the two firms prior to the merger.

b. Prepare a table that reports the profits of each profit center (SSH and GL) after allocating the overhead based on billable hours following the merger assuming that the cost savings and additional revenues are realized.

c. Based on the analyses in parts (*a*) and (*b*), discuss the likely outcome of the proposed merger talks. For example, will the attorneys in SSH and GL be equally enthused about the merger? Do you expect the merger to occur if put to a vote of all the lawyers in each firm?

d. What is the underlying cause for your prediction in part (*c*)?

P 7–28: Transmation

Transmation, with sales of more than $2.2 billion, builds and markets several of the world's leading brands of construction and agricultural equipment. Transmation has three operating divisions that are decentralized investment centers. While the three divisions produce and sell different lines of equipment to different customers, they do share a common R&D platform, corporate brand name, and many of the same marketing strategies, and operate in many of the same international jurisdictions. Currently, each division president is evaluated and rewarded based on the division's return on assets, defined as net income divided by total assets invested in the division. Net income is revenues generated by the division less operating expenses incurred by the division. The table below summarizes Transmation's annual operating results by division ($ millions).

	DIV A	DIV B	DIV C
Operating expenses	$300	$900	$800
Total divisional assets	$500	$500	$400
Revenues	$370	$1,050	$950

Required:

a. Calculate each division's ROA.

b. Each of the three Transmation divisions utilizes substantial corporate office resources. These include legal, marketing, information technology, human resources, and research and development. In addition to these corporate level services, Transmation incurs expenses for being a publicly traded firm (accounting, taxes, and the cost of corporate officers and director). These annual corporate-level expenses amount to $270 million, and currently each division is not being charged for these corporate expenses. The divisional operating expenses in the preceding table do not include any allocation of the $270 million corporate expenses. The corporate chief financial officer (CFO) argues that because each division has roughly equal amounts of total assets, each division should be allocated one-third of the $270 million corporate expenses. Calculate each division's ROA after allocating the corporate expenses using the CFO's proposed scheme.

c. Transmation's chief executive officer (CEO) likes the CFO's idea of allocating the corporate expenses to the divisions, but argues that each division does not consume equal corporate resources. Rather, each division's consumption of the various corporate resources is more likely proportional to the division's operating expenses. The CFO and CEO rule out more elaborate metering systems whereby each corporate resource, such as HR or IT, would keep track of the time they devote to each division. The CEO and CFO are convinced that such direct metering would be costly and generate much ill will between the divisions and the corporate departments. Calculate each division's ROA after allocating the corporate expenses using the CEO's proposed scheme.

d. Briefly describe how the relative profitability of the three divisions changes across the three scenarios calculated in parts (*a*), (*b*), and (*c*). Do NOT discuss the pros and cons of the various scenarios. Just describe how the numbers change.

e. Now describe the pros and cons of the three allocation scenarios [including part (*a*), where there are no allocations].

f. Which of the three allocation schemes would you recommend, or would you propose an alternative allocation scheme?

P 7–29: Symmetric Inc.

Symmetric Inc. has two profit centers (North and South) operating in different regions of the world. North and South divisions sell identical services to similar types of customers. However, because of their geographic separation, the two divisions do not share common customers. Most of the compensation of the senior management teams of North and South is tied to their division's profits, and the remainder is base salary. Annual profits in the two divisions depend heavily on the effort and skill of the senior management teams. Nonetheless, random shocks to each division's regional economy can cause its profits in any given year to add or subtract $100 million (each equally likely) from the profits the division would have earned absent the shock. For example, if the South Division would have earned $200 million absent the shock, after the shock it would have earned either $100 million or $300 million. Random economic shocks to North's profits are uncorrelated (independent) with random shocks to South's regional economy. Both divisions have the same expected profits.

The CFO of Symmetric wants to allocate $80 million of fixed corporate-level overhead costs to the two divisions, and is considering one of two possible allocation schemes: (1) allocate the $80 million based on the profits of the two profit centers, or (2) allocate the $80 million evenly; that is, $40 million to each division irrespective of the actual profits of the two profit centers.

Required:

Critically analyze the two alternative overhead allocation schemes and make a recommendation to senior management based on your analysis. Your recommendation should be supported by a rigorous quantitative analysis of the situation.

P 7–30: BFR Ship Building

BFR is a ship-building firm that has just won a government contract to build 10 high-speed patrol boats for the Coast Guard for drug interdiction and surveillance. Besides building ships for the government, BFR has a commercial vessel division that designs and manufactures commercial fishing and commuting ships. The commercial division and the government division are the only two divisions of BFR, and the Coast Guard contract is the only work in the government division.

The Coast Guard contract is a cost-plus contract. BFR will be paid its costs plus 5 percent of total costs to cover profits. Total costs include all direct materials, direct labor, purchased subassemblies (engines, radars, radios, etc.), and overhead. Overhead is allocated to the Coast Guard contract based on the ratio of direct labor expense on the contract to firmwide direct labor.

BFR can either purchase the engines from an outside source or build them internally. The following table describes the costs of the commercial division and the Coast Guard contract if the engines are built by BFR versus purchased outside.

BFR
Cost Structure
($ in Millions)

	Commercial Division	Coast Guard Contract (Engines Manufactured Internally)	Coast Guard Contract (Engines Purchased Externally)
Direct labor	$14.600	$22.800	$18.200
Direct material		32.900	25.900
Purchased engines		0.000	17.000

Overhead for BFR is $83.5 million and does not vary if the engines are purchased outside or manufactured inside BFR. Overhead consists of corporate-level salaries, building depreciation, property taxes, insurance, and factory administration costs.

Required:

    a. How much overhead is allocated to the Coast Guard contract if

        (1) The engines are manufactured internally?

        (2) The engines are purchased outside?

    b. Based on the total contract payment to BFR, will the Coast Guard prefer BFR to manufacture or purchase the engines?

    c. What is the difference in net cash flows to BFR of manufacturing versus purchasing the engines?

    d. Explain how cost-plus reimbursement contracts in the defense industry affect the make–buy decision for subassemblies.

Cases

Case 7–1: Phonetex

Phonetex is a medium-size manufacturer of telephone sets and switching equipment. Its primary business is government contracts, especially defense contracts, which are very profitable. The company has two plants: Southern and Westbury. The larger plant, Southern, is running at capacity producing a phone system for a new missile installation. Existing government contracts will require Southern to operate at capacity for the next nine months. The missile contract is a firm, fixed-price contract. Part of the contract specifies that 3,000 phones will be produced to meet government specifications. The price paid per phone is $300.

The second Phonetex plant, Westbury, is a small, old facility acquired two years ago to produce residential phone systems. Phonetex feared that defense work was cyclical, so to stabilize earnings, a line of residential systems was developed at the small plant. In the event that defense work deteriorated, the excess capacity at Southern could be used to produce residential systems. However, just the opposite has happened. The current recession has temporarily depressed the residential business. Although Westbury is losing money ($10,000 per month), top management considers this an investment. Westbury has developed a line of systems that are reasonably well received. Part of its workforce has already been laid off. It has a very good workforce remaining, with many specialized and competent supervisors, engineers, and skilled craftspeople. Another 20 percent of Westbury's workforce could be cut without affecting output. Current operations are meeting the reduced demand. If demand does not increase in the next three months, this 20 percent will have to be cut.

The plant manager at Westbury has tried to convince top management to shift the missile contract phones over to his plant. Even though his total cost to manufacture the phones is higher than at Southern, he argues that this will free up some excess capacity at Southern to add more government work. The unit cost data for the 3,000 phones are as follows:

	Southern	Westbury
Direct labor cost	$ 70	$ 95
Direct materials cost	40	55
Variable factory overhead*	35	45
Fixed factory overhead*	40	80
General burden†	10	20
Total unit cost	$195	$295

*Based on direct labor costs.

†Allocated corporate headquarters expense based on direct labor cost.

Westbury cannot do other government work, because it does not have the required security clearances. But Westbury can do the work involving the 3,000 phones. And it can complete this project in three months. "Besides," Westbury's manager argues, "my labor costs are not going to be $95 per phone. We are committed to maintaining employment at Westbury at least for the next three months. I can utilize most of my existing people who have slack. I will have to hire back about 20 production workers I laid off. For the three months, we are talking about $120,000 of additional direct labor."

Phonetex is considering another defense contract with an expected price of $1.1 million and an expected profit of $85,000. The work would have to be completed over the next three months, but Southern does not have the capacity to do the work and Westbury does not have the security clearances or capital equipment required by the contract.

Southern's manager says it isn't fair to make him carry Westbury. He points out that Westbury's variable cost, ignoring labor, is 33 percent greater than Southern's variable costs. Southern's manager also argues, "Adding another government contract will not replace the profit that we will be forgoing if Westbury does the telephone manufacturing. See my schedule."

Profits from Southern ($300 – 195)3,000		$ 315,000
Less: Profits from Westbury ($300 – 295)3,000		(15,000)
Forgone profits		$ 300,000
Profit in the next best government contract:		
Expected price		$1,100,000
Less:		
Direct labor	260,000	
Direct material	435,000	
Variable overhead	130,000	
Fixed factory overhead	150,000	
General burden	40,000	1,015,000
Expected profit		$ 85,000

Required:

Top management has reviewed the Southern manager's data and believes his cost estimates on the new contract to be accurate. Should Phonetex shift the 3,000 phones to Westbury and take the new contract or not? Prepare an analysis supporting your conclusions.

Case 7–2: Durango Plastics

SCX is a $2 billion chemical company with a plastics plant located in Durango, Colorado. The Durango plastics plant of SCX was started 30 years ago to produce a particular plastic film for snack food packages. The Durango plant is a profit center that markets its product to film producers. It is the only SCX facility that produces this plastic.

A few years ago, worldwide excess capacity for this plastic developed as a number of new plants were opened and some food companies began shifting to a more environmentally safe plastic that cannot be produced with the Durango plant technology.

Last year, with Durango's plant utilization down to 60 percent, senior management of SCX began investigating alternative uses of the Durango plant. The Durango plant's current annual operating statement appears in the accompanying table.

DURANGO PLANT
Income Statement, 2015
(Millions)

Revenue		$36
Variable costs	$21	
Fixed costs		
Plant administration (salaries and other out-of-pocket expenses)	17	
Depreciation	5	43
Net loss before taxes		$ (7)

One alternative use of the Durango plant's excess capacity is a new high-strength plastic used by the auto industry to reduce the weight of cars. Additional equipment required to produce the automotive plastic at the Durango plant can be leased for $3 million per year. Automotive plastic revenues are projected to be $28 million and variable costs are $11 million. Additional fixed costs for marketing, distribution, and plant overhead attributable solely to auto plastics are expected to be $4 million.

All of SCX's divisions are evaluated on a before-tax basis.

Required:

a. Evaluate the auto industry plastic proposal. Compare the three alternatives: (1) close Durango, (2) produce only film plastic at Durango, and (3) produce both film and auto plastic at Durango. Which of the three do you suggest accepting? (If Durango is closed, additional one-time plant closing costs just offset the proceeds from selling the plant.)

b. Suppose the Durango plant begins manufacturing both film and auto plastic. Prepare a performance report for the two divisions for the first year, assuming that the initial projections are realized and the film division's 2016 revenue and expenses are the same as in 2015. Plant administration ($17 million) and depreciation ($5 million) are common costs to both the film and auto plastics divisions. For performance evaluation purposes, these costs are assigned to the two divisions based on sales revenue. All costs incurred for the Auto Plastics division should be charged to that division.

c. Does the performance report in part (b) accurately reflect the relative performance of the two divisions? Why or why not?

d. In the year 2017, the Durango plant is able to negotiate a $1 million reduction in property taxes. Property taxes are included in the "plant administration account." In addition, the

Film Division is able to add $3 million in additional revenues (with $2.1 of additional variable cost) by selling film to European food packagers. Assuming that these are the only changes at the Durango plant between 2016 and 2017, how does the Auto Plastics Division's performance change between these two years? Allocate the common costs using the method described in part (*b*).

e. Write a short memo evaluating the performance of the Auto Plastics Division in light of the events in the year 2017 and describing how these events affect the reported performance of the Auto Plastics Division.

Chapter Eight

Cost Allocation: Practices

Chapter Outline

The previous chapter introduced the topic of cost allocations. Cost allocations are pervasive—most organizations, including profit, nonprofit, service, and manufacturing firms, allocate costs. Cost allocations serve numerous ends such as taxes, inventory valuation, cost-based reimbursements, and decision management and control.

In terms of creating incentives, cost allocations are like internal tax systems that cause decision makers to use less of the allocation base. Thus, the allocation bases chosen (what to tax) affect how resources are consumed inside the firm. Cost allocations also can create incentives to cooperate. Finally, noninsulating allocation methods help diversify the risk that managers bear. However, cost allocations can distort the reported performance of managers, divisions, products, and services being allocated the costs.

This chapter continues the discussion begun in the last chapter by first discussing a problem arising in most cost allocations—the death spiral—and then describing some specific methods used to allocate costs. Alternative methods for allocating service departments' costs are described in section C. Section D describes joint cost allocation, or allocating costs to multiple products produced from a single input. Finally, section E discusses segment reporting and joint benefits. An appendix describes reciprocal cost allocations for service department costs.

A. Death Spiral

Cost allocations involve apportioning common (or indirect) costs to cost objects. These common costs often arise because of economies of scale—it is more efficient to purchase the common resources centrally and share it among numerous users than for each user to acquire its own services. Hence, most common costs contain significant fixed costs. If the common cost is purely variable, each user could purchase their own amount and the resource becomes a direct cost to that user.

When common costs consist primarily of fixed costs and users have discretion over using the service being allocated, a death spiral can result. For example, consider an internal telecommunications department that provides telephones for inside users. The department purchases, installs, and maintains a central switch, a phone-mail system, and individual phone sets. Users are charged for their phones, the options used, and long-distance charges. There are substantial fixed costs for the central switch, local access charges, and maintenance of the phone-mail system.

Suppose the annual fixed costs are $600,000 and the annual cost of each of the 2,000 phone lines is $200. Most of the $600,000 represents depreciation of the existing equipment, which is largely a sunk cost. To recover all the costs from the users, each phone line is charged $500 (or $600,000 ÷ 2,000 + $200).

A local phone company will install private lines for $325 per year plus long-distance charges comparable to those available through the internal telecommunications department. Users start switching away from the telecommunications department to the outside phone company. At the end of the first year, 500 lines have been converted. To recover its costs, the telecommunications department raises its charge for the remaining lines to $600 (or $600,000 ÷ 1,500 + $200). This higher charge causes another 500 users to switch to the outside phone company and the cost rises to $800 per line ($600,000 ÷ 1,000 + $200). The final 1,000 users abandon the telecommunications department, citing exorbitant fees.

The death spiral results when utilization of a common resource (with significant fixed costs) falls, creating excess capacity. Average (full) cost transfer pricing charges the users for the common resource. The fixed costs are borne by the remaining users who have incentive to reduce utilization, further raising the average cost and causing additional defections.

Notice that the death spiral can occur whenever full cost transfer pricing is used, there are significant fixed costs, and the user has some discretion over the quantity of the

Managerial Application: Death Spiral in Corporate Jets	The annual operating cost of a corporate jet ranges between $40 and $50 million. Corporate flight departments routinely charge part or all of these costs to those internal departments using the aircraft. Allocating operating costs to internal users allows flight departments to justify the expense of the aircraft to top management, to apportion operating costs according to usage patterns, and to prevent overscheduling. Initially, only the direct operating costs (fuel and landing fees) were charged back to departments using the aircraft, while fixed costs were not (pilot salaries, maintenance costs, hangar rental, and insurance). When firms faced downturns in their business, a popular expense reduction target was to cut corporate jet usage by allocating the fixed costs along with the direct costs of operating the aircraft. Since fixed costs accounted for about 50 percent of the total cost at full utilization, usage rapidly shrank to the point where fixed costs rose to 85 percent of the total allocated cost. Jet usage dropped further, and each flight hour allocated became even more costly, sometimes approaching the cost of chartering a jumbo jet. This example illustrates how the "death spiral" can arise when substantial fixed costs exist and utilization falls. Fortunately, the term *death spiral* applies figuratively, and not literally, to corporate jets.

SOURCE: F. George, "Death Knell for Charge-Backs: Are the Days Numbered for Internal Billing for Use of Company Aircraft?" *Aviation Week: Business and Commercial Aviation*, October 2011, pp. 44–48.

common resource to use. As discussed in Chapter 5, one of the problems with full cost transfer pricing is underutilization of the common resource. Too few units are transferred.

There are several solutions to the death spiral. When excess capacity exists, users should be charged for only the variable cost of the resource. Alternatively, some of the fixed costs could be excluded from the transfer price. For example, the $600,000 in fixed costs (accounting depreciation of existing equipment) should be excluded because with excess capacity the opportunity cost of this equipment is zero.

Exercise 8-1

Clay Sprays produces a line of aerosol sprays for hospitals and clinics, including air fresheners, spot removers, disinfectants, rug cleaners, and polishes. The plant has substantial excess capacity. The following table presents Clay's current financial situation:

CLAY SPRAYS
Net Income—Current Year

Revenue (1,000,000 units @ $6/unit)	$6,000,000
Variable costs (1,000,000 units @ $3)	(3,000,000)
Fixed costs (manufacturing overhead)	(2,800,000)
Net income before taxes	$ 200,000

Clay Sprays carries no beginning or ending inventories. All the products have the same variable cost of $3 per unit, and the fixed cost of $2.8 million represents manufacturing overhead.

continued

Wendy Clay, CEO and owner, worries that the low volume is causing the remaining products to absorb more overhead per unit, driving up their costs and thereby making Clay Sprays's remaining products less competitive than they would be otherwise.

Clay asked her senior management team to find an acquisition that could add volume to the plant and thereby improve the overhead absorption problem. After analyzing several potential acquisition candidates, the team identified the Coronas Company. Also an aerosol manufacturer, Coronas's products are targeted at the household consumer. Coronas's products are produced by third-party custom-label manufacturers and Coronas has no manufacturing capacity—only a sales and marketing organization. Coronas, like Clay, is currently selling one million aerosol cans per year at an average wholesale price of $3 per can. Clay managers project that the variable cost of producing Coronas's aerosols will be $3 a can and that all of the Coronas volume can be handled by Clay's existing production facility without adding any additional fixed manufacturing overhead or affecting the current $3 variable cost of Clay's products.

Although purchasing Coronas and merging its volume into Clay does not add any incremental profits to Clay (since the wholesale price and the variable cost per can are both $3), Clay's management team still wants to proceed with the acquisition.

Mark Hendrickson, Clay's vice president of marketing, argues that Clay's products should appeal to its medical clients because of their high quality. But Clay's clients are switching to lower-quality, lower-priced manufacturers because of shrinking hospital budgets. Clay cannot lower its prices because doing so would erode margins (price less manufacturing cost). Acquiring Coronas, Hendrickson argues, will lower the overhead absorption by the Clay products, thereby allowing Clay to lower its prices on the medical market's aerosols without adversely affecting margins.

Required:

  a. Does Clay's acquisition of Coronas lower Clay's overhead rate on existing Clay products?

  b. Does Clay's profitability improve with the Coronas acquisition?

  c. Reconcile any apparent inconsistencies between your answers in parts (*a*) and (*b*).

  d. Is Mr. Hendrickson's analysis correct?

  e. Should Clay acquire Coronas?

  f. Why do you think Clay's management team is recommending the Coronas acquisition?

Solution:

  a. The Coronas acquisition lowers Clay's overhead rate on existing Clay products. The average cost of producing Clay's existing products is:

$$\text{Average cost} = \$3 + \frac{\$2,800,000}{1,000,000} = \$5.80$$

Following the acquisition of Coronas, this falls to:

$$\$3 + \frac{\$2,800,000}{2,000,000} = \$4.40$$

The average cost of Clay's existing products is now lower because the fixed cost of $2.8 million is spread over more aerosol cans.

b. Clay's profitability is not improved by the Coronas acquisition. Coronas is selling its aerosol products at $3 per can, which is variable cost. So Coronas is not adding any incremental profits to Clay.

Analysis of Clay's Profitability from Coronas Merger

	Clay Alone	Coronas Alone	Clay and Coronas Combined
Revenue	$6,000,000	$3,000,000	$9,000,000
Variable cost	3,000,000	3,000,000	6,000,000
Fixed cost	2,800,000	—	2,800,000
Net income before taxes	$ 200,000	$ 0	$ 200,000

Clay's profits remain at $200,000 both before and after the acquisition.

c. The answers to parts (a) and (b) appear inconsistent. While the overhead rate appears to have fallen after the acquisition, profits are not higher. The inconsistency is easily reconciled by noting the decline in average cost of Clay's existing products from $5.80 to $4.40. This decline in average cost does *not* represent a reduction in cash outlays. Rather, it represents a *shifting* of some of the fixed costs to the Coronas products. Suppose the $2.8 million fixed cost is allocated based on units. Then the following product line profitability analysis clearly shows the shifting of the fixed overhead.

CLAY AND CORONAS
Product Line Profitability
Pro Forma

	Clay Products	Coronas Products	Firm Total
Revenue	$6,000,000	$3,000,000	$9,000,000
Variable cost	3,000,000	3,000,000	6,000,000
Allocated fixed cost (based on units)	1,400,000	1,400,000	2,800,000
Net income (loss) before taxes	$1,600,000	$(1,400,000)	$ 200,000

The Clay products appear to be more profitable because half the overhead has been shifted to the Coronas products. But now the Coronas products appear to be losing $1.4 million. Overall, firm profitability has not changed.

d. Mr. Hendrickson is wrong. We know from economics that profit-maximizing prices are determined at the quantity where marginal cost equals marginal revenue. Fixed costs do not enter the pricing decision other than to determine whether or not to continue to produce at the optimum price. Mr. Hendrickson should not be setting Clay's

continued

aerosol prices based on average cost (or some cost-plus markup). To drive additional volume into the plant, instead of acquiring Coronas, Ms. Clay should carefully examine her pricing policies. By lowering her price, she will lose revenue from customers who would have bought at the higher price. But at a lower price, she will add more new customers. "Marginal revenue" is the difference between the revenue added from new customers purchasing at the lower price less the revenue lost from customers who would have paid the higher price. Clay should continue to drop its price until the marginal revenue from the last penny of price reduction equals $3, which is Clay's marginal cost.

e. If the desire to lower Clay's average fixed cost is the only reason to acquire Coronas, then the acquisition makes no economic sense. Coronas should be acquired only if *real* synergies exist. Real synergies include additional sales of Clay or Coronas aerosols as a result of the expanded markets or product lines. Or other synergies might arise if, by adding volume to the plant, operating efficiencies result and the variable cost of $3 per unit can be reduced.

f. Clay's management team might be interested in this acquisition because adding volume to the plant might mean additional job security.

Another way to resolve the death spiral is to use *practical capacity* instead of actual utilization in calculating the overhead rate. Practical capacity represents the amount of capacity the common resource (e.g., the telephone system) was expected to provide when it was purchased and used under normal operating circumstances. If the phone system was purchased to provide 2,500 phone lines, then 2,500 lines represents practical capacity. With practical capacity of 2,500 lines, each phone is charged $440. This $440 represents $240 of depreciation ($600,000 ÷ 2,500) plus $200 of variable cost. If only 1,200 lines are used, and each is charged $240 of the depreciation, then only $288,000 of the $600,000 depreciation is recovered ($240 × 1,200). The unused capacity (1,300 lines) of $312,000 is not charged to the remaining users, but rather is charged to a companywide expense. Practical capacity reduces the likelihood of a death spiral because the cost of unused capacity (e.g., $312,000) is not imposed on the remaining users of the common resource.[1]

Exercise 8–1 illustrates another effect of the death spiral. With excess capacity and substantial fixed costs, managers are tempted to add new products or services solely to lower the average fixed costs on existing products. The new products or services absorb some of the fixed costs, thereby lowering the fixed costs assigned to the existing products or services. However, as demonstrated by Exercise 8–1, this strategy is flawed. New products or services should be added only if they increase the present value of the firm's net cash flows after considering the cost of any additional capital necessary to add the new products or services.

---

[1]Chapter 9 introduces the concept of *normal volume:* the long-run average production volume of a plant or department. Practical capacity and normal volume represent equivalent concepts. They both compute overhead rates using a constant denominator volume that does not vary with actual utilization, thereby preventing the death spiral caused by rising overhead rates when actual utilization falls.

B. Allocating Capacity Costs: Depreciation

As seen in the previous section, a death spiral can result when a common resource with significant fixed costs and excess capacity is allocated to users who have discretion over utilization of the resource. In the telecommunications example, depreciation of the existing phone system is the principal fixed cost. One way to solve the death spiral is to not allocate some (or all) of the fixed cost. For example, allocate only the fixed cost of the capacity actually being used. If there is 40 percent excess capacity, allocate only 60 percent of the depreciation. However, this solution to the death spiral creates other concerns.

Notice that the death spiral, or underutilization of the common resource, is really a problem of how to use an existing resource. How much of the *existing* common resource should each agent use? If there is excess capacity, any charge discourages its use. However, prior to deciding how to allocate the available capacity among existing agents, the firm had to decide how much capacity to acquire. In the previous example, the firm had to decide how large a phone system to buy (how much phone-mail capacity, how many lines, how fast a switch, and so forth). The current fixed costs of the phone system (including depreciation) were "variable" costs prior to acquiring the capacity. Accounting depreciation (such as straight line) represents the annual historical cost of acquired capacity. Depreciation is the allocation of the asset's historical cost over time.

How much capacity should the firm acquire? The future users of that capacity usually have specialized, private knowledge of how intensively they will use the common resource. If these users know they will not be charged for their future use because fixed costs are not allocated, they will overstate their future use. If they are not charged for the excess capacity, they will still overstate their use if the common resource exhibits economies of scale (average cost declines as acquired capacity increases). Therefore, charging accounting depreciation is a commitment device.[2] Future users, knowing they will be charged for the historical cost of a durable asset, have less incentive to overstate their expected future utilization. Allocating accounting depreciation to users commits them to recovering at least the historical cost of the asset. (Allocating depreciation does not commit them to recovering the opportunity cost of capital tied up in the asset.)

In deciding whether to allocate depreciation on the common resource to its users, the firm makes a trade-off between the efficient investment in the common resource and its efficient utilization after acquisition. Charging depreciation helps control the overinvestment problem, but at the expense of underutilizing the asset after acquisition. Most firms charge users for depreciation. Thus, control of the overinvestment problem tends to dominate decision-making errors involving asset utilization (the death spiral). This is another example of how accounting systems tend to favor control when confronted with a choice between control and decision making.

C. Allocating Service Department Costs

Up to now, we have discussed allocating a single common cost to multiple users (either divisions or products). For example, Chapter 7 describes allocating personnel department costs and corporate-level costs to divisions. We now examine a more realistic situation in which a number of service departments exist whose costs are allocated to several

[2]See S. Sunder, *Theory of Accounting and Control* (Cincinnati, OH: South-Western Publishing, 1997), pp. 55–56; and R. Ball, S. Keating, and J. Zimmerman, "Historical Cost as a Commitment Device," *Maandblad voor Accountancy en Bedriifs-economie* (Netherlands), November 2000.

<table>
<tr><td>Managerial Application: Cost Allocations at IBM</td><td>During the 1980s and early 1990s, IBM had the policy of allocating costs from one line of business to another. Managers in those lines of business constantly argued that some of their overhead should be carried by other IBM businesses. IBM also typically allocated all of the R&D of a new technology to the line of business first using the technology, and subsequent users were able to utilize it for free. The cost allocation system masked the true profitability of many IBM businesses for years. IBM claimed it was making money in its PC business. But in 1992, "as IBM began to move away from its funny allocation system, IBM disclosed that its PC business was unprofitable." In 2004, IBM sold its PC division to China-based Lenovo Group for $1.75 billion.

Sources: P. Carroll, "The Failures of Central Planning—at IBM," *The Wall Street Journal*, January 28, 1993, p. A14; "IBM Sells PC Business to China's Lenovo," AP, December 8, 2004.</td></tr>
</table>

Figure 8-1

N service departments costs allocated to M operating divisions

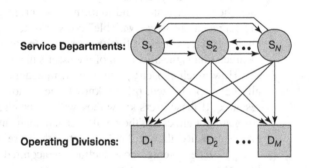

operating divisions. Figure 8–1 illustrates the general case of N service departments and M operating divisions. In a manufacturing plant, the service departments consist of purchasing, human resources, security, maintenance, information technology, engineering, and so forth. The operating divisions might be separate product lines or manufacturing functions such as parts manufacturing and assembly lines. In order to compute the manufacturing cost of the final products for inventory valuation, the cost of the service departments must be allocated to the operating divisions. The service departments are like buckets of water that must be emptied into the operating divisions. The arrows indicate the direction of the service flows. Complicating the allocation is the reciprocal use of services among the service departments. Service department S_1 not only provides service to operating divisions $D_1, D_2, \ldots D_M$, but it also provides service to the other service departments $S_2, S_3, \ldots, S_N$. For example, information technology (IT) provides IT service to purchasing, while purchasing is involved in buying computer hardware and software for information technology.

To illustrate the allocation of service department costs, consider just two service departments (telecommunications and information technology, IT) and two operating divisions (Cars and Trucks). Table 8–1 contains the percentage of each service department's capacity consumed by the various users.

Telecommunications consumes 10 percent of its own capacity internally and IT consumes 15 percent of its capacity internally. Also, each service department uses the other service department. The goal is to assign the costs of the service departments (telecommunications and IT) to the operating divisions (Cars and Trucks). Cars and Trucks make the final products, and their cost should include the telecommunications and IT costs.

TABLE 8-1 **Capacity of Service Departments Used**

	Telecommunications	IT	Cars	Trucks	Total
Telecommunications	10%	20%	40%	30%	100%
IT	25	15	35	25	100

FIGURE 8-2

Direct allocation method

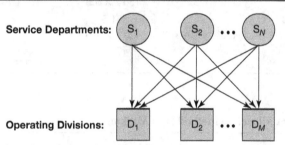

The following costs of the two service departments are to be allocated to Cars and Trucks:

Telecommunications	$2 million
IT	6 million
Total costs	$8 million

The $2 million and $6 million costs are costs incurred by the two departments and do not contain any costs allocated from the other service department.

There are several ways to allocate service department costs to the operating divisions: direct allocation, step-down allocation, and reciprocal allocation. These three methods and their advantages and disadvantages are discussed next.

1. Direct Allocation Method

Figure 8–2 illustrates the direct allocation of service department costs. Direct allocation ignores each service department's use of the other service departments. The allocation of S_1 is based only on the operating divisions' utilization of S_1. The fact that $S_2, S_3, \ldots, S_N$ also use S_1 is ignored. This greatly simplifies the allocation calculations, although we will see that inaccurate transfer prices for the services can result.

The divisional utilization rates in Table 8–1 are used to allocate service department costs. That is, the Cars division uses 40 percent of telecommunications and the Trucks division uses 30 percent. Together they use 70 percent. If 40 percent and 30 percent are used to allocate telecommunication's $2 million in costs, only $1.4 million of the total $2 million will be allocated to Cars and Trucks. The other $0.6 million remains unassigned. These results are shown in Table 8–2.

Allocating service department costs based on the divisions' actual use of each service department results in some of the service departments' costs remaining unallocated: $5 million of service department costs are to be allocated and $3 million remain unassigned. If all service department costs are to be allocated to Cars and Trucks, then each division's percentage of the total used by the divisions is the allocation rate. That is, the percentages are recomputed so that the Cars and Trucks divisions' shares sum to one. This method is termed direct allocation because the service department costs are allocated directly to the operating divisions rather than to the other service departments first and then to the operating divisions. The direct allocations are in Table 8–3.

TABLE 8-2 Service Department Percentages Used by Cars and Trucks ($ in Millions)

	Cars	Trucks	Total Allocated	Total Cost Incurred	Total Unallocated
Telecommunications	$0.8 (40% × $2)	$0.6 (30% × $2)	$1.4	$2.0	$0.6
IT	$2.1 (35% × $6)	$1.5 (25% × $6)	$3.6	$6.0	$2.4
Total			$5.0	$8.0	$3.0

TABLE 8-3 Direct Allocation Method ($ in Millions)

	Cars	Trucks	Total
Revised Shares, Direct Allocation Method			
Telecommunications	40%/(40% + 30%) = 4/7	30%/(40% + 30%) = 3/7	100%
IT	35%/(35% + 25%) = 7/12	25%/(35% + 25%) = 5/12	100%
Allocated Costs, Direct Allocation Method			
Telecommunications	4/7 × $2 = $1.143	3/7 × $2 = $0.857	$2
IT	7/12 × $6 = $3.500	5/12 × $6 = $2.500	$6
Total	$4.643	$3.357	$8

Since the revised shares in the first part of Table 8–3 sum to one, all the costs in telecommunications and IT are allocated to the two operating divisions and no costs remain unallocated. The allocated service department costs using these shares are in the bottom half of Table 8–3. Notice that the total cost of telecommunications and IT, $8 million, is now allocated to Cars and Trucks. However, this direct allocation method presents a problem in that the opportunity cost per unit of service is likely wrong. While we do not know the correct opportunity cost, we do know that the direct allocation method excludes the service departments' use of other service departments and therefore incorrectly states the opportunity cost of each service department.

Suppose that the Cars division increases its use of IT. This causes IT costs to rise, or, if the IT department is not expanded, its service is degraded. Since IT uses telecommunications, telecommunications' costs also rise when the Cars division uses more IT. But the direct allocation method does not charge IT for any telecommunications costs. Because each service department uses the other service department and the direct allocation method ignores these interactions, the cost allocated (i.e., the transfer price) is not the opportunity cost of the service department.

Another problem with the direct allocation method is that each service department will overuse the other service departments. Since each service department's costs are allocated only to the manufacturing departments, the other service departments view that service department as free. They are not charged for their use of other service departments and therefore have no monetary incentive to limit their use. Accordingly, nonfinancial methods, such as rationing, must be employed to control the excessive use of each service department by the other service departments.

FIGURE 8-3

Step-down allocation method

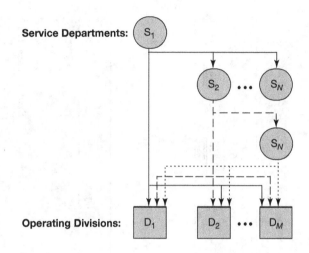

2. Step-Down Allocation Method

The **step-down method** partially overcomes the problems with direct allocations. The procedure begins by choosing a service department and allocating all of its costs to the remaining service departments and operating divisions. Then, a second service department is chosen and all of its costs (including its share of the allocated costs from the first service department) are allocated to the remaining service departments and operating divisions. This process continues until all service department costs are allocated. In this way, all service department costs cascade down through the service organizations and eventually are allocated to the operating divisions.

Figure 8–3 illustrates the step-down method. Service department S_1 is chosen first and all of its costs are allocated to S_2, S_3, . . ., S_N and D_1, D_2, . . ., D_M. The solid arrows indicate the first step of the process. Then all of S_2's costs plus S_2's share of S_1's costs are allocated to S_3, S_4, . . ., S_N and D_1, D_2, . . ., D_M. The dashed arrows indicate the allocation of S_2's costs. This continues until only service department S_N remains. All of its costs plus all of the costs allocated to S_N from the other service departments are allocated to the operating divisions as represented by the dotted arrows. Notice that half of the flows among service departments are captured by the step-down method. For example, S_2's use of S_1 is captured, although S_1's use of S_2 is not.

In our numerical example, the first service department to be allocated is telecommunications. The allocation shares are in the top half of Table 8–4, and the cost allocations are computed in the bottom half of the table. Telecommunications' costs are allocated to IT, Cars, and Trucks in the first step. Two-ninths of telecommunications are allocated to IT, 4/9 to Cars, and the remaining 1/3 to Trucks. In the first row of the bottom half of Table 8–4, these shares are used to allocate telecommunications' costs. IT receives $444,000, the Cars division receives $889,000, and the Trucks division receives $667,000. All $2 million of the telecommunications costs are allocated.

In the second step, IT costs plus data processing's share of the telecommunications costs are allocated to Cars and Trucks. Total IT costs to be allocated include IT's direct costs of $6 million plus the $444,000 allocated in the first step. The total $6,444,000 is allocated to Cars (7/12) and Trucks (5/12).

Notice that all $8 million of the service department costs are allocated (far right column, last row of Table 8–4). The Cars division receives $4.648 million and the Trucks division receives $3.352 million. By chance, the costs allocated to each division, Cars and Trucks, are about the same using either the direct method or the step-down method.

TABLE 8-4 Step-Down Allocation Method—Telecommunications First ($ in Millions)

	Information Technology	Cars	Trucks	Total
Telecommunications	20%/(20% + 40% + 30%) = 2/9	40%/90% = 4/9	30%/90% = 1/3	100%
IT	—	35%/60% = 7/12	25%/60% = 5/12	100%

Using these shares, the allocated costs are as follows:

	Costs to Be Allocated	Information Technology	Cars	Trucks	Total Allocated to Cars and Trucks
Telecommunications	$2	2/9 × $2 = $0.444	4/9 × $2 = $0.889	1/3 × $2 = $0.667	$1.556
IT	$6 + $0.444	—	7/12 × $6.444 = $3.759	5/12 × $6.444 = $2.685	6.444
			$4.648	$3.352	$8.000

TABLE 8-5 Step-Down Allocation Method—Information Technology First ($ in Millions)

	Telecommunications	Cars	Trucks	Total
IT	25%+(25% + 35% + 25%) = 5/17	35%/85% = 7/17	25%/85% = 5/17	100%
Telecommunications	—	4/7	3/7	100%

Using these revised shares, the allocated costs are:

	Costs to Be Allocated	Telecommunications	Cars	Trucks	Total Allocated to Cars and Trucks
IT	$6	5/17 × $6 = $1.765	7/17 × $6 = $2.470	5/17 × $6 = $1.765	$4.235
Telecommunications	$2 + $1.765	—	4/7 × $3.765 = $2.151	3/7 × $3.765 = $1.614	3.765
			$4.621	$3.379	$8.000

Managerial Application: Hospitals Use Step-Down Allocations	The U.S. Medicare system requires each hospital to file a Medicare Cost Report to get reimbursed for providing health care to Medicare patients. To file this report, all cost centers in the hospital (administration, finance, human resources) that supply services to other cost centers and major functional services, such as the emergency department, surgery, and maternity, are ordered in a step-down sequence. Each cost center allocates its cost using an allocation base. For example, nursing administration costs might be allocated using nursing hours or nursing salaries in each functional service. The Medicare Cost Report defines the order of the cost centers to be used in the step-down method but does allow each hospital some discretion. For example, administration and general costs are usually allocated last. However, some hospitals move it up in the list. The step-down method allocates the cost of each service center, as well as the costs stepped down to it, to the major functional services. Many hospitals use the data generated by the Medicare Cost Report to set prices and to negotiate third-party contracts. SOURCE: M. Muise and B. Amoia, "Step Up to the Step-Down Method," *Healthcare Financial Management*, May 2006.

The question arises as to the sequence of departments chosen in the step-down method. Had IT been chosen as the first service department in the sequence, the allocations in Table 8–5 would have been the result. In this example, the step-down method starting with the IT department results in a cost allocation pattern to the operating divisions that is about the same as the one produced by the direct allocation method.

3. Service Department Costs and Transfer Pricing of Direct and Step-Down Methods

The costs allocated to Cars and Trucks differ by only $27,000 depending on whether telecommunications (Table 8–4) or IT (Table 8–5) is chosen first. In Table 8–4, the Cars division is allocated $4.648 million, and in Table 8–5 the allocation is $4.621 million. The difference of $27,000 is less than 1 percent of the total costs allocated. Therefore, it would appear inconsequential as to whether telecommunications or IT is chosen over the direct allocation method. However, very different incentives result depending on which method is used. Allocated costs represent transfer prices. As we saw in Chapter 5, transfer pricing affects the quantity of the internal service demanded. If too high a transfer price is set, a death spiral can result when substantial fixed costs exist in the service department.

To illustrate the effect of the cost allocation method on transfer prices, we expand the telecommunications and IT example. Suppose the allocation base in telecommunications is the number of telephones in each department, and in IT the allocation base is the number of gigabytes of disk space used. Transfer prices are to be established for telephones and gigabytes. Allocated costs will be used to compute the transfer prices. The number of phones and gigabytes are as follows:

	Allocation Base
Telecommunications	3,000 telephones
IT	12 million gigabytes

The cost per phone will vary depending on the allocation method chosen. Part A of Table 8–6 computes the number of phones in each department, which is used in setting the allocated cost per phone. The Cars division has 40 percent of all telephones, or 1,200 phones. The Trucks division has 30 percent of all telephones, or 900 phones. Under direct allocation, only the phones in Cars and Trucks are used to allocate telecommunications costs. Hence,

TABLE 8-6   **Allocated Cost per Phone**

		Step-Down Allocation	
	Direct Allocation	*Telecommunications Chosen First*	*Information Technology Chosen First*
A. Number of Phones			
Number of phones:			
Telecommunications	—	—	—
IT	—	20% × 3,000 = 600	—
Cars	40% × 3,000 = 1,200	40% × 3,000 = 1,200	40% × 3,000 = 1,200
Trucks	30% × 3,000 = 900	30% × 3,000 = 900	30% × 3,000 = 900
Phones used to allocate costs	2,100	2,700	2,100
B. Cost per Phone			
Cost per phone*	$2M/2,100 = $ 952	$2M/2,700 = $ 741	$3.765M/2,100 = $1,793
Number of phones in Cars	1,200	1,200	1,200
Telecommunications charged to Cars	$1.143	$0.889	$2.151

*M denotes millions.

the allocation base is 2,100 phones. Under the step-down allocation with telecommunications chosen first, IT receives a charge for its phones. Thus, the number of phones used to allocate telecommunications costs rises to include the 600 phones in IT. On the other hand, if IT is chosen first in the step-down method, the number of phones in the allocation base is still 2,100 (those in Cars and Trucks) because the IT costs have already been allocated.

Part B of Table 8–6 reports the allocated cost per phone. The first line in part B is telecommunications costs divided by the total number of phones used to allocate costs (from part A). Notice that in the right column of part B, telecommunications costs are $3.765 million, the sum of the $2 million of telecommunications costs and the $1.765 million allocated to telecommunications when IT is allocated first (see Table 8–5). The last row reports the same cost allocations as in Tables 8–3, 8–4, and 8–5. For example, under the direct allocation method, the Cars division has 1,200 phones and will be charged $1.143 million. This is exactly the same charge as computed in Table 8–3. Likewise, the $0.889 million and $2.151 million in the last two columns correspond to the allocations computed in Tables 8–4 and 8–5, respectively.

The first row in Part B of Table 8–6 also shows the computation of the transfer price, or cost allocated per telephone, under the three allocation methods. The cost per phone varies from $741 to $1,793, depending on which allocation scheme is used. The high cost per phone of $1,793 in the right column occurs because some of the $6 million of IT costs is allocated to telecommunications before the cost per phone is calculated. The IT costs allocated to telecommunications increase telecommunications' costs and, ultimately, the allocated cost per phone.

Because the cost per phone (which represents the transfer price) varies depending on which allocation method is used, the cost allocation scheme affects the decision of each department to add or drop phones. The sequence of service departments in the step-down method can affect decision making because the last service department in the sequence will have a larger cost per unit of service. Remember that cost allocations are effectively internal tax schemes. How the taxes are applied will affect the "price" decision makers face in deciding to add or drop phones.

TABLE 8–7 **Allocated Cost per Gigabyte of Storage**

		Step-Down Allocation	
	Direct Allocation	*Telecommunications Chosen First*	*Information Technology Chosen First*
A. Number of Gigabytes (in Millions)			
Number of gigabytes:			
Telecommunications	—	—	$25\% \times 12 = 3.0$
IT	—	—	—
Cars	$35\% \times 12 = 4.2$	$35\% \times 12 = 4.2$	$35\% \times 12 = 4.2$
Trucks	$25\% \times 12 = 3.0$	$25\% \times 12 = 3.0$	$25\% \times 12 = 3.0$
Total gigabytes	7.2	7.2	10.2
B. Cost per Gigabyte (in Millions except Cost per Gigabyte)			
Cost per gigabyte	$\$6/7.2 = \$0.833$	$\$6.44/7.2 = \$0.895$	$\$6/10.2 = \$0.588$
Number of gigabytes in Cars	4.2	4.2	4.2
IT charged to Cars	$\$3.5$	$\$3.759$	$\$2.470$

The same conclusions hold for the information technology department. Table 8–7 presents the equivalent computations for the IT department, including the cost per gigabyte of storage across the various allocation methods. Again, note the wide variation in cost per gigabyte. The cost varies from $0.588 per gigabyte under the step-down method with IT chosen first to $0.895 under the step-down method with telecommunications chosen first. Also, note that the total charged to Cars (the last line) agrees with the previous calculations in Tables 8–3, 8–4, and 8–5.

We saw earlier that the various methods of allocating service department costs result in a difference of less than 1 percent of the total costs. However, these same methods can cause the cost-based transfer prices to vary by more than 140 percent for telephones ([$1,793 ÷ $741] ÷ $741) and more than 50 percent for gigabytes ([$0.895 ÷ $0.588] ÷ $0.588). Why the discrepancy? Refer back to Table 8–1. In this example, the Cars division uses roughly equal fractions of the two service departments (57 percent and 58 percent), and the Trucks division uses roughly equal fractions of the service departments (43 percent and 42 percent). Because these fractions are roughly the same in both departments, the total costs allocated to the divisions vary little across the various methods. However, the transfer prices per phone and gigabyte vary dramatically. In general, the allocation methods can yield substantial differences in amounts allocated. The numbers chosen for this example illustrate that transfer prices can vary greatly even when the cost allocation methods have little effect on the total amounts allocated.

The large variation in the cost-based transfer prices arises because the transfer prices in this setting are ratios. The numerator of the ratio is the sum of the department's direct costs and any costs allocated to the service department. The denominator of the ratio is the number of units in the remaining allocation base (number of phones or gigabytes). The first service department in the step-down sequence has no allocated costs in its numerator and a large number of users (and hence a large denominator). If this service department gets shifted from the first to the last in the sequence, its cost-based transfer price rises for two reasons. First, the ratio's numerator goes up by all of the other service department costs now being allocated to it. Second, its denominator goes down because the only users of its services that are included in the allocation base are the operating units. The other service departments are excluded from its denominator. Thus, the ratio changes a lot because the numerator goes up while the denominator goes down. For example, refer to the cost per phone in Table 8–6. With telecommunications first in the step-down sequence, the transfer price is $2M/2, 700 = $741. When it is last in the sequence, the cost per phone is $3.765M/2, 100 = $1,793. Notice that both the numerator and the denominator change as telecommunications is shifted from first to last in the sequence.

One criticism of the step-down method is that the sequence used is arbitrary and large differences can result in the cost per unit of service using different sequences. Also, the step-down method ignores the fact that although departments earlier in the sequence use service departments later in the sequence, earlier departments are not allocated these costs.

The death spiral, described in section A, can be a significant problem with step-down allocations if the service departments contain significant amounts of fixed costs. If transfer prices are established for these service department costs, then users have incentives to use less of the high-cost service departments. (The high-cost departments are those last in the step-down chain.) As usage falls, total costs do not fall proportionately because of the fixed costs. This causes the costs allocated to the remaining users to rise further, and these users will seek to replace the inside service with outside vendors that offer lower costs.

4. Reciprocal Allocation Method

Under the step-down method, the transfer price of phones and gigabytes can vary dramatically depending on the order selected for allocating the service departments' costs. The third allocation method, the reciprocal allocation method, is the most precise way to allocate service department costs when each service department uses other service departments. It captures all the service flows depicted in Figure 8–1. Under the reciprocal allocation method, a system of linear equations is constructed, one for each service department. Each equation contains the use of that department by all other service departments. If there are 20 service departments providing services to at least some of the other departments, there will be 20 equations with 20 unknowns. This system of equations is then solved to derive the cost shares for each operating department and the cost per unit of output in each service department. The appendix to this chapter illustrates the computations involved in the reciprocal method.

As demonstrated in the appendix, the reciprocal allocation method produces an allocated cost per phone of $1,492 and an allocated cost per gigabytes of $0.676. The following table compares these allocated costs with those of the direct and step-down allocation methods.

	Charge per Phone	*Charge per Gigabytes*
Direct method	$ 952	$0.833
Step-down:		
Telecommunications first	$ 741	$0.895
IT-first	$1,793	$0.588
Reciprocal method	$1,492	$0.676

The reciprocal allocation method produces neither the highest nor the lowest unit cost. By incorporating one service department's use of another service department, it avoids the distortions in unit allocated costs observed in the step-down method.

The cost per phone of $1,492 and the cost per gigabyte of $0.676 represent the opportunity cost of adding one more phone or using one more gigabyte assuming all the costs being allocated are variable. The phone charge reflects the fact that the additional phone uses some additional telecommunications and IT resources. Likewise, the gigabyte charge reflects the fact that one more gigabyte uses some additional IT and telecommunications resources. Therefore, the reciprocal method is more accurate in assessing the opportunity cost of service departments than either the direct or step-down allocations, assuming all service department costs are variable.

The reciprocal method produces a transfer price that can be compared with an outside price for the service. If the outside bid is less than the internal price, it should be accepted. This assumes that the inside costs of service (the $2 million and $6 million cost of telecommunications and IT, respectively) represent all variable costs. If any of these costs contain fixed costs and there is excess capacity, then the reciprocal method does not produce opportunity cost transfer prices.

In many service departments, fixed and variable costs are not distinguished. Total costs are accumulated and allocated to the operating divisions. Combining fixed costs with variable costs in the service departments can compromise the reciprocal method's ability to produce marginal cost transfer prices. To take full advantage of the reciprocal method's ability to estimate marginal cost transfer prices, only the variable costs in each service department should be allocated using the system of equations. The fixed costs in each service department are either not allocated or allocated based on each operating division's planned use of the service department's capacity.

Another critical assumption underlying all three allocation methods is that the utilization rates do not change with increases or decreases in scale. That is, if the firm doubles in size, will IT continue to utilize 20 percent of telecommunications? If this assumption is violated, then no method based on past utilization rates can yield accurate forecasts of opportunity cost.

While the reciprocal allocation method has certain theoretical advantages, it is not widely used. Why? First, calculating reciprocal allocations requires substantial computing power, especially when there are numerous service departments. Until recently, such problems could only be solved with very large computers. Now, spreadsheet software such as Excel can easily handle them. Second, few accountants were trained in solving systems of equations or how to formulate the problem. This conjecture seems implausible since many new innovations, such as derivative securities, suggest that financial managers quickly adopt new analytic procedures when it is in their interest to do so. Third, it is difficult (and hence costly) to intuitively explain the reciprocal method to nonfinancial managers in the firm. The reciprocal method appears as a "black box," and the managers being asked to bear the allocated costs do not fully understand how the charges were computed. This conjecture also seems implausible, especially if the benefits of the reciprocal method outweigh the costs. It also relies on the questionable assumption that certain groups are stupid. One would think that financial managers would be able to devise suitable tutorials to explain the calculations. Fourth, the dysfunctional aspects of the step-down method can be minimized by ordering the departments in the step-down sequence. That is, by judiciously choosing the order, the step-down method produces allocated costs that are very similar to those produced by the reciprocal method in terms of the ultimate decisions managers make using the allocated costs. While simple textbook examples can be constructed showing large deviations in allocated costs produced by the step-down and reciprocal methods—and, therefore, the potential for dysfunctional decision making—we have little evidence such differences exist in practice.

A final conjecture as to why reciprocal allocations are rarely used, and one consistent with other observed managerial accounting choices, is that the primary role of cost allocations is not decision making. If the primary function were decision making, then, since opportunity costs are the basis for decision making (and the reciprocal method approximates opportunity costs better than the other methods), we should observe fairly frequent use of the reciprocal method. The fact that we observe infrequent use of the reciprocal method suggests that accounting's primary focus is not decision making, but rather some other purpose such as decision control, financial reporting, or taxes. For example, using the step-down method affords managers considerable discretion in the resulting allocated costs because they can select the order of the departments. This discretion can be useful for strategic reasons, for financial reporting, to maximize cost-based reimbursements, or to minimize taxes.

5. Recap

There are three reasons to allocate service department costs (independent of which allocation method is chosen):

1. By charging a positive "price," users reduce their consumption from what it would be under a zero price (no cost allocations). Pricing the internal service helps allocate a scarce resource. At a zero price, demand usually exceeds supply. In the absence of a price mechanism to allocate department services, senior management will be confronted with requests to increase the amount of service via larger budgets and must devise nonprice priority schemes to manage the demand for service.

2. By allocating service department costs, senior management receives information about the total demand for the service at the allocated cost. This helps management to determine the optimum scale of the service department. For example, if the users are willing to pay a transfer price that recovers the cost of providing the service, then the service department is providing benefits to the users in excess of its costs.

3. By comparing the internal allocated cost with the outside external price of comparable services, senior management can assess the service department's operating efficiency. Gross inefficiencies are identified when the allocated cost per unit of service exceeds the external price.

Concept Questions		
	Q8–1	What is the death spiral and how is it prevented?
	Q8–2	What are some reasons to allocate service department costs, independent of which allocation method is chosen?
	Q8–3	What is step-down allocation? What are some criticisms of this allocation method?
	Q8–4	How do the direct allocation and step-down methods differ?
	Q8–5	How does the cost per unit of service vary over the sequence of service departments when the step-down method is used?

D. Joint Costs

A special case of cost allocations deals with allocating joint costs. A **joint cost** is incurred to produce two or more outputs from the same input. Joint products are produced from a single input. For example, hamburger and steak are joint products from a single joint input, the cow. In a mining operation, gold and silver are joint products from the joint input, ore. Usually, but not always, joint products are produced in fixed proportions, meaning that more gold cannot be produced if less silver is produced.

FIGURE 8-4 *Assembly and disassembly processes*

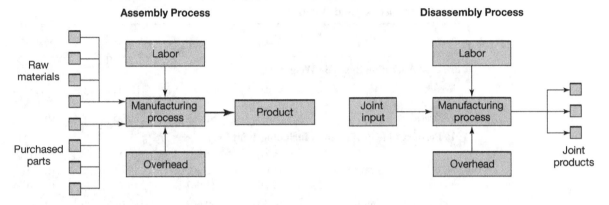

TABLE 8-8 **Relative Weight, Physical Volume, Relative Sales Value, and Net Realizable Value**

				Net Realizable Value		
	Weight (%)	*Volume (%)*	*Revenue of Final Product (%)*	*Costs*	*NRV**	*(%)*
A. Data						
Gasoline	60 lbs. (30%)	40 gals. (80%)	$60 (40%)	$50	$10	50%
Motor oil	40 lbs. (20%)	5 gals. (10%)	$60 (40%)	$54	6	30
Jet fuel	100 lbs. (50%)	5 gals. (10%)	$30 (20%)	$26	4	20
B. Allocated Joint Cost of $20 Barrel of Oil						
Gasoline	$ 30	$ 80	$ 40		$ 50	
Motor oil	20	10	40		30	
Jet fuel	50	10	20		20	
	$100	$100	$100		$100	

*NRV (net realizable value) = Revenue of final product - Costs. Costs are the additional costs required to produce the final product.

Firms convert one set of resources into another. Production is a process of assembling various factor inputs into a new combination. Many costs are thus common with other costs. Service department costs discussed in Section C are **common costs** of the various products manufactured. The fire insurance premium on the factory building used to manufacture various products in the plant is a common (and hence) inseparable cost of all the products manufactured in the building. Notice that joint costs and common costs are very similar in definition. The major distinction between the two is that common costs are incurred in both assembly and disassembly processes, but joint costs are incurred only in disassembly processes. In an assembly process, many inputs are assembled into a few final outputs. For example, an engine, a transmission, bumpers, tires, seats, and more are assembled to produce an automobile. In a disassembly process, a few inputs are disassembled into many final products. For example, a barrel of crude oil is disassembled into gasoline, motor oil, jet fuel, and asphalt. Figure 8–4 illustrates the difference between an assembly and a disassembly process.

There are many ways to allocate joint costs to joint products. For example, in an oil refinery, the cost of each barrel of crude oil can be allocated to the joint products based on physical weight, physical volume, relative sales value, or net realizable value. Table 8–8

TABLE 8-9   **Using Weight to Allocate Chicken Costs for Product Line Profitability of Fillets, Drumsticks, and Wings**

	Total	Fillets	Drumsticks	Wings
A. Cost Allocation Based on Weight				
Weight	32 oz.	16 oz.	12 oz.	4 oz.
Percentage of weight	100%	50%	37.5%	12.5%
Allocated cost	$2.00	$1.00	$0.75	$0.25
B. Product Line Profitability, Including Joint Costs				
Sales	$3.50	$2.40	$0.80	$0.30
Costs beyond split-off point	(1.00)	(0.80)	(0.04)	(0.16)
Joint costs (from above)	(2.00)	(1.00)	(0.75)	(0.25)
Profit (loss) per chicken	$0.50	$0.60	$0.01	$(0.11)

illustrates these various methods using a barrel of oil that is split into three products: gasoline, motor oil, and jet fuel. Part A provides the data used to allocate the $100 cost per barrel. Part B applies the percentages to allocate the barrel's $100 cost. Notice the wide variation in allocated costs across the various methods. The allocated cost of gasoline varies from $30 to $80. Jet fuel varies from $10 to $50.

Physical measures such as weight and volume are convenient allocation bases because they are easily observed. If selling prices are used (relative sales value method), they must be recorded; frequent changes in sales prices introduce variability into the allocated costs. The **net realizable value** method of allocating joint costs uses as the allocation base the difference between sales revenue and the additional costs (beyond the joint costs) required to process the product from the point at which the joint products are split off until they are sold. Net realizable value is described more fully next. When analyzing situations involving joint costs, the fundamental point to remember is that *joint cost allocations can cause a death spiral.* More on this next.

1. Joint Cost Allocations and the Death Spiral

To illustrate the analysis of joint products, consider a chicken processor who buys live chickens and disassembles them into fillets, wings, and drumsticks. Suppose live chickens cost $1.60 each. The variable cost to process the live chicken into parts is $0.40 per chicken. The *joint cost* per chicken is then $2. Once the parts are obtained, separate processing is necessary to obtain marketable fillets, drumsticks, and wings. Each separate part must be cleaned, inspected, and packaged, at a cost of $0.80 for fillets, $0.16 for wings, and $0.04 for drumsticks. The split-off point is the point in processing at which all joint costs have been incurred. These data and selling prices are displayed in Table 8–9 along with the joint cost allocations based on weight.

Part A allocates the $2 joint cost to the chicken parts based on weight. Part B adds these allocated joint costs to the cost of further processing the chicken parts. The numbers in part B show that a loss of $0.11 per chicken is incurred from further processing of the wings. Based on this report, management's inclination is to stop processing the wings because they appear to be losing money.

Suppose that wings are no longer processed and sold. Assume that the unprocessed wings are hauled away for free and that eliminating wings has no effect on the revenue for fillets and drumsticks. Product line profitability after allocating the joint costs among the remaining parts—fillets and drumsticks—is recalculated in Table 8–10.

Managerial Application: Allocating Joint Costs in Not-for-Profit Organizations	Not-for-profit organizations (NFPs) are under pressure to devote a large portion of their expenditures to accomplishing their mission. Outside ratings agencies use the percentage of expenses devoted to programming versus fundraising and administration as a key component in their formulas to rate and compare NFPs. For example, NFPs showing a higher fraction of their fundraising used for supporting their mission rather than for more fundraising and administration are rated higher, and presumably can attract additional donors.

NFPs conduct a host of activities such as events or publish newsletters that both serve their mission programs and generate fundraising opportunities. The costs related to these common activities must be allocated between program expenses, fundraising, and management and general expenses. Since this allocation often appears subjective, it has come under increased scrutiny. In the United States, the Financial Accounting Standards Board (FASB) has issued guidance regarding the appropriate methods for allocating joint costs. The FASB defines joint costs as "The costs of conducting joint activities that are not identifiable with a particular component of the activity" (ASC 958-720-20). The FASB guidance offers wide latitude in choosing how to allocate joint costs as long as it is rational and systematic, and leads to "reasonable" allocations.

Note that what the FASB calls "joint costs" are in fact "common" or "indirect" costs. NFPs do not produce joint products from a joint input such as a barrel of oil or a cow. Joint costs result from a disassembly process. NFPs are involved in an assembly process whereby numerous inputs are assembled to provide programs that support the NFPs' mission.

SOURCE: J. Cruitt, "How NFPs Should Allocate Joint Costs," *Journal of Accountancy,* October 2014, pp. 38–42.

TABLE 8-10 **Using Weight to Allocate Chicken Costs for Product Line Profitability of Fillets and Drumsticks (Wings Are Dropped)**

	Total	Fillets	Drumsticks
A. Cost Allocation Based on Weight			
Weight	28 oz.	16 oz.	12 oz.
Percentage of weight	100%	57.14%	42.86%
Allocated cost	$2.00	$1.14	$ 0.86
B. Product Line Profitability, Including Joint Costs			
Sales	$3.20	$2.40	$ 0.80
Costs beyond split-off point	(0.84)	(0.80)	(0.04)
Joint costs (from above)	(2.00)	(1.14)	(0.86)
Profit (loss) per chicken	$0.36	$0.46	$(0.10)

Total profits have fallen from $0.50 per chicken to $0.36 per chicken, and we are now losing $0.10 on drumsticks. If we believed the analysis in Table 8–9 and eliminated the wings, we must also eliminate the drumsticks because of the analysis in Table 8–10. Table 8–11 presents the profit statement per chicken if we eliminate the drumsticks along with the wings.

Now we are losing $0.40 per chicken. (But at least we do not have to worry about allocating joint costs to joint products, as we have dropped all but one of the joint products.)

348   *Chapter 8*

TABLE 8-11   Analysis of Processing Fillets Only

Sales	$ 2.40
Costs beyond split-off point	(0.80)
Joint costs	(2.00)
Profit (loss) per chicken	$(0.40)

FIGURE 8-5

Joint costs, costs beyond split-off, and selling prices

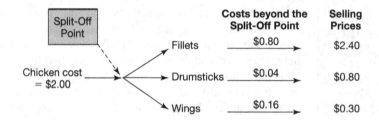

What is happening? Recall that joint cost allocations can cause a death spiral. The numbers in Tables 8–9 and 8–10 are misleading for decision making. The $2 joint cost of the chicken is fixed (sunk) with respect to further processing of the wings. If we no longer process and sell wings, we do not save $0.11 per chicken, as indicated by the reported loss in Table 8–9. It does not cost us $0.25 to get the wings in the first place because the wings are *free* once the chicken is processed. It costs us only the additional $0.16 per chicken incurred beyond the split-off point to process the wings to where we can sell them.

2. Net Realizable Value

What is the correct analysis? Apply the concept of opportunity costs from Chapter 2. What is the benefit forgone if wings are not processed further? The answer is the revenues of $0.30 less the costs incurred of further processing wings of $0.16, or $0.14. The allocated joint costs of the wings have already been incurred when the chicken is purchased and processed to the split-off point. The *only* benefit of further processing is the revenues less costs incurred to process further. The joint cost of the chicken is sunk at the time of the decision to process the wings.

Figure 8–5 illustrates the relation among joint costs, joint products, costs beyond the split-off point, and selling prices. Using the data from Table 8–9, Figure 8–5 portrays the joint products (fillets, drumsticks, and wings) that result from the joint input (the chicken). Once the joint products emerge after the split-off point, further costs are incurred before they can be sold. The costs beyond the split-off point are separable from the other joint product costs and will be incurred only if the particular joint product is processed further.

Relying on the graphic intuition in Figure 8–5, Table 8–12 presents the analysis using the net realizable value (NRV) allocation method. The relative profitability of each joint product depends only on its selling price less its costs beyond the split-off point. The difference between selling price and costs beyond the split-off point is called *net realizable value* and is analogous to contribution margin. If a particular joint product has negative net realizable value, it should not be processed further. However, if the cost of disposing of it is greater than its negative NRV, further processing is the least costly alternative.

Table 8–12 shows that all three chicken parts are yielding incremental revenues in excess of their further processing cost. For example, we can sell the wings for $0.30, yet the incremental cost (the cost of further processing) is only $0.16. Thus, the net realizable value of processing the wings is $0.14. Allocating joint costs using net realizable value as the allocation base does not distort product line profitability. In the footnote that accompanies Table 8–12, we see that fillets generate 64 percent of net realizable value and receive

Cost Allocation: Practices

349

TABLE 8-12   **Profits from Further Processing (Allocating Joint Costs Using Net Realizable Value)**

	Total	Fillets	Drumsticks	Wings
Sales	$3.50	$2.40	$0.80	$0.30
Costs beyond split-off point	(1.00)	(0.80)	(0.04)	(0.16)
Net realizable value from further processing	$2.50	$1.60	$0.76	$0.14
Less: Joint costs per chicken*	(2.00)	(1.28)	(0.61)	(0.11)
Profits	$0.50	$0.32	$0.15	$0.03

*Allocated based on net realizable value, as follows:

Net realizable value	$2.50	$1.60	$0.76	$0.14
Percentage of net realizable value	100%	64%	30.4%	5.6%
Joint cost	$2.00	$1.28	$0.61	$0.11

Managerial Application: Joint Costs in Sawmills	Processing a sawlog produces joint products: center boards, side boards, chips, and sawdust. The split-off point in sawmilling is where the sawlog is divided into these four joint products. A variety of joint cost allocation schemes are used in practice, and each method yields different costs for each product. In sawmilling, sales prices at the split-off point are usually not available, because the main products (i.e., center boards and side boards) are not sold without further processing. Many saw mills use physical measurement methods such as weight or volume to allocate the joint costs. These joint costs affect a product's profitability, transfer pricing decisions, and inventory valuation. For example, in the event of a fire, the loss covered by insurance will depend on the cost allocation method used.
	SOURCE: T. Tunes, A. Nyrud, and B. Eikenes, "Joint Cost Allocation in the Sawmilling Industry," *Forest Journal Products*, March, 2008.

64 percent of the joint costs. Wings generate only 5.6 percent of net realizable value and receive only 5.6 percent of the joint costs. Therefore, using net realizable value as the allocation base does not cause one product to bear a disproportionately larger percentage of joint costs than it generates in NRV.

After joint costs are allocated, wings show a "profit" of $0.03 per chicken. However, it is incorrect to say, "Wings generate $0.03 of profit per chicken." The correct statement is "Wings generate $0.14 of net cash flow per chicken if processed further."

Net realizable value does not distort product line profits because joint costs are allocated based on ability to pay. Products with the greatest contribution margins beyond the split-off point bear more of the joint cost. On the other hand, NRV allocation does not provide any additional information for decision making beyond whatever information is already contained in the net realizable value from further processing. That is, if a product is contributing positive cash flows beyond the split-off point, allocating joint costs to this product will not change the decision to process it further. Therefore, allocating joint costs using NRV is also irrelevant for product line profitability analysis. NRV allocations will not cause the wrong product line to be dropped, but they do not add anything for decision making beyond focusing the cash flows after the split-off point.

It is important to emphasize that when net realizable value is calculated, the costs beyond the split-off point must include only the direct costs associated with processing the joint product further. If no further processing is performed, then the firm should save all the costs beyond the split-off point. If costs beyond the split-off point contain any allocated fixed common costs, the decision to stop processing will not save the fixed common costs. For example, if costs beyond split-off contain allocated factory property taxes (because the further processing occupies shared factory space), the decision to stop further processing does not save these property taxes.

Exercise 8-2

New View produces two chemicals, V7 and AC, from a decomposition of M68JJ. Each batch of M68JJ, costing $22,000, yields 300 pounds of V7 and 400 pounds of AC. Each unit of V7 can be sold for $35, and each unit of AC can be sold for $25. Either intermediate product can be processed further. It costs $2,000 to convert 300 pounds of V7 into 240 pounds of V7HX. Likewise, it costs $1,500 to convert 400 pounds of AC into 320 pounds of AC92. Each pound of V7HX can be sold for $50, and each pound ofAC92 can be sold for $45. The $22,000–batch cost is allocated to the two intermediate products using pounds.

Required:

    a. Prepare a financial statement assuming V7 and AC are sold and not processed further. Calculate the profit per batch of each intermediate product that includes the allocated batch cost.

    b. If neither V7 nor AC is processed further, should New View produce V7 and AC?

    c. Should New View further process V7 into V7HX and/or AC into AC92? Justify your answer with supporting calculations.

Solution:

    a. Profits from producing just the intermediate products:

	V7	AC
Selling price of intermediate product	$ 35	$ 25
Number of intermediate pounds	× 300	× 400
Total revenue of intermediate product	$ 10,500	$ 10,000
Allocated joint cost*	$ 9,429	$ 12,571
Product line profit (loss)	$ 1,071	($ 2,571)

*$9,429 = $22,000 × (300 ÷ 700); $12,571 = $22,000 × (400 ÷ 700).

    b. New View should not produce the intermediate products, because the total revenue of the two intermediate products ($10,500 + $10,000 = $20,500) is less than the joint batch cost of $22,000.

    c. New View should sell V7 as an intermediate product and further process AC into AC92. This yields total net cash flow per batch of $1,400 ($10,500 + $14,400 – $22,000 – $1,500). Hence, it is now profitable to decompose batches of M68JJ into V7 and AC. The following table calculates the incremental cash flow of further processing each product.

	V7HX	AC92
Total revenue of intermediate product	$10,500	$10,000
Selling price of final product	$ 50	$ 45
Number of final product pounds	240	320
Total revenue of final product	$12,000	$14,400
Cost of further processing	$ 2,000	$ 1,500
Profit of further processing	$10,000	$12,900
Incremental profit of further processing versus selling the intermediate product	($ 500)	$ 2,900

	V7HX	AC92	Total
Sales of intermediate product	$10,500		$10,500
Sales of final product		$14,400	14,400
Cost of further processing		(1,500)	(1,500)
Joint cost			(22,000)
Total profit per batch			$ 1,400

Often, a manufacturing process, besides producing joint products (fillets, drumsticks, and wings), also yields by-products (gizzards and feet). These are joint products that have little commercial value or are not the primary products of the joint production process. Since management does not think of the by-products as being a managed part of the business, the sales revenue derived from them is subtracted from the joint costs. For example, suppose the by-products from each chicken (gizzard and feet) are sold for $0.07 and each chicken costs $1.67. Instead of treating the by-products as joint products and calculating a product line profit margin, management simply subtracts the $0.07 by-product revenue from the gross chicken cost of $1.67 to get the net chicken cost of $1.60. The net joint costs are then allocated to the joint products. This procedure allows management to focus on the major products being produced.

Historical Application: British Rail	After an analysis of profits by the various individual rail lines composing British Rail, management concluded that certain short trunk lines were unprofitable on a fully allocated cost basis. But after the unprofitable lines were closed, profits actually fell. Careful review of the facts revealed that labor was being charged to each rail line based on the amount of labor cost used on each line. But labor was a fixed, common cost. Labor union contracts prevented management from laying off employees when rail lines were closed. Rather, these employees were reassigned. Therefore, when lines were closed, revenues fell but the allocated common labor costs remained.

3. Decision Making and Control

Managers producing joint products must make two different, but interrelated, decisions: (1) which joint products to further process (and what prices to charge for them) and (2) given the answers in (1), whether to process any joint inputs (and how many). In step 1, managers decide whether to further process each joint product. A joint product should be further processed if its final sales price exceeds the additional processing cost plus its unprocessed sales value. Chicken wings should be processed further because their selling price of $0.30 exceeds the $0.16 additional processing cost (unprocessed wings have no value). Notice these decisions regarding further processing do not require any costs to be allocated.

In step 2, managers decide how many joint inputs (if any) to process. Here managers continue processing joint inputs (chickens) as long as the sum of the joint products' net realizable values (NRVs) exceeds all the costs up to and including the split-off point. The analysis in step 1 determines the profit-maximizing mix of joint products. If the sum of the NRVs doesn't cover the cost of the joint input plus the cost of operating the split-off point, don't produce. If the cost of chickens increases to $2.55, and the selling prices of the chicken parts remain the same, then the sum of the NRVs of $2.50 does not cover the joint cost of the chicken, and no chickens should be processed. Again, notice that cost allocations (even using NRV to allocate joint costs) play no role in making this decision.

Managers can make all the decisions regarding joint products without resorting to cost allocations. Joint cost allocations are not needed for decision making. Hence, given the pervasiveness of joint cost allocations, they must be serving other purposes such as inventory valuation for taxes and financial reporting or control.

Any joint cost allocation scheme other than net realizable value can lead to erroneous decisions regarding eliminating joint products. However, this does not mean that NRV is the best way of allocating joint costs. For the specific decision to eliminate a product, NRV is best because other allocation schemes distort the *incremental* profitability of the product or division. However, an allocation scheme other than NRV can be better for controlling agency problems.

Consider the case of an oil refinery producing gasoline and jet fuel, sold by two separate profit centers. If refinery costs, including the cost of crude oil, are assigned to the two profit centers using NRV, the relative profitability of each profit center is not distorted. Suppose the airline industry is expanding and the price of jet fuel rises relative to gasoline. The jet fuel profit center's NRV increases, as does its share of the joint costs. Likewise, gasoline's share of the joint costs falls and the allocated joint cost per gallon of gasoline falls. With a lower cost per gallon of gasoline, the gasoline division might lower its price. But the opportunity cost of a gallon of gasoline is not lower; in fact, it is likely to be higher to the extent that the refining process allows some substitution between jet fuel and gasoline production. Allocating the joint refinery costs using a physical measure such as gallons or pounds insulates each division from price fluctuations in the other division. Net realizable value is better for product line profitability decisions but may not be best for other decisions such as pricing or control. Management usually must trade off decision making and control. A single cost allocation procedure is unlikely to be best for both.

The discussion of joint products highlights the problems of assessing product line profitability when the profits include allocated joint costs. Only NRV allocations do not distort product line profitability. The same cautions apply to assessing product line profits that contain allocated common costs. Managers can make major strategic decision errors if they focus on product line profits after joint or common costs are allocated using anything other than net realizable value.

Concept Questions		
	Q8–6	What are joint costs? How do they differ from common costs?
	Q8–7	Describe some methods for allocating joint costs.
	Q8–8	What are the advantages and disadvantages of the net realizable method of allocating joint costs?

E. Segment Reporting and Joint Benefits

Chapter 7 described insulating versus noninsulating allocations within the context of reporting the profitability of business segments. This section expands on some additional issues involved in segment reporting.

Consider the router and disk drive divisions, which share a common cost. Some managers and accountants argue that each business segment report should be separated into those expenses that are controllable by the division and those expenses that are not controllable, but rather are allocated to the division. The following table illustrates segment reporting.

	April	
	Router Division	Disk Drive Division
Division revenues	$98,000	$103,000
Division controllable expenses	96,000	104,100
Controllable segment margin	$ 2,000	$ (1,100)
Allocated common costs*	(700)	(300)
Net income	$ 1,300	$ (1,400)

*Allocated based on square footage (70 percent to Router and 30 percent to Disk Drive).

In this statement, the router division is contributing $2,000 toward covering common costs, whereas the disk drive division is losing $1,100 before any common costs are allocated to the segment. Proponents of separating controllable from noncontrollable segment expenses believe this format is more informative of segment performance. Since segments cannot control common costs, they should not be held responsible for them. If a segment is contributing a positive contribution toward the common costs, it should be retained. This is, again, another application of the controllability principle. It is similar in spirit to the argument that fixed costs should be ignored in setting transfer prices and that joint costs are irrelevant in assessing product profitability.

Unfortunately, simple rules of thumb like dropping segments with negative controllable segment margins can be wrong in some situations. Consider the following examples. Suppose a segment such as the router division in the preceding table has a positive net income after all common cost allocations. Should it be retained? Not necessarily. The router division could be producing very low-quality routers that are adversely affecting the demand for the disk drives. Or the router division might be consuming so much of the attention of senior management that the other segments are suffering. In both of these cases, an apparently profitable segment based on its accounting statements should be dropped.

Now consider the example of a segment with a negative controllable segment margin such as the disk drive division. It appears this division should be dropped. Should it? Not necessarily. Suppose that the demand for disk drives and the demand for modems depend on each other because it is cheaper for customers to deal with one supplier of both disk drives and modems than two separate suppliers. Dropping either product adversely affects the demand for the other. The accounting segment report does not capture these interdependencies in demand.

In general, firms produce multiple products because there are synergies—in either production or demand. In Chapter 4, we argued that firms exist because they lower certain transactions costs below what it would cost to acquire equivalent goods or services in a series of market transactions. Firms have multiple segments because of synergies among segments. These synergies are "joint benefits" that are usually difficult to quantify, let alone allocate. Like joint costs, they cannot be allocated to segments in any meaningful way. Firms prepare segment reports as performance measures to help reduce agency costs. But to the extent there are large interdependencies among segments, these joint benefits make it very difficult to use the segment reports to decide which segments to drop without further analysis.

F. Summary

This chapter continues the cost allocation discussion begun in the previous chapter. Cost allocations can create a death spiral. The death spiral is a perverse problem that arises when (1) allocated costs contain fixed costs and (2) users reduce their demand for a service department in response to a high allocated cost. As usage falls, total costs do not fall proportionately because of the fixed costs. This causes the costs allocated to the remaining users to rise further, and the remaining users will seek to outsource the service to less expensive external vendors.

Two specific cost allocation situations are described: multiple service departments and joint costs. When the costs of several service departments are allocated to operating divisions, wide variations in transfer prices can result depending on how the service department costs are allocated and the order in which they are allocated if a step-down method is used. These variations in transfer price can then cause user departments to alter their consumption of service department resources.

Joint costs arise whenever a single joint input such as a barrel of oil is split into several joint products such as gasoline, motor oil, and jet fuel. Beware of all product line profitability studies that rely on allocated joint or common costs, unless these costs are allocated using net realizable value (revenues less the costs beyond the split-off point).

Chapters 9 through 13 expand the discussion begun in Chapters 7 and 8 by describing how costs are allocated to products. If a plant produces multiple products, the cost of each product must be computed for tax, inventory valuation, and decision management and control reasons. Chapters 9 through 13, based on the introductory material in Chapters 7 and 8, describe a number of complexities that arise in product costing within a manufacturing setting.

Appendix: Reciprocal Method for Allocating Service Department Costs

Section C of this chapter described various ways of allocating service department costs to operating divisions, including the direct allocation and step-down allocation methods. The reciprocal method was discussed, but its exact calculation was deferred to this appendix. To simplify the discussion, start by assuming that all costs in the service departments are variable.

TABLE 8-13   **Reciprocal Method of Allocating Service Department Costs to Operating Divisions ($ in Millions)**

| | Service Departments | | Operating Divisions | | |
	Telecommunications	Information Technology	Cars	Trucks	Total
Department providing service:					
Telecommunications	10%	20%	40%	30%	100%
IT	25%	15%	35%	25%	100%
Department costs before allocation of service costs	$ 2.000	$ 6.000			8.000
Service department allocated costs:					
Telecommunications	$ (4.475)*				$ (4.475)
	$ 0.448	$ 0.895	$1.790	$ 1.343	$ 4.475
IT		$(8.112)*			$ (8.112)
	$ 2.028	$ 1.217	$2.839	$ 2.028	$ 8.112
Total overhead allocated	$ 0.000	$ 0.000	$4.629	$ 3.371	$ 8.000
Overhead allocations bases:					
Allocated telecommunications costs	$ 0.448	$ 0.895	$1.790	$ 1.343	$ 4.475
÷ Number of phones	300	600	1,200	900	3,000
Cost per phone	$ 1,492	$ 1,492	$1,492	$ 1,492	$ 1,492
Allocated IT costs	$ 2.028	$ 1.217	$2.839	$ 2.028	$ 8.111
÷ Number of gigabytes (millions)	3.0	1.8	4.2	3.0	12.0
Cost per gigabyte	$ 0.676	$ 0.676	$ 0.676	$ 0.676	$ 0.676

*Two simultaneous equations with two unknowns must be solved:

Let

T = Total cost to be assigned from telecommunications

I = Total cost to be assigned from information technology

T = Initial cost incurred + 0.10T + 0.25I

T = $2.0 + 0.10$T$ + 0.25I (1)

I = Initial cost incurred + 0.20T + 0.15I

I = $6.0 + 0.20$T$ + 0.15I (2)

Solve equations (1) and (2). Start with equation (1) and collect terms:

0.9T = $2.0 + 0.25$I$

T = $2.0/.9 + (.25/.9)$I$

T = $2.222 + 0.278$I$ (3)

Now substitute the preceding equation into equation (2) and solve for I:

I = $6.0 + 0.20 ($2.222 + 0.278I) + 0.15I

I = $6.0 + 0.444 + 0.056$I$ + 0.15I

0.749 I = $6.444

I = $8.112

Substitute the value of I = $ 8.112 into equation (3) and solve for T:

T = $2.222 + 0.278($8.112)   (4)

T = $2.222 + $2.253

T = $4.475

When each service department uses the other service departments, the allocation of one service department's cost to another service department depends on the simultaneous utilization of each department. A simultaneous system of equations is needed to account for the reciprocal use among service departments. To illustrate the reciprocal method, the example of the telecommunications and information technology (IT) departments will be continued. Table 8–13 provides the computations of the reciprocal method.

The reciprocal method operates in two steps. The first step focuses on the interactions among the service departments (ignoring the operating divisions) and develops a total charge for each service department. The second step takes the total charge and allocates it across the service departments and operating divisions. The first two lines in Table 8–13 repeat the utilization percentages by users reported in Table 8–1. These utilization percentages among the service departments are used to form a system of two equations with two unknowns (see the footnote to the table). The total cost, T, of operating the telecommunications department includes telecommunication's own cost ($2.0) plus a proportion of its own cost and IT's costs and is given by the following equation:

$$T = \text{Initial cost incurred} + 0.10T + 0.25I$$

The initial cost in the telecommunications department is $2 million, which allows this equation to be written as

$$T = \$2.0 + 0.10T + 0.25I$$

Likewise, the total IT cost assigned, I, is given by the following equation:

$$I = \$6.0 + 0.20T + 0.15I$$

We have two equations with two unknowns. Using some simple algebra outlined in Table 8–13, we can solve for the two unknowns:

$$T = \$4.475 \text{ million}$$

$$I = \$8.112 \text{ million}$$

The second step of the reciprocal method allocates these revised total costs to all the service departments and operating divisions using the utilization rates in Table 8–13. The resulting allocations are also shown in the table. Using these allocations, a charge per phone and cost per gigabyte are computed. Each department and each division pays the same per phone and gigabyte.

It is important to understand the relation between the initial cost of the service department and the total cost to be assigned using the reciprocal method. Telecommunications incurs costs of $2 million, yet $4.475 million is being allocated. The reason that more is being allocated than incurred is because some of the allocated costs are assigned to the service departments. In order for all $2 million of telecommunications costs to be allocated to the operating divisions, the total allocated has to be increased by the amount that is charged to the service departments.

So far, the reciprocal method has been described as a system of two equations with two unknowns. Solving the two equations was straightforward: One equation was substituted into the other in order to solve for the remaining unknown. If there are more than three or four service divisions, this simple technique becomes very burdensome. Fortunately, Excel and other software provide convenient apps that can solve very large linear systems with N equations and N unknowns.

The preceding analysis assumes that all the service department costs ($2 million and $6 million) are variable. If the service department costs contain any fixed costs, only the variable cost portion is allocated using the simultaneous solutions method. The fixed costs can be allocated based on planned usage.

Self-Study Problem

Medical Center

Eastern University has a medical center consisting of a medical school and a hospital. The primary function of the medical school is education. To accomplish its mission, the hospital provides teaching opportunities for medical students and residents. In addition, medical research is conducted. Attracting top medical school faculty requires resources: good colleagues, good students, good research facilities, and competitive salaries. Faculty are expected to teach, conduct research, and provide medical care to patients. Good teaching requires knowledge of research and how to provide quality patient care. Patient care is enhanced by having faculty doing state-of-the-art research. Research is stimulated by inquisitive, bright students and actual patient cases. While the mix of activities varies substantially across faculty, a study of their time utilization reported the following averages:

	Percent of Time Devoted to
Teaching	30%
Patient care	25
Research	45

Recent pressures to reduce hospital costs have caused the medical center to take a close look at its cost structure. They have collected data on the medical center's operating revenues and expenses for the last fiscal year.

Medical Center Operating Revenues and (Expenses), Last Fiscal Year (Millions)

Direct patient care expenditures (nursing, pharmacy, laundry, etc.)*	$(297)
Direct research expenses (research supplies, lab technicians, etc.)*	(50)
Faculty salaries and benefits	(140)
Income from endowment	22
Medical school admissions and administration expenditures	(33)
Medical school tuition	82
Occupancy costs (utilities, maintenance, security, etc.)†	(80)
Patient revenues	370
Sponsored research funding	127

*Excludes faculty salaries.
†Square footage utilized:

Hospital	250,000
Medical school	50,000
Research labs	100,000

To help offset the high cost of medicine, the medical center solicits donations. The vast majority of the donations received are not specifically restricted to teaching, research, or hospital activities. Rather, most of the gifts are for the unrestricted use of the medical center. These contributions are invested in an endowment and the annual income from the endowment is a source of operating funds for the medical center.

Required:

a. Prepare a financial statement that reports separately the operating performance of teaching, research, and patient care for the medical center. Explain and justify any assumptions you make in preparing the statement.

b. Evaluate how accurately the report you have prepared reflects the financial performance of the three functions: teaching, research, and patient care. What inferences do you draw from your report in part (*a*)?

Solution:

a. This question illustrates the fundamental problems of trying to draw inferences about the profitability of joint products. The medical center produces three joint products: teaching, research, and patient care. All three are provided by the same organization rather than three separate organizations because synergies exist among the three. In addition to joint costs (faculty salaries), there are joint benefits (endowment income). Any attempt to try to

358 *Chapter 8*

allocate the joint costs (faculty salaries) and joint benefits (endowment income) is likely to lead to misleading inferences.

One way of evaluating performance is to allocate the faculty salaries based on time utilization. The occupancy costs are probably not entirely joint or common costs and these can be assigned based on square footage. Allocating the endowment income is problematic and arbitrary. There is no completely objective basis for allocating these joint benefits. The accompanying table allocates endowment income based on the same percentages used to allocate the faculty salaries. This assumes that what ultimately drives gifts to the medical center is the same as what drives the joint costs.

Medical Center Operating Performance by Function, Last Fiscal Year (Millions)

	Teaching	Research	Hospital	Total
Revenue	$82	$127	$370	$579
Direct expenses	33	50	297	380
Faculty salaries	42	63	35	140
Occupancy costs	10	20	50	80
Surplus (deficit) before endowment	$ (3)	$ (6)	$ (12)	$(21)
Endowment income*	7	10	6	22
Surplus (deficit)	$ 4	$ 4	$ (7)	$ 1

*Allocated based on faculty salaries. Numbers do not add to total because of rounding.

It is important to note that, after including the endowment income of $22 million, the medical center actually had a surplus of $1 million.

We see from the preceding table that all three functions are operating at a deficit before endowment income. But it appears that the hospital is losing the most money, $12 million out of the total $21 million deficit. After considering the endowment income, teaching and research are both showing a surplus and the hospital is showing a loss.

If the endowment income is allocated based on total revenues, teaching breaks even, research reports a $1 million deficit, and the hospital reports a $2 million surplus. For public relations and fund-raising purposes, the medical center would probably not want the hospital to report a surplus. Thus, endowment income would most likely not be allocated based on revenues.

b. One problem with the previous table is that it produces misleading product line profitability information. Because faculty salaries are a joint cost, any attempt to allocate these costs using other than net realizable values can be misleading. The following table recasts the preceding table using NRV as the allocation base for both faculty salaries and endowment income.

Medical Center Operating Performance by Function
Net Realizable Value Method, Last Fiscal Year (Millions)

	Teaching	Research	Hospital	Total
Revenue	$82	$127	$370	$579
Direct expenses	33	50	297	380
Occupancy costs	10	20	50	80
Net realizable value	$39	$ 57	$ 23	$119
% NRV	33%	48%	19%	100%
Joint costs*	39	57	23	118
Surplus (deficit)†	$ 0	$ 0	$ 0	$ 1

*Faculty salaries less endowment income.
†Numbers do not add to total because of rounding.

The results in this table indicate that all three activities are contributing cash flows toward covering the joint costs. Research appears to be providing the most cash flows at $57 million. However, even this table is misleading in one important aspect.

None of the three functions (teaching, research, and patient care) is separable from the others. Unlike the chicken example in the text, where the firm can decide to further process a chicken part, the medical center does not have this option. Closing the hospital will have a large impact on the demand for teaching services. Few top students will attend a medical school that does not offer clinical experience. Since the demand for the three functions is interdependent, changing the scale of one function affects the revenues of the others. This would be equivalent to the case in which the demand for chicken fillets depends on the availability of wings. If supermarkets want to offer their customers both fillets and wings and will only buy from chicken processors who offer a full product line, then eliminating one chicken part reduces the demand for the other parts. This interdependency among demands is a primary reason that the medical center offers all three services. It also renders any attempt to disaggregate the firm into separate subunits for decision-making purposes a dangerous exercise.

While it is tempting to provide a disaggregated product line performance report, such an exercise provides very little insight. The medical center is generating a small surplus of $1 million. The source of this surplus cannot be attributed to any one of the three functions because demands for the service and the production functions of each service are so highly interdependent.

The financial performance of each function is probably best measured by comparing each unit's actual costs and revenues with budgeted costs and revenues estimated prior to the start of the fiscal year.

Problems

P 8–1:   Swedish Hospital

Swedish Hospital uses a step-down method to allocate 25 indirect service department costs (information technology, laundry, security, records, food service, etc.) to the six direct patient care units (surgery, maternity, psychiatry, etc.). The Food Service (FS) department (patient and staff dining) currently is the third service department to be allocated in the step-down methodology. Swedish is revamping its step-down methodology and is considering moving FS from its 3rd place position to the 23rd position.

Required:

   a. FS costs are allocated based on the number of meals served. Does the FS allocated cost per meal served increase or decrease if FS moves from its 3rd place position to the 23rd position in the step-down methodology? Also, describe exactly what causes the allocated cost per meal to increase or decrease.

   b. Describe the issues that Swedish management should consider before moving FS from its 3rd place position to the 23rd position in the step-down methodology.

P 8–2:   Outback Opals

Outback Opals mines and processes opals from its Australian opal mines. The process consists of removing large chunks of stones, carefully splitting the stones and removing the opals, and then cutting and polishing the stones. Finally, the opals are sorted and graded (I, II, and III). The Grade I opals are sent to Outback's U.S. subsidiary for sale in the United States. The Graded II opals are sold through Outback's Hong Kong subsidiary in Hong Kong, and the Grade III opals are sold in Australia. It costs 35,000 Australian dollars (A$) to mine, cut, polish, and sort a batch of opals. The following table summarizes the number of stones in each batch mined, the additional costs to package and sell each stone after it is polished and graded, the selling price of each grade of stone (in Australian dollars), and the income tax rates that apply to any income derived from stones sold in the country of final sale.

	Grade I	Grade II	Grade III
Number of stones per batch	70	105	175
Additional costs to package and sell each stone	A$250	A$120	A$5
Selling price per stone	A$800	A$300	A$110
Income tax rate	30%	15%	45%
Country of final sale	U.S.	Hong Kong	Australia

Required:

a. Calculate the joint cost per stone of each grade of opal (I, II, and III) using the number of stones in each batch to allocate the A$35,000 joint mining, cutting, polishing, and sorting costs. (Round all decimals to four significant digits.)

b. Calculate the joint cost per stone of each grade of opal (I, II, and III) using the net realizable value of each grade of stones (before taxes) to allocate the A$35,000 joint mining, cutting, polishing, and sorting costs. (Round all decimals to four significant digits.)

c. Which method of allocating the joint cost of A$35,000 (number of stones or net realizable value) should Outback Opals use? Explain why.

P 8–3: Rose Hospital

Rose Hospital has two service departments (building services and food service) and three patient care units (intensive care, surgery, and general medicine). Building Services provides janitorial, maintenance, and engineering services, as well as space (utilities, depreciation, insurance, and taxes) to all departments and patient care units. Food Service provides meals to both patients and staff members. It operates a cafeteria and serves meals to patients in their rooms. Building services costs of $6 million are allocated based on square footage, and food service costs of $3 million are allocated based on number of meals served. The following two tables summarize the annual costs of the two service departments and the utilization of each service department by the other departments.

	Annual Cost * (Millions)
Building Services	$6.0
Food Service	3.0
Total overhead	$9.0

*Before allocated service department costs

Utilization Patterns

	Allocation Base	Building Services	Food Services	Intensive Care	Surgery	General Medicine	Total
Building Services	Square footage	2,500	15,500	10,000	20,000	40,000	88,000
Food Service	Meals	12,000	10,000	3,000	4,000	98,000	127,000

The following table summarizes the allocation of service department costs using the step-down method with Food Service as the first service department to be allocated:

Step-Down Method
(Food Service First) (Millions)

	Intensive Care	Surgery	General Medicine
Food Service	$0.09	$0.09	$2.52
Building Services	0.88	1.83	3.59
Total	$0.97	$1.92	$6.11

Required:

(Round all allocation rates and all dollar amounts to two decimal places.)

  a. Allocate the two service department costs to the three patient care units using the direct method of allocating service department costs.

  b. Same as part (a) except use the step-down allocation method with Building Services as the first service department allocated.

  c. Write a short, nontechnical memo to management explaining why the sum of the two service department costs allocated to each patient care unit in part (b) differs from the sum of the costs computed using the step-down method starting with Food Service.

P 8–4: Mystic Herbals

Mystic Herbals processes exotic plant materials into various fragrances and biological pastes used by perfume and cosmetic firms. One particular plant material, Xubonic root from the rain forest in Australia, is processed yielding four joint products: QV3, VX7, HM4, and LZ9. Each of these joint products can be sold as is after the joint production process or processed further. The following table describes the yield of each joint product from one batch, the selling prices of the intermediate and further processed products, and the costs of further processing each joint product. The joint cost of processing one batch of Xubonic root is $30,000.

	QV3	VX7	HM4	LZ9
Number of ounces per batch	100	80	125	195
Cost of further processing	$2,400	$400	$2,500	$2,800
Selling price of unprocessed intermediate product per ounce	$ 62	$ 49	$ 102	$ 47
Selling price of final product after further processing per ounce	$ 85	$ 57	$ 127	$ 61

Required:

  a. Allocate the $30,000 joint cost per batch to each of the joint products based on the number of ounces in each joint product.

  b. To maximize firm value, which of the joint products should be processed further and which should be sold without further processing?

  c. Based on your analysis in part (b) regarding the decisions to process further or not, should Mystic Herbals process batches of Xubonic root into the four joint products? Support your decision with a quantitative analysis and indicate how much profit or loss Mystic Herbals makes per batch.

  d. Suppose the joint cost of $30,000 is allocated using the net realizable value of each joint product. Calculate the profits (loss) per joint product after allocating the joint cost using net realizable value.

  e. Explain how the use of joint cost allocations enhances or harms the decision to process joint products.

P 8–5:　Berkman Financial

Berkman Financial is a regional bank that offers a variety of financial services to both retail and commercial customers. Berkman uses the step-down allocation method to allocate four service departments' costs (S1, S2, S3, and S4) to the three strategic business units (SBUs). Services provided by service departments are measured in "service units." The following table summarizes the cost of each of the four service departments and the number of service units used by the other service departments and SBUs:

Svc Dept	Svc Dept Cost (millions)	No. of Service Units Used						
		Service Departments				Strategic Bus Units		
		S1	S2	S3	S4	SBU1	SBU2	SBU3
S1	$3.50		43	6	2	30	40	28
S2	$6.20	28		4.2	7.2	39	78	12.5
S3	$8.30	4	6		15	22	43	52
S4	$4.20	17	3	2		63	22	9

In other words, Service Department S2 used 43 service units provided by S1 and SBU2 used 40 service units of S1. Likewise, S1 used 17 service units of S4 and SBU1 used 63 units of S4.

Required:

a. What is the cost per service unit of S1, and what is the cost per service unit of S2 if S1 is the first service department and S2 is the second department in the step-down order?

b. What is the cost per service unit of S1 and what is the cost per service unit of S2 if S2 is the first service department and S1 is the second department in the step-down order?

c. Describe briefly why the costs per service unit of S1 and S2 vary depending on the step-down allocation order.

d. Should S1 come before S2 or vice versa in the step-down order? In other words, what factors should management consider in ordering the four departments in the step-down allocation method?

P 8–6:　Joint Products, Inc.

Joint Products, Inc., produces two joint products, X and V, using a common input. These are produced in batches. The common input costs $8,000 per batch. To produce the final products (X and V), additional processing costs beyond the split-off point must be incurred. There are no beginning inventories. The accompanying data summarize the operations.

	Products	
	X	V
Quantities produced per batch	200 lb	400 lb
Additional processing costs per batch beyond split-off	$1,800	$3,400
Unit selling prices of completely processed products	$40/lb	$10/lb
Ending inventory	2,000 lb	1,000 lb

Required:

a. Compute the full cost of the ending inventory using net realizable value to allocate joint cost.

b. If the selling prices at the split-off point (before further processing) are $35 and $1 per pound of X and V, respectively, what should the firm do regarding further processing? Show calculations.

P 8–7: Upstate Growers

Upstate Growers (Upstate) is a cooperative corporation owned by 12 large apple farmers in New York State. Upstate is responsible for managing all 12 apple orchards, picking and sorting the apples, and producing the final apple products. Apples are washed and sorted into three grades: "large un-bruised apples," "large bruised apples," or "small apples." These three apple grades/categories comprise the final products produced and sold by Upstate. Large un-bruised apples are sold in supermarkets as whole "eating apples" after they are wrapped, packed, and shipped. Large bruised apples are peeled, cored, sauced, cooked, bottled, packed, and shipped to retailers as applesauce. And, small apples are juiced, cooked, filtered, and bottled as apple juice that is sold to supermarkets. Large un-bruised apples also can be converted into either applesauce or apple juice. Large bruised apples also can be juiced and bottled as apple juice like small apples, but cannot be sold as whole "eating apples." All three types of apples can be sold as is at $11 per 100 pounds of whole apples for use as livestock feed without incurring any additional costs.

All three types of apples (large bruised, large un-bruised, and small) are sorted into crates containing 100 pounds of apples. The cost of wrapping, packing, and shipping 100 pounds of large un-bruised apples is $12, which can be sold as whole apples for $31. The cost of peeling, coring, cooking, saucing, bottling, packing, and shipping 100 pounds of bruised large apples is $60, which can be sold as applesauce for $80. The cost of juicing, cooking, filtering, bottling, packing, and shipping 100 pounds of small apples is $28, which can be sold as apple juice for $34.

Upstate harvested, washed, and sorted 4.6 million pounds of apples. The cost of operating the 12 orchards was $274,000, and the cost of picking, washing, and sorting the apples was $48,000. These 4.6 million pounds of apples yielded 9,300 (100-pound) crates of large un-bruised apples, 14,200 (100-pound) crates of large bruised apples, and 22,500 (100-pound) crates of small apples. The orchards' operating costs and the costs of picking, washing and sorting the apples are allocated to three apple categories based on apple weight.

Required:

   a. Prepare a table that calculates the net profits of processing (1) a 100-pound crate of large un-bruised apples, (2) applesauce from a 100-pound crate of apples, and (3) apple juice from a 100-pound crate of apples after allocating the orchards' operating costs and the costs of picking, washing, and sorting the apples.

   b. Given the data in the problem, what should Upstate Growers do with each of the three sorted categories of apples harvested? In other words, to maximize firm value prepare a production plan for the large un-bruised apples (sell as whole "eating apples," whole apples to be used as livestock feed, applesauce, or apple juice), the large bruised apples (sell as whole apples to be used as livestock feed, applesauce, or apple juice), and the small apples (sell as whole apples to be used as livestock feed or apple juice)? Explain the logic underlying your production plan.

P 8–8: Murray Hill's Untimely Demise

Murray Hill was preparing the monthly report that allocates the three service department's (A, B, and C) costs to the three operating divisions (D1, D2, and D3) when he choked to death on a stale double cream-filled donut. You must step in and complete his step-down allocations. The three service departments (A, B, and C) have costs (before any cost allocation) of:

Service Department	Service Department's Own Cost
A	$600,000
B	300,000
C	200,000

364   *Chapter 8*

The following table provides the percentage of utilization of each service department by the other service departments and the operating departments:

	Service Departments			Operating Departments			
	A	B	C	D1	D2	D3	
A	5%	10%	20%	30%	15%	20%	100%
B	8	0	15	22	20	35	100
C	15	5	7	20	30	23	100

The step-down sequence is A, B, then C.

Poor Murray allocated only A's costs before the donut did him in. His incomplete spreadsheet is:

Service Department Cost		Service Departments			Operating Departments		
		A	B	C	D1	D2	D3
$600,000	A	$0	$63,158	$126,316	$189,474	$94,737	$126,316
	B						
	C						

Required:

a. Do Murray proud and complete the incomplete spreadsheet. Like Murray, round all cost allocations to the nearest dollar.

b. If the company wants the cost allocations to most accurately capture the opportunity cost of resources consumed by the operating divisions, how should the service departments be ordered in the step-down method?

P 8–9: Enzymes

Two genetically engineered enzymes are produced simultaneously from a series of chemical and biological processes: Q enzyme and Y enzyme. The cost per batch of Q and Y enzymes is $200,000, resulting in 300 grams of Q and 200 grams of Y. Before Q and Y can be sold, they must be processed further at costs of $100 and $150 per gram, respectively. Each batch requires one month of processing time and only one batch per month is produced.

The monthly demand for Q and Y depends on the price charged. The following table summarizes the various price-quantity combinations.

Quantity Sold	Price per Gram of Q	Price per Gram of Y
50	$1,200	$750
100	1,100	550
150	1,000	350
200	900	150
250	800	n.a.
300	700	n.a.

In the following analysis, the optimum price of Q is $900 per gram and the optimum price of Y is $750 per gram.

Cost Allocation: Practices

365

Quantity Sold	Price per Q	Revenue of Q	Total Cost of Q*	Total Profit	Price per Y	Revenue from Y	Total cost of Y†	Total Profit
50	$1,200	$ 60,000	$ 25,000	$35,000	$750	$37,500	$ 27,500	$10,000
100	1,100	110,000	50,000	60,000	550	55,000	55,000	0
150	1,000	150,000	75,000	75,000	350	52,500	82,500	(30,000)
200	900	180,000	100,000	80,000	150	30,000	110,000	(80,000)
250	800	200,000	125,000	75,000	n.a.			
300	700	210,000	150,000	60,000	n.a.			

*Cost per gram of Q = ($200,000/500) + $100 = $500/gram.
†Cost per gram of Y = ($200,000/500) + $150 = $550/gram.

Required:

a. Critically evaluate the analysis underlying the pricing decisions of $900 for Q and $750 for Y.

b. What should management do if the cost per batch rises to $225,000?

P 8–10: Sunder Toys

Sunder manufactures hard rubber pet toys. The purple dog chewy has a variable cost of $3.00 per unit. It is produced on a machine that is leased. The three models of this machine have three different capacities.

Maximum Daily Capacity (Units)	Daily Lease Cost
1,000	$10,000
1,200	10,800
1,400	11,200

The daily market demand for purple dog chewies at various prices is:

Price	Daily Quantity Demanded
$16.11	900
15.00	1,000
14.18	1,100
12.83	1,200
12.23	1,300
11.50	1,400

There is no uncertainty (daily variation) with respect to the daily demand for purple dog chewies. For example, if the price is set at $14.18, 1,100 chewies will be sold every day with certainty.

Required:

a. Given all the data, how many purple dog chewies should Sunder produce and sell? (Show calculations, neatly labeled.)

b. Suppose Sunder has the policy of not charging fixed costs to products whenever excess capacity exists. The manager of purple dog chewies receives a bonus based on the accounting profits from purple dog chewies. This manager has private knowledge of machine capacities, lease fees, and the demand for purple dog chewies, as well as the decision rights over how large a machine to lease. How big a machine will the manager lease and how many chewies will be produced and sold? (Show calculations, neatly labeled.)

c. Comment on Sunder's policy of not charging fixed costs to products whenever excess capacity exists.

P 8–11:   WWWeb Marketing

WWWeb Marketing is a decentralized firm specializing in designing and operating Internet marketing websites. The firm is four years old and has been growing rapidly, but it only shows a small profit. WWWeb has three profit centers: Design Division, Server Operations, and the Crawler Division. The Design Division devises Internet marketing strategies for external clients, including innovative websites and Web-based marketing strategies. Server Operations maintains the clients' websites on WWWeb's servers. The Crawler Division operates WWWeb's proprietary search engine that clients can use for Internet-based marketing research. In addition to these three profit centers, WWWeb has an IT group that maintains WWWeb's servers and telecommunication lines to the Internet.

The IT group is a cost center. The current annual IT budget is $548,000 for personnel, hardware and software leases for the servers, and telecommunication costs. The cost of the IT group is not allocated back to the three divisions. The CEO of WWWeb argues that the IT group is a common (shared) resource and is essentially a fixed cost. Adding another client website or performing a Web search does not generate any additional IT cost to the firm because WWWeb's IT group has excess capacity. WWWeb's CEO argues, "Any charge for IT back to the divisions will cause the divisions to avoid using our IT resources. As long as we have unused capacity on our systems we should be encouraging our people to use that capacity."

WWWeb currently uses about 80 percent of the capacity of its servers, routers, and fiber-optic high-speed lines to the Internet. The high-speed lines are the "pipes" through which all client server Web traffic flows. These high-speed lines are also used by WWWeb's e-mail traffic and the Crawler Divisions marketing research Web searches. Currently, the IT systems are performing well and WWWeb users experience few delays and minimal interference from other users. However, the three profit center managers are projecting growth in their businesses and expect to reach capacity on their servers and communication lines within the next 12 months. When this happens, the managers predict that they will experience significant service degradation.

Jose Coronas, head of WWWeb's IT group, has called a meeting of the three division managers to discuss the terrific deals being offered by telecom companies and hardware providers. Given the current slump in the economy, WWWeb can roughly double the capacity of its servers and high-speed access lines and lock in these low rates for two years. The incremental cost of doubling the IT group's capacity is to raise its hardware lease costs and access line costs by 20 percent. IT currently spends $18,000 a month on hardware leases and access lines. If it were to double its existing capacity, the total monthly cost would rise to $21,600. Mr. Coronas believes his existing IT personnel can handle the additional server and line capacity. Coronas and the three division managers recommend that WWWeb acquire the additional capacity and lock in these attractive rates.

Required:

a. Analyze WWWeb's current policy of how the three divisions are charged for IT costs and whether WWWeb should acquire the additional capacity.

b. Should WWWeb change its policy of how it charges IT costs to the divisions? If so, what changes would you recommend?

P 8–12:   ITI Technology

ITI Technology designs and manufactures solid-state computer chips. In one of the production departments, employees fabricate a six-inch circular wafer by laying down successive layers of silicon and then etching the circuits into the layers. Each wafer contains 100 separate solid-state computer chips.

After a wafer is manufactured, the 100 chips are cut out of the wafer, tested, mounted into protective covers, and attached to electrical leads. Then a final quality control test is performed.

The initial testing process consists of successive stages of heating and cooling the chips and testing how they work. If 99 percent of a chip's circuits work properly after the testing, it is classified as a high-density (HD) chip. If between 75 percent and 99 percent of a chip's circuits work properly, it is classified as a low-density (LD) chip. If fewer than 75 percent of the circuits work, it is discarded. Twenty wafers are manufactured in a batch. On average, 50 percent of each batch are HD, 20 percent are LD, and 30 percent are discarded. HD chips are sold to defense contractors and LD chips to consumer electronics firms. Chips sold to defense contractors require different mountings, packaging, and distribution channels than chips sold to consumer electronics firms. HD chips sell for $30 each and LD chips sell for $16 each.

Each batch of 20 wafers costs $29,100: $8,000 to produce, test, and sort, and $21,100 for mounting, attaching leads, and final inspection and distribution costs ($14,500 for HD chips and $6,600 for LD chips). The $29,100 total cost per batch consists of direct labor, direct materials, and variable overhead.

The following report summarizes the operating data per batch:

ITI Technology Operating Summary of HD and LD Chips

	Total	HD Chips	LD Chips	Scrap
Percentage of chips	100%	50%	20%	30%
Revenue	$36,400	$30,000*	$6,400†	$ 0
Total costs	29,100	14,550	5,820	8,730
Profit per batch	$ 7,300	$15,450	$ 580	$ (8,730)

*$30,000 = 50% × 20 wafers × 100 chips per wafer × $30/chip.
†$6,400 = 20% × 20 wafers × 100 chips per wafer × $16/chip.

The cost of scrap is charged to a plantwide overhead account, which is then allocated directly to the lines of business based on profits in each LOB.

Required:

    a. Critically evaluate ITI's method of accounting for HD and LD chips.

    b. What suggestions would you offer ITI's management?

P 8–13: Metro Blood Bank

Metro Blood Bank, a for-profit firm, collects whole blood from donors, tests it, and then separates it into two components: platelets and plasma. Three pints of whole blood yield two pints of platelets and one pint of plasma. The cost of collecting the three pints, testing them, and separating them is $300.

The platelets are sold for $165 per pint. But before they are sold they must be packaged and labeled. The variable cost of this additional processing is $15 per pint. Plasma is sold for $115 per pint after incurring additional variable processing costs of $45 per pint.

The selling prices of the platelets and plasma are set by competitive market forces. The prices of platelets and plasma quoted above are the current market prices, but they vary widely depending on supply and demand conditions. Metro Blood Bank ships its products nationwide to maximize profits. It has three operating divisions: blood collection and processing, platelets, and plasma. Collection and processing is a cost center, and platelets and plasma are profit centers.

Neither platelets nor plasma has any commercial value without further processing.

Required:

    a. Prepare two statements showing the profits per pint of platelets and plasma with collection and processing costs assigned using:

        (1) The number of pints of platelets and plasma produced from the whole blood.

        (2) The net realizable value of platelets and plasma.

    b. Discuss the advantages and disadvantages of each of the methods in part (*a*) for assigning collection and processing costs to the blood products.

P 8–14: Vigdor Wood Products

Vigdor processes cut trees into various wood products, veneers, lumber, wood chips, and so forth. Each of the products can be sold immediately upon processing the trees, or processed further and sold as a finished product. The following table lists the five products produced from each batch of trees, the tons of each product per batch, and the prices for the intermediate and finished products. The net cash outflow to convert each intermediate product into a finished product is $12 per ton. The net cash outflow to process one batch of trees into the five separate wood products is $800.

Outputs	Number of Tons per Batch	Intermediate Sales (Price/Ton)	Finished Sales (Price/Ton)
A342	1	$75	$88
A453	2	68	82
B691	4	62	73
B722	3	60	71
C132	6	40	57

Required:

    a. Given that Vigdor processes batches of trees into the five wood products, which of the five wood products should be sold as intermediate products (i.e., not processed further), and which ones should be sold as finished products (i.e., processed further)?

    b. If Vigdor's cost to process trees into the five wood products is $800, should Vigdor process trees?

    c. Assuming that the quantities and prices in the preceding table do not change, how high can the $800 cost to process one batch rise before Vigdor stops processing trees into the five wood products?

    d. Assuming that the cost to process trees into the five wood products is $800, and given your decisions in part (*a*), calculate the profit *per ton* of each of the five wood products after allocating the $800 processing cost to the five wood products using:

        (1) Tons of wood products produced.

        (2) Net realizable value of wood products produced.

    e. Given the allocations of the $800 cost of processing trees in part (*d*), would you want to change any of your decisions in part (*a*), assuming your objective is to maximize the net cash flows for Vigdor?

    f. Describe how the allocation of the $800 cost of processing trees into the five wood products affected your decisions in parts (*a*) and (*b*).

P 8–15: Advanced Micro Processors

Advanced Micro Processors (AMP) has designed a new dual-core microprocessor, dubbed DUALxl. DUALxl microprocessors are produced on silicon wafers with 100 chips per wafer. Once fabricated, the wafer is cut into individual microprocessors (also called "chips"). Then each chip is mounted on a base encased in a protective epoxy coating and tested. Because of slight impurities in the silicon and other compounds used in producing the wafers, as well as small perturbations in the manufacturing equipment, 60 microprocessors meet the rigorous testing and can be sold as a DUALxl microprocessor. Thirty microprocessors have small defects that prevent them from being sold as DUALxl chips. But these microprocessors can be sold as MAXV microprocessors. Of the 100 chips, 10 are of no commercial value and are scrapped.

Two hundred wafers are produced in each batch that costs $270,000. Each batch of 20,000 chips yields 12,000 DUALxl's and 6,000 MAXV's, and 2,000 chips are scrapped. The $270,000 batch cost is entirely variable. That is, producing one additional batch generates an "out-of-pocket" cash outflow of $270,000.

The following table summarizes AMP's operations for the current year:

	DUALxl	MAXV
Chip fabrication cost per unit*	$ 15	$ 15
Variable selling and distribution costs per unit	$ 55	$ 8
Fixed selling and distribution costs per unit[†]	$ 6	$ 4
Quantity (chips) per batch	12,000	6,000
Actual number of batches this year	6	6
Actual quantity produced this year	72,000	36,000
Selling price	$ 120	$ 25
Budgeted batches per year	5	5
Budgeted units this year	60,000	30,000
Fixed selling and distribution costs	$360,000	$120,000
Units sold	69,000	31,000

*Calculated as $270,000 / (12,000 DUALxl chips + 6,000 MAXV chips).
[†]Based on expected number of DUALxl chips of 60,000 and expected number of MAXV chips of 30,000.

AMP sells the DUALxl chips for $120 and the MAXV chips for $25. The DUALxl and MAXV microprocessors are sold through separate selling and distribution channels that are separate organizations.

Actual fixed selling and distribution costs were the same as budgeted total fixed selling and distribution costs ($360,000 and $120,000); the actual chip fabrication cost was the same as the budgeted chip fabrication cost ($270,000); and the actual variable selling costs were the same as the budgeted amounts ($55 and $8). There were no beginning inventories of DUALxl or MAXV microprocessors.

Required:

a. Prepare individual income statements for DUALxl and MAXV microprocessors for the current year.

b. What are the inventory balances of DUALxl and MAXV microprocessors on AMP's balance sheet at the end of the current year?

c. Analyze the relative profitability of the DUALxl and MAXV microprocessors based on their respective income statements prepared in part (a). What advice would you offer management?

P 8–16: Jason Rocks

Jason Rocks is a small rock quarry that produces five different sizes of stones, from small crushed stones (#1 stones) to large (three-inch) rocks (#5 stones). The stones are first mined and sorted into the five grades. Once the stones are mined and sorted, they can be sold to a local distributor either washed or unwashed. Jason Rocks mines and sorts 500 tons of stone each day and is a price taker in the local stone market. The following table contains the percentage of each type of stone quarried each day and the market prices at which Jason Rocks can sell its five types of stones as either washed or unwashed:

Type of Stone	% of Daily Production	Selling Prices (per Ton)	
		Unwashed	*Washed*
#1	10%	$210	$219
#2	20	185	192
#3	20	150	170
#4	35	145	155
#5	15	160	165

The daily cost of mining and sorting the stones is $75,000, which includes the salaries and benefits of the employees who quarry and sort the stones, the depreciation on the equipment used in the process, the royalty payments to owners of the quarry for the stone removed, and an allocation of the utilities, insurance, property taxes, and administrative costs of the entire quarry operation. Washing any of the five types of stone costs $8 per ton, and delivering the stone to the local distributor costs $7 per ton. Jason Rocks allocates the mining and sorting costs based on the tons of each type of stone produced.

Jason Rocks does not have to sell all of the types of stones it produces. Any unsold stones are left in the quarry at no additional cost after they have been mined and sorted. The owners of Jason Rocks want to maximize the quarry's net cash flows.

Required:

    a. For each of the five stone types, calculate the total cost of one ton of unwashed stones in inventory.

    b. For each of the five stone types, calculate the total cost of one ton of washed stones in inventory.

    c. What is the reported profit per ton of each type of unwashed stone that is sold?

    d. What is the reported profit per ton of each type of washed stone that is sold?

    e. Which of the five stone types should be sold as washed stones, and which stone types should be sold as unwashed stones? Which stone type(s) should not be sold?

    f. The owners of Jason Rocks learn that new environmental and safety regulations have been enacted that will raise its operating costs to $85,000 per day. The owners do not expect these regulations to affect the selling prices of the washed and unwashed stones, nor do they expect them to affect the costs of washing and delivering the stones. Given this new information, how do your answers in part (*e*) change?

P 8–17: Ferguson Metals

Ferguson Metals is a decentralized mining, smelting, and metals company with three divisions: mining, lead, and copper. The mining division owns the ore mine that produces the lead and copper that occur in the vein. Mining removes the ore, crushes it, and smelts it to separate the metals from the crushed rock. It then sells the two products to the other two divisions: lead and copper. Each batch mined yields 50 tons of lead and 25 tons of copper. (One ton is 2,000 pounds.) The metals are transferred from mining to the lead and copper divisions at cost plus a small profit to give mining an incentive to produce.

The current market price for copper is roughly $0.60 per pound; for lead it is $0.30 per pound. But these prices are for substantially purer copper and lead than the mining division has the ability to produce. Mining could sell its lead in the market at its current purity level for $0.17 per pound. Since the metal divisions are currently incurring the cost to refine the metals to the purity levels they require, management does not believe it is equitable to charge the divisions the current market prices for the unrefined metals. If the metals were transferred at market prices, the lead and copper divisions would be paying twice for the refining process, and the mining division would be rewarded for a level of purity it is not providing.

Table 1 shows the mining division's income statement per batch.

The variable mining and smelting costs per ton of lead and copper are based on the fixed yields of the two metals. Production last year at mining was 100 batches, and both the lead and copper divisions had no change in inventory levels.

TABLE 1   **Mining Division Income Statement per Batch**

	Lead	*Copper*
Revenue	$42,000	$21,000
Costs:*		
Mining	22,000	11,000
Smelting	16,000	8,000
Profits per batch	$ 4,000	$ 2,000

*Based on a normal volume of 100 batches per year.

TABLE 2   **Metal Division Income Statement ($000s)**

	Lead	*Copper*
Sales	$ 6,600	$ 6,700
Variable costs:		
Metal costs*	5,000	2,200
Other costs	500	700
Contribution margin	$ 1,100	$ 3,800
Fixed costs	800	1,100
Net income before taxes	$ 300	$ 2,700
Net investment	$10,000	$14,000
Return on assets	3%	19%

*The metal costs exceed the costs of the mining division because some metals are purchased on the open market to expand capacity and to smooth production of the downstream industrial products.

The lead and copper divisions further process the two metals into industrial products. Because of increasing foreign competition, the lead division has been showing a negligible return on investment. Table 2 shows income statements for the two metal divisions for last year.

All of the fixed costs in both the lead and copper divisions represent separable annual cash outflows to maintain current capacity. They are not common costs. Ferguson's top management has the opportunity to invest in what appears to be a highly profitable joint mining venture, which promises very high returns. Ferguson's share of the net present value of the venture is around $30 million, discounted at the firm's before-tax cost of capital of 12 percent. To finance this project, the company is considering divestiture of the lead division. A foreign company looking to gain a foothold in the U.S. market has offered $5 million for this division. While Ferguson's net investment in this division is $10 million, management reasons it can use the proceeds to undertake the joint venture.

Required:

Should management sell the lead division to the foreign company? Present an analysis supporting your conclusions.

P 8–18:   Polymtech

Polymtech uses advanced laser technology to manufacture polymers for a variety of applications. One of their processes produces four separate polymers (N200, HV87, HMT45, and V989) in one batch containing 1,000 grams of final product. The proportion of each polymer produced in the batch is fixed by the chemistry of the process and cannot be altered. Each of the four polymers produced in the batch can either be sold as is or further processed and sold at a higher price. Each batch producing the four polymers costs $2090.00 per batch before further processing any of the four polymers. The following table summarizes the output per batch, the selling price per gram with and without further processing, and the cost of further processing.

Products	N200	HV87	HMT45	W989
Total grams per batch	200	300	150	350
Sales price/gram without further processing	$1.89	$2.93	$3.30	$0.76
Cost/gram of further processing	$0.73	$0.53	$0.82	$0.37
Sales price/gram with further processing	$3.65	$3.44	$4.10	$2.17

Required:

   a. Which of the four polymers should be processed further and then sold, and which polymers should be sold immediately without further processing?

   b. Should Polymtech be producing batches of these four polymers?

   c. What is the maximum cost per batch (excluding any further processing costs) that Polymtech is willing to incur before Polymtech stops producing batches of these four polymers? Assume that all selling prices and further processing costs do not change.

   d. To analyze the relative profitability of the four polymers, allocate the batch production cost of $2,090 to each of the four polymers using the number of grams of each polymer produced in the batch as the allocation base. Which polymer is the most and which polymer is the least profitable after allocating the $2,090 batch cost?

   e. Based on your analysis in part (*d*), recommend actions that management can take to improve the profitability of producing batches of these four polymers.

P 8–19:   RBB Brands

You are working on a special assignment as a financial analyst for the president of household products of RBB Brands. RBB Brands is a large $4 billion diversified consumer products firm. RBB has two divisions, household products and foods, each headed by a president. Each division is evaluated as a profit center. The senior managers of each division receive bonuses paid out of a pool equal to 1 percent of the division's accounting profits. Both divisions receive services from two corporate service departments: engineering and maintenance.

The president of household products attended a meeting at which the corporate controller made a presentation proposing that the two divisions' accounting profits be charged for engineering and maintenance services. Table 1 summarizes each division's use of the two service departments, as well as each service department's use of the other service department (as well as its own use).

The controller then distributed Tables 2 and 3. He explained that each division would be charged for the hours of maintenance and engineering it actually used. The charge per hour would be based on the allocated cost of the service department. Table 2 reports the allocation of service department costs using the step-down allocation method starting with maintenance costs. Table 3 reports the allocation of service department costs using the step-down allocation method but starting with engineering costs. The controller's office is considering adopting one of these two methods and is seeking input from the divisions.

TABLE 1   RBB Brands
Summary of Service Department Utilization (All Numbers, Except Dollars, Are 1,000 Hours)

Service Departments	Service Departments		Profit Centers			
	Engineering	Maintenance	Household Products	Foods	Total	Total Cost (Millions)
Engineering	500	100	900	1,200	2,700	$67.50
Maintenance	800	900	1,600	2,900	6,200	$55.80

Cost Allocation: Practices **373**

TABLE 2   RBB Brands

Allocation of Service Department Costs Using Step-Down Allocation First Department Allocated: Maintenance (Millions of Dollars Except Cost per Hour)

Service Departments	Service Departments		Profit Centers		
	Engineering	Maintenance	Household Products	Foods	Total
Maintenance hours consumed	800		1,600	2,900	5,300
Percentage of maintenance cost	15%		30%	55%	100%
Cost per maintenance hour					$ 10.53
Allocated cost of maintenance department	$ 8.42		$16.85	$30.53	$ 55.80
Engineering operating cost	67.50				$ 67.50
Total cost to be allocated	$75.92				$ 75.92
Engineering hours consumed			900	1,200	2,100
Cost per engineering hour					$ 36.15
Engineering costs allocated to profit centers			$32.54	$43.38	$ 75.92
Maintenance and engineering costs allocated to profit centers			$49.38	$73.92	$123.30

TABLE 3   RBB Brands

Allocation of Service Department Costs Using Step-Down Allocation First Department Allocated: Engineering (Millions of Dollars Except Cost per Hour)

Service Departments	Service Departments		Profit Centers		
	Engineering	Maintenance	Household Products	Foods	Total
Engineering hours consumed		100	900	1,200	2,200
Percentage of cost		4.55%	40.91%	54.55%	100%
Engineering operating cost	$67.50				$ 67.50
Cost per engineering hour					$ 30.68
Allocated cost of engineering department		$ 3.07	$27.61	$36.82	$ 67.50
Maintenance operating cost		55.80			$ 55.80
Total cost to be allocated		$58.87			$ 58.87
Maintenance hours consumed			1,600	2,900	4,500
Cost per maintenance hour					$ 13.08
Percentage of maintenance			35.56%	64.44%	100%
Maintenance costs allocated to profit centers			$20.93	$37.94	$ 58.87
Maintenance and engineering costs allocated to profit centers			$48.54	$74.76	$123.30

Required:

Analyze and critically evaluate the controller's proposal in a position paper to the president of household products. In addition, provide a series of key points that the president can raise at the next meeting with the corporate controller and corporate management.

P 8–20:   Karsten Mills

Karsten Mills is one of the premier carpet manufacturers in the world. It manufactures carpeting for both residential and commercial applications. Home sales and commercial sales each account for about 50 percent of total revenue. The firm is organized into three departments: manufacturing, residential sales, and commercial sales. Manufacturing is a cost center and the two sales departments are profit centers. The full cost of each roll of carpeting produced (including fully absorbed overhead) is transferred to the sales department ordering the carpet. The sales departments are evaluated as profit centers; the full cost of each roll is the transfer price.

The current manufacturing plant is at capacity. A new plant is being built that will more than double the capacity. Within two years, management believes that it can grow Karsten's businesses such that most of the excess capacity will be eliminated. When the new plant comes on line, one plant will produce exclusively commercial carpeting and the other will produce exclusively residential carpeting. This change will simplify scheduling, ordering, and inventory control in both plants and will create some economies of scale through longer mill runs. Nevertheless, it will take a couple of years before these economies of scale can be realized.

Each mill produces carpeting in 12-foot-wide rolls of up to 100 yards in length. The output of each mill is measured in yards produced. Overhead is assigned to carpet rolls using carpet yards produced in the mill. The cost structure of each plant is as follows:

	Old Plant	New Plant
Normal machine hours per year	6,000	5,000
Normal carpet yards per hour	1,000	1,400
Normal capacity	6 million yards	7 million yards
Annual manufacturing overhead costs		
excluding accounting depreciation	$15,000,000	$21,000,000
Accounting depreciation per year	$ 6,000,000	$21,000,000

Besides being able to run at higher speed, producing more carpet yardage per hour, the new mill will use 15 percent less direct material and direct labor because the new, more automated machines produce less scrap and require less direct labor per yard. The cost of a job run at the old mill is

Carpet A6106: (100-Yard Roll)	
Direct materials	$ 800
Direct labor	600
Direct costs	$1,400

Although the new mill has lower direct costs of producing carpeting than the old mill, the higher overhead costs per yard at the new mill have the sales department managers worried. They are already lobbying senior management to have the old mill assigned to produce their products. The commercial sales department manager argues, "More of my customers are located closer to the old plant than are residential sales' customers. Therefore, to economize on transportation costs, my products should be produced in the old plant." The residential sales department manager counters with the following argument: "Transportation costs are less than 1 percent of total revenues. The new plant should produce commercial products because we expect new commercial products to use more synthetic materials and the latest technology at the new mill is better able to adapt to the new synthetics." Senior management is worried about how to deal with the two sales department managers' reluctance to have their products produced at the new plant. One suggestion put forth is for each plant to produce about half of commercial sales products and about half of residential sales products. But this proposal would eliminate most of the economies of scale that would result from specializing production in each plant to one market segment.

Required:

a. Calculate the overhead rates for the new plant and the old plant, where overhead is assigned to carpet based on normal yards per year.
b. Calculate the expected total cost of carpet A6106 if run at the old mill and if run at the new mill.
c. Put forth two new solutions that would overcome the resistance of the residential and commercial sales department managers to the new plant. Discuss the pros and cons of your two solutions.

P 8–21:   Impact Designs

Impact Designs embroiders corporate and sports logos on clothing using state-of-the-art multiple-head digital embroidering machines. Impact Designs is considering adding a new machine to enter the college and university market for athletic clothing (sports jerseys, jackets, caps, etc.). The client would buy the clothing and ship it to Impact Designs for embroidering. Impact Designs would only charge the client for embroidering the college's graphic design. The following table summarizes the price-quantity relation Impact Designs expects to face if it enters this college athletic gear market.

Number of embroideries per month	3,600	3,000	2,570	2,250
Price per embroidery	$14.00	$14.75	$15.50	$16.25

(Assume that all graphic designs that colleges use are of equal complexity and hence embroidering services can be priced per embroidery.)

Impact Design can lease various machines that provide different embroidering capacities. The following table summarizes the monthly lease fee, operating costs, and capacities of the various embroidering machines. The lease contract requires Impact Designs to lease the equipment for five years.

Monthly Lease Cost of Machine	Number of Embroideries per Month	Variable Cost per Embroidery
$30,000	3,600	$3.90
$24,000	3,000	$4.15
$21,000	2,570	$4.20
$20,000	2,250	$4.50

Required:

a. What size of machine will a firm-value-maximizing owner of Impact Designs lease, and what price will the owner set for an embroidery? Support your answer with clearly labeled computations. Assume that the market demand for embroideries at the various prices is perfectly certain over the life of the lease.
b. Impact Designs is organized into operating divisions. Each division manager is paid a fixed salary plus a bonus that depends in part on his/her division's profits. Impact Designs excludes fixed manufacturing capacity costs from the calculation of division profits whenever the division has excess capacity. Discuss possible reasons it might be beneficial for

376   *Chapter 8*

Impact Designs to have this policy of excluding fixed manufacturing capacity costs from the calculation of division profits whenever excess manufacturing capacity exists.

c. The manager of the newly created college athletic gear market will be paid a fixed salary plus a bonus that depends in part on the college athletic gear division's profits. Impact Designs excludes fixed manufacturing capacity costs from the calculation of division profits whenever the division has excess capacity. The corporate executive and owners of Impact Designs do not know how the quantity of embroideries demanded by the market may vary with the price of an embroidery. This information is only known by the college athletic gear division manager. What size machine will the college athletic gear division manager lease? Support your answer with clearly labeled computations. Assume that the market demand for embroideries at the various prices is perfectly certain over the life of the lease.

d. Discuss why your answers in parts (*a*) and (*c*) are either the same or differ.

P 8–22:   Littleton Medical Center

Littleton Medical Center (LMC) has three service departments (accounting, human resources, and janitorial/maintenance) and two patient units (hospital and an outpatient clinic). The following table summarizes the operations of LMC for the last fiscal year.

Service Departments	*Service Department Cost (000)*
Human resources	$1,200
Accounting	$1,600
Janitorial/maintenance	$2,400

These department costs are allocated to the two patient units (hospital and clinic). The following table summarizes the allocation bases used to allocate each service department and the utilization of each allocation base.

	Service Departments			**Patient Units**		
Service Departments	*HR*	*Acctg*	*Jan/Maint*	*Clinic*	*Hospital*	*Allocation Base*
Human resources		50	150	2,000	3,000	Employees
Accounting	50		100	6,000	4,000	Transactions(000)
Janitorial/maintenance	8,000	9,000		150,000	400,000	Square feet

Required:

a. Allocate the three service departments' costs (HR, Accounting, and Janitorial/Maintenance) to the two patient units (Clinic and Hospital) using the direct allocation method.

b. Allocate the three service departments' costs (HR, Accounting, and Janitorial/Maintenance) to the two patient units (Clinic and Hospital) using the step-down allocation method. The order of the three departments is: (1) HR, (2) Accounting, and (3) Janitorial/Maintenance.

c. What are the primary advantages of the step-down method compared to the direct allocation method?

P 8–23: Aurora Medical Center

Aurora Medical Center (AMC), located outside Phoenix, has an inpatient hospital and outpatient clinic. Because it is located in a retirement area, a substantial fraction of its patients are elderly, and hence their medical insurance is provided through the Medicare program of the federal government. Medicare outpatient clinic care is reimbursed by the federal government at cost. Each clinic with Medicare outpatients submits a reimbursement form to Medicare reporting the costs of treating these patients. Medicare inpatient reimbursement is based on predetermined rates depending on the diagnosis. For example, all Medicare-paid hip replacements in Phoenix are reimbursed at $14,800 per patient, regardless of the hospital's cost.

AMC has two administrative departments that provide services to both the hospital and the clinic: accounting and information management (IM). The accompanying tables summarize the service levels provided by these two departments:

	Administrative Departments	
	Accounting	*IM*
Total cost	$3,800,000	$4,800,000
Allocation base	Number of transactions	Disk space (gigabytes)
	Service Levels	
	Transactions	*Gigabytes*
Accounting		8
IM	40,000	
Hospital	1,100,000	7
Clinic	600,000	9
Total	1,740,000	24

Accounting department costs are distributed to users based on the number of transactions posted to the general ledger generated by that user. IM costs are distributed to users based on the gigabytes of storage dedicated to the user. Medicare guidelines allow these allocation bases to be used. Medicare also provides some discretion to hospitals in the methods used to allocate costs, as long as they are reasonable and generally accepted.

Required:

a. Design a report for assigning the accounting and IM costs to the hospital and clinic. How much of the costs of accounting and IM should be allocated to inpatients and outpatients?

b. Justify your design in part (*a*). Explain why AMC should follow your suggestions.

P 8–24: Grove City Broadcasting

Grove City Broadcasting owns and operates a radio station and a television station in Grove City. Both stations are located in the same building and are operated as separate profit centers with separate managers, who are evaluated based on station profits. Revenues of both the radio and the TV station are from advertising spots. The price of a standard 30-second ad is based on audience size, which is measured by an independent outside agency. The radio station sells a 30-second ad for $100. (Assume that all 30-second ads sell for $100 regardless of the time of day they air.) The $100 price is based on an expected audience size of 20,000 listeners. If the listener audience were to double, the 30-second ad would sell for $200. In other words, each radio listener is worth $0.005 ($100 ÷ 20,000) of advertising revenue per 30-second ad. Each TV viewer is worth $0.008 per 30-second ad. The radio station sells 3,550 ads per month, and the TV station sells 3,200 ads per month.

Sports Wire has approached both the radio and television managers about subscribing to its service, which brings all sports scores, sports news, and sports analyses to the station via an on-line computer system over the Internet. The radio and/or TV stations' sports announcers could download scores and news directly into sports scripts and read them over the air. Sports Wire is more comprehensive and contains more sports stories than the current general news wires that Grove City is receiving. If one of the two stations buys Sports Wire, the price is $30,000 per month. For an extra $5,000 per month, both the radio and the TV station can use Sports Wire. If both stations use Sports Wire, the $5,000 additional fee includes an extra computer terminal that allows two users to be on the system at the same time.

Sports Wire will not increase the number of ads each month, just the revenue per ad. The Grove City radio manager believes that purchasing Sports Wire would increase his audience by 1,500 listeners per ad. The television manager believes her audience size would increase by 500 viewers per ad.

Required:

a. If the two managers did not cooperate but rather each made a decision assuming he or she was the sole user of the system, would either buy Sports Wire? Support your answer with detailed calculations.

b. If the owner of Grove City Broadcasting had all the facts available to the two managers, would the owner buy Sports Wire?

c. The costs of the current wire services that Grove City purchases are allocated to the two stations based on the number of stories aired each month from the wire services. The owner of Grove City Broadcasting decides to purchase Sports Wire for both stations and to allocate its $35,000 cost based on the number of Sports Wire stories aired each month. During the first month, the radio station uses 826 Sports Wire stories and TV uses 574. Allocate the Sports Wire cost to the radio and TV stations.

d. What is the allocated cost per Sports Wire story in the first month?

e. Given the allocation of the Sports Wire cost, what behaviors can you predict from the radio and TV station managers?

f. Design an alternative allocation scheme that will avoid the problems identified in part (e). Discuss the advantages and disadvantages of your allocation scheme.

P 8–25:   Gemini Logistics

Gemini Logistics (GL) offers packaging and shipping solutions to small and medium-sized companies in the greater metropolitan New York City region that do not have scale economies to do in-house packaging and shipping, and yet have special requirements preventing them from utilizing UPS pack/ship services. GL runs a fleet of trucks in the NYC area collecting parcels and next-day-delivery pouches. The GL warehouse is near the Newark, New Jersey, airport, which is used for shipping all GL packages. GL negotiates bulk discount rates with FedEx, UPS, and DHL for the final delivery of GL packages to end customers of GL clients. For example, an online seller of used DVDs receives domestic orders for DVDs. This online seller has GL pick up, package, label, and ship the DVD to the end user.

GL has three operating divisions (profit centers): Domestic Parcel, Domestic Pouch (next-day-delivery), and International. Each operating division serves a different customer set and hence has its own direct sales organization. However, all three divisions share the same common resources of its Newark warehouse and the GL truck fleet.

Currently, GL uses bar coding to uniquely identify, label, and track shipments through GL's system and the carrier (UPS, FedEx, or DHL). Radio-frequency identification (RFID) is starting to substitute for bar coding technology. RFID involves a small electronic tag the size of a postage stamp that emits radio waves to transfer data between a reader and the tag attached to the item being shipped. Each item being shipped will have its own unique identifying number, allowing GL more accurate packaging, labeling, and shipping. UPS, FedEx, and DHL already deploy RFID tagging. Each tag costs $0.09 per shipped package.

GL estimates that a fully deployed RFID system in its warehouse will allow each division to generate additional net operating margins by allowing the GL division to raise its shipping fees, attract new customers wanting this new technology, and lower its operating costs from shipping errors and lower handling costs in the warehouse. The following table presents estimates of the additional net operating margin and the total number of shipments in the three divisions if RFID technology is deployed by GL.

	International	Domestic Parcel	Domestic Pouch
Current net operating margin before RFID	$4,800,000	$7,300,000	$5,600,000
Percentage of additional net operating margin from RFID	7%	5%	3%
Total number of shipments (after RFID)	96,000	608,333	700,000

In other words, the international division currently has net operating margins of $4.8 million, and this will rise by 7 percent if RFID is adopted. Net operating margin is shipping fees received by the GL division less all direct costs incurred by the division (such as labor costs of employees assigned to the division and payment to the carriers [UPS, FedEx, DHL]), but excludes the allocation of any common shared resources (such as the cost of the truck fleet, warehousing costs, corporate offices, marketing, etc.).

In addition to the RFID tags required on each package, a fully functional RFID system requires RF readers, middleware to filter RFID data, upgrades to GL's enterprise warehouse management systems and networks, and other IT hardware. GL estimates the additional annual fixed cost of a RFID system (not including the cost of the individual tags) to be $450,000.

Each GL division (Domestic Parcel, Domestic Pouch, and International) is a profit center and is evaluated (and rewarded) based on net operating margin *less* its allocated cost of all shared common resources such as the truck fleet, warehousing costs, and the costs of the RFID technology (if adopted). All shared common costs (including the total cost of the RFID system) are allocated based on the number of packages shipped by the division.

Required:

a. The chief information technology officer of GL proposes that GL adopts RFID and that each of the divisions pay its share of the technology using GL's usual method for allocating shared common costs. Each division can choose to opt in or opt out of the RFID system. Will all three divisions of GL be in favor of the new RFID technology? Support your answer with an analysis of the costs and benefits of RFID for each of the three divisions.

b. If one or two of the divisions decide to opt out of the RFID system, will the remaining division(s) continue to pursue the RFID system? Again, support your answer with an analysis of the costs and benefits of RFID to the division(s) that favored the RFID system in part (a).

c. Suppose senior management makes the decision to adopt RFID rather than allowing the three divisions to choose to opt in or opt out, would senior management adopt RFID (assuming they want to maximize firm value)? Support your answer with an analysis of the costs and benefits of RFID to GL.

d. Gemini Logistics has the policy of decentralizing decision making to the three operating divisions and then rewarding the divisions based on their operating results (after charging the divisions for all the direct and indirect costs incurred by the divisions). Discuss some possible reasons most firms have the policy of charging their operating divisions for common shared resources (such as the RFID system) and the problems such a policy can create.

e. Write a short memo describing what, if any, changes you recommend to GL regarding its policy of charging divisions for their share of common shared resources.

380   *Chapter 8*

P 8–26: Tariffs Inc.

Tariffs Inc. manufactures two product lines in the same plant: AllDomestic and SomeDomestic. Both product lines are sold in Tariff Inc.'s home country. AllDomestic is produced entirely from parts either manufactured by Tariffs Inc. or purchased from outside vendors that are domiciled in Tariffs Inc.'s home country. SomeDomestic consists of parts manufactured both inside and outside Tariffs Inc.'s home country. Tariffs Inc.'s home country has tariff regulations that require all manufacturers of products sold in the home country to pay a sizeable tariff unless the domestic content of the product is at least 50 percent of the total cost of the product. In other words, if a product sold in Tariffs Inc.'s home country has foreign content of 50 percent, then a sizeable tariff must be paid by the manufacturer (i.e., Tariffs Inc.). If the product has foreign content of 49.99 percent, then no tariff is assessed. Foreign content is measured by the ratio of costs incurred outside the home country to total costs incurred (foreign plus domestic costs). For purposes of computing costs, foreign and domestic costs include both the direct *and* indirect costs.

The following table summarizes the total direct foreign and total direct domestic costs of Tariff Inc.'s two product lines.

Direct Costs	AllDomestic	SomeDomestic
Domestic content	$1,300	$1,500
Foreign content	$ 0	$2,600

Besides the domestic direct costs Tariffs Inc. incurs to manufacture the two product lines, it also has domestic indirect (common) costs. These domestic indirect costs are in two service departments: S1 and S2. S1 and S2 are domiciled in Tariffs Inc.'s home country and, hence, are treated as domestic costs in tariff calculations. The total cost of operating S1 is $500 and the total cost of operating S2 is $2,000. (Note: These figures do not include any allocated costs from the other service department.) AllDomestic and SomeDomestic require the services of each of these two service centers as part of their manufacturing process. Moreover, each service department uses the services of the other service department. The following table summarizes the number of service units consumed of each service department by the other service department and by the two product lines, AllDomestic and SomeDomestic.

	Service Units Consumed			
	S1	S2	AllDomestic	SomeDomestic
S1	0	100	300	600
S2	400	0	250	50

In other words, S2 consumes 100 service units of S1 and AllDomestic consumes 300 service units of S1.

Required:

a. Allocate the costs of S1 ($500) and S2 ($2,000) to the AllDomestic and the SomeDomestic product lines using the direct allocation method.

b. Allocate the costs of S1 ($500) and S2 ($2,000) to the AllDomestic and the SomeDomestic product lines using the step-down allocation method where S1 is allocated first and S2 is allocated second.

c. Allocate the costs of S1 ($500) and S2 ($2,000) to the AllDomestic and the SomeDomestic product lines using the step-down allocation method where S2 is allocated first and S1 is allocated second.

d. Which allocation method (*a, b,* or *c*) should Tariffs Inc. use? Explain why. Assume Tariffs Inc. does not use indirect cost allocations to measure and reward the performance of managers in Tariffs Inc., the allocated costs are not used for any decision-making purposes, and Tariffs Inc. pays no other taxes other than possible tariffs.

e. Assume the tariff rate is 20 percent of the total cost of manufacturing the product (domestic content cost plus foreign content cost including all allocated indirect cost). How much tariff will Tariffs Inc. pay based on your recommended allocation method in part (*d*)?

P 8–27: Thompson Instruments

Thompson Instruments (TI) has proprietary technology and produces products for three market segments: commercial, defense, and international. Thompson has three profit centers organized by the same three market segments. After each profit center produces its products, they are sent to a centralized TI testing lab for final testing and certification. The TI testing lab, which is treated as a cost center, has the following cost structure: fixed costs of $240,000 per month and variable costs of $30 per testing hour performed. The $240,000 of fixed costs consists almost entirely of historical cost depreciation of the testing equipment.

Outside testing firms can also be used to test TI products produced by the three profit centers. Each outside testing firm can only test products for one TI market segment (commercial, defense, or international). Geographic and technical differences among the outside testing vendors prevent the defense vendor from testing commercial or international TI products. Likewise, the defense vendor can only test TI defense products. And so forth.

The following table summarizes the prices charged by the outside testing vendors and the number of testing hours budgeted for each month for Year One. (Assume that all 12 months in each year are identical.)

Profit Centers	International	Commercial	Defense
Outside testing vendor price per test hour	$75.00	$80.00	$92.00
Budgeted testing hours per month	1,000	2,000	3,000

Thompson Instruments has the policy of recharging the testing department's fixed and variable costs through a single overhead rate set at the beginning of the year based on the budgeted testing hours of all three profit centers. Each profit center has the decision-making authority to have its products tested internally by TI's testing department or by the external vendor. Assume the only difference between TI's testing department and the outside testing vendors is price. Quality, timeliness, confidentiality, and so forth, are identical between inside and outside testing.

Required:

a. Calculate the testing department's overhead rate per testing hour for Year 1.

b. Given the testing department's overhead rate computed in part (*a*) for Year 1, which profit centers will choose TI's testing for their products, and which profit centers will use the outside vendor?

c. Before Year 2 begins and before the TI testing department lab overhead rate is set for Year 2, TI's defense profit center loses a government contract that involves 1,000 testing hours per month. Calculate the testing department's overhead rate per testing hour for Year 2, assuming that the other two profit centers continue to have the same number of testing hours they used in Year 1 and that the TI testing department's fixed cost and variable cost per hour do not change.

d. Given the testing department's overhead rate computed in part (*c*) for Year 2, which profit centers will choose TI's testing for their products, and which profit centers will use their outside vendor?

e. Based on your answer to part (*d*), and assuming: (1) the TI testing department's fixed cost and variable cost per hour do not change, (2) Defense does not regain the lost contract, and (3) the Year 3 overhead rate set in the testing department is based on the number of testing hours performed by the testing department in Year 2, calculate the testing department's overhead rate in Year 3.

f. Given the testing department's overhead rate computed in part (*e*) for Year 3, which profit centers will choose TI's testing for their products, and which profit centers will use their outside vendor?

g. Based on your answer to part (*f*), and assuming: (1) the TI testing department's fixed cost and variable cost per hour do not change, (2) Defense does not regain the lost contract, and (3) the Year 4 overhead rate set in the testing department is based on the number of testing hours performed by the testing department in Year 3, calculate the testing department's overhead rate in Year 4.

h. Given the testing department's overhead rate computed in part (*g*) for Year 4, which profit centers will choose TI's testing for their products, and which profit centers will use their outside vendor?

i. Given the sequence of events that have occurred over Years 1 through 4, what problem does TI face? Propose (and then critique) **TWO** possible solutions to resolve the problem.

P 8–28:   Columbine Granite

Columbine Granite produces a number of different granite products from its granite quarry in Georgia. The production process begins when a 50-foot-tall block of solid granite is excavated from the mountain quarry. These huge blocks of granite are drilled and broken into movable smaller blocks for processing into building materials. The smaller blocks are cut into granite slabs of desired thickness and the granite slabs are then polished using abrasives and diamond polishing wheels to enhance the beauty of the granite. The slabs are then sorted by size. Some slabs will be cut to smaller dimensions due to natural imperfections in the stone. The larger pieces that cannot be used in slabs are broken up for decorative stone. Sand and stone dust result from cutting the 50-foot blocks out of the mountain, cutting these into smaller blocks, cutting these smaller blocks into slabs, and from producing the decorative stones. A 50-foot-tall block of granite produces the following finished products:

	Tons/Batch	Cubic Feet/Batch (volume)
Sand and stone dust	330.0	7,500
Decorative stone	577.5	5,000
Small 2″ slabs (4′ × 8′)	412.5	8,750
Large 2″ slabs (4′ × 12′)	330.0	3,750

The cost of removing the 50-foot block from the mountain, cutting it into smaller blocks, and then the cost of cutting the slabs is $183,000. A 50-foot block produces, on average, 937.5 4′ × 8′ slabs and the cost of polishing one 4′ × 8′ slab is $96. A 50-foot block produces, on average, 500 4′ × 12′ slabs and the cost of polishing one 4′ × 12′ slab is $144. The cost of finishing and packaging the 330 tons of sand and stone dust is $500, and the cost of further grinding and packaging the 577.5 tons of decorative stones is $2,500.

Once each of the four products is finished (i.e., the sand and stone dust is finished and packaged and the slabs are polished), they are sold for the following amounts:

	Price/Ton	Price/Slab
Sand and stone dust	$25.00	
Decorative stone	$75.00	
Small 2″ slabs (under 4′ × 8′)		$320.00
Large 2″ slabs (4′ × 12′)		$480.00

Required:

    a. Allocate the $183,000 cost of removing the 50-foot block from the mountain, cutting it into smaller blocks, and cutting the smaller blocks into slabs to the four products using tons of each product produced from the 50-foot block as the allocation base.

    b. Calculate the total profits of producing each of the four products and the total profit of processing a 50-foot block after allocating the $183,000 cost to the four products using tons of each product produced from part (*a*).

    c. Allocate the $183,000 cost of removing the 50-foot block from the mountain, cutting it into smaller blocks, and cutting the smaller blocks into slabs to the four products using the cubic feet (volume) of each product produced from the 50′ × 20′ × 20′ block as the allocation base.

    d. Calculate the total profits of producing each of the four products and the total profit of processing a 50-foot block from the mountain after allocating the $183,000 cost to the four products using cubic feet (volume) of each product produced from part (*c*).

    e. Which of the four products (i.e., sand and stone dust, decorative stones, the 4′ × 8′ slabs, and the 4′ × 12′ slabs) should Columbine sell and which ones should not be sold? Assume that the products Columbine decides not to sell can be used as fill material in the quarry. There is no cost of hauling the unsold products back to the quarry, and any unsold products do not incur the additional processing costs (i.e., the sand and stone dust does not require any packaging, the decorative stones do not require further grinding and packaging, or the 4′ × 8′ and 4′ × 12′ slabs do not require any polishing). Justify your answer.

    f. Should Columbine Granite use tons or cubic feet (volume) to allocate the $183,000 cost of removing the 50-foot block from the mountain, cutting it into smaller blocks, and cutting the smaller blocks into slabs to the four products? Justify your recommendation based on well-reasoned arguments.

P 8–29: Palabora Mining

Palabora Mining owns and operates a copper mine. Besides producing copper, the mine also produces magnetite, vermiculite, and titanium dioxide. To extract the ore and to separate the four minerals (copper, magnetite, vermiculite, and titanium dioxide) costs $680,000 per batch and yields 175 tons of unprocessed copper, 2,400 tons of unprocessed magnetite, 1,600 tons of unprocessed vermiculite, and 320 tons of unprocessed titanium dioxide. Each batch produced yields the same proportions of the four minerals and the proportions cannot be varied by changing mining operations. The $680,000 cost per batch consists of the direct, out-of-pocket costs to mine and separate the four minerals.

Each unprocessed mineral can be sold unprocessed or processed further and sold as a more refined product. The following table summarizes for each of the four minerals the tons per batch, the price per ton if sold after further processing, the price per ton if sold unprocessed, and the additional costs to process further. In other words, all 175 tons of copper can be sold without further processing for $6,200 per ton or it can be sold for $8,000 per ton if further processed. But to process the entire 175 tons of copper that are in the batch costs an additional $383,000.

	Tons per Batch	Price/Ton after Further Processing	Price/Ton without Further Processing	Additional Costs to Process Further
Copper	175	$8,000	$6,200	$383,000
Magnetite	2,400	$200	$145	$130,000
Vermiculite	1,600	$325	$280	$220,000
Titanium dioxide	320	$2,400	$1,600	$180,000

Required:

    a. Which of the four minerals should be sold unprocessed and which should be processed further and then sold? Provide detailed calculations supporting your recommendations.

b. Based on your decisions in part (*a*), should Palabora Mining continue to produce batches of the four minerals if each batch costs $680,000? Provide detailed calculations supporting your recommendations.

c. Palabora Mining allocates the $680,000 batch cost to the four minerals based on tons of each mineral in the batch. Prepare a table that allocates the $680,000 batch cost to the four minerals based on tons of each mineral in the batch and the profits (revenues less any costs to process further if the mineral is processed further less allocated batch cost) of each mineral.

d. Which mineral is the most profitable, and which is the least profitable based on your analysis in part (*e*)?

e. Based on your analyses in parts (*a*) through (*d*), what advice would you give to the managers of Palabora Mining regarding processing of each of the four minerals and the current method described in part (*c*) used to allocate the $680,000 batch cost?

P 8–30: Sydney Mira

Sydney Mira provides two financial services through two separate operating divisions (O1 and O2). These two operating divisions require the services of three internal service departments (S1, S2, and S3). The costs of the three service departments last month and the use of each service department by the two operating divisions are:

	S1	*S2*	*S3*
Service Department cost (000s)	$400	$500	$600
Service units used by			
O1	70	60	80
O2	90	80	50

Each service department (S1, S2, and S3) meters the use of its services to other service departments and operating divisions (O1 and O2) in Sydney Mira via "service units." Each of the three service departments has a different method of determining service units it supplies, but collectively all three service departments report service units and these service units are used to allocate the service departments' costs to the users of the service department. For example, service department S1 provided 70 service units to operating division O1 last month.

In addition to providing services to the two operating divisions, O1 and O2, the service departments provide services to the other service departments. The following table summarizes the service units consumed last month by the service departments.

	S1	*S2*	*S3*
S1 use		50	60
S2 use	20		40
S3 use	15	25	

Last month, S2 used 50 service units supplied by S1, and S1 used 20 service units supplied by S2.

Required:

a. Using the direct allocation method, calculate the allocated cost per service unit provided by S1, S2, and S3.

b. Using the direct allocation method, calculate the costs of S1, S2, and S3 that are allocated to O1 and O2.

c. Using the step-down allocation method, calculate the allocated cost per service unit provided by S1, S2, and S3. The order of the departments in the step-down is S1 first, S2 second, and S3 last.

   d. Using the step-down allocation method, calculate the costs of S1, S2, and S3 that are allocated to O1 and O2. The order of the departments in the step-down is S1 first, S2 second, and S3 last.

   e. Using the step-down allocation method, calculate the allocated cost per service unit provided by S1, S2, and S3. The order of the departments in the step-down is S3 first, S2 second, and S1 last.

   f. Using the step-down allocation method, calculate the costs of S1, S2, and S3 that are allocated to O1 and O2. The order of the departments in the step-down is S3 first, S2 second, and S1 last.

   g. Discuss the advantages and disadvantages for Sydney Mira of using the direct allocation method, the step-down method (S1 first, S2 second, and S3 last), and the step-down method (S3 first, S2 second, and S1 last).

P 8–31: Vista View Wines

Vista View Wines (VVW) is a large vineyard that produces a host of varietal wines (premium reds and whites) and fortified wines. Fortified wines such as brandy, vermouth, sherry, madeira, and port consist of wine with additional distilled products. Besides sourcing grapes for its wines from its own vineyard, VVW purchases grapes from surrounding vineyards. VVW is organized around two profit centers: Wines (all of the premium wines) and Ports (all of the fortified wines). A case of wine or fortified wine is sold as soon as it is produced. Each profit center faces its own demand curve as depicted below, and each profit center has different and distinct marketing and distribution channels. Wines sells its products by private labeling them to hotels, whereas Ports sells its fortified wines to liquor stores.

WINES		PORTS	
Number of Cases	Price	Number of Cases	Price
(000s)	per Case	(000s)	per Case
160	$103.00	60	$90.00
170	$ 99.75	70	$85.00
180	$ 96.50	80	$80.00
190	$ 93.25	90	$75.00
200	$ 90.00	100	$70.00
210	$ 86.75	110	$65.00
220	$ 83.50	120	$60.00

   VVW purchased 5,000 tons of grapes that were then crushed and the juice from the first and second pressings was used by Wines and the juice from the third and fourth pressings was used by Ports. Each subsequent pressing applies more pressure, and the resulting juice contains more impurities. The cost of the grapes (including pressing) amounted to $5 million and these costs are recovered from Wines and Ports using predetermined rates based on the budgeted number of juice gallons used in the cases produced (and sold). Based on their budgeted gallons used and cases produced, Wines is charged $19 per case and Ports $13 per case to recover the grape and pressing costs of $5 million. (Grape and pressing cost is charged to each of the two profit centers.)

   In addition to the grape and pressing cost, Wines and Ports incur variable costs to ferment, age, bottle, package, and distribute their products. Wines incurs variable costs of $25 per case and Ports incurs $20 of variable costs per case. Wines and Ports have separate fermenting, packaging, marketing, and distribution channels and incur their own fixed costs ($6.3 million by Wines and $2.8 million by Ports). The managers of Wines and Ports are compensated based on the profits of their individual operation, which is calculated based on their own revenues, variable and fixed costs, and the grape and pressing costs.

Required:

   a. How many cases of wines do you expect Wines to produce, and how many cases of fortified wines do you expect Ports to produce?

   b. Based on your calculations in part (a), how much profit will Wines and Ports report?

386   *Chapter 8*

    c. If central management has the same knowledge of the demand conditions as Wines and Ports and makes the Wines and Ports price-quantity decisions to maximize firm profits instead of allowing each division to make its own price-quantity decision, would the same price-quantity decisions be made? Justify your answer with supporting calculations and analyses.

    d. Explain why your answers in part (*a*) and (*c*) are the same or different.

    e. Assuming that VVW continues to maintain its decentralized organizational structure and continues to compensate its Wines and Ports managers based on their own profits as described in the problem, what, if any, changes would you recommend VVW make in the way profits of each profit center is calculated?

Cases

Case 8–1:   Carlos Sanguine Winery

Carlos Sanguine, Inc., makes premium wines and table wines. Grapes are crushed and the free-flowing juice and the first-processing juice are made into premium wines. The second- and third-processing juices are made into table wines.

Table 1 summarizes operations for the year, and Table 2 breaks down manufacturing overhead expenses into general winery costs and production facilities costs.

Based on Tables 1 and 2, the accounting department prepared the report in Table 3.

Management is concerned that the table wines have such a low margin. Some of the managers urge that these lines be dropped. Competition keeps the price down to $7 per case, which causes some managers to question how the competition could afford to sell the wine at this price.

Before making a final decision, top management asked for an analysis of the fixed and variable costs by product line and their break-even points. When management saw Table 4, the president

TABLE 1   **Summary of Operations for the Year**

Tons of grapes	10,000	
Average cost per ton	$190	
	Premium Wines	*Table Wines*
Number of cases produced and sold	400,000	70,000
Selling price per case	$11.00	$7.00
Revenues	$4,400,000	$490,000
Grape costs*	1,650,000	250,000
Packaging costs	1,000,000	140,000
Labor	200,000	35,000
Selling and distribution†	400,000	35,000
Manufacturing overhead	400,000	87,500
Operating profit (loss)	$ 750,000	$ (57,500)

*Grape costs represent the cost of the juice placed into the two product categories and are calculated as

	Gallons of Juice Used in Each Product	% of Juice	×	Total Grape Costs	=	Grape Cost per Product
Premium wines	13,200,000	86.84%		$1,900,000		$1,650,000
Table wines	2,000,000	13.16		1,900,000		250,000
Total	15,200,000	100.00%				$1,900,000

Note: A greater quantity of juice is required per case of premium wine than per case of table wine because there is more shrinkage in the premium wines.

†Each product has its own selling and distribution organization. Two-thirds of S&D expenditures vary with cases produced; the remainder of the expenditures do not vary with output.

Cost Allocation: Practices

TABLE 2   **Manufacturing Overhead by Products**

	Premium Wines	Table Wines	Total
General winery costs*	$212,800	$37,200	$250,000
Production facilities costs†			
(depreciation and maintenance)	187,200	50,300	237,500
Manufacturing overhead	$400,000	$87,500	$487,500

*General winery costs do not vary with the number of cases or the number of product lines and are allocated based on cases produced.

†Premium and table wines have separate production facilities. One-fourth of each of their production facilities costs varies with cases produced. The remainder are fixed costs previously incurred to provide the production capacity.

TABLE 3   **Product Line Cost Structure per Case**

	Premium Wines		Table Wines	
Net sales		$11.00		$7.00
Variable costs				
Grapes	$4.13		$3.57	
Packaging	2.50		2.00	
Labor	0.50		0.50	
Selling and distribution	1.00	8.13	0.50	6.57
Margin		$2.87		$ 0.43
Less manufacturing overhead		1.00		1.25
Operating profit (loss)		$1.87		$(0.82)

TABLE 4   **Fixed and Variable Costs per Product and Product Break-Even Points**

	Premium Wines		Table Wines	
Sales		$11.00		$ 7.00
Less variable costs				
Grapes	$ 4.13		$3.57	
Packaging	2.50		2.00	
Labor	0.50		0.50	
Selling and distribution	0.66		0.33	
Manufacturing overhead	0.12*	7.91	0.18†	6.58
Contribution margin		$ 3.09		$ 0.42
Less unitized fixed costs per unit				
Selling and distribution	0.33		0.17	
Manufacturing overhead	0.88	1.21	1.07	1.24
Profit (loss)		$ 1.88		$ (0.82)
Break Even				
Fixed costs (400,000 × $1.21)	$484,000		(70,000 × $1.24)	$86,800
÷ Contribution margin	3.09			0.42
Number of cases to break even	156,634			206,667

*($187,200 × 25%) ÷ 400,000 cases.
†($50,300 × 25%) ÷ 70,000 cases.

388   *Chapter 8*

TABLE 5   Effects of Discontinuing Table Wines

1. No effect on the sale of premium wines is expected.
2. The juice being used in the table wines can be sold to bulk purchasers to use in fruit juices for $150,000 per year.
3. The table wine production facilities (tanks, refrigeration units, etc.) have no use in premium wine production. These can be sold for $350,000, net of disposal costs.
---

remarked, "Well, this is the final nail in the coffin. We'd have to almost triple our sales of table wines just to break even. But we don't have that kind of capacity. We'd have to buy new tanks, thereby driving up our fixed costs and break-even points. This looks like a vicious circle. By next month, I want a detailed set of plans on what it'll cost us to shut down our table wines." Table 5 summarizes the shutdown effects.

Based on the facts presented in the case, what should management do?

Case 8–2: Wyatt Oil

Wyatt Oil owns a major oil refinery in Channelview, Texas. The refinery processes crude oil into valuable outputs in a two-stage process. First, it distills a barrel of crude oil at a variable cost of $2 per barrel into two types of outputs: light distillates (such as gasoline, jet fuel, diesel fuel, and kerosene) and heavy distillates. The light distillates are sold for $48 per barrel. The heavy distillates can either be sold for $30 per barrel or fed into a catalytic cracking unit ("cat cracker") at a variable cost of $3 per barrel to be converted into light distillates and sold, for $48 per barrel. The diagram in Figure 1 illustrates the refining process.

Wyatt's Channelview refinery can distill 60 million barrels of oil per year and feed 30 million barrels of heavy distillate a year into the cat cracker. It can process either light, sweet crude from Texas (such as West Texas Intermediate) or heavy, sour crude from the Middle East (such as Kuwait Export), depending on the market prices of the two types of crude. More valuable products are distilled from a barrel of light, sweet crude than from a barrel of heavy, sour crude (see Figure 2). Light, sweet crude currently costs $34 per barrel and heavy, sour crude costs $30; however, the price

FIGURE 1

Crude oil distillation: The first step

SOURCE: http://www.eia.doe.gov/pub/oil_gas/petroleum/analysis_publications/oil_market_basics/Refining_text.htm#Crude%20Oil%20Quality.

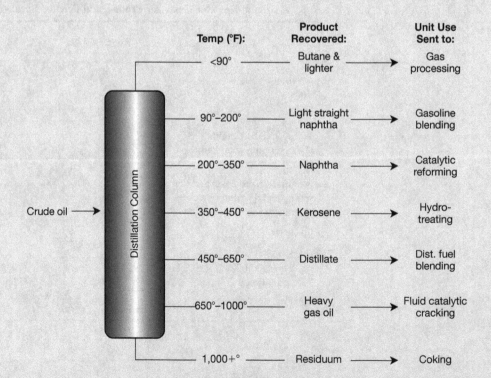

FIGURE 2

Product yield from simple distillation

NOTE: Arab Light is slightly lighter and sweeter than Kuwait Export. West Texas Intermediate is lighter than Kuwait Export (specific gravity of 40.8 for WTI versus 31.4 for Kuwait Export) and sweeter than Kuwait Export (sulfur percentage of 0.34% for WTI versus 2.52% for Kuwait Export).
SOURCE: http://www.eia.doe.gov/pub/oil_gas/petroleum/analysis_publications/oil_market_basics/Ref_image_Simple.htm.

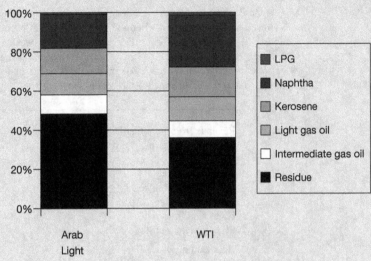

FIGURE 3

Price difference between light crude oil and heavy crude oil, 1988–2001

NOTE: Light crude oil is defined here as having an API gravity of 40.1 or greater, and heavy crude oil is defined as having an API gravity of 20.1 or less.
SOURCE: http://www.eia.doe.gov/emeu/perfpro/ref_pi2/fig5.htm.

TABLE 1

	West Texas Intermediate	Kuwait Export
Light distillates	30 million bbls./year	20 million bbls./year
Heavy distillates	30 million bbls./year	40 million bbls./year
Total	60 million bbls./year	60 million bbls./year

TABLE 2

	Distilling Crude Oil	Cracking Heavy Distillates
Variable cost	$2 per bbl.	$3 per bbl.
Annual fixed cost	$180 million	$90 million
Annual capacity	60 million bbls.	30 million bbls.

differential is volatile, as noted in Figure 3. The output from 60 million barrels of West Texas Intermediate and 60 million barrels of Kuwait Export is shown in Table 1.

The fixed and variable costs and capacities associated with distilling crude and cracking the heavy distillates are shown in Table 2.

Until recently, Wyatt's Channelview refinery processed West Texas Intermediate, but it switched to Kuwait Export when the price differential between the two reached $3.50 per barrel. Kim Quillen, manager of the refinery, is concerned because the switch to heavy, sour crude has resulted in the refinery selling only 50 million barrels of light distillates instead of 60 million—because the refinery has capacity to crack only 30 million barrels of heavy distillates. The refinery's projected accounting income for the year is shown next.

Revenue from light distillates	$960,000,000
Revenue from processed heavy distillates	1,440,000,000
Revenue from sold heavy distillates	300,000,000
Cost of crude oil	(1,800,000,000)
Variable distilling costs	(120,000,000)
Variable cracking costs	(90,000,000)
Fixed distilling costs	(180,000,000)
Fixed cracking costs	(90,000,000)
Net income	$ 420,000,000

Buying an additional cat cracker to increase cracking capacity by 10 million barrels would cost $900 million. It would last for 20 years, increasing the refinery's annual fixed costs by $45 million per year. Quillen has asked his accountant, John Hanks, to evaluate the investment, and Hanks has contemptuously dismissed the project. His analysis appears next.

Sales value of light distillates	$48.00 per bbl.
Cost of heavy distillates*	(35.00) per bbl.
Additional cat cracker accounting costs**	(7.50) per bbl.
Capital charge***	(13.50) per bbl.
Residual income (loss)	$(8.00) per bbl.

* $\frac{\$180,000,000}{60,000,000 \text{ bbls.}} + \$2 \text{ per barrel} + \$30 \text{ per barrel}$

** $\frac{\$45,000,000}{10,000,000 \text{ bbls.}} + \$3 \text{ per barrel}$

*** $\frac{\$900 \text{ million} \times 15\%}{10,000,000 \text{ bbls.}}$

Hank concludes his evaluation by saying, "What an awful project! Our residual income decreases by $8 on every barrel. Not to mention the possibility that we might switch back to using West Texas Intermediate sometime. Then we would have excess cat cracker capacity, which would just rust away over time since expanding our distilling capacity is not feasible. There is no way we should pursue this project."

Quillen is puzzled, for he knows that many other refineries have been installing additional cat cracker capacity in response to the growing price differential between sweet, light crude and sour, heavy crude. Fortunately, he has just hired you to evaluate the capital investment.

Required:

a. Allocate the projected $420 million accounting income of the Channelview refinery among its three activities—light distillates, processed heavy distillates, and sold heavy distillates—by allocating joint costs on the basis of (1) physical volume and (2) net realizable value. Compare the ratio of accounting profit to net realizable value of the three activities under both methods.

Cost Allocation: Practices

b. Did Quillen make the right decision to switch from West Texas Intermediate to Kuwait Export when the price differential reached $3.50 per barrel? Assuming there are no switching costs, find the optimal decision rule as a function of the price differential.

c. Would your decision rule be different if you were to expand the cracker capacity to 40 million barrels? Find the optimal switching rule if the refinery can crack 40 million barrels of heavy distillates each year.

d. Assume the price differential between West Texas Intermediate crude and Kuwait Export crude remains the same at $4 per barrel. Should Quillen expand the refinery's cat cracking capacity?

e. Now consider the possibility of changes in the price differential. Suppose that this year's price differential is $4, but next year's price differential could be anywhere between 75 percent and 125 percent of the current year differential (equally likely, so next year's price differential can be thought of as a random variable uniformly distributed on the interval [$3, $5]). Each succeeding year, the price differential follows the same pattern: between 75 percent and 125 percent of the prior year price differential. Should Quillen expand capacity? Why or why not?

SOURCE: R. Sansing.

Chapter Nine

Absorption Cost Systems

Chapter Outline

Chapter 1 described the function of the internal accounting system as providing information for decision making and control. Chapters 2 and 4 provided the underlying economic framework for decision management and decision control. Chapters 7 and 8 introduced the topic of cost allocations and discussed various reasons firms allocate costs. These reasons included decision management, decision control, cost-plus pricing contracts, financial reporting, and taxes. This chapter continues the discussion of cost allocations by describing a particular costing system widely used in manufacturing called *absorption costing.*

Absorption cost systems ensure that all manufacturing costs are directly traced or allocated to the various products made. The cost objects are the products. If it costs $32 million to operate a factory that manufactures 620,000 cell phones (16 different models), including units still in inventory, then an absorption cost system either directly traces or allocates the $32 million among the 620,000 cell phones. Absorption cost systems display the same trade-off between decision making and control, but most of the discussion of this trade-off is deferred to the next two chapters; this chapter focuses on the mechanics of these cost systems.

Absorption cost systems are widely used in financial reporting for calculating the book value of inventory and cost of goods manufactured. These systems evolved in manufacturing firms. However, the same concepts have been applied to the service sector, including financial institutions and service firms such as financial institutions, law firms, hospitals, advertising agencies, and telecommunication firms. To keep the chapter focused, absorption cost systems in service industries are not described, although several problems at the end of this chapter and in other chapters illustrate absorption costing in nonmanufacturing settings. Actually, nonmanufacturing accounting systems are simpler in that they do not have work-in-process and finished goods inventories. On the other hand, defining the "product" to which costs are allocated is often more difficult. For example, in a bank that offers a wide range of services from loans to bank accounts, many of which involve numerous common costs, the list of products is not always clear cut. Nonetheless, since there are no substantive differences in absorption costing in manufacturing versus nonmanufacturing settings (except for inventories in manufacturing firms), the concepts described in this chapter should be mastered regardless of the actual organizational context.

There are different types of manufacturing processes:

- Job shops (customized production to a customer's specification).
- Batch manufacturing (standardized products manufactured in batches of given lot sizes either to meet customer orders or for inventory).
- Assembly processes (finished parts and subassemblies assembled into a finished product).
- Continuous flow processing lines (such as oil refineries and chemical processing plants).

Plants often consist of different production processes. For example, parts may be manufactured in batches in one department and assembled into finished products in another department. These different production processes usually require slightly different accounting systems to accumulate the costs and assign them to products. There are basically two types of absorption systems: job order systems and process cost systems. **Job order costing** is used in departments that produce output in distinct jobs (job order production) or batches (batch manufacturing). Job order costing is also widely used in assembly processes. A job might consist of a single unit, such as the construction of an office building, or a batch of units, such as 200 windshield wiper motors for automobiles. In a service organization, a job might be handling a client's lawsuit or processing a loan application at a bank. The cost of each job is tracked separately, and job order cost systems accumulate costs by jobs. Alternatively, some assembly processes and continuous flow production processes use **process costing**. Production in these settings (e.g., soft-drink producers and oil refining) is continuous and distinct batches do not exist. Costs are assigned to the production processes and ultimately to the products flowing through the various processes. With either system, all manufacturing costs are assigned to the products produced.

In practice, there is great diversity in how firms' accounting systems assign costs to products, jobs, or activities. Even within batch processing departments, no two systems are exactly the same. Many plants use hybrids of job order and process costing. Each accounting system is tailored to the peculiarities of the department or plant. However, there are similarities across all these systems that are addressed in this chapter. Section A describes job order costing. Section B describes how job order costs flow through the manufacturing T-accounts. The central problem addressed in cost systems is how to treat costs that cannot be traced directly to the product, job, or service. The allocation of these indirect (overhead) costs to products/ production is often a key design issue in costing systems, and section C describes how overhead is allocated to manufacturing jobs. Section D discusses permanent versus temporary volume changes, and section E describes the use of single versus multiple overhead rates for allocating overhead to jobs. Process costing is addressed in section F. Section G summarizes the chapter. Appendix A provides a more in-depth discussion of the mechanics of process costing. Appendix B illustrates the relations among volume, average costs, and prices.

A. Job Order Costing

To illustrate job order costing in a manufacturing setting, consider a plant that produces multiple products. Each product is produced in a batch requiring different raw material inputs and different classes of direct labor. Moreover, the products utilize various combinations of common resources such as machines, supervisors, engineers, and factory space. Every job manufactured passes through a common machining process. The time spent in this machining center is recorded for each job and used to allocate overhead costs to the job. Each job has a job order cost sheet that records the costs attached to the products produced in the batch and the number of machine hours spent processing the job. A typical job order cost sheet appears in Table 9–1. The job sheet in Table 9–1 is the underlying source document in the job order cost system. Prior to computers, manufacturing firms maintained job order cost sheets manually. Today, job order cost sheets are electronic records in computer systems.

The job sheet records all direct materials issued for the job, including the type, quantity, and cost of materials. Each day, factory employees record the time they spent working on particular jobs and the hours they were idle or in a training program. All direct labor worked on job #5167 is posted to the job order sheet. Notice that different types of labor were used on the job. Job #5167 was started on March 10, completed on May 28, and yielded 1,560 completed units. It accumulated $14,147 of direct materials costs and $17,422 of direct labor costs.

Also recorded on the job sheet are the number of machine hours used by the job. In this plant, machine hours are used to allocate overhead costs at the rate of $25 per machine hour, a predetermined rate. (How overhead rates are determined is discussed later in this chapter.) Job #5167 used 213 machine hours. Multiplying 213 machine hours times $25 per hour yields $5,325 of overhead charged to this job. The total charges for this job amount to $36,894. Since there were 1,560 units in the job, the average cost was $23.65 per unit.

The allocation basis for indirect manufacturing costs accumulated in the overhead account is machine hours. Remember from Chapter 7 that using machine hours as the allocation base taxes machine hours and creates incentives to substitute other inputs for machine hours.

Job #5167 illustrates several important features of job order costing:

- The items being produced by the job are the objects being costed.
- All direct costs of manufacturing the job are traced directly to the job.
- Each job is charged for some indirect manufacturing overhead.

TABLE 9–1　**Job Order Cost Sheet**

Job Number 5167　　　　　　　　　　**Date Started** 3/10

　　　　　　　　　　　　　　　　　　Date Completed 5/28

Raw Materials					Direct Labor			
Date	Type	Quantity	Amount	Machine Hours	Date	Type	Hours	Amount
3/13	103a	205	$ 6,305	13	3/13	a65	15	$ 265
3/14	214	106	5,210	111	3/14	a68	20	596
4/1	217	52	786	45	4/18	b73	81	811
4/23	878	229	1,187	28	4/23	c89	368.5	7,370
5/23	331	113	659	16	5/28	c89	419	8,380
Totals			$14,147	213				$17,422

SUMMARY OF COSTS:

Total direct materials	$14,147
Total direct labor	17,422
Overhead (213 machine hours @ $25/hr)	5,325
Total job cost	**$36,894**
Divided by: Number of units in batch	1,560
Average cost per unit produced	$ 23.65

- An input measure, machine hours, is used to allocate overhead costs to jobs. An input measure is the allocation base.
- The overhead rate (here, the rate per machine hour) is set at the beginning of the year, before the first jobs are started. This overhead rate is the ratio of expected factory overhead for the year divided by the expected machine hours for the year.
- Reported product costs are average rather than variable or marginal costs. Each job is assigned a portion of the overhead. Since overhead contains both variable and fixed costs, overhead distributed to jobs contains some fixed costs.

Historical Application: Job Order Cost Sheets and United States Steel

In the 1870s, Andrew Carnegie built the Thompson Steel Works in Pittsburgh, which later became U.S. Steel. One of Carnegie's many management innovations—and his obsession—was a detailed cost accounting system. Each department in the steel works listed the amount and cost of labor and materials used by each job as it passed through the department. Carnegie received daily reports showing the direct costs of the products produced and would repeat, "Watch the costs and the profits will take care of themselves."

Carnegie's cost sheets were called a marvel of ingenuity and careful accounting. He required his people to explain the most minute change in unit costs. Carnegie and his managers used these data to evaluate the performance of his people, maintain the quality and mix of raw materials, evaluate improvements in process and product, and price products. New orders would not be accepted until costs had been carefully checked.

SOURCE: A. Chandler, *The Visible Hand: The Managerial Revolution in American Business* (Cambridge, MA: Harvard University Press, 1977), pp. 267–68.

B. Cost Flows through the T-Accounts

Job order cost sheets allow the assignment of all factory costs to the jobs flowing through the factory. As jobs enter the factory and remain in process, direct labor costs and direct materials costs are posted to job sheets via the computer system.

Table 9–1 illustrated the job order cost sheet for one job. Modern factories can have hundreds or even thousands of jobs in various stages of completion in the factory at any one time. The accounting system tracks the costs charged to each job by posting them to ledger accounts (T-accounts) via the usual mechanics of double-entry bookkeeping. As costs are charged to individual jobs, they are also entered in a work-in-process inventory account, which contains all the dollars of jobs in process, including the direct materials, direct labor, and overhead allocations. As raw materials move from the storeroom to the factory floor for individual jobs, their dollars are transferred out of the raw materials account and into the work-in-process account.

Figure 9–1 diagrams the flow of costs among the various T-accounts. When a job is finished and transferred to finished goods inventory, the total job cost from the job order cost sheet is transferred out of the work-in-process T-account and into the finished goods T-account. Similarly, when the goods are sold, the dollars flow out of the finished goods T-account and into the cost-of-goods-sold T-account.

The overhead T-account contains all indirect labor (supervisors as well as factory workers who are not working on jobs because they are either in training programs, setting up or maintaining machines, or idle), indirect materials (supplies not directly assignable to particular jobs), and other factory costs. Other factory costs include insurance, property taxes, depreciation, accounting costs, purchasing, security, general factory management,

FIGURE 9-1

Schematic of a job order cost system

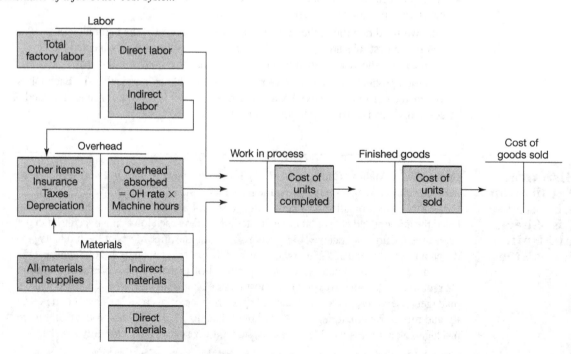

and utilities. These costs represent the common resources used by all jobs. In a typical plant, direct labor is about 30 percent of total factory costs, direct materials is another 30 percent, and overhead is 40 percent. However, these percentages can vary widely. Direct labor can be as low as 1 percent of total manufacturing costs and overhead as high as 80 percent. The overhead T-account is a control account. It is used to temporarily accumulate and then distribute the indirect costs to the jobs. At the end of the accounting period, any remaining balance in this account must be charged to a balance sheet or income statement account.

Management must decide which inventory flow assumption to use in making the transfers between the various T-accounts. Should the costs follow a first-in, first-out (FIFO); last-in, first-out (LIFO); or specific identification flow? This decision is discussed in financial accounting, particularly with regard to the tax implications of the LIFO/FIFO choice. (In periods of rising costs, LIFO reduces reported income and hence taxes by taking the most recent and thus highest costs to the income statement.) However, the inventory accounting decision affects both decision making and control. For example, if LIFO is used, the most recent prices flow through the accounts and old prices remain in inventory. LIFO produces more timely (current) information regarding price changes than FIFO. In particular, LIFO-based product costs are computed using the most recent raw material prices and usually more closely reflect replacement costs.

To the extent replacement costs are good proxies for opportunity cost, LIFO is usually better for decision making. However, LIFO also creates control problems. Performance evaluation systems based on accounting profits create incentives for managers close to retirement or with a short horizon in the firm to liquidate old LIFO inventory levels, thereby generating large accounting profits (but also large tax liabilities). The choice of inventory flow assumptions is important because it affects taxes, financial statements (and the external contracts based on them), internal decision making, and control. To simplify the discussion, for the remainder of this text we assume that the firm uses the specific identification inventory valuation method, unless otherwise stated.

Table 9–2 illustrates the various T-accounts in Figure 9–1 used in constructing the firm's income statement. The cost of goods sold in the income statement consists of the change in finished goods inventory plus the cost of goods manufactured during the period, which in turn is composed of direct labor, direct materials, and overhead. Table 9–2 shows sales of $2.2 million. The cost of goods sold is $1.362 million, calculated by taking the sum of the beginning inventory and cost of goods manufactured and deducting the ending inventory. The cost of goods manufactured, calculated in the footnote to Table 9–2, consists of direct materials and labor and overhead plus the change in work-in-process inventories.

Concept Questions	Q9–1	What are the two distinct absorption systems?
	Q9–2	Describe the flow of costs through the T-accounts in a job order cost system.
	Q9–3	Suppose that during the production of a particular job, a machine malfunctions, destroying $2,750 of raw materials. How should the cost of these materials be handled? Should they be charged to the job in process?

TABLE 9-2   Income Statement for a Manufacturing Firm

SAMPLE COMPANY
Income Statement
($000s)

Sales		$2,200
Cost of goods sold:		
Finished goods—Jan. 1	$ 217	
Cost of goods manufactured*	1,337	
Cost of goods available for sale	1,554	
Less finished goods—Dec. 31	(192)	
Cost of goods sold		(1,362)
Gross profit		$ 838
Less		
Selling and administrative expense		
Variable	$ 216	
Fixed	349	(565)
Net income		$ 273

*Cost of goods manufactured:

Direct materials		
Materials inventory—Jan. 1	$ 13	
Purchases	232	
Material available for use	245	
Less materials inventory—Dec. 31	(20)	
Material used		$ 225
Direct labor		480
Manufacturing overhead		665
Total manufacturing costs incurred		$1,370
Add work in process—Jan. 1		90
Total in process		$1,460
Less work in process—Dec. 31		(123)
Cost of goods manufactured		$1,337

C. Allocating Overhead to Jobs

The previous two sections illustrated how a job order cost system accumulates product costs and how the accounting system tracks manufacturing costs through the various T-accounts. This section describes the mechanics of using overhead rates to distribute indirect costs to jobs. The use of prospective overhead rates (those estimated at the beginning of the year) results in over- or underabsorbed overhead at the end of the year, and this section discusses how this over/underabsorption is treated. The concept of flexible budgeting is reintroduced and applied to calculating overhead rates. This section concludes by describing alternative ways of estimating budgeted volume.

1. Overhead Rates

The most interesting aspect of job costing is its treatment of overheads because it involves management's judgment and offers managers discretion in product costing and income determination. If all resource utilization and factory costs could be traced directly to the products consuming those resources, then cost accounting would be nothing more than arithmetic. The innovation of job order costing is the accumulation of all indirect costs in an overhead account and the subsequent distribution of these costs to individual jobs through the use of an overhead rate. An overhead allocation base is chosen to allocate the indirect costs to jobs. Machine hours are used as the overhead allocation base in Table 9–1. As work is performed on the job, overhead is charged to the job based on total machine hours used. A *prospective* overhead rate, set at the beginning of the year, allows jobs to be costed as they are produced.

Most firms use prospective, not actual, overhead rates. Suppose overhead is charged to jobs based on the total actual machine hours used in the plant for the entire year. Then, the total cost of each job (including overhead) is unavailable until the end of the year. The overhead costs for the first job cannot be determined until all the jobs are finished. For example, suppose the first job completed in the year uses 1,000 machine hours and overhead is assigned based on actual machine hours. Overhead on the first job could be 1 percent of actual overhead if actual total hours for the year end up being 100,000 hours or 2 percent if the final number of machine hours is 50,000 hours. Using a prospective overhead rate allows more timely reporting of total costs, including indirect costs.

Notice in Table 9–1 that factory volume is measured in machine hours, not units of production. That is, volume is being measured with an *input* measure, not an *output* measure. This practice is common in most plants. Inputs are used to measure volume because most plants produce heterogeneous products. If a factory manufactures small pumps and large pumps, the number of pumps manufactured can give a misleading measure of plant output. Plant volume can actually fall while the total number of pumps increases if there is a shift from large to small pumps. Therefore, an input measure rather than an output measure captures volume in plants manufacturing heterogeneous products.

The input measure selected (machine hours, direct material dollars, direct labor hours, direct labor dollars) is usually the one that has the greatest association or cause-and-effect relation with overhead. That is, the allocation base is the factor input most correlated with overhead. Overhead consists of both fixed and variable indirect costs. In the long run, fixed costs can be adjusted to changes in volume.

Most firms select allocation bases where a logical or statistical association exists between the allocation base and overhead. For example, as plant output expands,

<table>
<tr><td>**Managerial Application: Absorption Costing in China**</td><td>Management accounting and costing practices in China employ many of the same techniques as those employed in the West. A survey of 200 Chinese companies found:

- 94 percent of firms allocate overhead to products manufactured.
- More than 50 percent of firms use direct labor or direct labor cost as the overhead allocation base, and the others use raw material cost, machine hours, or predetermined percentages.
- To avoid overstating their reported profits, Chinese accounting regulations require that overhead be allocated based on actual costs, rather than a predetermined application rate.
- Overhead cost is only about 6 percent of total cost for the median company in the sample.

SOURCE: R. Lawson, "How Accurate Are Chinese Costing Practices?" *Strategic Finance*, May 2009, pp. 41–46.</td></tr>
</table>

400   *Chapter 9*

additional supervisors must be hired. Therefore, the cost driver of supervision can be either the number of machine hours or the number of direct labor hours. If overhead costs vary with direct labor hours, then direct labor hours is the volume measure. In Chapter 7, overhead rates were shown in certain circumstances to serve as a proxy for hard-to-observe opportunity costs. If the overhead rate (which is the average cost) is less than or equal to the marginal cost imposed on the firm when output expands by one more unit, allocating overhead is better than not allocating it. The factor input used as the volume measure then becomes "taxed," and the choice of volume measure becomes, in essence, a decision regarding which factor input to tax. Usually, management wants to tax the input that imposes externalities on other parts of the organization. Ideally, the overhead rate provides an estimate of the opportunity cost of using one more unit of the allocation base.

Four points of this discussion and Figure 9–1 are worth noting:

1. The overhead rate equals annual budgeted overhead divided by budgeted volume. This measure averages out seasonal variability in monthly expenditures and volume. Each completed job can be costed, even though the total overhead and actual volume for the year are not known.

2. Budgeted volume is measured using an input, such as direct labor, instead of output. Typical volume measures are direct labor hours, direct labor dollars, direct material dollars, and machine hours.

3. The measure of volume chosen as the allocation base is usually the one that has the greatest association with overhead.

4. The choice of the overhead volume measure is critical; because it is the taxed input, managers will seek to reduce its use.

Point 2 above suggests that direct labor and machine hours are common overhead allocation bases. Most manufacturing firms use direct labor (direct labor hours or direct labor costs) to allocate at least a portion of factory overhead as a way to control labor costs. Machine hours and direct material dollars are other commonly employed allocation bases. While the predominant overhead allocation base in many plants is direct labor, it is not uncommon for manufacturing overhead cost to exceed direct labor cost by a factor of two. Direct labor costs are thus being used to allocate a pool of costs twice the size of the allocation base. Chapter 11 addresses whether such a scheme makes sense.

2. Over/ Underabsorbed Overhead

Suppose a plant manufactures aluminum cans of different sizes. Machine hours in the aluminum extrusion machine are used to measure volume. At the end of the year, the overhead account likely contains a balance amount:

Overhead Account		
Actual overhead incurred	Total overhead absorbed to units in production	= Budgeted overhead rate × Volume measure (machine hours)
Underabsorbed	Overabsorbed	

Historical Application: Absorption Costing and Economic Darwinism	As early as 1690, some British companies used a single accounting system, based on double-entry bookkeeping, to generate both financial statements and detailed cost reports for internal decision making and control. Analyses of company archives reveal that by the mid-1800s, most UK firms were following absorption costing techniques whereby manufacturing overheads were being absorbed into the cost of the products produced. Internally transferred intermediate products were costed at average full cost—and sometimes at market price. The fact that today's absorption costing systems can be traced back more than 150 years suggests that they have survived the test of time, and, based on Economic Darwinism, they are yielding benefits in excess of their costs.

Source: T. Boyns and J. Edwards, "The Construction of Cost Accounting Systems in Britain to 1900: The Case of the Coal, Iron and Steel Industries," *Business History* 39, pp. 1-29

Total overhead absorbed is the budgeted overhead rate times the volume produced. The firm has 100,000 budgeted machine hours, which is the budgeted volume for the aluminum can plant for the year. Annual budgeted overhead is $2,500,000. The budgeted overhead rate is thus $25 per machine hour. Suppose that, at the end of the year, 103,000 machine hours have been used. The amount of overhead absorbed is $103,000 \times \$25 = \$2,575,000$. If actual overhead incurred was $2,565,000, then there is $10,000 of overabsorbed overhead in the overhead account.

Overhead Account

Actual overhead incurred: $2,565,000	Total overhead absorbed: $103,000 \times \$25$ $= \$2,575,000$
	$10,000 Overabsorbed

The overhead T-account shows a $10,000 overabsorbed balance at the end of the year. Recall that the reason a balance remains in the overhead account is because the overhead rate is set at the beginning of the year—before either the actual overhead or the actual volume are known. The accounting system charged work in process with $10,000 more overhead than was actually incurred by the plant. This can arise because actual overhead differs from budgeted overhead and/or because the volume measure (machine hours) differs from budgeted volume. Chapter 13 describes how over/underabsorbed overhead is analyzed to determine the cause of the variance.

There are three ways of disposing of the over/underabsorbed balance at year-end. First, write it off to cost of goods sold. Suppose overhead absorbed is $3 million. If actual overhead incurred is $2.9 million, $100,000 of overhead that was not incurred was still charged to work-in-process (WIP). When this $100,000 of overabsorbed overhead is written off to cost of goods sold, cost of goods sold is reduced and income rises by $100,000 (before taxes). If, on the other hand, actual overhead incurred is $3.2 million, overhead is underabsorbed by $200,000. In this case, $200,000 of overhead was incurred but not charged to WIP. Writing off this $200,000 of underabsorbed overhead causes cost of goods sold to increase and income to fall by $200,000 (before taxes).

Historical Application: Over- and Under-absorbed Overhead Understood by 1910

By 1910, most large U.S. manufacturing companies had come to use overhead accounts to accumulate and distribute these costs to products. One writer described the typical accounting treatment as follows:

> The overhead account is charged each month . . . with the items composing the indirect expenses, and is credited through the fixed overhead percentage with the total amount applied to the various production orders and cost sheets. The balance, if a debit, shows the undistributed portion of the overhead, which means that the fixed percentage added to the labor cost was not sufficient to cover the indirect expenses. When there is a credit balance, however, it shows that the percentage allowed was more than sufficient.

Absorption cost systems, including the use of prospective overhead rates, have survived more than 100 years in a variety of firms, absent government regulations. The survival of those systems in firms that operate in competitive markets is evidence that absorption cost systems are providing benefits that exceed their costs.

SOURCE: J. Nicholson, Cost Accounting—Theory and Practice (New York: The Ronald Press Co., 1913), p. 197. Quoted by P. Garner, *Evolution of Cost Accounting to 1925* (Montgomery, AL: University of Alabama Press, 1954), p. 176

The second method of disposing of over/underabsorbed overhead is to allocate (prorate) it among work-in-process, finished goods, and cost-of-goods-sold T-accounts based on the amount of overhead in these categories. For example, in the previous example there was $100,000 of overabsorbed overhead. Suppose that of the $3 million of overhead absorbed, $0.5 million is still in work-in-process, $1.0 million remains in finished goods inventory, and $1.5 million is in cost of goods sold. Then the following illustrates the proration of the $100,000 of overabsorbed overhead:

	Work-in-Process	Finished Goods	Cost of Goods Sold	Total
Overhead absorbed	$500,000	$1,000,000	$1,500,000	$3,000,000
Percentage of overhead absorbed	16.67%	33.33%	50%	100%
Overabsorbed overhead prorated	$(16,670)	$ (33,330)	$ (50,000)	$ (100,000)
Overhead before proration	500,000	1,000,000	1,500,000	3,000,000
Overhead after proration	$483,330	$ 966,670	$1,450,000	$2,900,000

The third method of disposing of over/underabsorbed overhead involves recalculating the cost of each job using actual overhead incurred and actual volume to compute a revised, end-of-year overhead rate. The second and third methods produce similar net income and inventory valuations. The third method is the most expensive in terms of bookkeeping and data processing costs, especially if a large number of jobs have been manufactured and each one is to be recosted. One reason to choose the third alternative of recosting all jobs is that the firm has cost-plus contracts whereby some of the firm's revenues are tied to reported costs. In this case, recosting each job can change the amount of overhead assigned to products manufactured under cost-plus contracts, thereby changing the firm's revenues, profits, and cash flows.

Usually the magnitude of the over/underabsorbed overhead is small, and thus disposing of the balance is not material. Writing small balances off to cost of goods sold is expedient, and senior managers do not concern themselves with such technical accounting

Managerial Application: Overhead Allocations and GAAP	One reason manufacturing overhead is allocated to work-in-process and therefore to product costs is for inventory valuation for external financial reports. Generally accepted accounting principles (GAAP) require: The primary basis of accounting for inventories is cost, which has been defined generally as the price paid or consideration given to acquire an asset. As applied to inventories, cost means, in principle, the sum of the applicable expenditures and charges directly or indirectly incurred in bringing an article to its existing condition and location. It is understood to mean acquisition and production cost, and its determination involves many considerations. Variable production overheads are allocated to each unit of production based on the actual use of the production facilities. However, the allocation of fixed production overheads to the costs of conversion is based on the normal capacity of the production facilities. Normal capacity refers to a range of production levels. Normal capacity is the production expected to be achieved over a number of periods or seasons under normal circumstances, taking into account the loss of capacity resulting from planned maintenance. Some variation in production levels from period to period is expected and establishes the range of normal capacity. Unallocated overheads shall be recognized as an expense in the period in which they are incurred. Thus, GAAP allows management significant discretion. It can either take over/underabsorbed overhead to the income statement by writing it off to cost of goods sold or allocate it among the inventory accounts. SOURCE: This is from FASB Accounting Standards Codifications ASC 330.10.30-1 at tps://asc.fasb.org/section&trid=2127012&search_marker=searchresult&query=dGhlK3ByaW1hcnkrYmFzaXMrb2YrYWNjb3VudGluZytmb3IraW52ZW50b3JpZXM=

issues. However, large balances remaining in the overhead account attract senior managers' and the external auditors' attention. The decision to write off all or some of the over/underabsorbed overhead to cost of goods sold depends on the effect of the various alternatives on net income. If writing off the entire balance versus prorating the balance results in roughly the same net income amounts such that typical users of the financial statements would not alter their investment or lending decisions, then the over/underabsorbed overhead disposition decision is immaterial to the typical user. In this case, writing off the balance in the overhead account being most expedient would be chosen. However, if the typical user of the financial statements would alter his or her investment decision if over/underabsorbed overhead is written off entirely to cost of goods sold versus prorated, then proration would be the method chosen.

3. Flexible Budgets to Estimate Overhead

As described previously, most firms use prospective overhead rates, or those estimated before the fiscal year begins. This requires managers to forecast next year's overhead rate. A flexible budget provides one way to forecast the overhead rate (Chapter 6). The first step requires estimating budgeted annual overhead.

$$\text{Budgeted annual overhead} = \text{Fixed overhead} + \text{Variable overhead}$$
$$= FOH + VOH \times BV$$

where

FOH = Fixed overhead
VOH = Variable overhead per unit of volume
BV = Budgeted volume

404   *Chapter 9*

Historical Application: Behavior of Overhead Costs	It is well known that overhead costs contain both a fixed and a variable component:
	[Overhead costs] refer to costs that cannot be traced home and attributed to particular units of business in the same direct and obvious way in which, for example, leather can be traced to the shoes that are made of it. And most of the real problems involve one other fact; namely, that an increase or decrease in output does not involve a proportionate increase or decrease in cost.
	SOURCE: J. Clark, *Studies in the Economics of Overhead Costs* (Chicago: University of Chicago Press, 1923), p. 1.

Suppose that fixed overhead is projected at $500,000, variable overhead is projected at $20 per machine hour, and 100,000 machine hours are budgeted. Then, budgeted annual overhead is

$$\text{Budgeted annual overhead} = \$500,000 + \$20 \times 100,000 \text{ machine hours}$$
$$= \$500,000 + \$2,000,000$$
$$= \$2,500,000$$

The second step involves calculating the budgeted annual overhead rate:

$$\text{Budgeted overhead rate} = \frac{\$2,500,000}{100,000 \text{ machine hours}}$$
$$= \$25/\text{machine hour}$$

Flexible budgets allow budgeted annual overhead to vary with volume. Overhead is not treated as a purely fixed cost but rather as a mixture of fixed and variable costs. Analyzing how total overhead varies with volume should lead to a more accurate estimate of budgeted overhead.

Chapter 6 described the budgeting process. One important function of that process is estimating the budgeted overhead rate. This occurs prior to the beginning of the year. Hence, the budgeted overhead rate is a prospective rate. To simplify the terminology, throughout the remainder of this book, whenever the term *overhead rate* is used, it refers to the "budgeted overhead rate" unless otherwise specifically stated.

Exercise 9-1

The Rosen Company has two manufacturing departments, production and assembly. Each department has separate overhead rates. Rosen made the following estimates for its production and assembly departments for the current calendar year:

	Production	*Assembly*
Factory overhead	$ 300,000	$100,000
Direct labor cost	$1,000,000	$210,000
Machine hours	1,500	6,250
Direct labor hours	50,000	10,000

continued

The company uses a budgeted overhead rate to apply overheads to orders. Machine hours are used to allocate overhead in the production department and direct labor hours are used to allocate overhead in the assembly department.

Required:

a. Calculate the overhead rate for each department.

b. A summary of job #77 follows:

	Production	Assembly
Direct materials used	$3,000	$2,000
Direct labor costs	$11,000	$15,500
Machine hours	100	250
Direct labor hours	500	750

What are overhead costs for job #77?

c. Actual operating results for the current year are:

	Production	Assembly
Factory overhead	$325,000	$65,000
Direct labor cost	$900,000	$230,000
Machine hours	1,550	6,250
Direct labor hours	47,000	10,500

Calculate the over/underapplied overhead for each department.

Solution:

a. Overhead rate:

For the Production Department

$$\frac{\text{Factory overhead}}{\text{Machine hours}} \quad \frac{\$300,000}{1,500} = \$200.00 \text{ per machine hour}$$

For the Assembly Department

$$\frac{\text{Factory overhead}}{\text{Direct labor hours}} \quad \frac{\$100,000}{10,000} = \$10.00 \text{ per direct labor hour}$$

b. Overhead costs for job #77:

Production Department	$200 × 100 machine hours	= $20,000
Assembly Department	$10 × 750 direct labor hours	= $ 7,500
Total overhead cost		$27,500

c. The over/underapplied overhead per departments are:

	Production	Assembly
Actual overhead	$325,000	$ 65,000
Overhead applied		
1,550 × $200/machine hour	$310,000	
10,500 × $10/direct labor hour		$105,000
	$ 15,000 U	$ 40,000 O

NOTE: U = Underapplied; O = Overapplied.

Chapter 9

4. Expected versus Normal Volume

Previous sections have described prospective overhead rates as the ratio of budgeted overhead to budgeted volume. Budgeted volume can be determined in two ways. Budgeted volume can be estimated as either the volume expected for the coming year (**expected volume**) or the long-run average volume. Long-run average volume is called **normal volume,** or the average volume over both upturns and downturns in the economy.

The following example motivates the important difference between expected volume and normal volume. Fast Change offers automobile oil changes at $30 each. This is the only service provided. The variable cost ($20) of providing an oil change includes both direct labor and supplies (oil and oil filter). The fixed cost of $4,000 per month includes advertising, the manager's salary, rent, utilities, insurance, and so forth. Table 9–3 summarizes last month's operations.

Last month, Fast Change had net income before taxes of $1,000 on 500 oil changes, and the full (average) cost of an oil change as shown in the table was $28.00 ($20 of variable cost plus $8.00 = $4,000 ÷ 500 of fixed cost).

This month, the price of an oil change ($30) remains constant, as does the variable cost and fixed cost. However, the number of oil changes falls from 500 to 350. Table 9–4 summarizes operations for this month.

Fast Change lost $500 this month. Notice that the average cost of an oil change has risen from $28.00 to $31.43 ($20 of variable cost plus $11.43 = $4,000 ÷ 350 of fixed cost). The accounting system reports that the cost of an oil change increased. A manager's natural tendency when confronted by a cost increase is to raise prices. But in Fast Change's case, average costs rose because volumes fell. The out-of-pocket costs (the variable cost) of the service did not change. The cost of doing one more oil change is still $20. The opportunity cost of an oil service has not changed. Therefore, the price of an oil change should not be raised. In fact, the price probably should be lowered because the demand for oil changes has dropped. For example, if a new competitor has opened up down the street and is offering oil changes at lower prices, Fast Change will also have to lower its prices. Appendix B illustrates the relations among shifts in demand, changes in fixed costs, and price changes.

The preceding Fast Change example illustrates an important point. Basing overhead rates on short-run fluctuations in volume causes accounting costs, but not opportunity costs, to rise when volume falls and causes them to fall when volume rises. This occurs because overhead contains some fixed costs. The example demonstrates that overhead costs per unit rise when volume declines and vice versa. This sends inappropriate signals to managers to raise prices when demand falls and to lower prices when demand rises. Profit-maximizing managers want to do just the opposite. To avoid incorrect pricing

TABLE 9-3   **Fast Change Summary of Operations Last Month**

Price per oil change	$30
Variable cost per service	$20
Number of oil changes	500
Revenue	$ 15,000
Variable cost	(10,000)
Fixed cost	(4,000)
Net income	$ 1,000
Total cost	$ 14,000
Number of oil changes	÷500
Cost per oil change	$ 28.00

TABLE 9-4   **Fast Change Summary of Operations This Month**

Price per oil change	$30
Variable cost per service	$20
Number of oil changes	500
Revenue	$10,500
Variable cost	(7,000)
Fixed cost	(4,000)
Net loss	$ 500
Total cost	$11,000
Number of oil changes	÷350
Cost per oil change	$ 31.43

decisions, managers should be wary of altering overhead rates due to short-run fluctuations in volume. To calculate an overhead rate that does not fluctuate with volume, use *normal volume* as the allocation base. Normal volume is the long-run average volume during good and bad years. Often, normal volume is the volume projected when the plant was built.

Suppose a firm has two identical plants: one in Rochester, Minnesota, and one in Chicago. Suppose further that volume falls by half and that management decides to shut down the Chicago plant. There are ongoing unavoidable fixed costs in the Chicago plant of $1 million per month, including property taxes on the closed plant. In most cases, it would be inappropriate to charge these fixed costs of $1 million to the Rochester plant and increase the Rochester overhead rate. Now suppose that the two plants are located next to each other in Rochester and one is closed. It is still inappropriate to charge the remaining plant's overhead account with the unavoidable $1 million continuing costs. By the same logic, if there is only one plant and its volume falls by 50 percent, one should not increase the overhead charge on the remaining production. Allowing the overhead rate to rise as volume falls creates a potential death spiral (Chapter 8). If volume falls, the unallocated overhead costs should be charged directly to profits, not to the remaining products produced. This is the logic underlying normal volume. To prevent overhead rates and reported product costs from varying with volume, the base volume used in the denominator to compute the overhead rate should be the long-run normal volume.

Using normal volume rather than expected volume to set overhead rates creates underabsorbed overhead when actual volume is less than normal volume. Work-in-process, finished goods, and cost of goods sold, collectively, do not contain all of the overhead incurred. When this underabsorbed overhead is written off to cost of goods sold, cost of goods sold rises and net income falls. When actual volume exceeds normal volume, overabsorbed overhead results; more overhead is included in product costs than is actually incurred. This overabsorbed overhead, when written off, causes cost of goods sold to fall and net income to rise. However, in both cases the amount of overhead charged to individual products remains the same—it is based on normal volume. The costs of individual products do not vary inversely with volume.

Using normal volume improves decision management, particularly the pricing decision. For decision control reasons, however, senior managers might not want to use normal volume and may not want to have over/underabsorbed overhead charged to cost of goods sold. Managers responsible for managing the overhead have less incentive to control it if over/underabsorbed overhead is not charged to product costs. Overhead tends to grow over time and is difficult to control. When overhead rates vary with expected volume, managers responsible for specific overhead items often encounter pressure to reduce overhead growth. Downstream managers (e.g., marketing) who receive product costs with overhead included will pressure upstream managers to control their overhead expenditures. There is increased monitoring of upstream managers by downstream managers. This mutual monitoring is stronger if overhead rates rise when volume falls (i.e., normal volume is not used). However, if volume increases, overhead rates fall and downstream managers have less incentive to monitor overhead costs.

Using normal volume, managers have more discretion in managing earnings because setting normal volume is more subjective than setting expected volume. Expected volume can be compared to current volume, but normal volume is the average over the long term. How long is the long term? Again, normal volume is poorer for decision control.

The choice between using normal volume (long-run average volume) and next year's expected volume for calculating overhead rates depends on whether decision management or decision control is the primary concern. Using normal volume enhances decision management. Using next year's expected volume enhances decision control. Again, we see the trade-off between decision management and decision control in making a design choice about the internal accounting system. Most firms use expected, not normal, volume. Thus, it appears that decision control is more important than decision management.

Exercise 9-2

Pacemakers Inc. manufactures and distributes pacemakers that are implanted into patients to regulate their heart rate. The projected overhead rate is based on a flexible budget. Overhead is applied to pacemakers based on direct labor hours. The following table contains management's forecasts of fixed overhead, variable overhead per direct labor hour, and projected annual volume for the next three years, 2016 to 2018. Projected annual volume is estimated by summing the expected number of each pacemaker to be manufactured in each of the next three years times the amount of direct labor hours in that pacemaker.

	2016	2017	2018
Fixed overhead	$2,200	$2,300	$2,500
Variable overhead per DLH	$ 1.10	$ 1.15	$ 1.20
Projected annual volume (DLH)	800	1,200	1,000

DLH = direct labor hours.
NOTE: Fixed overhead and projected annual volume in 000s.

Management forecasts that the plant's average, long-run volume over the next three years will be 1 million direct labor hours per year.

Required:

    a. Calculate the projected overhead rates for 2016 to 2018 using *expected* volume.

    b. Calculate the projected overhead rates for 2016 to 2018 using *normal* volume.

    c. Even though actual overheads for 2016 to 2018 are not known yet, using your estimated overhead rate based on *expected* volume from part (*a*), forecast Pacemakers' over/underabsorbed overhead for 2016 to 2018.

continued

d. Even though actual overheads for 2016 to 2018 are not known yet, using your estimated overhead rate based on *normal* volume from part (*b*), forecast Pacemakers' over/underabsorbed overhead for 2016 to 2018.

Solution:

a. b.

	2016	2017	2018
Fixed overhead	$2,200	$2,300	$2,500
Variable overhead per DLH	$ 1.10	$ 1.15	$ 1.20
Projected annual volume (DLH)	800	1,200	1,000
Normal annual volume (DLH)	1,000	1,000	1,000
Flexible overhead budget:			
Based on expected volume	$3,080*	$3,680	$3,700
Based on normal volume	$3,300†	$3,450	$3,700

*$2,200 + 800 × $1.10
†$2,200 + 1,000 × $1.10

Projected overhead rate/DLH:			
Based on expected volume	$3.85*	$3.07	$3.70
Based on normal volume	$3.30†	$3.45	$3.70

*$3,080 ÷ 800
†$3,300 ÷ 1,000

c.

Projected overhead incurred	$3,080	$3,680	$3,700
Projected over/underabsorbed overhead based on expected volume			
Projected overhead absorbed based on expected volume	$3,080	$3,680	$3,700
(Over)/underabsorbed overhead	$ 0	$ 0	$ 0

NOTE: Projected overhead incurred is based on the flexible budget = FOH + VOH × Expected volume. Projected overhead absorbed is based on expected volume = OHR × Expected volume. Where OHR = [FOH + VOH × Expected volume] ÷ Expected volume, Over- or underabsorbed overhead = [FOH + VOH × Expected volume] − OHR × Expected volume = 0.

d.

Projected overhead incurred	$3,080	$3,680	$3,700
Projected over/underabsorbed overhead based on normal volume			
Projected overhead absorbed based on normal volume	$2,640*	$4,140†	$3,700‡
(Over)/underabsorbed overhead	$ 440	$(460)	$ 0

*$3.30 × 800
†$3.45 × 1,200
‡$3.70 × 1,000

Concept Questions	Q9–4	Why are prospective overhead rates used to assign overhead costs to jobs?
	Q9–5	Give a reason you might have overabsorbed overhead at the end of the year.
	Q9–6	Describe three ways to eliminate the balance in the overhead account at the end of the year.
	Q9–7	Why are input measures used in calculating prospective overhead rates?
	Q9–8	How are flexible budgets used in absorption cost systems?

D. Permanent versus Temporary Volume Changes

As discussed previously, basing overhead rates on normal volume (long-run average volume) prevents reported unit costs from falling when volume increases and from rising when volume falls. Instead, when actual volume exceeds normal volume, overhead is usually overabsorbed. When this overabsorbed overhead is written off to cost of goods sold, income increases. The opposite usually occurs when normal volume exceeds actual volume. Underabsorbed overhead, when written off to cost of goods sold, reduces income.

With normal volume, unit costs do not vary with economic booms and busts. Accounting profits still vary with volume, but accounting product costs do not vary. When the decision is made to acquire physical capacity (e.g., build a plant), implicit assumptions are made regarding normal volume. However, once the capacity is in place, long-run average volume may very well differ from anticipated volume used to justify acquiring the capacity. For example, managers might underestimate entry by competitors. Suppose a plant is built on the assumption of 100,000 machine hours of output per year for 15 years. In the fifth year, a competitor enters the market, lowering normal volume to 75,000 machine hours. If managers base the overhead rate on a volume of 75,000 machine hours, unit costs will rise, giving a misleading signal that marginal costs have increased and that perhaps a price hike is in order. However, this is probably the wrong signal for the accounting system to send.

If long-run normal volume drops 25 percent (a permanent reduction), then management might consider taking a one-time 25 percent write-off of the historical cost of facilities. In addition, they might want to treat 25 percent of the other fixed overhead costs (such as property taxes) as a period cost to avoid distorting product costs. Similarly, if normal volume increases by 25 percent (a permanent increase), and the plant has the excess capacity to handle this larger volume, then the depreciable life of the plant and equipment can be shortened. This will increase the depreciation expense charged to overhead, offsetting the higher volume so that depreciation per unit of product does not fall.

While, in theory, managers can reduce the book value of plant and equipment for permanent reductions in volume, thereby reducing the overhead charges, managers are reluctant to make the write-off for other reasons. Such a write-off is a public admission by the managers that they overinvested in capacity, which can be damaging to their careers. Moreover, write-offs can provide competitors with useful strategic information to the extent that they are uninformed about the exact amount of the excess capacity.

In summary, temporary changes in volume are assumed to average out over the business cycle, and no asset write-offs or other accounting changes are necessary. However, to prevent dysfunctional pricing decisions, fixed asset write-offs can accompany permanent

Managerial Application: Customer Profitability Analysis	Once the firm has a reliable product costing system that computes accurate product costs, managers can then analyze individual customer profitability. A profit and loss statement can be prepared that reports the revenues generated for each customer less the cost of the products sold (from the absorption costing system) less all other costs incurred to service the customer. These other costs include overnight deliveries, the cost of excessive change orders, the extra time spent by engineers or sales people servicing the customer, the extra costs incurred by purchasing to process short-lead-time orders, and so forth.
	One study found that the least profitable 20 percent of customers can reduce profits by 80 percent, while the most profitable 20 percent of customers can generate 150 percent of a company's profit. Another consultant asserts that 30 percent of customers of many firms are not profitable—and two-thirds of those will never be profitable. Hence, it becomes important for firms to identify and take actions to either drop the unprofitable customers or convert them into profitable ones (raise prices or cut extra services) and to further cement solid relations with the profitable customers so they don't leave. One management consultant advocates creating "customer operating partnerships" to boost business. In these partnerships, suppliers and their profitable customers integrate their supply chains to gether. The supplier operates deep inside the customer's business. This creates a barrier to entry for potential rivals.
	However, at the heart of any customer profitability analysis and customer operating partnerships is the firm's absorption costing system that accurately tracks costs generated by each customer.
	SOURCE: J. Hyatt, "Future Tense," *CFO*, January 2009, pp. 50–54.

declines in volume, thereby preventing overhead rates and hence unit costs from rising. In fact, generally accepted accounting procedures require firms to write down the book value (and hence the subsequent depreciation) if the book value cannot be recovered and is less than its fair value.[1]

Concept Questions	Q9–9	Why should normal volume be used to determine overhead rates?
	Q9–10	Why should one-time write-offs of fixed capital be used in absorption cost systems?

E. Plantwide versus Multiple Overhead Rates

This section describes alternative methods of aggregating overhead costs and allocating them to products. Figure 9–2 schematically represents a single, plantwide overhead rate, which is the method used in the examples so far. All of the overhead costs are first accumulated in a single overhead account or cost pool—a collection of accounts accumulated

---

[1]See FASB, "360-10-35-17 Measurement of an Impairment Loss," https://asc.fasb.org/home.

412   *Chapter 9*

FIGURE 9-2

Single plantwide overhead rate

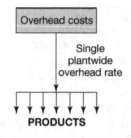

FIGURE 9-3

Multiple overhead rates based on overhead categories

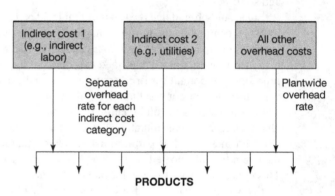

for the purpose of allocating the costs in the pool to activities, products, or processes—and then allocated to products using a single plantwide overhead rate.

A slightly more complicated way to allocate overhead costs is to use multiple overhead rates for different overhead cost items. In this case, each component of overhead is treated as a separate cost pool. Figure 9–3 illustrates this method.

For example, suppose the overhead account is composed of the following three categories:

Indirect labor	$ 750,000
Utilities	650,000
All other costs	1,100,000
Total overhead	$2,500,000

Each category is then allocated to jobs through separate allocation bases. For example,

Overhead Category	Allocation Base	Budgeted Volume
Indirect labor	Direct labor dollars	$3 million direct labor
Utilities	Machine hours	100,000 hours
All other costs	Direct materials dollars	$4 million direct materials

A third method of accumulating overhead cost pools and allocating them to products involves developing different overhead rates by departments. Instead of being allocated by cost category, overhead costs are first grouped by departments. Each department is a separate cost pool. Separate allocation bases are developed for each department, and then overhead costs are allocated to products. Figure 9–4 illustrates this two-step procedure.

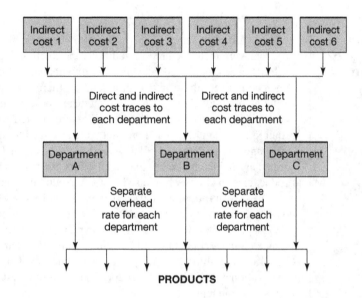

FIGURE 9-4

Two-stage allocation of departmental overhead rates

Suppose the factory contains three departments: machining, painting, and assembly. The $2.5 million of total overhead costs is broken down into three different departments:

Department	Department Costs	Allocation Base
Machining	$ 900,000	Machine hours
Painting	750,000	Dollars of paint used
Assembly	850,000	Direct labor dollars
Total overhead	$2,500,000	

Under this method, all overhead costs are first accumulated by departments. Often, step-down allocations (discussed in Chapter 8) are used to assign service department costs (indirect cost pools) to manufacturing departments. These department costs are then allocated to jobs based on one of three allocation bases: machine hours for machining department costs, dollars of paint used for painting department costs, and direct labor dollars for assembly department costs.

Choosing to use a single plantwide overhead rate, multiple rates, or departmental rates depends on the plant's organization, the incentive systems in place, management's demand for accurate cost data for decision making, and the incremental cost of using more complex cost systems. A plantwide overhead rate is acceptable if the plant has a single homogeneous production process. In this case, a single plantwide overhead rate likely captures the *average* cause-and-effect relation between volume and overhead. Most manufacturing firms in the United States or overseas use separate overhead rates for manufacturing departments, work centers, or machine cells. But single, plantwide overhead rates are also common.

It is commonly believed that a plantwide rate is a less accurate measure of the cause-and-effect relation in plants composed of several heterogeneous processes. Suppose a plant has three departments (parts fabrication, assembly, and testing) with overhead rates of $30, $50, and $100 per direct labor hour, respectively. To simplify the example, assume that each department has the same number of total direct labor hours per year. The simple

<table>
<tr><td>

**Managerial
Application:
Duriron
Pumps**

</td><td>

Duriron Company Pump Division produces centrifugal pumps. Originally, the plant's products were manufactured in traditional production departments that were organized by function. Parts moved between departments depending on the operations required. When completed, they waited for assembly. Increased competition and new manufacturing technology changed the manufacturing process, how it was organized, and the accounting systems. "Focused factories" were created within the plant. The machines required for assembling each product were arranged to allow the product to flow from one stage to another. Component parts, produced in highly automated cells, were located around the assembly line to introduce the parts where they were required. Each product class had its own focused factory. Productivity and profitability improved.

   The accounting system also changed. Each focused factory allocated its overhead costs based on the number of units produced in the particular focused factory.

   Chapter 1 describes the integral role played by the accounting system in the firm's organizational architecture and how the organizational architecture changes in response to environment shifts in competition and technology. Duriron illustrates how one firm's organizational architecture (including its accounting system) adapted to changes in the firm's environment.

Source: www.entrepreneur.com/tradejournals/article/16358994_2html.

</td></tr>
</table>

average (the plantwide overhead rate) is $60, or ($30 + $50 + $100) ÷ 3. Suppose a particular job uses 500 direct labor hours in each of the first two departments and 2,000 hours in the third department. A plantwide overhead rate would charge this job $180,000 of overhead ($60 × 3,000 hours). Individual department overhead rates would charge the job $240,000 (or $30 × 500 + $50 × 500 + $100 × 2,000). However, if overhead consists of large amounts of fixed historical costs, such as depreciation, then neither plantwide overhead rates nor individual department rates accurately reflect the opportunity cost of capacity. If the plant is organized into production departments, separate departmental overhead rates usually are more useful for performance evaluation purposes.

   It is often implicitly assumed that multiple overhead rates for different classes of overhead costs are more accurate estimates of product costs than a single plantwide overhead rate. Using multiple overhead rates requires that each overhead item be analyzed and that the volume measure most closely associated with the variation in the overhead cost item be used as the allocation base. That is, the cost driver for each overhead category must be identified. Disaggregating overhead allocations using different allocation bases presumably results in more accurate estimates of product costs.[2] Activity-based costing (ABC), discussed in Chapter 11, uses multiple overhead rates to presumably derive more accurate product costs.

   No costing system can accurately measure opportunity costs. All cost systems approximate the opportunity cost of making products. The accuracy of a product costing system depends on how costs vary with various decisions. Varying the production levels of existing products will cause overhead costs to vary in one particular way. But adding or dropping product lines can cause overheads to vary in a different way. For example, suppose that increasing production of an existing product adds 20,000 machine hours in a particular department, which causes overhead costs to increase. But if 20,000 machine hours are

[2]S. Datar and M. Gupta, "Aggregation, Specification, and Measurement Errors in Product Costing," *Accounting Review* 69 (October 1994), pp. 567–92. This article demonstrates that adding more cost pools and more overhead rates does not necessarily increase the accuracy of product costs.

added because a new product line is introduced, overheads in this department will likely be even larger. More engineering time, scrap, tooling, and so on are required to add a new product than to increase the volume of an existing product. Therefore, allocating individual overhead accounts using separate cost drivers might give more accurate product costs when volume changes for existing products. On the other hand, a firmwide overhead rate may be just as accurate for estimating product costs when new products are introduced.

Concept Questions	Q9–11	Why will using multiple overhead rates produce more accurate estimates of product costs?
	Q9–12	There are three general methods of allocating overhead costs: plantwide rates, rates for each expense category, and departmental rates. Describe when each is the most useful.

F. Process Costing: The Extent of Averaging

Job order cost systems are employed when production occurs in batches of distinct jobs. But some manufacturing processes have continuous flow production. For example, an oil refinery is a continuous flow production process with no jobs. Crude oil is fed in and various petroleum products, from gasoline to asphalt, are produced in (roughly) continuous streams. If the production process does not have jobs, how are costs accumulated? In such continuous flow production processes, all costs are averaged via an allocation process, not unlike overhead allocations in a job order cost system.

All costing systems average costs over products. Job order costing calculates the cost of separate jobs whereby all the units in the job are assumed to receive the average amount of direct materials and direct labor. Taking the total direct labor and direct materials in the job and dividing by the number of units assumes that each unit receives the average amount of direct labor and materials. Job order cost systems do not track the amount of direct labor or materials for each individual unit produced; it is not cost beneficial to collect this level of detail. Likewise, overhead costs are first allocated to jobs and then assumed to be incurred uniformly over all the units in the job.

Process costing is an extreme case of averaging. It is job order costing with one job. Since the production process is a continuous flow operation, discrete jobs do not exist. In process costing, costs are assigned to identical products that undergo a series of manufacturing processes in a continuous flow. These processes are usually organized as separate cost centers. Costs are assigned to products flowing through each process. Total manufacturing costs must be allocated among units still in work-in-process, as well as units transferred out of the plant to finished goods inventory or cost of goods sold. Appendix A describes the mechanics of process costing accounting in greater detail.

Process costing is inherently simpler and less costly to maintain than job order costing because one does not have to account for separate jobs. On the other hand, the information provided is far more aggregate and often less useful for decision making. In particular, costs for individual jobs are not available and hence cannot be used to evaluate cost trends across different jobs of similar products.

Concept Question	Q9–13	What is process costing? Is it useful for decision making? What are its limitations?

G. Summary

This chapter describes the mechanics and logic of absorption costing systems. These widely used manufacturing cost systems generally distribute all factory costs to the products produced. Absorption cost systems are also prevalent in service industries. There are two basic types of absorption costing systems: job order cost systems and process cost systems. Job order costing computes an average unit cost for each batch or job produced, whereas process costing computes an average unit cost for each product produced in a given time period (week, month, or quarter). Both systems distribute all factory costs to units manufactured.

The salient facts about absorption costing systems include the following:

1. Absorption cost systems attach bits of "costs" to units of inventory as these units move through the manufacturing process. The historic costs incurred by the factory are attached to all the units produced in the factory during the period the costs are incurred, except for under/overabsorbed overhead.

2. Absorption cost systems are backward-looking in that they track historical costs to individual products; they are not necessarily opportunity costs.

3. Indirect (common) costs are assigned to products based on an overhead cost allocation scheme.

4. The overhead allocation base (volume measure) is usually the one with the greatest association with the common costs being allocated. That is, the volume measure selected is usually the most important cost driver of the overhead costs being allocated.

5. An overhead rate is estimated as the ratio of the budgeted overhead expenses to the budgeted (normal or expected) volume measure.

6. Adjusting overhead rates because of short-run changes in volume can cause dysfunctional decisions. If overhead rates are changed in response to short-run changes in volume, overhead rates rise as volume falls and vice versa. These are the wrong cost signals to send throughout the firm as the firm moves through expansionary and recessionary business cycles.

7. At the end of the year, any over/underabsorbed balance in the overhead account usually is written off to cost of goods sold.

8. Instead of using a single plantwide overhead rate, management can develop overhead rates for each overhead expenditure category or overhead department in the factory. However, these multiple overhead rates may or may not provide a more accurate estimate of opportunity cost than a single plantwide rate.

The ability of absorption costing systems to support decision making and control is discussed in the next two chapters.

Appendix A: Process Costing

A process cost system is based on equivalent units. An equivalent unit is the amount of output stated in terms of completed units. For example, if three units are one-third complete, this is equivalent to one complete unit. Or, if 200 units of product are in work-in-process at the end of the month and these units are 75 percent complete, then these 200 units represent 150 equivalent units $(200 \times 75\%)$.

Process cost systems track direct materials and conversion costs (labor and overhead). A major function of all absorption cost systems, including process costing, is to divide total costs incurred into two pieces: those costs still in process and those that have completed manufacturing and thus are in either finished goods inventory or cost of goods sold. Computing the cost of ending work in process and the cost transferred to finished goods requires several distinct calculations. An average cost per equivalent unit of work is computed for materials and conversion costs. These average costs per equivalent unit are used to allocate the material and conversion costs among work-in-process inventory, finished goods inventory, and cost of sales.

TABLE 9-5 Cajun Peanut Butter Inc. Operating Data for March

There was no beginning inventory in process on March 1. The following summarizes the operating data for the month of March:

	Dollars	*Quantity*
Peanuts purchased and entered in process	$32,000	20,000 lb
Ending inventory in process (30% complete)	not available	1,200 lb
Cajun spices	$4,000	
All other factory costs (conversion costs)	$15,000	

Process cost systems view production as consisting of three batches of product: the beginning work-in-process inventory, units started and finished this period, and the ending work-in-process inventory. Consider the following example.

Cajun Peanut Butter Inc. uses process costing to compute product costs for inventory and cost of goods sold. This firm has discovered and patented a peanut butter machine that makes Cajun-flavored peanut butter through a continuous flow process whereby peanuts are dumped into the machine at the beginning of the process and Cajun flavoring is added at the very end. Conversion costs are incurred continuously and evenly throughout the conversion process. The relevant information for March is presented in Table 9–5. All conversion costs (labor and overhead) are assumed to be incurred uniformly during the process. To simplify the discussion, we begin the analysis by assuming no beginning inventories (although later we will illustrate the case with beginning inventories).

Table 9–6 decomposes the mechanics of process costing into four steps. Step 1 summarizes the physical flow of the units and calculates the equivalent units of work in the physical flows. The summary of the physical flows is based on the accounting identity:

$$\text{Beginning inventory} + \text{Units started} = \text{Units transferred out} + \text{Ending inventory}$$

In step 1, this equation becomes

$$0 + 20{,}000 = 18{,}800 + 1{,}200$$

Since the ending inventory is 1,200 pounds and 20,000 pounds were started, 18,800 pounds must have been finished and transferred. These equations hold under the assumption of no spoilage. To simplify the calculations, we assume there is no spoilage or waste at Cajun Peanut Butter Inc.

Costs and the amount of work done are accumulated for each of the two batches: (1) *ending work-in-process (WIP) inventory* and (2) *transferred out* in March. Consider the batch of ending work-in-process inventory. In step 1, there are 1,200 pounds of ending WIP inventory, which are 30 percent complete with respect to conversion costs. This inventory was started in March. Conversion costs were incurred to produce this level of completion, requiring 360 equivalent units of work (1,200 lb @ 30 percent). All the peanuts are added at the beginning, so there are 1,200 equivalent units of peanuts in the ending WIP inventory. On the other hand, since all the Cajun spices are added at the end of the process, the ending work-in-process inventory contains no equivalent units of spices. All the units transferred out (18,800) are complete with respect to conversion, peanuts, and spices, so there are 18,800 equivalent units of these items.

Step 2 in Table 9–6 computes the cost per equivalent unit for the conversion costs, peanuts, and spices. Total equivalent units are the sum of the equivalent units in the ending WIP inventory and units transferred out in March. The three cost categories (conversion, peanuts, and Cajun spices) have different equivalent units. For conversion costs, 19,160 equivalent units were produced. For peanuts, 20,000 equivalent units were produced. For Cajun spices, 18,800 equivalent units were

TABLE 9-6   **Cajun Peanut Butter Inc.—Calculation of Ending Work-in-Process and Cost of Units Transferred Out for March**

	Units	Conversion	Peanuts	Spices	Total
		Equivalent Units			
Step 1					
Physical flow:					
Units started	20,000				
Units to account for	20,000				
Ending work-in-process (30%)	1,200	360	1,200	0	
Transferred out	18,800	18,800	18,800	18,800	
Units accounted for	20,000				
Step 2					
Equivalent units		19,160	20,000	18,800	
Costs per unit:					
Total costs		$15,000	$32,000	$ 4,000	
Cost per equivalent unit		$0.7829	$1.6000	$0.2128	$2.5957
Step 3					
Total costs to account for:					
Conversion costs	$ 15,000				
Peanuts purchased	32,000				
Cajun spices	4,000				
Total costs	$ 51,000				
Step 4					
Ending work-in-process	$ 2,202	$282	$1,920	0	
		$0.7829 × 360	$1.60 × 1,200	$0.2128 × 0	
Transferred out (18,800 × $2.5957)	48,798				
Total costs	$ 51,000				

produced. The cost per equivalent unit is an average cost calculated as the ratio of the total costs incurred in the cost category and the number of equivalent units of work performed in that category. Costs per equivalent unit for conversion, peanuts, and spices are $0.7829, $1.6000, and $0.2128, respectively. The total cost of a complete pound of peanut butter is the sum of the conversion, peanuts, and spice costs ($2.5957).

Step 3 lists all the costs to be assigned to either the ending WIP inventory or the units transferred out, totaling $51,000. Step 4 uses the costs per equivalent unit to value work in process and units transferred out. Costs are assigned to the ending WIP inventory by taking the equivalent units in ending WIP inventory for each cost category and multiplying by the cost per equivalent unit in the same cost category. These are then summed across categories to get the cost of the ending WIP inventory. For example, the ending WIP inventory of $2,202 is composed of $282 of conversion costs (360 equivalent units times $0.7829 per equivalent unit) and $1,920 of peanuts (1,200 equivalent units times $1.60 per equivalent unit). There is no Cajun spice cost in the ending WIP inventory because these spices are only added when the process is finished. The cost of the units transferred out is $48,798 (18,800 × 2.5957).

TABLE 9-7 Cajun Peanut Butter Inc.
Revised Operating Data for March (Including Beginning Inventories)

	Dollars	*Quantity*
Beginning inventory in process (40% complete)	$ 3,600*	2,000 lb
Peanuts purchased and entered in process	$32,000	20,000 lb
Ending inventory in process (30% complete)	not available	1,200 lb
Cajun spices	$ 4,000	
All other factory costs (conversion costs)	$15,000	

*Composed of $600 conversion cost ($0.75 per equivalent unit × 2,000 lbs. × 40% complete) plus $3,000 peanut cost ($1.50 per equivalent unit × $2,000 × 100% complete).

While highly simplified, the preceding example illustrates the key concepts in a process costing system. All costs incurred in March, $51,000, are either assigned to WIP or transferred out to finished goods. Like job order costing, process costing fully absorbs all manufacturing costs to units produced or in inventory.

We now make the example more realistic and complicated by introducing beginning inventories. With beginning inventories comes the decision of whether to use FIFO, weighted average, or LIFO. That is, do we assume the beginning inventory costs flow out first (FIFO), are averaged in with the costs incurred in March (weighted average), or are still in the ending inventory (LIFO)? The remainder of this appendix illustrates the FIFO and weighted average methods. LIFO is not illustrated, but it can be calculated by building LIFO layers from the beginning and ending inventories.

Table 9–7 provides the raw data, including the beginning inventory data. All the data are the same as before, except the beginning inventory of 2,000 pounds is 40 percent complete with respect to conversion costs and has a cost of $3,600.

Table 9–8 illustrates the computations assuming a FIFO cost flow. The first change to notice is that the units transferred out are different from those in Table 9–6. From the earlier accounting identity, solving for units transferred out yields

$$\text{Units transferred out} = 2,000 \text{ lb} + 20,000 \text{ lb} - 1,200 \text{ lb} = 20,800 \text{ lb}$$

Given the revised transferred out amount, the equivalent units for conversion, peanuts, and spices are calculated in step 1 of Table 9–8. Under FIFO costing, the goal is to compute the cost per equivalent unit of only the work done in March. The equivalent units in the beginning WIP inventory (800 equivalent units of conversion costs) are subtracted out under step 2 to make sure the equivalent units computed are for work done in March only. The beginning inventory contains equivalent units of work done in prior periods.

Step 2 also computes the cost per equivalent unit: $0.7367 for conversion costs, $1.60 for peanuts, and $0.1923 for spices. Total costs to account for now include the beginning WIP inventory ($3,600) plus the costs incurred in March (see step 3). The unit costs from step 2 are used to compute the ending amount of work in process ($2,185) in step 4. Ending WIP inventory ($2,185) is composed of the equivalent units of conversion, peanuts, and spices in the ending WIP inventory multiplied by the respective cost per equivalent unit of conversion ($0.7367) and peanuts ($1.60). (Remember, since spices are added at the end of the process, WIP contains no spice costs.)

In step 4, the cost of units transferred to finished goods consists of the beginning WIP inventory ($3,600), the costs to complete the beginning WIP inventory ($884 of conversion and $385 of spices), and the cost of units started and completed in March ($47,545).

420   *Chapter 9*

TABLE 9-8   **Cajun Peanut Butter Inc. Revised Calculation of Ending Work-in-Process and Cost of Units Transferred Out for March**
(FIFO Cost Flow)

	Units	Equivalent Units			
		Conversion	*Peanuts*	*Spices*	*Total*
Step 1					
Physical flow:					
Beginning work-in-process (40%)	2,000				
Units started	20,000				
Units to account for	22,000				
Ending work-in-process (30%)	1,200	360	1,200	0	
Transferred out	20,800	20,800	20,800	20,800	
Units accounted for	22,000				
Step 2					
Less equivalent units in beginning WIP		(800)	(2,000)	0	
Equivalent units of work done in March		20,360	20,000	20,800	
Costs per unit:					
Total costs incurred in March		$15,000	$32,000	$ 4,000	
Cost per equivalent unit		$0.7367	$1.6000	$0.1923	$2.5290
Step 3					
Total costs to account for:					
Beginning work-in-process	$ 3,600				
Conversion costs	15,000				
Peanuts purchased	32,000				
Cajun spices	4,000				
Total costs	$ 54,600				
Step 4					
Ending work-in-process	$ 2,185	$265	$1,920	0	
		$0.7367 × 360	$1.60 × 1,200	$0.1923 × 0	
Transferred out:					
Beginning work-in-process	$ 3,600				
Cost to complete beginning WIP	884	60% × 2,000 × 0.7367			
	385			2,000 × 0.1923	
Started and completed:					
20,800 − 2,000 =					
18,800 × $2.5290	47,545				
Total costs	$54,600*				

*Rounding error.

Table 9–8 illustrates the FIFO method. Table 9–9 illustrates the weighted average method. FIFO calculates an average cost per equivalent unit using only the costs incurred this period and the equivalent units produced this period. The weighted average method calculates the average cost per equivalent unit using both the beginning inventory and current production. The weighted average

TABLE 9-9   **Cajun Peanut Butter Inc. Revised Calculation of Ending Work-in-Process and Cost of Units Transferred Out for March**
(Weighted Average Cost Flow)

	Units	Conversion	Peanuts	Spices	Total
		Equivalent Units			
Step 1					
Physical flow:					
Beginning work-in-process (40%)	2,000				
Units started	20,000				
Units to account for	22,000				
Ending work-in-process (30%)	1,200	360	1,200	0	
Transferred out	20,800	20,800	20,800	20,800	
Units accounted for	22,000				
Step 2					
Equivalent units of work done to date		21,160	22,000	20,800	
Costs per unit:					
Beginning work-in-process		$ 600	$3,000		
Current costs added		15,000	32,000	$ 4,000	
Total cost		$15,600	$35,000	$ 4,000	
Cost per equivalent unit		$0.7372	$1.5909	$0.1923	$2.5204
Step 3					
Total costs to account for:					
Beginning work-in-process	$3,600				
Conversion costs	15,000				
Peanuts purchased	32,000				
Cajun spices	4,000				
Total costs	$54,600				
Step 4					
Ending work-in-process	$2,174	$265	$1,909	0	
		$0.7372 × 360	$1.5909 × 1,200	$0.1923 × 0	
Transferred out:					
20,800 × $2.5204	52,424				
Total costs	$54,600*				

*Rounding error.

cost includes not just the cost of work performed this period but also the costs incurred in previous periods that are still in the beginning inventory. Total equivalent units are the sum of both the beginning WIP inventory equivalent units and the equivalent units worked this period. For example, equivalent units of peanuts (22,000) consist of 1,200 units in the ending inventory plus 20,800 units transferred out. These 22,000 units include the peanuts in the beginning inventory. The total cost in step 3 is the sum of the costs in the beginning WIP inventory and costs incurred this period. Thus, the cost per equivalent unit is a weighted average of the costs in the beginning WIP inventory and those incurred this period.

Comparing Tables 9–8 and 9–9 reveals that the FIFO and weighted average methods give very similar numbers for the ending inventory and transferred-out costs. Whenever the beginning and ending inventories are a small fraction of the units started or finished, most of the cost incurred is transferred out.

Many continuous flow plants are composed of a series of production stages, each treated as a separate process costing unit. For example, an oil refinery consists of a crude splitter, various distillers, and refractors. Intermediate products flow from one stage to another. Each stage tracks beginning and ending work-in-process inventories and transferred-out costs for material and conversion costs. The costs of units transferred out of one stage become the transferred-in costs for the next stage downstream. Thus, stringing together a series of statements similar to Table 9–8 or 9–9 lets management compute each stage's separate costs as well as the entire plant's costs.

Finally, if the process has considerable scrap or waste, it is often accounted for and reported separately, which adds to the complexity of the calculations. But the conceptual issues remain: Process cost systems assign all costs to units. These systems report average unit costs, which are a mixture of fixed and variable costs—not measures of marginal or opportunity costs.

Appendix B: Demand Shifts, Fixed Costs, and Pricing

This appendix illustrates that when volumes drop, causing average costs to rise, prices usually should be lowered, not raised. A photocopy store owner expects long-run average volume (normal volume) to be 175,000 copies per month. The store is leased for $1,000 per month, employees are paid $2,000 per month, and a copier is leased for $500 per month plus $0.005 per copy. Paper costs also are $0.005 per sheet. Each copy requires one page of paper (i.e., there is no two-sided copying). The store lease and employee costs do not vary with copy volume.

The store completes a customer order for 5,000 flyers at $0.04 per page, or $200. Assuming that taking this job did not require forgoing another job—that is, equipment and labor had excess capacity—the opportunity cost of this job was $50 (the paper at $0.005 per page and the additional copier fee at $0.005 per page). But the accounting cost of this order is $150, which incorporates some allocated overhead. The amount of overhead allocated to this job is the sum of the overhead items (store rental, labor, and copier rental) divided by normal volume for the year, multiplied by the volume for this job, or:

	Overhead Costs per Month
Office rental	$ 1,000
Labor	2,000
Copier rental	500
	$ 3,500
Divided by normal copy volume	175,000
Overhead costs per normal copy	$ 0.020
Plus: Paper costs	0.005
Additional copier charge per page	0.005
Total cost per page	$ 0.030
Times number of pages in job	5,000
Total job cost	$ 150

What does the $0.03 total cost per page represent? It is the long-run average cost. That is, at a normal volume of 175,000 copies per month, the store must charge at least $0.03 per page to break even over time. Suppose that copy volume this month falls from 175,000 copies to 100,000 copies. Overhead costs per copy increase to $0.035 (or $3,500 ÷ 100,000). Should prices be increased?

The profit-maximizing price occurs at the quantity that equates marginal cost and marginal revenue. Has marginal cost changed? No, it is still $0.01 per page. Has marginal revenue changed? Maybe—it depends on how the demand curve has shifted. Figures 9–5 and 9–6 illustrate the typical case in which price should be lowered when demand falls.

In Figure 9–5, the demand curve labeled Normal demand corresponds to 175,000 copies being demanded at a price of $0.04 per copy. This demand curve has a marginal revenue curve, Normal marginal revenue. Equating the marginal cost of $0.01 to normal marginal revenue yields the profit-maximizing copy volume (175,000 copies) and price ($0.04).

Suppose that demand has shifted to the Low demand curve in Figure 9–6. At a price of $0.04, there is now demand for only 100,000 copies. (Take the price of $0.04 and move horizontally to the Low demand curve; then move down the vertical line and read off the quantity of 100,000.) In other words, if the demand curve shifts down and the price remains at $0.04 per copy, only 100,000 copies will be sold per month.

If demand is now represented by the Low demand curve in Figure 9–6, what is the profit-maximizing price to charge? Is it higher or lower than $0.04? Remember, profit maximization occurs at the quantity where marginal revenue equals marginal cost. Marginal cost has not changed; it is still $0.01 per copy. Marginal revenue for the Low demand curve is the dashed line in Figure 9–6 called Low marginal revenue. The Low marginal revenue and Marginal cost curves intersect at the output

FIGURE 9-5

Photocopy store example

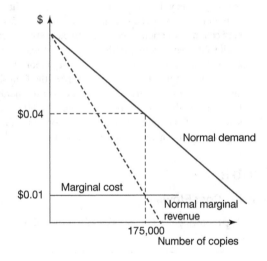

FIGURE 9-6

Photocopy store example: Reduce price when demand falls

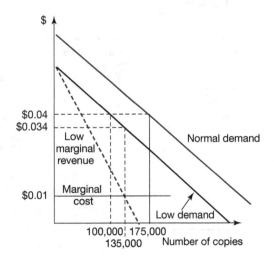

424   *Chapter 9*

TABLE 9-10   Photocopy Store Profits (Loss) at a Price of $0.04 per Copy versus $0.034 per Copy

	Price = $0.04 Copies = 100,000	Price = $0.034 Copies = 135,000
Revenue	$4,000	$4,590
Variable costs	(1,000)	(1,350)
Fixed costs	(3,500)	(3,500)
Loss	$ (500)	$ (260)

---

level of 135,000 copies per month. Following this quantity level up to the Low demand curve yields a price of about $0.034 per copy. Therefore, to maximize profits under the low demand situation, the copy store must *lower* the price from $0.04 to $0.034.

Table 9–10 compares total profits at the price of $0.04 and volume of 100,000 copies with the profits at a price of $0.034 and volume of 135,000 copies. Under both pricing scenarios, the store is losing money. However, the loss is smaller when the price is cut to $0.034 per copy. Notice that in both cases fixed costs remain constant at $3,500. Since fixed costs do not vary (by definition) between the two pricing scenarios, fixed costs are irrelevant for the *pricing decision*. But they are not irrelevant when it comes to the *shutdown decision*. Suppose the store lease and copier rental ($1,500 a month) are paid a year in advance but labor ($2,000 a month) is paid at the end of each month. Assuming that the store cannot be sublet, the firm should continue to operate until the current store and copier leases expire. It should then cease operations unless demand has increased sufficiently. Even though the store is not recovering all its fixed costs, fixed costs that have already been paid are sunk costs. Continuing to operate the store until the fixed costs (lease, copier rental, and labor) are payable again generates a positive cash flow.

Self-Study Problems

Self-Study Problem 1:   Cost Flows

The following is a job cost sheet for a special product:

Job Number 711   **Date Started**   5/26

                                                                           Date Completed 6/15

	Raw Materials				Direct Labor		
Date	*Type*	*Cost*	*Qty.*	*Amount*	*Cost/Hr.*	*Hours*	*Amount*
5/26	130	$30	6	$180	$18	5	$90
6/15	248	10	20	200	15	10	150
				$380		15	240

Total direct materials $380

Total direct labor   240

Overhead (15 direct labor hours @ $10/hour)   150

Total job cost $770

Overhead is allocated based on direct labor hours (DLH). The raw materials were in inventory before being used on job #711. The product is sold on 7/10. Identify the cost flows on each of these dates: 5/26, 6/15, and 7/10.

Solution:

Cost flows:

On 5/26: $180 from "Raw materials inventory" to "Work-in-process"
  $90 from "Labor" to "Work-in-process"
  $50 from "Overhead" to "Work-in-process" for overhead-related to direct labor hours (5 DLH × $10/DLH)

On 6/15: $200 from "Raw materials inventory" to "Work-in-process"
  $150 from "Labor" to "Work-in-process"
  $100 from "Overhead" to "Work-in-process" for overhead related to direct labor hours (10 DLH × $10/DLH)

On 6/15: $770 from "Work-in-process" to "Finished goods"

On 7/10: $770 from "Finished goods" to "Cost of goods sold"

Self-Study Problem 2:   R&R Chairs, Inc.

R&R Chairs, Inc., manufactures two types of ergonomic chairs (the basic and the executive) in two departments (frame fabrication and cushion fabrication). In planning for the coming year, the managers would like to know the production cost of each chair. The main difference between the two chairs is additional padding in the executive chair. Budgeted direct costs for each department are as follows:

Budgeted Chair Production and Cost Data

	Frame Fabrication	Cushion Fabrication	Total
Basic			
Number of chairs			225,000
Direct labor/chair	$ 7.40	$ 6.40	
Direct materials/chair	6.70	2.40	
Total	$14.10	$ 8.80	$ 22.90
Executive			
Number of chairs			192,000
Direct labor/chair	$ 7.50	$ 8.70	
Direct materials/chair	6.80	6.20	
Total	$14.30	$14.90	$ 29.20

Currently, the company uses a single plantwide overhead rate based on direct labor dollars to assign overhead costs to products. Budgeted overhead costs for the year are shown in the accompanying table.

Budgeted Overhead Costs

Rent	$1,680,000
Indirect labor	1,660,000
Indirect materials	1,125,000
Equipment lease payments	1,665,000
Total overhead	$6,130,000

426   *Chapter 9*

Required:

a. Given planned production rates of 225,000 basic chairs and 192,000 executive chairs, prepare a statement calculating the fully absorbed cost for each chair in each department.

b. Management is considering switching to departmental overhead rates. Overhead costs in frame fabrication are assigned to chairs based on direct labor dollars, whereas cushion fabrication overhead costs are assigned based on direct material dollars. Calculate separate departmental overhead rates and prepare a new statement of the fully absorbed cost per chair given the following information:

Budgeted Overhead Costs

	Frame Fabrication	*Cushion Fabrication*
Rent	$ 500,000	$1,180,000
Indirect labor	650,000	1,010,000
Indirect materials	470,000	655,000
Equipment lease payments	280,000	1,385,000
Total overhead	$1,900,000	$4,230,000

c. Explain the difference in costs between the two methods. Comment on which allocation scheme is likely to produce more accurate estimates of production costs.

Solution:

a. Plantwide overhead rate:

Total overhead	$6,130,000
Divided by direct labor dollars*	÷ $6,215,400
Overhead rate/direct labor dollar	$ 0.986

*$6,215,400 = 225,000 × ($7.40 + $6.40) + 192,000 × ($7.50 + $8.70)

	Frame Fabrication	*Cushion Fabrication*	*Total*
Basic			
Direct labor/chair	$ 7.40	$ 6.40	$13.80
Direct materials/chair	6.70	2.40	9.10
Overhead ($0.986/DL$)	7.30	6.31	13.61
Total	$21.40	$15.11	$36.51
Executive			
Direct labor/chair	$ 7.50	$ 8.70	$16.20
Direct materials/chair	6.80	6.20	13.00
Overhead ($0.986/DL$)	7.40	8.58	15.97*
Total	$21.70	$23.48	$45.17*

*$.01 rounding difference.

b. Separate departmental overhead rates:

	Frame Fabrication	Cushion Fabrication
Total overhead	$1,900,000	$4,230,000
Total direct labor dollars	÷ $3,105,000*	
Total direct material dollars		÷ $1,730,400†
Overhead rate	$ 0.612	$ 2.445

	Frame Fabrication	Cushion Fabrication	Total
Basic			
Direct labor/chair	$ 7.40	$ 6.40	$13.80
Direct materials/chair	6.70	2.40	9.10
Overhead ($0.612/DL$)	4.53		4.53
Overhead ($2.445/DM$)		5.87	5.87
Total	$18.63	$14.67	$33.30
Executive			
Direct labor/chair	$ 7.50	$ 8.70	$16.20
Direct materials/chair	6.80	6.20	13.00
Overhead ($0.612/DL$)	4.59		4.59
Overhead ($2.445/DM$)		15.16	15.16
Total	$18.89	$30.06	$48.95

*$3,105,000 = $7.40 × 225,000 + $7.50 × 192,000
†$1,730,400 = $2.40 × 225,000 + $6.20 × 192,000

c. Going from a single plant overhead rate to separate department rates causes the basic chair's expected cost to fall $3.21 per chair and the executive chair's expected cost to rise $3.78 per chair. The basic chair's cost falls about 9 percent and the executive chair's cost rises about 8 percent. The reason for these changes is as follows. Cushion fabrication contains much of the overhead of the factory. Executive chairs contain a higher fraction of direct materials cost than direct labor cost. If all the overhead is allocated based on direct labor dollars, basic chairs bear a larger fraction of the overhead costs than if more of the overhead, in particular the cushion fabrication costs, is assigned to executive chairs. If cushion fabrication costs vary more with direct materials than direct labor, then the separate department overhead rates give a more accurate estimate of product costs than a single plantwide rate. However, if direct labor is the overhead cost driver in the cushion fabrication department, then a single overhead rate is likely to be more accurate.

Problems

P 9–1: Equivalent Units (See Appendix A)

Department 100 is the first step in the firm's manufacturing process. Data for the current quarter's operations are as follows:

	Number of Units
Beginning work-in-process (70% complete)	30,000
Units started this quarter	580,000
Units completed this quarter and transferred out	550,000
Ending work-in-process (60% complete)	60,000

Chapter 9

Required:

Materials are added at the beginning of the process. Conversion costs (labor and capital costs) are incurred uniformly. The firm uses the FIFO method of inventory accounting. How many equivalent units of conversion cost were used in the current quarter in Department 100?

P 9–2: Allington Screen Plant

The Allington Screen Plant of Allington Windows manufactures new and replacement screens. The plant produces more than 500 different screen sizes and offers four different aluminum frame colors. Plant overhead is absorbed to each screen produced using the square inches of the screen as the allocation base. (For example, a screen with dimensions $20\frac{7}{32}$ width $\times$ $38\frac{21}{32}$ height has 781.581 square inches.) The single plantwide overhead rate, estimated before the year begins, is based on a flexible budget (budgeted fixed overhead plus budgeted variable overhead) divided by budgeted volume. Volume is measured in square inches of the screens produced. The following table summarizes operations for the year:

Budgeted variable overhead (per sq. in.)	$0.01
Actual overhead incurred	$4,287,482
Budgeted fixed overhead	$3,594,240
Overabsorbed overhead	$797,759
Actual volume (sq. in.)	141,256,700

Required:

Calculate the budgeted volume amount (in screen square inches) Allington Screen Plant used in computing the plantwide overhead rate for the year.

P 9–3: Durnstein Schnapps

Durnstein Schnapps produces three types of schnapps from locally grown Austrian pears, plums, and cherries. Schnapps is a clear, colorless beverage distilled from fermented fruit that normally contains about 40 percent alcohol. The pear and plum schnapps are produced using an identical process whereby the pears and plums are fermented and then distilled. The cherry schnapps employs a similar production process but requires more direct labor to produce the unique and highly prized Durnstein Cherry Schnapps. Each variety of schnapps (pears, plums, and cherries) is produced in batches of 500 liters and then bottled.

Durnstein Schnapps uses an absorption costing system to assign overhead to its three products for inventory costing. A single, predetermined, plantwide overhead rate is computed using a flexible manufacturing overhead budget. Variable manufacturing overhead is budgeted to be €16.00 per direct labor hour and fixed manufacturing overhead is budgeted to be €845,000 for the year. The following table summarizes budgeted and operating data for the last fiscal year.

	Pear	*Plum*	*Cherry*
Actual batches	520	370	210
Budgeted number of batches	500	400	200
Actual direct hours per batch	17	15	34
Budgeted direct labor hours per batch	18	18	35

Durnstein Schnaps incurred actual manufacturing overhead last year of €1,250,500.

Required:

a. Calculate Durnstein Schnapp's plantwide overhead rate for last year.

b. One batch of plum schnapps used 20 direct labor hours. How much manufacturing overhead was absorbed by this one batch?

c. How much over/underabsorbed overhead did Durnstein Schnapps have last year?

d. Recommend/discuss how Durnstein Schnapps is likely to account for the over/underabsorbed overhead you calculated in part (c).

P 9–4: MacGiver Brass

MacGiver Brass is a brass plating firm with sales of $8 million and profits before taxes of $625,000. MacGiver has a loan outstanding at its local bank for working capital purposes. As the loan officer reviewing MacGiver's loan application, you are charged with making a recommendation as to whether the $608,000 loan should be renewed for another year.

Upon reviewing MacGiver's most recent annual report, you find the following footnote: "Underabsorbed overhead of $462,000 was prorated to inventories (2/3) and cost of goods sold (1/3)."

Required:

a. How should you evaluate MacGiver's annual report in light of this footnote? In particular, how does this footnote affect your recommendation regarding the loan?

b. In preparing for your meeting with MacGiver's president and chief financial officer, what questions do you want to ask regarding this footnote?

P 9–5: Pool Scrubbers

Pool Scrubbers manufactures three different models of swimming pool cleaners (710, 720, and 830). These are sophisticated, computer-controlled, programmed cleaners that scrub and vacuum the pool's bottom, walls, and steps and provide supplemental filtration of pool water. The three models differ in their capacity and programmability.

Pool Scrubbers uses an absorption costing system that absorbs manufacturing overhead to the three models based on direct labor hours. The single plantwide manufacturing overhead rate is predetermined before the beginning of the fiscal year using a flexible manufacturing overhead budget. Variable manufacturing overhead is budgeted to be $3.00 per direct labor hour, and fixed manufacturing overhead is budgeted to be $1.4 million. Direct labor is budgeted at $25 per direct labor hour. The following table summarizes the budgeted and actual results of operation for the year:

	Models		
	710	*720*	*830*
Actual number of units produced	5,100	3,900	2,200
Actual DL hours per unit	3.10	4.20	5.90
Budgeted wholesale price	$550	$750	$1,050
Budgeted direct labor hours per scrubber	3.00	4.00	6.00
Budgeted direct materials	$95	$125	$175
Budgeted production (units)	5,000	4,000	2,000
Budgeted DL cost (@ $25 per DL hour)	$75	$100	$150

Required:

a. Calculate the firmwide overhead rate for the year (round to four decimals). The overhead rate is calculated before the fiscal year begins.

b. A batch of 100 units of model 720 is produced using 405 direct labor hours. How much overhead is absorbed by this batch of 100 model 720s?

c. Actual overhead incurred during the year was $1,520,500. Calculate the amount of over- or underabsorbed overhead for the year.

d. Scrubbers writes off any over/underabsorbed overhead to cost of goods sold. What is the effect on earnings of writing off the over/underabsorbed overhead calculated in part (c) on net income? In other words, does net income increase or decrease relative to what net income was prior to the write-off of the over/underabsorbed overhead calculated in part (c)?

430   *Chapter 9*

P 9–6:   Thermalloy

Thermalloy makes extruded aluminum heat sinks that are small devices that help cool semiconductors and printed circuit boards. Thermalloy uses an absorption costing system whereby all fixed and variable manufacturing overhead is absorbed to manufactured products via a single plantwide overhead rate that is estimated at the beginning of the year using a flexible manufacturing budget. Volume is measured in direct labor hours. The following data summarize Thermalloy's operations for the year:

Overabsorbed overhead	$121,402
Budgeted variable overhead/DL hour	$9.00
Actual direct labor hours	183,500
Budgeted fixed overhead	$3,500,000
Actual overhead incurred	$5,200,098
Budgeted direct labor hours	???

Required:

Calculate Thermalloy's budgeted direct labor hours.

P 9–7:   Lys Wheels

Lys Wheels manufactures high-performance mountain bikes. Lys uses a predetermined overhead rate based on direct labor hours to absorb overhead to mountain bikes. For the last fiscal year, the firm had the following operating data:

Actual direct labor hours	19,000
Underabsorbed overhead	$ 7,000
Actual overhead incurred	$197,000
Budgeted overhead	$210,000

Required:

What was Lys's budgeted volume last year?

P 9–8:   Ware Paper Box

Ware Paper Box manufactures corrugated paper boxes. It uses a job order costing system. Operating data for February and March are as follows:

Job	Date Started	Date Finished	Date Sold	Total Manufacturing Cost as of 2/28	Total Manufacturing Cost in March*
613	1/28	2/5	2/15	$12,500	
614	2/5	2/17	2/20	17,200	
615	2/20	2/27	3/5	18,500	
616	2/25	3/10	3/20	10,100	$13,400
734	2/21	3/15	4/1	4,300	8,200
735	2/27	4/1	4/9	9,100	2,400
736	3/2	3/22	4/19		16,300
617	3/15	3/20	3/26		19,200
618	3/22	4/5	4/15		14,400

*Manufacturing costs incurred only in March. Does not include any manufacturing costs incurred in prior months.

The factory was closed due to a labor strike prior to January 28, when job #613 was started. There were no other jobs in the plant at that time.

Required:

Calculate the following amounts:

    a. Work-in-process inventory as of 2/28.

    b. Work-in-process inventory as of 3/31.

    c. Finished goods inventory as of 2/28.

    d. Finished goods inventory as of 3/31.

    e. Cost of goods sold for February.

    f. Cost of goods sold for March.

P 9–9: DeJure Scents (See Appendix A)

DeJure Scents manufactures an aftershave and uses process costing. All materials are added at the beginning of the process, and conversion costs are incurred uniformly over time. In May, DeJure started 15,000 gallons. There was no beginning inventory. May's ending inventory of work-in-process was 2,000 gallons, which were 50 percent complete with respect to conversion costs.

    In May, conversion costs were $28,000 and materials costs were $45,000.

Required:

    a. Calculate the equivalent units of conversion and materials.

    b. Calculate the cost per equivalent unit of conversion and materials.

    c. Calculate the cost of the ending inventory and the cost transferred to finished goods inventory.

P 9–10: Chemtrex (See Appendix A)

Chemtrex is an agricultural chemical producer. Process costing is used in its mixing department. At the beginning of July, Chemtrex had 700,000 gallons 70 percent complete in work-in-process. During July, it started another 4,000,000 gallons and produced 3,700,000 gallons. One million gallons of ending work-in-process were 60 percent complete at the end of July. Conversion costs are incurred uniformly over the mixing process.

Required:

Calculate the number of equivalent units of conversion work performed during July.

P 9–11: Media Designs

Media Designs is a marketing firm that designs and prints customized marketing brochures. The design department designs the brochure and the printing department prints and binds it. Each department has separate overhead rates. The following estimates for the two departments were made for the calendar year 2017.

	Design	Printing
Overhead	$800,000	$500,000
Direct labor cost	$3,250,000	$410,000
Direct materials cost	$8,500	$250,000
Direct labor hours	50,000	10,000

    Media Designs uses a budgeted overhead rate to apply overhead to jobs. Direct labor hours are used to allocate overhead in the design department, and direct materials cost is used to allocate overhead in the printing department.

432   *Chapter 9*

Required:

    a. What are the overhead rates for the design and printing departments?

    b. A summary of the Matsui job follows:

	Design	Printing
Direct materials used	$3,000	$12,000
Direct labor costs	$46,200	$28,500
Direct labor hours	700	750

What are overhead costs for the Matsui job?

    1. Actual operating results for 2017 are

	Design	Printing
Overhead	$802,000	$490,000
Direct labor cost	$3,193,000	$451,500
Direct materials cost	$ 11,550	$230,000
Direct labor hours	51,500	10,500

Calculate the over/underapplied overhead for each department.

P 9–12:   Simple Plant

Simple Plant manufactures DNA test strips. Manufacturing overhead is applied to units produced using direct labor dollars as the allocation base. The overhead rate is calculated prior to the beginning of the fiscal year that runs January 1 to December 31. Simple Plant has one manufacturing employee, J. Kusic, and one overhead expense besides indirect labor, property taxes. J. Kusic's salary and fringe benefits for next year are forecast to be $50,000. Kusic is expected to work 2,000 hours at a cost of $25 per hour ($50,000/2,000). Eighty percent of Kusic's time is budgeted to be direct labor, and the remainder is budgeted to be indirect labor. Property taxes are projected to be $110,000. There was no beginning balance of work-in-process on January 1.

Required:

    a. Calculate Simple Plant's overhead rate for next year.

    b. On January 2, the first working day of the new fiscal year, Kusic works eight hours (five hours on manufacturing test strips and three hours waiting for raw materials to arrive). Each day, Simple Plant posts all entries (transactions) to the accounts. What are the balances in the Overhead account and the Work-in-Process account at the close of business on January 2?

    c. At the end of the year, Kusic's salary and benefits are $50,000, with $44,000 of the total charged to test strips manufactured. Kusic worked 2,000 hours during the year. Property taxes paid during the year amounted to $103,000. What, if any, is the balance in the overhead account before an adjusting entry is made to transfer the balance to other accounts?

P 9–13:   Rick's Bags

Rick's Bags manufactures both golf bags and tennis totes. Fixed manufacturing overhead is budgeted to be $187,200, variable manufacturing overhead is budgeted to be $1.10 per direct labor hour, and fixed selling and administration costs are budgeted to be $346,000. Each golf bag is expected to use 2.5 direct labor hours and each tennis tote is expected to use 1.8 direct labor hours. Planned production consists of 12,000 golf bags and 18,000 tennis totes.

During the year, 34,060 direct labor hours are used to make golf bags and 16,250 direct labor hours are used to make tennis totes. Manufacturing overhead incurred during the year was $207,500. Overhead is absorbed into products using actual direct labor hours.

Required:

    a. Calculate the manufacturing overhead rate used to absorb overhead to golf bags and tennis totes.

    b. A batch of tennis totes is produced in May. The batch uses 1,900 direct labor hours. How much overhead is charged to this batch of tennis totes?

    c. Calculate the amount of over/underabsorbed overhead at the end of the year.

    d. Describe in nontechnical terms what the over/underabsorbed overhead calculated in part (*c*) means.

P 9–14: Unknown Company

Compute the unknowns:

Sales	$100,000
Direct materials used	29,000
Direct labor	10,000
Variable selling and administration expenses	16,000
Fixed manufacturing overhead	30,000
Fixed selling and administration expenses	9,000
Gross profit	?
Opening material inventory	3,000
Closing material inventory	10,000
Variable manufacturing overhead	?
Purchase of direct material	?
Cost of goods manufactured	?
Net income	1,000

There is no opening or closing finished goods or work-in-process inventory.

P 9–15: Luxor Fashions

Luxor Fashions manufactures very high-quality traditional men's suits that are sold in exclusive men's stores around the world. Luxor opened a new factory in Italy two years ago to employ the best Italian tailors to cut, assemble, and stitch high-fashion mens' business attire. The business plan for the new factory called for 250 tailors, each working 2,000 hours per year. Overhead is allocated to individual suits based on the number of direct labor hours in the suit. Luxor uses a flexible overhead budget to estimate its overhead rate. Fixed manufacturing overhead next year is budgeted at 26.05 million euros, and variable manufacturing overhead is budgeted at 20 euros per direct labor hour. The following table provides next year's production schedule and the number of expected (budgeted) direct labor hours per suit style:

Luxor Fashions
Planned Production Schedule and Budgeted
Direct Labor Hours per Suit Style Next Year

Suit Model	Production Budget Model (Number of Suits)	Budgeted Direct Labor Hours per Suit
#108	17,000	2.0
#211	43,000	3.0
#243	62,000	1.0
#368	49,000	4.0
#789	40,000	2.5

434   *Chapter 9*

Required:

    a. Calculate Luxor's overhead rate for next year using expected volume.

    b. Calculate Luxor's overhead rate for next year using normal volume.

    c. Discuss the advantages and disadvantages of using expected volume in calculating factory overhead rates.

    d. Which method (expected or normal volume) is more widely used?

    e. What conclusions do you draw from your answer in part (*d*)?

P 9–16:   Advanced Medical

Advanced Medical (AM) manufactures four different blood oxygen level monitors (A300, B400, C500, and D600) at its Denver plant. The Denver plant opened four years ago and was built with the expectation of producing annually 4,000, 5,000, 6,000, and 7,000 of the A300, B400, C500, and D600 monitors, respectively. However, a recession has reduced the demand for all medical devices. The following table reports the number of units of each monitor AM has sold (Last Year and This Year) and expects to sell Next Year.

Production (units)	A300	B400	C500	D600
Last Year	3,700	4,600	5,800	6,900
This Year	3,500	4,500	6,400	6,800
Next Year	3,400	4,400	5,500	6,700

AM uses a flexible budget to estimate its manufacturing overhead and manufacturing overhead rate. Overhead is assigned to the four monitors using direct labor dollars (i.e., manufacturing volume is measured as direct labor dollars). For Next Year, AM budgets $6.5 million for fixed manufacturing overhead and $0.90 per direct labor dollar for variable overhead. Budgeted direct labor dollars per monitor are $25, $24, $23, and $22 for the A300, B400, C500, and D600 monitors, respectively.

Required:

    a. Calculate AM's budgeted manufacturing volume for Next Year.

    b. Using your budgeted manufacturing volume in part (*a*), compute AM's manufacturing overhead rate for Next Year.

    c. Discuss how you chose Next Year's budgeted volume in part (*a*). In other words, what are the advantages and disadvantages of the method you used to compute Next Year's budgeted manufacturing volume?

P 9–17:   Dead Eye Putters

Dead Eye Putters manufactures golf putters in three models: P450, Q550, and R650. Manufacturing overhead is assigned to each putter model using a predetermined overhead rate and the direct labor hours actually used in manufacturing each putter model. The firm calculates the overhead rate before the year begins using a flexible budget. Budgeted volume is measured using direct labor hours.

The following data summarize the budgeted and actual production for the fiscal year:

	P450	Q550	R650
Budgeted production (units)	60,000	50,000	40,000
Budgeted direct labor hours per unit	0.75	1.00	1.25
Actual production (units)	58,000	51,000	35,000
Actual direct labor hours per unit	0.77	1.10	1.18

After the fiscal year ends, Dead Eye Putters reports $884,713 underabsorbed overhead and actual overhead incurred of $25,875,026. Variable overhead was budgeted to be $3.50 per direct labor hour.

Required:

    a. Compute Dead Eye Putter's manufacturing overhead rate used during the year.

    b. What budgeted fixed overhead did Dead Eye Putters use in computing its manufacturing overhead rate for the year?

P 9–18: Welding Robots

The frame-welding department of a large automotive company welds car frames as they pass down the assembly line. Four computer-controlled robots make the welds on each frame simultaneously. When installed last year, each robot was expected to have a five-year useful life before becoming obsolete and being replaced by newer, faster models with more advanced electronics. Over its life, each robot is expected to make 100 million welds. The robots cost $8 million apiece and have no salvage value at the end of their useful lives after the cost of dismantling and removing them is taken into consideration.

The firm has a traditional absorption costing system that costs each frame. The accounting system supports decision making and control. Straight-line depreciation is used for both internal and external reporting, and accelerated depreciation is used for taxes. As frames move through the welding stations, they are charged based on the number of welds made on each frame. Different car frames require different numbers of welds, with some frame models requiring up to 1,000 welds. Welds cost $0.11 each. This charge is set at the beginning of the year by estimating the fixed and variable costs in the welding department. Accounting determines the expected number of welds projected for the year by taking the projected number of frames times the number of welds per frame. The expected number of welds is used to estimate total costs in the welding department. The cost per weld is then the ratio of the projected welding costs to the expected number of welds. Seventy-two million welds were projected for the current year.

The following statement illustrates the computation of the charge per weld:

Charge per Weld, Current Year

	Variable Costs (at 72 Million Welds)	Fixed Costs	Total Costs
Depreciation*		$ 6,400,000	$ 6,400,000
Welding rods	$ 700,000		700,000
Engineering services	300,000	200,000	500,000
Electricity	180,000		180,000
Factory overhead	85,000	55,000	140,000
Total	$ 1,265,000	$ 6,655,000	$ 7,920,000
÷ Expected number of welds	72,000,000	72,000,000	72,000,000
Cost per weld	$ 0.0176	$ 0.0924	$ 0.1100

*Depreciation per year = 4 robots × $8 million per robot ÷ 5-year life.

After reviewing the preceding statement, Amy Miller, manager of the body fabricating division (which includes the welding department), made the following remarks:

I know we use straight-line depreciation to calculate the depreciation component of the cost per weld now. But it would seem to make a lot of sense to compute robot depreciation using units-of-production depreciation. Each robot cost $8 million and was expected to perform 100 million welds over its useful life. That comes to 8¢ per weld. Thus, we should charge each weld at 8¢ plus the remaining fixed and variable costs as calculated on this statement. If I back out the $6.4 million depreciation from the earlier figures and recompute the fixed costs per weld at

72 million welds, I get $255,000 divided by 72 million, or $0.00354. Add this to the variable cost per weld of $0.0176 plus the 8¢ depreciation and our cost per weld is $0.1011 per weld, not the 11¢ now. This reduces our costs on our complicated frames by as much as $10.

The real advantage of using units-of-production depreciation, in my opinion, is that depreciation becomes a variable cost. This has real advantages because, when you lower your fixed costs, your break-even point is lower. Operating leverage is lower, and thus the company's overall risk is reduced.

I think we should go to the plant controller and see if we can convince him to use a more realistic basis for calculating the depreciation costs of the robots.

Required:

Do you agree with Amy Miller's proposal?

P 9–19:   HexBugs

HexBug manufactures and sells small robotic creatures that change direction when they encounter obstacles in their path. These battery-powered toys, some radio-controlled, sell for retail prices ranging from $6 to $25. HexBugs come in three styles: nanos (about an inch long), antes (about two inches long), and crabs (about three inches long). All three HexBugs are manufactured in a common manufacturing site. HexBug uses an absorption costing system that absorbs manufacturing overhead to the three styles based on direct material dollars. The single plantwide manufacturing overhead rate is predetermined prior to the beginning of the fiscal year using a flexible manufacturing overhead budget. Variable manufacturing overhead is budgeted to be $0.720 per direct material dollar, and annual fixed manufacturing overhead is budgeted to be $6.5 million. All three styles of Hexbugs are produced in batches of 1,000 bugs. The following table summarizes the budgeted and actual results of operation for the year:

Hexbug Styles	Nano	Ante	Crab
Actual number of units produced (000s)	7,100	4,400	2,200
Budgeted variable distribution cost per 1000	$100	$250	$310
Budgeted production (000s)	6,350	4,800	2,300
Budgeted direct labor per 1000	$50	$150	$200
Price per 1000	$2,200	$6,300	$7,200
Actual direct material per unit per 1000	$740	$1,800	$2,300
Budgeted direct material per 1000	$750	$1,730	$2,130

Required:

   a. Calculate the firmwide overhead rate for the year.
   b. A batch of 1,000 Antes was produced in March that incurred $145 of direct labor and $1,650 of direct materials. How much overhead is absorbed by this batch of Antes produced in March?
   c. Actual overhead incurred during the year was $23,586,000. Calculate the amount of over- or underabsorbed overhead for the year.
   d. HexBug writes off any over/underabsorbed overhead to cost of goods sold. What is the effect on earnings of writing off the over/underabsorbed overhead calculated in part (c) on net income? In other words, does net income increase or decrease relative to what net income was prior to the write-off of the over/underabsorbed overhead calculated in part (c)?

P 9–20:   Specialized Surgical Instruments

Specialized Surgical Instruments (SSI) manufactures four surgical implants. SSI uses an absorption costing system to allocate manufacturing overhead to its four products. Direct labor hours are used as the allocation base. The annual budgeted overhead rate is predetermined using a flexible budget. Fixed overhead is budgeted at $580,000 for the current year. The following table summarizes the budgeted number of units of each of the four implants, the budgeted number of direct labor hours per implant, and the actual direct labor hours used to produce each of the four implant models for the current year.

	(Current Year)			
	VX4	*VX8*	*CMA*	*ALX*
Budgeted direct labor hours per unit	3	2	4	5
Budgeted units	5,000	4,500	3,500	2,400
Actual volume (direct labor hours)	13,950	8,500	14,250	10,800

At the end of the current year, actual manufacturing overhead incurred was $1,258,300 and manufacturing overhead was underabsorbed by $184,800.

Required:

What was SSI's budgeted variable overhead rate per direct labor hour in the current year? (Show calculations.)

P 9–21: Pebble Beach Sandals

Pebble Beach Sandals has designed and patented a luxury golf sandal for both men and women. The unique handmade designs include spikes and cleats to prevent the golfer from slipping during the swing. The sandal is made from sheepskin, creating comfortable and distinctive footwear sold directly to wholesalers who then sell them to exclusive golf shops for retail prices starting at $400.

The sandals are manufactured in the United States and sold in the United States and Europe through two dedicated sales divisions. The United States and EU sales divisions are organized as separate profit centers with decision rights to set prices in their respective geographic territories. The U.S. factory is a cost center that produces the sandals and transfers them to the two sales divisions. Each sales division is charged the full manufacturing cost of the sandals (direct labor, direct materials, and overhead). All the sandals produced, both men's and women's styles, and all the various models contain similar amounts of direct labor and direct material. The only difference between the U.S. and EU sandals is the sizing and the size labels stitched into the sandals. Hence, volume in the plant is measured as pairs of sandals manufactured.

This year's manufacturing cost of Pebble Beach sandals is given by the following table:

Direct labor	$ 38
Direct material	44
Variable overhead	9
Allocated fixed manufacturing overhead*	39
Total cost	$130

*Based on expected volume of 17,400 sandals and fixed manufacturing overhead of $678,600.

The U.S. plant was built with a capacity to produce between 16,000 and 20,000 sandals per year and a long-run expected volume of 18,000 sandals.

The U.S. sales division faces the following demand curve for sandals:

Price*	Quantity
$260	7,200
255	7,600
250	8,000
245	8,400
240	8,800
235	9,200

*Price = 350 − (1/80) equality.

Besides paying the manufacturing plant's transfer cost of the sandals ($130 per pair), the U.S. sales division has its own variable costs of $20 per pair and incurs fixed costs per year of $700,000.

Required:

a. In order to maximize its own profits (after paying the manufacturing plant's transfer cost of $130), how many pairs of sandals will the U.S. sales division order and expect to sell this year? Show calculations.

b. Next year, the U.S. sales division expects its variable costs per pair to remain at $20 and its fixed costs to remain at $700,000 per year. However, due to a sharp reduction in EU demand caused by a recession, the projected combined demand from the U.S. and EU sales divisions for sandals falls from the current level of 17,400 sandals to 14,200. The plant's budgeted direct labor, direct materials, variable overhead, and fixed overhead will remain the same as this year's amounts, but the allocated fixed overhead per pair of sandals will rise due to the lower projected volumes. Compute next year's allocated fixed manufacturing overhead per pair of sandals and the total cost that will be used as the transfer cost based on next year's projected volume. (Round all costs to the nearest dollar.)

c. Using the transfer cost you computed in part (b), how many pairs of sandals will the U.S. sales division order next year? Show calculations.

d. Does the number of pairs of sandals ordered by the U.S. sales division maximize the profits (net cash flows) of Pebble Beach Sandals? Explain why or why not.

e. What suggestions would you offer management to increase Pebble Beach Sandals' shareholder value?

P 9–22: NerfyGuns

NerfyGuns manufactures and sells battery-powered guns that shoot soft pelts retailing for prices ranging from $6 to $25. NerfyGuns come in three styles: pistols, rifles, and assaults. All three NerfyGuns are manufactured in a common manufacturing site. NerfyGuns uses an absorption costing system that absorbs manufacturing overhead to the three styles based on direct material dollars. The single plantwide manufacturing overhead rate is predetermined prior to the beginning of the fiscal year using a flexible manufacturing overhead budget. Variable manufacturing overhead is budgeted to be $0.720 per direct material dollar, and annual fixed manufacturing overhead is budgeted to be $6.5 million. All three styles of NerfyGuns are produced in batches of 1,000 guns. The following table summarizes the budgeted and actual results of operation for the year:

NerfyGuns Styles	Pistol	Rifle	Assault
Actual number of units produced (000s)	7,100	4,400	2,200
Budgeted variable distribution cost per 1000	$100	$250	$310
Budgeted production (000s)	6,350	4,800	2,300
Budgeted direct labor per 1000	$50	$150	$200
Price per 1000	$2,200	$6,300	$7,200
Actual direct material per unit per 1000	$740	$1,800	$2,300
Budgeted direct material per 1000	$750	$1,730	$2,130

Required:

a. Calculate the firmwide overhead rate for the year.

b. A batch of 1,000 Rifles was produced in March that incurred $145 of direct labor and $1650 of direct materials. How much overhead is absorbed by this batch of Rifles produced in March?

c. Actual overhead incurred during the year was $23,586,000. Calculate the amount of over- or underabsorbed overhead for the year.

d. NerfyGuns writes off any over/underabsorbed overhead to cost of goods sold. What is the effect on earnings of writing off the over/underabsorbed overhead calculated in part (c) on net income? In other words, does net income increase or decrease relative to what net income was prior to the write-off of the over/underabsorbed overhead calculated in part (c)?

P 9–23:   Maya Jewelry

Maya Jewelry is a not-for-profit firm in Miami that employs recent immigrants from Guatemala to produce Mayan-style jewelry that is sold exclusively in the United States. Profits from Maya Jewelry support the immigration, settlement, support, education, and housing of Guatemalans in the United States. Maya produces two types of products: bracelets and necklaces, both made from silver and semi-precious stones. Guatemalan artisans hand-assemble the jewelry using native Central American Indian motifs by Guatemalan designers.

Although each bracelet and necklace is unique and slightly different depending on the precious stones and the crafter, each bracelet and necklace should conform to the following budgeted costs for next year:

(per jewelry item)	Bracelet	Necklace
Budgeted variable selling cost	$11.50	$17.35
Budgeted direct materials	$53.85	$78.25
Budgeted direct labor hours	3	7

Maya expects to produce 4,550 bracelets and 1,720 necklaces next year, and budgets direct labor cost (i.e., its artisans who produce both bracelets and necklaces) of $16.00 per direct labor hour. Fixed manufacturing overhead is budgeted at $675,000, and fixed selling costs are budgeted at $125,000. Variable manufacturing overhead is budgeted at $1.75 per direct labor hour. Maya uses a flexible budget to estimate budgeted manufacturing overhead, and computes a plantwide overhead rate using direct labor hours as the allocation base.

Required:

a. Compute Maya's overhead rate for next year.

b. During the first week of the next year, Maya produces 85 bracelets and 37 necklaces. The bracelets required 268 direct labor hours, and the necklaces required 264 direct labor hours. How much manufacturing overhead will be absorbed into Work-in-Process inventories during the first week of next year?

c. During the year, Maya produced 4,800 necklaces using, on average, 3.12 direct labor hours and 1,670 necklaces using, on average, 6.82 direct labor hours per necklace. Total manufacturing overhead incurred during the year amounted to $733,756. Calculate the over- or underabsorbed overhead for the year.

d. Early in January, an Australian jewelry company with 28 stores in Australia comes to Maya with an offer to purchase 500 bracelets for $130 each and 250 necklaces for $215 each. Moreover, the Australian company is prepared to sign a contract that it will not resell the Maya jewelry back into the United States. Maya determines that it has enough capacity to accept the Australian offer and that accepting the offer does not alter any of Maya's budgeted costs. Moreover, because Maya sells its jewelry directly to the Australian company, it will not have to incur any selling expenses. Should Maya accept the offer? (Provide computations to support your decision.)

P 9–24:   Kitchen Rite

Kitchen Rite is considering outsourcing the production of a steel chassis that is used in a kitchen appliance. Two thousand chassis are produced per month. An outside vendor will supply an identical chassis for $9.90. The chassis is manufactured in two steps. A stamping press punches out the part from sheet metal, bends the sides, and cuts holes in it, all in one operation. Then a welding machine welds the corners. Both the welding and stamping machines are used to produce only this one chassis model. The following job order cost sheet summarizes the costs of producing a single chassis.

	Cost per Unit
Steel plate	$ 4.75
Direct labor:	
Stamping ($20/hour)	1.60
Welding ($30/hour)	2.50
Overhead:	
Stamping (depreciation)	3.60
Welding (lease payment)	2.15
General plant	5.90
	$20.50

The stamping machine is old and has little economic value. A used equipment dealer is willing to remove the machine and haul it away at no cost. The stamping machine was purchased 13 years ago for $1,728,000. For both tax and reporting purposes, it is being depreciated using a 20-year life, straight-line method, and it has zero salvage value. The welding machine is leased for $4,300 per month, and the lease can be canceled at any time and the machine returned. However, an early termination penalty of $1,800 per month for the next 42 months must be paid.

General plant overhead consists primarily of the allocated cost of depreciation on the plant, property taxes, and fire insurance on the plant. Kitchen Rite currently has excess plant space. The manufacturing space freed up if the chassis is outsourced has no other use.

Employees are unionized and have a clause in their contract that prevents the firm from firing them if their jobs are eliminated due to outsourcing. The employees working on the stamping machine will be placed on indefinite furlough at 75 percent of their current pay. The employees operating the welding machine can be reassigned to other positions in the firm as job openings occur. Given the high demand for welders, these reassignments will occur within a few weeks of outsourcing the chassis.

Kitchen Rite has a tax loss for the current and the previous two years.

Required:

Should Kitchen Rite outsource the chassis? Support your recommendation with a clear financial analysis of the facts.

P 9–25:   Frames Inc.

Frames Inc. manufactures two types of metal frames: large and small. Steel angle iron is first cut to the appropriate sizes; the pieces are then welded together to form the frames. The process involves a high degree of automation. There is considerable indirect labor by skilled technicians and engineers who maintain the automated equipment. There are two manufacturing departments: cutting and welding. The following report details the actual costs of production for the year:

FRAMES INC.
Year Ending 12/31

Direct Costs			
Frame Type	*Units Produced*	*Direct Labor*	*Direct Materials*
Large	10,000	$ 480,000	$950,000
Small	30,000	1,140,000	800,000

Overhead Costs by Department

Overhead Costs	Cutting	Welding	Total
Utilities	$ 58,000	$174,000	$ 232,000
Indirect labor	430,000	480,000	910,000
General factory costs			150,000
Total overhead costs			$1,292,000

Kilowatt-Hours (000s)

Frame Type	Cutting	Welding	Total
Large	530	1,040	1,570
Small	910	1,200	2,110
Total kilowatt-hours	1,440	2,240	3,680

Required:

a. Compute the unit costs of large frames and small frames for the year using a single factorywide overhead rate. The factorywide overhead allocation base is direct labor cost.

b. Compute the unit costs of large frames and small frames for the year using different overhead rates for utilities, indirect labor, and general factory costs. Utility costs and indirect labor costs are allocated to frames using kilowatt-hours. General factory costs are allocated to frames using direct costs (the sum of direct labor and direct materials).

c. Compute the unit costs of large frames and small frames for the year using departmental overhead rates for the cutting and welding departments. General factory overhead costs are evenly divided between the two departments before departmental overhead is allocated to the frames. Cutting department overhead costs are allocated based on direct materials costs; welding department overhead costs are allocated based on kilowatt-hours in the welding department.

d. Analyze why different unit costs result from the different methods of allocating overhead costs to the products. Which method is best?

P 9–26:   Hurst Mats

Hurst Mats manufactures custom replacement floor mats for automobiles. The floor mats are made of spun nylon on highly automated, expensive machinery. Hurst manufactures two mat styles: Plush and Deluxe. Hurst's unionized work force makes it difficult for Hurst to compete on price. So far, it has been able to successfully compete on quality, innovative design, and delivery schedule. However, the leaders of Hurst's union are aggressive and are seeking additional work-related job guarantees. Hurst management would like to reduce its dependence on unionized labor.

Hurst's manufacturing process is overhead-driven; most of the overhead arises from the common machinery that produces the Plush and Deluxe floor mats. Nonunionized engineers and technicians maintain the equipment. Expensive lubricants and filters are required to operate the machines, which require large amounts of electricity and natural gas. Each mat style is produced in batches that consist of 10 mats per batch. Plush and Deluxe do not put differential demands on the equipment other than through the amount of machine time required to produce each batch of mats. The following table summarizes the operating data for each mat style:

	Plush	Deluxe
Machine minutes per batch of 10 mats	12	9
Direct labor per batch of 10 mats	$4	$6
Direct material per batch of 10 mats	$7	$5
Number of batches per year	14,000	9,000

442   *Chapter 9*

Overhead is allocated to the two mat styles using a predetermined overhead rate estimated from a flexible budget at the beginning of the year. Fixed overhead is estimated to be $680,000, and variable overhead is estimated to be $1.50 per machine minute. Management is debating whether to use machine minutes or direct labor cost as the overhead allocation base to allocate overhead to the two mat styles.

Required:

a. Calculate two overhead rates. The first uses machine minutes as the allocation base, and the second overhead rate uses direct labor cost as the allocation base. Round both overhead rates to two decimals.

b. Calculate the *total* product cost per batch of Plush and Deluxe mats using the two overhead rates calculated in part (*a*).

c. Discuss the advantages and disadvantages of using machine minutes or direct labor cost as the allocation base for assigning overhead to the two mat styles.

P 9–27: Mutual Fund Company

Mutual Fund Company (MFC) is considering centralizing its overnight mail function. Five departments within MFC use overnight mail service: trades processing, trades verifications, securities processing, accounts control, and customer service. Although these departments send different types of packages (weight and content), they often send packages to the same destinations. Currently, each of these departments independently contracts for overnight mail service. The five departments' present rates are:

Present Rates per Package

	Number of Pounds in Package				
Department	*1*	*2*	*3*	*4*	*5*
Trades processing	$ 7.25	$ 8.50	$ 9.75	$11.00	$12.25
Trades verifications	7.75	8.75	9.75	10.75	11.75
Securities processing	8.00	9.50	11.00	12.50	14.00
Accounts control	10.00	12.00	14.00	15.50	16.50
Customer service	16.00	18.00	20.00	22.00	24.00

MFC has requested that each of the five departments submit an estimate of its overnight mail for the coming year. The departments' estimates are as follows:

Usage Estimates

	Packages per Day	*Annual Number of Packages**	*Average Weight per Package*	*Pounds per Year*
Trades processing	100	25,000	5 lbs.	125,000
Trades verifications	100	25,000	3 lbs.	75,000
Securities processing	100	25,000	2 lbs.	50,000
Accounts control	50	12,500	5 lbs.	62,500
Customer service	10	2,500	1 lb.	2,500
Total	360	90,000		315,000

*Based on 250 days per year.

Using these volume estimates, MFC was able to negotiate the following corporate rates with EXP Overnight Express:

Corporate Rates per Package

Weight (Pounds)	Rate	Weight (Pounds)	Rate
1	$ 7.75	6	$12.55
2	8.70	7	13.55
3	9.65	8	14.50
4	10.65	9	15.45
5	11.60	10	16.45

The centralized overnight mail unit would be run as a cost center. All expenses would be charged back to the five departments. The chargebacks would have two components:

1. The corporate rate per package charged by EXP (based on weight).
2. An overhead allocation per package.

MFC plans to use a prospective overhead rate. Pounds per package will be used as the allocation base. As each package comes in, overhead will be charged. The rate will be set at the beginning of the year, allowing the overnight mail service to be costed as it is used. The common costs that make up overhead are labor, supervision, and other expenses as follows:

Overhead Expenses

3 employees @ $11,000 per person, per year	$33,000
1 supervisor @ $18,000 per year	18,000
Other costs (rent, utilities, etc.)	24,000
Total overhead	$75,000

At this time, there is much controversy and skepticism about the centralization of the overnight mail function. The managers of trades processing and trades verifications are most opposed to the proposed system. They claim not only that it is unfair but also that the annual cost savings created by this centralized system do not justify a change.

Required:

a. Calculate the overhead allocation rate that would be used with the centralized system.
b. Calculate the estimated overall cost and department cost of MFC's overnight mail service under both the present system and the proposed centralized system.
c. Discuss why the managers of trades processing and trades verifications are opposed to the proposed centralized system. Do you agree with their criticisms?
d. Evaluate the proposed method of allocating overhead under the centralized system. Is there a better method for allocating cost? If so, what is it?
e. Do you think the proposed centralized system can be improved? If so, how?

P 9–28: Amalfi Texts

Amalfi Texts specializes in printing textbooks for high school science classes. Publishing companies like McGraw-Hill contract with authors to prepare the manuscript, which is then copyedited and typeset. Amalfi receives the typeset manuscript electronically and then prints and binds the textbook. The Printing Department prints the pages and the Binding Department assembles the book and attaches the cover. Each department has its own overhead rate. Overhead rates in both departments are based on expected volume. Volume in the Printing Department is measured by the total number of pages printed in the year, and volume in the Binding Department is measured by the total number of books bound in the year. The following table summarizes expected volume, fixed overhead in each department, and the expected variable overhead per unit of volume in each department.

	Printing	*Binding*
Fixed overhead (millions)	$3.60	$1.46
Volume measure	Number of pages	Number of books
Variable overhead per unit of volume	$0.02	$1.25
Expected number of pages	240,000,000	
Expected number of books		400,000

Required:

    a. Calculate the overhead rates Amalfi Texts will use for the year in the Printing and Binding departments.

    b. During the year, Amalfi prints and binds 10,000 copies of Zhang's *Modern Biology.* Each copy of the Zhang text has 550 pages. Direct labor in the Printing and Binding departments for the Zhang book was $13,500 and $19,000, respectively, and direct materials in the Printing and Binding departments were $61,000 and $21,500, respectively. Calculate the total cost of producing the Zhang book.

    c. Amalfi's total production for the year (including the Zhang book) was 410,000 books with 250 million pages. Actual overhead incurred in the Printing and Binding departments amounted to $8.82 million and $2.185 million, respectively. Calculate the over- or underabsorbed overhead in each department and for the entire firm for the year.

    d. Instead of using expected volume, had Amalfi used normal volume (288 million pages and 480,000 books), how much over- or underabsorbed overhead would Amalfi have for the year?

    e. Discuss the various factors (reasons) why Amalfi might want to use normal versus expected volume in calculating its overhead rates.

P 9–29: Pyramid Products

Pyramid Products manufactures a large number of home and commercial cleaning products at its plant in Oshkosh, Wisconsin. This plant, which employs about 450 people, produces floor waxes, cleaners, bathroom and kitchen cleaners, aerosol air fresheners, disinfectants, and laundry detergents. The products are sold under their own brand name (Pyramid) to supermarkets and home and garden centers. Over time, competition from national brands and price pressure from mass merchandisers such as Walmart have eroded Pyramid sales to the point that the Oshkosh plant has substantial excess capacity—approaching 40 percent of the plant's historical capacity 25 years ago when the plant was built. Pyramid has tried a variety of strategies to increase sales of its existing products, but so far none seem to be yielding dramatic effects.

In an effort to build volume in the plant and to increase the demand for its existing products, management has begun an acquisition strategy and engaged an investment banking firm to find suitable acquisition targets. A suitable target would be in the home cleaning industry with products complementary to Pyramid's, with production that could be shifted to the Oshkosh plant. A complementary product would not duplicate existing Pyramid products and would have a distribution channel that could be used to enhance the sales of other Pyramid products. The investment banker has identified two candidates, Zapp and Kleann. Each produces a branded product for the home cleaning market and both offer Pyramid about the same synergies in terms of increasing the demand for Pyramid's existing products. Both could be acquired for about the same price, but because Pyramid has limited capital and limited access to the capital markets, it can acquire only one of the two companies, not both.

Pyramid's investment banker has provided the following summary data for both targets:

	Zapp	Kleann
Price per case	$ 45.00	$ 37.50
Variable cost per case	$ 33.00	$ 27.50
Annual volume (cases)	80,000	60,000
Direct labor hours per case	0.20	0.60

Besides reviewing the price and variable cost information in the preceding table, the Oshkosh plant manager and her chief financial officer have visited both Zapp and Kleann. They estimate that the Oshkosh plant will have to incur additional fixed annual overhead costs of $600,000 if Zapp is acquired and $400,000 if Kleann is acquired. These additional annual fixed costs include such items as additional leased equipment and additional personnel in quality control, engineering, and purchasing.

The Oshkosh plant uses a single plantwide overhead rate to assign plant overhead to products. Currently, the factory's fixed overhead is $3 million and its current volume is 50,000 direct labor hours. There is negligible variable factory overhead in the Oshkosh plant. Fixed factory overhead is absorbed to products based on direct labor hours.

Required:

    a. Calculate the Oshkosh plant's current fixed manufacturing overhead rate (before the acquisition of either Zapp or Kleann).

    b. Calculate what the Oshkosh plant's fixed manufacturing overhead rate will be if Zapp is acquired. Assume that the additional fixed overhead of $600,000 needed to bring Zapp into the Oshkosh plant is added to the existing plant overhead and the total pool is assigned to all products (including Zapp).

    c. Calculate what the Oshkosh plant's fixed manufacturing overhead rate will be if Kleann is acquired. Assume that the additional fixed overhead of $400,000 needed to bring Kleann into the Oshkosh plant is added to the existing plant overhead and the total pool is assigned to all products (including Kleann).

    d. Pyramid's management does not know what final negotiated price Pyramid will have to pay for each target. The investment banker thinks that both Zapp and Kleann can be purchased for about the same price. However, management must decide which one to pursue first. The plant manager is most interested in Kleann. She argues that her plant's largest problem is overhead absorption. The existing products in the plant are bearing an increasingly larger charge for overhead as volume drops. Kleann, she argues, will absorb more factory overhead than Zapp because it requires three times as much direct labor hours per case and Zapp requires less additional fixed overhead than Kleann. Critically evaluate the plant manager's argument as to why Pyramid should first evaluate Kleann rather than Zapp. Assume that both Zapp and Kleann offer Pyramid's existing products about the same benefits in terms of new channels of distribution for Pyramid's products.

P 9–30: Magic Floor

Magic Floor produces and sells a complete line of floor care products: wax strippers, floor soaps, and floor waxes. All of these products are packaged on a new high-speed bottling fill line. Empty bottles (pints, quarts, half gallons, or gallons) are automatically removed from their boxes and placed on the line. The empty bottles are then filled, sealed with a foil closure, capped with a screw, and labeled. The filled, sealed, capped, and labeled bottles go to a weigh station to ensure each bottle has the correct amount of fill, and the nonrejected packaged bottles are placed in boxes and a bar-coded shipping label is attached. The fill line requires minimal direct labor once it is programmed for the bottle size, contents, and the bar-coded labels. The decision to purchase the

446   *Chapter 9*

fill line in 2014 was justified under the assumption that the line would run 7 hours a day, 5 days a week, and 50 weeks a year.

The 2017 budget for the fill line is:

Maintenance	$ 77,000
Indirect labor	182,000
Depreciation	127,000
Utilities	29,000
Indirect supplies	27,000

Magic Floor's 2017 budgeted production is:

Filled Bottles	Pints	Quarts	Half-Gallons	Gallons
Wax stripper	40,000	50,000	60,000	47,000
Soap	48,000	62,000	79,000	70,000
Wax	44,000	55,000	68,000	49,000

Magic Floor allocates the fill line costs to the various bottled products using a predetermined overhead absorption rate calculated based on budgeted costs divided by budgeted volume. Budgeted volume is measured in seconds on the fill line. Pints are filled in 3 seconds, quarts in 5 seconds, half-gallons in 9 seconds, and gallons in 17 seconds.

During 2017, the following times (in seconds) were recorded for filling bottles on the fill line:

	Pints	Quarts	Half-Gallons	Gallons
Wax stripper	118,000	246,000	542,000	800,000
Soap	145,000	305,000	703,000	1,180,000
Wax	130,000	270,000	608,000	840,000

Actual overhead costs incurred in 2017 on the fill line are:

Maintenance	$ 76,000
Indirect labor	179,000
Depreciation	127,000
Utilities	28,000
Indirect supplies	25,000

Required:

a. Calculate the expected volume of the bottling fill line for 2017.

b. Calculate the normal volume of the bottling fill line for 2017.

c. Calculate the overhead absorption rate for the bottling fill line for 2017 based on expected volume (round overhead rate to four decimals).

d. Calculate the overhead absorption rate for the bottling fill line for 2017 based on normal volume (round overhead rate to four decimals).

e. Calculate the over/underabsorbed overhead amount for the bottling fill line for 2017 based on expected volume.

f. Calculate the over/underabsorbed overhead amount for the bottling fill line for 2017 based on normal volume.

g. Explain in intuitive terms why your answers in parts (*e*) and (*f*) differ.

Case

Case 9–1: Portable Phones Inc.

Portable Phones Inc. manufactures and sells wireless telephones for residential and commercial use. Portable Phones' plant is organized by product line, with five phone assembly departments in total. Each of these five phone assembly departments is responsible for the complete production of a particular phone line, including manufacturing some parts, purchasing other parts, and assembling the unit.

Each of the five phone assembly department managers reports to a product-line manager who has profit responsibility for his/her product. These five product-line managers have authority over pricing, marketing, distribution, and production of their product. Each of the five phone assembly departments is a cost center within its respective product-line profit center.

A key component of each phone is the circuit board(s) containing the integrated circuit chips. Each phone assembly department purchases from outside vendors the basic boards and chips to be attached to its board(s). The board department of the plant receives the boards and chips in kits from each phone assembly department and assembles them into completed boards ready for assembly into the phones. The board department (with a cost structure that is 80 percent fixed and 20 percent variable) uses a single highly automated assembly line of robotic insertion machines to precisely position each chip on the board and soldering machines to solder the chips onto the board. The board department is a common resource for the plant; all five of the phone assembly departments use the board department to assemble some or all of their boards. Since the board department has a single assembly line, it can only assemble boards for one type of phone at a time. The assembly departments have authority to seek the most competitive supplier for all their parts and services, including circuit board assembly.

The board department's assembly schedule is determined at the beginning of each month. The five assembly departments request a time during the month when they plan delivery of particular kits to the board department and specify the number of boards to be assembled. The manager of the board department then takes these requests and tries to satisfy the assembly departments' requests.

However, the board department manager finds that she has a peak load problem; the assembly departments tend to want their boards assembled at the same time. The only way to satisfy these requests is to work overtime shifts during these peak periods even though the board department has excess capacity at other times of the month.

The total monthly costs of the board department (equipment depreciation, maintenance, direct labor, supervision, and engineering support) are assigned to the phone assembly departments based on an hourly rate. The board department's total monthly costs are divided by the number of hours of capacity in the month (e.g., if a particular month has 22 working days, this is equivalent to 352 hours or 22 days × 2 shifts × 8 hours per shift) to arrive at a charge per hour. To give the phone assembly departments incentives to have their kits (boards and chips) delivered to the board department in a timely manner, the phone assembly department is charged for the time from when the last job (a batch of boards assembled for a phone assembly department) was finished by the board department until the time when the next job is finished. For example, suppose phone assembly department A's phones were finished at 9:00 a.m. and that department B delivered its kits at 1:00 p.m. and they were completed at 7:00 p.m. the same day. Department B would be charged for 10 hours of the board department's costs even though the board department was idle for 4 of the 10 hours.

When first installed, the board department was expected to be operating at full capacity, two shifts per day, six days per week. But due to increased competition and outsourcing of some models, the board department is now operating at about 70 percent of the initial planned capacity.

Required:

a. If you manage a phone assembly department, when during the month would you tend to request that your phone circuit boards be assembled by the board department (everything else being held constant)? Explain why.

b. Identify various dysfunctional behaviors likely to occur among the phone assembly departments and the board department.

c. What management changes would you suggest? In particular, what changes would you make in the accounting system? Explain why each change should be made.

Chapter Ten

Criticisms of Absorption Cost Systems: Incentive to Overproduce

Chapter Outline

A. Incentive to Overproduce

    1. Example

    2. Reducing the Overproduction Incentive

B. Variable (Direct) Costing

    1. Background

    2. Illustration of Variable Costing

    3. Overproduction Incentive under Variable Costing

C. Problems with Variable Costing

    1. Classifying Fixed Costs as Variable Costs

    2. Variable Costing Excludes the Opportunity
       Cost of Capacity

D. Beware of Unit Costs

E. Summary

> Traditional cost data tend to be irrelevant and mischievous. These systems of simple proportional divisions followed by allocations and reallocations do not provide data appropriate for managerial use in planning or controlling operations. Moreover, they tend to put such data as do exist in an inaccessible form. Unless other purposes for such data exist, the systems should be discontinued to save the clerical costs of operating them.[1]

The last chapter described traditional absorption cost systems. These systems have been widely used for hundreds of years, and some elements of them have been traced back to the beginning of the Industrial Revolution. For as long as these systems have been used, they have been criticized for producing misleading information and creating incentives that are inconsistent with maximizing the value of the firm. The quotation above is just one example of the charges leveled at traditional cost accounting systems. Despite such criticism, absorption cost systems remain in wide use today. Moreover, nonmanufacturing systems employ elements of absorption cost systems. This chapter and the next chapter examine some common complaints and present some alternatives to solve the problems.

As described in Chapter 1, cost systems serve numerous functions, including decision making, control, and external reporting. No single system can satisfy all the requirements of each function, so trade-offs must be made. Managers constantly revise their costing systems as technology and their firms' organizational architecture change. Examining the well-known problems in costing systems provides a greater appreciation of how to implement them and how to become a more intelligent user of their data. Also, one must be careful not to reject a particular type of cost system (e.g., absorption costing) merely because a particular firm or industry implements it badly.

Section A of this chapter describes how absorption cost systems can create incentives for managers to produce more than they sell (the incentive to overproduce). Section B presents an alternative to absorption costing called *variable costing* that purportedly eliminates the incentive to overproduce. However, there are still incentives to overproduce under variable costing in some situations. Furthermore, variable costing creates other dysfunctional incentives, which are described in section C. The lesson of this and the following chapter is described in section D, "Beware of unit costs." All cost systems generate product costs (average unit costs) that are inaccurate to some extent and inappropriate for some decisions because all cost systems rely on historical costs, not opportunity costs. The degree of inaccuracy varies across products and decisions. The concept of unit cost implies a relation between the unit cost figure and volume. When a unit cost figure is reported—say, $5.12—the first reaction is that it will cost $5.12 to produce one more unit. But in many (if not most) cases, unit costs are mixtures of variable and fixed costs and thus do not represent the incremental cost of producing one more unit.

Chapters 10 and 11 illustrate that all cost systems produce misleading information for some decisions and that average unit costs are misleading because costs per unit implies that these are the variable (or marginal) costs of production. A unit cost figure unlikely measures both the opportunity cost of producing one more unit (marginal cost) and the opportunity cost of doubling output. Producing one more unit unlikely requires additional capacity, while doubling output most likely requires adding more (costly) capacity. Reported unit costs can be long-run average costs, short-run marginal costs, or neither. Without detailed knowledge of the production process and accounting system, it is easy to misinterpret unit cost data.

---

[1]B. Goetz, *Management Planning and Control: A Managerial Approach to Industrial Accounting* (New York: McGraw-Hill, 1949), p. 143.

A. Incentive to Overproduce

Absorption cost systems include both job order and process cost systems. These systems are designed to *absorb* all manufacturing costs into product costs. All costs incurred by the factory are absorbed by products. Some complaints about these systems arise from their full absorption character. In particular, absorption cost systems often create incentives to overproduce.

1. Example

To illustrate the incentive to overproduce, consider a department with $10,000 of fixed costs and constant variable costs of $5 per unit. Assume that (1) the department produces a single homogeneous product and (2) actual overhead incurred equals overhead absorbed and actual production is the same as budgeted production. The first assumption allows volume to be measured in units produced. The second assumption ensures that there is no over/underabsorbed overhead. These assumptions greatly simplify the arithmetic of the example without altering any of the basic conclusions.

The firm sells 2,000 units at $12 per unit but can produce 2,000, 2,200, or 2,400 units. There is no beginning inventory. Table 10–1 shows how reported profits vary with different production levels.

Sales revenue is constant at $24,000, but production varies from 2,000 units to 2,400 units. Variable costs for the 2,000 units sold remain constant at $10,000. Fixed costs are allocated to units sold using overhead absorption:

$$\text{Fixed costs absorbed to units sold} = \frac{\text{Fixed costs}}{\text{Units produced}} \times \text{Units sold}$$

Notice that the overhead rate is lower when more units are produced. Also, while sales, variable costs per unit, and fixed costs remain constant, profits increase as production (not sales) increases.[2] Why? The fixed costs charged off to income for the 2,000 units sold decline from $10,000 when production equals 2,000 units to $8,333 when production equals 2,400 units. When more units are produced than sold, some of the fixed costs are inventoried. When the number of units in inventory is increased, the fraction of fixed costs in inventory increases. With more fixed costs in inventory, fewer fixed costs are transferred to the income statement. Absorption costing systems spread all the manufacturing

TABLE 10-1 **Reported Profits Increase with Production**

	Production (Units)		
	2,000	*2,200*	*2,400*
Sales revenue (2,000 @ $12)	$ 24,000	$ 24,000	$ 24,000
Variable costs (2,000 @ $5)	(10,000)	(10,000)	(10,000)
Fixed costs ($10,000/2,000) × 2,000	(10,000)		
($10,000/2,200) × 2,000		(9,091)	
($10,000/2,400) × 2,000			(8,333)
Profit	$ 4,000	$ 4,909	$ 5,667

---

[2]This example allocates fixed costs to products using actual production instead of budgeted production. Because we are assuming actual and budgeted fixed costs are equal (as are units produced and budgeted units), using actual data gives the same allocations as using budgeted data.

TABLE 10-2   **Fixed and Variable Costs in Inventory**

	Production (Units)		
	2,000	*2,200*	*2,400*
Units in inventory	0	200	400
Fixed costs in inventory: ($10,000/2,000) × 0	$ 0		
($10,000/2,200) × 200		$ 909	
($10,000/2,400) × 400			$ 1,667
Fixed costs charged to profits (from Table 10–1)	10,000	9,091	8,333
Total fixed costs	$10,000	$ 10,000	$ 10,000
Total inventory:			
Variable costs (@ $5/unit)	$ 0	$ 1,000	$ 2,000
Fixed costs (from above)	0	909	1,667
Inventory	$ 0	$ 1,909	$ 3,667

costs (including fixed manufacturing costs) against all the units worked on. When production is increased (holding sales constant), average unit costs fall and reported accounting profit per unit sold increases.

Table 10–2 illustrates that as more units are produced with sales held constant, a greater fraction of the fixed manufacturing costs flows into inventory. The total dollars of fixed costs remain constant; they are just shifted from the income statement to the balance sheet. The amount added to inventory increases from zero to $3,667 at a production level of 2,400 units. However, building inventories to shift fixed costs to the balance sheet is not costless. Additional cash is needed to pay the variable costs. When 2,400 units are produced, the firm must find financing for the $2,000 variable costs in inventory.

Managers rewarded on total profits calculated using absorption costing can increase reported profits by increasing production (holding sales constant). A major criticism of absorption costing is that it creates incentives for managers to overproduce, thereby building inventories.

This analysis makes the critical assumption that variable cost *per unit* remains constant as production is increased. If marginal cost (and hence variable cost) per unit rises faster than average fixed costs fall as production increases, then average unit costs actually increase. An increasing marginal cost reduces the incentives of managers to overproduce with absorption costing. Unless stated otherwise, the remainder of this chapter assumes that marginal (and variable) cost per unit is constant as volume changes.

Exercise 10–1

Velazquez Designs, a wholly owned subsidiary of Tura Products, manufactures wallpaper. Managers are paid quarterly bonuses based on net income. Management at Velazquez expects sales next quarter to be 10,000 rolls of wallpaper at $8 per roll. Velazquez has limited inventory of wallpaper on hand, and the managers want to increase the inventory. Velazquez uses a traditional absorption costing system where product costs contain both fixed and variable manufacturing costs. The following table shows how costs are expected to behave at various production levels.

continued

452   *Chapter 10*

	Alternative Production Levels				
Production (rolls of wallpaper)	10,000	11,000	12,000	13,000	14,000
Fixed manufacturing cost	$40,000	$40,000	$40,000	$40,000	$40,000
Variable manufacturing cost	$30,000	$35,900	$41,600	$48,270	$55,900

Required:

Based on the data, what level of production do you expect management to choose?

Solution:

The following table shows that operating income is maximized at a production level of 13,000 rolls:

	Alternative Production Levels				
Sales	10,000	10,000	10,000	10,000	10,000
Production	10,000	11,000	12,000	13,000	14,000
Revenue	$80,000	$80,000	$80,000	$80,000	$80,000
Cost of goods sold	$70,000	$69,000	$68,000	$67,900	$68,500
Operating margin	$10,000	$11,000	$12,000	$12,100	$11,500
Fixed cost	$40,000	$40,000	$40,000	$40,000	$40,000
Total variable cost	$30,000	$35,900	$41,600	$48,270	$55,900
Total cost	$70,000	$75,900	$81,600	$88,270	$95,900
Average variable cost	$3.00	$3.26	$3.47	$3.71	$3.99
Average fixed cost	$4.00	$3.64	$3.33	$3.08	$2.86
Average total cost	$7.00	$6.90	$6.80	$6.79	$6.85

This exercise illustrates that even though average fixed costs continue to fall as production increases, average variable cost starts to increase faster than average fixed cost falls beyond 13,000 rolls.

Managerial Application: Intel Overproduces to Boost Earnings

Intel, one of the world's largest producers of computer chips, tried to boost profits by overproducing. Manufacturing computer chips requires substantial fixed manufacturing costs. By overproducing and building inventory, the average cost of the chips sold falls. This increases gross margins (sales less cost of goods sold) and profits. Intel had been reporting gross margins of 53 percent. But an outside analyst following Intel predicted that shares of Intel were headed for a fall. He reasoned that Intel's high margins resulted mostly from a buildup in inventory, not sales to end users. When Intel announced its gross margin fell to 49 percent, Intel's stock price plummeted.

SOURCE: G. Morgenson, "Far from Wall Street, Intel's Bad News Was No Surprise," *The New York Times*, June 9, 2002.

2. Reducing the Overproduction Incentive

There are several ways to mitigate the incentive to overproduce. The first is to charge managers for inventory holding costs. That is, inventory values are increased by the cost of capital plus warehousing costs. Managers oppose this policy because inventory holding costs then have to be backed out of profits for external reporting, which increases accounting and data processing complexity and causes division profits (with the inventory holding costs) to be lower than firm profits (without the holding costs). If a manager is evaluated based on residual income instead of net income, managers are charged the cost of capital for holding inventory. Remember from Chapter 5 that residual income is net income less the firm's cost of capital times the amount of investment during the year, including inventories. If the manager overproduces, inventories increase and residual income falls.

For instance, consider the example in Tables 10–1 and 10–2. Suppose the manager is evaluated and rewarded based on residual income. Furthermore, assume that the only asset is inventory and the firm's cost of capital is 20 percent. Table 10–3 illustrates how residual income varies with production.

We see from Table 10–3 that at a cost of capital of 20 percent, residual income does not eliminate the incentive to overproduce. It does, however, make it less profitable to the manager. For example, by producing 2,400 units, the manager raises profits from $4,000 to $5,667. Residual income cuts the gain from over producing from $1,667 (or $5,667 – $4,000) to $934 (or $4,934 – $4,000).

A second method of reducing the overproduction incentive is a strict senior management policy against building inventories. Compensation plans can contain a clause that bonuses tied to net income will not be paid if inventories exceed a certain amount. However, such strict constraints are cumbersome and generate influence costs. Circumstances exist when increasing inventories maximizes firm value (e.g., new product introductions, unexpected market shocks to supply or demand, or growing sales). Therefore, it is difficult to know at the beginning of the year what upper bound to place on inventory levels.

Third, in a single-plant, publicly traded firm, compensation can be based on stock prices instead of on accounting earnings, which removes the incentive for managers to overproduce. For example, awarding the plant manager stock or stock options forces the manager to bear the consequences of decisions that do not maximize firm value. However, this method imposes additional risk on managers for general marketwide events. In publicly traded firms with many plants, any plant manager's overproduction has a small effect on the value of the firm. Hence, free-rider problems in multiplant firms decrease the ability of stock-based compensation to eliminate the overproduction incentive.

A fourth possibility is to use just-in-time (JIT) production systems to reduce inventory levels. (Chapter 14 describes JIT in greater detail.) In a JIT system, manufacturing does not typically begin until the part or final product is ordered by a customer. Intermediate products flow immediately from one stage of production to another with little work-in-process inventories. If the production schedule is determined by demand, then the plant manager

TABLE 10-3   **Residual Income and Overproduction**

	Production (Units)		
	2,000	*2,200*	*2,400*
Profits (from Table 10–1)	$4,000	$4,909	$5,667
Inventory (from Table 10–2)	0	1,909	3,667
Cost of inventories (@ 20%)	0	382	733
Residual income	4,000	4,527	4,934

454   *Chapter 10*

or product-line manager does not have the discretion to set production levels in excess of demand. In essence, a JIT system removes from managers the decision rights to set production levels. These decision rights are replaced by demand-driven market orders. JIT systems can reduce inventories and thus the incentive to overproduce in order to increase reported profits. A final option is to change the costing system. Variable costing systems, discussed next, reduce the incentive to overproduce.

Concept Questions		
	Q10–1	What is the danger in viewing unit costs as variable costs?
	Q10–2	How can managers increase profit artificially when an absorption cost system is used?
	Q10–3	Name four ways to mitigate the incentives for managers to overproduce.

B. Variable (Direct) Costing

Variable costing (sometimes called *direct costing*) is claimed to eliminate the incentive to build inventories, although, as we will see later, it is not entirely successful.

1. Background

Under **variable costing**, all fixed costs are written off against income in the year they are incurred. Fixed manufacturing costs are not absorbed into product costs and do not flow through the inventory accounts. Product costs contain only the variable components. Fixed manufacturing costs are treated as period costs and are written off. Thus, the only difference between absorption costing and variable costing is in the treatment of fixed manufacturing costs. Fixed manufacturing costs are included as part of product costs under absorption costing and written off as period expenses (and not included in product costs) under variable costing. The purported advantages of variable costing are that it eliminates distortions to income and product costs when volume changes, and it reduces the dysfunctional incentives to overproduce.

Variable costing attracted much attention in the 1950s and 1960s. A few companies still use it. We discuss it here because it helps us to better understand absorption costing systems. Also, variable cost transfer pricing is similar to variable costing. The transfer price consists of only the variable costs. The same weaknesses of variable cost transfer pricing also apply to variable costing (see Chapter 5).

2. Illustration of Variable Costing

As an example of variable costing versus absorption costing, consider the data in Table 10–4. The same assumptions made earlier continue to apply: A single homogeneous product is produced, budgeted volume equals actual volume, and variable cost per unit

---

TABLE 10-4   Data for Direct Costing and Absorption Costing Example*

Price			$11/unit sold
Direct materials and labor (all variable)			$2/unit produced
Flexible overhead budget			$40,000 + $3/unit produced

	Sales	*Production*	*Overhead*
Year 1	10,000 units	10,000 units	$70,000
Year 2	10,000 units	11,000 units	$73,000

*To simplify all examples, assume there are no beginning inventories.

TABLE 10-5   **Absorption Costing and Variable Costing Income Statements for Years 1 and 2**

	Year 1		Year 2	
A. Absorption Costing Net Income				
Sales		$110,000		$110,000
Direct materials and labor	(20,000)		(20,000)	
Overhead absorbed:				
$\dfrac{\$70,000}{10,000} \times 10,000$	(70,000)	(90,000)		
$\dfrac{\$73,000}{11,000} \times 10,000$			(66,364)	(86,364)
Net income		$ 20,000		$ 23,636
B. Variable Costing Net Income				
Sales		$110,000		$110,000
Direct materials and labor	(20,000)		(20,000)	
Variable overhead	(30,000)		(30,000)	
Fixed overhead	(40,000)	(90,000)	(40,000)	(90,000)
Net income		$ 20,000		$ 20,000

does not increase as production is expanded. In Table 10–4, the company sells 10,000 units each year and produces 10,000 units in year 1 and 11,000 units in year 2. Actual overhead costs in both years are the same as predicted by the flexible budget ($70,000 in year 1 and $73,000 in year 2).

Table 10–5 provides the absorption costing and variable costing income statements for the two years. In part A, net income under absorption costing rises in year 2 even though sales are flat, because some of the fixed costs are inventoried.

In part B, all of the fixed overhead of $40,000 is written off each year, and net income is the same across the two years. All overhead costs are written off to the income statement under variable costing. Inventoried units are charged for variable overhead costs under both absorption and variable costing. Only the fixed overhead is treated differently. Under variable costing, in year 2 only variable overhead of $30,000 is written off to income. The

---

Historical Application: A Nineteenth-Century Example of Variable Costing

Two very influential nineteenth-century English accountants, Garcke and Fells, recognized the problems of letting fixed costs enter unit costs. Garcke was a managing director of British Electric Traction Co., and Fells was the general manager of Salt Union Limited. They argued that fixed overhead charges should be written off to net income:

> [Fixed overheads] do not vary proportionately with the volume of business. . . . [They] are, in the aggregate, more or less constant, while the manufacturing costs fluctuate with the costs of labor and the price of materials. To distribute the charges over the articles manufactured would, therefore, have the effect of disproportionately reducing the cost of production with every increase, and the reverse with every diminution of business. Such a result is to be deprecated.

SOURCE: E. Garcke and J. Fells, *Factory Accounts*, 4th ed. (London: Crosby, Lockwood, and Son, 1893), p. 73. Quoted by P. Garner, *Evolution of Cost Accounting to 1925* (Montgomery: University of Alabama Press, 1954), p. 124.

456 *Chapter 10*

remaining $3,000 of variable overhead (1,000 units × $3 of variable overhead) remains in inventory along with the other $2 of direct cost per unit. Two points should be noted from this example:

1. When production and sales are equal, absorption costing and variable costing give identical profit amounts (assuming no beginning inventories). When production and sales are equal, both costing methods write off all fixed costs to income.
2. Absorption cost net income is higher in year 2 than in year 1 because some of the fixed costs in year 2 end up in inventory. In contrast, variable cost net income is constant over the two years.

Exercise 10-2

Matson manufactures a metal dog cage that has variable cost of $50 per cage. Budgeted and actual fixed manufacturing overhead are $900,000. Cages sell for $60 each.

Required:

Calculate variable cost net income and absorption cost net income under each of the following independent cases:

a. Sales and production are 100,000 cages.

b. Sales are 90,000 cages and production is 100,000 cages.

c. Sales are 100,000 cages and production is 90,000 cages. The beginning inventory consists of 20,000 units manufactured last year. Last year, 100,000 units were manufactured, 80,000 were sold, variable costs were $50 per cage, and fixed manufacturing overhead costs were $900,000. For inventory valuation purposes, all of this year's production is sold and 10,000 units in the beginning inventory are sold (LIFO is used to value inventories).

Solution:

a. Sales equal production:

	Absorption Costing	Variable Costing
Revenue (100,000 @ $60)	$6,000,000	$6,000,000
Variable cost (100,000 @ $50)	5,000,000	5,000,000
Fixed manufacturing overhead	900,000	900,000
Net income	$ 100,000	$ 100,000

b. Sales less than production:

	Absorption Costing	Variable Costing
Revenue (90,000 @ $60)	$ 5,400,000	$5,400,000
Variable cost (90,000 @ $50)	4,500,000	4,500,000
Fixed manufacturing overhead		900,000
$900,000 × (90,000 ÷ 100,000)	810,000	
	$ 90,000	$ 0

c. Sales greater than production:

	Absorption Costing	Variable Costing
Revenue (100,000 @ $60)	$ 6,000,000	$ 6,000,000
Variable cost (100,000 @ $50)	5,000,000	5,000,000
Fixed manufacturing overhead		900,000
90,000 units × ($900,000 ÷ 90,000)	900,000	
10,000 units × ($900,000 ÷ 100,000)	90,000	
Net income	$ 10,000	$ 100,000

3. Overproduction Incentive under Variable Costing

In Table 10–5, note that under variable costing, profits do not vary with production volume changes. Proponents claim that variable costing eliminates the incentives of managers to show higher profits by overproducing. However, this claim is not entirely accurate. To illustrate, the example is modified slightly in Table 10–6. Actual overhead incurred is no longer the same as that predicted by the flexible budget ($70,000 in year 1 and $73,000 in year 2), but rather is $17,000 higher in both years ($87,000 in year 1 and $90,000 in year 2).

The issue becomes whether this $17,000 of additional overhead is variable or fixed. At the beginning of the year, the flexible budget is a useful tool to forecast total overhead as a function of volume. But at the end of the year, any deviation between actual spending and the flexible budget can be due to changes in fixed costs, changes in the variable cost per unit of volume, or both. In the absence of specific knowledge regarding whether the $17,000 budget variance is a fixed cost or a variable cost, managers can use their discretion to manage earnings. If the $17,000 is treated as a variable cost, then even under variable costing, managers have an incentive to overproduce. Table 10–6 presents the revised net income numbers with the additional $17,000 of overhead.

As displayed in parts A, B, and C of Table 10–6, net income is always $3,000 when production volume and sales are the same. (See year 1.) When production exceeds sales (as in year 2), absorption costing shows higher income in year 2 than in year 1 (part A). Under absorption costing, managers can show larger profits by overproducing. In part B, the extra $17,000 is treated as an additional fixed cost under variable costing. These additional dollars are written off in both years and net income is the same in both years.

Under variable costing, with the $17,000 of additional overhead classified as a variable cost (part C), the variable overhead per unit is composed of two pieces. There is the original $3 of variable overhead per unit plus the $17,000 of extra overhead (assumed to be variable), which is converted to a per-unit amount by dividing by the number of units produced. When unit production exceeds units sold, some of the extra variable overhead is inventoried.

In the preceding example, management has discretion over classifying the additional $17,000 as either a fixed or variable cost. If each component of overhead—such as depreciation, utilities, property taxes, or indirect labor—is separately classified as fixed or variable, then at the end of the year management has no discretion to classify the over- or underabsorbed overhead as either fixed or variable. For example, suppose indirect labor is classified as variable overhead and at the end of the year indirect labor is underabsorbed. Then management has no discretion in classifying this underabsorbed indirect labor. It is a variable cost. However, some overhead components are mixed costs—they contain both fixed and variable elements. For example, utilities contain a fixed amount for turning on the lights and heat in the plant and a variable component for operating the machinery.

TABLE 10-6   Net Income under Absorption Costing and Variable Costing with an Additional $17,000 of Overhead

	Year 1		Year 2	
A. Absorption Costing				
Sales		$ 110,000		$ 110,000
Direct labor and materials	(20,000)		(20,000)	
Overhead absorbed:				
$\dfrac{\$87,000}{10,000} \times 10,000$	(87,000)	(107,000)		
$\dfrac{\$90,000}{11,000} \times 10,000$			(81,818)	(101,818)
Net income		$ 3,000		$ 8,182
B. Variable Costing, with $17,000 Treated as Additional Fixed Cost				
Sales		$110,000		$110,000
Direct labor and materials	(20,000)		(20,000)	
Variable overhead	(30,000)		(30,000)	
Fixed overhead ($40,000 + $17,000)	(57,000)	(107,000)	(57,000)	(107,000)
Net income		$ 3,000		$ 3,000
C. Variable Costing, with $17,000 Treated as Additional Variable Cost				
Sales		$ 110,000		$110,000
Direct labor and materials	(20,000)		(20,000)	
Variable overhead:				
$\left(\$3 + \dfrac{\$17,000}{10,000}\right) \times 10,000$	(47,000)			
$\left(\$3 + \dfrac{\$17,000}{11,000}\right) \times 10,000$			(45,455)	
Fixed overhead	(40,000)		(40,000)	
		(107,000)		(105,455)
Net income		$ 3,000		$ 4,545

At the end of the year, the total bill for utilities is a mixture of both fixed and variable costs. In this case, management can exercise discretion by classifying any budget variance in the total utility bill as either a fixed or variable cost.

C. Problems with Variable Costing

1. Classifying Fixed Costs as Variable Costs

The principal benefit of variable costing is it eliminates (or reduces) the incentive to over-produce as a way to boost reported earnings. However, the preceding example illustrates a potential problem with variable costing. How does one determine which costs are fixed and which costs are variable *at the end of the year?* At the beginning of the year, the fixed and variable components can be estimated. At the end of the year, however, when total overhead is known and is probably different from that forecast by the flexible budget, it is difficult and time-consuming to sort out whether the difference is due to a change in fixed costs, variable costs, or both. By classifying all of the excess overhead costs as variable, managers using variable costing can *inventory* some of these extra costs by overproducing.

Therefore, even under variable costing, building inventories can result in higher reported profits whenever actual overhead exceeds the flexible budget amount. The use of variable costing introduces another element of discretion into the accounting system. Someone must have the decision rights to determine at the end of the year how much of the actual overhead was fixed and how much was variable. This additional discretion, if exercised by the individuals being monitored by the accounting system, reduces the system's value as a control device. The managers responsible for the day-to-day operations that generate the overhead usually have more information regarding what causes actual overhead to exceed budget than their superiors. These managers can often argue more persuasively than their superiors about the causes of the excess overhead and whether it should be classified as a fixed or variable cost. Determining the fixed and variable portions of overhead is often arbitrary and creates incentives for the people being monitored to manipulate the classification. While the incentive to overproduce is lessened under variable costing as compared with absorption costing, the tendency to build inventories must still be monitored.

Exercise 10-3

Filters Plus manufactures filters for swimming pools. It uses an absorption costing system and writes off over/underabsorbed overhead to cost of goods sold. Overhead is applied to products at the rate of $6.30 per direct labor hour (DLH). Total variable overhead is budgeted at $72,600 and 22,000 hours were expected. The income statement is:

FILTERS PLUS
Income Statement (Absorption Costing) Year Ending 12/31

Sales		$824,500
Cost of goods sold		571,400
Gross margin		$253,100
Selling and administrative costs		
Variable	$172,900	
Fixed	67,600	240,500
Net income		$ 12,600

Filters Plus had no beginning inventories of filters. The ending inventory as of 12/31 consists of 1,400 filters, each of which required 2 direct labor hours to manufacture.

Required:

What would Filter Plus's net income be under variable costing? (Show calculations and explain the logic of your methodology.)

Solution:

The first step is to calculate the budgeted fixed overhead per direct labor hour (DLH):

$$\text{Overhead rate} = \$6.30 = \text{Budgeted fixed overhead/DLH} + \frac{\$72,600}{22,000}$$

$$\text{Budgeted fixed overhead} = \$3.00 \text{ DLH}$$

continued

Since there are 1,400 filters in inventory and each has 2 DLH, then the total fixed overhead in inventory is $8,400 (1,400 × 2 DLH × $3/DLH).

Net income under variable costing is lower by the $8,400 of fixed costs included in inventory under absorption costing, or:

Net income (absorption costing)	$12,600
Less: fixed cost in inventory	(8,400)
Net income variable costing	$ 4,200

2. Variable Costing Excludes the Opportunity Cost of Capacity

Another problem with variable costing is that it produces misleading unit cost figures. The opportunity cost of manufacturing a given product includes the direct costs and the forgone opportunities of using the plant and equipment in other ways. Inside the firm, market prices do not exist to guide the allocation of scarce resources. Management must devise alternative accounting and administrative systems to allocate scarce resources. (See Chapter 4.) Unit cost data are a substitute inside the firm for the lack of market prices. If variable costing is used, unit cost figures do not contain any amount for the opportunity cost of the production capacity. Full absorption costs, while not an exact measure of opportunity costs, can be a better measure than variable costs especially when the firm is capacity-constrained. If fixed costs are ignored, managers have incentives to overconsume the fixed capacity resources.

On the other hand, if the firm has excess capacity, including fixed charges in unit costs overstates opportunity cost and discourages use of the excess capacity. In extreme cases, a death spiral can be induced (Chapter 8). To the extent that the economy is growing and surviving firms in general are growing, firms face capacity constraints. Then, these firms will want to include fixed costs in product costs to proxy for the opportunity cost of capacity. Is variable costing better than absorption costing? Economic Darwinism (the marmot-and-bear parable) suggests that commonly used procedures such as absorption costing probably yield benefits in excess of their costs. Since variable costing is not widely used,

Managerial Application: Throughput Accounting: Old Wine in New Bottles

FIAMA, a Brazilian textile firm, uses throughput accounting to assess product profitability and to make better pricing and operating decisions. Throughput accounting doesn't allocate costs to products. Rather, throughput is the rate at which the firm generates money. Throughput per unit is price less variable cost per unit. (In Chapter 2, price less variable cost was defined as "contribution margin.") Firm profits are the sum of each product's throughput times the number of units sold less operating expenses (all costs required to generate the total throughput). If a cost isn't variable, then it is included in operating expense. Thus, by definition, "operating expenses" must include fixed overhead.

Throughput accounting sounds a lot like variable (direct) costing. New terminology and a new name do not alter the fact that throughput accounting is old wine in new bottles. Nor do the new name and terminology avoid the problems associated with variable costing.

SOURCE: T. Corbett, "Three-Questions Accounting," *Strategic Finance*, April 2006, pp. 48–55.

its benefits are probably less than its costs. Also, variable costing is rarely used for external reporting. Generally accepted accounting principles, financial accounting standards, and the U.S. Internal Revenue Service require the allocation of fixed manufacturing costs to products. If variable costing is used for internal reports and absorption costing is used for external reports, internal and external reporting systems will produce different numbers. As discussed in Chapter 1, reconciling the different numbers is time-consuming and diverts senior managers' attention from more important issues.[3]

Concept Questions		
	Q10–4	What is the major difference between absorption costing and variable costing?
	Q10–5	Give two claimed advantages of variable costing. Give two potential problems with variable costing.

D. Beware of Unit Costs

All cost systems, whether absorption or variable systems, produce unit cost figures. Such product costs are used for both decision making (pricing, outsourcing, product mix) and decision control (transfer pricing, performance evaluation). This section presents an example of how unit-based costs can be wrong for some decisions.

A glass bottle producer makes only two types of bottles: gallon wine jugs and quart juice bottles. Only one input, natural gas, is used to make both bottles. Labor, capital, and silica are all free. Natural gas is purchased for an annual fixed fee of $100,000 plus $0.20 per cubic yard up to 500,000 yards and then $0.30 per cubic yard thereafter. The only fixed cost is the $100,000 annual fee to purchase gas for $0.20 per cubic yard up to 500,000 cubic yards. The following table summarizes how much natural gas is needed to produce the two bottles:

	Natural Gas
100 gallon jugs	9 cubic yards
100 quart bottles	3 cubic yards

Current production consists of 3 million gallon jugs and 7 million quart bottles.

Table 10–7 summarizes production, gas used, and the variable and fixed costs. To arrive at a full absorption cost per bottle, the fixed gas cost is allocated based on gas used. Gallon jugs use 270,000 ÷ 480,000 or 56.25 percent of the gas, and quart bottles use the remaining 43.75 percent. Allocating the fixed cost of gas in these proportions yields $56,250 assigned to gallon jugs and $43,750 assigned to quart bottles. Table 10–8 summarizes the full cost and variable cost of the two bottles.

The full cost per bottle is about twice the variable cost. Both the full and variable cost figures lead to inappropriate conclusions for some decisions. For example, suppose a

---

[3]A prevalent argument holds that managers typically prefer variable costing but are forced to use absorption costing because generally accepted accounting principles (GAAP) require full costing of inventories for external reporting. An alternative view posits that if an overwhelming majority of firms wanted to use variable costing for GAAP, they could influence the standard-setting process to allow such a change. In other words, GAAP reflects what most managers consider preferred accounting practices.

TABLE 10-7   **Bottle Production and Gas Utilization**

	Gallon Jugs	Quart Bottles	Total
Current production (in bottles)	3,000,000	7,000,000	
Current production (in 100 units)	30,000	70,000	
Gas per 100 units (cubic yards)	9	3	
Gas used (cubic yards)	270,000	210,000	480,000
Gas cost:			
Fixed cost			$100,000
Variable cost (@ $0.20/cubic yard)	$54,000	$42,000	$ 96,000

TABLE 10-8   **Full Cost and Variable Cost per Bottle**

	Gallon Jugs	Quart Bottles
Variable cost	$ 54,000	$ 42,000
Allocated fixed cost	56,250	43,750
Total cost	$ 110,250	$ 85,750
÷ Bottles produced	3,000,000	7,000,000
Full cost/bottle	$ 0.03675	$ 0.01225
Variable cost/bottle	$ 0.01800	$ 0.00600

customer asks to purchase 1 million additional gallon jugs at $0.022. The variable cost of $0.018 is less than the price. It appears we should accept the offer. However, since we are currently using 480,000 cubic yards of gas, the additional production pushes gas purchases above the 500,000-cubic-yard limit and we have to purchase additional gas at $0.30 per cubic yard instead of $0.20 per cubic yard.

The additional gallon jugs require 90,000 cubic yards of gas (1,000,000 jugs ÷ 100 bottle lots × 9 cubic yards per 100-bottle lot). The cost of this gas is

Cost of first 20,000 cubic yards @ $0.20	$ 4,000
Cost of last 70,000 cubic yards @ $0.30	21,000
Incremental cost	$25,000
Number of gallon jugs	÷ 1,000,000
Incremental cost per jug	$0.0250

Notice that neither the variable cost nor the full cost figures accurately estimate the opportunity cost of the additional 1 million gallon jugs. The reason is that neither the full cost nor the variable cost estimates include the higher gas cost per cubic yard when more than 500,000 cubic yards are required. Both full and variable costing rely on historical costs. If the firm expands or contracts into areas of its cost curve where it has not been before, there is no historical information regarding the level of costs in these unexplored regions.

By now, you should have acquired a healthy skepticism of accounting costs, particularly *unit* costs. One writer summarized absorption costing over 65 years ago as follows:

> (Accounting) product costs are never actual costs, but leveled, smoothed, or "normal" costs. It should be clear, then, that product costs are the result of specific tracing of some cost items (direct costs) plus the assignment of indirect (variable and fixed) costs by the use of average-expected or "normal" indirect cost rates. The unit costs thus computed are technically compiled average costs; they are "normal" costs—never actual costs.[4]

Not only are unit costs not actual costs; they are not marginal costs. Although stated in terms of dollars per unit, unit costs do not tell us the cost of producing one more unit.

E. Summary

This chapter discusses one of the criticisms of traditional absorption costing systems: Absorption cost systems create incentives to overproduce. By producing more units than the firm can sell, some of the fixed costs are absorbed to units in inventory. These fixed costs in inventory are not in the cost of products sold. As long as variable costs per unit do not rise faster than average fixed costs fall as more units are produced, then the average full unit cost falls and the profits on these units rise. This creates the incentive to overproduce.

A firm can reduce (but not eliminate) the incentive to overproduce by adopting variable (direct) costing systems. Variable costing writes off all fixed manufacturing costs as a period cost. As a result, profits cannot be increased by overproducing and thereby spreading these fixed costs over more units.

While variable costing systems reduce the incentives to overproduce, these systems are not generally observed in practice, which suggests that their total costs exceed their total benefits. There are alternative mechanisms for controlling managers' incentives to overproduce, such as flat prohibitions on increasing inventory levels, charging managers for inventory holding costs, and just-in-time production scheduling. Moreover, writing off all fixed costs gives managers an additional degree of discretion over their performance evaluation system. They often have discretion over classifying expenditures as fixed or variable. Also, if fixed costs are written off, product costs are distorted to the extent that they do not reflect the opportunity cost of the plant's capacity.

Self-Study Problems

Self-Study Problem 1:   Dial Cards

A plant with $1 million of fixed manufacturing overhead costs makes decks of playing cards with a variable manufacturing cost per deck of $1.00. The plant only makes playing cards and allocates

---

[4]W. Vatter, *Managerial Accounting* (New York: Prentice Hall, 1950), p. 402.

464   *Chapter 10*

all the fixed costs to the product by the number of decks produced. The firm can sell 200,000 decks a year for $10.00 each. There is no beginning inventory. The plant manager has the opportunity to make 200,000 decks, 220,000 decks, or 240,000 decks. Handling excess inventory costs $0.10/deck. Handling costs are expensed in the year they are incurred. Which production level causes the highest reported income for the year?

	Production Levels		
	200,000	*220,000*	*240,000*
Fixed manufacturing costs	$1,000,000	$1,000,000	$1,000,000
Variable manufacturing cost ($1/unit)	200,000	220,000	240,000
Total costs	$1,200,000	$1,220,000	$1,240,000
Average cost per deck	$6/deck	$5.5454/deck	$5.1667/deck
Revenues (200,000 decks)($10/deck)	$2,000,000	$2,000,000	$2,000,000
Cost of goods sold			
(200,000 decks)($5.5454/deck)	(1,200,000)		
(200,000 decks)($5.1667/deck)		(1,109,080)	
(240,000 decks)($5.17/deck)			(1,033,340)
Excess inventory handling costs	0		
(220,000 – 200,000)($.10/deck)		(2,000)	
(240,000 – 200,000)($.10/deck)			(4,000)
Net income	$ 800,000	$ 888,920	$ 962,660

Self-Study Problem 2:   Kiddo Inc. (A)

Kiddo Incorporated manufactures running shoes. Recently, it added a new line of pump sneakers. Over the past two years, sales of both the Runner and the Pump have been flat at 5,000,000 and 2,400,000 pairs, respectively. However, in anticipation of increased sales, production was increased from 5,140,000 to 5,200,000 for the Runner and from 3,000,000 to 3,564,000 for the Pump from year 1 to year 2.

Production costs for the two sneakers are very different. Materials cost $14.00 per Runner and $17.75 per Pump. Labor costs are $4.60 and $5.00 and variable overhead costs are $6.60 and $7.30 for the Runner and the Pump, respectively. Fixed overhead costs are $50 million and are allocated based on direct labor cost. Kiddo uses LIFO. Round ratios to two decimal digits.

Required:

  a. Based on revenues of $32 per Runner and $46 per Pump, prepare an income statement for each year.

  b. Explain the change in net profit from year 1 to year 2. Be sure to explain any differences between the Runner and the Pump.

Solution:

  a. Income statements for years 1 and 2 are the following:

	Runner	*Pump*	*Total*
Year 1			
Revenue	$160,000,000	$110,400,000	$270,400,000
Expenses:			
Material	70,000,000	42,600,000	112,600,000
Labor	23,000,000	12,000,000	35,000,000
Variable overhead	33,000,000	17,520,000	50,520,000
Fixed overhead*	29,650,000	15,480,000	45,130,000
Net income	$ 4,350,000	$ 22,800,000	$ 27,150,000
Year 2			
Revenue	$160,000,000	$110,400,000	$270,400,000
Expenses:			
Material	70,000,000	42,600,000	112,600,000
Labor	23,000,000	12,000,000	35,000,000
Variable overhead	33,000,000	17,520,000	50,520,000
Fixed overhead†	27,550,000	14,376,000	41,926,000
Net income	$ 6,450,000	$ 23,904,000	$ 30,354,000

*Year 1

	Runner	*Pump*	*Total*
Direct labor per pair	$ 4.60	$ 5.00	
× Units produced	5,140,000	3,000,000	
Direct labor cost	$23,644,000	$15,000,000	$38,644,000
Fixed overhead rate per direct labor dollar			
($50,000,000/$38,644,000)			$1.29
Direct labor per pair	$ 4.60	$ 5.00	
× Fixed overhead rate	1.29	1.29	
Fixed overhead per pair	$ 5.93	$ 6.45	
× Number of pairs sold	5,000,000	2,400,000	
Allocated fixed overhead	$29,650,000	$15,480,000	$45,130,000

†Year 2

	Runner	*Pump*	*Total*
Direct labor per pair	$ 4.60	$ 5.00	
× Units produced	5,200,000	3,564,000	
Direct labor cost	$23,920,000	$17,820,000	$41,740,000
Fixed overhead rate per direct labor dollar			
($50,000,000/$41,740,000)			$1.20
Direct labor per pair	$ 4.60	$ 5.00	
× Fixed overhead rate	1.20	1.20	
Fixed overhead per pair	$ 5.51	$ 5.99	
× Number of pairs sold	5,000,000	2,400,000	
Allocated fixed overhead	$27,550,000	$14,376,000	$41,926,000

b. Net income increased from year 1 to year 2 even though sales were constant. This change
results from increased production. The fixed costs are allocated based on direct labor cost.
Increasing production decreases the fixed cost per pair of sneakers, thereby increasing
profits per pair sold. In year 1, 90.26 percent of the $50 million of fixed overhead was
included in profits. This fell to 83.85 percent, causing year 2 profits to increase.

466   *Chapter 10*

Problems

P 10–1: Federal Mixing

Federal Mixing (FM) is a division of Federal Chemicals, a large diversified chemical company. FM provides mixing services for both outside customers and other Federal divisions. FM buys or receives liquid chemicals and combines and packages them according to the customer's specifications. FM computes its divisional net income on both a fully absorbed and variable costing basis. For the year just ending, it reported

	Net Income
Absorption costing	$13,800,000
Variable costing	12,600,000
Difference	$ 1,200,000

Overhead is assigned to products using machine hours.

There is no finished goods inventory at FM, only work-in-process (WIP) inventory. As soon as a product is completed, it is shipped to the customer. The beginning inventory based on absorption costing was valued at $6.3 million and contained 70,000 machine hours. The ending WIP inventory based on absorption costing was valued at $9.9 million and contained 90,000 machine hours.

Required:

Write a short nontechnical note to senior management explaining why variable costing and absorption costing net income amounts differ.

P 10–2: Hurricane Safe

Hurricane Safe produces an LED rechargeable flashlight torch that it sells online through various websites. It has the following cost structure.

	Fixed	*Variable*	*Total*
	Cost*	**Cost**	**Cost**
Advertising	$2.20	$ 2.70	$ 4.90
Distribution	1.70	1.25	2.95
Direct labor		4.50	4.50
Direct material		11.00	11.00
Manufacturing overhead	4.20	5.50	9.70
Selling	1.20	0.90	2.10
Total cost	$9.30	$25.85	$35.15

*Fixed cost at 100,000 units per year

Required:

  a. If the flashlight torch sells for $50, how many torches must Hurricane sell each year to break even?

  b. Hurricane Safe had no inventory of torches at the beginning of the year but had 1,000 torches at the end of the year. Hurricane Safe uses variable costing to value ending inventories. What is Hurricane Safe's ending inventory value of torches?

P 10–3: Varilux

Varilux manufactures a single product and sells it for $10 per unit. At the beginning of the year, there were 1,000 units in inventory. Upon further investigation, you discover that units produced last year had $3 of fixed manufacturing costs and $2 of variable manufacturing costs. During the year, Varilux produced 10,000 units of product. Each unit produced generated $3 of variable manufacturing cost. Total fixed manufacturing cost for the current year was $40,000. Selling and administrative costs consisted of $12,000 of variable costs and $18,000 of fixed costs. There were no inventories at the end of the year.

Required:

Prepare two income statements for the current year: one on a variable cost basis and the other on an absorption cost basis. Explain any difference between the two net income numbers and provide calculations supporting your explanation of the difference.

P 10–4: Zipp Cards

Zipp Cards buys baseball cards in bulk from the companies that produce them. Zipp buys sheets of 48 cards, then cuts the sheets into individual cards, and sorts and packages them, usually by team. Zipp then sells the packages to large discount stores. The accompanying table provides information regarding operations for 2016 and 2017.

Zipp Cards—Summary of Operations

	2016	2017
Unit sales (of 48 cards)*	50,000	48,000
Price	$ 5.00	$ 4.90
Production in units (budgeted = actual)	50,000	75,000
Variable cost	$ 1.00	$ 1.00
Fixed manufacturing overhead	$160,000	$160,000

*One unit equals 48 cards.

Volume is measured in terms of 48-card sheets processed. Budgeted production and actual production in 2016 were both 50,000 units. There were no beginning inventories on January 1, 2016. In 2017, budgeted and actual production rose to 75,000 units.

At the beginning of 2017, the president of Zipp was pleasantly surprised when the accountant showed her the income statement for the year 2016. The president remarked, "I'm surprised we made more money in 2017 than 2016. We had to cut prices and we didn't sell as many units, yet we still made more money. Well, you're the accountant and these numbers don't lie."

Required:

a. Prepare income statements for 2016 and 2017 using absorption costing.

b. Prepare a statement reconciling the change in net income from 2016 to 2017. Explain to the president why the firm made more money in 2017 than in 2016.

P 10–5: TransPacific Bank

You are working as a loan officer at TransPacific Bank and are analyzing a loan request for a client when you come across the following footnote in the client's annual report:

Inventories are priced at the lower of cost or market of materials plus other direct (variable) costs. Fixed overheads of $4.2 million this year and $3.0 million last year are excluded from inventories. Omitting such overhead resulted in a reduction in net income (after taxes) of $720,000 for this year. Our tax rate is 40 percent.

In preparing to present the loan application to the bank's loan committee, write a brief paragraph in nontechnical terms describing what this footnote means and how it affects the bank's evaluation of the financial condition of the borrower.

P 10–6: Zeflax Bottles

Zeflax manufactures insulated plastic bottles for bikes that the company sells for $4.00 per bottle. Last year, the company produced 230,000 bottles and sold 200,000 bottles. This year, Zeflax produced 200,000 bottles and sold 230,000 bottles. In both years, Zeflax's fixed manufacturing cost was $500,000 and its variable manufacturing cost was $1.00 per bottle. The president of Zeflax commented, "I don't understand these crazy financial statements. Our prices and costs didn't change, we sell more bottles this year, and we show lower income. Something has got to be wrong."

Required:

a. Prepare income statements for Zeflax for last year and this year using absorption costing. Assume that Zeflax's only costs are the fixed and variable manufacturing costs given in the problem.

b. Prepare income statements for Zeflax for last year and this year using variable costing. Assume that Zeflax's only costs are the fixed and variable manufacturing costs given in the problem.

c. Explain to the president of Zeflax in nontechnical terms why the financial statements prepared by the accountant in part (a) are not in error. In other words, explain to the president why net income fell this year from last year even though Zeflax sold more bottles.

P 10–7: Alliance Tooling

Alliance Tooling produces a single product in its plant. At the beginning of the year, there were no units in inventory. During the year, Alliance produced 120,000 units and sold 100,000 units at $26.75 per unit. Variable manufacturing costs are $13.50 per unit. Alliance pays $2.70 per unit for sales commissions and shipping. It has fixed costs of $720,000 for selling and administration. Its tax rate is 40 percent.

Required:

a. Prepare an income statement for Alliance Tooling using absorption costing.

b. Prepare an income statement for Alliance Tooling using variable costing.

c. Explain why the net income figures computed in parts (a) and (b) differ.

P 10–8: Aspen View

Aspen View produces a full line of sunglasses. This year it began producing a new model of sunglasses, the Peak 32. It produced 5,300 pairs and sold 4,900 pairs. The following table summarizes the fixed and variable costs of producing Peak 32 sunglasses. Aspen View uses variable costing to value its ending inventory.

	Fixed Cost	Variable Cost	Total Cost
Direct labor		$ 3.50	$ 3.50
Direct material		7.50	7.50
Manufacturing overhead	$3.20	4.50	7.70
Advertising	1.20	1.70	2.90
Distribution	.70	.25	.95
Selling	1.20	.90	2.10
Total cost	$6.30	$18.35	$24.65

Required:

a. What is Aspen View's ending inventory value of Peak 32 sunglasses?

b. Aspen View is considering switching from variable costing to absorption costing. Would this year's net income from Peak 32 sunglasses be higher or lower using absorption costing? Explain.

    c. Suppose Aspen View uses absorption costing. If, instead of producing 5,300 pairs of Peak 32s it produced only 5,000, would net income from Peak 32 sunglasses be higher or lower from the smaller production compared to the larger production? Explain.

    d. Aspen View has an opportunity cost of capital of 20 percent. What is the cost of producing 5,300 pairs of Peak 32s instead of 4,900 pairs?

P 10–9:   CLIC Lighters

CLIC manufactures two types of cigarette lighters: Basic and Super. A new plant began producing both lighter models this year. The following variable costing statement summarizes the first year of operations:

CLIC LIGHTERS
Income Statement—Manufacturing
For the Year Ended December 31

	Products		
	Basic	Super	Total
Number of units produced	200,000	160,000	
Number of units sold	180,000	110,000	
Selling price	$ 0.50	$ 0.70	
Sales revenue	$ 90,000	$ 77,000	$167,000
Cost of goods sold	18,000	22,000	40,000
Manufacturing margin	$ 72,000	$ 55,000	$127,000
Fixed overhead			103,000
Income from manufacturing			$ 24,000

    For internal control purposes, variable costing is used. Management also wants income from manufacturing calculated using absorption costing. Fixed overhead is allocated to the two lighters using actual machine minutes. Each Basic lighter requires 1.1 machine minutes and each Super lighter requires 1.2 machine minutes.

Required:

    a. Calculate the fixed overhead rate per machine minute.

    b. Calculate the plant's income from manufacturing for both Basic and Super lighters and for the entire plant using absorption costing.

    c. Prepare a table that reconciles the difference in income from manufacturing reported using variable costing and absorption costing.

    d. Explain in one or two sentences why income from manufacturing differs depending on whether variable costing or absorption costing is used.

P 10–10:   Medford Mug Company

The Medford Mug Company is an old-line maker of ceramic coffee mugs. It imprints company logos and other sayings on mugs for both commercial and wholesale markets. The firm has the capacity to produce 50 million mugs per year, but the recession has cut production and sales in the current year to 15 million mugs. The accompanying table shows the operating statement for 2016.

MEDFORD MUG COMPANY
Income Statement
Year Ending 2016 ($ in Millions)

Sales (15 million @ $2)		$ 30.0
Less costs of goods sold		
Variable cost (15 million @ $0.50)	(7.5)	
Fixed cost	(20.0)	(27.5)
Gross margin		$ 2.5
Less selling and administration		(4.0)
Operating profit		$ (1.5)

At the end of 2016, there was no ending inventory of finished goods.

The board of directors is very concerned about the $1.5 million operating loss. It hires an out-side consultant who reports back that the firm suffers from two problems. First, the president of the company receives a fixed salary, and because she owns no stock, she has very little incentive to worry about company profits. The second problem is that the company has not aggressively mar-keted its product and has not kept up with changing markets. The current president is 64, and the board of directors makes her an offer to retire one year early so that they can hire a new president to turn the firm around. The current president accepts the offer to retire, and the board immediately hires a new president with a proven track record as a turnaround specialist.

The new president is hired with an employment contract that pays a fixed wage of $50,000 a year plus 15 percent of the firm's operating profits (if any). Operating profits are calculated using absorption costing. In 2017, the new president doubles the selling and administration budget to $8 million (which includes the president's salary of $50,000). He designs a new line of "politically correct" sayings to imprint on the mugs and expands inventory and the number of distributors han-dling the mugs. Production is increased to 45 million mugs, and sales climb to 18 million mugs at $2 each. Variable costs per mug remain at $.50 and fixed costs at $20 million in 2017.

At the end of 2017, the president meets with the board of directors and announces he has accepted another job. He believes he has successfully gotten Medford Mug back on track and thanks the board for giving him the opportunity. His new job is helping to turn around another struggling company.

Required:

   a. Calculate the president's bonus for 2017.

   b. Evaluate the performance of the new president in 2017. Did he do as good a job as the numbers in part (*a*) suggest?

P 10–11:   Kothari Inc.

The telecom division of Kothari Inc. produces and sells 100,000 line modulators. Half of the modu-lators are sold externally at $150 per unit, and the other half are sold internally at variable manu-facturing costs plus 10 percent. Kothari uses variable costing to evaluate the telecom division. The following summarizes the cost structure of the telecom division.

	Variable Manufacturing Costs
Materials	$ 27.00
Labor	12.00
Overhead	4.00
Total manufacturing cost	$ 43.00
Fixed manufacturing overhead	$1,700,000
Variable period costs (per units)	$18.00
Fixed period costs	$1,900,000

Required:

a. Calculate the net income of the telecom division (before taxes) using variable costing.

b. Telecom can outsource the final assembly of all 100,000 modulators for $9.00 per modulator. If it does this, it can reduce variable manufacturing cost by $1.00 per unit and fixed manufacturing overhead by $700,000. If the managers of the telecom unit are compensated based on telecom's net income before taxes, do you expect them to outsource the final assembly of the modulators? Show calculations.

c. What happens to the net cash flows of Kothari Inc. if the final assembly of the modulators is outsourced?

P 10–12: Mystic Mugs

Sanjog and Rajiv Gupta have started a business that manufactures and sells thermal mugs. Users personalize the mugs by plugging them into a laptop and downloading their favorite images from a digital camera. The company makes two mug sizes: 16 and 24 ounce mugs. This is its first year of business. The following data summarize operations for the first year.

	16 oz. mug	24 oz. mug	Total
Selling price	$9.75	$11.20	
Direct materials/unit	$1.10	$ 1.45	
Direct labor/unit	$0.60	$0.80	
Variable overhead/unit	$0.30	$0.40	
Variable selling and distribution/unit	$1.65	$1.75	
Units sold	22,500	16,400	
Units produced	24,000	16,400	
Fixed manufacturing overhead			$ 85,000
Fixed selling and distribution			$148,000

There were no beginning inventories. Overhead is assigned to products using direct labor dollars.

Required:

a. Calculate Mystic Mugs's net income before taxes using absorption costing.

b. Calculate Mystic Mugs's net income before taxes using variable costing.

c. Prepare a table that reconciles any difference between the two net income figures calculated in parts (*a*) and (*b*).

d. Write a short memo explaining in lay terms any difference between the two net income figures calculated in parts (*a*) and (*b*).

P 10–13: Avant Designs

Avant Designs designs and manufactures polished-nickel fashion bracelets. It offers two bracelets: Aztec and Mayan. The following data summarize budgeted operations for the current year:

AVANT DESIGNS
Summary of Budgeted Operations
Current Year

	Aztec	Mayan
Sales price/unit	$12	$15
Variable cost/unit	$4	$5
Units sold	30,000	20,000
Machine minutes/unit	2	3
Beginning inventory	0	0
Ending inventory	3,000	1,000

Budgeted fixed manufacturing overhead for the year was $258,000.

Required:

    a. Prepare the budgeted income statement for the year using variable costing.

    b. Prepare the budgeted income statement for the year using absorption costing. Budgeted fixed manufacturing overhead is allocated to the two bracelets using machine minutes.

    c. Explain the difference in the two net income figures computed in parts (*a*) and (*b*). That is, reconcile any difference in earnings and explain why it occurs.

P 10–14:   Taylor Chains

Taylor designs and manufactures high-performance bicycle chains for professional racers and serious amateurs. Two new titanium chain sets, the Challenger and the Tour, sell for €110 and €155, respectively. The following data summarize the cost structure for the two chain sets:

	Challenger	Tour
Number of units budgeted and produced	43,000	55,000
Number of units sold	40,000	52,000
Direct labor hours per unit	2	3
Direct labor cost per hour	€22	€22
Direct materials per unit	€45	€61

Taylor uses an absorption costing system. Overhead is applied to these two products based on direct labor hours using a flexible budget to calculate the overhead rate before production begins for the year. Taylor budgeted (and produced) 43,000 Challenger chains and 55,000 Tour chains. Fixed manufacturing overhead was estimated to be €1.65 million and variable manufacturing overhead was estimated to be €1.75 per direct labor hour. Actual overhead incurred amounted to €2.1 million. Any over- or underabsorbed overhead is written off to cost of goods sold.

Required:

    a. Calculate the overhead rate Taylor used to absorb overhead to the chains.

    b. Using the predetermined overhead rate you calculated in part (*a*), and assuming any over- or underabsorbed overhead is written off to cost of goods sold, calculate Taylor Chains' net income before taxes for both the Challenger and Tour chains and for the entire firm.

    c. Instead of using absorption costing, use variable costing to calculate Taylor Chains' net income before taxes for both the Challenger and Tour chains and for the entire firm. Assume that any over- or underabsorbed overhead is treated as a fixed cost and is written off to cost of goods sold.

    d. Explain why the net income numbers calculated in parts (*b*) and (*c*) differ, and reconcile the difference numerically.

    e. Suppose that next year Taylor incurs total manufacturing overhead of €2.3 million and sells all the chains it produces next year as well as the 6,000 chains it had in inventory from the first year of production. How much manufacturing overhead will appear on Taylor's income statement if the company uses (i) absorption costing or (ii) variable costing?

P 10–15:   Conner Coffees

The Breckenridge, Colorado, plant of Conner Coffees roasts, grinds, and packages premier coffees for upscale coffee cafés. The manager of the Breckenridge plant is evaluated and rewarded based on absorption costing net income of her plant. The Breckenridge plant sells its coffees in five-pound vacuum-sealed foil packs for $60 per five-pound pack. Each pack has a variable manufacturing cost of $30. Annual total fixed manufacturing cost is $48,000. The Breckenridge plant expects to sell 10,000 packs this year, and the manager can choose to produce 10,000, 11,000, or 12,000 packs. Variable cost per pack of $30 will not change if the plant manager produces between 10,000 and 12,000 packs. Assume there are no beginning inventories, fixed and variable period costs are zero, and the corporate income tax rate is zero.

Required:

a. If the manager of the Breckenridge plant has the discretion to set the production level and seeks to maximize her bonus, what production level (10,000, 11,000, or 12,000) will be chosen, and how much absorption costing net income will be reported?

b. Instead of evaluating the Breckenridge manager based on absorption costing net income, the Breckenridge manager is evaluated based on absorption costing residual income of her plant using a 12 percent weighted-average cost of capital. What production level (10,000, 11,000, or 12,000) will the Breckenridge manager select, and how much absorption costing residual income will be reported?

c. Critically analyze the statement: "The use of residual income solves the overproduction problem created by absorption costing." Under what conditions is this statement true, and under what conditions is it false?

P 10–16:   Milan DiElectrics

Milan DiElectrics (MDE), an Italian firm founded by Frank and Florence Potestio 25 years ago, produces a unique class of ruggedized capacitors for military, aerospace, and industrial applications. Ruggedized solid-state components must be able to withstand extreme temperatures and vibration. The Potestios built MDE into a multimillion-euro firm before they sold it last year to BTX, a large Dutch conglomerate. The Potestios agreed to stay with MDE for one year to ensure the smooth integration of MDE into BTX. The sale agreement between the Potestios and BTX set aside a significant portion of the purchase price for MDE that would be paid out to Frank and Florence if certain net income targets were achieved in the year following the sale. The higher the reported income of MDE, the more of the set-aside Frank and Florence receive. The contract specified that generally accepted accounting procedures (including MDE's existing absorption costing system) would be used to calculate MDE's net income for determining the amount of the set-aside returned to the Potestios.

MDE's existing absorption costing system allocates fixed manufacturing overhead to units produced, using the number of capacitors produced. While MDE produces several different models of capacitors with different electrical specifications, there are negligible differences in the variable costs and manufacturing facility resource demands of the various models. So volume is measured in terms of capacitors produced. MDE incurs annual fixed manufacturing overhead of €30 million. Because of the scarcity of certain precious metals and the limited supply of highly skilled technicians to achieve the demanding standards required of MDE capacitors, MDE faces the following variable cost per unit schedule:

Quantity Manufactured per Year (000s)	Variable Cost per Unit (euros)
300	50.0000
350	54.2857
400	60.0000
450	73.3333
500	90.0000

All MDE capacitors sell for €200. Based on detailed conversations with their customers, Frank and Florence are highly certain they will sell 300,000 capacitors this year and for the next several years. However, this is private information known only to the Potestios and not to BTX. The sale agreement does not specify any inventory holding costs or any penalties for excessive ending inventories.

Assume that MDE had no beginning inventories and the only costs (expenses) MDE incurs are the fixed and variable manufacturing costs described earlier.

Required:

a. Given the information provided, how many capacitors do you expect the Potestios will produce this year? Justify your answer with clearly labeled numerical calculations and a short essay explaining how you arrived at your conclusion.

474   *Chapter 10*

b. Assume that the managers of BTX have all the private knowledge held by the Potestios, the BTX managers are in control of MDE, and the BTX managers want to maximize the net cash flows of MDE. What production level will the BTX managers choose? (Assume it is costly to hold inventory and there is no uncertainty regarding expected capacitor sales.) Justify your answer with clearly labeled numerical calculations and a short essay explaining how you arrived at your conclusion.

c. Before starting the current fiscal year, the Potestios are approached by another electronics manufacturing and testing company, ADZ, that proposes the following outsourcing arrangement between ADZ and MDE. ADZ will provide the final manufacturing steps in producing MDE capacitors, testing the completed units, packaging, and shipping them to MDE customers. MDE will pay ADZ €90 per capacitor manufactured. This will allow MDE to reduce its fixed manufacturing cost by €25 million annually, and MDE can reduce its variable manufacturing cost by €10 per capacitor. ADZ is a very high-quality firm, and so the Potestios and BTX have no concerns about the impact of outsourcing some of the manufacturing processes and testing to ADZ. Do you expect the Potestios to accept the ADZ outsourcing proposal? Assume selling price and expected sales do not change if MDE accepts the ADZ proposal. Justify your answer with clearly labeled numerical calculations and a short essay explaining how you arrived at your conclusion.

d. Assume that the managers of BTX have all the private knowledge held by the Potestios, the BTX managers are in control of MDE, and the BTX managers want to maximize the net cash flows of MDE, do you expect the BTX managers to accept the ADZ outsourcing proposal? Justify your answer with clearly labeled numerical calculations and a short essay explaining how you arrived at your conclusion.

e. Explain why your answers to parts (c) and (d) either are the same or different.

P 10–17: Navisky

Navisky designs, manufactures, and sells specialized GPS (global positioning system) devices for commercial applications. For example, Navisky currently sells a system for environmental studies and is planning systems for private aviation and fleet management. The firm has a design team that identifies potential commercial GPS applications and then designs and develops prototypes. Once a prototype is deemed successful and senior management determines that a market exists for the new application, the new design is put into production, and the firm markets the new product through independent salespeople, direct marketing, trade shows, or whatever channel is most appropriate for that market.

Currently, Navisky has one very successful system in production (for environmental studies) and several others in development. Navisky, located in Austria, is one of nine wholly owned subsidiaries of a large Swiss conglomerate. Andreas Hoffman, president of Navisky, expects to retire next year. He receives a fixed salary and a bonus based on reported accounting earnings. The bonus is 5 percent of earnings in excess of €850,000 for actual earnings between €850,000 and €1,400,000. If actual earnings exceed €1,400,000, the bonus is capped at €27,500 (5% × €[1,400,000 − €850,000]). (Earnings, both actual and target, are before taxes.)

The following data summarize Navisky's current operations (in euros).

	Annual Fixed Costs	Variable Costs/Unit
Development costs	€ 900,000	
Selling and administration costs	1,100,000	€300
Manufacturing overhead	2,700,000	190
Direct materials		140
Manufacturing labor		50
Total	€4,700,000	€680
Selling price/unit	€5,500	

Senior management at Navisky, including Mr. Hoffman, expects to sell about 1,200 units of the environmental GPS device this year. However, they have considerable discretion in setting production levels. Their plant has excess capacity and can produce up to 1,500 environmental devices without seeing any increase in the variable manufacturing costs per unit.

Navisky uses a traditional absorption costing system to absorb manufacturing overhead into product costs for inventory valuation and to calculate earnings for internal compensation purposes as well as external reporting. At the beginning of the current fiscal year, there was no beginning inventory of the environmental GPS devices.

Required:

a. How many units of the environmental GPS device would Mr. Hoffman like to see Navisky produce if he expects to sell 1,200 devices this year?

b. Suppose Mr. Hoffman's bonus calculation was based on net income after including a charge for inventory holding costs at 20 percent of the ending inventory value. In other words, his bonus is 5 percent of net income in excess of $850,000 up to $1,400,000 where net income includes a 20 percent inventory holding cost. How many units of the environmental GPS device would Mr. Hoffman like to see produced if he expects to sell 1,200 devices this year?

c. Explain why your answers in parts (b) and (c) differ, if they do.

d. How many units of the environmental GPS device would Mr. Hoffman like to see produced, assuming he expects to sell 1,200 devices this year if Navisky's net income is calculated using variable costing and net income includes a 20 percent inventory holding cost?

P 10–18:   DIM

Diagnostic Imaging & Medical (DIM) has introduced a revolutionary new magnetic resonance imaging (MRI) device that it sells to hospital radiology departments. Their new device has a much larger chamber that reduces patients' claustrophobic reactions compared to current machines. The following table displays how total cost per year varies with annual production. In other words, if DIM produces nine machines, the nine machines have a total manufacturing cost of $2.93 million.

Units	Total Manufacturing Cost
0	$1,000,000
1	1,500,000
2	1,800,000
3	1,950,000
4	2,050,000
5	2,170,000
6	2,314,000
7	2,486,000
8	2,690,000
9	2,930,000
10	3,210,000
11	3,534,000
12	3,906,000
13	4,330,000
14	4,810,000
15	5,350,000

To simplify the analysis, assume DIM has no period costs, only the product costs in the preceding table. Management receives a bonus based on reported profits, where profits are calculated using absorption costing.

Required:

 a. At a selling price of $500,000 per MRI, management expects to sell six units next year and plans to produce a few extra machines. The extra units are for training, marketing, and temporary spare parts in case an installed MRI fails and spare parts are needed. Management has financing and production capacity to vary production between 6 and 10 units. How many MRIs do you expect management to produce? Show your analysis that leads to this conclusion.

 b. Instead of expecting to sell six units at $500,000 each as in part (*a*), management expects to sell 11 units at $400,000 per unit. With expected sales at 11 units and a price of $400,000, DIM has the resources to produce between 11 and 15 MRIs. How many MRIs do you expect management to produce if expected sales are 11 units? Show your analysis that leads to this conclusion.

 c. Describe the differences and similarities in your answers to parts (*a*) and (*b*). Pay particular attention to the relation between units sold [6 in part (*a*) and 11 in part (*b*)] and expected units produced, and how this relation differs or does not differ between parts (*a*) and (*b*). Also, explain what is causing your answers in parts (*a*) and (*b*) to differ or not differ.

 d. Provide some plausible explanations of why average costs may increase beyond a certain quantity of production.

P 10–19: Easton Plant

The Easton plant produces sheet metal chassis for flat-panel televisions. The chassis are manufactured on a computerized, numerically controlled (NC) machine that cuts, drills, and bends the metal to form the chassis for the television set. Two different chassis are produced: HX–3 and DX–55.

Easton has a single plantwide overhead account. Actual machine minutes on the NC machine are used to distribute overhead to the two products. There were no beginning inventories of work in process or finished goods. The following table summarizes the planned and actual production data for the year:

	HX–3	*DX–55*
Planned unit production	6,500	3,400
Budgeted machine minutes per unit	× 6.2	× 9.8
Expected machine minutes	40,300	33,320
Actual units produced	7,200	3,900
Actual volume (machine minutes)	44,640	38,220

The following data summarize the flexible overhead budget:

	Fixed	*Variable (per Minute)*
Depreciation	$695,000	
Indirect labor		$0.80
Indirect materials		1.00
Property taxes	28,000	
Utilities	55,000	0.90
Other	42,000	0.30
Total	$820,000	$3.00

At the end of the year, the following overhead amounts had been incurred:

	Actual
Depreciation	$ 695,000
Indirect labor	71,288
Indirect materials	84,860
Property taxes	31,000
Utilities	133,074
Other	68,858
Total	$1,084,080

Any over- or underabsorbed overhead is written off to cost of goods sold. The ending finished goods inventory consists of 2,000 units of HX–3 and 1,000 units of DX–55, representing 13,400 minutes and 10,300 minutes of actual machine time, respectively.

Required: (Round all dollars, including overhead rates, to two decimal places.)

    a. Calculate the overhead absorption rate set at the start of the year.

    b. Calculate the over- or underabsorbed overhead for the year.

    c. The firm is considering switching to variable costing. What effect would this decision have on Easton's reported profit for this year? To implement variable costing at the end of the year, variable overhead is calculated as $3.00 per machine minute times the actual number of machine minutes. Fixed overhead is the difference between total actual overhead and variable overhead.

    d. Instead of defining fixed overhead as all overhead in excess of variable overhead as in part (*c*), assume the following: Fixed overhead is budgeted fixed overhead ($820,000), and variable overhead is the difference between total actual overhead and budgeted fixed overhead. What is the difference between absorption net income and variable costing income given these new assumptions?

P 10–20: Promotional Products

Promotional Products (PP) manufactures and sells electronic accessories such as smartphone cases, flash drives, etc. PP uses a traditional full absorption costing system for financial reporting and has a risk-adjusted weighted-average cost of capital of 18 percent when making capital investment decisions.

    PP recently added a new, proprietary, one-terabyte flash drive key chain called "MegaFlash" to its product line. It has hired a product line manager, Karva Dewan, to manage this new one-terabyte product. Dewan can buy 150,000 to 230,000 of the internal circuit boards from one particular Asian producer for $25 per drive. She then has to incur another $5 per drive to mount the circuit board into the key chain. To purchase more than 230,000 one-terabyte circuit boards, she will need to use a second manufacturer that charges $35 per one-terabyte circuit board. Rather than using LIFO or FIFO, PP uses average cost to value inventories.[5]

    To insert the circuit board into the key chain and produce a finished MegaFlash requires fixed manufacturing overhead (leased equipment, plant space, utilities, etc.) of $1,500,000 per year. Karva expects to sell 200,000 one-terabyte key chains per year at the profit maximizing price of $50 per drive to both Internet (Amazon) and brick-and-mortar retailers (Walmart and Target). Ms. Dewan receives a bonus based on the reported profits from MegaFlash, calculated as revenues less fully

---

    [5]The average cost per unit is computed as: Total manufacturing costs incurred ÷ Total units manufactured.

478   *Chapter 10*

absorbed cost of goods sold. Fully absorbed cost of goods sold includes both fixed and variable manufacturing costs.

Required:

a. How many units of MegaFlash do you expect Ms. Dewan will produce in the first year if she wishes to maximize her first-year bonus? Support your answer with a rigorous data analysis.

b. Is Dewan's decision in part (*a*) maximizing Promotional Product's value? Why or why not?

c. Provide two suggestions as to how the owners of PP can change Ms. Dewan's performance measure to better align the owners' interest with that of Ms. Dewan. Describe how each of your suggested changes helps better align the owners' interest with that of Ms. Dewan.

d. Describe any potential problems/pitfalls that might arise in each of your two suggested changes in part (*c*).

P 10–21:   Ceramtics

Ceramtics manufactures a high-speed ceramic switch used in the telecommunications industry. Data about Ceramtics's operations for 2017 and 2018 are presented below:

Ceramtics
Summary of Operations
2017 and 2018

	2017	*2018*
Sales price/switch	$4,400	$4,400
Number of switches sold	2,000	2,000
Number of switches produced	2,400	1,600
Fixed manufacturing costs	$2.4 million	$2.4 million
Variable manufacturing costs per switch	$2,800	$2,800

Ceramtics had no beginning inventories in 2017. To simplify the computations, assume Ceramtics has only manufacturing expenses (i.e., there are no selling, administration, distribution, or interest expenses and no taxes). Ceramtics uses the FIFO method for inventory costing. Assume that budgeted volume and actual volume are the same, budgeted fixed and actual fixed overhead are the same, and budgeted variable and actual variable overhead per switch are the same. In other words, at the end of the year there is no over- or underabsorbed overhead.

Required:

a. Prepare income statements for 2017 and 2018 using absorption costing.

b. Prepare income statements for 2017 and 2018 using variable costing.

c. Reconcile any differences in income for 2017 and 2018 between absorption costing and variable costing from parts (*a*) and (*b*). That is, explain why absorption and variable costing give different net income numbers in 2017 and 2018.

P 10–22:   GrwnPwr

GrwnPwr, a privately held startup company, designs and manufacturers patented electrodes for electric-powered vehicle batteries. GrwnPwr's patented electrodes allow battery makers to produce lighter and more powerful batteries for electric vehicles (cars, trucks, heavy equipment, etc.) because of GrwnPwr's unique electrode design and chemical composition. Each electrode consists of a proprietary metal alloy that is precisely machined in a four-axis computer numerical controlled (CNC) gang mill that can produce the extremely tight tolerances needed for lighter and more powerful batteries. Battery manufacturers then assemble from three to six electrodes to form a complete battery unit.

You work as a financial analyst for a private equity firm that is considering making a direct investment in GrwnPwr. Your boss has asked you to analyze the firm's current financial condition. But before starting your analysis, your boss notices that GrwnPwr is using variable costing rather than traditional absorption costing. During GrwnPwr's first year of operations, it produced and sold two different electrodes, the X759 model and the Z200 model. GrwnPwr's variable costing income statement for its first year of operations is provided below. Note there were no beginning inventories of models X759 and Z200.

	X759	Z200	Total
Revenue	$537,600	$533,200	$1,070,800
Direct materials	(31,360)	(31,820)	(63,180)
Direct labor	(32,480)	(26,660)	(59,140)
Fixed manufacturing overhead			(632,000)
Selling, general, admin expenses			($420,000)
Net income before taxes			($103,520)

The footnotes to the financial statements read as follows: "Finished goods inventory under variable costing at year end consisted of $31,920 of X759 and $25,160 of Z200."

Your boss isn't quite sure what the difference is between variable and absorption costing and doesn't know how the reported net income before taxes would change if GrwnPwr used absorption costing. He asks you to prepare a statement showing what GrwnPwr's net income before tax would have been if it had used absorption costing. You contact GrwnPwr's CFO and learn the following additional facts:

- Each X759 electrode sold for $48.
- Each Z200 electrode sold for $62.
- Each X759 electrode required 13.5 minutes of milling time.
- Each Z200 electrode required 18.2 minutes of milling time.
- There is no variable overhead in GrwnPwr's manufacturing process. That is, manufacturing costs consist only of direct materials and labor (the variable costs) and fixed manufacturing overhead. Fixed manufacturing overhead consists entirely of lease payments on equipment, the factory rent, and other cash expenses.
- You conclude that milling minutes is the most appropriate way to absorb fixed manufacturing overhead to the electrodes.

Required:

a. Prepare a statement showing what GrwnPwr's net income before tax would have been if GrwnPwr had used absorption costing.

b. Write a memo to your boss (i) explaining why the absorption costing and variable net income before tax amounts do or do not differ and (ii) discussing how your absorption costing net income before tax should (or should not) be used in your private equity firm's decision to invest in GrwnPwr. In particular, how should your private equity firm's valuation of GrwnPwr change (or not change) based on your absorption costing statement prepared in part (*a*)?

480 *Chapter 10*

P 10–23: Sants Brakes Co.

The current year's income statement for Sants Brakes Co. on a variable costing basis appears in the accompanying table.

SANTS BRAKES COMPANY
Income Statement—Manufacturing
For the Year Ended December 31 ($000s)

	Product Lines			
	G-226	G-348	G-714	Total
Number of units sold (in thousands)	650	280	120	—
Sales revenue	$7,800	$2,240	$1,920	$11,960
Cost of goods sold	5,200	840	480	6,520
Manufacturing margin	$2,600	$1,400	$1,440	$ 5,440
Fixed overhead				3,600
Income from manufacturing				$ 1,840

Inventories of finished stock were increased during the year in anticipation of increases in sales volume in the current year. Inventories in units of product for the beginning and end of the year follow.

	Beginning Inventory	Ending Inventory
G-226	20,000	90,000
G-348	50,000	90,000
G-714	20,000	50,000

The budgeted operating level for assigning fixed overhead to production is 1.8 million machine hours. One-half hour is required to produce a unit of G-226, two hours are required for a unit of G-348, and four hours are required for a unit of G-714.

Required:

a. Recast the income statement on an absorption costing basis.

b. Explain why the income from manufacturing on the absorption costing statement differs from the income on the variable costing statement. Show your computations.

Case

Case 10–1: Joon

Joon manufactures and sells to retailers a variety of home care and personal care products. Joon has a single plant that produces all four of its product lines: Stick Goods (brooms and mops), Floor Care (strippers, soaps, and waxes), Brushes (hair brushes and shoe brushes), and Aerosols (room deodorizers, bug spray, furniture wax). The following statement summarizes Joon's financial performance for the most recent fiscal year.

	Stick Goods	Floor Care	Brushes	Aerosols	Total
Quantity (000 cases)	20	35	15	30	
Direct labor hours/case	1.5	1	2	1.6	
Total direct labor hours (000)	30	35	30	48	143
Manufacturing cost per case:					
Direct material	$ 51.00	$ 21.00	$ 31.00	$ 11.00	
Variable overhead	5.25	3.50	7.00	5.60	
Direct labor cost	31.50	21.00	42.00	33.60	
Fixed overhead	46.50	31.00	62.00	49.60	
Total cost per case	$ 134.25	$ 76.50	$ 142.00	$ 99.80	
Selling price per case	$ 165.00	$ 122.00	$ 189.00	$ 145.00	
Total revenue (000)	3,300	4,270	2,835	4,350	$14,755.00
Operating margin per case	30.75	45.50	47.00	45.20	
Total operating margin (000)	615	1,592.5	705	1,356	$ 4,268.50
Selling, general, and administrative (000):					
Fixed					(1,350.00)
Variable (20% of revenues)					(2,951.00)
Net income (loss) (000)					$ (32.50)

Direct labor costs $21 per hour. Fixed manufacturing overhead of $4.433 million is allocated to products based on direct labor hours. Last year, the fixed manufacturing overhead rate was $31 per direct labor hour ($4.433 million/143,000 direct labor hours). Variable manufacturing overhead is $3.50 per direct labor hour. Selling, general, and administrative (SG&A) expenses consist of fixed costs ($1.35 million) and variable costs ($2,951 million). The variable SG&A is 20 percent of revenues.

The Joon plant has considerable excess capacity. Senior management has identified a potential acquisition target, Snuffy, that sells a line of automotive products (car waxes, soaps, brushes, and so forth) that are complementary to Joon's existing products and that can be manufactured in Joon's plant. Snuffy does not have any manufacturing facilities, but rather outsources the production of its products to contract manufacturers. Snuffy can be purchased for $38 million. The following table summarizes Snuffy's current operating data:

Snuffy Operating Data
Most Recent Fiscal Year

	Car Care
Quantity (000 cases)	60
Direct labor hours per case	1.9
Direct material per case	$18
Selling price per case	$138
Additional fixed manufacturing overhead	$450,000
Additional fixed SG&A	$400,000

Senior management argues that the reason Joon is currently losing money is that volumes have fallen in the plant and that the remaining products are having to carry an increasingly larger share of the overhead. This has caused some Joon product managers to raise prices. Senior managers realize that they must drive more volume into the plant if Joon is to return to profitability.

Since organic growth (i.e., growth from existing products) is difficult due to a very competitive marketplace, management proposes to the board of directors the purchase of Snuffy as a way to drive additional volume into the plant. With volume of 60,000 cases and 1.9 direct labor hours per case, Snuffy's car care product line will add 114,000 direct labor hours to the plant and increase volume about 80 percent (114,000/143,000). This additional volume will significantly reduce the overhead the existing products must absorb and allow the product managers to lower prices. To incorporate Snuffy's manufacturing and distribution into Joon's current operations, Joon will have to incur additional fixed manufacturing overhead of $450,000 per year for new equipment and $400,000 per year for additional SG&A expenses.

Required:

a. Prepare a pro forma financial statement that shows Joon's financial performance (net income) for the most recent fiscal year assuming that Joon has already acquired Snuffy's car care products and has incorporated them into Joon's manufacturing and SG&A processes. In preparing your analysis, make the following assumptions:

   i. Snuffy's products have the same fixed and variable cost structure as Joon's existing lines (i.e., variable overhead is $3.50 per direct labor hour, and variable SG&A is 20 percent of revenues).

   ii. The addition of Snuffy products does not change the demand for Joon's existing products.

   iii. There are no positive or negative externalities in manufacturing from having the additional Snuffy volume in the plant.

   iv. There is sufficient excess capacity in the plant and the local labor markets to absorb the additional Snuffy volume without causing labor rates or raw material prices to rise.

b. Based on your financial analysis in part (*a*), should Joon acquire Snuffy?

c. Evaluate management's arguments in favor of acquiring Snuffy.

d. What other advice would you offer Joon's management?

Chapter Eleven

Criticisms of Absorption Cost Systems: Inaccurate Product Costs

Chapter Outline

The last chapter described a specific problem with absorption cost systems. Since absorption cost systems allocate some fixed manufacturing costs to products, producing extra units causes these fixed costs to be spread over more units. As long as variable cost per unit does not increase, average cost falls with higher production levels. Holding sales constant, managers can increase profits by overproducing. Profit margins increase because some of the fixed manufacturing cost is now in inventory rather than charged to net income.

This chapter describes a second criticism of absorption costing: It can produce misleading product costs. In most absorption cost systems, overheads are usually allocated based on direct labor or direct material. However, overheads can vary in other ways—for example, with machine setups. If the cost allocation system does not use allocation bases that represent the cause-and-effect relations with overhead, then inaccurate product costs are generated. Section A describes this problem in greater detail. Section B presents activity-based costing (ABC) as an alternative to traditional absorption costing.[1] Activity-based costing seeks to derive more accurate product costs. However, activity-based costing also comes with its own limitations. These are described in section C. Section D summarizes how most firms use activity-based costing.

A. Inaccurate Product Costs

Some cost accounting systems fail to track the physical activities that consume resources and generate costs. For example, the accounting system records the labor costs of setting up machines (financial flows). But in many plants, the accounting system does not record the number of setups or what caused them. The accounting system records the costs incurred in the purchasing department but not usually what is driving the costs of purchasing, such as part numbers, number of purchases, and inspections.

Consider the following example. Procter & Gamble (P&G) has several plants, each producing a number of laundry soaps (Tide, Cheer, and Oxydol, among others). Tide is produced for a few days; then another product is produced. Suppose that P&G has just two plants. The plants are the same size and have identical equipment. Plant S produces 10 million pounds per year of a single soap: Tide. Plant M also produces 10 million pounds per year but of multiple brands of soap: 3 million pounds of Tide, 2 million pounds of Cheer, 1 million pounds of Oxydol, half a million pounds of private store labels, and numerous specialty soaps. Twenty different brands are produced in plant M over the course of a year. To simplify the example and highlight the essential point, assume that the cost of the raw material in each brand of soap is the same. Moreover, assume that producing a pound of soap requires the same direct labor and machine hours at both plants. Each pound of soap, regardless of the brand, has direct labor and direct material costs of $0.34.

Are the plants' operations the same? That is, could a visitor distinguish between the two plants without resorting to looking at the actual soap brands produced? Plant M will have a larger support staff for scheduling production, inspecting purchased items, purchasing and handling different inventory items, and making engineering changes. Plant M is handling more transactions (purchase orders, inspections, material movements, order tracking) than plant S. Therefore, plant M will have larger overhead expenditures than

---

[1]Strictly speaking, activity-based costing (ABC) is not an alternative to absorption costing. ABC, like absorption costing, ultimately traces all overhead to cost objects. The difference between traditional absorption and ABC, as explained later in the chapter, involves the complexity of allocations and how the cost allocation bases are chosen.

Managerial Application: ABB Robots	ABB, a Swiss-Swedish engineering conglomerate, allocated overhead costs to manufacturing industrial robots using direct labor and material costs. Since it took about the same amount of direct labor and materials to make a robot tailored to a customer's needs as a standard robot that is manufactured in high volumes, both robots were allocated roughly the same overheads. However, the customized robot places more demands on the engineers, purchasers, and inspectors than a mass-produced standard robot. ABB found it was understating the cost of the customized robot and overstating the cost of the standard one.

SOURCE: "Activity-Based Costing," *The Economist*, June 29, 2009, www.economist.com/node/13933812.

plant S. Suppose plant S has total annual factory overhead of $1.4 million, and plant M has $1.8 million of overhead.

Now consider how a traditional absorption costing system will cost the soaps produced in the two factories. Because each pound of soap has the same direct labor, direct materials, and machine time, each pound in plant M will have the same reported cost, which will be higher than the cost reported in plant S. Tide in plant M will show a higher accounting cost than the identical Tide in plant S because of the higher overhead in plant M. The accounting cost of the soaps in the two plants is as follows:

Cost of One Pound of Soap in Plants S and M

	Plant S	Plant M
Direct labor and materials	$0.34	$0.34
Overhead*	0.14	0.18
Total cost	$0.48	$0.52

	Plant S	Plant M
*Factory overhead (millions)	$ 1.4	$ 1.8
Volume (millions)	10	10
Overhead per pound	$0.14	$0.18

Both plants have the same direct costs. If overhead is assigned to soap using direct labor, direct materials, or machine hours, then each pound of soap in both factories will receive one ten millionth of its plant's overhead.

A competitive market for laundry soap will drive the price of soap down toward the cost in plant S, which is $0.48. Suppose the market price for soap becomes $0.51. Plant S is making an accounting profit of $0.03 per pound. Plant M managers, relying on their accounting system's reported cost, will appear to be incurring a loss of $0.01 per pound. Assuming that customers are willing to pay higher prices for specialty products, plant M's small-volume specialty soaps can be priced higher and will appear more profitable. Plant M will deemphasize Tide and further differentiate its product line by adding more specialty soaps. But doing so will drive up overhead costs as production becomes more complex with the additional resources required for scheduling, purchasing, and managing even more different soap inventories.

Exercise 11-1

O'Reilly Manufacturing produces three models of a product: Super, Supreme, and Ultra. These models are basically the same design, but different quality standards are applied in the production process. Frequent production line stops, adjustments, and startups cause a certain amount of scrap costs. Also, scrap occurs when inspectors reject a product for not meeting specifications. Once rejected, the product has no commercial value and is hauled away. All costs incurred to produce a scrapped product are charged to a scrap account, which is part of overhead. The budgeted operating statement for the firm, by product, follows.

O'REILLY MANUFACTURING
Budgeted Operating Statement

	Super	Supreme	Ultra	Total
Unit volume	85,000	42,000	13,000	
Selling price	$205	$225	$235	
Revenue	$17,425,000	$9,450,000	$3,055,000	$29,930,000
Less:				
Raw materials	$ 8,500,000	$4,200,000	$1,300,000	$14,000,000
Direct labor*	5,312,500	3,150,000	975,000	9,437,500
Overhead†	3,478,245	2,062,395	638,360	6,179,000
Total cost	$17,290,745	$9,412,395	$2,913,360	$29,616,500
Profits	$ 134,255	$ 37,605	$ 141,640	$ 313,500

*Direct labor cost is $25 per hour.

†Overhead costs are allocated to products based on direct labor dollars.

Overheads consist of:

Depreciation	$3,500,000
Indirect labor	450,000
Scrap	1,679,000
Other	550,000
Total	$6,179,000

	Super	Supreme	Ultra
Direct labor hours per unit	2.5 hours	3 hours	3 hours
Total scrap	$850,000	$504,000	$325,000
Profits per unit	$1.58	$0.90	$10.90

Management is concerned about the relatively low profit per unit of Supreme as compared to the Ultra line and is considering a variety of marketing strategies to increase sales of Ultra because its profit margins are substantially higher.

Required:

Critically analyze management's conclusion that profits are substantially higher on Ultra. Present supporting figures to back up your analysis and conclusions.

Solution:

Management is incorrect in concluding that Ultra is more profitable than Super and Supreme. They are being misled by the allocation of overhead costs, including the treatment of scrap costs. All the scrap costs are charged to overhead and then allocated to the products based on direct labor costs. But Super and Supreme have substantially lower scrap rates per unit of good product than Ultra, as the following table indicates:

	Scrap	Units	Dollars Scrap per Unit
Super	$850,000	85,000	$10
Supreme	504,000	42,000	12
Ultra	325,000	13,000	25

A less cost-distorting treatment of the scrap cost is not to assign scrap to the overhead account and then allocate it back to the products based on direct labor dollars but rather to assign it directly to each product as follows:

	Super	Supreme	Ultra	Total
Revenue	$17,425,000	$9,450,000	$3,055,000	$29,930,000
Less:				
Raw materials	$ 8,500,000	$4,200,000	$1,300,000	14,000,000
Direct labor	5,312,500	3,150,000	975,000	9,437,500
Scrap costs	850,000	504,000	325,000	1,679,000
Overhead*	2,533,113	1,501,987	464,900	4,500,000
Total cost	$17,195,613	$9,355,987	$3,064,900	$29,616,500
Profits (loss)	$ 229,387	$ 94,013	$ (9,900)	$ 313,500
Unit costs	$ 202.30	$ 222.76	$ 235.76	
Profits per unit	$ 2.70	$ 2.24	$ (.76)	

*Allocate the remaining overhead using direct labor dollars:

Total overhead	$6,179,000
Less: Scrap	(1,679,000)
Overhead to be allocated	$4,500,000
Divided by: Direct labor dollars	÷ $9,437,500
Overhead rate per direct labor dollar	$ 0.476821

By directly tracing the scrap costs to the products, Ultra is now showing a loss, and Super and Supreme are showing a larger profit than before.

Even though Ultra shows a loss, we cannot conclude that it should be discontinued because we have not analyzed how the other overhead costs (e.g., indirect labor) vary across the different products. If the remaining overhead costs include common costs, then dropping one product does not reduce the firm's total costs by the amount of overhead assigned to this dropped product. Remember the adage—"Beware of product line profitability analyses that include allocated joint or common costs."

The problem in plant M is the way the traditional absorption costing system allocates costs. Even though producing Tide in both factories uses the same resources, plant M has higher overhead costs than plant S. Many costs in a plant are driven not so much by the number of units produced as by the number of transactions, such as machine setups, purchase orders, or shipments. Allocating these transaction-based costs using unit volume causes products with large production volumes to be assigned too large a share of these costs.

When managers and accountants speak of inaccurate product costs, they mean that overhead costs are not being tracked to the activities causing the costs (such as setups). Rather, these costs are being combined with other cost pools (such as maintenance), and these overly aggregated cost pools are then being allocated to products using allocation bases (like direct labor) that do not capture the actual cause-and-effect relation driving the particular costs in the overly aggregated cost pool. In the preceding example, Tide does not really cost more to produce in plant M than in plant S. However, the accounting system inaccurately reports this. Overhead costs are higher in plant M because of the additional products produced. If Tide were the only soap produced in plant M, its cost would be the same as in plant S. Thus, the accounting system in plant M inaccurately charges Tide for some overhead costs that should be assigned to those products in plant M that are causing the higher costs.

Traditional absorption systems can be modified to provide more accurate product costs in plant M. An activity-based cost system is one such modification. Whether activity-based systems are truly alternatives to absorption systems or simply modifications is a legitimate question, although such questioning ultimately deteriorates into a semantic debate. The important point, however, is that managers seeking to control costs must manage the cost drivers. Controlling costs requires identifying and managing the key factors that generate costs, not massaging the cost numbers or cost allocation procedures. Activity-based cost systems (described next) are intended to provide more accurate product costs and to give managers the data to manage the cost drivers. Activity-based costing recognizes that overhead costs vary not only with volume but also with the range of items manufactured—that is, their diversity and complexity. Finally, examining activity-based systems furthers our understanding of costing systems in general.

| **Concept Questions** | Q11–1 | Why does traditional absorption costing often yield inaccurate product costs? |
| | Q11–2 | In a plant producing multiple products, would absorption costing overcost or undercost the more complex products? Why? |

B. Activity-Based Costing

This section describes a type of absorption costing called *activity-based costing* (ABC). While a manufacturing setting is chosen to describe activity-based costing, this technique has also been applied in insurance and banking institutions, nonprofit organizations, and the marketing and distribution departments of firms.

Activities are repetitive tasks performed by each specialized group or activity center within the firm. Activity centers are cost centers (see Chapter 5). Costs are assigned to activities (i.e., cost centers) in the initial step of the process, and then these activity center costs are either directly traced or allocated to products. In this sense, activity-based cost systems are very similar to the two-stage allocation procedure depicted in Figure 9–4. However, activity-based cost systems differ from more traditional absorption cost systems in terms of the choice of allocation bases used to allocate department/activity center costs.

An entire vocabulary has developed surrounding activity-based costing, including activity-based management, activity drivers, resource drivers, cost driver analysis, and value-chain costing. Since the purpose of this section is to introduce the concepts of activity-based costing, not to treat the subject comprehensively, the terminology used in this chapter is simplified from that found in practice.[2]

1. Choosing Cost Drivers

Installing an activity-based cost system begins with an analysis of the types of transactions that generate costs in each support department (e.g., purchasing, engineering, maintenance, and quality control). Cost analysts examine each department to understand what drives the costs in that support department. Examples of typical cost drivers are the number of inspections or testings, receipts of raw materials and parts, the number of part numbers in inventory, machine setups, and engineering change orders. For each support department studied, the primary cost driver is identified.

Once the cost driver is determined, it can be classified into one of four mutually exclusive categories: unit level, batch level, product level, or capacity sustaining. Figure 11–1 illustrates these four categories in an activity-based costing system. **Unit-level costs** arise from activities that are performed at least once for each unit of product. For example, machining a surface, drilling a hole, or attaching a subassembly must be done for each and every unit produced. These costs include direct labor and material and variable overhead.

Batch-level costs arise from activities performed once for each batch or lot of products. For example, machine setups, cleanup, and moving the batch to the next step in the production process depend on the number of batches rather than the number of units in each batch. Purchase orders and inspections are also examples of batch-level activities. They occur once for each batch, independent of how many units are in the batch.

Product-level costs arise from activities to support the production of the product type or model. For example, engineering support costs for process modifications and product design depend on the existence of the product line and do not vary with the number of units or number of batches produced. Other examples of product-level costs include the costs of engineering change orders, product enhancement, and packaging costs unique to the product.

Finally, **capacity-sustaining costs** arise from all remaining activities required for the overall productive capacity of the factory. For example, plant security, maintenance, administration, insurance, depreciation, utilities, and property taxes are incurred to maintain the production capability of the plant and do not depend on the number of units, batches, or product lines produced. These are common costs, shared by all the products

FIGURE 11-1

Activity-based cost system categorization and allocation of indirect costs

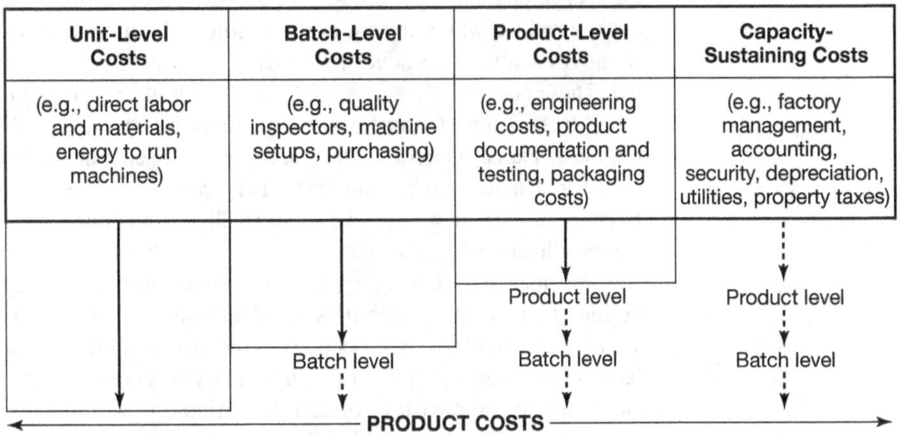

Unit-Level Costs	Batch-Level Costs	Product-Level Costs	Capacity-Sustaining Costs
(e.g., direct labor and materials, energy to run machines)	(e.g., quality inspectors, machine setups, purchasing)	(e.g., engineering costs, product documentation and testing, packaging costs)	(e.g., factory management, accounting, security, depreciation, utilities, property taxes)
		Product level	Product level
	Batch level	Batch level	Batch level

← PRODUCT COSTS →

[2]The interested reader is referred to R. Kaplan and S. Anderson, *Time-Driven Activity-Based Costing: A Simpler and More Powerful Path to Higher Profits* (Boston: Harvard Business School Publishing, 2007).

490   *Chapter 11*

Managerial Application: AT&T and ABC	The business billing center of AT&T, with $30 million annual expenses, prints, sorts, and mails invoices to business customers. Its activities include monitoring the billing process, editing and checking the data, and correcting errors. It installed ABC to control costs. First, a thorough analysis of the process revealed the underlying cost drivers for each activity (number of customers tested, change requests, service orders, and pages printed). Second, costs were assigned to cost objects based on the cost drivers.
	Armed with the new cost data, management benchmarked their operations with billing centers in other companies. In two years, AT&T's billing center reduced operating expenses 26 percent even though billable minutes increased 46 percent.

SOURCE: T. Hobdy, J. Thompson, and P. Sharman, "Activity-Based Management at AT&T," www.focusedmanagement. com/knowledge_base/articles/fmi_articles/middle/at&t.htm.

produced. These capacity-sustaining costs are not caused by, and hence cannot be tracked to, any particular product, batch, or product line.

Some writers suggest splitting out additional levels such as process-level costs, which arise from the engineering activities necessary to maintain a particular production process, or customer-sustaining costs, which arise from sales or engineering activities required to support a particular customer. Conceptually, these are similar to product-level activities. To simplify the exposition, only four cost levels are discussed here. (In practice, the number of levels used by a particular system depend on the firm's specific circumstances.)

In Figure 11–1, direct costs that are unit-level costs are traced directly to the units produced. Other costs, such as indirect labor to set up machines or to purchase materials for each batch, cannot be traced directly to units; they depend not on the number of units in the batch, but only on the number of batches. For example, the work load in the purchasing department usually depends on the number of purchase orders issued, receipt of the order, and inspection of the order. The amount of work is about the same whether 100 units or 10,000 units are in the order. Once these batch-level costs are traced to a batch, they can be allocated to the product by dividing by the number of units in the batch.

Product-level costs, such as engineering costs and some maintenance costs, are incurred only if the particular product line exists. These costs vary with the number of distinct products in the plant, not with the number of batches or units. For example, the number of engineers needed to maintain the product line often depends on the complexity of the product, which in turn is a function of the number of different parts in the product. Some firms allocate product-level costs based on the number of different parts in the product. These costs are then averaged over the number of units produced.

All remaining factory costs that cannot be traced directly to units, batches, or product lines, such as general factory management, accounting department costs, and property taxes, are capacity-sustaining costs. They can be allocated to units by first allocating them to product lines, then to batches, and finally to the units in the batches. Alternatively, they can be allocated directly to units using direct labor or machine hours.

When each cost is segregated into one of these four categories, the factory is broken up into distinct sets of activities, or identifiable operations that consume resources. Costs are accumulated by activity centers. Cost drivers should accurately reflect the underlying factors that cause a particular overhead activity's costs to vary. Cost drivers (both financial and nonfinancial measures of activity) mimic how products consume resources in activity centers. ABC attempts to refine the set of internal "tax rates" (Chapter 7) used to tax externalities inside the firm. Instead of taxing direct materials for purchasing department costs, purchase orders or part numbers are the cost drivers and become the taxed activity.

Exercise 11-2

Southridge is a 200-bed hospital and has the following cost structure: $250 per bed per day for nursing care, food, linen, and janitorial services; $50 per bed per day for occupancy costs such as depreciation, administration, and utilities; and $120 per patient for admission in the admitting department and social work discharge planning. The bed cost of $250 varies with the number of bed days. Occupancy cost represents the cost of providing capacity and does not vary with bed days. The $120 admission cost varies with the number of patients admitted. Each patient, regardless of the number of days in the hospital, must be admitted and then discharged. Two years ago, the average patient stayed seven days. Now, the average patient stays four days. To simplify the illustration, assume all hospital beds are always occupied. Note that prescription drugs and medical procedures such as X-rays and lab tests are billed directly to patients and are not included in Southridge's operating costs.

Required:

a. What was the total annual cost of operating Southridge two years ago?

b. What is the total annual cost of operating Southridge today?

c. Describe why total costs increased from two years ago to today.

d. How has the average cost of a patient stay changed?

e. Categorize the three cost categories above using the ABC labels: unit-level, batch-level, product-level, and capacity-sustaining costs.

Solution:

a. Calculating the total annual cost two years ago first requires determining the number of admissions per year:

Bed days per year	365
Bed days per admission	÷7
Admissions per bed per year	52.14
Number of beds	× 200
Admissions per year	10,428

Total cost (millions):

Variable bed cost (200 beds × $250 × 365 days)	$18.25
Occupancy cost (200 beds × $50 × 365 days)	3.65
Costs of admission (10,428 admissions × $120)	1.25
Total annual cost	$23.15

b. Total annual cost today:

Bed days per year	365
Bed days per admission	÷4
Admissions per bed per year	91.25
Number of beds	× 200
Admissions per year	18,250

Total cost (millions):

Variable bed cost (200 beds × $250 × 365 days)	$18.25
Occupancy cost (200 beds × $50 × 365 days)	3.65
Costs of admission (18,250 admissions × $120)	2.19
Total annual cost	$24.09

continued

---

c. Total operating cost increased about $940,000 (7,822 additional admissions × $120 per admission) because average length of stay has fallen from seven to four days, and the number of patients admitted has increased. To service the increased number of admissions requires more admission and discharge resources.

d. The average cost of a patient stay two years ago was $2,220 ($23.15 million ÷ 10,428 patients). The average cost of a patient stay today is $1,320 ($24.09 million ÷ 18,250 patients). The average cost per patient has decreased because length of stay (and hence the cost that varies with days) is lower. However, total hospital costs are higher because Southridge is incurring more costs admitting and discharging the greater volume of patients.

e. Unit-level costs: The $250 per bed per day cost for nursing and so forth. These costs vary with the number of patient bed days.

Batch-level costs: The $120 per admission cost. Each patient admitted consumes some admissions and social work costs, regardless of the patient's length of stay.

Product-level costs: Lab tests, X-rays, and surgical departments are like production-sustaining costs. These costs are accumulated in the various service areas, and then patients are charged for the medical services they use.

Capacity-sustaining costs: The $50 per bed per day occupancy cost. Even though these costs are being allocated based on bed days, they do not vary with either bed days or the number of admissions. Occupancy costs provide the basic capacity to serve the 200 patients per day.

Activity-based cost systems can be related back to the discussion of cost curves in Chapter 2. Chapter 2 presented a linear cost curve of the form

$$TC = VC \times Q + FC$$

where

TC = Total cost
VC = Variable cost per unit
Q = Number of units produced
FC = Fixed cost

That is, total cost, *TC,* can be disaggregated into variable costs, $VC \times Q$, and fixed cost, *FC.* Fixed costs, by definition, do not vary with *Q,* units produced.

Under activity-based costing, a more complex cost function is assumed to exist—namely,

$$TC = VC \times Q + BC \times B + PC \times L + OC$$

where

TC = Total cost
VC = Variable cost per unit
Q = Number of units produced
BC = Cost per batch
B = Number of batches
PC = Cost per product line
L = Number of product lines
OC = All other costs that do not vary with some activity measure

| **Historical Application: Activity-Based Costing in the Railroads** | In the 1870s, the railroads developed a sophisticated unit-cost measure: the cost of hauling a ton of freight one mile. The accounts were segregated into four groups: |

1. Maintenance of the roadway and general management.
2. Station expenses.
3. Movement expenses.
4. Interest on the capital investment.

The first group involves costs that do not vary with volume of traffic. Group 2 contains costs that vary with volume of freight. Group 3 contains costs that vary with the number of trains run. The last group represents interest on the capital investment. Three cost drivers were used to allocate the four cost pools:

- Average number of tons transported over one mile of road per year (groups 1 and 4).
- Length of haul (2).
- Average number of tons of freight in each train (3).

This complex calculation of cost per ton-mile resembles current activity-based costing systems that separate costs into unit-level, batch-level, product-level, and capacity-sustaining-level costs. Unit-level costs are roughly the movement expenses (3). Batch-level costs are like station expenses (2). Product-line costs resemble maintenance of roadway expenses (1). And interest on capital investment is required to sustain the entire system.

SOURCE: A. Chandler, *The Visible Hand: The Managerial Revolution in American Business* (Cambridge: Harvard University Press, 1977), pp. 116–19.

In addition,

$$FC = BC \times B + PC \times L + OC$$

That is, some fixed costs, *FC,* that do not vary with units produced do vary with the number of batches and product lines.

The more complex ABC cost function recognizes that costs vary due to more than just changes in units produced, *Q.* Costs also vary with the number of batches and the number of product lines. To the extent batches and product line variables (*BC* and *PC*) correctly capture how batch and product line costs vary in the particular factory under study, ABC will have more explanatory power and will be more accurate than simple unit-based systems.

While the ABC cost function captures more of the complexity in the factory, it still makes a number of simplifying assumptions that potentially reduce its accuracy. For example, every batch is assumed to cost $*BC* regardless of the number of units in the batch, the types of products in the batch, and what was produced before the current batch. Also, each product line is assumed to cost $*PC* regardless of the complexity of the product lines.

Activity-based costing tries to identify the factors that drive cost and then use these factors to allocate overhead costs. The following exercise illustrates an ABC system.

Exercise 11-3

A tree nursery with 50 varieties of trees is considering a change in product mix in its inventory. The manager wants to estimate the effect of each type of tree on indirect costs. Indirect costs are identified and estimated for the following activities: watering, repotting (transferring trees to larger pots), and administration. Total estimated annual costs for each activity, the cost driver for each activity, and the expected annual usage of each cost driver are as follows:

Activity	Estimated Costs	Cost Driver	Estimated Usage of Cost Driver
Watering	$100,000	Number of trees	500,000
Repotting	200,000	Number of repots	200,000
Administration	45,000	Number of different types of trees	50

Required:

a. What are the application rates for each of the activities?

b. Given the choice of cost driver, determine the activity level (unit-level, batch-level, product-level, production-sustaining level) of each of the activities.

c. What are the indirect costs of 100 weeping birches, each of which requires repotting once a year?

Solution:

a. The application rate for each activity is calculated by dividing the estimated costs of the activity by the estimated usage of its respective cost driver:

Activity		Application Rate
Watering	$100,000/500,000	$0.20/tree
Repotting	$200,000/200,000	$1.00/repot
Administration	$45,000/50	$900/type of tree

b. Both watering and repotting are unit-level activities because their cost drivers vary with the number of units. Administration is treated as a product-level activity because each product receives the same indirect costs.

c. The indirect costs traced to the 100 weeping birches are as follows:

Activity	Application Rate	Usage	Costs
Watering	$0.20/tree	100	$ 20
Repotting	$1.00/repot	100	100
Administration	$900/type of tree	1	900
Total annual indirect costs			$1,020

2. Absorption versus Activity-Based Costing: An Example

Following is an example that compares a single unit-based allocation system and activity-based costing. The term *single unit-based allocation system* refers to an absorption cost system whereby all manufacturing overhead is allocated using only allocation bases that vary with units produced, such as direct labor, direct material, or machine hours. VBL Co. manufactures three DVD players and two DVD recorders in its plant. The players and recorders make up two separate product lines, each with its own engineering department. The five models are manufactured in separate batches.

The following table contains the production and direct costs for each model.

	DVD Models				
	Players			**Recorders**	
	105	*205*	*305*	*801*	*901*
Number of units/year	80,000	100,000	60,000	40,000	20,000
Cost/DVD unit					
Direct labor	$34.00	$35.00	$36.00	$42.00	$44.00
Direct material	$60.00	$64.00	$65.00	$80.00	$85.00
Number of units/batch	200	100	150	50	50
Number of batches/year	400	1,000	400	800	400

The plant's overhead consists of the following items and amounts.

Factory Overhead Costs
($ in Millions)

Testing, setups, and supplies		$ 9.30
Product-line costs:		
Four-head models	$5.40	
Six-head models	4.20	9.60
Other factory costs		2.98
Total overhead costs		$21.88

The following tables calculate the total manufacturing cost per unit by model using a single unit-based allocation scheme. Overhead is assigned to models by a plantwide overhead rate using direct labor dollars as the allocation base.

The first step is to calculate the plantwide overhead rate based on direct labor costs.

	DVD Models					
	105	*205*	*305*	*801*	*901*	*Total*
Number of DVDs	80,000	100,000	60,000	40,000	20,000	
Direct labor/unit	$34.00	$35.00	$36.00	$42.00	$44.00	
Total direct labor cost (millions)	$2.72	$3.50	$2.16	$1.68	$0.88	$10.94
Total factory overhead (millions)						$21.88
Overhead rate (percentage of direct labor cost)						200%

496   *Chapter 11*

FIGURE 11-2

DVD player unit-based cost system

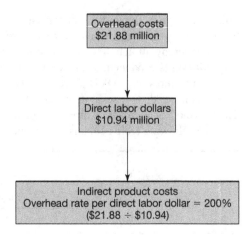

Using the estimated plantwide overhead rate of 200 percent of direct labor cost, the absorption cost of each product line is calculated next.

Model Costs per DVD
(Absorption Costing)

	Models				
	105	*205*	*305*	*801*	*901*
Direct labor	$ 34.00	$ 35.00	$ 36.00	$ 42.00	$ 44.00
Direct material	60.00	64.00	65.00	80.00	85.00
Overhead (200% of direct labor)	68.00	70.00	72.00	84.00	88.00
Total cost per DVD	$162.00	$169.00	$173.00	$206.00	$217.00

Under this costing scheme, the unit cost of the DVDs ranges from $162 to $217. Figure 11–2 illustrates the unit-based costing computation. All the overhead costs of $21.88 million are allocated to the DVDs using direct labor dollars as the sole allocation base.

VBL Co. was concerned that using a single, plantwide overhead allocation base might distort product costs. An activity-based costing study reveals that the cost of manufacturing a batch consists of indirect labor for machine setups and testing and supply costs. There are 3,000 batches per year. Product-line costs consist of engineering and equipment specialized in each particular product line. Other factory costs consist of plant administration and general maintenance of the plant.

Using the preceding data, overhead is assigned to the models using an activity-based costing system with three cost pools: batch-related costs, product-line costs, and capacity-sustaining costs. Batch-related costs and product-line-related costs are assigned to models based on the number of batches. Capacity-sustaining activities consist of other factory costs of $2,980,000. These costs are allocated to models based on direct labor cost.

The following tables illustrate the activity-based costing overhead cost assignment. The first step in the activity-based costing method is to calculate the application rate for each of the three activity cost drivers.

1. Batch-related costs: \$9.3 million ÷ 3,000 batches = \$3,100 per batch

	Models				
	105	*205*	*305*	*801*	*901*
Batch-related costs per batch	\$3,100	\$3,100	\$3,100	\$3,100	\$3,100
Batch size	÷ 200	÷ 100	÷ 150	÷ 50	÷ 50
Batch-related costs per DVD	\$15.50	\$31.00	\$20.67	\$62.00	\$62.00

2. Product-line-related costs:

	Players	*Recorders*
Product-line costs	\$5,400,000	\$4,200,000
Number of batches	÷ 1,800	÷ 1,200
Product-line costs/batch	\$ 3,000	\$ 3,500

	Models				
	105	*205*	*305*	*801*	*901*
Product-line cost per batch	\$3,000	\$3,000	\$3,000	\$3,500	\$3,500
Number of DVDs per batch	÷ 200	÷ 100	÷ 150	÷ 50	÷ 50
Product-line cost per DVD	\$15.00	\$30.00	\$20.00	\$70.00	\$70.00

3. Capacity-sustaining costs:

Other factory costs	\$2,980,000
Total direct labor cost	÷ \$10,940,000
Overhead rate per direct labor dollar	27.24%

Given the three cost drivers, the activity-based cost of each DVD is calculated in the following table.

Model Costs per DVD
(Activity-Based Costing)

	Models				
	105	*205*	*305*	*801*	*901*
Direct labor	\$ 34.00	\$ 35.00	\$ 36.00	\$ 42.00	\$ 44.00
Direct material	60.00	64.00	65.00	80.00	85.00
Overhead:					
Batch-related costs	15.50	31.00	20.67	62.00	62.00
Product-line-related costs	15.00	30.00	20.00	70.00	70.00
Capacity-sustaining costs					
(27.24% of direct labor)	9.26	9.53	9.81	11.44	11.99
Total cost	\$133.76	\$169.53	\$151.47	\$265.44	\$272.99
Ratio of activity-based cost to absorption cost	−17%	0%	−12%	+29%	+26%

FIGURE 11-3

DVD player plant's activity-based costing system

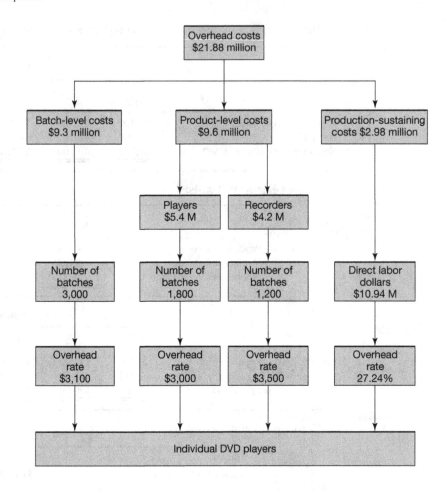

Under activity-based costing, the unit cost of the DVDs ranges from $133.76 to $272.99. Figure 11–3 illustrates the activity-based costing computation.

Notice that all manufacturing overhead costs are allocated under both unit-based and activity-based costing. There is no distinction between fixed and variable costs. All costs are viewed as being variable in the long run and assigned to the products.

Under activity-based costing, the players' costs are 0 to 17 percent lower than under a plantwide overhead rate, and the recorders costs are 26 to 29 percent higher. The product-line costs under unit-based costing are assigned to models using direct labor costs. Since the players require about 77 percent of the direct labor dollars [($2.72 + $3.50 + $2.16) ÷ $10.94], they are assigned 77 percent of the $9.6 million of product-line costs. However, the players account for only 56 percent of the product-line costs ($5.4 ÷ 9.6). Thus, unit-based costing assigns more product-line costs to the players than does activity-based costing.

This example illustrates how traditional unit-based costing can overcost high-volume models and undercost low-volume models. Since the recorders are more complex, they require more product-line costs per unit than the players. Unit-level allocation bases (e.g., direct labor) overcost the less complex products and undercost the more complex, more resource-consuming products.

Concept Questions	Q11–3	What are the usual four mutually exclusive cost pools used in activity-based cost accounting?
	Q11–4	Does activity-based costing allocate more or less total manufacturing costs to products than unit-based costing?

C. Analyzing Activity-Based Costing

Having described activity-based costing (ABC) and how cost drivers are selected, this section discusses some of the reasons firms adopt it, why most firms do not, and the costs and benefits of ABC.

1. Reasons for Implementing Activity-Based Costing

An interesting study compares product costs computed using a traditional unit-based absorption costing system with product costs computed using an activity-based system.[3] The site is an electronics factory producing more than 800 different electrical instruments. The factory manufactures the circuit boards and assembles them into a completed instrument, which is then tested. The traditional unit-based costing system assigned all overhead costs to one of the two overhead cost pools. One pool was allocated to individual products based on direct materials and the other pool was allocated based on direct labor. Direct materials averaged 65 percent of total product costs, direct labor averaged 2 percent of total product costs, and overhead averaged 33 percent of product costs. Six-month product volumes range from 1 to 4,826 units; half of the products have volumes of fewer than 50 units every six months. Thus, the plant produces both high- and low-volume products.

The factory converted to an activity-based costing system, which identified 14 different activity centers and accumulated the costs in each center separately. The new system identified cost drivers for each activity center such as the number of parts per instrument and the number of batches. Instead of just two allocation bases (direct labor and direct materials), 14 allocation bases are used to allocate overhead costs.

The traditional unit-based cost of each product is compared with its activity-based cost by computing the ratio of activity-based cost to unit-based cost for each product. Fifty percent of the activity-based product costs are within about 10 percent of the traditional unit-based costs. Fewer than 20 percent of the product costs vary by more than 50 percent. These data indicate that for most of the products, activity-based costing and traditional unit-based costing generate roughly comparable product costs. But for a few products, dramatic changes in product costs result when computed under activity-based costing. One percent of the products has activity-based costs equal to five times their traditional unit-based costs

The authors of the study find that (1) high-volume products have lower-activity-based unit costs relative to unit-based costs and (2) low-volume products tend to have higher activity-based costs than unit-based costs. Traditional unit-based costing systems tend to assign more costs to large-volume jobs relative to small-volume jobs, particularly when overhead contains a high fraction of indirect costs that do not vary with units produced but do vary with batches and product lines. When these batch and product-line costs are allocated to jobs based on a volume measure such as units or direct materials, large-volume jobs bear a high fraction of these costs.

---

[3]G. Foster and M. Gupta, "Implementation of an Activity Accounting System in the Electronics Industry," in *Measuring Manufacturing Performance,* ed. R. Kaplan (Boston: Harvard Business School, 1989).

500   *Chapter 11*

Managerial Application: Insteel Industries	Insteel manufactures and markets concrete-reinforcing products such as industrial wire, fasteners, nails, and mesh. Its South Carolina plant produced 477 individual products. About 20 percent of its products accounted for 85 percent of its revenues, and 20 percent of its customers accounted for 95 percent of its revenues. Senior managers at this plant formed an ABC team that identified 80 cost pools and appropriate cost drivers for these pools. For example, materials-handling costs were assigned to products based on the number of moves required by each product. Based on the new ABC cost data, management at this plant undertook a series of profit-enhancing actions: They discontinued unprofitable products, increased prices on other unprofitable items, and dropped unprofitable customers. After the success of ABC at its South Carolina plant, Insteel implemented ABC at its other plants. SOURCE: V. Narayanan and R. Sarkar, "The Impact of Activity-Based Costing on Managerial Decisions at Insteel Industries—A Field Study," *Journal of Economics and Management Strategy*, Summer 2002, pp. 257–88.

Managerial Application: Acxiom Corporation	Acxiom, a publicly traded firm, provides interactive marketing services to *Fortune* 500 companies. Its services include market databases, mailing list processing, data warehousing, and facilities management. Acxiom owns InfoBase, the largest consumer database in the United States, covering more than 500 million consumers. Acxiom uses activity-based costing to trace costs to activities and processes. A software project involves the following activities: planning the project, designing software, writing code, and testing code. Acxiom's ABC system accumulates the costs of these activities and assigns them to products, projects, and customers. This allows Acxiom to assess customer and product profitability and to hold its people accountable. It also allows it to further decentralize decision making because lower-level employees, knowledgeable of the firm's cost structure, can make decisions about changing a project's specification without approval by higher-level managers. SOURCES: www.Acxiom.com. N. Singer, "Mapping and Sharing the Consumer Genome," *NY Times*, June 16, 2012.

This study of a plant that converted to an activity-based costing system shows that activity-based costing does make a difference in reported product costs, although for most products the unit cost changes are not terribly large.

Activity-based costing systems claim to offer several advantages. ABC increases the percentage of product costs directly traced to individual products. Also, ABC provides an understanding of how costs are consumed by individual products, the activities required to produce them, the direct and indirect costs in the various activity centers, and how indirect costs are generated by cost drivers. Activity-based cost systems focus cost control at the activity level and the product design level. Allocating overhead costs using direct labor encourages managers to reduce the direct labor content in products. Activity-based systems focus managers' attention on controlling costs in the activity center and reducing the content of the cost drivers in the products.

Activity-based costing systems are promoted as a way to develop more accurate product or product-line costs. *Accuracy* means that changes in product volume, batch size, or product design characteristics (number of parts, manufacturing complexity, etc.) cause reported cost changes to be more highly correlated with changes in opportunity cost. Besides being more accurate, ABC changes the incentives of operating managers.

Identifying the underlying cost drivers allows managers to focus their attention on them. For example, product designers will change the way products are designed and manufactured to reduce the reported ABC costs. ABC systems tax different things (recall the discussion in Chapter 7 that cost allocations are de facto internal tax systems). To the extent that the chosen cost drivers are in fact associated with the factors that cause costs to change, an activity-based cost system taxes different activities and hence will cause managers to change their behavior and thus reduce actual costs incurred.

But these managers must have the *decision rights* to alter the levels of the cost drivers and there must be a *performance evaluation system* that gives them incentives to minimize cost. Adopting an activity-based costing system is a change in the *performance measurement system*. For behavior to be changed in the desired way, the other two parts of the organizational architecture (performance reward and decision-right partitioning) must encourage the appropriate changes. (Recall from Chapter 4 that all legs of the organization's three-legged stool must be coordinated with one another.)

Once the cost system has been converted to ABC, managers presumably have more accurate product cost information to make pricing decisions and to improve operating efficiencies. **Activity-based management (ABM)** is a process whereby business activities are identified and evaluated for potential streamlining or elimination. Using the ABC costs, each activity is evaluated based on those that add value to the product and those that don't add value. Value-enhancing activities are improved while activities that do not enhance value are eliminated. The ABC cost data help managers identify those products to produce, the profitable customers to retain, and the value-increasing activities to use in producing the products or servicing the customer.

2. Benefits and Costs of Activity-Based Costing

Most proponents argue that activity-based costing provides more accurate product cost data for decision making (decision management). A central tenet of activity-based costing is that more accurate product costs are always preferable to less accurate product costs and that accuracy generally increases with the number of cost drivers.

Adding more cost drivers allows more of the factors that cause overhead to vary (such as the number of batches, the number of part numbers, or the number of product lines) to be included in the ABC system. This increases the accuracy of the product cost numbers generated by the accounting system and, presumably, better operating, pricing, and resource utilization decisions result. However, adding additional cost pools and cost drivers for these pools is not free. Separate cost pools for each cost driver must be developed and data on each cost driver must be collected. At some point, the cost of adding more cost pools and cost drivers exceeds the benefit, in terms of better decisions resulting from the additional accuracy. Hence, it is unlikely that the ABC system ever achieves 100 percent accuracy. The solid curve in Figure 11–4 depicts the net benefits (benefits less costs) as a function of the number of cost drivers. Up to N^* cost drivers, the net benefits are increasing. But beyond N^*, the net benefits decline.

So far, the analysis has focused exclusively on how the costs and benefits of decision making vary with the number of cost drivers. Now let us introduce decision control. As more cost drivers are introduced, lower-level managers have more discretion in choosing the "cost drivers" because they usually have specialized knowledge of the factors driving costs in their departments. Increasing the number of cost drivers means giving more discretion over the cost system to the managers whose performance is being measured by these systems. Increasing the discretion of these managers usually reduces the ability of the system to monitor their behavior.

The costs of ABC systems include both the direct costs of collecting data on the activity levels and the costs incurred from the loss of control arising from less effective

502   *Chapter 11*

FIGURE 11-4

*Net benefits versus
number of cost
drivers (decision
making only and
decision making and
control)*

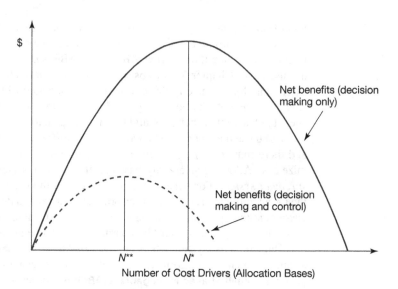

Number of Cost Drivers (Allocation Bases)

monitoring of managers involved in the choice of the cost drivers. Some of this discretion will be exercised opportunistically by these managers to manipulate their performance measures. When this second set of costs is included, the net benefits curve is lower, and the optimum number of cost drivers becomes N^{**} in Figure 11–4.

The dashed line in Figure 11–4 suggests that fewer cost drivers—and, hence, less accurate product costs—can be desirable. More accurate product cost knowledge is undesirable if it leads to poorer decision control. For example, some firms prefer to bias their costs upward to prevent the sales force from shaving margins by setting prices so low that they cover only variable costs.[4] This is partly a problem with the performance reward system and partly a problem with how product costs are measured. Nonetheless, some managers are reluctant to report lower product costs for decision control reasons.

Other companies systematically understate product costs, as in targeting costing, which is described more fully in Chapter 12. Many Japanese firms, in particular, set cost targets based on what the item should cost in order for the firm to compete. Such target costs are well below the costs that the firm can currently achieve. However, low target costs encourage innovation and cost improvement. Other incentive-control reasons can cause firms to choose less accurate cost systems. Zytec simplified its cost system to just one cost driver: time to manufacture the product (cycle time). While such a system produces less accurate product costs than multiple-cost-driver ABC systems, senior management wanted to focus employee attention on what it believed was the single most important cost reduction factor in the firm.

Finally, recall the discussion in Chapter 1 that accounting costs are not necessarily opportunity costs. Accounting costs are based on the historical cost of past resource acquisition. In particular, accounting depreciation is the periodic write-off of fixed assets acquired in prior periods. ABC provides an alternative allocation of these historical costs. ABC does not allocate opportunity costs. To the extent that these historical costs are reasonable approximations of opportunity cost, then ABC can improve decision making. However, to the extent that product costs contain significant amounts of accounting depreciation and the accounting depreciation grossly misstates the opportunity cost of the

---

[4]K. Merchant and M. Shields, "When and Why to Measure Costs Less Accurately to Improve Decision Making," *Accounting Horizons*, June 1993, pp. 76–81.

Managerial Application: The Costs of ABC Exceed the Benefits at an Agilent Technologies Plant	Many Agilent Technologies plants have successfully implemented ABC, but not the Colorado Springs Division. This division produced test and measurement equipment. A six-person team spent one and one-half years designing and implementing an ABC system. Wages, benefits, occupancy costs, and depreciation were largely fixed and comprised 85 percent of total costs. By treating these costs as though they were largely variable, the ABC system was not useful in managing short-term cost fluctuations. The ABC system had numerous cost drivers, one for just about every activity in a process. In pursuit of accurate costs for extremely heterogeneous products, the system became unwieldy trying to explain the monthly variance reports. Employees constantly tweaking the driver rates created an administrative "nightmare" for the accounting system. Finally, the division simplified the accounting system by allocating overhead using material dollars, thereby eliminating two people in the cost accounting function.

SOURCE: S. Landry, L. Wood, and T. Linquist, "Can ABC Bring Mixed Results?" *Management Accounting*, March 1997, pp.28–33; www.Agilent.com

capacity, then ABC is no more an accurate estimate of opportunity cost than traditional absorption costing methods. Consider another example. The firm produces a variety of products at a plant site where it owns the building and land. Accounting depreciation on the building is included in both ABC and traditional unit-based costing. However, both systems ignore the opportunity cost of the land. If this land is very valuable, both product costing methods understate the opportunity cost of the products produced at this site.

Hence, an inherent contradiction exists in ABC. ABC is promoted as better for decision making. But decision making requires opportunity costs, not historical costs. However, ABC does not measure opportunity costs. It offers a different way to allocate historical cost, which may or may not be useful for decision making. Remember the old adage in computer science called "GIGO" or "garbage in, garbage out." ABC's ability to measure opportunity cost is only as good as historical cost (that is being reallocated) is at capturing opportunity cost.

3. ABC Measures Costs, Not Benefits

Suppose a firm produces a single product in its only plant. Such a firm is not likely to use ABC because all the indirect costs are being incurred to support this single product. There is no need to allocate these indirect costs across multiple products. As we have seen, product costing becomes more challenging in multiproduct plants that produce a variety of low- and high-volume products that place differential demands on the plant's common resources (purchasing, setup, engineering, etc.). Presumably, ABC provides a more accurate representation of how each product consumes common factory resources. However, ABC does not capture the benefits of producing and selling multiple products.

As discussed in Chapter 4, firms sell multiple products if they can do so more economically than separate single-product firms. Multiproduct plants can be low-cost producers due to demand- or supply-side synergies. For example, because product quality information is expensive for consumers to acquire, firms develop brand-name capital that allows them to offer broad product lines. Toyota can introduce and sell a new small sports utility vehicle (SUV) at lower cost than can a new startup company because the marketplace already knows the Toyota name and its overall quality reputation. A startup company would need to invest billions of dollars to assure the consumer of its SUV's quality.

Another example of a demand-side benefit of being a multiproduct firm is offering consumers one-stop shopping. Catalog companies such as L.L.Bean include many clothing

504   *Chapter 11*

<table>
<tr><td>Managerial Application: ABC Can Be Costly</td><td>The British government employed activity-based costing to measure the cost of policing and law enforcement in England and Wales. Government officials used the ABC data to assess productivity by relating all input costs to outputs and to allocate resources among the various law enforcement agencies. After using the system for four years, a review concluded that ABC was a costly, inefficient, and expensive national exercise; was difficult to implement; was a poor value; and alternative methods should be used. The review recommended that ABC be replaced with a less costly, easier to use alternative that has greater impact on productivity. This conclusion was based on the following observations:</td></tr>
</table>

- ABC is not user friendly and is not usable by managers running the police service. ABC required experts to extract and interpret the data.
- ABC generated spurious variations because the data are only collected twice a year. Comparisons of costs of crime and detections by type of crime are subject to data errors.
- ABC imposed significant bureaucratic burdens by requiring that redundant data be collected.

SOURCE: "Final Report of the Independent Review of Policing," February 2008, Homeoffice.gov.uk.

items, often arranged in outfits that allow the consumer to order matching pants, shirt, and sweater. This reduces consumers' transaction costs of assembling a coordinated outfit.

On the supply side, producing multiple products in the same plant allows the firm to capture economies of scope, learning curve effects, or smoothing production over time. For example, some tire companies produce both snow tires and all-weather tires in the same plant because separate plants would be too small to provide low-cost production. Or, if one plant produced only snow tires, they would have to be inventoried during spring and summer until they could be sold in fall and winter.

Although ABC systems capture how different products consume resources, they are unable to capture the joint benefits of having multiple products. For example, an ABC analysis might demonstrate that producing a particular sunglasses model has an ABC cost greater than its price. However, if this sunglasses model is worn by movie stars (which increases the sales of the firm's other sunglasses models), then this "loss leader" provides significant brand-name marketing benefits.

Likewise, suppose a new product allows the firm to smooth production and utilize excess capacity. An ABC analysis might still show this product is unprofitable. Suppose an engineering department requires five engineers to support peak production, which occurs over nine months. In the three months that are off peak, two engineers could be let go, but because it is too expensive to recruit and train new engineers, they are retained. A new product is added to utilize the two engineers and other excess capacity in the off-peak period. Three or four years after this product is added, it is unlikely that anyone remembers why the product was added to the plant. Hence, an ABC analysis probably charges this new product the full cost of the two engineers, which could cause the firm to drop the product. Adding the new product did not increase the number of engineers. The plant had two "extra" engineers in the off-peak period to staff the peak period.

Finally, recall the discussion of joint costs in Chapter 8, which described the futility of allocating joint costs to joint products. All joint cost allocation schemes, other than net realizable value, distort product costs for decision making. If the cost of the chicken

Historical Application: A Nineteenth-Century Example of ABC	Founded around 1813, the Boston Manufacturing Co. produced equipment for cotton and silk mills. This firm's cost accounting system is described in the following passage: There was a painstaking tabulation of all direct costs, together with a careful allocation of such costs to the department in which they were incurred. . . . A definite attempt was made to charge many overhead costs to the production accounts. An outstanding example of this attempt to assign such costs to the department in which they were incurred is provided by the company's treatment of executive salaries. The salaries of Paul Moody and Patrick Tracy Jackson were spread over several different accounts, and the allocations were varied from period to period as the supervisory attention of these men shifted. Presumably the basis employed in making these charges was the number of hours . . . devoted by the agent and the treasurer to the various phases of the business. SOURCE: G. Gibb, *The Saco-Lowell Shops* (Cambridge: Harvard University Press, 1950), pp. 50–51, quoted in P. Garner, *Evolution of Cost Accounting to 1925* (Montgomery: University of Alabama Press, 1954), p. 84.

is allocated to the wings based on weight, the cost of wings is distorted. Wings might be dropped even though they provide incremental net cash flow. Analogously, multiple products can yield joint benefits from the demand or supply side. ABC, like all cost allocation schemes, ignores these benefits by focusing on allocating costs. And even if these joint benefits are identified, they cannot be allocated meaningfully. Suppose L.L.Bean offers a matching shirt and sweater in its catalog. If each is offered without the other, L.L.Bean sells either 1,000 shirts or 1,000 sweaters. By offering both as an outfit, they sell 1,200 of each, or 400 outfits more in total. How should the additional joint benefits of these 400 be allocated? They shouldn't be allocated because any attempt to do so will likely distort the relative profitability of both the shirt and the sweater.

D. Acceptance of Activity-Based Costing

Many people have the impression that activity-based costing is a recent invention. However, over 50 years ago Peter F. Drucker, a well-known management consultant, wrote that absorption costing systems can produce misleading product cost data.[5] Professor Goetz advocated activity-based costing principles in 1949 when he wrote:

Each primary (overhead) class should be homogeneous with respect to every significant dimension of managerial problems of planning and control. Some of the major dimensions along which (overhead) may vary are number of units of output, number of orders, number of operations, capacity of plant, number of catalogue items offered.[6]

Firms in the United States and Europe installed *activity-based systems* in the 1970s before the term *activity-based costing* was coined.

Many firms have experimented with activity-based costing systems but have not integrated the activity-based cost data into their accounting systems. The activity-based cost systems are primarily stand-alone supplemental analyses conducted as special studies.

---

[5]P. Drucker, "Managing for Business Effectiveness," *Harvard Business Review,* May–June 1963, pp. 53–60. Also, see C. Horngren, "Management Accounting: This Century and Beyond," *Management Accounting Research,* September 1995, pp. 281–86.

[6]B. Goetz, *Management Planning and Control: A Managerial Approach to Industrial Accounting* (New York: McGraw-Hill, 1949), p. 142.

They are off-line and are updated once or twice a year to produce revised product cost data for strategic analysis, not for product costing and periodic internal reporting.

Most firms adopting ABC use it for decision making outside the accounting function. In one article, the authors conjecture: "Thousands of companies have adopted or explored the feasibility of adopting ABC. However, we estimate that no more than 10 percent of them now use activity-based management in a significant number of operations. The other 90 percent have given up, or their programs are stagnating or floundering."[7] The evidence suggests that firms implementing ABC use it for decision making, not control, because firms rarely incorporate the ABC cost allocation bases into their financial reporting of inventories and cost of goods sold.

One study reports that as many as 60 percent of all U.S. organizations have attempted to implement ABC, but only 20 percent have done so. Eight percent continue to use traditional unit-based costing methods.[8] A survey of 2,800 large U.S. firms found that extensive ABC use is associated with higher quality levels and operating efficiency. However, extensive ABC use had no significant association with return on assets. But since firms adopting ABC also adopted new performance measurement systems, quality improvement programs, and just-in-time production methods, one cannot conclude that ABC caused the higher quality and operating efficiencies.[9]

Several problems exist in implementing ABC.[10] First, to implement ABC, cost analysts use interviews, time logs, and direct observation of the time people spend on various activities to estimate the resource expenses assigned to an activity. Interviewing and surveying employees to get their time allocations is time-consuming and costly. One money center bank required 70,000 employees at more than 100 facilities to submit monthly surveys of their time. The bank had 14 full-time people managing the ABC data collection and processing. The high cost to maintain the ABC model has caused many firms to update the information infrequently, leading to out-of-date activity cost driver rates and inaccurate estimates of product and customer costs. Consequently, most ABC models are often not maintained, their cost estimates soon become obsolete, and the firm abandons ABC.

A second problem involves the complexity of many ABC systems. To generate accurate ABC cost estimates, more cost drivers are added to capture the underlying complexity of the various processes performed by the firm. This dramatically increases the demands on the computer systems used to store and calculate the cost estimates. One company uses 150 activities to cost 600,000 cost objects (products and customers); running the model monthly requires data estimates, calculations, and storage for more than 2 billion items. The systems often take days to process one month's data.

The third problem encountered in ABC is the increased ability of employees and managers to game the numbers. To the extent that ABC numbers are used to evaluate performance or decide which processes or products to outsource, employee welfare is affected. ABC requires people to estimate how they spend their time and identify specific cost drivers. These inherently subjective estimates are difficult to verify objectively and can lead to inaccurate estimates of activity-based costs. ABC's inherent subjectivity makes it susceptible to gaming and hence lowers its value in decision control.

[7]J. Ness and T. Cucuzza, "Tapping the Full Potential of ABC," *Harvard Business Review,* July–August 1995.
[8]P. Sharman, "The Case for Management Accounting," *Strategic Finance,* October 2003, pp. 43–47.
[9]C. Ittner, W. Lanen, and D. Larcker, "The Association between Activity-Based Costing and Manufacturing Performance," *Journal of Accounting Research* 40 (June 2002), pp. 711–26.
[10]The first two problems are described in Kaplan and Anderson (2007).

Managerial Application: Time-Driven Activity-Based Costing: Old Wine in New Bottles	To repair major criticisms of ABC, "time-driven ABC" is being promoted as a new and innovative methodology. Under time-driven ABC, firms estimate the time required to perform an activity and the cost per unit of time. If resource consumption is not time-based, but rather volume-based (e.g., a distribution center), the cost is allocated via the volume consumed (e.g., cost per cubic foot). Time-based ABC computes activity costs at planned capacity and any unused capacity creates a "cost variance" that is not allocated to individual products.

While time-driven ABC has been promoted as simpler, less expensive, less subjective, and more powerful than traditional ABC implementations, it has been criticized along the following lines:

1. Time-based ABC is not new. Time- or event-driven ABC has existed in various forms for decades.

2. Traditional ABC includes the cost of unused capacity, whereas time-driven ABC excludes unused capacity costs in computing individual product costs. Firms use their cost system for a variety of purposes, including taxes. Tracking and identifying unused capacity, and how this capacity should be incorporated into reported costs, varies from firm to firm. Obviously, whether unused capacity should be included in product costs depends on each firm's particular circumstances, and one-size-fits-all mandates likely are wrong for some firms.

3. The time-driven ABC model is not easier to develop and maintain. ABC, time-driven ABC, and other costing methodologies are prone to error. All costing methods require updating as processes and costs change. Both ABC methods require resurveying activity costs every time underlying processes, products, and services change.

4. Time-driven ABC does not drive faster, better business decisions. Time-driven ABC focuses on time standards to the exclusion of other cost factors. Focusing on time standards can direct too much attention to reducing the wait time in the activity cost driver, instead of investigating other, more effective ways to reduce cost. One manufacturer using time-driven ABC to identify cost-cutting opportunities spent a lot of time reducing the time standard before redesigning the product.

Few calls for activity-based costing are based on decision control reasons. The trade-off between decision management and decision control described in Chapter 1 helps to predict some of the observed tendencies:

1. Proponents of activity-based costing are operating managers who want better information for decision making.

2. Most ABC systems are stand-alone off-line systems. Firms are reluctant to change accounting systems, which are primarily for decision control.

3. Most of the resistance to ABC comes from corporate management and the accounting staff. ABC systems tend to sacrifice decision control for decision management, thereby reducing the usefulness of accounting numbers for decision control.

Managerial Application: Simplify Operations versus ABC	A small family-owned manufacturing company formed a team of 15 employees to implement ABC. Two years of study and $200,000 later, the team discovered that low-volume products cause more overhead than high-volume products. However, before fully implementing ABC, this company was bought by Illinois Tool Works, which had a different strategy in mind. Instead of trying to come up with better cost allocations, ITW decided to simplify and eliminate non-value-added activities. Instead of implementing ABC, ITW converted the plant to just-in-time (JIT) production, redesigned its production processes, eliminated certain overhead costs, converted indirect costs into direct costs, and dropped low-volume products. The switch to JIT eliminated most setups. The plant adopted a flatter organizational structure by decentralizing more decision-making authority to lower levels and eliminating some levels. The plant now uses direct costing and has eliminated most arbitrary cost allocations. The profitability of the plant has improved.
	SOURCE: L. Tatikonda, D. O'Brien, and R. Tatikonda, "Succeeding with 80/20," *Management Accounting*, February 1999, pp. 40–44, www.ITW.com.

While much has been written about the benefits of activity-based costing for decision management, few proponents have gone back to ABC adopters to follow up on the outcomes and understand why the ABC systems were not fully implemented. In one firm, activity-based costing was implemented and abandoned after a year. The controller explained that under the old system, with just a few unit-based cost drivers, everyone understood the weaknesses of the system and accepted its faults. With the new system, managers were constantly arguing over the appropriate cost drivers. To stop the bickering, the controller abandoned ABC.

Many firms have redesigned their products and production processes, thereby converting formerly indirect costs into direct costs. These companies set up machines more rapidly. Faster setups mean more setups. These plants have fewer workers associated with overhead costs such as moving, storing, inspecting, and expediting. Production is more of a continuous flow process, eliminating the need for work to stop, start, and wait. With less common costs, activity-based systems are far less valuable. More of the cost is directly traceable to the products. When a high fraction of the total cost of the production process is directly traceable to the products, product costs are more accurate. In addition, when multiple products are produced, firms design cost centers around product lines rather than by functions. Costs are then reported by product line, which avoids allocating costs to individual products within the product line. Activity-based costing systems in these settings add little value over simpler traditional unit-based costing systems.[11] Finally, in firms where fixed factory overhead is a small fraction of total product cost, reallocating a small cost pool using more accurate cost drivers does not cause individual product costs to vary. Firms facing little competition are able to price their products above cost, so that inaccurate average unit costs are not as critical as when competition is driving prices down to or even below average cost. Activity-based costing systems will not be adopted everywhere, and the value of ABC is not the same across all plants.

---

[11]See M. Sakurai, "The Influence of Factory Automation on Management Accounting Practices: A Study of Japanese Companies," in *Measuring Manufacturing Performance,* ed. R. Kaplan (Boston: Harvard Business School, 1989). "Japanese managers and academics actually prefer simple methods for allocating overhead to the more complex activity accounting allocation methods advocated by several U.S. academics" (p. 43).

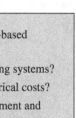

Criticisms of Absorption Cost Systems: Inaccurate Product Costs **509**

Concept Questions		
	Q11–5	What are two purposes for implementing activity-based costing?
	Q11–6	What are some advantages of activity-based costing systems?
	Q11–7	What problems are associated with tracking historical costs?
	Q11–8	How does the trade-off between decision management and decision control affect the form that an absorption cost system takes within a particular firm?
	Q11–9	Under unit-based absorption costing systems, are high- or low-volume products overcosted? Why?

E. Summary

This chapter discusses the second of two major criticisms of traditional absorption costing systems: They can, in some circumstances, produce misleading or inaccurate estimates of product costs. Inaccurate estimates of product costs become especially serious in multiproduct plants producing both high- and low-volume products or where products vary in their complexity. Traditional absorption cost systems typically allocate overhead using unit-level allocation bases, such as direct labor or direct materials. However, overhead costs also vary with the number of batches, number of customers, and the number of product lines. Products using relatively greater proportions of batch and product-line costs will be undercosted if unit-level allocation bases are chosen.

Activity-based costing (ABC) attempts to provide more accurate estimates of the resources consumed by the various products manufactured. ABC systems presumably generate more accurate product costs by identifying what drives individual indirect cost pools. Overhead costs are grouped into activity centers (cost pools), and specific overhead cost drivers are chosen that best capture cost consumption in that activity center. These activity-center-specific cost drivers are used to allocate the costs in the activity center to the products using that activity center.

The primary advantage of ABC systems is more accurate product costs that aid in decision making. However, these activity-based systems are costly to design and implement. They can be prone to gaming by constantly revising the cost pools or cost drivers. Moreover, ABC costs do not capture any customer-side synergies from producing a variety of products. ABC might better reflect product costs, but not product "benefits" that arise from lowering customer transaction costs when a customer purchases different products. Finally, ABC systems do not measure opportunity costs. These systems, like traditional absorption costing, allocate historical costs of plant and equipment (and not land costs) to the products.

Numerous firms have experimented with activity-based costing systems. Yet a minority have adopted ABC and changed their performance evaluation systems to incorporate the new cost system.

Self-Study Problem

Kiddo Inc. (B)

(For the basic data, refer to Chapter 10 self-study problem Kiddo Inc. [A].) Further analysis of Kiddo's production process has allowed it to allocate costs using activity-based costing. Engineering costs, rework expenses, and equipment maintenance and depreciation were estimated for each production line. Product-line costs for the Runner and Pump sneakers are $5 million and $12 million,

510 *Chapter 11*

respectively. Setup costs for each batch are $2,500. The batch size for the Runner is 1,000 pairs of sneakers. The batch size for the Pump in year 1 is 500 pairs and 600 pairs for year 2. Remaining fixed overhead costs total $5,150,000 and were allocated based on direct labor cost.

Required:

    a. Prepare a revised income statement for each year using activity-based costing.

    b. Explain changes in the net profit between the original cost allocation system and activity-based costing.

Solution:

    a. Here are income statements for years 1 and 2 under activity-based costing:

Year 1

	Runner	Pump	Total
Revenue	$160,000,000	$110,400,000	$270,400,000
Expenses:			
Material	70,000,000	42,600,000	112,600,000
Labor	23,000,000	12,000,000	35,000,000
Variable overhead	33,000,000	17,520,000	50,520,000
Gross margin	$ 34,000,000	$ 38,280,000	$ 72,280,000
Batch costs*	12,500,000	12,000,000	24,500,000
Product-line costs†	4,863,813	9,600,000	14,463,813
Fixed overhead‡	3,065,159	1,599,213	4,664,372
Net profit	$ 13,571,028	$ 15,080,787	$ 28,651,815

	Runner	Pump	Total
*Batch Costs			
Cost per batch	$ 2,500	$ 2,500	
× Units sold	5,000,000	2,400,000	
÷ Units per batch	1,000	500	
Allocated batch costs	$12,500,000	$12,000,000	
†Product-Line Costs			
Total product-line costs	$ 5,000,000	$12,000,000	
÷ Units produced	5,140,000	3,000,000	
× Units sold	5,000,000	2,400,000	
Allocated line costs	$ 4,863,813	$ 9,600,000	
‡Fixed Overhead Costs			
Remaining fixed overhead			$ 5,150,000
Units produced	5,140,000	3,000,000	
× Direct labor per pair	$4.60	$5.00	
Total labor cost	$23,644,000	$15,000,000	$38,644,000
Fixed overhead per direct labor $			$ 0.1333
Direct labor of units sold	$23,000,000	$12,000,000	
Fixed overhead allocated			
(× $0.1333)	$ 3,065,159	$ 1,599,213	

Year 2

	Runner	Pump	Total
Revenue	$160,000,000	$110,400,000	$270,400,000
Expenses:			
Material	70,000,000	42,600,000	112,600,000
Labor	23,000,000	12,000,000	35,000,000
Variable overhead	33,000,000	17,520,000	50,520,000
Gross margin	$ 34,000,000	$ 38,280,000	$ 72,280,000
Batch costs*	12,500,000	10,000,000	22,500,000
Product-line costs†	4,807,692	8,080,808	12,888,500
Fixed overhead‡	2,837,805	1,480,594	4,318,400
Net profit	$ 13,854,502	$ 18,718,598	$ 32,573,100

	Runner	Pump	Total
*Batch Costs**			
Cost per batch	$ 2,500	$ 2,500	
× Units sold	5,000,000	2,400,000	
÷ Units per batch	1,000	600	
Allocated batch costs	$12,500,000	$10,000,000	
†Product-Line Costs			
Total product-line costs	$ 5,000,000	$12,000,000	
÷ Units produced	5,200,000	3,564,000	
× Units sold	5,000,000	2,400,000	
Allocated line costs	$ 4,807,692	$ 8,080,808	
‡Fixed Overhead Costs			
Remaining fixed overhead			$ 5,150,000
Units produced	5,200,000	3,564,000	
× Direct labor per pair	$ 4.60	$ 5.00	
Total labor cost	$23,920,000	$17,820,000	$41,740,000
Fixed overhead per direct labor $			$ 0.1234
Direct labor of units sold	$23,000,000	$12,000,000	
Fixed overhead allocated			
(× $0.1234)	$ 2,837,905	$ 1,480,594	

b. Profits are higher in both years 1 and 2 under activity-based costing than under traditional absorption costing. Under the original allocation system, profits increase in year 2 since more of the fixed overhead was inventoried. Now, the $50 million fixed overhead is split so that a greater portion goes to the Pump line. Since more of the Pump shoes are inventoried than the Runner shoes, more of the overhead is also inventoried. Consider the costs per unit for the two years under both allocation systems:

Per-Unit Summary	Runner	Pump
Price	$32.00	$46.00
Material	14.00	17.75
Labor	4.60	5.00
Variable overhead	6.60	7.30
Gross margin	$ 6.80	$15.95

512   *Chapter 11*

Per-Unit Summary	Runner	Pump
Year 1		
Absorption costing:		
Fixed overhead*	$ 5.93	$ 6.45
Net profit	$ 0.87	$ 9.50
ABC costing:		
Gross margin	$ 6.80	$15.95
Batch costs	2.50	5.00
Product-line costs	0.97	4.00
Fixed costs	0.61	0.67
Total costs	$ 4.08	$ 9.67
Net profit	$ 2.72	$ 6.28
Year 2		
Gross margin	$6.80	$15.95
Absorption costing:		
Fixed overhead	5.51	5.99
Net profit	$ 1.29	$ 9.96
ABC costing:		
Gross margin	$ 6.80	$15.95
Batch costs	2.50	4.17
Product-line costs	0.96	3.37
Fixed costs	0.57	0.62
Total costs	$ 4.03	$ 8.16
Net profit	$ 2.77	$ 7.79

*From Chapter 10, Kiddo Inc. (A)

For both years under both systems, the direct costs and selling price remain constant, providing margins of $6.80 and $15.95 for the Runner and the Pump, respectively. The fixed overhead in cost of goods sold is divided by number of units sold to calculate fixed overhead per unit for both years under the original system. Under that system, net profits increase from $0.87 to $1.29 per Runner and $9.50 to $9.96 per Pump. When the overhead is divided into product-line and batch costs, the cost structure changes significantly. The Runner's net profits jump to $2.72 and $2.77 for the two years. Profits on the Pump in turn drop to $6.28 and $7.79.

Problems

P 11–1:   The Maui Seminar

Your boss, the vice president of corporate accounting, has just returned from a two-week seminar in Maui on activity-based cost accounting. He says he wants to completely overhaul the company's existing absorption-based accounting system. "Activity-based costing is the wave of the future and will allow us to make better product-line decisions and therefore be more competitive in the market-place," he asserts.

He wants you to start implementation immediately, but he would like your comments before you begin. How do you respond?

SOURCE: L. McGinn.

P 11–2:   GAMMA

GAMMA produces over a hundred different types of residential water faucets at its Delta, Florida, plant. This plant uses activity-based costing to calculate product costs. The following table summarizes the plant's overhead for the year and the cost drivers used for each activity center:

Summary of Plant Overhead and Activity Centers

Activity Center	Total Cost (Millions of Dollars)	Cost Driver	Amount of Cost Driver	Activity Cost per Unit of Cost Driver
Materials handling	$20.8	Direct materials	$130 million	$0.16
Purchasing	13.8	Part numbers	800	$17,250
Set-up labor	6.8	Batches	500	$13,600
Engineering	10.9	Number of products	125	$87,200
Occupancy	16.2	Direct labor	$90 million	$0.18
Total plant overhead	$68.5			

One faucet model GAMMA manufactures is Explorer. Its total product cost is as follows:

	Amount of Cost Driver	Activity Cost per Unit of Cost Driver	Total Cost
Direct labor			$121,700
Direct materials			90,500
Materials handling	$ 90,500	$0.16	14,480
Purchasing	9	17,250	155,250
Setup	8	13,600	108,800
Engineering	1	87,200	87,200
Occupancy	$121,700	$0.18	21,906
Total cost			$599,836
Number of units manufactured			12,500
Product cost per unit			$ 47.99

Required:

Calculate the product cost per unit of the Explorer faucet using absorption costing where plant overhead is assigned to products using direct labor dollars.

P 11–3:   ABC and Volume Changes

Required:

- a. What differentiates unit-level costs, batch-level costs, product-line costs, and capacity-sustaining costs? Give examples.
- b. "One advantage of an activity-based cost system is that it prevents unit costs from rising when volumes fall and unit costs from falling as volumes rise." True or false? Discuss why.

514   *Chapter 11*

P 11–4:   Milan Pasta

At its Lyle Avenue plant, Milan Pasta produces two types of pasta: spaghetti and fettuccine. The two pastas are produced on the same machines, with different settings and slightly different raw materials. The fettuccine, being a wider noodle and more susceptible to curling edges, requires more inspection time. The total daily cost of inspection is $500. Here are daily production data for the two products:

	Spaghetti	*Fettuccine*
Pounds produced	6,000	2,000
Machine minutes per pound	0.20	0.40
Inspection hours per product line	8	24

Required:

 a. Calculate the inspection cost per pound of pasta using traditional absorption costing with number of machine hours as the allocation base.

 b. Calculate the inspection cost per pound of pasta using activity-based costing. Assume inspection time is the cost driver.

 c. Analyze why inspection costs differ between the methods used in parts (*a*) and (*b*).

P 11–5:   LifeCam Medical

LifeCam Medical produces various titanium orthopedic bone plates for trauma injuries. It has three different product lines (TS1, IFO, and Xpan) and uses activity-based costing to compute the cost of the three product lines. The ABC system employs three indirect cost pools. One pool is based on the grams of titanium in each product. Another pool is based on the number of machine milling minutes used to produce each product. And the third cost pool is allocated based on the amount of direct labor dollars in each product. The following table summarizes the operating data and the computation of ABC product costs:

	TS1	*IFOR*	*Xpan*
Number of units produced	2,300	1,200	900
Grams of titanium per unit	40	25	30
Milling minutes per unit	12	28	37
Direct materials per unit	$85.00	$130.00	$185.00
Direct labor per unit	$48.00	$83.00	$102.00
Allocated cost per gram of titanium	$17.00	$17.00	$17.00
Allocated cost per milling minute	$72.00	$72.00	$72.00
Overhead rate/Direct labor $	$2.53	$2.53	$2.53
ABC Unit Manufacturing Cost	*TS1*	*IFOR*	*Xpan*
Direct labor	$48.00	$83.00	$102.00
Direct material	85.00	130.00	185.00
Allocated cost based on grams of titanium	680.00	425.00	510.00
Allocated cost based on milling minutes	864.00	2,016.00	2,664.00
Overhead cost based on direct labor $	121.44	209.99	258.06
Total ABC cost per unit	$1,798.44	$2,863.99	$3,719.06

The three cost pools in the ABC system have three ABC rates that were computed by taking all the costs in the cost pool divided by the total cost driver in the pool (i.e., total grams of titanium). So, for example, the cost pool based on grams of titanium per unit has an ABC rate of $17.00 per gram of titanium. Product TS1 has 40 grams of titanium per unit, so each unit of TS1 is allocated $680 (40 × $17). TS1 is charged for the milling cost pool at $72 per milling minute. Since each unit of TS1 requires 12 milling minutes, TS1's milling cost is $864 (12 × $72). All factory overheads not included in the gram and milling ABC cost pools are assigned to products at the rate of $2.53 per direct labor dollar. TS1 has $48 direct labor dollars, so its cost includes $121.44 of other overheads ($48 × $2.53).

The current ABC system has been under development and refinement for the last three years. The CFO is tired of all the bickering over how many cost pools to use, what are the right cost drivers, and which costs should be included in the cost pools. She decides to eliminate the ABC system and return to the simpler system where all factory costs are allocated to the three products using a single factorywide allocation base of direct labor dollars.

Compute the unit manufacturing cost of the three products using a single overhead rate where the allocation base is direct labor dollars.

P 11–6:   Astin Car Stereos

Astin Car Stereos manufactures and distributes four different car stereos. The accompanying table summarizes the unit sales, selling prices, and manufacturing costs of each stereo.

ASTIN CAR STEREOS
Summary of Operations
Current Fiscal Year

	A90	B200	B300	Z7
Sales price	$100	$120	$140	$180
Manufacturing cost (all variable)	$ 80	$ 90	$100	$120
Units sold	15,000	13,000	12,000	9,000

Selling and distribution (S&D) expenses are $1,270,000. They are treated as a period cost and written off to the income statement. To assess the relative profitability of each product, S&D expenses are allocated to each product based on sales revenue.

Upon further investigation of the S&D expenses, half are shown to be for marketing and advertising. Each product has its own advertising and marketing budget, administered by one of four marketing managers. Z7, the premier product, is advertised heavily. Forty percent of the marketing and advertising budget goes toward Z7, 30 percent to B300, 20 percent to B200, and 10 percent to A90.

The remaining S&D expenses consist of distribution and administration costs (25 percent) and selling costs (25 percent). The distribution and administration department is responsible for arranging shipping and for billing the customers. (Customers pay transportation charges directly to the common carrier.) It also handles federal licensing of the car radios. Upon analysis, each product line places equal demands on the distribution and administration department, and each consumes about the same resources as the others. Selling costs consist primarily of commissions paid to independent salespeople. The commissions are based on gross margin (sales revenue less manufacturing cost).

Required:

    a. Allocate all S&D expenses based only on sales revenue. Identify the most and least profitable products.

    b. Allocate all S&D expenses based only on the advertising and marketing budget. Identify the most and least profitable products.

    c. Allocate all S&D expenses. Use the advertising and marketing budget for advertising and marketing costs, the demand for these resources by product for distribution and administration costs, and commissions for selling costs. Identify the most and least profitable products.

    d. Discuss the managerial implications of the various schemes. Why do the different schemes result in different product-line profits? Which product is really the most profitable? The least profitable?

P 11–7: DVDS

DVDS manufactures and sells DVD players in two countries. It manufactures two models—Basic and Custom—in the same plant. The Basic DVD has fewer options and provides lower-quality output than the Custom DVD. The basic model is sold only in a developing country and the custom model is sold only in a developed country. DVDS pays income taxes to the country where the final sale of the DVD player takes place. The following table summarizes DVDS operations.

DVDS
Summary of Operations
Current Year

	Basic	Custom
Quantity produced and sold	60,000	70,000
Price	$75	$140
Direct labor/unit	$15	$30
Direct materials/unit	$40	$80
Income tax rate	15%	35%

Besides direct materials and direct labor, manufacturing overhead amounts to $2 million and is currently assigned to products based on direct labor dollars. Manufacturing overhead is a fixed cost (does not vary with the number of units produced).

Required:

    a. Calculate the unit manufacturing costs of the Basic and Custom DVD models using traditional absorption costing. Manufacturing overhead is allocated based on direct labor dollars.

    b. DVDS hires a consulting firm to analyze its costing methods. After performing an extensive review, the consultants determine that the vast majority of the $2 million of overhead varies with the number of different parts in the two DVD models. The number of parts drives purchasing department activities. More engineering time is spent on the more complex Custom DVD models. More accounting depreciation of assembly and testing equipment is incurred producing the Custom DVD model than the Basic DVD model. The Basic DVD has 140 different parts and the Custom DVD model has 160 different parts. Calculate the unit manufacturing costs of the Basic and Custom DVD models using activity-based costing.

    c. Should DVDS change its costing methodology from its traditional absorption costing to ABC? Explain why it should or should not.

P 11–8: SPP

SPP (Secure Payment Processing) is the dominant technology firm that provides end-to-end secure Internet transaction processing. SPP offers its e-tailers the best security of their customer personal information in the industry. Its clients include many large and smaller e-tailers selling online products. When an online consumer purchases a product on an SPP client website, the storage of the customer's credit card information and processing the transaction is done by SPP—all of which is invisible to the e-tailer's customer. SPP uses its proprietary encryption software to store the customer's account information on its own servers, not on the e-tailer's server.

SPP is organized into two groups: Set-up Group and Transaction Processing Group. After acquiring a new client or after an existing client revises it Web portal, SPP assigns a team of its software engineers in the Set-up Group to customize SPP's software that links the e-tailer's website to SPP's servers. These SPP software engineers also run diagnostics to ensure the e-tailer's website is secure and is optimized to SPP's software.

SPP charges e-tailer's a set-up charge of $12,000 for its Set-up Group's software engineers to customize the SPP software, optimize the client's site, and test the client's firewalls. Then, the e-tailer is charged a fee of $0.13 per transaction processed each time a customer makes a purchase on the e-tailer's website. The following table summarizes SPP operations for the last 12 months:

Total operating costs	$28,696,143
Annual number of transactions processed	280,510,000
Number of new or existing client set-ups	350

Required:

   a. SPP calculates the cost of processing a transaction as the ratio of total operating cost divided by the number of transactions processed. Compute the cost of processing a single transaction.

   b. The newly hired CFO of SPP worries that the current method of calculating the cost of processing a transaction [as described in part (*a*)] is too simplistic. After some further analysis, the CFO determines that 39 software engineers (with an average cost of $139,000) work exclusively on new client set-ups. In addition to the wages and benefits of $139,000 per software engineer, the Set-up Group has additional costs of $8,408,143 (occupancy costs, travel, administration, equipment, software licenses, etc.). Both the Set-up Group's wages and additional costs are included in the Total operating costs of $28,696,143. Based on the preceding information, compute the cost of processing a transaction and the cost of a client set-up.

   c. Should SPP compute the cost of processing a transaction using the method described in part (*a*) or the method you used in part (*b*)? Explain.

P 11–9:   Friendly Grocer

Friendly Grocer has three departments in its store: beverages, dairy and meats, and canned and packaged foods. Each department is headed by a departmental manager. Operating results for the last month (in thousands) are given in the table.

	Beverages	Dairy and Meats	Canned and Packaged Foods	Total
Sales	$250.00	$470.00	$620.00	$1,340.00
Direct costs:				
Cost of goods sold (COGS)	200.00	329.00	527.00	1,056.00
Indirect costs:				
SG&A (20% of COGS)	40.00	65.80	105.40	211.20
Operating income	$ 10.00	$ 75.20	$(12.40)	$ 72.80

The direct costs consist of the cost of goods sold. Indirect costs consist of selling, general, and administrative (SG&A) costs and are allocated to each department at the rate of 20 percent of costs of goods sold. Based on the preceding report, beverages had operating income of $10,000, dairy and meats had operating income of $75,200, and canned and packaged foods lost $12,400.

Senior management is concerned that the allocation of costs might be distorting the relative profitability of the three departments. Further analysis of the SG&A account yields the following breakdown:

Shelf space costs	$ 90.00
Handling costs	20.00
Coupon costs	15.00
Shrinkage	28.00
Other indirect costs	58.20
Total	$211.20

Shelf space costs consist of store occupancy costs such as depreciation on the building and fixtures, utilities, store maintenance, property taxes, and insurance. Beverages make up 25 percent of the shelf space, dairy and meats make up 35 percent of the space, and canned and packaged goods make up 40 percent of the shelf space.

Handling costs consist of the labor required to stock the shelves and remove outdated products. The beverage suppliers (Coca-Cola, Pepsi, etc.) provide the labor to shelve their products (i.e., the beverage delivery people stock their products on the shelf). Dairy and meats' labor costs for stocking are three-quarters of the handling costs; canned and package foods' labor and handling costs are one-quarter of the total.

Coupon costs consist of the labor costs to process the redeemed coupons. Dairy and meats do not have any coupons. Twenty percent of the coupons redeemed are for beverages and 80 percent are for packaged and canned foods.

Shrinkage consists of the cost of products spoiled, broken, and stolen. Shrinkage by product category comes to

Beverages	$ 1
Dairy and meats	21
Canned and packaged foods	6

The remaining indirect costs are allocated based on cost of goods sold.

Required:

a. Apply an activity-based costing system and recalculate the operating income of the three departments.

b. Based on the statement you prepared in part (*a*), write a short memo to management discussing the revised operating income of the three departments and which statement (yours or the one in the question) management should use.

P 11–10:   Houston Milling

Houston Milling is a subcontractor to Pratt & Whitney, which makes jet engines. Houston Milling makes two different fuel pump housings for two Pratt & Whitney jet engines: the A11 housing and the D43. These pump housings are received from Pratt & Whitney, which buys them from an outside (independent) foundry and ships them to Houston for precision machining. Houston performs two machining operations on the housings. These are performed in two separate machining departments (Department 1 and Department 2). Both housings, A11 and D43, require machining in both Departments 1 and 2. Before the parts are machined, the machines must first be set up, which includes cleaning the machine, checking the tools in the machine, adjusting the tolerances, and then finally machining some trial parts. Houston's current accounting system tracks the number of setups and direct labor hours used by each part. Table 1 summarizes the indirect costs of producing A11 and D43. (The direct costs such as direct labor and materials are ignored to simplify the computations.)

Setup and machine hours in the two departments are pooled into two cost pools: setup and machining. Table 1 allocates the costs in these two pools to the two products. Under this accounting

Criticisms of Absorption Cost Systems: Inaccurate Product Costs **519**

system, A11 has indirect costs of $8,600 and D43 has indirect costs of $6,400. Management believes that the current accounting system is not producing accurate costs for the two products because the two cost pools are too aggregated. They decide to disaggregate the data and use four cost pools. They collect some additional data, which are summarized in Table 2.

Required:

    a. Calculate revised cost allocations based on the disaggregated data in Table 2. Number of setups is used to allocate the indirect cost of setups in both Departments 1 and 2 and direct labor hours are used to allocate the machining costs in Departments 1 and 2.

    b. Prepare a short memo describing the pros and cons of the revised allocated indirect costs in part (*a*) compared to those in Table 1.

    c. After completing the analysis in parts (*a*) and (*b*), some additional data are collected from a special study of setup hours and machine hours in the two departments. These data are presented in Table 3. In particular, setup hours and machine hours are collected in the two departments. Management now believes that setup hours and machine hours more accurately reflect the true cause-and-effect relations of setup costs and machining costs in Departments 1 and 2 than number of setups and direct labor hours, respectively.

        Based on the data presented in Table 3, calculate revised cost allocations for A11 and D43. Setup costs in Departments 1 and 2 are to be allocated based on setup hours, and machining costs in Departments 1 and 2 are to be allocated based on machine hours.

    d. Compare the total product costs for A11 and D43 in Table 1 and parts (*a*) and (*c*). What conclusions can you draw?

TABLE 1   Houston Milling Allocated Indirect Costs of Producing Parts A11 and D43

	Functions		
	Setup	*Machining*	*Total*
Indirect cost	$5,000	$10,000	$15,000
Allocation base	Number of setups	Direct labor hours	
Usage: A11	10	66	
D43	15	34	
Total	25	100	
Allocation rate	$200/setup	$100/DL hr.	
Allocations: A11	$2,000	$ 6,600	$ 8,600
D43	3,000	3,400	6,400
Total	$5,000	$10,000	$15,000

TABLE 2   Houston Milling Disaggregated Cost Pool Data

	Setup		Machining		
	Department 1	*Department 2*	*Department 1*	*Department 2*	*Total*
Total cost	$3,000	$2,000	$8,000	$2,000	$15,000
Allocation base	Number of setups	Number of setups	Direct labor hours	Direct labor hours	
Usage: A11	7	3	32	34	
D43	13	2	18	16	
Total	20	5	50	50	

520   *Chapter 11*

TABLE 3   **Houston Milling Setup Hours and Machine Hours in Departments 1 and 2**

	Department 1		**Department 2**	
	Setup	*Machining*	*Setup*	*Machining*
Total cost	$3,000	$8,000	$2,000	$2,000
Allocation base	Setup hours	Machine hours	Setup hours	Machine hours
Usage: A11	15	115	6	120
D43	15	85	4	80
Total	30	200	10	200

P 11–11:   Sanchez Gadgets

Sanchez Gadgets purchases innovative home kitchen gadgets from around the world (such as a kitchen torch, a pasta maker, and an automatic salad spinner) and sells them to specialty cooking retail stores. Sanchez has a marketing department that locates and purchases the innovative gadgets and prepares price lists and catalogs for Sanchez's direct selling force. Sanchez's salespeople are assigned geographic sales territories and are responsible for all the specialty kitchen stores in their geographic territories.

Management at Sanchez is concerned that with more than 450 different items available, it is currently carrying too many different SKUs (SKUs are "stock keeping units"). Management is currently looking for a methodology to eliminate unprofitable SKUs. To focus on developing that methodology, assume that Sanchez has just four SKUs: SKU1, SKU2, SKU3, and SKU4. The following data summarize the current sales, selling prices, and cost (purchase price plus freight) for each SKU:

	SKU 1	*SKU 2*	*SKU 3*	*SKU 4*
Wholesale price (to retailer)	$51.00	$13.00	$85.00	$7.00
Cost (including all freight)	$29.00	$8.00	$49.00	$5.00
Sales volume	12,000	25,000	8,000	30,000

Sanchez purchases items for sale and inventories them. The cost of inventorying each item (including the opportunity cost of financing the item) is 20 percent of the annual cost of the item. So if 100 units of a gadget are sold each year, and the cost of the item is $4, Sanchez's inventory holding cost is $80 (20% × 100 × $4).

The annual cost of the marketing department is $135,000. This amount consists of the salaries and fringe benefits of the employees who purchase the products and prepare the catalogs and price lists. Management determines that marketing department costs vary with the number of SKUs.

The annual cost of the direct sales force is $350,000. This amount consists of the salaries, fringe benefits, and travel expenses of the salespeople who call on the retail specialty kitchen stores to sell Sanchez gadgets. After extensive conversations with the salespeople, management believes that the salespeople spend their time in proportion to the sales volume of the gadgets. In other words, if a particular gadget accounts for 10 percent of Sanchez's total revenue, then the sales force spends about 10 percent of its time selling that item.

Required:

     a. Design a reporting methodology that identifies possible SKUs that Sanchez should consider dropping from its product mix. Using your methodology, compute the profitability of each of the four SKUs.

b. Based on your analysis in part (*a*), which SKUs should Sanchez drop? Which ones should Sanchez retain?

c. Discuss the critical assumptions underlying your analysis in part (*a*).

P 11–12:   Rextera

Rextera produces a line of skin care products. It has two product lines: Young Skin and Moisturizer. Young Skin is a patented, heavily promoted, and proprietary cream that removes wrinkles and "makes you look ten years younger." Moisturizer is a cream that moisturizes the skin. Rextera sells its two products lines only through its website. Its strategy is to drive consumers to its website via articles in fashion and health magazines, other web sites, and blogs about Young Skin. Although many customers initially are drawn to Rextera's site because of these Young Skin stories, only a small fraction of Rextera website visitors buy Young Skin (due to its high price).

The following data summarize the operating data on the two product lines.

	Young Skin	*Moisturizer*	*Total*
(per ounce)			
Price	$800	$50	
Variable cost	$100	$30	
Separable fixed manufacturing overhead	$200,000	$600,000	
Common fixed marketing costs			$1,000,000
Number of ounces sold	900	70,000	

Variable cost consists of both variable manufacturing cost and variable selling and distribution (shipping) cost. Young Skin and Moisturizer are produced in separate factories, each with its own separable fixed manufacturing overhead. Both product lines share the same common marketing costs (primarily the cost of maintaining the website and advertising the website via articles placed in fashion and health magazines, other websites, and blogs).

Product-line profits are not used in calculating any Rextera manager bonus or compensation. Rextera only sells its products in the United States.

Required:

a. Prepare a report showing product-line profits for Young Skin and Moisturizer after allocating the common fixed marketing costs of $1,000,000, using total revenue on each of the two product lines.

b. Rextera management worries that using revenues to allocate the common fixed marketing costs as in part (*a*) is distorting the relative profits of the two product lines. They believe a more accurate way to allocate these costs is to analyze how customers utilize the Rextera website. After analyzing the various Web pages downloaded by website visitors after coming to the Rextera home page, the following Web views were generated by visitors to the Rexera website during the last six months:

Number of Young Skin Web page views	603,250
Number of Moisturizer Web page views	31,750

Prepare a report showing product line profits for Young Skin and Moisturizers after allocating the common fixed marketing costs using Web page views as the allocation base.

c. Which of the two reports prepared in parts (*a*) and (*b*) best captures the profitability of Young Skin and Moisturizer?

P 11–13:   Routers Inc.

Routers Inc. manufactures and sells two types of high-speed, secure wireless routers: a home router and a commercial router. Routers Inc. purchases components (printed circuit boards, antennas, power supplies, plastic cases), assembles complete units and tests and boxes them in its plant. The following table summarizes operations for the last fiscal year.

	Home	*Commercial*
Number of units produced	12,000	5,000
Direct labor minutes per unit	9	21
Direct material cost per unit	$6.50	$23.00

In other words, management budgeted and produced 12,000 home routers last year and budgeted and produced 5,000 commercial routers. Each direct labor minute cost the firm $0.40, and manufacturing overhead last year amounted to $426,000. Routers Inc. employs a traditional absorption costing system to allocate manufacturing overhead to products using direct labor minutes as the allocation base.

Required:

a. What was the manufacturing overhead rate Routers Inc. calculated last year assuming that actual and budgeted overheads and volumes were identical? (In other words, budgeted volume and actual volumes were the same, and budgeted and actual manufacturing overheads were the same.)

b. Compute the total unit manufacturing costs of the home and commercial routers for last year.

c. Some senior managers at Routers Inc. questioned using direct labor minutes to allocate the $426,000 of manufacturing overhead arguing (i) it is too coarse and (ii) a more nuanced (sophisticated) approach was required. An extensive study of the manufacturing overheads revealed that the annual manufacturing overhead of $426,000 consists of two components: batch-related costs of $308,000 and product-line related costs of $118,000. Each time a batch is produced, components must be ordered in advance, inspected and stocked when received, and moved to the assembly department before production commences. Then, the assembly line must be prepared for the batch, and a few routers produced and tested to insure the assembly process is performing properly. During the year, 40 batches of home routers were assembled (each with 300 home routers per batch) and 100 batches of commercial routers were assembled (each with 50 commercial routers per batch). The product-line related costs of $118,000 consist of engineering and technician expenses devoted to revising the technical specifications of the components used in the two product lines to comply with the various government agencies regulating wireless devices. Each product line consumes half of the product-line related costs of $118,000. Given the data revealed in the cost study (discussed earlier), compute the manufacturing overhead that should be assigned to the home router and the commercial router.

d. The people conducting the manufacturing overhead cost study argue that using the new manufacturing overhead allocations will increase the accuracy of the cost of producing home routers and commercial routers, and hence should be adopted. You are hired as a consultant to the chief financial officer (CFO). Write a brief memo recommending how the CFO should proceed. Should the CFO stay with the existing absorption costing system, switch to the new system, or gather additional information (and what information should be gathered)?

P 11–14:   Wedig Diagnostics

Wedig Diagnostics manufactures two laser photometers that are used in preparing DNA tests. The U.S. model is designed for use in the United States, and the EU model is designed to meet the specifications in most of the European Union. Both models are manufactured in the United States. The EU models are shipped to Wedig's wholly owned European subsidiary, which sells them. All units manufactured are sold. The following table summarizes the selling prices, direct materials and labor, and number of units sold.

	U.S. Model	*EU Model*
Selling price/unit	$2,500	$2,200
Direct materials/unit	$235	$260
Direct labor/unit	$560	$500
Number of units sold annually	15,000	16,800

The EU units are sold in U.S. dollars. Wedig has total manufacturing overhead of $39 million annually. This overhead is allocated to both U.S. and EU models using total direct labor dollars. Wedig transfers its EU model to its European subsidiary at full cost (direct materials and labor plus allocated overhead). Assume that Wedig pays U.S. taxes only on the profits it makes on sales in the United States, and the Wedig EU subsidiary pays taxes only on the profits it makes on sales in the EU. The U.S. income tax rate is 30 percent, and the Wedig European subsidiary has a tax rate of 15 percent.

Wedig hires a consulting firm to perform an ABC analysis of its overhead costing methodology. This analysis reveals that the $39 million of overhead consists of three cost pools: batch-related costs ($12 million), parts-related costs ($9 million), and direct labor–related costs ($18 million). Each model is produced in batches, and batch-related costs consist of engineering, quality control, and machining costs that vary with the number of batches produced. The U.S. model is produced in 45 batches each year, and the EU model is produced in 55 batches a year.

The U.S. and EU models differ in terms of the number of different parts in each unit. The U.S. model has 40 different part numbers, and the EU model has 80 different part numbers. Parts-related costs consist of the costs of operating the purchasing department (excluding the costs of the parts purchased), inspecting the parts upon arrival, inventorying the parts, and managing the parts inventory. Parts-related costs vary with the number of part numbers in each product. Finally, the direct labor-related costs consist of human resources, accounting, and other overhead costs that vary with the amount of direct labor in each model.

Required:

 a. Calculate the unit manufacturing cost of the U.S. and EU models using total direct labor dollars to allocate the $39 million of manufacturing overhead.

 b. Calculate the unit manufacturing cost of the U.S. and EU models using the ABC analysis to allocate the $39 million of manufacturing overhead.

 c. Prepare income statements (including income tax expense) for Wedig and its European subsidiary using the unit manufacturing costs calculated in part (*a*) (overhead is allocated using total direct labor dollars).

 d. Prepare income statements (including income tax expense) for Wedig and its European subsidiary using the unit manufacturing costs calculated in part (*b*) (overhead is allocated using the ABC analysis).

 e. Discuss the advantages and disadvantages of using direct labor versus ABC to allocate the $39 million of overhead.

P 11–15:   Toby Manufacturing

Toby Manufacturing produces three different products in the same plant and uses a job order costing system to estimate product costs. A flexible budget is used to forecast overhead costs. Total budgeted fixed factory overhead is $450,000 and variable overhead is 120 percent of direct labor dollars.

524   *Chapter 11*

Projected volumes, selling prices, and direct costs for the three products for the next calendar year are as follows:

	Product AAA	Product BBB	Product CCC
Projected number of units	6,000	3,000	1,000
Direct materials per unit	$22	$25	$30
Direct labor per unit	$11	$12	$16
Selling price	$98	$115	$140

Upon closer analysis of the overhead account, warehousing costs are determined to be a major fraction of overhead. The manufacturing process requires six operations. Between operations, intermediate products are moved and warehoused until the next production stage. Each product requires 10 days of processing time to complete all six operations. But the products have different total cycle times because of different waiting times between operations. Cycle time is the total time from when the product is started in production until it is completed and shipped. Product AAA has the shortest cycle time (20 days) because the large volume allows more accurate forecasts and more continuous scheduling of production. Product BBB has a total cycle time of 40 days; product CCC has a total cycle time of 50 days. Products BBB and CCC have longer warehousing times of work in process because of more frequent scheduling changes and supplier delays.

Half of what is currently treated as fixed overhead cost is involved in the warehousing function.

Required:

a. Prepare a pro forma income statement by product line for the year based on full absorption costing. Product costs should include overhead assigned on direct labor cost.

b. Prepare a revised pro forma income statement by product line using activity-based costing.

c. Comment on the differences.

P 11–16:   Kay Enterprises

Kay Enterprises is a small, family-owned and managed business. It has a patented production process for manufacturing a digital switch used in large telephone switches. It manufactures two models in its plant in Atlanta, Georgia. The U.S. model is sold to U.S.-based telephone companies, and the European switch is transferred to Kay's wholly owned subsidiary in Ireland, where it is sold to European telephone companies. U.S. switches are sold only in the United States, and European switches can be sold only in Europe. One brother, Lloyd Kay, manages the U.S. company, and his brother, Colin Kay, manages the Irish firm. The two switches share the same proprietary production process but have different design specifications to match the different telephone systems.

All switches manufactured are sold; Kay does not have any work-in-process or finished goods inventories. Because of the patented nature of the production process, Kay faces very little competition for its switches either in the United States or Europe. This allows the firm to set a relatively high price above its costs.

The following table summarizes the annual number of U.S. and European switches produced and the costs of manufacturing each switch. All manufacturing overhead of $24 million is a fixed cost that does not vary with the number of switches produced. Overhead is allocated to units produced based on direct labor dollars.

	Switches	
	European	*United States*
Units produced (000s)	1,000	900
Units transferred (000s)	1,000	N/A
Final selling price*	$30	$32
Direct labor per unit	$2.00	$3.00
Direct material per unit	$8.00	$9.00

N/A not applicable.

*Final selling price to the external market, not to the Irish company.

Because Kay operates in two countries, it must calculate and report income by country. Assume that the United States has a 35 percent income tax rate on U.S.-derived income. Profits of firms in Ireland are taxed at 10 percent to encourage foreign investment. In recent years, the U.S. and Irish tax authorities have scrutinized Kay's full-cost transfer pricing policy. The tax authorities become suspicious if a different transfer price is used for taxes than for other purposes. Kay transfers the European switches at full accounting cost (direct labor, direct material, and allocated overhead).

Required:

a. Prepare separate income statements for each country for Kay Enterprises for the current operating year using direct labor dollars to allocate manufacturing overhead to the switches.

b. Kay is considering switching to activity-based costing for allocating overhead to the two models of switches. Upon analysis of the production process, it is determined that most of the $24 million of manufacturing overhead varies with the number of batches produced. The equipment is set up between batches; raw materials are ordered and inspected on a batch basis. The quality control department checks five units per batch. Packing and shipping costs vary with the number of batches. After conducting this analysis, Kay decides to switch to ABC for allocating manufacturing costs. European switches are produced in batch sizes of 20,000, and U.S. switches are produced in batch sizes of 30,000. Prepare separate income statements for each country for Kay Enterprises for the current operating year using ABC to allocate manufacturing overhead to the switches.

c. Which set of income statements [those in part (a) or (b)] should Kay Enterprises use?

P 11–17: Goodstone Tires

Goodstone Tires designs, manufactures, and sells automotive tires through three profit centers (divisions): Passenger Vehicles, Industrial Vehicles, and Racing. The Racing Division develops state-of-the-art high-performance racing tires for NASCAR, grand prix, and Indy cars. Racing, while a small part of Goodstone's total revenues and profits, provides much external visibility and a proving ground for Goodstone's future generation of passenger and industrial tires. Racing's motto is "What's winning today is on tomorrow's cars and trucks."

The following table summarizes the revenues and variable and fixed expenses (in millions of dollars) of the three divisions:

	Racing	*Passenger*	*Industrial*	*Total*
Revenue	$135.00	$2,900.00	$2,400.00	$5,435.00
Division variable expenses	81.00	1,160.00	1,200.00	2,441.00
Division fixed expenses	13.50	580.00	480.00	1,073.50

526   *Chapter 11*

Each division operates as a decentralized organization with its own manufacturing, distribution, marketing, administrative, and sales organizations. Corporate headquarter costs of $1,400 million are allocated to the three divisions based on divisional sales.

Required:

a. Prepare a report detailing divisional performance based on net income after allocating corporate overhead using divisional sales as the allocation base.

b. Discuss the pros and cons of the report you prepared in part (*a*).

c. Upon further reflection, the chief financial officer (CFO) believes that allocating corporate overhead using divisional revenues is too simplistic. Corporate overhead consists of the following:

R&D	$ 420.00
Corporate image advertising	330.00
Interest	370.00
Corporate office	280.00
Corporate overhead	$1,400.00

All research and development for the divisions is conducted at the corporate R&D lab. The lab's total spending of $420 million is spent on projects directed specifically at one of the three divisions. As a percentage of total R&D spending, Racing has 50 percent, Passenger 30 percent, and Industrial 20 percent.

Corporate image advertising amounts to $330 million. While the content of the ads varies, each ad contains images of Goodstone's Racing, Passenger, and Industrial products. The general corporate directive, based on market research, is that each print or television corporate image ad should, on average, contain 60 percent of the images or messages drawn from Racing, 30 percent drawn from Passenger, and 10 percent drawn from Industrial.

Corporate borrows to finance the operations (current assets and fixed assets) of the three divisions. No division seeks long-term external financing. Of the total current and fixed assets financed externally by the corporate office, 30 percent are in Racing, 50 percent are in Passenger, and 20 percent are in Industrial.

Finally, "Corporate Office" of $280 million consists of the CEO, CFO, chief legal counsel, chief information officer, chief human resource officer, and their staffs. The CFO polled each of the senior officers in the Corporate Office asking them how much of their time and their staff's time was devoted to each of the three divisions. Based on the data, the CFO decided that Corporate Office expenses should be allocated to the three divisions as follows: 40 percent to Racing, 45 percent to Passenger, and 15 percent to Industrial.

Based on the preceding information, prepare a revised divisional performance report that satisfies the CFO's request for a less simplistic, more accurate allocation of corporate overhead.

d. Discuss the pros and cons of the performance report prepared in part (*c*).

e. The corporate strategy of using the Racing Division both as a way to promote Goodstone's Passenger and Industrial products and also as a way to develop and perfect the next generation of tires was tested when an external consulting firm was hired to estimate the impact on Passenger and Industrial sales from having the Racing Division. Using both longitudinal and cross-sectional data from Goodstone and the tire industry, the consultant concluded that at the current scale of the Racing Division, Racing increases Passenger and Industrial revenues by 10 percent and 5 percent, respectively. Moreover, the consultant concluded that the benefits from corporate image advertising and centralized R&D permeate the entire organization and enhance recruiting and retaining personnel. For example, the R&D lab can attract better engineers and scientists to work on Passenger and Industrial projects because they also work on state-of-the-art racing projects. Corporate R&D projects, while directed specifically at a particular division, provide significant spill-over effects for the other divisions. Lab equipment purchased for Passenger or Industrial projects often is used later on racing projects. And research findings generated on Racing projects almost always have implications for Passenger and Industrial products. In fact, when choosing among R&D projects, the head of the lab selects projects that have maximum corporatewide benefits.

Based on the findings of the external consultants, prepare another divisional performance report for the three operating divisions.

f. Discuss the pros and cons of the report developed in part (*e*).

P 11–18: Hospital Admissions Office

The admissions office of a large hospital has an annual operating budget of $700,000. These costs are distributed to inpatient departments (surgery, medicine, pediatrics, psychiatry) and to outpatient departments (drug treatment, prenatal care, dialysis). In the past, the admissions office's costs have been allocated to inpatients and outpatients based on the number of patients processed. But now hospital management is seeking some alternative ways to distribute these costs.

The following data for the last 12 months summarize the number of patients, average days per stay, average patient bill, and average number of minutes to register inpatients and outpatients.

	Number of Patients	Average Days per Patient Stay	Average Patient Bill	Average Minutes to Register a Patient
Inpatient	25,000	6.50	$8,200	12
Outpatient	120,000	1.00	700	8

Required:

a. Allocate the admissions office's annual operating budget to inpatient and outpatient categories based on

  (*i*) Total number of patients.
  (*ii*) Total number of patient days.
  (*iii*) Total patient billings.
  (*iv*) Total minutes used registering.

b. Discuss the managerial implications of these various alternative ways to distribute the admissions office's costs. Which method should the hospital adopt?

P 11–19: ABC and Taxes

A plant manufactures two products, Hi-V and Lo-V. Hi-V is the high-volume product that represents most of the plant's revenue. It is produced 10 times per year, inventoried, and shipped to customers twice a month. Lo-V is a specialty product. It is made to order in small but frequent batches (usually once a week) and shipped immediately to customers. The plant uses an absorption costing system that assigns manufacturing overhead to products based on direct labor hours.

528 *Chapter 11*

This table summarizes the annual cost structure and operating data for the plant.

		Hi-V	Lo-V
Direct materials	4 @ $13	$ 52	
	10 @ $2		$ 20
Direct labor	.75 hr @ $12	9	
	.25 hr @ $12		3
Overhead	.75 hr @ $40	30	
	.25 hr @ $40		10
Total cost per unit		$ 91	$ 33
Selling price		$ 95	$ 100
Ending inventory		700	0
Production (units)		12,000	4,000
Setups per year		10	40
Manufacturing overhead:			
Fixed overhead			$390,000
Variable overhead per direct labor hour			$ 1
Budgeted volume:			
Hi-V (12,000 × .75)			9,000
Lo-V (4,000 × .25)			1,000
Budgeted direct labor hours			10,000
× Variable overhead per hour			$ 1
Variable overhead			$ 10,000
Fixed overhead			390,000
Budgeted overhead			$400,000
÷ Budgeted volume			10,000
Overhead rate			$ 40

A careful analysis of the plant's fixed overhead reveals that $350,000 of the $390,000 varies with the number of setups. The remaining $40,000 of fixed overhead will still be allocated to products based on direct labor hours. There were no beginning inventories.

Required:

    a. Compute product costs per unit of Hi-V and Lo-V using activity-based costing.

    b. Prepare a table that compares the *profits of the two product lines* using the current absorption costing allocation method and activity-based costing.

    c. Income taxes are 50 percent. Calculate the plant's total tax liability under absorption costing and under activity-based costing.

    d. In general, will switching to activity-based costing lower a firm's taxes? Describe the general conditions necessary for activity-based costing to lower taxes.

P 11–20: Familia Insurance Company

Familia Insurance Company (FMC) specializes in offering insurance products to the Hispanic community. It has its own direct sales organization of agents that sells three lines of insurance: life insurance, auto insurance, and home insurance. FMC is organized around three profit centers (Life, Auto, and Home) and several cost centers (Sales, Accounting and IT, Human Resources, and Underwriting and Claims). Each agent sells all three insurance lines. Accounting and IT processes all transactions, including customer billing, claims, payroll, and so forth. Human Resources hires employees and manages the employee benefits plans. Underwriting and Claims sets the rates for the three types of policies, calculates the insurance premiums for each policy written, and processes insurance claims.

The three profit center managers are responsible for designing their marketing materials, training the common sales force to sell their policies, and designing their policies to appeal to their market demographics. Each profit center manager is compensated based on net income before taxes in their profit center.

The sales strategy of FMC is to heavily market the auto insurance and then sell the customer life and home insurance products. The following statement (in millions of dollars) summarizes operations for the last fiscal year:

	Life Insurance	Home Insurance	Auto Insurance	Total
Premium revenue	$ 500.00	$ 900.00	$ 600.00	$ 2,000.00
Investment income	87.50	157.50	105.00	350.00
Total revenue	$ 587.50	$1,057.50	$ 705.00	$ 2,350.00
Expenses:				
Insurance losses and loss adjustments	$ (300.00)	$ (540.00)	$(560.00)	$(1,400.00)
Policy acquisition expenses	(112.50)	(202.50)	(135.00)	(450.00)
Operating and administrative expenses	(100.00)	(180.00)	(120.00)	(400.00)
Net income before taxes	$ 75.00	$ 135.00	$(110.00)	$ 100.00

Policy premiums are invested in securities, and income from these investments is reported as "Investment income." "Insurance losses and loss adjustments" represent the actual insurance claims paid plus anticipated losses not yet paid for policies written that year. "Policy acquisition expenses" are the costs of the direct sales force. Operating and administrative expenses (in millions) consist of the following:

Operating and Administrative Expenses

Underwriting and claims	$ 90.00
Accounting and IT	70.00
Human resources	40.00
Advertising	120.00
Profit center expenses	30.00
Corporate office	50.00
Total O&A expenses	$400.00

In the statement of operations for last year, "Investment income," "Policy acquisition expenses," and "Operating and administrative expenses" are allocated to the three profit centers based on premium revenues. "Insurance losses and loss adjustments" are based on the actual and estimated losses on each policy written as calculated by the actuaries in the Underwriting and Claims department.

Profit center expenses consist of the salaries and benefits of the management and staff operating the profit centers and other direct costs incurred by the profit center. The $30 million consists of $6 million in the Life Insurance profit center, $15 million in the Home Insurance profit center, and $9 million in the Auto Insurance profit center. Corporate office expense consists of FMC's senior managers and their staff. They oversee all the profit and cost centers and design FMC's advertising campaigns.

FMC management and the board of directors worry about the large losses being reported in the Auto Insurance profit center and question the methodology being used to allocate both the investment income and the expense items. A consultant hired by senior (corporate) management to analyze these items finds the following relations:

- Investment income generated by each insurance line depends on the difference between premium revenues and insurance losses and loss adjustments.
- Policy acquisition expenses are driven by the time each agent spends on selling a particular line of insurance. Based on a questionnaire sent to FMC's agents, the consultant reports that, on average, agents spend 30 percent of their time selling auto policies, 30 percent selling home policies, and 40 percent selling life policies.
- Underwriting and Claims expenses are driven by the number of policies in each area. There are 150,000 life policies, 375,000 home policies, and 225,000 auto policies.
- The number of policies in each insurance line is a reasonable approximation of what causes resource consumption in Accounting and IT.
- Human resource costs are driven by the number of employees at FMC. Most of the employees at FMC are in either "Policy Acquisition expenses" or "Profit Center expenses." A reasonably accurate proxy for human resources consumed by employees is salary and benefit expenses of the direct sales force (policy acquisition expenses) plus the profit center expenses.
- Advertising and Corporate office expenses represent firmwide common resources. All FMC ads promote the FMC brand and not individual lines of insurance. After much discussion, management agrees the most commonly accepted allocation scheme for these two expense items is premium revenue.

Required:

a. Based on the consultant's recommendations, prepare a revised statement of operations for the current year that reports revised net income before taxes for each of the three profit centers.

b. Should FMC replace its current methodology for computing net income before taxes with the statement of operations you prepared in part (*a*)? Present the advantages and disadvantages of the two methodologies, and make a recommendation.

P 11–21: Brickley Chains

Brickley Chains produces five different styles of silver chains, A, B, C, D, and E, in a highly automated batch machining process. The following table summarizes the production and cost data for the five products.

Product	Annual Volume	Direct Labor per Unit	Direct Material per Unit
A	5,000	$2.00	$4.00
B	3,000	2.50	4.50
C	1,000	3.00	5.00
D	800	4.00	6.00
E	500	5.00	7.00

Annual overhead is $80,000.

Required:

a. Compute the unit cost of each chain, A–E, using absorption costing. Overhead is assigned to individual products using direct labor cost.

b. Upon further analysis, you discover that the annual overhead of $80,000 consists entirely of the highly automated machining process. Each chain type is produced in batches with chains of the same type. Each batch requires the same amount of machine time. That is, producing a batch of 100 style A chains requires the same amount of machine time as a batch of 25 style E chains. The following table summarizes the batch size for each type of chain:

Product	Batch Size
A	100
B	100
C	50
D	40
E	25

Compute the unit cost of each chain, A–E, using activity-based costing.

    d. Prepare a table comparing the activity-based cost and absorption cost of each product. Discuss why the product costs differ between the two costing methods.

Cases

Case 11–1: Tilist Golf

Tilist Golf is a premier producer of golf clubs and golf balls. The Ball Division makes two types of balls: a professional ball (the "Masters") played by professional and top amateur players and a mass-market ball (the "Distance") that targets weekend players. Although most golf balls are very similar in construction and performance, slight differences exist between them. The Masters ball is a little softer and allows skilled players to put more spin on the ball for control. The Distance ball is a little harder with a more durable cover. While the two balls perform similarly, many golfers perceive the differences are larger than they really are, especially across ball manufacturers. Most golfers have a favorite brand of ball. Golf ball manufacturers compete over ball design (dimples, cover, core composition), price, and marketing. The principal way balls are marketed is through the endorsements of major professional golfers. Tilist pays professional golfers up to $500,000 per year to wear Tilist hats or shirts during tournaments, to allow Tilist to use their image in commercials, and to play Tilist balls (which are provided free to the professional) in all tournaments.

Tilist's Ball Division has separate profit centers managing each type of ball. The following table summarizes the operations of the Ball Division for last year.

	Masters	Distance
Price per dozen	$26	$7
Variable cost per dozen	$12	$3
Quantity sold	300,000	25,000,000

In addition, the Ball Division has $61.429 million of overhead, consisting of sponsorships, promotions, R&D, and so forth.

Required:

    a. Prepare income statements for the two ball types after allocating the $61.429 million of overhead based on revenue.

b. Senior management of the Ball Division has undertaken a review of the cost allocation methodology used in part (*a*). They hired an ABC consultant and formed an ABC task force to design a new allocation scheme that better allocates the $61.429 million overhead to the two ball types. The overhead consists of the following items:

Promotional samples	$ 1,075,000
Sponsorships	18,500,000
Advertising	34,837,000
R&D	3,450,000
Ball Division headquarters expenses	3,567,000
Overhead	$61,429,000

Promotional samples consist of Tilist balls given away to touring pros under Tilist sponsorships, marketing opportunities, and charity events. $950,000 of Masters and $125,000 of Distance balls comprise the $1,075,000 of promotional samples.

The $18.5 million of sponsorships consists of payments to touring professional golfers expected to do well in televised tournaments. Sponsored pros are paid to play Tilist balls and wear the Tilist name on their hats or shirts. Sponsorships are aimed at increasing Tilist's name recognition across all types of golfers. Senior managers and the ABC task force believe the sponsorships expenditure is best assigned to the two divisions based on the number of balls sold.

The advertising expenditure of $34,837,000 covers television and print ads ($1.35 million for Masters and $33.487 million for Distance).

Tilist has a research lab where it designs new balls by experimenting with different dimple patterns, covers, and cores. About one-third of the R&D effort is devoted to improving the Masters, and two-thirds of the R&D effort is directed toward improving the Distance.

After an extensive study of the various functions of the Ball Division's headquarters expenses, including the time spent by the various personnel in the two ball divisions, the ABC task force has agreed that 40 percent of the $3.567 million headquarters expenses should be allocated to Masters and the remainder to Distance.

Prepare income statements based on the findings of the ABC task force.

c. Based on the income statements prepared in part (*a*) (overhead allocated using revenues) and part (*b*) (ABC overhead allocations), what conclusions can you draw about the relative profitability of the two ball types?

Case 11–2: SnapOn Fasteners

SnapOn makes snap-together button fasteners (a male top and female bottom) for designer clothes. Each top and bottom consists of several metal parts that, when attached to the garment, allow the shirt, jacket, or pants to be closed without the use of a zipper. The top of each button consists of a shiny or painted metal surface, usually embossed with the designer's logo or design. Fashion design houses contract with manufacturers to produce their fashion lines. The fashion house specifies the particular SnapOn fasteners the manufacturer will use. The manufacturer then purchases the top and bottom sections of the fasteners and leases SnapOn attaching machines to attach the fasteners to the garments. Because each fastener is designed specifically for a particular designer, SnapOn attaching machines must be tailored to each fastener so that the fastener can be attached to the garment without scratching or marring the snap, and the machine can operate reliably without jamming. Each machine is specialized to a particular fastener by the tooling in the machines, which have tight tolerances for the particular fastener shape, size, and finish. This tooling is the materials handling device that moves the various components of the tops and bottoms through the machine and positions them in the correct location so that the machine can then compress the metal parts and fabric together.

SnapOn has achieved a good reputation among top design houses for producing high-quality, unique fasteners and a line of attaching machines that do not jam and do not mar the fastener. SnapOn has a staff of service technicians who maintain the attaching equipment 24/7. If a machine malfunctions, SnapOn guarantees that it will repair it within 24 hours, anywhere in North America. This service is very important to SnapOn's customers because fashion designers operate on short cycle times. Once they design their spring, summer, fall, or winter lines and show them to the buyers, the designers have eight weeks to produce and deliver the lines. Keeping their designs secret until they are released keeps other fashion houses and knock-off producers from copying their designs. The top fashion designers are willing to pay premium prices for high-quality fasteners that can be attached using highly reliable equipment.

SnapOn has two product lines (fasteners and attaching machines) and produces both lines in the same plant. Separate managers are responsible for the two product lines. Each manager receives 50 percent of his/her bonus based on reported net income of his/her product line, and 50 percent of his/her bonus based on SnapOn's total net income. All manufacturing overhead of $59.615 million is applied to all products (attaching machines and fasteners) using direct labor dollars. All selling and service costs of $47.210 million are allocated to fasteners and attaching machines based on revenue dollars generated by each product line. The following table summarizes the operations of SnapOn (in millions) for the most recent fiscal year.

SNAPON FASTENERS
Summary of Operations
Last Fiscal Year

	Machines	Fasteners
Revenue	$95.750	$132.895
Direct labor	22.650	43.680
Direct materials	24.640	21.840

Required:

a. Prepare income statements for SnapOn's two lines of business (fasteners and attaching machines) that include manufacturing overhead and selling and service expenses allocated to each business line using the methodology described previously. Assume there are no beginning or ending inventories of either attaching machines or fasteners.

b. Senior management is concerned that its current costing methodology of allocating manufacturing overhead based on direct labor dollars is too simplistic and is not producing unit manufacturing costs that accurately reflect the true consumption of indirect manufacturing overheads. Since manufacturing overhead is about 50 percent of total manufacturing cost (direct labor, direct materials, and manufacturing overhead), small errors in cost allocations could materially affect the calculated unit manufacturing costs. Some foreign competitors are entering SnapOn's traditional fashion markets and are offering fasteners at prices below SnapOn's unit manufacturing costs. Garment manufacturers who use these foreign fasteners have to lease attaching machines from other U.S. manufacturers because the foreign fastener-makers do not provide their own attaching machines. SnapOn will not allow non-SnapOn fasteners to be used in SnapOn attaching equipment.

Senior management organizes a task force to study SnapOn's manufacturing overhead and selling and service costs and asks the task force to devise a better methodology for tracing these costs to individual products and the two lines of business. After three months of analysis, the task force presents the following breakdown of last year's manufacturing overhead amount:

	Manufacturing Overhead Amount	Cost Driver
Purchasing	$ 9.812	Direct materials
Depreciation of machinery	17.611	Traced directly
Supervision	3.665	Direct labor
Occupancy	19.873	Square footage
Engineering	8.654	Traced directly
Total	$59.615	

The task force determines that costs in the purchasing department are driven by the dollars spent on direct materials. The depreciation of machinery should be charged to the two product lines based on the machinery used by the two product lines. Since attaching machine production and fastener production use different equipment, the depreciation of the manufacturing equipment can be directly traced to the two product lines. Of the $17.611 million of total depreciation, 70 percent is for equipment used to manufacture the attaching machines and 30 percent is for equipment used to manufacture fasteners. Employees are supervised either manufacturing attaching machines or manufacturing fasteners. So direct labor dollars are the cost driver of supervision expenses. The production of attaching machines occupies 75 percent of the total manufacturing space (square footage) and fastener production occupies the remaining 25 percent. Hence, occupancy costs (depreciation of the building, property taxes, property insurance, and utilities) should be assigned to products using square footage as the cost driver. Finally, engineers are assigned exclusively to either attaching machine production (60 percent of the engineering costs) or fastener production (40 percent).

The task force also examined the selling and service costs and determined that $11.850 million of the total $47.210 million consisted of service costs for the attaching machines (salaries, travel, and parts to maintain the attaching machines in the field). The task force also determined that selling costs of $35.36 million vary with revenues.

Using the task force's findings, prepare revised income statements for SnapOn's two lines of business (attaching machines and fasteners) for the last fiscal year. Assume there are no beginning or ending inventories of either attaching machines or fasteners.

c. Briefly describe any changes in the relative profitability of the two lines of business after implementing the task force's analysis.

d. Should SnapOn stay with its current costing system as portrayed in part (*a*), or should SnapOn convert to the new costing methodology based on the task force's analysis as portrayed in part (*b*)? Be sure to justify your recommendation based on the advantages and disadvantages of each alternative.

Case 11–3: Dyna Golf

Joe Bell, president and chief executive officer of Dyna Golf, has called a meeting of the executive committee of his board of directors. He is concerned about the price competition and declining sales of his golf wedge line of business. Bell summarizes the current situation by saying,

As you know, we set target prices to maintain a gross margin on sales of 35 percent. On some products, such as our drivers, we have been able to achieve the target price. We have been able to achieve higher prices on our putters than a target 35 percent gross margin would dictate. But our wedges are a totally different story.

Our factory is among the most efficient in the world. I think that some foreign companies are dumping wedges in the U.S. market, driving down prices and unit sales. We've been reluctant to further cut our prices for fear of what this will do to our gross margins. Fortunately, we've been able to offset the decline in sales of wedges by significantly raising the price of our putters. We were pleasantly surprised when our customers readily accepted the price increases of our putters, and we haven't experienced much reaction from our competitors on the putter price increases.

Steve Barber, an outside director on the board, asks:

Joe, I don't pretend to know a lot about the golf club business, but how confident are you in your cost data? If your costs are off, won't your prices be off as well?

Joe Bell responds:

That's a good point, Steve, and one I've been worried about. We've been modernizing our production facilities and I've asked our controller, Phil Meyers, to look into it and report back after he has undertaken a thorough analysis. My purpose for calling this meeting was to update you on our current situation and let you know what we are doing.

Background

Dyna Golf has been in business for 15 years. Its one plant manufactures three different types of golf clubs: drivers, wedges, and putters. Dyna does not produce a complete club with a shaft and grip. It makes the metal head that is sold to other companies that assemble and market the complete club. Dyna holds four patents on a unique golf club head design that forges together into one club head three different metals: steel, titanium, and brass. It also has a very distinctive appearance. These three metals weigh different amounts, and by designing a club head with the three metals, Dyna produces a club with unique swing and feel properties. While the Dyna club is unique and covered by patents, other manufacturers have recently introduced similar technology using comparable manufacturing methods.

The Dyna driver is sold to a single distributor that adds the shaft and grip and sells the driver to retail golf shops. Dyna first made its reputation with its driver. It became an "instant hit" with amateurs after a professional golfer won a tournament using the Dyna driver. Based on the name recognition from its driver, Dyna introduced a line of putters and then wedges. The wedges are sold to three different distributors and the putters to six different distributors. Specialty, high-end putters like Dyna's have a retail price of $120 to $180 and drivers a retail price of $350 to $500. Golfers like to experiment with new equipment, especially when they are playing badly. Therefore, it is not uncommon for golfers to own several putters and switch among them during the year. Putter manufacturers seek to capitalize on this psychology with aggressive advertising campaigns. It is less common for players to switch among wedges as they do with putters. Since it takes several rounds of golf playing with a new wedge to get its feel and distance control, most players don't experiment as much with wedges as with putters, or even drivers.

TABLE 1   Dyna Golf Basic Product Information

	Drivers	*Wedges*	*Putters*
Production	10,000 units in 1 run	15,000 units in 3 runs	5,000 units in 10 runs
Shipments	10,000 units in 1 shipment	15,000 units in 5 shipments	5,000 units in 20 shipments
Selling prices:			
Target	$162.61	$134.09	$ 81.31
Actual	162.61	125.96	105.70

Production process

All three clubs (drivers, wedges, and putters) use the same manufacturing process. Each of the three clubs consists of between 5 and 10 components. A component is a precisely machined piece of steel, brass, or titanium that Dyna buys from outside suppliers. The components are positioned in a jig, which is placed in a specially designed computer-controlled machine. This machine first heats the components to a very high temperature that fuses them together, then cools them, and polishes the finished club.

The factory is organized into five departments: Receiving, Engineering, Setup, Machining, and Packing. Before a production run begins, Receiving issues a separate order for each component comprising the club head and inspects each order when it arrives. Engineering ensures that the completed club heads meet the product's specifications and maintains the operating efficiency of the machines. Because of the preciseness of the production process, Engineering is constantly having to issue Engineering change orders in response to small differences in purchased components. Setup first cleans out the machine and jigs, adjusts the machine to the correct settings to produce the desired club head, and then makes a few pieces to ensure the settings are correct. Machining contains several machines, any of which can be used to manufacture drivers, wedges, or putters once it is equipped with the proper jigs and tools. Packing is responsible for packaging and shipping completed units.

Table 1 summarizes the basic product information for the three products: production, shipments, target prices, and actual prices. For example, Dyna manufactured all 10,000 drivers in a single production run and shipped them all out in a single shipment. The 5,000 putters were manufactured in 10 separate runs and shipped in 20 shipments. Dyna set a target price for drivers to be $162.61 (wholesale price) and achieved it. However, it was not able to achieve its target price for wedges ($134.09 versus $125.96), but it exceeded its target price for putters ($105.70 versus $81.31).

Accounting system

Table 2 summarizes raw material, setup and run labor, and machine time for each of the three products. Each product is produced in the machining department by assembling the metal components. Drivers require 5 components, whereas wedges and putters require 6 and 10 components, respectively. Before the production begins, the machine must be set up, requiring setup labor. Then to produce clubs, operating the machines requires both machine time and run labor time. Both setup and run labor cost $20 per hour. Machining has a total budget of $700,000, consisting of the depreciation on the machine, electricity, and maintenance. Drivers take more run labor time than machine time because several operators are required to operate the machinery when drivers are produced. During putter machining, the operator can be operating two machines at once.

Table 3 summarizes the overhead accounts.

Phil Meyers, Dyna's controller, and Joe Bell meet a week after the executive committee meeting of the board of directors. Joe Bell asks Phil to report on what he has found. Phil begins,

> Joe, as you know, our current accounting system assigns the direct material costs of the components and the direct labor for run time to the three products. Then it allocates all overhead costs, including setup time and machine costs, to the three products based on direct run labor dollars. Setup labor is considered an indirect cost and is included in overhead. Based on these

TABLE 2   **Dyna Golf Production Information**

	Drivers	*Wedges*	*Putters*
Raw material	5 components @ $4 each = $20	6 components @ $5 each = $30	10 components @ $1 each = $10
Labor ($20/hr)			
Setup labor	10 hr per production run	10 hr per production run	11 hr per production run
Run labor	1/2 hr per driver	1/3 hr per wedge	1/4 hr per putter
Machine time	1/4 hr per driver	1/3 hr per wedge	1/2 hr per putter

TABLE 3   **Dyna Golf Overhead**

Receiving department	$ 300,000
Engineering department	500,000
Machining department	700,000
Packing department	200,000
Setup department	3,000
	$1,703,000

procedures we calculate our product costs for drivers, wedges, and putters to be $105.70, $87.16, and $52.85, respectively.

I've been looking at our system and have become worried that our overhead rate is getting out of line. It's now over 750 percent of direct labor cost. Since we've introduced more automated machines, we're substituting capital or overhead dollars for labor dollars. The Engineering department schedules its people based on change orders it receives. Drivers are pretty standard and only generate 25 percent of the change orders and wedges about 35 percent. Putters are our most complex production process and require the remainder of the change orders.

I'm thinking we should refine our accounting system along the following lines. First, we should break out setup labor from the general overhead account and assign that directly to each product. We know how much time we are spending setting up each machine for each club-head run. Second, we should stop allocating receiving costs based on direct labor dollars but rather on raw material dollars. And third, the remaining overhead (excluding setup and receiving) should be allocated based on machine hours. If we make these three changes, I think we'll get a more accurate estimate of our products' costs.

Joe Bell responded,

These seem to be some pretty major changes in our accounting system. I'll need some time to mull these over. Let me think about it and I'll let you know in a few days how to proceed.

Required:

What advice would you offer Joe Bell?'

Chapter Fourteen

Management Accounting in a Changing Environment

There is no shortage of management gurus writing books professing how to make organizations function better. They speak of organizational innovations such as *benchmarking, six sigma, total quality management, reengineering, lean manufacturing, the virtual corporation, downsizing, brainstorming,* and *corporate culture*. Most of these prescriptions are not directed specifically at improving firms' internal accounting systems. However, if implemented, most of these organizational changes require significant changes in the accounting system because the accounting system is an integral part of most firms' organizational architecture.

Chapter 1 described the forces that motivate changes in accounting and organizational architecture. This framework provides a useful way for understanding when a particular organizational innovation, such as total quality management (TQM), should be introduced and the accounting implications of such a change.

Previous chapters of this book described and analyzed management accounting systems. Besides being used for both decision making and control, these accounting systems support external reporting for shareholders, taxes, and government regulations. Thus, one of the central themes of this text is that trade-offs arise when the accounting system is designed for multiple purposes. In addition to providing a better understanding of the internal uses of the accounting system, this book reinforces the importance of viewing the accounting system as part of the firm's organizational architecture. This analytic structure helps readers better understand, use, and design accounting systems, as well as other systems that evaluate and reward performance and partition decision rights.

This final chapter applies the analysis in the previous chapters to some recent internal accounting system innovations. Section A reviews many of the key points raised in earlier chapters and expands Chapter 1's integrative framework in which accounting is an integral part of the firm's organizational architecture. This framework is used in section B to analyze recent organizational innovations (total quality management, just-in-time production, six sigma, lean manufacturing, and the balanced scorecard) and how accounting systems have responded to them. Section C discusses when accounting systems should be changed. Finally, section D offers a few concluding thoughts.

Over the course of your career, you will see numerous proposals to modify your firm's internal accounting system. Successful managers are those who can identify and implement firm-value-increasing proposals and avoid value-destroying changes. The four organizational innovations discussed in section B offer good case studies for applying what has been learned thus far. They also help review the strengths and weaknesses of the traditional accounting systems studied earlier.

A. Integrative Framework

As described in Chapter 4, firms arise because they can produce goods and services more cheaply than single proprietors transferring intermediate products in market transactions. But with firms come agency problems because the employees tend to care more about their own personal welfare than about the owners' welfare. Organizational architectures arise to control these agency costs: Decision rights are partitioned and performance is evaluated and rewarded. A critical task is linking the decision rights with the knowledge required to make the decision. It may be easier to transfer the decision rights to the person with the knowledge than to transfer knowledge to the person with the decision rights.

Figure 14–1 expands Chapter 1's integrative framework for understanding the usefulness of accounting systems in the firm's organizational architecture. Starting at the top, two external factors (technological innovation and market conditions) affect the firm's business strategy (described next). The business strategy then interacts with the firm's organizational

FIGURE 14-1

The determinants of business strategy, organizational architecture, and firm value

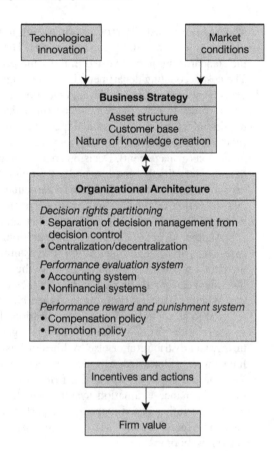

architecture to provide incentives for managers and employees. These incentives affect the actions taken, which in turn affect the value of the firm. Thus, Figure 14–1 emphasizes that external factors like technology and market conditions affect investments, organizational architecture, incentives, actions, and ultimately the value of the firm.

1. Organizational Architecture

The box labeled organizational architecture in Figure 14–1 outlines the three major elements of the firm's organizational architecture described in Chapter 4. The first element, decision rights partitioning, consists in part of separating decision management from control. In particular, each decision is decomposed into the following sequence of requests and approvals:

Decision Step	Control or Management
1. Decision initiation	Management
2. Decision ratification	Control
3. Decision implementation	Management
4. Decision monitoring	Control

The individual with the decision rights for decision management usually does not have the decision rights for control. This separation of decision management from control reduces the agency problem in organizations. For example, as described in Chapter 12, standard-setting usually requires input from individuals who will have their performance judged, at least in part, by these standards. Therefore, the decision rights to set or change the standards are not all vested in the same people who will be judged by the standards. The cost accounting department, industrial engineering, and senior management retain the decision control rights to ratify and monitor the standard costs.

In order to make decisions (for either decision management or control), managers require information. One would expect the information used for ratifying and monitoring (control) to be qualitatively different from the information used in initiation and implementation (management). Decision control information is likely to be more aggregate, less detailed, less timely, and less under the control of the manager being monitored than is decision management information. In particular, the manager being monitored should have less discretion to alter the information system being used for control than the manager using the information for decision management.

Another aspect of decision rights partitioning involves assigning various decisions to particular parts of the organization. For example, the decision rights to set the prices of the firm's products could be assigned to the sales department that has the knowledge of individual customers' demand curves, or they could be set by the vice president of marketing. Whether decision rights are assigned higher up or lower down in an organization is referred to as centralization–decentralization. The location of decision rights affects the structure of the firm—whether the firm is organized functionally by marketing, manufacturing, and distribution or else by lines of business. In all cases, decision rights must be linked with the knowledge needed for decision making.

The second component of a firm's organizational architecture in Figure 14–1 is the performance evaluation system, which includes the accounting system. Besides using accounting-based measures of performance, firms also develop nonaccounting-based measures: the firm's stock price, customer complaints, quality, and percentage of deliveries on time.

The third component of a firm's organizational architecture is the performance reward system. This consists of the firm's compensation and promotion policies. If performance can be measured easily and with little error, such as by counting the number of units produced by the employee, then more of the employee's pay varies directly with performance (piece rate). Otherwise, more of the employee's compensation is relatively fixed and is not tied directly to measured performance.

2. Business Strategy

Why do firms have different organizational architectures, including different accounting systems? What factors cause firms to modify their organizational architectures? The top three boxes in Figure 14–1—labeled technological innovation, market conditions, and business strategy—outline the factors affecting a firm's organizational architecture.

Each firm faces different investment opportunities, which are the investment projects available to the firm today and in the future.[1] The investment projects available to and selected by the firm comprise its **business strategy**. Some firms, such as consumer electronics firms, have large R&D programs that create many new product ideas, some of which are profitable. Other firms, such as utilities, have very few new investment projects; regulatory agencies limit the types of services they can provide, and their investment

---

[1]The following papers present evidence regarding the interdependencies among organizational architecture, capital structure, and accounting choice outlined in this section and summarized in Figure 14–1. C. Smith and R. Watts, "The Investment Opportunity Set and Corporate Financing, Dividend, and Compensation Policies," *Journal of Financial Economics* 32 (1992). Also see J. Brickley, C. Smith, and J. Zimmerman, *Managerial Economics and Organizational Architecture*, 6th ed. (New York: McGraw-Hill/Irwin, 2016).

Managerial Application: Business Strategy and Customer Base at Xerox	Xerox's traditional customer was the manager of the client's central reprographics department (CRD). Most large photocopier users had CRDs with high-volume, light-lens copiers. CRDs were pretty similar, with operators feeding hard-copy originals and producing large copy volumes. But digital technology allows users to network computers directly to printers. The customers of this digital technology are no longer CRD managers but computer centers and information technology managers. Xerox sales representatives now must have more technical expertise in computer systems and networking and more specialized knowledge of the customer's business and document processing needs. Each Xerox device performs multiple functions (scanning, printing, finishing, and faxing). The changing nature of Xerox's customers and the increasing complexity of its products compelled Xerox to change how its sales force is organized. Instead of being organized geographically and by size of customer, the sales force is organized along industry lines and products. Some Xerox salespeople specialize by client industry (education, law firms, manufacturing) and others by product line (color specialists, high-volume specialists, and so forth).
Managerial Application: Technology and Banking	Secure Internet connections and computers have made possible automated teller machines (ATMs) and online banking. These innovations have reduced the need for numerous local branch banks. Economies of scale in ATM networks and online banking—and, hence, the need for fewer branch banks—is one reason driving bank mergers. A corporate merger is an example of how companies change their organizational architecture.

opportunities consist of maintaining their current power-generating capacity. Public utilities rely on increases in consumer demand for electricity and heat to grow the utility's business, and most of their value derives from their existing assets in place (power plants and distribution systems). Firms such as consumer electronics firms and pharmaceuticals, however, have significant amounts of future growth options because of their R&D investments.

One important existing asset that generates future investment opportunities is the firm's *brand-name capital,* which provides consumer name recognition that lowers the information costs of introducing new products. Pepsi is recognized worldwide. When Pepsi introduced Diet Pepsi, consumers already had an expectation of taste and quality before sampling the new product. Its existing brand-name capital gives Pepsi a cost advantage that new entrants do not have when introducing a new product. Thus, brand-name capital affects the types of new investments a firm will undertake.

Business strategy affects the firm's organizational architecture because it determines the firm's asset structure, its customer base, and the nature of knowledge creation and dissemination within the firm. Each of these in turn affects and is affected by the firm's organizational architecture. (Notice the two-way arrow in Figure 14–1.) Not only does the firm's business strategy affect how the firm is organized, the organizational architecture affects the ability of the firm to generate and implement new profitable investment opportunities and hence new business strategies. For example, Corning, a glass company primarily making dishes and glassware (Corning Ware and Pyrex) invented fiber-optic cable active matrix LCDs and ceramic substrate for automobile catalytic converters. These innovations caused significant changes in Corning's organizational architecture. Likewise, successful organizational architecture generates new investment opportunities that can be commercially exploited.

Managerial Application: Evolving Role of Managerial Accounting in China	In 1979, China replaced its centrally planned economy with a market economy. Under the old system, the prices of companies' inputs and outputs, as well as their production targets, were set by the government. The cost of firms' inputs and the price of their outputs were fixed by the central government, and managers were measured on production. With a market economy, prices are set by markets, while firms determine what to produce and in what quantities, and how to produce it in order to maximize profits.

Before 1979, management accounting did not exist in China. Under a planned economy, accountants were accumulators and reporters of financial data to government central planners who set production quotas and prices for each firm's output. Accountants were viewed as bookkeepers. Following the reforms, companies eliminated their accounting functions that reported financial data to central planners. Management accountants in China today resemble their Western counterparts. Chinese management accountants now describe their most important functions as providing financial information to other managers for decision making and cost management and control.

This example illustrates how changes in market conditions (replacing a centrally planned economy with a market economy) in Figure 14–1 cause firms to change their strategy (from maximizing output to maximizing profits) and also change their organizational architectures. The role of accountants changed in Chinese firms.

SOURCES: R. Lawson, "Moving Ahead: The Evolving Role of the Finance and Accounting Function in China," *Strategic Finance*, March 2009, pp. 27–33; and L. Yuen, "Opportunities and Challenges for Management Accounting in Mainland China," *Financial Management*, July 7, 2013.

Business strategy consists of the following:

1. *Asset structure.* The firm's business strategy determines its asset structure. Pharmaceutical company assets are primarily drug patents and brand-name drugs, whereas Internet provider assets are primarily fiber-optic cable lines and servers. If the firm's assets consist of buildings and machinery, the performance evaluation systems are more likely based on accounting measures. If the firm's assets consist of future growth options, as in an oil and gas exploration firm, the firm is more likely to tie executives' compensation to market-based performance such as stock price.

2. *Customer base.* The business strategy determines the type of customer and the geographic dispersion of customers, which in turn affect how the firm is organized to service its customer base. For example, franchised retail stores like fast-food outlets are an alternative to company-owned stores when the customer base is geographically dispersed. The franchised store is operated by an independent owner who has more incentive to acquire specialized knowledge of the local market and to maximize profits than would an employee of the parent company. But to monitor the quality of the franchised outlets, the franchiser requires a field organization to inspect the outlets, which in turn dictates how the franchiser is organized (including performance evaluation and reward systems for the field group).

3. *Knowledge creation.* The nature of knowledge creation is determined by the business strategy selected. If the firm is in very stable markets in which knowledge is not created quickly, a more centralized organizational architecture can be adopted. Certain kinds of knowledge (like sales figures) can be converted to numerical representation that can easily be communicated to others in the firm. But other types of knowledge, such as customer preferences in particular markets, are more difficult to write down and convey to others. Easily communicated knowledge allows decision rights to be vested higher in the firm, meaning

that lower-level performance evaluation and reward systems can be simpler. Therefore, the investments chosen by the firm determine how and where knowledge is generated, which affects the partitioning of decision rights. At Xerox, understanding the customer's document processing needs is much more important with a digital, networked printer than with the older, light-lens copier.

3. Environmental and Competitive Forces Affecting Organizations

The top two boxes in Figure 14–1 indicate that the firm's business strategy depends on technological innovations and changes in market conditions. New technology such as fiber optics causes relative prices of competing technologies to change, which in turn causes some investment projects to become more valuable and others less valuable. For example, fiber optics helped to create the Internet, which allows e-mail. E-mail, in turn, reduces the demand for fax and regular postage services (snail mail). Technological change affects the costs of transmitting knowledge and monitoring performance. Manufacturing plants use beepers and cellular phones to monitor maintenance personnel. Restaurants use beepers to alert wait staff that orders are ready and to let customers know that their table is available. Technological change sets off a chain reaction that causes not only the investment opportunities but also the firm's knowledge base, asset structure, customer base, and organizational architecture (including its internal accounting systems) to change.

A similar chain reaction is set off when market conditions change. Increased global competition has forced many firms that once enjoyed protected domestic markets to become more cost competitive. Instead of making products domestically, firms now source parts and subcomponents globally, causing organizational changes. Market conditions change for a variety of reasons, including changes in government regulations and taxation policies. Changes in tax rates cause the profitability (after taxes) of investment opportunities to change, thus affecting which projects are accepted. The North American Free Trade Agreement (NAFTA) reduced tariffs among Canada, Mexico, and the United States. As a result of NAFTA, companies relocated production sites in search of lower costs. Not only has the flow of trade increased among the three countries, but the geographic dispersion of company operations has changed. Emerging markets in the People's Republic of China and the former Soviet Union also have set off chain reactions within firms seeking to expand into these markets. Their investment opportunities (business strategies) have changed, prompting modifications in organizational architecture.

It is important to emphasize that the preceding discussion and Figure 14–1 do not represent a complete overview of a very complex set of interactions. Many other important corporate policies such as capital structure, information technology, and marketing strategy have been excluded to simplify the discussion. However, the important point should not be missed—the internal accounting system is related to a larger set of other corporate policies.

4. Implications

Successful firms (and managers) will be those who adapt quickly to changing markets and technologies. New profitable investments will appear and some previously profitable investments will become unprofitable. Successfully implementing profitable projects requires organizational architectures that link decision rights and knowledge and that create incentives for managers to use their knowledge to take actions that capture the value in the investments undertaken.

While this book has focused on the firm's internal accounting system, it is important to understand the larger setting into which the accounting system fits. Figure 14–1 gives the big picture and highlights how external shocks to the firm from technological innovation and changing market conditions affect its value by working through the interdependencies between organizational architecture (including the choice of accounting systems) and the firm's business strategy. Senior managers are constantly trying to adapt to these external shocks by modifying their business strategy and organizational architecture. Figure 14–1 provides two important observations:

1. Alterations in the firm's organizational architecture, including changes in the accounting system, are likely to occur in response to changes in the firm's business strategy caused by external shocks from technology and shifting market conditions.
2. Changes in the accounting system rarely occur in a vacuum. Accounting system changes generally occur at the same time as changes in the firm's business strategy and other organizational changes, particularly with regard to the partitioning of decision rights and the performance evaluation and reward systems.

Three significant managerial implications are derived from these two observations. First, before implementing an accounting or other organizational change, it is important to understand what is driving the change. Second, a new accounting system should not be adopted merely because other firms are doing so; they may be reacting to a different set of external shocks. Third, an accounting system should not be changed without concurrent, consistent changes in the way decision rights are partitioned, as well as in the performance reward systems. All three parts of the organization's architecture must be internally consistent and coordinated.

Concept Questions		
	Q14–1	Define the firm's business strategy.
	Q14–2	Describe how the firm's business strategy affects its organizational architecture.
	Q14–3	Describe why technological innovation and changes in market structure cause firms to change their organizational architecture.
	Q14–4	Is it a good idea for managers to copy organizational changes adopted by other firms?

B. Organizational Innovations and Management Accounting

Firms have pursued a number of organizational innovations: total quality management, just-in-time production, six sigma, lean manufacturing, and the balanced scorecard. This section describes these innovations and their effect on management accounting and illustrates how to apply the framework presented in Figure 14–1 to better understand the innovations in terms of what causes firms to adopt them and whether they will be successful.

1. Total Quality Management (TQM)

Quality is a major issue in both the profit and nonprofit sectors of the economy. In attempting to improve quality, managers have had to grapple with what it means. There is considerable debate surrounding what constitutes Total quality management (TQM) and how to define quality. Nonetheless, to most experts, TQM encompasses both improving the tangible aspects of product quality (performance, reliability, conformance to specification, durability, serviceability, and perceived quality) and enhancing the efficiency of the organization (lowering costs and increasing productivity). TQM seeks to improve all aspects of the company: its products, processes, and services. Managers must also design measurement systems to report improvements in quality. This section describes various definitions of quality, discusses some quality measurement systems, and analyzes these systems within the framework presented in Figure 14–1.

While quality can be measured in many ways, the two most common methods involve meeting customer expectations and reducing defects.

Customers have expectations with respect to all of a product's attributes, including delivery schedules, reliability, operating characteristics, and service. These expectations include means, variances, and options. For example, a customer might expect a service technician to arrive, on average, within two hours of making the service call, with a standard deviation of one hour. If the service representative arrives within one hour, on average, but with a standard deviation of two hours, the firm has met one customer expectation (mean arrival time) but has not met another expectation (arriving dependably within one hour).

Defining quality as meeting customer expectations requires knowledge of the entire set of customer expectations, the actual realized values, and the importance customers attach to particular expectations. Each customer views deviations from some expectations to be more important than deviations from other expectations. For example, missed delivery schedules might be more important than missed service times for some customers. Preferences over product attributes vary across customers. Understanding customer preferences for product attributes is important specialized knowledge to acquire. Customers include external customers for the firm's products and services, as well as internal customers. For example, the maintenance department might not have external customers, but it has internal customers.

The traditional approach to ensuring product quality was extensive inspection of raw materials, purchases, and manufactured products. Quality assurance inspectors were added along the production line to weed out inferior products. Statistical sampling methods draw random samples from a batch and rejects the entire batch if that sample contains a statistically large number of defective units. Notice that this process implicitly defines quality as low variance—meeting a certain set of specifications, which might or might not be of interest to the consumer. Firms built into their operating budgets and standard costs a normal allowance for scrap and rework. In some cases, if market demand exceeded production in a period, marginally defective products were released. Defective products reaching the market were corrected by the field service organization under warranty arrangements. Most firms' accounting systems ignored the opportunity cost of inferior quality.

By the 1980s, two key factors combined to change the traditional approach to quality in many industries. First, the cost of detecting problems and monitoring production via computer instrumentation fell relative to the cost of maintaining quality via inspectors. Instead of manually detecting and correcting defects after production, improved instrumentation allowed earlier detection and correction of problems, often while the

| **Managerial Application: ISO 9000** | The International Organization of Standards (ISO) establishes quality standards. Its ISO 9000 standard has different levels of certification depending on the complexity of the manufacturer's operations. To become ISO certified, a manufacturer must document that it relies on written policies, procedures, and quality methods. Independent external registrars then visit the plant requesting ISO certification to ensure the applicant has the necessary documentation, quality manuals, and procedures in place (including continual improvements). Semiannual reviews and reaudits every three to four years are necessary to maintain certification. ISO does not guarantee that quality end products are being manufactured; rather, it certifies that policies exist that allow quality products to be manufactured.

SOURCE: http://en.wikipedia.org/wiki/ISO_9000 |

Managerial Application: Saia's Xtreme Guarantee	Saia Inc., a U.S. trucking company, seeks to provide total customer satisfaction through its Xtreme Guarantee. Saia guarantees: • Pick-Up Performance—Pick up shipment on day promised. • On-Time Delivery—Delivered on time as posted in our published transit times. • Claims-Free Service—Delivered without exception. • Claims under $1,000 Settled within 30 Days—Resolution in writing within 30 days of a claim. • Invoicing Accuracy—Accurate invoice the first time. • Proof of Delivery Turnaround within 5 Minutes. If the company fails to provide these services, the entire invoice will be refunded. SOURCE: http://www.saia.com.

product was in production. Second, worldwide competition expanded to such nonprice forms of competition as quality. Once the Japanese automobile and electronics companies gained price competitiveness against their American competitors, they turned their attention to achieving quality advantages. Both the lower cost of detecting defects and increased global competition fostered quality improvements. Notice that in terms of Figure 14–1, both technological innovation and changed market conditions created the TQM movement.

To reduce defects, companies redesigned their products to require fewer vendors, making it easier to maintain tighter controls on the quality of their suppliers. Product designers redesigned parts that failed. Production processes were redesigned to reduce defects by installing monitoring equipment to ensure more uniform production. Firms adopted TQM programs. While many TQM programs were initially started to improve the tangible aspects of product and service quality, TQM programs evolved to enhance products, prices, and services for both internal and external customers. Major changes in the organization's architecture also occurred, including modifying the performance evaluation and reward systems and the partitioning of decision rights. Decision rights were pushed down lower in the firm, where the knowledge of customer preferences and the production process often resides.

With highly competitive world markets, companies now must compete not only on price but also on delivery schedules, service, and other product attributes valued by their customers. In general, quality has come to mean giving customers what they want. Notice that when firms compete on quality, many different dimensions of quality come into play. TQM programs emphasize the multidimensional aspects of quality.

In terms of Figure 14–1, both technological innovations (computer instrumentation) and market conditions have forced companies to change both their business strategy and their organizational architecture. Central to TQM programs is knowing what the customer wants and how to produce it at lower cost. If knowledge of customer preferences and production processes resides lower down in the organization with the people who have direct contact with customers, then the theory in Chapter 4 says to place the decision rights with those employees. Most TQM programs argue for empowering employees to improve quality. Empowerment is another way of saying that decision rights are transferred to people with the specialized knowledge of customer preferences and production processes. Therefore, an important component of TQM is changing the firm's organizational architecture by decentralizing certain decision rights to lower-level managers.

Of course, if decision rights are repartitioned, then performance evaluation and reward systems also must change.

TQM programs also require accounting systems. Defect rates, on-time delivery, and customer complaints are easy for managers to understand and easy to measure. Without a corresponding accounting system, however, these diverse measures are difficult to aggregate. Managers do not know how to make trade-offs among quality decisions. For example, is it more costly to design and manufacture a product with fewer defects or to focus on inspection and correcting defects from initial production? Is it cheaper to install monitoring equipment or stay with manual inspections? Managers require cost data to make these comparisons for decision management purposes.

Total quality programs define a series of quality measures, including product design (number of new parts, total number of parts), vendor rating systems (number of defects, on-time delivery), manufacturing (defect rates, scrap, rework, on-time delivery), and customer satisfaction (surveys, warranty expense). The framework in Figure 14–1 predicts that if other parts of the organization's architecture are being modified, the accounting system will be, too. This is the case in TQM. Besides tracking the nonfinancial measures of quality listed earlier, some firms report the cost of quality. Quality costs can be categorized into four groups:

1. Prevention costs incurred to eliminate defective units before they are produced (reengineering products or production processes and employee training).
2. Appraisal costs incurred to eliminate defective units before they are shipped (inspecting and testing both raw material and work-in-process).
3. Internal failure costs (the costs of defective units in manufacturing).
4. External failure costs, including the cost of returns, warranty work, and product liability claims, as well as the opportunity cost of lost sales from reputation effects.[2]

These various costs are dispersed throughout the firm, usually in numerous overhead accounts. Aggregating these costs into a single cost-of-quality report brings them to the attention of senior managers. However, the opportunity costs of forgone sales caused by a reputation for low-quality products often represent the largest quality cost. These opportunity costs are unobservable, and hence not captured by the accounting system.

Part of the TQM philosophy is that improved quality can actually be less costly to the organization. The opportunity cost of selling defective products and not satisfying customers can be very high. Errors must be corrected and disgruntled customers mollified. Dissatisfied customers will seek other suppliers of the service or product. A reputation for shoddy workmanship is often the death knell for organizations. Even if a defect is discovered before being sent to a customer, the cost of handling and fixing the problem can be quite high. In many cases, the defective product cannot be fixed and must be junked. However, as discussed a bit later, "Quality is not free." Improving the quality of the firm's products or services requires resources; hence enhancing quality is costly. The question is, "Do the benefits of improving quality exceed the costs?" Figure 14–2 illustrates how quality costs likely behave as the firm seeks to improve quality. As the percentage of defects increases, the costs of internal and external failure also increase. However, higher defect rates usually result from low appraisal and prevention costs. Total quality costs will exhibit the usual U-shape, indicating that there is an optimum quality level. Trying to further reduce defect rates below this optimum costs more in prevention and appraisal costs than can be saved by lower internal and external failure costs.

---

[2]G. Wang, Z. Gao, and T. Lin, "Integrating the Quality Cost Report," *Cost Management*, January/February, 2007, pp. 42–47.

FIGURE 14–2

Optimum quality cost

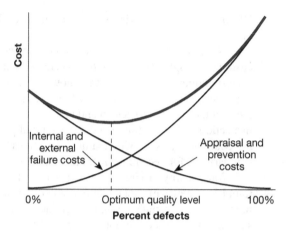

Although numerous firms initiated quality improvement programs, not all achieved their objectives. Studies show that many executives claim that quality is top priority, yet only one-third claim their programs are effective. Several companies, including McDonnell Douglas aircraft and Florida Power & Light, abandoned their TQM programs. Some 60 to 70 percent of senior managers in one survey believe that their TQM programs have not boosted their ability to compete. Another survey concluded that "many businesses may waste millions of dollars a year on quality-improvement strategies that don't improve their performance and may even hamper it."[3] This evidence supports the notion of an optimum level of investment in quality as depicted in Figure 14–2. Firms can over- or underinvest in quality.

Managerial Application: Measuring Health Care Quality	A central pillar in the Affordable Care Act of 2010 (the ACA or "Obamacare") involves tying more Medicare payments to the quality, not the quantity of health care by 2018. In 2014, 33 federal programs required providers to submit data on 1,675 quality measures, and state, local, and private health plans mandate hundreds more. Not unexpected, a fierce debate rages on how to measure quality. Many doctors, hospitals, and insurers prefer broader quality measures that assess patient outcomes rather than the current myriad quality metrics that largely measure processes such as tracking the percentage of patients with chest pain who get an aspirin in the emergency room. But some critics doubt whether such broad measures can actually measure quality. The executive director of the American Medical Association argues that few high-quality outcome measures exist to drive improvement. Some doctors grumble that whether patients get better is often out of their control and outcome metrics might drive doctors to avoid treating the sickest patients. The federal government reports that more than 2,600 hospitals will see their Medicare payments cut between 1 and 3 percent in 2015, or a total of $428 million, for not reducing 30-day readmissions sufficiently. The fight over measuring health care quality will only intensify as the ACA rolls out. Stay tuned. SOURCE: M. Beck, "Debate Heightens Over Measuring Health-Care Quality," *The Wall Street Journal*, January 30, 2015.

[3]*The Wall Street Journal,* October 1, 1992, p. B7; M. Beer, "Why Total Quality Management Programs Do Not Persist: The Role of Management Quality and Implications for Leading a TQM Transformation," *Decision Sciences,* Fall 2003, p. 623.

2. Just-in-Time (JIT) Production

Another organizational innovation is just-in-time (JIT) production. In a JIT plant, production and demand are synchronized because production does not start until an order is received. Products are *pulled* through the plant by customer orders, rather than *pushed* through by a master production schedule designed to keep the plant operating at full capacity. The goal of a JIT plant manager is to reduce the time the product spends in the plant. To accomplish this goal, the plant is reorganized so that raw materials and purchased parts are delivered to the factory right before they are entered into the production process, resulting in no intermediate work-in-process inventories. Units flow from one production cell to another with no interruptions. Units spend time in the factory only when actual work is being expended on them. Of course, this describes an ideal JIT installation. Few actual JIT plants achieve the ideal.

Throughput time is the total time from when a product starts the production process until it is ready for sale. Throughput is the sum of processing time, time waiting to be moved or worked on, time spent in transit, and inspection time. The goal of JIT is to drive the last three items (waiting, transit, and inspection time) to zero. The sum of the last three items is referred to as *wasted* or *non-value-added time*. The benefits of reducing throughput time include smaller in-process inventories, leading to

- Lower capital costs of holding inventories.
- Less factory and warehouse space and cost savings.
- Reduced overhead costs for material movers and expediters.
- Reduced risk of obsolescence.
- Faster response time to customers and reduced delivery times.

Achieving reduced throughput time requires the following changes:

1. *Increase quality.* To prevent production downtime, the quality of raw materials and the quality of the manufacturing process must be improved. Increased material and process quality eliminates the need to stop processing because of defects.
2. *Reduce setup times.* If machines can be set up quickly for a new production run, then parts do not have to wait for processing to begin. Moreover, inventories do not accumulate in front of the machine while it is being set up.
3. *Balance flow rates.* The rate of production in the various manufacturing cells must be the same or else work-in-process inventories will build up after the cells with the faster flow rates.
4. *Improve factory layout.* Redesign the factory to reduce travel time. Do not group machines that perform the same function in one department. Instead, organize machines by how the products are sequenced through them. The factory becomes organized around dedicated JIT production lines producing a single type of product, sometimes called **dedicated flow lines**.
5. *Change performance measurement and reward systems.* No longer must employees be evaluated and rewarded on the number of units produced. Individuals are no longer rewarded for maximizing flow rates. Such a performance measure encourages workers to build inventories and to have inventories in front of their station as buffer stocks. The performance measure in a JIT system is throughput time divided by process time. As this ratio approaches 1, non-value-added time decreases.

One important aspect of JIT involves changing the firm's relationship with its suppliers. In the past, managers believed that having several suppliers of each input increased competition and kept prices down. Firms had policies of dividing total purchases among several sources, which required each arriving order to be inspected to ensure quality. Having multiple suppliers made it more difficult to coordinate timely delivery of supplies. In a JIT environment, firms have drastically reduced their number of suppliers. The purchasing firm benefits from lower prices due to volume discounts, lower ordering costs (since only a single-relationship contract is required), and higher quality ensured by audits of the supplier's process rather than inspection of each shipment. Transportation costs are usually lower because suppliers can use long-term contracts with shippers. Through electronic data interchange (EDI), buyers and sellers integrate their computer systems so that purchase orders are also received JIT.

However, sole-sourcing is not a universal panacea. Sourcing from a single supplier and specializing purchases from a single supplier create incentives for the parties to the contract to behave opportunistically.[4] For example, in the early days of General Motors, GM bought all of its auto bodies from the independent firm of Fisher Body. GM frames and Fisher bodies were specialized to each other and there were incentives for one party to try to exploit the other. The solution was for GM to buy Fisher Body.

Accounting in a JIT production environment becomes much simpler. It takes on many aspects of a process costing system described in Chapter 9. In a JIT organization, job order costing, in which costs are accumulated for each job or batch, is no longer desirable. Having production employees update job order sheets as work is performed is non-value-added time. Also, because products are in work-in-process for such a short time, there is less need to worry about valuing partially completed products. In JIT accounting systems:

- Labor and overhead are combined into a single account (conversion costs).
- As much as possible, general factory overhead is traced directly to dedicated JIT lines (e.g., utilities, machine depreciation, and maintenance).
- Material costs are charged directly to products.
- Conversion costs are assigned based on machine (or cell) time.
- Detailed work-in-process accounting is eliminated because WIP inventories vanish.
- A single inventory account, raw and in-process materials (RIP), is used.
- All raw materials and purchases issued to production are charged to RIP.
- As units are finished, RIP is reduced by the materials costs and finished goods inventory is charged for the materials.
- Conversion costs are charged directly to finished goods (not RIP).

Managerial Application: Does JIT Work?	A study of 200 companies adopting JIT found the following results. Compared to a matched sample of 200 non-JIT adopters, inventory turnover ratios increased following JIT adoption. Moreover, the JIT adopters show improved ROA, relative to their non-adopting counterparts. JIT users' inventory turnover (Cost of sales ÷ Average inventory) climbed from 3.5 to 4.4 in the three years following adoption, whereas the nonadopters' inventory turnover remained relatively flat.
	Source: M. Kinney and W. Wempe, "Further Evidence on the Extent and Origins of JIT's Profitability Effects," *Accounting Review*, January 2002, pp. 203–25.

---

[4]B. Klein, R. Crawford, and A. Alchain, "Vertical Integration, Appropriable Rents, and the Competitive Contracting Process," *Journal of Law & Economics,* October 1978, pp. 297–326.

Firms adopting JIT accounting systems have significantly reduced the number of accounting transactions. Some firms have reduced their journal entry volume twentyfold because detailed payroll posting to jobs has been eliminated and jobs no longer need to be tracked through the work-in-process accounts as they move from department to department.

However, JIT also has drawbacks. Holding everything else constant, decreasing throughput time (like increasing quality or productivity) is unambiguously good because it increases firm value. However, everything else is not usually held constant. Redesigning the factory layout, reducing setup times, and requiring suppliers to increase quality and provide JIT deliveries can potentially increase costs. A sole supplier of a specialized input has some monopoly power and can use this position to extract higher prices. Accounting systems that measure throughput time without charging managers for the costs of improving throughput will cause throughput time to fall, but other costs might rise.

Moreover, firms hold inventories to smooth out fluctuations in supply or demand. If there is a labor strike, or bad weather prevents delivery of raw materials, or demand increases unexpectedly, inventories allow the firm to avoid the opportunity cost of lost sales. Reorganizing the factory, improving product and process quality, and changing purchasing relationships with suppliers can smooth out some of the fluctuations in production but cannot eliminate all the shocks to the system. After an earthquake in Kobe, Japan, Toyota's sole source of brake shoes for its cars could not operate for several weeks, causing Toyota to halt production at most of its plants in Japan. Toyota lost production of 20,000 cars, costing it an estimated $200 million in revenue. In another case, Toyota had to shut down two-thirds of its assembly lines after a fire at one of its major suppliers. Random fluctuations outside management's control, such as weather-related and demand-related shocks, cause the firm to carry some inventories as a buffer against losing sales.

While much has been written extolling the virtues of JIT accounting, other commentators warn of the system's weaknesses. Few firms have been able to completely eliminate raw materials inventory. After JIT was installed at one plant, raw materials inventory ranged from a two-day to a five-day supply on hand and finished inventory on hand fell from a 2.8-month supply to a 1.3-month supply. But since production tripled, the actual dollar value of inventory on hand increased. The number of accounting entries at this plant fell drastically. However, the accounting system was no longer able to track inventory levels, which meant that physical counts of inventory (some every six weeks) were required to provide information on specific inventory levels. Inconsistent with the basic JIT philosophy, these inventory counts are non-value-added activities that disrupt the production process by forcing employees to stop producing and count the inventory.

Adopting JIT causes the plant to change its organizational and even physical structure. The organizational changes require changes in performance measurement systems, including the internal accounting systems. Thus, accounting system changes follow and support changes in the physical and organizational structure of the plant.

In terms of Figure 14–1, technological advances in computer-aided manufacturing have been one impetus allowing factories to be redesigned along continuous flow JIT lines. Suppliers' computers are now linked electronically to their customers' computers, and electronic order processing is commonplace. These technological advances have made JIT production possible. Likewise, market conditions are changing. Customers are demanding that their purchases be delivered in continuous, small-order lot sizes, providing further incentives for manufacturers to adopt JIT techniques. Thus, two shocks to the firm's business environment have caused changes in the physical and organizational architecture of plants. Accounting systems, as part of the organizational architecture, are not exempt from these changes and have also been modified, as evidenced by simplified JIT accounting systems described earlier.

Managerial Application: Harley-Davidson and JIT	Harley-Davidson manufactures motorcycles. Over the years, direct labor has shrunk to about 10 percent of a motorcycle's product cost. In the past, each employee had to keep track of every product worked on in the course of the day. For an average employee, this meant about 20 bikes. Each day, the accounting system had to record 10,000 entries. However, management was not using this information for any decision making. When direct labor was a larger fraction of product costs, managers tracked direct labor variances more carefully. After introducing JIT, Harley-Davidson changed the accounting system. Direct labor was no longer treated as a direct cost but rather it and overhead were treated as conversion costs. Conversion costs were assigned to individual products based on how many hours the product was in the manufacturing process. This change greatly simplified the accounting process because all the individual labor transactions were no longer entered daily.

SOURCES: W. Turk, "Management Accounting Revitalized: The Harley-Davidson Experience," in *Emerging Practices in Cost Management*, ed. B. Brinker (Boston: Warren, Gorham & Lamont, 1990), pp. 155–66; and J. Schinwald, "Case Study: Harley-Davidson," July 28, 2005, www.webpronews.com/topnews/2005/07/28/case-study-harley-davidson.

3. Six Sigma and Lean Production[5]

This section explores two more recent management innovations: six sigma and lean production (sometimes referred to as "lean manufacturing" or just "lean").

Six sigma

Previously, total quality management (TQM) was described as a management approach, centered on quality and based on the participation of all the firm's employees with the goal of enhancing customer satisfaction. TQM became fashionable in the 1980s and 1990s in the United States, but it fell out of favor as many companies found that it did not generate the advertised benefits. In the late 1990s and 2000s, six sigma came to replace TQM. Six sigma is a set of practices, first popularized by Motorola, to systematically improve internal processes by eliminating defects and hence the quality of products and services. The term "six sigma" refers to the ability to produce products at defect levels below about three defects per million.

Like TQM, six sigma involves a structured, project-based approach with an executive-level six sigma committee that identifies potential projects such as procurement, manufacturing, logistics, sales, marketing, and distribution. Project teams, led by internal six sigma experts (called black belts), are formed and follow a well-developed methodology of defining the process improvement goals, measuring the current process and collecting relevant data, analyzing the causal factors, improving the process based on the analysis, and controlling any variances before they result in defects. Six sigma is a refined version of TQM.

But six sigma is not without its critics. Noted quality guru Joseph Juran claims that six sigma is "a basic version of quality improvement," stating that "there is nothing new there." In one study of the 58 large companies that announced six sigma programs, 91 percent underperformed the stock market.

---

[5]This section is based on the following references: M. Holweg, "The Genealogy of Lean Production," *Journal of Operations Management*, March 2007, pp. 420–37; *http://en.wikipedia.org/*; B. Morris, "New Rule: Look Out, Not In," *money.cnn.com*, July 11, 2006; F. Rudisill and D. Clary, "The Management Accountant's Role in Six Sigma," *Strategic Finance*, November 2004, pp. 35–39; and A. van der Merwe and J. Thomson, "The Lowdown on Lean Accounting," *Strategic Finance*, February 2007, pp. 26–33.

Managerial Application: Six Sigma at Caterpillar	Caterpillar, the world's largest global manufacturer of construction and mining equipment with more than 113,000 employees and revenues in excess of $40 billion, uses an extensive six sigma program to improve operating efficiencies. Senior managers at Caterpillar decided to apply its six sigma techniques to streamline and improve its accountings systems that had become overly burdensome. The old accounting systems focused about 75 percent of its resources on tax, legal, and regulatory compliance and only 25 percent on insightful analysis. Scattered throughout the firm were numerous multiple business ledgers and software packages, causing thousands of monthly reconciling journal entries, significant overtime hours by the staff, low morale of the finance and accounting staff, and less than optimal business decisions. Numerous six sigma teams were created, one in each business unit, to implement an integrated, transparent financial reporting system. To provide incentives and signal that senior management believes in six sigma, Caterpillar tied compensation to specific results for those who participated in the six sigma process. The outcome was an integrated financial reporting system linking financial reporting directly with results for product lines while eliminating the need for reconciling journal entries. SOURCE: K. Jones and C. Chen, "The Pervasive Success of 6 Sigma at Caterpillar," *Strategic Finance,* April 2010, pp. 29–33.

Lean production

JIT was described previously as a management approach whereby raw materials and supplies are delivered to a manufacturing operation just as they are needed to meet demand. Although JIT was first used by Ford Motor Company in the 1920s and 1930s, it was really the adoption, refinement, and promotion of JIT by Toyota in the 1970s and 1980s that popularized the technique. High land values forced Japanese manufacturers to reduce inventories, thereby lowering the cost to warehouse parts and finished products. But like other management fads, JIT failed to provide the overly hyped promises.

When JIT fell from favor, it was replaced with lean production. Lean production seeks to eliminate all non-value-added activities from the firm's value chain. The value chain consists of all primary and support activities that an organization performs to convert inputs into value-added outputs for its external customers. Typical activities in a value chain include research and development, design and engineering, production, distribution, and customer service. Lean production identifies and then eliminates non-value-added activities in demand planning, inventory planning, supply chain planning, and other capabilities that increase responsiveness to customers, reduce cycle time, and control costs.

Lean consists of a wide variety of efficiency and cost-trimming techniques dating back to the first "efficiency experts" in the early 1900s. In fact, many firms, such as Caterpillar and Textron, employ both six sigma and lean techniques to improve quality, cut processing times, eliminate waste, and cut costs. The latest term is "lean six sigma." Consistent with Figure 14–1, lean production has spawned "lean accounting," whereby the accounting system is modified to report all revenues and expenses for each of the firm's value chains in order to better identify non-value-added activities.

The chapter has described four management innovations: TQM, JIT, six sigma, and lean production. Management gurus and consultants refine old concepts and seek to differentiate their techniques by inventing new terminology. TQM and six sigma are management approaches centered on quality that aims to continually lower costs and improve the provision of services and products to customers. JIT and lean production seek to drive non-value-added activities (such as inventories) out of the process. Important lessons

626   *Chapter 14*

emerge from understanding past and current management innovations such as TQM, JIT, six sigma, and lean production:

- Firms are always looking for new ways to improve operating efficiencies, cut costs, and improve customer satisfaction.

- Successful management innovations require a careful and coordinated change in the firm's organizational architecture (decision rights assignments, performance measurement, and performance rewards). Announcing a new program on the company's website or in an e-mail rarely provides significant long-run improvements.

- Many new management innovations are fads. They are "old wine in new bottles." Once discredited, the same innovation eventually resurfaces with a refined set of techniques and a new name.

4. Balanced Scorecard

Beginning in the 1990s, many large firms, such as AT&T, KPMG, Bank of Montreal, Allstate, Tenneco, Mobil, and Citicorp, adopted a **balanced scorecard**. In Figure 14–1, successful firms develop a strategy that delivers goods or services to their customers at prices that exceed the costs of providing these products. The strategy of an organization provides a direction for the organization, such as goals for the introduction of new products, customer satisfaction, market share in specific areas, and efficiencies in production. Some companies, such as Amazon and McDonald's, have chosen *operational excellence*. Others have chosen *customer intimacy* (Home Depot) or *product leadership* (Intel and Apple). Highly successful firms excel at one while maintaining high standards on the other two.

A strategy, however, is seldom specific enough to describe the steps necessary to achieve the goals. A more detailed plan identifying the inputs necessary to implement the strategy is required. A balanced scorecard translates the strategy into a plan of action that identifies specific objectives and performance drivers to help determine if the organization is moving in the right direction.

A balanced scorecard links the firm's strategy to performance drivers, thereby providing a comprehensive view of the organization.[6] A balanced scorecard relates key performance indicators, such as on-time deliveries, to those actions required of employees to successfully achieve the firm's strategy and hence maximize firm value. In terms of Figure 14–1, the balanced scorecard is designed to identify those **key performance indicators** used to focus employees on those actions required to implement the firm's strategy.

Most balanced scorecards combine both decision management and decision control. Decision management is provided by identifying the sequence of objectives and the key performance indicators that allow the organization to achieve its goals. The balanced scorecard also provides decision control by establishing performance measures and targets for each objective. It articulates the strategy of the organization and communicates this strategy in a commonly understood language.

The balanced scorecard derives its name from the balance it attempts to achieve among the firm's strategy (objectives) and key performance indicators. Many observers of corporate culture lament the emphasis on short-term performance measures in corporations. Quarterly earnings announcements appear to have undue influence on the actions of the managers of a corporation. Focusing on short-term performance measures can reduce the value of the organization because of a reluctance to invest in activities that benefit the

---

[6]R. Kaplan and D. Norton, *Strategy Maps: Converting Intangible Assets into Tangible Outcomes* (Boston: Harvard Business School Press, 2004). Also see R. Kaplan and D. Norton, "Transforming the Balanced Scorecard from Performance Measurement to Strategic Management: Parts I and II," *Accounting Horizons,* March and June 2004, pp. 87–104 and 147–60.

FIGURE 14-3   *The balanced scorecard's four perspectives*

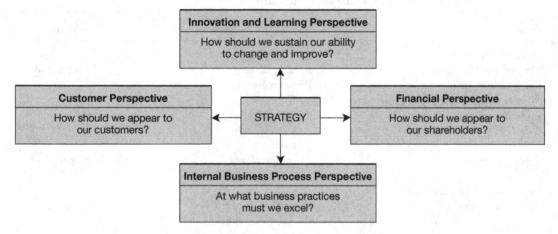

organization in the long run. Research and development, plant maintenance, and employee training are examples of expenditures that harm the short-term financial measures, but benefit the organization in the long run. Balanced scorecards tend to include both short- and long-term performance indicators.

The ultimate objective of profit organizations is to generate value for the owners of the organization. But value for owners results from satisfying customers, operating efficiently, and having the infrastructure necessary to accomplish all of those activities. Therefore, most firms do not rely solely on financial performance indicators. Financial performance indicators occur periodically and may not be very timely. Clearly, nonfinancial performance indicators such as customer satisfaction and employee turnover are also important.

Balanced scorecard's four perspectives

Advocates of the balanced scorecard argue that it recognizes the multiple stakeholders of an organization. These stakeholders include the shareholders or owners, customers, suppliers, employees, and society. Balanced scorecard proponents contend that the organization's objectives should reflect the interests of these stakeholders. Many corporate mission statements mention these stakeholders. Objectives related to the stakeholders are captured in the balanced scorecard through four perspectives: financial, customer, internal business processes, and innovation and learning. Each of these perspectives has objectives, performance indicators, targets, and initiatives.

Figure 14–3 illustrates these four perspectives:

Innovation and learning perspective   The innovation and learning perspective focuses on the infrastructure of the organization. To achieve its goals, an organization requires the right people and systems, as well as facilities to support them. Without learning and innovation in the organization, the organization cannot adapt to a dynamic environment. To adapt, an organization must continually retrain its employees, improve its technology and information systems, and adapt to evolving customer demands. Performance indicators include employee training efforts, information system implementations, and equipment and facility purchases.

Customer perspective   The customer perspective of the balanced scorecard is concerned with adding customer value. Customer value can be achieved through innovative and high-quality products and services and low prices. The balanced scorecard should highlight the organization's strategy for adding customer value. Typical performance indicators for the customer perspective include customer satisfaction surveys and market share, on-time delivery, and reduced defects.

TABLE 14-1   **An Insurance Company's Balanced Scorecard**

Objective	Performance Indicators	Targets
Financial Perspective		
Efficient use of assets	Return on assets	17% per year
Grow underwriting	Premium growth	4% per year
Innovation and Learning Perspective		
Employee training	Percent of employee hours spent in training	5% per year
Employee retention	Percent employee turnover	6% per year
Internal Business Process Perspective		
Reduce error rates	Percent of time employees spend correcting errors	2% per year
Automate customer inquiries	Growth in percent of customers logging on to company website	18% per year
Customer Perspective		
Grow market share	Increase in number of under-35 insurance buyers	3% per year
Customer satisfaction	Percent of customers saying they are "very satisfied" on customer surveys	80%
Fast response to loss claims	Days to process loss claims	95% of all claims processed within three days

Financial perspective   The financial perspective of the balanced scorecard represents the shareholders/owners of the organization. The objectives from the financial perspective in a for-profit organization are oriented toward providing shareholders a return on their investment. Typical performance indicators include profit, sales growth, and measures of risk. Nonprofit organizations would also have financial objective indicators such as balancing revenues and expenditures.

The objectives of the financial perspective in the balanced scorecard coincide with creating firm value in the framework of Figure 14–1. Increases in firm value come from the other perspectives: customers, internal business processes, and learning and growth.

Internal business process perspective   The objectives of the internal business process perspective deal with issues of efficiency and quality. Six sigma, information technology, and lean are processes that support this perspective. Activities should be analyzed to determine whether they add value and how they can be most efficiently performed. For example, supplier relations are critically important to the success of retail and manufacturing firms. Using business-to-business Internet transactions to speed purchases from suppliers increases on-time deliveries to customers and improves quality. Typical performance indicators for the internal business process perspective include number of defects, throughput time, and on-time delivery.

Table 14–1 presents an example of a balanced scorecard for an insurance company. For each of the four perspectives, objectives, performance indicators, and targets are specified. Each responsibility center in the organization then derives its own balanced scorecard.

Managerial Application: The Balanced Scorecard at Philips Electronics	Philips Electronics, with more than 250,000 employees in 150 countries, adopted the balanced scorecard as a way to communicate the firm's business strategy and vision throughout the firm. Four critical success factors are competence (knowledge, technology, leadership, and teamwork), processes (drivers for performance), customers (value propositions), and financial (value, growth, and productivity). At Philips, the balanced scorecard starts at the corporate level and then cascades down to the divisions and the business units. At the corporate level is the strategy scorecard. The divisions have operations-review scorecards, and the business units have their own scorecards. Each lower-level scorecard must articulate with the next higher-level card in the sense that when the lower-level unit achieves its scorecard targets this furthers the next higher-level unit's targets. A typical business-unit scorecard contains the following metrics:

- Financial: Economic profit realized, income from operations, working capital, operational cash flow, inventory turns.
- Customers: Rank in customer survey, market share, repeat order rate, complaints.
- Processes: Percentage reduction in process cycle time, number of engineering changes, capacity utilization, order response time, process capability.
- Competence: Leadership, percentage of patent-protect turnover, training days per employee, quality improvement team participation.

SOURCE: I. Pandey, "Balanced Scorecard: Myth and Reality," *Vikalpa*, January–March 2005, pp. 51–66.

Relations among perspectives The four perspectives of the balanced scorecard should relate to each other. The strategy of the organization is the starting point and dictates the financial perspective objectives. To achieve the financial perspective objectives, the organization must look at its relations with its customers and determine how it can add value to its customers. Adding value to customers comes from efficient and quality operations of internal processes. But processes cannot operate efficiently without the appropriate learning and innovation within the organization. Identifying these links is critical to implementing a successful balanced scorecard. For example, an insurance company might determine that improving its information systems and training employees lead to faster insurance claims processing for its policyholders. This leads to increased customer satisfaction, more loyal customers, and eventually, better financial results.

Assessing the balanced scorecard

The balanced scorecard concept is consistent with Figure 14–1 because it links the firm's strategy with the cause-and-effect relationships among the various performance indicators. However, many balanced scorecard implementations focus only on identifying the various key performance indicators and are silent about how these are linked to compensation. Moreover, balanced scorecard advocates do not address updating other parts of the organizational architecture in response to the new strategy. Thus, decision rights assignments and compensation plan changes are often ignored. While many firms are embracing this approach, there are several conceptual and practical problems with balanced scorecards.

Telling managers to maximize firm value is like telling a sports team to win. More concrete strategies and objectives are required. Balanced scorecards help communicate to managers how to implement value-maximizing strategies. Problems begin to arise when the scorecards are used as performance measures.[7] As performance measurement systems,

630 *Chapter 14*

FIGURE 14-4

Relation between customer satisfaction and firm value

balanced scorecards produce dysfunctional behaviors. Suppose a football quarterback has a very simple balanced scorecard consisting of number of completed passes, yards gained by running, and games won. Suppose the quarterback is paid on each measure. Clearly, the objective of the team is to win. Passing and running contribute to winning. But, if the quarterback thinks that a passing play has a greater chance of succeeding than a running play, even though the latter might win the game, the quarterback will in some circumstances choose the passing play.

Similarly, customer satisfaction is usually related to firm value. More satisfied customers are more loyal and willing to pay higher prices for the firm's goods and services. However, how far should managers go in maximizing customer satisfaction? Figure 14–4 illustrates the typical relationship between firm value and customer satisfaction. Firm value increases up to customer satisfaction level C*. But customer satisfaction levels beyond C* reduce firm value because it costs more to increase customer satisfaction than these more satisfied customers return in additional purchases. Giving managers balanced scorecards that include customer satisfaction (or employee turnover, market share, product quality, and so forth) can create incentives for managers to reduce firm value.

Balanced scorecards often contain 10 to 30 performance indicators. However, you can only maximize one variable at a time. Telling managers to simultaneously maximize 20 balanced scorecard indicators provides that manager with no guidance as to the relative trade-off among the indicators. It is an impossible task. Suppose you are told to maximize your grade in managerial accounting and to maximize your physical fitness. You can't do both simultaneously. Because there are only 24 hours in a day, you must make trade-offs.

If managers receive compensation based on numerous balanced scorecard performance measures, they will choose those measures easiest to achieve and ignore more difficult tasks.[8] Firm value will almost certainly suffer. Balanced scorecards are not balanced in the sense of specifying how managers should make trade-offs between the various performance indicators. They do not tell managers when to stop producing more customer satisfaction because firm value falls beyond that point. Most balanced scorecards suggest that more of each performance indicator is preferred to less. Moreover, balanced

---

[7]M. Jensen, "Value Maximization, Stakeholder Theory, and the Corporate Objective Function," *Business Ethics Quarterly* 12 (January 2001).

[8]See Brickley, Smith, and Zimmerman, 2016, p. 514.

Managerial Application: A Balanced Scorecard Failure	The U.S. retail banking operations of a leading international bank adopted a balanced scorecard and abandoned it three years later. What went wrong?

The firm has hundreds of branches located throughout North America. Prior to installing the balanced scorecard, each branch manager received a bonus based on achieving specific performance objectives. This bonus system had grown so complex that a 78-page manual described it. Upper-level managers were frustrated with the system because branch managers were gaming the system to earn bonuses without delivering financial results.

A balanced scorecard was introduced with five imperatives: achieving good financial results, delivering for customers, managing costs, managing risk, and having the right people in the right jobs. Extensive training programs accompanied the rollout of the scorecard system. Each branch was measured on about 40 different metrics such as customer attrition, customer satisfaction, assets under management, training and staff development, and so forth. But unlike the earlier formula-based bonus system, branch managers under the balanced scorecard received *subjective* performance measures. While proponents of the balanced scorecard provide little guidance on how each metric in the scorecard should be linked to compensation, they usually conjecture that subjective, rather than objective, compensation should be used because it is "easier and more defensible to administer . . . and also less susceptible to game playing."[†]

Under the new subjective performance evaluation scheme, each branch manager reports directly to an area director who assesses the branch manager's quarterly performance as being "below par," "at par," or "above par." Area directors were allowed to incorporate whatever factors they thought were important into the managers' performance "par" ratings. Quarterly bonuses were awarded based on the par ratings after the area directors' recommendations were discussed among all the region's area directors and approved by the region's president.

After analyzing the ratings, the subjectivity in weighting the balanced scorecard measures in the bonus plan allowed supervisors to ignore many performance measures, change criteria from quarter to quarter, ignore measures that predicted future financial performance, and weight measures that were not predictive of desired results.

After implementing the balanced scorecard, surveys of the branch managers revealed little change in the branch managers' understanding of the firm's strategic goals or their connections to the managers' actions. Only 32 percent were satisfied with the scorecard process, while 45 percent were dissatisfied. Many branch managers felt the process was unfair and did not cover the important aspects of their job and that their bonuses did not accurately reflect their performance. One branch manager wrote, "I hate the new process. Favoritism comes too much into play." Three years later, the balanced scorecard was abandoned in favor of a more objective, commission-style system based on the branch revenues.

One must be careful not to generalize the results of this single balanced scorecard failure to other settings. This firm might have implemented the scorecard poorly, in the sense of not choosing the appropriate performance indicators or the use of subjective, rather than more objective, compensation schemes. Maybe the area directors received inadequate training in assessing "par" performance. Perhaps the regional presidents did not supervise their area directors. What is clear from this case study is the close linkage between performance evaluation (the balanced scorecard) and performance reward (subjective evaluation by the area directors), as depicted in Figure 14–1. This firm rolled out a balanced scorecard that included both new performance metrics and a

Managerial Application: A Balanced Scorecard Failure (*Contd.*)	new bonus system. The combined system failed and was replaced. We cannot establish which piece caused the failure. However, we see that the two pieces are really inseparable and that each must be internally consistent and coordinated with both the decision rights assignment and the firm's strategy. SOURCE: Based on C. Ittner, D. Larcker, and M. Meyer, "Subjectivity and the Weighting of Performance Measures: Evidence from a Balanced Scorecard," *Accounting Review* 78 (july 2003), pp. 725–58.

scorecards are not scorecards in the usual sense of indicating who is winning and losing. They are statistical summaries of the game. They do not provide a single comprehensive measure of performance like, say, EVA.

One critic claims that many managers embrace balanced scorecards because "it is easier for people to engage in intense value claiming activities at the expense of value creation."[9] The balanced scorecard gives managers multiple criteria for measuring their success and thus reduces their accountability for destroying shareholder value. Some reduction in shareholder value becomes acceptable if some other stakeholder is shown to have benefited.

Concept Questions	Q14–5	Describe four different definitions of *quality*.
	Q14–6	If *quality* is defined as meeting customer expectations, what does measuring quality require?
	Q14–7	Total quality costs can be categorized into four groups. What are they?
	Q14–8	How does cost accounting become easier in a just-in-time environment?
	Q14–9	What are some of the problematic aspects of a JIT environment?
	Q14–10	Describe which parts of Figure 14–1 are affected by a firm's adoption of a balanced scorecard approach.
	Q14–11	Describe two criticisms of the balanced scorecard.

C. When Should the Internal Accounting System Be Changed?

There is no single ideal management accounting system. Each organization faces different technologies and market conditions and hence seeks to develop its own unique business strategy. Because each firm has a unique business strategy, no two firms will share the same organizational architecture or have the same management accounting system. Also, accounting must continually deal with trade-offs among external users wanting information describing firm performance and internal users wanting information for decision making and control. Surviving organizations must meet the demands of changing technologies and markets by revising their business strategies and organizational architectures

---

[9]Jensen, 2001.

(Figure 14–1). Because firms are in a constant state of flux, the accounting system must evolve.[10]

Certain signs indicate that the internal accounting system is not working well. One sign is dysfunctional behavior on the part of managers because of poorly chosen performance measures. Managers will make decisions to positively influence performance measures. If those performance measures are not consistent with the goals of the organization, management will make decisions that do not further the organization's goals. Another sign of problems with the accounting system is poor operating decisions. If product mix and pricing decisions based on management accounting are not adding to firm value, then the accounting system is either providing inaccurate estimates of opportunity costs and/or creating dysfunctional incentives.

Often, changes in customers' organizational architectures cause suppliers to change their architecture (and accounting systems). For example, when the large automakers switched to JIT, firms supplying auto parts switched to JIT. If your major customers are modifying their organizational architectures, they are likely responding to technological and market conditions. The way in which knowledge is generated and disseminated has probably changed. These changes likely affect your firm's organizational architecture.

Managers should not necessarily look to the latest management accounting fads to give them direction in changing their management accounting systems. Activity-based costing (ABC), for example, is only appropriate for certain types of organizations. Each organization must continually evaluate and improve its management accounting system to meet the challenges of a changing environment and a changing organization.

D. Summary

The chapter analyzed several organizational innovations. These innovations illustrate that internal accounting systems are an integral part of the organization's architecture. When managers change the architecture of their organization by decentralizing decision rights and empowering employees via TQM programs because the firm's business strategy changes, accounting systems are likewise modified. Similarly, after installing JIT production systems, accounting system changes follow. Firms adopt balanced scorecards to better link performance measures to their business strategy.

This text has emphasized the dual role of internal accounting systems for decision making and control. Because the internal accounting system is performing two separate roles (it is also being used for taxes and financial reporting), trade-offs between these roles must be made. In its decision-making role, the accounting system is the first place managers turn to for help in estimating opportunity costs. However, accounting numbers are not forward-looking opportunity costs. Accounting systems record historical costs, which are backward looking. Therefore, accounting numbers are useful for decision making only under very strong assumptions, primarily that the future will look like the past.

Because the same system is being used for decision-making and control functions, it is not surprising that if the accounting system is used primarily for decision control, operating managers seeking information for decision making usually find the accounting data wanting. Likewise, if the accounting system is being used primarily for decision making

---

[10]See G. Cokins, "Top 7 Trends in Management Accounting," *Strategic Finance,* Part I, December 2013, and Part 2, January 2014.

634   *Chapter 14*

(e.g., pricing), then it is likely under greater control by the manager and will not prove very useful for control (performance evaluation).

As industries restructure in reaction to technological change and changing market conditions via downsizing, mergers, leveraged buyouts, spinoffs, and recapitalizations, alternative organizational architectures such as outsourcing are being used to control agency problems. If agency problems are being reduced by these alternative organizational architectures, then internal accounting systems should move from a decision control function to a decision management function. Because changing the organization's architecture has reduced the agency costs, the internal accounting system becomes more oriented toward decision making. This may explain why certain firms adopt activity-based costing systems, which are designed primarily to improve decision making, not control. In fact, the analysis in this text predicts that firms changing to agency-cost–reducing organizational architectures such as leveraged buyouts are more likely to emphasize decision management rather than decision control in their management accounting systems.

Self-Study Problem

Self-Study Problem: Gilbert Foods

Gilbert Foods manufactures food seasonings and packaged dry sauce mixes for sales in grocery stores. Gilbert started a quality improvement program in 2016. It expanded its training and quality assurance programs and began monitoring employee satisfaction and estimating lost sales due to quality problems. The data in the following table summarize the quarterly results of operating its six sigma program over the last two years.

GILBERT FOODS
Quality Costs
2016–2017
(Millions)

	2016				2017			
	Q1	*Q2*	*Q3*	*Q4*	*Q5*	*Q6*	*Q7*	*Q8*
Customer complaint dept.	$ 3.90	$ 3.45	$ 3.03	$ 2.76	$ 2.50	$ 2.27	$ 2.14	$ 2.01
Inspection	1.40	1.56	1.75	1.95	2.39	2.96	3.63	4.46
Lost sales	49.20	40.31	33.11	28.42	24.45	21.08	19.20	17.44
Process engineering	2.20	2.46	2.76	3.11	3.87	4.86	6.13	7.58
Quality assurance administration	6.20	6.52	6.86	7.19	7.93	8.74	9.61	10.53
Returns	26.90	21.09	16.35	13.53	11.32	9.50	8.43	7.52
Rework	15.80	12.65	10.03	8.49	7.25	6.16	5.56	5.00
Scrap	17.60	14.48	11.92	10.32	8.92	7.72	7.00	6.34
Testing	1.60	1.72	1.85	1.99	2.29	2.62	3.01	3.45
Training	13.10	14.39	15.90	17.46	21.12	25.50	30.37	36.35

Required:

a. Prepare a cost-of-quality report that classifies each expense as being in one of four categories: appraisal, prevention, internal failure, or external failure.

b. What conclusions can you draw from the data presented about Gilbert Foods's six sigma program?

Management Accounting in a Changing Environment   **635**

Solution:

  a. The following table reclassified the cost-of-quality expenses:

GILBERT FOODS
Quality Costs
2016–2017
(Millions)

	2016				2017			
	Q1	*Q2*	*Q3*	*Q4*	*Q1*	*Q2*	*Q3*	*Q4*
Quality assurance administration	$ 2.20	$ 6.52	$ 6.86	$ 7.19	$ 7.93	$ 8.74	$ 9.61	$ 10.53
Training	13.10	14.39	15.90	17.46	21.12	25.50	30.37	36.35
Process engineering	2.20	2.46	2.76	3.11	3.87	4.86	6.13	7.58
Prevention	$ 21.50	$ 23.37	$ 25.52	$ 27.76	$ 32.92	$ 39.10	$ 46.11	$ 54.46
Inspection	$ 1.40	$ 5.56	$ 1.75	$ 1.95	$ 2.39	$ 2.96	$ 3.36	$ 4.46
Testing	1.60	1.72	1.85	1.99	2.29	2.62	3.01	3.45
Appraisal	$ 3.00	$ 3.28	$ 3.60	$ 3.94	$ 4.68	$ 5.58	$ 6.64	$ 7.91
Rework	$ 15.80	$ 12.65	$ 10.03	$ 8.49	$ 7.25	$ 6.16	$ 5.56	$ 5.00
Scrap	17.60	14.48	11.92	10.32	8.92	7.72	7.00	6.34
Internal failure	$ 33.40	$ 27.13	$ 21.95	$ 18.81	$ 16.17	$ 13.88	$ 12.56	$ 11.34
Returns	$ 26.90	$ 21.09	$ 16.35	$ 13.35	$ 11.32	$ 9.50	$ 8.43	$ 7.52
Customer complaint dept.	3.90	3.45	3.03	2.76	2.50	2.27	2.14	2.01
Lost sales	49.20	40.31	33.11	28.42	24.45	21.08	19.20	17.44
External failure	$ 80.00	$ 64.85	$ 52.49	$ 44.71	$ 38.27	$ 32.85	$ 29.77	$ 26.97
Total costs	$137.90	$118.63	$103.56	$ 95.22	$ 92.04	$ 91.41	$ 95.08	$100.68

  b. From the preceding data, we see that prevention and appraisal costs are increasing while internal and external failure costs have been decreasing. The following graph plots three series: prevention and appraisal costs, failure costs, and total quality costs.

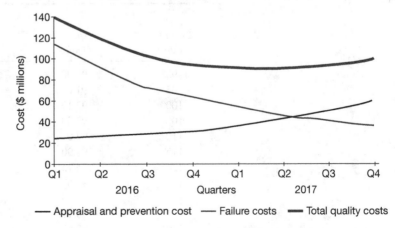

A preliminary conclusion from the graph is that Gilbert Foods is probably now spending too much on trying to improve quality. Assuming that the underlying production processes have not changed

636   *Chapter 14*

over time, quality costs were minimized in the second quarter of 2017. Since then, the additional money spent on appraisal and prevention has yielded smaller internal- and external-failure cost savings.

Problems

P 14–1: British Airways

British Airways (BA) has implemented the balanced scorecard. Match the following performance indicators:

Return on invested capital	On-time arrivals
Earnings growth	Percent empty seats
Lost baggage	Employee turnover
Employee training hours	Number of frequent flyers (25,000 miles on BA)

to these four balanced scorecard perspectives:

Financial	Innovation and learning
Customer	Internal business processes

Note: Performance indicators may be used for more than one perspective.

P 14–2: Chateau Napa

Chateau Napa purchased a small vineyard and is now producing magnum bottles (1.5 liters) of Redwood Cabernet Sauvignon. This wine is much sought after, and bottling the wine in larger bottles enhances its quality, prestige, and demand. Because of the limited size of the vineyard, the quantity of wine produced is fixed. The only decision variable is the quality of the wine produced. Quality is a function of a host of factors: the quality of oak barrels used to age the wine, the ability of the oenologist (winemaker), the length of time it is aged, and so forth. In general, the more money spent on quality, the higher the price of the wine. Several experts rate wines, and the *Wine Spectator*'s rating has become the industry standard. The following table summarizes how quality (as measured in expected *Wine Spectator* points with a scale of 0–100) varies with the amount of spending on quality and how various quality levels translate into price:

Cost of Quality	Expected Quality	Wholesale Price Received
$ 90	90.00	$570.20
95	91.08	576.44
100	92.10	582.34
105	93.08	588.00
110	94.01	593.38
115	94.90	598.52
120	95.75	603.44
125	96.57	608.17
130	97.35	612.69
135	98.11	617.08
140	98.83	621.24
145	99.53	625.28

Note: Magnums are produced in two-bottle sets. So if $115 is spent on enhancing the quality of a two-bottle set, a quality rating of 94.90 is expected and a final wholesale price Chateau Napa expects to receive is $598.52 per two-bottle set.

The managers producing and marketing the Redwood Cabernet Sauvignon are evaluated and compensated based on the balanced scorecard. Just two metrics are used in their scorecard: actual quality achieved and profits per two-bottle set. Half the bonus is based on quality achieved using the following formula:

$$\text{Quality bonus} = \text{Maximum } (0, \text{quality achieved} - 90) \times 5\%$$

In other words, the managers must receive a quality rating of at least 90 points before any bonus is paid. If they achieve a perfect rating of 100 points, they receive 50 percent of their bonus [$5\% \times (100 - 90)$]. The other 50 percent of their bonus is tied to profits achieved from selling the two-bottle sets. Profits consist of the wholesale selling price less quality costs less all other operating costs ($450 per two-bottle set[11]). The profit bonus is based on the following formula:

$$\text{Profit bonus} = \text{Maximum } (0, \text{profit} - \$30) \times 10\%$$

Managers are expected to achieve profits between $30 and $35. For every dollar of profit they generate above $30, they receive 10 percent of their bonus. So if they have profits of $33.15 per set, they receive 31.5 percent [$10\% \times (\$33.15 - \$30)$] of their bonus. (All bonus computations are rounded to three significant digits, i.e., 46.7 percent.)

Required:

a. Given the balanced scorecard incentive scheme being used to reward the Redwood Cabernet Sauvignon managers, how much do you expect them to spend on quality? What quality level do they expect to achieve? How much profit per two-bottle set do they expect to earn, and what is their expected total bonus (in percent)?

b. To maximize firm value, how much would Chateau Napa want the managers of Redwood Cabernet Sauvignon to spend on quality? What quality level would this spending likely yield? And how much profit does this quality level produce?

c. Explain why your answers in parts (*a*) and (*b*) are either the same or different.

d. Using the setting in the problem, explain what is meant by the saying "You can only maximize in one dimension at a time."

P 14–3: Fiedler International

You work on a team that reports to the chief financial officer of Fiedler International, a consumer products company that manages a variety of consumer beauty brands (shampoos, facial soaps, deodorants). Your team evaluates possible acquisitions. You are currently analyzing the possible purchase of Lush, a manufacturer of face moisturizers with UV sun blockers. Lush is a small publicly traded company that has no single large shareholder. Most of the stock is held by institutional investors and Lush managers hold a small percentage of the stock.

The materials you have received from Lush include information about its senior management performance evaluation and incentive compensation plans. Lush uses a balanced scorecard to evaluate and reward senior managers. Managers can earn up to 50 percent of their salary as a bonus depending on four balanced scorecard metrics: customer service, human resources and innovation, operational efficiency, and financial performance. Each of the four metrics is scaled between 0 and 1. Senior managers receive up to 25 percent of their bonus for each metric. If the customer service metric is 0.67, and a particular manager's salary is $400,000, then for customer service that manager receives $33,500 ($50\% \times \$400,000 \times 0.67 \times 25\%$). The compensation committee of Lush's board of

---

[11]Other operating cost of $450 per two-bottle set is a constant and does not vary with the amount spent on quality.

directors sets the scale for each of the four metrics. For example, the financial performance metric is economic value added, or EVA. Last year's EVA was $13 million. The compensation committee sets the lower and upper bound of EVA as $12 million and $16 million. Hence, if the current year's EVA is $12 million, the financial performance metric is 0. If EVA is $15 million, the metric is 0.75 [($15 – $12)/($16 – 12)], and the manager earning the $400,000 salary would receive a bonus of $37,500 (50% × $400,000 × 0.75 × 25%).

Fourteen separate metrics are used to compute the four metrics. The following metrics are computed and then aggregated to form the four metrics:

Customer Service	Human Resources and Innovation	Operational Efficiency	Financial Performance
Returns	New products	On-time production	EVA
Customer complaints	Percent of new products developed on time and on budget	Unit manufacturing cost	
On-site customer training seminars	Employee satisfaction	Safety accidents	
Shipping errors	Employee turnover	Dollars of scrap	
	Employee training		

Lush has been using the balanced scorecard for three years and the achieved levels of each metric for the last three years are:

	Customer Service	Human Resources and Innovation	Operational Efficiency	Financial Performance
2015	0.86	0.77	0.76	0.79
2016	0.92	0.91	0.82	0.73
2017	0.95	0.94	0.94	0.69

Write a memo to your acquisition team describing balanced scorecards and the primary reasons they are used, and the likely effect of Lush's use of the balanced scorecard in terms of how Fiedler should be evaluating Lush. Specifically: (*a*) briefly describe balanced scorecards and why firms use them, and (*b*) analyze Lush's use of the balanced scorecard and how this might affect Fiedler's evaluation of Lush as a possible takeover target.

P 14–4: Guest Watches

Guest Watches is a division of Guest Fashions, a large, international fashion designer. Guest Watches manufactures highly stylish watches for young adults (age 18 to 30) who are fashion conscious. It is a profit center and its senior management's compensation is tied closely to the reported profits. While Guest Watches has succeeded in capturing the fashion market, product dependability is eroding these gains. A number of retailers have dropped or are threatening to drop the Guest watch line because of customer returns. Guest watches carry a one-year warranty and 12 percent are returned, compared with an industry average of 4 percent. Besides high warranty costs and lost sales due to reputation, Guest Watches has higher-than-industry-average manufacturing scrap and rework costs.

Senior management, worried about these trends and the possible erosion of its market dominance, hired a consulting firm to study the problem and make recommendations for reversing the situation. After a thorough analysis of Guest Watches's customers, suppliers, and manufacturing facilities, the consultants recommended five possible actions ranging from the status quo to a complete Total Quality Management, Zero Defects program (level IV). The accompanying table outlines the various alternatives for Guest Watches. (Dollar figures are in thousands.)

	Additional Training Cost*	*Additional Prevention/ Compliance*†
Status quo	$ 0	$ 0
Level I	80	180
Level II	200	240
Level III	350	340
Level IV	550	490

* Includes the annual costs of training employees in TQM methods.
† All annual costs, including certifying suppliers, redesigning the product, and inspection costs to reduce defects.

The consultants emphasized that while first-year startup costs are slightly higher than in subsequent years, management must really view the above cost estimates as annual ongoing costs. Given employee turnover and supplier changes, training, prevention, and compliance costs are not likely to decline over time.

The consulting firm and the newly appointed vice president for quality programs estimated that under level IV, rework and scrap would be $25,000 and warranty costs zero. Level IV was needed to get the firm to zero defects. A task force was convened and after several meetings generated the following estimates of rework/scrap and warranty costs for the various levels of firm commitment:

	Total Rework/ Scrap Cost*	*Total Warranty Costs*†
Status quo	$500	$350
Level I	300	280
Level II	150	140
Level III	75	80
Level IV	25	0

* The costs of manufacturing scrap and rework.
† The costs of repairing and replacing products that fail in the hands of customers.

There was considerable discussion and debate about the quantitative impact of increased quality on additional sales. While no hard and fast numbers could be derived, the consensus view was that the total net cash flows (contribution margin) from additional sales as retailers and customers learn of the reduced defect rate would be the following:

	Contribution Margin on Additional Sales
Status quo	$ 0
Level I	600
Level II	1,000
Level III	1,200
Level IV	1,300

Required:

a. Assuming that the data as presented are reasonably accurate, what should Guest Watches do about its deteriorating quality situation? Should it maintain the status quo or should it adopt the consultants' recommendation and implement level I, II, III, or IV?

b. Evaluate the analysis underlying your policy recommendation in part (*a*). Will the senior management of the Watch Division make the same decision as the senior management of Guest Fashions?

P 14–5: Applying TQM in Manufacturing versus Administration

One large company that has been successful in applying total quality management (TQM) principles in manufacturing reports that it has had less success in applying the same techniques in improving administrative functions such as order taking, distribution, and human resources. This company (which has won several quality awards and has significantly improved its product quality) used state-of-the-art TQM methods to train all of its employees in how to apply TQM. However, the company has not been able to achieve the same cost reductions and service quality enhancements in administrative areas as it has in the manufacturing area. Assuming that this phenomenon extends to other companies, why do you think that TQM works better in manufacturing than in nonmanufacturing/service areas?

P 14–6: Email from Suresh Batik

I received the following email from a former student.

I hope you are doing well.

I took your Managerial Accounting class ten years ago and have a question on how to do costing in a service-based business. Currently, I am working for a firm that manufactures various products used in pipelines (torque wrenches, flange pullers, bolts and flanges, grinding machines, etc.). Five years ago we began servicing pipelines in refineries, offshore/onshore platforms, nuclear plants, etc. Our services include joint integrity, leak sealing, and leak-free bolted connections. Our service technicians go to customers to service their pipelines and charge the customers an hourly fee. In servicing these customers, our technicians often sell these customers our various manufactured products. The company is organized around functions and not as separate profit centers.

Currently, our cost accounting system only calculates the costs of physical products we manufacture, not the cost of our servicing side of the business. While we charge our customers a fee for our various services, our accounting system does not track the actual costs of providing these services, nor does it track the products our customers purchase because our technicians require these products to complete their servicing functions. Rather, the cost of field technicians is "overhead," and hence our profitability is all over the place. In slack periods, the utilization of our field technicians is low and our profitability is low, while in peak periods the utilization of our technicians is high and our overall profitability rises. We should (but we don't) account for time and utilization rate of technicians, cost and utilization of tools used, training costs, and the revenues of the products sold during the servicing. These latter revenues are treated as revenues to the entire corporation, not revenues to the servicing end of the business. We don't know the profitability of our servicing business, although we are confident it is very profitable.

Before jumping to any conclusions, I would like to know how to proceed about possible changes in our accounting systems and any advice you might offer regarding how to better evaluate the profitability of our new (and growing) service business. Thank you for your time.

Best Regards
Suresh Batik

Required:
What advice/guidance would you offer Suresh?

P 14–7:   The Pottery Store

The Pottery Store is a chain of retail stores in upscale malls that sells pottery, woodcarvings, and other craft items. The typical customer is shopping for a gift and spends between $50 and $200. Buyers in the corporate office contact artists around the country and buy inventory for the stores. Corporate headquarters sets the final selling price for each item and determines when to mark them down for sales. Each store manager is responsible for store staffing and layout. Store managers do not have responsibility for choosing the merchandise, store hours (set by the mall), or pricing decisions.

Required:
   a.   Design a balanced scorecard for the store managers.
   b.   How would your answer to part (*a*) change if the store managers also had decision-making responsibilities for both selecting the merchandise to carry in the store and pricing?

P 14–8:   Software Development Inc.

Software Development Inc. (SDI) produces and markets software for personal computers, including spreadsheet, word processing, desktop publishing, and database management programs. SDI has annual sales of $800 million.

Producing software is a time-consuming, labor-intensive process. Software quality is an extremely important aspect of success in computer software markets. One aspect of quality is program reliability. Does the software perform as expected? Does it work with other software in terms of data transfers and interfaces? Does it terminate abnormally? In spite of extensive testing of the software, programs always contain some bugs. Once the software is released, SDI stands behind the product with phone-in customer service consultants who answer questions and help the customer work around problems in the software. SDI's software maintenance group fixes bugs and sends out revised versions of the programs to customers.

SDI tracks the relation between quality costs and quality. The quality measure it uses is the number of documented bugs in a software package. These bugs are counted when a customer calls in with a complaint and the SDI customer service representative determines that this is a new problem. The software maintenance programmers then attempt to fix the program and eliminate the bug. To manage quality, SDI tracks quality costs. It has released 38 new packages or major revisions in existing packages in the last three years. The accompanying table reports the number of defects (bugs) documented in the first six months following release. Also listed in the table are total product cost and quality cost per software package release.

Product costs include all the costs incurred to produce and market the software, excluding the quality costs in the table. Quality costs consist of three components: training, prevention, and software maintenance and customer service costs. Training costs are expenditures for educating the programmers and updating their training. Better-educated programmers produce fewer bugs. Prevention costs include expenditures for testing the software before it is released. Maintenance and customer service costs include (1) the programmers charged with fixing the bugs and reissuing the revised software and (2) the customer service representatives answering phone questions. The training and prevention costs are measured over the period the software was being developed. The number of defects and maintenance and service costs are measured in the first six months following release.

SDI Defects and Quality Costs by Program Release*

Program Release	Number of Defects	Product Cost	Training Cost	Prevention Cost	Software Maintenance and Customer Service Cost	Total Costs
1	66	$3,455	$442	$ 770	$2,160	$6,827
2	86	3,959	428	447	2,658	7,492
3	14	3,609	417	1,167	687	5,880
4	73	3,948	211	655	2,334	7,148
5	17	3,104	290	1,013	544	4,951
6	48	3,179	253	547	1,556	5,535
7	80	3,112	392	508	2,633	6,645
8	41	3,529	276	577	1,563	5,945
9	50	3,796	557	634	1,666	6,653
10	67	3,444	365	947	2,140	6,896
11	42	3,922	453	869	1,444	6,688
12	64	3,846	378	1,108	1,942	7,274
13	71	3,014	555	762	2,384	6,715
14	1	3,884	301	773	423	5,381
15	18	3,183	378	1,080	857	5,498
16	85	3,475	528	1,010	2,572	7,585
17	17	3,445	357	666	631	5,099
18	50	3,203	285	427	1,546	5,461
19	22	3,839	239	1,080	891	6,049
20	73	3,060	540	1,054	2,309	6,963
21	52	3,182	329	1,079	1,867	6,457
22	75	3,075	395	832	2,697	6,999
23	35	3,456	447	969	1,518	6,390
24	53	3,987	355	651	2,042	7,035
25	25	3,836	309	1,160	1,036	6,341
26	6	3,886	234	794	252	5,166
27	78	3,846	418	833	2,800	7,897
28	82	3,106	409	1,092	2,871	7,478
29	39	3,506	448	899	1,342	6,195
30	47	3,545	450	442	1,450	5,887
31	30	3,376	456	784	1,260	5,876
32	17	3,740	542	420	607	5,309
33	67	3,479	411	821	2,018	6,729
34	51	3,773	351	1,145	1,873	7,142
35	74	3,034	497	671	2,389	6,591
36	25	3,768	268	887	1,094	6,017
37	14	3,168	356	645	837	5,006
38	77	3,561	492	1,167	2,597	7,817
Average	48	$3,509	$390	$ 826	$1,671	$6,395

* Per 100,000 lines of computer code.

All the numbers in the table have been divided by lines of computer code in the particular program release. Programs with more lines of code cost more and also have more bugs. Prior studies find that using lines of code is an acceptable way to control for program complexity. Thus, the numbers in the table are stated in terms of defects and cost per 100,000 lines of code.

The following figure plots the relation between total cost and number of defects. The vice president of quality of SDI likes to use it to emphasize that costs and quality are inversely related. She is fond of saying, "Quality pays! Our total costs fall as the number of defects declines. The more we spend on quality, the lower our costs."

SDI total costs by defects

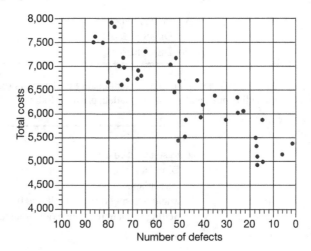

Required:

Critically evaluate the vice president's analysis.

P 14–9: Stirling Acquisition

You are working for an investment banking firm. One of your clients is examining the possibility of purchasing Stirling Manufacturing, a parts supplier (specifically, tail-light assemblies) to the automobile industry.

Your client has asked your firm to evaluate Stirling (a privately held company) and indicate how much should be paid for Stirling. Stirling has a batch-manufacturing process. Raw materials inventories are held until they are placed into production. Batches of between 2,000 and 2,500 tail-light assemblies are manufactured. These are then delivered daily, 100 to 150 at a time, to satisfy Stirling's customers' demand for just-in-time (JIT) deliveries. Your client is considering installing JIT production methods at Stirling if the acquisition is completed.

Your boss asks you to write a memo that outlines the various likely results if Stirling adopts JIT production techniques and the likely impact on Stirling's cash flows and eventual market value. Your memo will provide background information for your colleagues who are actually estimating Stirling's current price and future value after acquisition. Your client is planning on making a number of changes at Stirling. JIT is just one of them. Your memo will assist the analysts in your firm and should direct them in their data gathering and valuation efforts. Your memo should describe specifically what additional data your colleagues should collect in order to estimate JIT's cash flow effects.

P 14–10: TQM at the Stowbridge Division

The Stowbridge Division is analyzing expanding its total quality management program. It already has a TQM program in place. However, one of its customers, Amlan Equipment, is asking all suppliers to become ISO 9000 qualified, a process that certifies that the firm meets various standards. Once suppliers are ISO 9000 qualified, Amlan can reduce its inspection costs. Not all of the suppliers will be certified, and those that are will receive more business from Amlan.

Amlan purchases a stainless steel rotor from Stowbridge. After earning ISO 9000 certification, Stowbridge estimates that it will have to incur the following annual incremental costs as long as it wants to maintain its certification:

Annual Incremental Costs to Be ISO 9000 Certified

Training	$74,000
Inspection	$96,000
Prevention	$62,000
Direct materials	+10%
Direct labor	+15%

To manufacture the current quality of the rotors (before ISO 9000 certification), the budgeted selling price and standard cost data per rotor follow.

Selling price	$14.00
Less standard costs:	
Direct materials	$ 4.30
Direct labor	2.40
Manufacturing overhead (all fixed)	2.05
Selling and administrative (all variable)	1.60
Unit cost	$10.35
Unit profit	$ 3.65

Unless Stowbridge receives ISO 9000 certification, it will lose Amlan's business of 120,000 units per year. Management estimates that the higher quality of the rotor that meets quality criteria will allow Stowbridge to add 14,000 rotors to its existing sales from new and continuing customers. Stowbridge is currently selling 480,000 rotors per year, including the Amlan sales. The 480,000 current sales amount to 63 percent of plant capacity. The additional 14,000 units sold can be manufactured without exceeding plant capacity. The higher-quality process after ISO 9000 certification is received would apply to all the rotors produced.

Required:

Should Stowbridge seek ISO 9000 certification? Support your recommendation with an analysis of the costs and benefits of certification.

P 14–11: Warren City Parts Manufacturing

Warren City, with sales of $2 billion, produces and sells farm equipment. The manufacturing division produces some parts internally; purchases other parts from external suppliers; and assembles farm equipment, including tractors, combines, and plows. Within the manufacturing division is parts manufacturing, which fabricates a large variety of parts. Parts manufacturing is further subdivided into 12 departments, including screw products, metal stamping and fabrication, plastic injection molding, and steel castings. Each of these parts departments is headed by a department manager whose performance is evaluated along several dimensions: meeting budgeted costs, meeting delivery schedules, improving quality, achieving affirmative action and employee satisfaction goals, and minimizing inventory adjustments.

Inventory adjustments occur twice a year after internal auditors conduct a physical inventory of the parts department's work-in-process and compare it with the amount of inventory as reported in the work-in-process (WIP) account. For example, if on June 30 the auditors take a physical inventory count and find $130,000 of physical WIP inventory in the steel castings department, but the WIP account reports an inventory balance of $143,000, then a negative inventory adjustment of −9.1 percent (−$13,000 ÷ $143,000) is made. Any inventory adjustment, positive or negative, reflects unfavorably on the parts department manager's performance and results in a reduction in the manager's bonus. The parts department manager is expected to maintain a tight control of WIP inventories, including ensuring the integrity of his or her department's accounting reports of WIP. Large inventory adjustments indicate that the manager does not have good control of WIP.

Four years ago, Warren City adopted JIT production procedures. The result has been a drastic reduction of WIP inventories. For example, the following data illustrate the steel castings department's WIP account balance before adjustments, inventory adjustment, and throughput for the last seven years.

Warren City Steel Castings Department

Year	WIP (as of 12/31)	Inventory Adjustment	Throughput
2002	$1,920,000	12.0%	$76,550,000
2003	1,780,000	−12.9	82,130,000
2004	1,690,000	13.2	69,780,000
2005	1,550,000	13.6	73,290,000
2006	1,480,000	17.9	88,360,000
2007	1,430,000	−17.8	91,080,000
2008	1,390,000	19.5	93,960,000

*Deflated by 12/31 WIP.

Throughput is the total dollar cost of parts manufactured in the year. It is the sum of the beginning inventory plus direct labor and materials and overhead, less ending inventory. Warren City uses a standard cost system and all inventories are valued at standard cost. When a batch of parts completes production, the WIP inventory is reduced by the standard cost of the part times the standard number of parts in the batch. Each part is manufactured in standard lot sizes.

Inventory adjustments can result for a number of reasons:

1. *Different batch sizes.* The department manager decides to deviate from standard batch sizes. Unless a special entry is recorded, the accounting system assumes that the number of units in the batch is the standard number. Sometimes the manager has some excess production capacity and decides to increase the standard batch size. In some cases, the manager produces fewer parts than called for by the standard lot size because of machine breakdowns or bottlenecks. For example, suppose a certain part calls for a standard batch size of 150, but the manager decides to produce 200 parts and keep 50 as spares, but he fails to update the WIP account for the additional 50 units. The WIP account contains only 150 at standard cost, but the auditors count 200, causing a positive inventory adjustment.

2. *Timing differences.* The accounting system charges some expenses in a different time period than the department manager expects. This causes the dollar amount of the WIP balance to differ from standard cost.

3. *Standard cost revisions.* The standard cost of a part is revised, and the auditors use a different standard cost in valuing the ending WIP inventory than was used in the WIP account.

4. *Audit mistakes.* The internal auditors make mistakes in counting the final physical WIP inventory.

The first two reasons are by far the most prevalent causes of inventory adjustments.

Required:

    a. Management is concerned that the magnitude of the inventory adjustment has increased over time. What are some likely reasons that the absolute value of the inventory adjustment has grown?

    b. Evaluate the use of the inventory adjustment described earlier to measure a parts department manager's performance.

P 14–12:   Secure Servers Inc.

Secure Servers Inc. (SSI) is one of the largest software and service providers directed at providing high levels of backup and security for computer servers to the financial community, military, and other clients requiring off-site backup and security systems. SSI's software packages include encryption, downloading, and data warehousing of large amounts of data to various SSI sites in dedicated locations. SSI backup locations are designed to survive virtually all natural disasters and terrorist attacks.

SSI employs 6,000 people in Dayton, Ohio. Being one of Dayton's largest employers, it has a deep commitment to the community and supports local educational, cultural, and philanthropic activities. SSI also believes strongly in both customer and employee satisfaction. To achieve these objectives, SSI employs a balanced scorecard to evaluate and reward senior managers. One-fourth of each senior executive's bonus is tied to the following objectively determined performance measures:

- Community engagement (independent survey of local leaders).
- Customer satisfaction (independent survey of customers).
- Employee satisfaction (independent survey of employees).
- Corporate profit (audited net income before taxes).

The annual surveys of local leaders, customers, and employees are conducted by an independent opinion survey firm that reports directly to the board of directors. Corporate profit is the firm's reported net income before taxes as audited by an international public accounting firm. SSI's senior management team believes strongly in the concept of the balanced scorecard and accepts it as a valid and productive performance measurement and incentive tool.

Senior management is tasked with determining how much to spend on further improvements in community engagement, customer satisfaction, and employee satisfaction. The following table captures the relations among additional spending in each area and the expected improvements from such expenditures (in millions).

Additional Expenditure	Customer Satisfaction	Employee Satisfaction	Community Rating
$0.50	60%	75%	40%
1.00	75	80	50
1.50	80	85	60
2.00	85	90	70
2.50	90	95	80
3.00	95	100	90

For example, by spending an additional $3 million on customer service (improved call centers, training, etc.), a 95 percent customer satisfaction can be achieved. Or, by spending an additional $2 million on employee-related activities (improved child care, athletic facilities, fringe benefits), a 90 percent employee satisfaction can be achieved. Or spending $1 million on additional community projects can raise SSI's community rating survey to 50 percent.

Besides raising the satisfaction scores as detailed earlier, making additional expenditures on these three areas also generates additional net cash flows to the firm. The following table estimates the additional cash flows SSI receives from making the additional expenditures.

	Customer Satisfaction		Employee Satisfaction		Community Rating	
Additional Expenditure	Index	Additional Cash Flow	Index	Additional Cash Flow	Index	Additional Cash Flow
$0.5	60%	$0.9	75%	$0.7	40%	$0.75
1.0	75	1.5	80	1.3	50	1.50
1.5	80	2.1	85	1.5	60	2.25
2.0	85	2.7	90	1.8	70	3.00
2.5	90	3.1	95	2.0	80	4.00
3.0	95	3.5	100	2.1	90	4.00

For example, spending $3 million for community projects yields a community rating index of 90 percent and additional cash flows of $4.0 million, which increases net income before taxes by $1.0 million ($4.0 − $3.0).

To convert audited net income into a percentage index that can be averaged with the other three survey metrics, SSI uses the following formula:

$$\text{Profit index} = -3 + 0.05 \times \text{Net income}$$

So, if net income is $74 million, the profit index for use in the balanced scorecard is 70 percent $[-3 + (0.05 \times 74)]$.

The four indexes are averaged to get an overall index for determining the bonus for each senior executive of SSI. For example, the following four indexes yield a balanced scorecard of 79.75 percent:

Customer satisfaction	76.00%
Employee satisfaction	88.00
Community rating	85.00
Profit index	70.00
Average	79.75%

SSI expects audited net income before taxes for the year before making any additional expenditures on customer satisfaction, employee satisfaction, and community engagement to be $72 million.

Required:

a. What levels of additional spending do you expect the senior management team of SSI will select for:

(1) Customer satisfaction.

(2) Community engagement.

(3) Employee satisfaction.

Be sure to justify your answers with appropriate analysis.

b. Given the levels of additional spending on the three items you recommended in part (*a*), what is the expected balanced scorecard index? That is, calculate the average balanced scorecard management expects to generate if they make the expenditure decisions you predict in part (*a*). Show calculations.

c. What level of spending would you expect a profit-maximizing owner of SSI to select for:

(1) Customer satisfaction.

(2) Community engagement.

(3) Employee satisfaction.

What is the expected balanced scorecard resulting from these spending levels?

P 14–13:   Kollel Hospital

Kollel is a private hospital that operates in a large metropolitan area. The hospital admits "regular" patients and "private" patients. Regular patients are admitted and treated by staff doctors who are full-time employees of Kollel Hospital. Private patients are admitted and treated by private physicians (physicians in private practice who have admitting privileges to Kollel). To maintain its leadership role in the community, Kollel is deeply committed to its total quality management program. Management and staff form multidisciplinary teams to study various hospital functions. This year, one team reviewed a hospital unit that exclusively treated a particular type of medical admittance. (All patients of this type of admittance were treated in this unit.) The team found that patients preferred to be discharged sooner rather than later and that, overall, the patients felt that they were kept in the hospital too long.

The specific unit under review consists of 16 beds. Last year, the unit treated 300 patients. The patients were heterogeneous with respect to their level of illness. Properly diagnosed and treated, patients should have been discharged in an average of 16 days. Nevertheless, the TQM study showed that patients remain in the hospital an average of 19 days. Furthermore, research showed that the average stay of regular patients was shorter than the average stay of private patients, even though the private physicians did not handle more difficult cases at the time of admission. The study found that private doctors took longer to diagnose their patients and spent less time with them during treatment. As a result, these doctors did not promptly recognize whether a treatment was working or whether the patient was ready to be discharged.

In order to increase the quality of care, hospital management is studying plans to lower the average stay of these patients. One alternative being considered is preventing the private doctors, who are keeping their patients in the unit the longest, from admitting patients into the unit. Some, but not all, of these patients can be replaced by patients admitted by staff doctors. The trade-off between the number of patients admitted and the length of a patient's stay is shown in the following table. Last year, 150 regular and 150 private patients were admitted. The average stay was 16 days for regular patients and 22 days for private patients, making an overall average of 19 days per patient.

Admissions as a Function of Reducing Length of Stay

	Status Quo	1 Day	2 Days	3 Days	4 Days
Regular patients' stays (days)	16	16	16	16	16
Regular patients admitted	150	153	160	173	185
Private patients' stays (days)	22	21	20	19	18
Private patients admitted	150	145	135	117	95

For this specific type of admittance, the hospital collects $10,000 per stay from the insurance companies, regardless of whether the patient is admitted regularly or privately. This amount is used to cover the unit's fixed cost of $1,752,000 per year (365 days) and a variable cost of $150 per patient per day. Note that the charges for the doctor's services are handled separately and are not considered for purposes of this analysis.

Required:

a. Calculate the average hospital stay for all patients under each scenario listed in the table. Also, for each case calculate the occupancy rate (percentage of beds filled on average). Discuss the relation between the average length of stay and the occupancy rate.

    b. Prepare an income statement showing the net income for each scenario, separating the margin earned on regular and private patients. Where is profit maximized? What are the components of the change in net income?

P 14–14: Tagway 4000

Tagway 4000 is a computer manufacturer based in Montana. One component of the computer is an internal battery that keeps track of the time and date while the computer is turned off. Tagway produces the batteries in-house. The division that produces the batteries (one million each year) is treated as a cost center. The manager of the division is compensated based on her ability to keep total costs low and meet quality control measures of numbers of defects and delivery time. She has a base salary of $144,000. She is eligible for a $34,000 bonus if total costs do not exceed $2 million, not including her compensation. She is eligible for a $40,000 bonus if there are 32 or fewer defects per one million units produced. Finally, she is eligible for a $22,000 bonus if she delivers batteries on time. *On time* is defined as averaging two days between the order from the assembly department and delivery to the assembly department.

    The basic cost of producing a battery is $1.55. However, current methods have an inherent defect rate of 1,032 defects per million (approximately four standard deviations or 4 sigma). The cost of improving the defect rate involves using higher-quality materials and more experienced labor. Down to 32 defects per million (approximately five sigma), the costs are linear. (Based on currently available inputs, improving the defect rate below 32 per million is impossible.) For every additional $450, one defect per million can be removed. In other words, the cost to reduce defects to the desired level of 32 per million is $450,000.

    The current production method delivers the batteries in an average of four days. The cost of overtime necessary to lower the average to three days is $90,000. The cost of speeding up delivery another day is $95,000, making the cumulative cost of lowering the average to two days $185,000. The marginal cost of reducing the average delivery a third day is $115,000, making the total cost of reducing the average delivery time to one day $300,000.

Required:

    a. Create a table showing the production costs for defect rates of 1,032, 500, 100, 50, and 32 per million and average delivery times of one to four days. Do not include the manager's salary. Note the minimum cost.

    b. Create a table showing the manager's compensation for defect rates of 1,032, 500, 100, 50, and 32 and average delivery times of one to four days. Note the maximum compensation level.

    c. Comment on the ideal number of defects and delivery times necessary to achieve the minimum costs and the maximum compensation level.

    d. Assume that the company as a whole can measure the financial losses related to defects and late deliveries. The costs would include warranty costs, express delivery charges, lost sales, and lost goodwill. These costs do not affect the manager's compensation. The cost for each defect is $460. The cost for each day above one-day average delivery is $500,000 per day late. That is $0 for one-day average delivery, $500,000 for two days, and so on. Create a table showing the firm's total costs— including production costs, costs of defects, costs of delays, and the cost of the manager's compensation (including applicable bonus)—for defect rates of 1,032, 500, 100, 50, and 32 per million and average delivery times of one to four days. Note the minimum cost.

    e. Comment on the optimum delivery times and number of defects necessary to achieve the minimum costs to the firm and the maximum compensation level now that the firm's total costs are considered.

650 *Chapter 14*

Cases

Case 14–1: Global Oil[12]

In 1995, Global Oil Corporation's Marketing and Refining (M&R) Division was the fifth largest U.S. refiner with 7,700 Global-branded service stations selling about 23 million gallons per day, or 7 percent of the nation's gasoline. All the service stations are company owned. In 1990, M&R ranked last among its peers in profitability and was annually draining $500 million of cash from the corporation.

In 1993, M&R reorganized from a centralized functional organization (Refineries, Transportation, Warehousing, Retail, and Marketing) into 17 geographic business units (sales and distribution) and 14 service companies. The functional organization was slow to react to changing market conditions and the special customer needs that differed across the country. The new decentralized organization was designed to better focus on the customer. New marketing strategies could be better tailored to local markets by giving local managers more decision-making authority.

A new corporate strategy to focus on the less price-sensitive customer who would not only buy Global gas but also shop in its convenience gas-store outlets was implemented simultaneously with the reorganization. Global's new strategy was to redesign its convenience stores so they would become a "destination stop," offering one-stop shopping for gas and snacks.

The old organization used a variety of functional measures: manufacturing cost, sales margins and volumes, and health and safety metrics. After changing its corporate strategy and organizational structure, M&R decided to change its performance metrics and began investigating the balanced scorecard.

Balanced scorecard (BSC) at M&R

M&R formed project teams of managers to design performance metrics for its operations. Thirty-two different metrics were identified. These included Financial (ROA, cash flow, volume growth, etc.), Customer (share of segment, mystery shopper, etc.), Internal (safety incidents, refinery ROA, inventory level, etc.), and Learning (strategic skills accumulation, quality of information system, etc.). The "mystery shopper" is a third-party vendor who purchases gas and snacks at each station monthly. During each visit, the mystery shopper rates the station on 23 items related to external appearance, rest rooms, and so forth. A brochure describing the BSC was prepared and distributed to M&R's 11,000 employees in August of 1994. Extensive meetings with employees explained the new metrics and the BSC concept.

Compensation plans

All salaried employees of M&R received up to a 10 percent bonus if Global ranked first among its seven competitors on ROA and earnings per share (EPS) growth. In addition to this existing plan, a new program was added that awarded bonuses of up to 20 percent to managers. The size of the bonus depends on the average performance of three factors:

- *Global's competitive ranking on ROA and EPS growth.*
- *M&R's balanced scorecard metrics.*
- *Own business unit's balanced scorecard.*

In 1995, M&R generated more income per barrel of oil than the industry average, and its ROA exceeded the industry's average.

Required:

   a. Critically evaluate M&R's implementation of the balanced scorecard. Identify any strengths and weaknesses of the program.
   b. Was the adoption of the balanced scorecard at M&R responsible for the turnaround in its financial performance?

---

[12]This case is based on R. Kaplan, "Mobil USM&R(A): Linking the Balanced Scorecard," Harvard Business School Case 9–197–025 (May 7, 1997).

Case 14–2: Productivity Measures

Background

Economists and managers have long recognized the importance of productivity in determining an organization's success. Productivity is the relation between the firm's output of goods and services and the inputs necessary to produce that output. If a firm is able to produce more output with the same inputs, we say it has improved its productivity. Likewise, if two firms produce the same quantity of goods and services but one firm uses less input, that firm is called more productive. Countries that produce more output per person generate more consumable wealth. Economists keep productivity statistics, and these numbers are reported in the financial press as measuring the competitiveness and well-being of that country.

In the 1970s, many of the largest U.S. firms became interested in productivity and better ways to measure and improve their firms' productivity. Largely driven by foreign competition, these American firms were losing market share to Japanese and European rivals. Japanese auto companies were producing cars with fewer employee hours per car than American companies, thus offering lower-priced and often higher-quality cars than U.S. automakers. Foreign steel producers were more productive than their U.S. counterparts. Concerned about their declining relative productivity in 1977, large U.S. firms financed the formation of the American Productivity Center (later the American Productivity and Quality Center). To become more productive, some firms experimented with various productivity measures.

In its most basic form, productivity is defined as:

$$\text{Productivity} = \frac{\text{Output}}{\text{Input}}$$

If the firm uses a single input (steel) to produce a single homogeneous product (horseshoes) that never changes over time, then the measure of productivity is the units of output per quantity of input, or the number of horseshoes per pound of steel. If steel waste is reduced, more horseshoes can be produced with the same amount of steel. One measure of productivity is the ratio of horseshoes to steel, in terms of physical volume. Steel is not the only input to making horseshoes. Labor is also an input, and labor is usually the input of most interest to managers. Productivity is usually thought of as the amount of output per unit of labor. Most managers want to know the number of horseshoes produced per person and how this number changes over time and compares to the competition.

Proponents of productivity measurement systems argue that managers should focus on productivity instead of accounting profits. A firm can appear profitable but can be experiencing declining productivity if selling prices are rising faster than input prices. Productivity measures help identify these cases. Managers control the physical aspects of the manufacturing process, such as the amount of steel scrap in making horseshoes, but they cannot control the price of steel or the price of horseshoes. For the most part, managers cannot influence prices but must take them as a given and try to produce more output from a given physical input or the same output using less physical input.

Proponents of productivity measures argue that basing managerial performance on productivity, which does not include uncontrollable price changes, yields a better indicator of the manager's performance. They argue that traditional accounting measures, such as net income, include many factors that managers cannot control and do not focus enough attention on factors that managers can control such as labor productivity. The following example illustrates productivity measurement systems in more detail.

Measuring productivity

If the firm produces several types of outputs (large and small horseshoes) and the mix of output varies over time, then the productivity measure must somehow aggregate the quantities of outputs into a single aggregate quantity. Likewise, several inputs must be aggregated to derive a homogeneous

652   *Chapter 14*

input measure. The measure of productivity (outputs/inputs) must aggregate the multiple inputs and the multiple outputs.

To measure firmwide productivity when multiple inputs and outputs exist, prices are used as the weighting factors. The productivity measure with two outputs and three inputs becomes:

$$\text{Productivity} = \frac{\text{Output}_1 \times \text{Price} + \text{Output}_2 \times \text{Price}_2}{\text{Input} \times \text{Cost}_1 + \text{Input}_2 \times \text{Cost}_2 + \text{Input}_3 \times \text{Cost}_3}$$

Output i ($i = 1$ or 2) and input j ($j = 1$, 2, or 3) denote the physical quantities of the ith output and the jth input. Price i and cost j are the corresponding output prices and input costs. If one then compares how productivity changes over time, this aggregate measure of productivity will vary with changes in both physical quantities and relative prices. But productivity measures should exclude noncontrollable price and cost changes, thereby focusing managers' attention on physical quantities.

To exclude price and cost changes from the performance measure, yet still have a way to aggregate multiple inputs and outputs, the following scheme is used:

1. Choose a base period year and use that year's prices and costs as the weights for future years. The base year should be one of high production, and a new base year should be chosen about every five years as the structures of production and prices change.
2. Weight the physical quantity of each input and output using the base period cost or price for that input or output.
3. Divide the weighted outputs by weighted inputs to compute the productivity index for the year.
4. Divide this year's productivity index by last year's to get the change in productivity.[13]

A simple example with two inputs (steel and labor) and two outputs (small and large horseshoes) illustrates the mechanics of the computations.[14] Table 1 summarizes operations for the last two years:

TABLE 1   **Physical Quantities**

Inputs/Outputs	Base Year Prices	Last Year	This Year
Outputs:			
Small horseshoes	$2	500	600
Large horseshoes	$3	500	550
Inputs:			
Steel	$1	1,000	300
Labor	$4	300	320

---

[13]J. Kendrick and D. Creamer, *Measuring Company Productivity,* Conference Board (1969). For an alternative scheme to measure productivity within a more usual standard cost system, see R. Banker, S. Datar, and R. Kaplan, "Productivity Analysis and Management Accounting," *Journal of Accounting, Auditing and Finance,* 1989. Also see E. Adam, J. Hershauer, and W. Ruch, *Productivity and Quality: Measurement as a Basis for Improvement* (Englewood Cliffs, NJ: Prentice-Hall, 1981); and B. Gold, *Productivity, Technology, and Capital: Economic Analysis, Managerial Strategies, and Government Policies* (New York: Lexington Books, 1979).

[14]The example and discussion gloss over the thorny issue of including capital as an input. See Kendrick and Creamer (1969) for one possible treatment.

Based on these data, the productivity measures are calculated as shown in Table 2:

TABLE 2

Inputs/Outputs	Last Year	This Year
Outputs:		
Small horseshoes	$1,000	$1,200
Large horseshoes	1,500	1,650
Total outputs	$2,500	$2,850
Inputs:		
Steel	$1,000	$1,200
Labor	1,200	1,280
Total inputs	$2,200	$2,480
	$2,500	$2,850
Productivity	$2,200	$2,480
	= 1.136	= 1.149

Increase in productivity $\dfrac{1.149 - 1.136}{1.136} = 1.1\%$

Total productivity increased from 1.136 last year to 1.149 this year, or a 1.1 percent increase. Using base period prices, the productivity measure indicates that more output was produced using relatively less input.

In a study of productivity systems in Canada, few firms were found to measure aggregate firm-wide productivity as the ratio of firm outputs to firm inputs.[15] Instead, firms develop a few distinct nonfinancial measures that capture the essential strategic elements of their business. For example, a steel company tracks tons of steel shipped divided by tons of iron purchased and tons of steel shipped divided by number of employees. In an insurance company, the number of policies processed per employee in a particular department is reported. Other companies measure yield rates, defect rates, and production rates. The study concludes (p. 132), "We believe that productivity measures are *operational aids* in the strategic process that helps organization members keep track of what is required for the organization to achieve its long-run goals."

Required:

a. Critically analyze the productivity calculations in Table 2. Did the managers of the firm perform better this year compared with last year, as the productivity measures indicate?

b. Discuss some plausible reasons why comprehensive productivity systems have not been widely adopted by organizations.

c. Consider the situation of Burk Wheels. Burk Wheels manufactures aluminum automobile wheels (onto which rubber tires are mounted). The owner, Gerry Burk, is worried about increased competition from foreign countries (with lower labor costs) and is seeking to increase the productivity of her workers. She decides to implement a bonus system for direct line supervisors and department managers to reward them for improving labor productivity. In particular, supervisors will receive bonuses if they improve their department's

---

[15]H. Armitage and A. Atkinson, *The Choice of Productivity Measures in Organizations: A Field Study of Practice in Seven Canadian Firms* (Hamilton, Ontario: Society of Management Accountants of Canada, 1990). A study of U.S. firms reported that fewer than 15 percent used or planned to use total productivity measures; see J. Kraus, *How U.S. Firms Measure Productivity* (New York: National Association of Accountants, 1984).

labor productivity, defined as Output ÷ Labor hours. The casting department is the primary production process whereby molten aluminum is poured into molds, cooled, and then removed to form the wheels. Operating data for the casting department for the last two months prior to announcing the labor productivity incentive program are:

	March	April
Wheels cast	1,680	1,710
Direct labor hours	722	701
Aluminum used (pounds)	14,616	15,219
Direct labor wages/hour	$23.10	$23.75
Price of aluminum/pound	$ 0.92	$ 0.91

Solutions to Concept Questions

Q1–1: One system cannot be designed to maximize two conflicting objectives better than two systems each maximizing one objective. If a single system is used for both decision management and decision control, trade-offs must be made to create a balanced system that maximizes profits for the firm.

Q1–2: An internal accounting system provides managers and executives with key cost information regarding their business. Examples include financial budgets, inventory costs, product costs, factory costs, and overhead costs.

Q1–3:
- a. External reports (taxes, financial statements).
- b. Performance evaluations. (How well did a manager meet profit expectations for a given year?)
- c. Decision making. (Does continuing to produce a given product line maximize firm profit?)

Q1–4: An internal accounting system should have the following characteristics:
- a. It should provide information necessary to identify the most profitable products and at what volumes they should be produced.
- b. It should provide information in such a way that production inefficiencies are detected.
- c. In combination with the performance evaluation and reward systems, the internal accounting system should create incentives for managers to maximize firm value.
- d. It must support the financial and tax accounting functions.
- e. Its cost-to-benefit ratio must be less than 1.

Q1–5: Few firms have multiple systems. Typical reasons include:
- a. There are additional costs required to maintain multiple systems, including additional data processing and bookkeeping costs.
- b. There is confusion surrounding different measures. Managers wonder which system has the "right" number. The natural tendency is to reconcile the difference. Reconciliation is costly in terms of time.
- c. With one system, the external auditor can also be used to monitor and control the internal reporting system at little additional cost.

Q1–6: Surviving firms in competitive industries tend to use administrative procedures whose benefits net of costs are at least as high as their competitors'. In a competitive world, if surviving organizations are using some operating procedure over long periods of time, then it is likely that this procedure is yielding benefits in excess of costs.

Q1–7: The chief financial officer's major responsibilities involve providing all the accounting reports for both external parties and management, tax administration, budgeting, treasury including financing, investments, and internal audit.

Q2–1: The opportunity cost consists of the receipts from the most valuable forgone alternative when making a decision or choice among many options.

Q2–2:
- a. Opportunity costs are not necessarily the same as payments.
- b. Opportunity costs are forward-looking.
- c. Opportunity costs can be dated at the moment of final decision.

Q2–3: The $8,325 is an accurate estimate of the opportunity cost if we can resell the material for that amount, or we can replace the material and the future price is expected to be $8,325. In general, historical costs can be reasonably accurate estimates of opportunity costs if the current market price has not changed and there is a ready market to buy and sell the material.

Q2–4: Sunk costs are costs incurred in the past that cannot be recovered and are, therefore, irrelevant for future decision making. An example of a sunk cost is a firm's purchase of 100 pounds of a material required in a one-time project. Sixty pounds are used in this project. The remaining 40 pounds have no market value. Using the opportunity cost concept, the historical cost of the remaining 40 pounds is sunk and irrelevant for future uses of this material.

Q2–5: Avoidable costs are those costs that will not be incurred if an existing operation is closed or changed. Avoidable costs are the opportunity costs. Unavoidable costs are costs that will continue to be incurred regardless of the decision.

Q2–6: Mixed costs are cost categories that cannot be classified as being purely fixed or purely variable. An example is utilities.

Q2–7: A step cost is a cost that is fixed over a given range of output level. For example, supervisory personnel cost is a step cost.

Q2–8: A fixed cost is a cost that does not vary with the number of units produced. Although fixed with respect to volume changes, fixed costs can still be managed and reduced.

Q2–9: A variable cost is the additional cost incurred when output is expanded. Labor and materials are usually two variable costs. A variable cost is not necessarily a marginal cost. A marginal cost is the cost of the last unit produced, while variable cost is the portion of the total cost that varies with the quantity produced. If the variable cost is linear, then marginal cost per unit equals variable cost per unit and is constant as volume changes. If variable cost is not linear, marginal cost will be nonconstant.

Q2–10:

   a. Price and variable cost per unit must not vary with volume.

   b. It is a single-period analysis.

   c. It assumes a single-product firm.

Q2–11: The major benefit of CVP analysis is that it forces managers to understand how costs and revenues vary with changes in output. Its limitations include:

   a. Price and variable cost must not vary with volume.

   b. It is a single-period analysis (no time value of money).

   c. It assumes a single-product firm.

Q2–12: Estimating opportunity costs requires the decision maker to formulate all possible alternative actions and the forgone net receipts from those actions. This is a costly and time-consuming process. Furthermore, the opportunity cost changes as the set of alternative actions changes.

Q2–13: Direct costs are those costs that are worth tracing to the unit being costed. Cost–benefit analysis requires one to determine whether tracing the cost has a benefit greater than its costs.

Q2–14: Overhead costs include indirect labor and materials and other general manufacturing costs that cannot be directly traced to the units produced. Overhead costs are usually allocated using a base that most closely approximates those factors that cause overhead to vary in the long run.

Q2–15: Period costs consist of all nonmanufacturing costs, including selling, distribution, general, and administrative costs. Period costs are not included in the cost of the products that are in inventory. Period costs are written off to the income statement when incurred.

Q2–16: Motion and time studies break each labor task down to its basic movements and then time each movement. These studies have two objectives: (1) to estimate direct labor costs of a particular job and (2) to reduce these costs by redesigning the way employees perform or redesigning the product to reduce labor input.

Q2–17: Fixed costs do not directly enter the pricing decision. Fixed costs (if not incurred yet) only enter the decision to produce or not produce the good or service.

Q3–1: Even for riskless investments, a dollar today can be deposited in the bank and start earning interest so that in the future it will have grown to more than a dollar.

Q3–2: If expenses are paid after they are deducted for accounting purposes, then the present value of the expenses is smaller than the cost recognized on the income statement causing an accounting loss. However, if the discounted expenses are less than the revenue, then there is an economic profit. For example, suppose a product is sold for $10, costs $9 to manufacture, and has a three-year warranty. The expected warranty cost is $1.10, which is expected to be paid at the end of three years. The accounting loss is $0.10 because the warranty expense is recognized when the product is sold, not when the warranty cost is paid. If the interest rate is 12 percent, then the present value of the warranty expense is $1.10 \div (1.12)^3 = \$0.78$ and the economic profit is $0.22 (or $10.00 − 9.00 − $0.78).

Q3–3: Present value is the amount of money needed today that, when invested at the prevailing interest rate, will grow to the future amount.

Q3–4: Future value is the amount of money available at a future date by taking the present amount and investing it at the prevailing interest rate.

Q3–5: Compound interest is the interest earned on money invested, including principal and reinvested interest.

Q3–6: Perpetuities are infinite streams of equal payments while annuities are finite streams of equal payments.

Q3–7: Net present value is the discounted value of future cash flows minus initial investment.

Q3–8: The monthly interest rate compounds interest more frequently than an annual interest rate. If the monthly interest rate is one-twelfth of the annual interest rate, savers would have more interest at the end of the year with monthly compounding. So to equate the total interest received under monthly and annual interest rates, the monthly interest rate must be smaller than one-twelfth the annual rate.

Q3–9: Accounting depreciation is an allowable deduction in calculating taxable income and taxes payable. Being able to depreciate fixed assets reduces taxes and increases net cash flows after taxes.

Q3–10: The real interest rate is composed of the risk-free rate and a risk premium.

Q3–11: The nominal interest rate is composed of the risk-free rate, a risk premium, and an inflation rate.

Q3–12: Three flaws with IRR are that (1) it does not take into account the magnitude of investment (a larger dollar amount earning a lower return may be worth more than a smaller dollar amount earning a higher return), (2) some projects result in multiple IRRs, making investment decisions unclear, and (3) the IRR method incorrectly assumes that intermediate cash flows are reinvested at the project's internal rate of return.

Q3–13: A dollar invested in buildings is depreciated and thereby lowers taxes and increases cash flows. However, a dollar invested in land or working capital cannot be depreciated and provides no tax shield.

Q3–14: Accounting earnings contain accruals and deferrals and, as such, are not the same as cash flows. Only cash flows can be invested and earn interest; earnings cannot be invested until cash is realized.

Q4–1: Agency costs are the decline in value resulting from agents pursuing their own interests instead of the principal's interests. Differences among risk tolerances, working horizons, and excessive job perquisites all contribute to agency costs. Agency costs also arise when agents seek to manage larger organizations, to increase either their job security or their pay.

Q4–2: Agency costs are reduced by monitoring and bonding activities. Agency costs are limited by the existence of a labor market for managers, competition from other firms, and the market for corporate control.

Q4–3: Goal incongruence means simply that agents and principals have different utility functions.

Q4–4: By restructuring the agent's incentive scheme, the agent's and principal's objectives can be made more congruent.

Q4–5: Because knowledge is valuable in decision making, the right to make a decision should reside with the person who has the specific knowledge for the decision.

Q4–6:
  a. Measuring performance.
  b. Rewarding and punishing performance.
  c. Partitioning decision rights to their highest-valued use.

Q4–7: Influence costs consist of the forgone opportunities arising from employees trying to affect decisions by politicking and other potentially nonproductive influence activities. Influence costs arise when employees waste valuable time trying to influence decisions.

Q4–8: The firm, defined as a locus of contracts, exists because each resource owner is better off contracting with the firm than either contracting separately with all the resource owners individually or not contracting at all. Each resource owner, by contracting with the firm, is implicitly contracting with all others contracted with the firm. The firm economizes on repetitive contracting and transaction costs are reduced.

Q4–9: *Decision management* refers to those aspects of the decision process whereby the manager either initiates or implements a decision (e.g., a supervisor requesting an additional employee to make her department run more efficiently).

Decision control refers to those aspects of the decision process whereby managers either ratify or monitor decisions (e.g., the supervisor's boss ratifying the decision and allowing her to hire an additional employee).

Q4–10: All organizations must construct:
  a. Systems that partition decision rights. Decision rights lie initially with the board of directors. The rights are then assigned throughout the organization.
  b. Systems that measure performance. The system developed must measure the performance of variables over which the agent has been given decision rights.
  c. Systems that reward and punish performance. The system must be matched to the performance variables being measured.

Q4–11: The four steps in the decision process are:
  a. *Decision initiation*—the beginning of the decision process. This step is usually performed by the person with the specific knowledge; a decision management function.
  b. *Decision ratification*—reviewing and approving the request; a decision control function.
  c. *Decision implementation*—usually associated with the individual(s) who initiated the process; a decision management function.
  d. *Decision monitoring*—evaluating the implementation; a decision control function.

The separation of management and control helps reduce agency costs. The separation is structured so that the decision makers do not measure their own performance.

Q5–1: Responsibility accounting dictates that decision rights are linked with the specialized knowledge necessary to exercise the decision rights and that the performance measurement system (e.g., the accounting system) measures the performance of outcomes that depend on the decision rights assigned to agents.

Q5–2: The internal accounting system is most useful in decision monitoring and is an important part of the separation of decision management and control. Accounting departments, being independent of operating management, are part of the firm's internal contracting system designed to reduce agency costs. Accounting reports are one measure of an agent's performance.

Q5–3: Responsibility centers differ in their assigned decision rights and their performance management system.

  • *Cost center.* This center's goal is either to maximize output given a fixed amount of resources or to minimize input costs given a fixed output. The performance measures are (1) actual versus budgeted output and (2) actual versus budgeted cost.

If measured on total cost, the quality of the output may be a problem. If measured on average cost, the incentive to increase inventory exists.

- *Profit center.* Profit centers are given a fixed amount of capital; they control pricing and the input mix. The performance measure is the center's budgeted versus actual profit. Managers have the incentive to build inventories and request more capital assets as long as they are not charged the opportunity cost of the assets.
- *Investment center.* Investment centers have all the decision rights of profit centers plus some control over the amount of capital invested. The performance measure is either ROI or residual income. There are two problems with ROI. First, ROI is not a measure of the center's economic rate of return, creating a potential horizon problem. Second, managers have the incentive to reject profitable projects if the expected ROI is less than the mean ROI for the center. Residual income also has its shortcomings. Primarily, it too suffers from the horizon problem. Residual income is an absolute number and cannot be used to compare centers of different size.

Q5–4: EVA and residual income are based on the same formula. EVA might adjust accounting earnings, uses weighted-average cost of capital, and links performance measurement (EVA) to compensation.

Q5–5: The controllability principle holds managers responsible for only those decisions they have the authority to affect. One limitation is that while managers may have little control over the likelihood of some event, if they can influence the costs (or benefits) of the event, they should still be held accountable. The second limitation is that the performance of managers can often be better gauged by comparing it with the performance of others (relative performance evaluation) even though the managers being evaluated may have no control over others' performance.

Q5–6: All performance measurement schemes, including accounting-based schemes, are likely to produce misleading results and induce dysfunctional behavior if used mechanically and in isolation from other measures. The second point is that no system is perfect. The question to ask is this: Is the proposed system better than the next best alternative?

Q5–7:

- a. International taxation.
- b. Incentives and performance measurement of profit or investment centers.

Q5–8:

- a. *Market price:* Given a competitive external market for the good, the transfer price is determined by the external market price.

- b. *Variable cost:* Transfer price is determined by the variable cost of manufacturing the good.
- c. *Full cost:* Transfer price is determined by the full (fixed and variable) cost of manufacturing the good.
- d. *Negotiated price:* A negotiated price is determined by negotiations between the purchasing and selling divisions.

Q5–9: No. Changing transfer pricing methods does more than shift income among divisions. The method used can change the profitability of the firm as a whole because the buying/selling division changes its scale of operations in response to the transfer price.

Q6–1: Budgets are developed using "key planning assumptions" or "basic estimating factors."

Q6–2: Key planning assumptions represent those factors that are to some extent beyond management control and that set a limit on the overall activities of the firm. They must be forecast based on past experience, field estimates, and/or statistical analysis.

Q6–3: A budget variance occurs when actual expenses do not match budgeted expenses exactly or when budgeted revenues do not match actual revenues exactly.

Q6–4: Budgets are part of both. Most managers are evaluated in part on how well they are able to meet the budgeted expectations of their department, division, and so on. Budget variances are indicators of whether managers are meeting expectations. A large unfavorable variance may cause a manager to be demoted or lose his job.

Q6–5: Budgets provide:

- a. A communication device involving both vertical and horizontal information transfers.
- b. A negotiation and internal contracting procedure.
- c. A role in the performance evaluation and reward system.
- d. A role in partitioning decision rights.

Q6–6: Budgets separate decision management from decision control. Managers have the decision management rights (i.e., budget preparation and operating decisions). The board of directors has the decision control rights (i.e., budget review and approval and financial statement review).

Q6–7: The budgeting process serves as a communication device in a large firm. The process gives managers incentives to share their specific knowledge, thus transmitting this knowledge vertically and horizontally throughout the firm. Key planning assumptions are shared and developed in this process as well. The information-sharing process also serves as a negotiation and contracting procedure between different subunits within the firm. Review of the prior year's budget is a part of this process, and therefore budgeting is part of the performance evaluation and reward and punishment system. These processes partition decision rights within the firm.

Q6–8: This is just another example of the trade-off between decision making and control. The budget system transfers specialized knowledge about key planning assumptions. However, if the budget is also used for control and provides incentives for meeting the budget, then managers will "shade" their forecasts to enhance their performance whenever performance is measured by comparing actual results with budget.

Q6–9: A bottom-up budgeting system means that lower levels in the organization prepare the initial budgets because they have the specialized knowledge, and as the budget winds its way through the decision ratification process, higher levels in the organization review the budget and bring to bear additional knowledge.

Q6–10: The *ratchet effect* refers to basing next year's budget on this year's actual performance if this year's actual performance exceeds this year's budget. If, in this year actual performance falls short of budget, next year's budget is not reduced. Budget ratcheting causes employees to reduce output this year to avoid being held to a higher standard in future periods.

Q6–11: Participative budgeting occurs when the person ultimately held responsible for meeting the target makes the initial budget forecast.

Q6–12: A short-run budget is a one-year budget. Like all budgets, it forces managers with specific knowledge to communicate their forecasts and becomes the internal contract between the manager and the firm. A long-run budget projects from 2 to 10 years into the future and is a key part of a firm's strategic planning process. A short-run budget involves both decision management and decision control, while a long-run budget is primarily for decision management.

Q6–13: Line-item budgets authorize a manager to spend only up to a specific amount on each line item. These budgets are an extreme form of control; decision rights to substitute resources are denied. The benefit of such control is a reduction of agency costs. The disadvantage of these budgets is that managers are disinclined to look for savings because they cannot transfer the savings to another line item. If coming in under budget reduces the next year's budget for that line item, then the manager has no incentive to search for savings.

Q6–14: Budget lapsing provides tighter controls on managers than budgets that do not lapse. The primary purpose is to prevent certain agency problems from occurring. The opportunity cost of lapsing budgets is usually less efficient operations. Managers will devote time at year-end to ensure that the budget is fully spent, thereby protecting future budget levels.

Q6–15: A static budget is a budget that does not change with volume, while a flexible budget changes with volume. The major reason for using flexible budgets is to better measure the actual performance of a person or entity after controlling for volume effects, assuming that the person/entity being evaluated cannot control the volume changes. However, if a manager can influence the effect of the volume change, then it is unwise to shield the manager from the volume changes.

Q6–16: With incremental budgeting, each lower-level manager submits a budget by making incremental changes to each line item. Detailed explanations justifying the incremental changes are submitted and reviewed by the organization. Base budgets are taken as given.

Zero-based budgeting (ZBB) resets each line item in the budget to zero and the entire amount must be justified. ZBB, in principle, maximizes firm value by identifying and eliminating expenditures whose total costs are greater than total benefits, whereas inefficient base budgets can still exist with incremental budgeting. However, ZBB often degenerates to incremental budgeting. The same justifications are submitted to support the incremental changes. The volume of reports under ZBB is larger than under incremental budgeting, causing senior managers to focus on changes.

Q7–1: Some of the reasons for allocating costs are taxes, external financial reporting, third-party reimbursement, and solving the organizational problem.

Q7–2: Cost allocations can affect cash flows if the firm has contracts tied to reported costs (e.g., defense contractors using cost-plus contracts). Cost allocations can also affect taxes and thus cash flows. For example, allocating costs can affect product costs and thus the amount of cost of goods sold.

Q7–3: Allocating costs causes an increase in the reported costs of using the resource being allocated. For example, if property taxes are allocated using square footage, then floor space becomes taxed. These cost allocations are like taxes on these resources. Like all taxes on consumption items, the tax discourages use of the item levied with the tax.

Q7–4: Externalities are costs or benefits imposed on other individuals without their participation in the decision-making process and without compensation for the cost or benefits imposed on them (e.g., air pollution).

Q7–5: A negative externality causes others to bear some cost as the result of a decision made that is beyond their control. A positive externality causes others to receive some benefit as the result of a decision made that is out of their control.

Q7–6: One way to reduce an externality is to impose a tax on the use of the resource or the decision that creates the externality.

Q7–7:

a. *Ra,* the overhead rate at volume level a, is greater than *MCa,* the marginal cost at a. Under this condition, the cost allocation overstates the marginal cost of the externality. Therefore, taxing might cause more harm than good.

b. *Rb = MCb.* Under this condition, the cost allocation and the marginal cost are equal. In this case the cost allocation perfectly reflects the amount of tax to apply.

c. *Rc < MCc.* Under this condition, the cost allocation rate is less than the marginal cost of the externality. Taxing under this condition is better than no tax.

Q7–8: If common costs are not allocated, managers have less incentive to invest in the specialized knowledge necessary to determine the optimal level of the common costs. Furthermore, if the decision rights over the level of the common costs do not reside with a manager and are not allocated back to the manager's department, the manager will always demand more common costs.

Q7–9: A noninsulating allocation method causes the performance measure (e.g., divisional profits) to depend on the performance of another division. If other divisions improve their performance, your division bears fewer allocated costs and hence will show better performance (after receiving allocated costs). Noninsulating allocation methods create incentives for managers to cooperate and mutually monitor each other to protect their interest.

Q7–10: Factor prices do not represent the total cost to the firm of the input factor. "Distorted" factor prices represent an attempt by senior managers to proxy the total cost.

Q8–1: The death spiral can result whenever transfer prices include fixed costs and users shift away from the internal common resource. This further increases the full cost transfer price, causing further users to reduce their demand. Death spirals can be avoided by using variable cost transfer pricing and cost allocations.

Q8–2:

a. Taxing the users with some positive price causes them to reduce their consumption from what it would be under a zero price (no allocation).

b. By allocating the costs, senior management gets information about the total demand for the service at the allocated cost.

c. By comparing the internally allocated cost with the external market price of comparable services, senior management is able to assess the operating efficiency of the service department.

d. Taxing the internal service helps allocate a scarce resource. At a zero price, demand will almost always exceed supply. In the absence of a price

mechanism to allocate department services, senior management will be confronted with complaints to increase the amount of service via larger budgets and must devise nonprice priority schemes to manage the queue waiting for service.

Q8–3: Step-down allocation is an allocation method that recognizes that service departments use each other's services. The process begins by choosing one service department and allocating its cost to the remaining services and operating departments. The process is repeated for each of the remaining service departments. A major criticism of the step-down method is that the sequence is arbitrary and large differences in the cost per unit of service across different sequences are possible. The step-down method also ignores the fact that departments earlier in the sequence use service departments later in the sequence.

Q8–4: The direct allocation method ignores service departments using each other's services in allocating costs. The step-down method allocates service department costs to other service departments later in the sequence.

Q8–5: The first service department in the step-down sequence has a smaller cost per unit than if it is the last department in the sequence. The reason is twofold: (1) there are fewer costs to allocate, and (2) there are more users over which to allocate the costs.

Q8–6: Joint costs are costs incurred in the production of two or more outputs from the same production process in fixed proportion. Joint products are produced in fixed proportions. Common costs arise in production settings where there can be substitution among outputs. More of one output can be produced by reducing the output of another product.

Joint costs are associated with disassembly processes where a joint input is disassembled into several products. Common costs usually describe assembly processes where numerous inputs including some common resources are assembled to form the output.

Q8–7: Three common methods to allocate joint costs are (1) physical measures, (2) relative sales value method, and (3) net realizable value method. The fundamental point to remember when analyzing situations involving joint costs is that any joint cost allocated to final products is meaningless for assessing product-line profitability.

Q8–8: The advantage of NRV is that it does not distort the relative profitability of product-line costs and hence is better for decision making. The disadvantage of NRV is that it is costly to collect selling prices and costs beyond the split-off point.

Q9–1:

a. Job order costing.

b. Process costing.

Q9–2:

a. Direct labor, direct materials, and overhead allocations are charged to "work-in-process" while the job remains in process.

b. When a job is finished, the total cost of the job is transferred from "work-in-process" to "finished goods inventory."

c. When the goods are sold, the total cost of the job is transferred from "finished goods inventory" to "cost of goods sold."

Q9–3: The $2,750 cost of materials should be charged to the overhead account as indirect materials. Machines occasionally malfunction and destroy raw materials. This is not unusual and is a normal part of the manufacturing process. To charge the current job that happens to be in production at the time overstates the cost of this job. Charging the $2,750 to overhead and then allocating it to all jobs does not misrepresent the cost of the current job in production.

Q9–4: Using a prospective overhead rate allows more timely reporting of total costs because actual total overhead costs cannot be determined until the end of the year.

Q9–5: Overabsorbed overhead can be the result of higher volume produced during the year than budgeted. Overabsorbed overhead also can result if less overhead cost was incurred than budgeted.

Q9–6:

a. Charge it off to cost of goods sold.

b. Allocate it among work-in-process, finished goods, and cost of goods sold based on the amount of overhead in these categories.

c. Recalculate the cost of each job using actual overhead incurred and actual volume to compute a revised overhead rate.

Q9–7: Manufacturing plants produce a wide variety of products that are measured in different units. Input measures, however, are common to any product. Therefore, an input measure that is common to all manufacturing units and has the greatest association with the overhead is used to calculate the prospective overhead rate.

Q9–8: Flexible budgets split overhead into fixed and variable components as in the formula

Budgeted OH = Fixed OH + Variable $OH \times EV$

Using a flexible formula allows a firm to derive an estimate of the total overhead that varies with volume.

Q9–9: Absorption costs represent average costs and are often used in the pricing decision. Fluctuations in sales volume may or may not cause marginal costs to change. Overhead rates based on normal volumes prevent incorrect pricing decisions based on temporary volume fluctuations.

Q9–10: Unforeseen circumstances that lower volume do not necessarily increase marginal costs. An increase

in unit costs will give a misleading signal to raise prices. Managers make capital investments using assumptions of normal volume. Unit costs are also developed using these assumptions. If these assumptions are incorrect, then the capital investment should be written off as a period expense and the unit costs recalculated using the new estimate of normal volume.

Q9–11: Multiple overhead rates do not necessarily always produce more accurate estimates of product costs. It often depends on the particular decision context. For some decisions using multiple overhead rates for different classes of overhead costs, each overhead item can be analyzed and the most representative cost driver for each overhead category can be identified and used as the allocation base.

Q9–12:

a. Single factorywide overhead rate. This method is useful when the plant has a single homogeneous production process.

b. Separate overhead rate for each indirect cost item. This method is useful when different products consume varying amounts of indirect costs but the plant is not organized into production departments.

c. Separate overhead rate for each department. This method is useful when different products consume varying amounts of indirect costs and the plant is organized into production departments.

Q9–13: Process costing is used in continuous-flow production processes. Costs are averaged because there are no discrete batches. Information is more aggregate in form and therefore not very useful in decision making.

Q10–1: Viewing unit costs as variable costs implies that there is causality between unit cost figures and volume produced. In many cases unit costs are mixtures of variable and fixed costs and thus do not represent the incremental cost of producing one more unit.

Q10–2: By producing more units than are sold, some of the fixed costs are inventoried instead of being assigned to the income statement.

Q10–3:

a. Charge inventory holding costs against profits or adopt variable costing.

b. Implement rules against adding to or building inventories.

c. Use stock-price-based incentives for managers instead of accounting numbers for compensation. This will only work in a single-plant, publicly traded firm.

d. Use JIT production systems.

Q10–4: The major difference is how they treat fixed manufacturing overhead. Under absorption costing, overhead is treated as part of the product costs. Using variable costing, fixed overhead is written off as a period expense.

Q10–5: Two claimed advantages of variable costing are:
- *a.* It eliminates the distortions to income and product costs when volume changes.
- *b.* It reduces the dysfunctional incentives to overproduce.

Two potential problems with using variable costing are:
- *a.* It is difficult to determine which costs are fixed and which are variable.
- *b.* It produces unit cost figures that contain no estimate of the opportunity cost of capacity.

Q11–1: Traditional absorption costing can lead to inaccurate product costs if the allocation bases chosen do not capture the underlying overhead cost drivers. In other words, the allocation bases used to allocate overhead to products do not accurately reflect the factors that cause overhead to vary.

Q11–2: Complex products are usually undercosted by absorption cost systems because the factors that cause one product to be more complex than another are not used to allocate overhead. Unless the more complex products use proportionately more direct labor than less complex products, then too little overhead is allocated to the more complex products.

Q11–3:
- *a.* Unit level.
- *b.* Batch level.
- *c.* Product level.
- *d.* Production-sustaining level.

Q11–4: Both allocate the same total costs to products.

Q11–5:
- *a.* To develop more "accurate" product or product-line costs.
- *b.* To change incentives of operating managers.

Q11–6:
- *a.* An increase in the percentage of product costs directly traced to individual products.
- *b.* A better understanding of how costs are consumed by individual products and what activities are required to produce individual products.
- *c.* A better understanding of the direct and indirect costs in the various activity centers.
- *d.* A better understanding of how indirect costs are generated by the cost drivers.

Q11–7: The physical activities that consume resources and generate costs are not tracked through historical costs; the cost drivers cannot be discerned from the accounting numbers. Managers must be able to identify and manage the cost drivers to successfully control costs.

Q11–8: The form of an absorption system is audience dependent. If the collected information is to be used for decision management, then the form of the absorption system will lean toward an ABC system where the underlying drivers can be measured. If the information is primarily for decision control, then ABC is less useful. Multiple systems are costly; therefore, in choosing a system, trade-offs between decision management and decision control usually must be made.

Q11–9: High-volume products tend to be overcosted in unit-based absorption costing because much of the factory overhead is due to managing the number of products and batches in the plant. The low-volume products cause just as many transactions to occur in the plant (such as purchase orders and setups).

Q12–1: Standard costs are a set of benchmarks used to measure the performance of the firm with respect to controlling costs and for internal repetitive contracting.

Q12–2:
- *a.* Product pricing decisions.
- *b.* Make-versus-buy decisions.
- *c.* Plant resource allocation decisions.

Q12–3: Yes. For example, the standard cost of an hour of machine time in the lathe department is a proxy for the opportunity cost of using one hour of lathe time. This standard cost conveys to other managers throughout the firm the opportunity cost of using lathes.

Q12–4: If managers with the specific knowledge for updating the standard have part of their performance evaluation based on the difference between actual performance and the standard, this creates an incentive for them to update standards to levels that they feel are achievable.

Q12–5: Target costing is a top-down approach. It begins with a target price established by marketing. The firm's required return on investment is subtracted from the target price to derive the target product cost. This cost is then exploded into its subcomponents, which become the standards to be met if the firm is to meet its desired market penetration and required return. Traditional standard costing is a bottom-up approach and is less product/market driven.

Q12–6:
- *a.* Direct labor variances.
- *b.* Direct materials variances.
- *c.* Overhead variances.

Q12–7:
- *a.* Wage variance.
- *b.* Efficiency variance.

Q12–8: Large favorable variances could be the result of replacing the standard-quality material with substandard-quality material, yielding a favorable price variance.

Q12–9:
- *a.* Price variance.
- *b.* Quantity variance.

Q12–10:
a. Incentive to build inventories and/or lower quality.
b. Externalities.
c. Discourage cooperation.
d. Mutual monitoring incentives.
e. Satisficing behavior.

Q12–11: In seeking favorable price variances, the purchasing department has incentives to buy materials in large lot sizes to secure quantity discounts.

Q12–12: The purchasing department can impose costs on manufacturing by purchasing low-quality materials. Manufacturing can impose costs on the purchasing department by requesting rush deliveries or by changing the specifications of purchased parts.

Q12–13: There are two organizational reasons for writing variances off to cost of goods sold. First, prorating the variances creates incentives for managers to manipulate reported income. Second, prorating variances back to inventories will change the product costs incurred by the manager responsible for selling these inventories. The first reaction will be to change prices, an action he or she should not take. Of course, marginal costs can and do change, and standards must be updated to correctly reflect any changes.

Q12–14: Standard cost systems are expensive in terms of the opportunity cost of a manager's time to investigate cost variances and to oversee the development and maintenance of the standards. The benefit of standard costs comes from the development of specialized knowledge created by the manager in his or her investigations.

Q12–15: Many cost systems were developed as a means to measure and control direct labor costs. The fraction of direct labor in modern factories has decreased, thus lowering the benefits of a standard cost system. Also, modern factories have frequent changes in products and/or processes. Numerous changes cause the costs of maintaining a standard cost system to increase.

Q13–1:
a. *Budgeted volume.* The production volume used in calculating the overhead rate.
b. *Standard volume.* The production of volume that the plant would have generated if each unit of product manufactured used precisely the standard unit of volume allowed.
c. *Actual volume.* The actual production volume generated.

Q13–2: *Budgeted volume* can be estimated using either the projected number of units times their standard volume per unit (*expected volume*) or the long-run average units of volume (*normal volume*). Expected volume more accurately estimates next year's actual volume, but it causes overhead rates to vary inversely with volume. Normal volume is likely to cause larger over- or underabsorbed overhead, but overhead rates do not vary with volume.

Q13–3:
a. At the beginning of the year, estimate the flexible budget for the year.
b. Convert expected overhead into an overhead absorption rate.
c. Apply overhead to production using standard volume.
d. At the end of the year, compute overhead variances.

Q13–4:
a. *Overhead efficiency variance.* The difference in flexible budgets using actual volume and standard volume.
b. *Overhead volume variance.* The difference between the flexible budget at standard volume and overhead applied.
c. *Overhead spending variance.* The difference between how much overhead was actually incurred versus how much overhead should have been incurred for the actual volume worked.

Q13–5:
a. Unexpected changes in prices of variable overhead items.
b. Unexpected changes in fixed costs.
c. Unexpected changes in the plant's production technology cause costs to vary in ways different from those captured by the flexible budget.

Q13–6: The difference between budgeted revenues and actual revenues can be disaggregated into a *price variance* and a *quantity variance*. The quantity variance can be further disaggregated into *mix* and *sales* variances.

Q13–7: The *mix variance* reports how much of the *quantity variance* is due to the change in product mix because of substitution across products, holding constant the number of units sold. The *sales variance* reports how much of the *quantity variance* is due to actual quantity sold differing from budget, holding the mix constant.

Q14–1: The firm's business strategy is all the investment projects available to the firm today and into the future. The business strategy arises from the nature of the business the firm is in and the amount and type of spending on R&D.

Q14–2: Business strategy affects the organizational structure in three ways. The types of investments affect the way specialized knowledge is created and thus how decision rights are partitioned. The investments affect the physical asset structure and how the firm must be organized for decision making and control of these assets. Finally, the investments affect the type and nature of the customer base, which again causes the firm to adopt organizational structures to service this customer base.

The organizational structure in turn affects the business strategy. The ability of the firm to generate profitable investment ideas and implement them requires an organizational structure with incentives and controls conducive to maximizing firm value.

Q14–3: Technological and market structure changes cause firms' investment opportunities (strategy) to change. Some previously profitable projects disappear and new profitable projects emerge. These changes in investment opportunities prompt changes in organizational architecture.

Q14–4: Maybe. Other firms adopting organizational changes are often reacting to a change in either technology or market conditions. Such changes should cause management to reexamine its firm's policies. But to simply mimic the other changes is not a good idea. Other firms have different investment opportunities and different organizational architectures. They may be changing organizational policies not because of some change in technology or market condition but because they realized their old system could be improved. Also, sometimes managers make mistakes and adopt value-reducing organizational changes, which should certainly not be mimicked.

Q14–5:

a. High mean (e.g., Rolls-Royce versus Toyota).

b. Low variance (McDonald's hamburgers versus local diner).

c. Larger number of options.

d. Meeting customer expectations.

Q14–6:

a. Knowledge of customer expectations.

b. Measures of actual realized value.

c. Weights to combine the various deviations from expectations.

Q14–7:

a. Prevention costs—incurred to eliminate defective units before they are produced.

b. Inspection costs—incurred to eliminate defective units before they are shipped.

c. Scrap/waste costs—the costs of defective units in manufacturing.

d. Failure costs—costs of returns, costs of warranty work, and opportunity cost of lost sales from reputation effects.

Q14–8: JIT takes on many aspects of a process costing system; there are no batches or discrete jobs. Instead, separate accounts, labor, and overhead are charged to a conversion costs account, and materials costs are charged to products. Finished goods inventory is charged for conversion costs and for materials as units are completed. The materials charge for completed units is backflushed, reducing the raw and in-process inventory account.

Q14–9: Decreasing throughputs has some dysfunctional aspects. Increased costs are incurred in factory redesign, setup time reduction, and JIT delivery of raw material. Accounting systems focused on throughput time do not charge managers for these costs. Consequently, managers measured on throughput will do things that may decrease throughput but at the expense of firm profits.

Q14–10: The balanced scorecard seeks to better link the boxes in Figure 14–1 on business strategy and the performance evaluation system. A balanced scorecard translates the strategy into a plan of action that identifies specific objectives and performance drivers to help determine if the organization is moving in the right direction.

Q14–11: Balanced scorecards can be useful if they cause managers to identify the underlying value drivers that create firm value and communicate these inside the firm. However, balanced scorecards have several drawbacks. First, balanced scorecards ignore changes in other parts of the firm's organizational architecture, such as decision rights assignments and compensation plans. Changing just one leg of the three-legged stool can create dysfunctional results. Second, telling managers to simultaneously maximize 20 balanced scorecard indicators provides no guidance as to the relative trade-off among the indicators. It is an impossible task. You can only maximize one variable at a time. Third, if their pay is based on multiple metrics, managers will choose those measures that are easiest to achieve and ignore more difficult tasks. Fourth, by giving managers multiple criteria for measuring their success, the balanced scorecard reduces their accountability for destroying shareholder value.

Glossary

Absorbed Overhead. See *Applied Overhead.*

Absorption Cost System. A cost system designed to allocate all manufacturing costs into product costs. All direct and indirect manufacturing costs, including overheads incurred in the period, are assigned to products produced or still in progress.

Accelerated Depreciation. Any depreciation method that depreciates an asset faster than the straight-line depreciation method. See *Double-Declining-Balance Depreciation as an example.*

Activity Base. See *Cost Driver.*

Activity-Based Costing (ABC). A process of identifying activities that cause indirect costs and choosing cost drivers to apply those indirect costs to different products and services.

Activity-Based Management (ABM). The management processes that use activity-based costing information to improve firm performance by eliminating non-value-added activities, making better pricing and product-mix decisions, improving manufacturing and administrative processes, and designing better products.

Actual Expenses. The expenses incurred during a given budget period.

Actual Overhead Costs. Indirect costs incurred by the organization.

Actual Revenue. The revenue generated during a given budget period.

Actual Usage. The number of times an allocation base is used during the period.

Actual Volume. The amount of the volume produced during a period of time.

Agency Cost. The cost of agents pursuing their own interests instead of the principal's. Cost includes the reduction in the value of the firm and all resources expended to reduce the divergence of interest.

Alienability. The right to sell something and receive the proceeds from the sale.

Alienable Right. The right of an individual or a firm to take an action with a specific object, including selling the object.

Allocation Base. The unit of measure used to allocate costs. For example, direct machine hours would be an allocation base used for distributing indirect manufacturing costs.

Annuity. A stream of equal cash flows for a fixed number of periods.

Applied Overhead. Overhead costs allocated to products based on an overhead absorption rate. Also called *absorbed overhead.*

Appraisal Costs. Costs related to identifying defective units before they are shipped to customers.

Asset Structure. The nature and geographic dispersion of assets held by the organization.

Average cost. The total costs of production divided by the number of units produced.

Avoidable Product and Service Costs. Those costs that are no longer incurred if a product or service is dropped.

Balanced Scorecard. A set of performance measures that provide a comprehensive view of the organization by recognizing the goals of shareholders, the satisfaction of customers and employees, and methods to improve the firms internal processes.

Basic Estimating Factors. Forecasts of strategic elements faced by the firm, such as selling prices and input costs.

Batch-Level Costs. Indirect costs that are associated with the number of batches of a particular product or service.

Benchmarking. Comparison of an organization's processes, products, or services with those of other firms in the industry.

Benefit. Aspects of a decision that help the organization achieve its goals.

Benefit-Cost Ratio. The ratio of benefits divided by costs of a project, program, or decision. If the ratio is greater than 1, the benefits outweigh the costs. If the ratio is less than 1, costs outweigh the benefits. If the ratio equals 1, costs and benefits are equal.

Beta. The systematic (nondiversifiable) risk of a firm's stock. Beta is an estimate of the sensitivity of the firm's stock in relation to the market. If a firm's beta is greater than 1, the firm's stock varies more than the average stock in the market. If a firm's beta is less than one, it is less risky than the average stock in the market. A stock with a beta equal to 1 is of average riskiness. Beta is estimated as the slope coefficient from regressing a firm's stock returns on the market returns.

Book Value. Purchase price minus accumulated depreciation for a depreciable asset.

Bottleneck. The process of an organization that has the least capacity.

Break-Even Analysis. The process of identifying the number of units that must be sold to achieve zero profit.

Break-Even Point. The number of units needed to sell in order for total revenues to equal total costs.

Budget. A forecast of the revenues and/or expenses expected to occur within a future time period. Budgets are an integral part of the organization's performance evaluation and decision rights partitioning system.

Budget Lapsing. A type of budgeting that does not allow managers to carry over budget surpluses from one year into the next year. Under a budget lapsing system, funds not spent are lost at the end of the budget period.

Budget Variance. A budget variance occurs when actual expenses differ from budgeted expenses or when budgeted revenues differ from actual revenues.

Budgeted Expenses. The forecast of expenses expected to be incurred in a given time period.

Budgeted Overhead. Total overhead predicted to be incurred during a period, including fixed and variable overhead at budgeted volume.

Budgeted Overhead Costs. See *Budgeted Overhead*.

Budgeted Revenue. The forecast of revenue expected to be generated in a given time period.

Budgeted Volume. The amount of production expected to occur during the year, usually stated in terms of a common input measure such as direct labor hours. Budgeted volume can be estimated as expected volume for next year or normal volume over the long run.

Budgeting. Process of gathering information to assist in making forecasts.

Business Strategy. How the firm creates value in terms of products offered, markets served, technology utilized, and the nature of the firm's asset structure, including the investment projects available today and in the future.

By-Product. A joint product of a manufacturing process that has either little commercial value or is not of sufficient interest to management to maintain separate cost and revenue reports.

Capacity. Maximum output of the operation of an organization.

Capacity-Sustaining Costs. Costs that arise from sustaining the overall operation of the factory, such as depreciation, utilities, property taxes, and insurance.

Capital Budgeting. The process of choosing an investment project by comparing the future cash flows from the project with its investment.

Carrying Costs. See *Holding Costs*.

Common Cost. A cost that is shared by two or more products or users.

Compound Interest. Interest earned on money invested, including principal and reinvested interest.

Computer-Aided Manufacturing (CAM). Use of programmable robots and other programmable devices to assist in the manufacturing of products.

Contribution Margin. Revenues less variable costs.

Contribution Margin per Unit. The sales price minus the variable cost per unit.

Control System. Those procedures that help ensure self-interested agents of the organization maximize the value of the organization.

Controllability Principle. Holding managers responsible for only those decisions for which they are given authority.

Controllable Costs. Costs that are affected by a particular manager's decisions.

Controller. The person in charge of both management accounting and financial accounting in an organization; usually the chief accountant. Also called *comptroller*.

Conversion Costs. All manufacturing costs other than direct material costs.

Cost. Cash or other assets that must be surrendered or future claims that must be given in order to achieve a specific goal.

Cost Accounting. The calculation and reporting of actual or predicted costs of products, services, or processes.

Cost Allocation. The distribution or assignment of indirect, common, or joint costs to different departments, processes, or products within an organization.

Cost Application. The distribution (or assignment) of indirect, common, or joint costs to different products, as distinguished from cost allocation, which broadly covers departments, activities, or products.

Cost/Benefit Analysis. The process of making decisions by comparing the costs and benefits of alternative choices.

Cost Center. A type of organizational subunit in which managers have decision rights over a set of costs and are evaluated in part on achieving cost targets.

Cost Driver. The physical measure of activity, such as machine setups or number of purchase orders, that is most highly associated with total costs in the activity center.

Cost Object. A product, process, department, or program that the organization wishes to cost.

Cost of Capital. The opportunity cost of funds invested in a particular project, or the minimum required rate of return necessary for a potential project to be considered.

Cost of Goods Sold. The historical cost of products sold as reported in the income statement.

Cost of Quality. Cost of preventing, identifying, and correcting quality problems. Also includes external costs such as the cost of lost sales and lost goodwill due to failing to meet customers' expectations of quality.

Cost Pools. The accumulation of costs related to an indirect activity.

Cost–Volume–Profit (CVP) Analysis. The process of estimating profit assuming fixed and variable costs and a constant price over all rates of output.

Current Cost. The cost of replacing current resources using the prices of identical or similar resources available in the market.

Customer Base. The type and geographical location of customers.

Death Spiral. A situation occurring when transfer prices include fixed costs and users reduce their use of the internal product or service. This further increases the transfer price (based on average cost) and more users reduce their demand.

Decentralization. Assignment of decision-making rights to lower operating levels of an organization. Decreases cost of transferring specific knowledge needed to make decisions, but increases the cost of controlling behavior.

Decision Control. Those aspects of the decision process in which managers either ratify or monitor decisions.

Decision Management. Those aspects of the decision process where managers either initiate or implement decisions.

Decision Model. Methodical routine, such as a mathematical formula, for comparing alternative actions.

Decision Rights. The duties that a particular individual in an organization is expected to perform.

Dedicated Flow Line. The factory is organized by product line, and workers and machines are arranged to produce a single type of product. Products usually are not produced in batches but rather in single units.

Denominator Volume. The production level used to determine the budgeted overhead absorption rate.

Depreciation. The reduction in the historical cost of a fixed asset over time.

Depreciation Tax Shield. The reduction in taxes due to depreciation's reducing taxable income.

Differential Cost. See *Incremental Cost.*

Direct Allocation Method. A method of allocating service department costs directly to operating departments. This method ignores service departments providing services to other service departments.

Direct Costing. See *Variable Costing.*

Direct Costs. Costs that can be easily traced or metered directly to a product or service.

Direct Labor. Labor costs that can be identified with a specific product or service.

Direct Labor Variance. Difference between actual labor cost incurred and standard labor cost; a variance that occurs as the result of a combination of two variances: wage variance and efficiency variance. The wage variance is the difference between the actual and standard wage multiplied by the actual number of hours worked. The efficiency variance is the difference between the actual and standard number of hours worked multiplied by the standard wage rate.

Direct Materials. Parts and raw materials of a product.

Direct Materials Variance. Difference between actual materials cost incurred and standard material cost; a variance that occurs as the result of a combination of two variances: price variance and quantity variance. The materials price variance is the difference between the actual and standard materials price multiplied by the actual quantity of materials. The materials quantity variance is the difference between the actual and standard materials quantity multiplied by the standard price.

Discount Factor [$1/(1+r)^t$]. r is the discount rate and t is the number of years until the cash flow is received. The present value of $1 received at a future date.

Discount Rate (r). Interest rate used to calculate the present or future value of cash flows. See *Cost of Capital.*

Discounted Cash Flow (DCF). Multiplying future cash flows by discount factors to obtain a present value.

Double-Declining-Balance Depreciation. Form of accelerated depreciation in which the depreciation rate ($2/n$, where n is the useful life) on the book value in each year is equal to double what the first year's depreciation rate would be under straight-line depreciation.

Dysfunctional Decision Making. When the benefits from a decision are smaller than the costs for the firm as a whole.

Economic Darwinism. Differential variations among firms' organizational architectures, decision processes, or technologies that affect firms' chances of survival in a competitive environment. Natural selection is the process whereby those differential variations that increase an organization's chances of survival will tend to be imitated and become more prevalent in other firms. Managers will not imitate management practices of failing firms but those of successful firms.

Economic Order Quantity. The order size that minimizes inventory ordering and holding costs.

Economic Value Added (EVA®). A performance measure calculated by taking adjusted accounting earnings and subtracting the weighted-average cost of capital times total capital employed. Similar to *Residual Income.*

Electronic Data Interchange (EDI). The direct exchange of data such as purchase orders and invoices between organizations via computer networks.

Employee Empowerment. The delegation of greater decision rights to members of the organization.

Engineered Costs. Costs that result as a direct technological relation between inputs and outputs.

Enterprise Resource Planning (ERP). An integrated, automated, computer-based system that tracks production by job, work center, and activity and then shares the information enterprisewide in real time.

Equivalent Units. The amount of output stated in terms of complete units. For example, if 200 units of product are in work-in-process at the end of the month and these units are 75 percent complete, then these 200 units represent 150 equivalent units ($200 \times 75\%$).

Ethics. The process of determining standards and procedures for dealing with judgmental decisions affecting other people.

Expected Overhead. The fixed overhead plus the variable overhead multiplied by the expected volume.

Expected Volume. The amount of production expected to occur during the period, usually stated in terms of a common input measure such as direct labor hours.

Experience Curve. Theory that production costs per unit decrease as output increases because workers learn how to make the product more efficiently.

External Failure Costs. Costs incurred when a customer receives a defective product.

Externality. Costs or benefits imposed on other individuals without their participation in the decision-making process and without compensation for the cost or benefits imposed on them.

Facility-Related Costs. Indirect costs that are common to multiple products and services.

Failure Costs. The costs of returns, warranty work, and opportunity cost of lost sales from reputation effects when the product fails to meet customer expectations.

Favorable Variances. The amount that budgeted costs are greater than actual costs or budgeted revenues are less than actual revenues.

Financial Accounting. Accounting for the revenues, expenses, assets, liabilities, and equities of an organization, concentrating on external users (shareholders, lenders, and government). Constrained by FASB rulings and other generally accepted accounting principles.

Financial Accounting Standards Board (FASB). An independent board that is responsible for the establishment of *generally accepted accounting principles* (GAAP) used in external reporting.

Financial Leverage. The amount of debt in the firm's capital structure. Measured as the ratio of debt to equity or debt to total assets. The greater the firm's financial leverage, the more variable are the firm's profits and the more likely the firm will be forced into bankruptcy for a given downturn in sales.

Firm. A locus of contracts between individuals and resource owners.

First-In, First-Out (FIFO). An inventory flow that assumes that the oldest units in inventory are sold first.

Fixed Cost. The cost of initiating production, which does not vary with the number of units produced.

Flexible Budget. A budget that is stated as a function of some volume measure, such as units produced. Flexible budgets adjust for changes in volume.

Flexible Overhead Budget. The flexible overhead budget consists of fixed overhead plus variable overhead multiplied by volume.

Full Cost. The sum of all costs incurred in the production of a product or service.

Future Value. Value of cash flows at a future date, taking into account interest accumulated between when the cash flow occurred and the future date.

Goal Incongruence. When agents of the firm maximize their personal utility, not the principal's. See *Agency Cost.*

Gross Margin. Sales less cost of goods sold, sometimes stated as a percentage of sales.

Historical Costs. The actual costs incurred to acquire resources. Accounting systems measure historical costs, not opportunity costs.

Holding Costs. Costs including insurance, labor, interest on capital investment, and storage space necessitated by storing inventory.

Implementation. The step in the decision process to carry out the plans of the organization.

Incremental Analysis. Basing a decision on changes in cash flows that result from that decision. Also called *incremental approach.*

Incremental Budgeting. A system whereby only the anticipated change in expenditures or revenues over last year must be justified to senior management.

Incremental Cost. The cost difference between two viable alternatives.

Indirect Cost Pool. All costs that cannot be directly traced to the product and that are similar are combined into a single amount and allocated to products or processes using a single allocation base.

Indirect Costs. Costs that are shared by two or more products or users.

Inflation. Decline in the purchasing power of money due to the average increase in prices.

Information System. A network, usually within an organization, by which information is generated and circulated. This network involves computer systems as well as other mechanisms, such as payroll records, purchasing documents, and managers' impressions and specific knowledge.

Initiation. The step in the decision process to identify areas of improvement within the organization.

Inspection Cost. Cost incurred to eliminate defective units before they are shipped; for example, testing costs.

Insulating Allocation. A method allocating costs in such a way that the performance of one division or subunit of the organization is unaffected by the performance of others. See *Noninsulating Allocation.*

Intermediate Product. Product passed from one segment of an organization to another for further work before it is ready for sale. May require transfer price.

Internal Accounting System. The accounting system that collects, aggregates, and generates and distributes budgeted and actual financial and cost information within the firm for use by executives and managers for both decision making and control.

Internal Auditor. A person within the organization who monitors various divisions and departments of the organization to determine whether prescribed operational procedures are being followed.

Internal Control System. A system of checks and balances within the organization that help the organization achieve its goals.

Internal Failure Costs. Costs incurred when a defect is discovered before being received by a customer.

Internal Rate of Return (IRR). Interest rate that equates the present value of future cash flows to the current outlay, or the discount rate that produces a zero net present value.

Internal Revenue Service (IRS). An agency of the U.S. government responsible for administering and collecting taxes.

Inventoriable Costs. See *Product Costs.*

Inventory. Depending on classification, direct materials, work-in-process, or finished goods, includes cost of materials, costs of producing incomplete units, or costs of producing complete, unsold units.

Inventory Ordering Costs. Handling costs, including the purchasing department and inspection costs resulting from ordering inventory.

Investment Center. A subunit of the firm that has decision rights over the amount of capital to be invested, the prices of its products, and the manufacturing process and is usually composed of several profit centers.

Investment Opportunities. All the investment projects available to the firm now and in the foreseeable future.

Job Order Costing. Products are produced in distinct batches or jobs, and the costs of each specific batch are tracked separately using a job order cost sheet.

Job Order System. A system of recording costs for a particular job, which could be a single unit or a batch.

Joint Cost. The cost of the input and process that yields two or more products in fixed proportions as a result. For example, the cost of the barrel of oil and of splitting it into gasoline and motor oil is a joint cost.

Joint Products. Products generated from the splitting of a single material input.

Just-in-Time Production. A production system in which each item on the production line is produced immediately as needed by the next step in the process, thereby reducing raw materials and in-process inventories.

Just-in-Time Purchasing. The purchasing department can only order materials as they are needed for production. Usually, the purchasing department has a blanket purchase order with the vendor calling for daily deliveries.

Key Performance Indicators. Those actions and activities required for the firm to achieve its strategy and hence maximize its value.

Key Planning Assumptions. Those factors that are to some extent beyond management control and that set a limit on the overall activities of the firm. See *Basic Estimating Factors.*

Labor Efficiency Variance. The actual number of hours worked minus the standard number of hours, multiplied by the standard wage rate.

Last-In, First-Out (LIFO). An inventory flow that assumes that the newest units in inventory are sold first.

Lean Accounting Systems. Lean Accounting primarily seeks to support lean production and thereby provide information to managers that improves all the various processes in the firm. Lean accounting systems are simple and straightforward and provide data to better understand customer value and waste in the current processes. Such systems often shun traditional accounting methods such as variance reporting, standard costs, and ABC as too complicated and wasteful.

Lean Production. Consists of a wide variety of efficiency and cost-trimming techniques that seek to reduce all non-value activities from the firm's value chain by identifying and then eliminating non-value-added activities in demand planning, inventory planning, supply chain planning, and other capabilities that increase customer responsiveness, reduce cycle time, and control costs.

Line Item Budget. A budget that authorizes the manager to spend only up to the specified amount budgeted for each particular expense item listed in the budget.

Line Personnel. Production supervisors, workers, and other employees with direct responsibility for manufacturing (or for another firm objective).

Linear Programming. A mathematical technique for finding the optimal decision given a linear objective function and multiple linear constraints.

Management Accounting. The accounting system used within the organization to help the organization achieve its goals.

Management by Exception. The practice of focusing on operating activities that show results that significantly differ from expected standard results.

Managerial (Management) Accounting. The internal use by managers of the accounting system for decision making and control. Also called *internal accounting*.

Marginal Cost. The incremental cost of the last unit produced, which in most cases varies as volume changes.

Marginal Revenue. The incremental revenue added by the last unit sold, which in most cases varies as volume changes.

Market Price. The price or value of a good or service received in an exchange between two independent parties.

Master Budget. A document that integrates all the estimates from the different departments to establish guidelines and benchmarks for the whole organization.

Materials Price Variance. The difference between the actual price and standard price of raw materials times the actual quantity used or purchased.

Materials Quantity Variance. The difference between the actual and standard quantity of materials used times the standard price.

Materials Requirement Planning (MRP). Computer programs that allow organizations to quickly ascertain resource requirements to make a product.

Microeconomics. The study of the behavior of consumers and firms in competitive, oligopolistic, and monopolistic markets using the underlying theories of supply and demand.

Mixed Cost. Cost that cannot be classified as being purely fixed or purely variable; for example, utilities.

Mix Variance. Captures the effect of substitution among the products, holding constant the number of units sold.

Modified Accelerated Cost Recovery System (MACRS). Allowed depreciation expense for tax purposes based on tax regulation that classifies depreciable assets into different recovery periods that have various patterns of depreciation.

Monitoring. The step in the decision process to make sure that plans are implemented as designed.

Monitoring Cost. The cost of observing members of the organization directly or indirectly.

Multistage Cost Allocation. The process of allocating costs to cost objects followed by the allocation of costs from those cost objects to other cost objects.

Mutual Monitoring. When one agent observes and reports on dysfunctional/nonoptimal decisions made by another agent.

Negative Externality. A cost imposed on individuals that is the result of a decision that took place without their participation in the decision-making process and without compensation.

Negotiated Price. A transfer pricing method whereby the transfer price is determined through negotiations between the purchasing and selling division managers.

Net Income. The excess of all revenues and gains over all expenses and losses for a specific period of time.

Net Present Value (NPV). Discounted value of future cash flows less initial investment. Method for evaluating capital investment projects.

Net Realizable Value. Revenues less direct and separable costs for each product.

Nominal Interest Rate. Interest rate observed in the market, composed of two elements: the real interest rate and expected inflation.

Noninsulating Allocation. A noninsulating method bases cost allocations on the performance of all divisions' actual performance in aggregate. Therefore, the cost allocated to a division is, in part, dependent on the performance of the remaining divisions. See *Insulating Allocation.*

Non-Value-Added Cost. Cost of an activity that does not improve a product or process and may be eliminated without changing the level of function, form, or volume of the product or process. See *Value-Added Cost.*

Normal Costing. In setting overhead rates, expected volume is set at long-run average volume to prevent product costs from rising in downturns and falling in upswings.

Normal Volume. The long-run average production volume of a plant or department.

Operating Leverage. The ratio of fixed costs to total costs. The higher a firm's operating leverage, the greater will be the variability of profits for a given change in sales.

Opportunity Cost. The receipts from the next most valuable forgone alternative when making a decision or choice among many options.

Opportunity Cost of Capital. The forgone opportunity of using cash for another purpose such as earning interest in a bank account.

Organizational Architecture. The structure of an organization. Consists of (1) the assignment of decision rights within the organization, (2) the methods of rewarding individuals, and (3) the systems to evaluate the performance of both individuals and business units.

Outlay Cost. A cost that requires a cash disbursement. Also called *out-of-pocket cost.*

Outsourcing. Choosing to have an outside supplier rather than an internal subunit of the organization provide a product or service.

Overabsorbed Overhead. The amount of overhead applied is greater than actual overhead cost incurred.

Overhead. All manufacturing costs that cannot be directly traced to a product. Overhead includes indirect labor and materials, plant depreciation, insurance and property taxes, plant management salaries, and so forth. See *Indirect Cost Pool.*

Overhead Absorbed. The overhead rate multiplied by standard units of volume.

Overhead Absorption Rate. Budgeted overhead divided by budgeted volume. Also called *overhead application rate.*

Overhead Costs. Indirect costs of products or services.

Overhead Efficiency Variance. The difference between flexible budgets using actual volume and standard volume. It is an estimate of the additional overhead incurred

or saved as a result of the inefficient or efficient use of the plant or department.

Overhead Spending Variance. Actual overhead cost incurred less the flexible budget at actual volume. It is an estimate of how much actual overhead incurred differs from the amount of overhead that should have been incurred given the actual volume in the plant or department.

Overhead Volume Variance. The flexible budget at standard volume less the overhead applied. It is an estimate of the unused or overused fixed plant capacity.

Participative Budgeting. Eliciting opinions from affected managers in establishing a budget.

Payback Method. Method of evaluating a project by measuring the time until the investment is recovered. Although very easy to compute, this method ignores time value of money and cash flows after payback, making it a poor measure of profitability.

Payback Period. The time required to generate cash inflows equal to the initial investment.

Performance Measure. Direct or indirect measures of actions of individuals or groups of individuals within the organization.

Performance Reports. Evaluation tool used for comparing budgeted and actual performance.

Period Costs. Costs that are expensed in the period in which they are incurred because they are not part of the product's costs. Includes interest expense, advertising, selling, administrative and distribution expenses, and research and development costs.

Perpetuity. An infinite stream of equal payments received each period and invested at a given discount rate.

Physical Measure Method. A procedure of dividing joint costs based on a physical characteristic of the joint products.

Planning. Establishing goals and preparing possible budgets to achieve those goals.

Positive Externality. A benefit seen by individuals that is the result of a decision that took place without their participation in the decision-making process and for which they do not pay.

Practical Capacity. The expected output rate the organization can operate when the capacity was purchased and used under normal operating conditions.

Present Value. The amount of money that, if invested today, would grow to a designated future amount. Discounted value of future cash flows.

Prevention Costs. Costs incurred to prevent defective units before they are produced. For example, reengineering products or production processes.

Pricing Decision. The choice of a price for a product or service.

Prime Cost. Direct materials plus direct labor costs.

Process Costing. A method of costing products produced in a continuous process in which costs cannot be accumulated by the batch or job.

Product Costs. All costs incurred in the manufacturing process that can be traced or allocated to a given product and inventoried. Unlike period costs, product costs are accrued to the period in which they are sold.

Product-Level Costs. Costs associated with a product, but not with a particular unit or batch of the product.

Product Mix Decision. A decision on the types and proportions of products and services to offer.

Product or Service Cost. The forgone opportunity of using resources to provide a product or service.

Profit Center. A subunit of the firm with the decision rights over prices and manufacturing processes to maximize profit. Profit centers are evaluated on meeting target profits and are composed of several cost centers.

Pro-Forma Financial Statements. Financial statements based on forecasted data.

Projected Costs. Costs forecasted for a future time period.

Proration. The process of dividing over- or underabsorbed overhead into finished inventory, cost of goods sold, and work-in-process.

Qualitative Factors. Elements that are not measurable using numerical means.

Quality. Measure of a product's conformance to prespecified standards for both qualitative and quantitative factors as perceived by the customer.

Ratification. The step in the decision process to determine whether a proposal is consistent with the goals of the organization.

Real Interest Rate. Interest rate that would occur with no inflation. The real interest rate is composed of a risk-free interest rate plus a risk premium.

Reciprocal Allocation Method. A method of allocating service costs that explicitly recognizes all interactions among the service departments.

Relative Performance Evaluation. Instead of basing performance on absolute performance, performance is judged relative to some benchmark, usually other individuals' performance as a group, to help control for random events outside the control of the manager being evaluated.

Relative Sales Value Method. A procedure of dividing joint costs based on the gross sales value of the joint products.

Relevant Range. The range of output levels over which variable costs are reasonable approximations of opportunity costs.

Required Rate of Return. See *Cost of Capital.*

Residual Income. A performance measure for investment centers that subtracts the opportunity cost of the investment from the income generated by the assets of the investment.

Responsibility Accounting. The process of recognizing subunits within the organization, assigning decision rights to managers in those subunits, and evaluating the performance of those managers.

Return on Investment (ROI). A performance measure calculated by dividing the income from an investment by the size of the investment.

Risk Premium. Expected additional return that compensates for the uncertainty involved with an investment.

Risk-Free Interest Rate. The guaranteed interest rate that can be earned loaning money to the federal government. Government securities define the risk-free rate since they are the only investments considered to be free of default risk.

Robinson-Patman Act. A federal law that prohibits charging customers different prices if it is injurious to competition in the market.

Sales Variance. Captures the effect of quantity sold holding the mix of products sold constant.

Satisficing Behavior. Employees seeking to achieve satisfactory levels of performance, but not trying to excel.

Securities and Exchange Commission (SEC). A federal commission, established through the Securities Exchange Act of 1934, which administers the securities laws and regulates purchases and sales of securities, including financial disclosure.

Segment. Any part of an organization that can be separated out for purposes of investment, profit, and/or cost evaluation. See also *Cost Center, Investment Center,* and *Profit Center.*

Semivariable cost. See *Mixed Cost.*

Separable Costs. Separable costs are not part of the joint production process but rather are beyond the point at which the joint costs are incurred. Separable costs can be directly traced to individual products.

Setup Costs. Costs, including labor and materials, necessary to prepare a machine to begin a production run.

Shutdown Costs. Costs incurred in shutting down a division or product line. These costs are only incurred if the shutdown decision is made.

Six Sigma. A structured management approach that identifies potential projects throughout the organization and then defines the process improvement goals, measures the current process and collects relevant data, analyzes the causal factors, determines that all factors have been considered, improves the process based upon the analysis, and controls any variances before they result in defects.

Split-Off Point. The point in processing at which all joint costs have been incurred.

Staff Personnel. The employees of an organization who provide services such as purchasing, sales, and maintenance to support line personnel.

Stakeholders. Parties that are affected by an organization.

Standard Costs. Costs that are predetermined on a per-unit basis. Standard costs are used as a benchmark for evaluating performance. These costs are often used in or are the output from the budgeting process.

Standard Volume. The amount of volume the plant would have generated if each unit of product manufactured used precisely the standard unit of volume allowed.

Static Budgets. Budgets that don't adjust for volume.

Step Cost. A cost that is constant over ranges of production and increases by discrete amounts as volume increases from one interval to the next.

Step-Down Method. A method of allocating costs whereby one service department's cost is allocated to all remaining service departments and operating departments, and so on, until all service department costs are allocated to final products.

Straight-Line Depreciation. Depreciation method in which the amount taken to depreciation expense each year is constant and equal to $1/n$ times the depreciable amount, where n is the depreciable life of the asset.

Strategic Planning. The process whereby managers select the firm's overall objectives and the tactics to achieve those objectives.

Suboptimal Decision Making. See *Dysfunctional Decision Making*.

Sunk Costs. Costs that were incurred in the past, cannot be recovered, and are therefore irrelevant for decision making.

Target Costing. The process of designing a quality product at a sufficiently low cost to be able to sell the product at a competitive price and still yield a sufficient profit.

Tax Accounting. The accounting system used to calculate taxable income and report to government taxing authorities.

Theory of Constraints. A process of identifying and managing constraints in the making of products or in the provision of services.

Throughput Time. The total time from when a product starts the production process until it is ready for sale, including processing time, time waiting to be moved or worked on, time spent in transit, and inspection time. Also called *cycle time*.

Total Overhead Variance. The difference between total actual and applied overhead.

Total Quality Management (TQM). A philosophy of continually lowering costs and improving the provision of services and products to customers.

Transfer Price. The cost charged by one segment of an organization for a product or service supplied to another segment of the same organization.

Transferred-in-Cost. The total cost of production from previous processing that is transferred to the next department in which the product is scheduled for processing.

Treasurer. Manager or officer responsible for cash management.

Tubs on Their Own Bottoms. An expression used to refer to operating units in a nonprofit organization in order to avoid the term "profit center."

Underabsorbed Overhead. When actual overhead incurred is higher than overhead assigned to products during the year.

Unfavorable Variances. The amount by which budgeted costs are less than actual costs or by which budgeted revenues are greater than actual revenues.

Unit-Level Costs. Costs that arise from activities that are performed at least once for each unit of product. Direct labor and materials are unit-level costs.

Value Chain. Flow of business functions where value (function, form, or volume) is increased at each stage. Examples would be R&D, Manufacturing, Marketing, Sales, Distribution, and Service.

Value-Added Activities. Activities that provide value to the customer.

Value-Added Cost. Cost related to an activity that improves the function, form, or volume of a productor process, and may not be eliminated without changing the product or process. See *Non-Value-Added Cost*.

Variable Costs. Additional costs incurred when unit production increases. Variable costs per unit usually are assumed not to vary with volume.

Variable Costing. A cost system that excludes fixed costs from product costs and writes off all fixed costs against income in the year that the costs are incurred. Also called *direct costing*.

Variance. The difference between budgeted and actual costs or standard and actual costs. May relate to price or quantity for labor, materials, or overhead.

Wage Variance. The actual wage per hour minus the standard wage multiplied by the actual number of hours worked.

Waste Costs. The costs of defective units in manufacturing.

Weighted-Average Cost. A per-unit product cost determined by taking the weighted average of the cost of all units in inventory.

Zero-Based Budgeting. A system in which each budgeted line item must be justified and reviewed in total each year. That is, each year the budget for each line item is set to zero and the total has to be justified to senior management before the budget is approved.

Index